6

MW00577679

Our Covenant Heritage

Blessed be the LORD God, the God of Israel,
Who only does wondrous things!
And blessed be His glorious name forever!
And let the whole earth be filled with His glory.
Amen and Amen.

Psalm 72:18-20 NKJ

Our Covenant Heritage

*The Covenanters' Struggle
for Unity in Truth as Revealed in
the Memoir of James Nisbet
and Sermons of John Nevay*

Edwin Nisbet Moore

Illustrated by Brenda Newman and Linda Rhoden

Christian Focus Publications Ltd
Ross–shire, Scotland

Copyright
© 2000 Edwin Nisbet Moore

Published by Christian Focus Publications Ltd.
Geanies House
Fearn, Tain
Ross – shire
IV20 1TW
Scotland, UK

Printed by W S Bookwell in Finland

All Scripture quotations, unless otherwise indicated, are
from the King James Bible or from source materials. Where
indicated, the Holy Bible, New King James Version Copyright 1982 by Thomas Nelson, Inc. was used with permission.

ISBN 1 85792 6188
G02 – Church History
CHM/CHL/CHS

Publisher's Cataloging-in-Publication
(Provided by Quality Books, Inc.)

Moore, Edwin Nisbet.

   Our Covenant Heritage : the Covenanters'
struggle for unity in truth as revealed in the
memoir of James Nisbet and sermons of John Nevay
/ Edwin Nisbet Moore ; illustrated by Brenda
Newman and Linda Rhoden. – 1st ed.
   p. cm.
   Includes bibliographical references and index.

1. Covenanters. 2. Covenant Theology–History.
  3. Reformation–Scotland–History–17th century.
  4. Nisbet, James, 1667–1728. 5. Nevay, John, d.
  1672. 6. Covenanters–Persecutions–Scotland.
Title.

BX9801.M66 2000   285.241
                  QB100-500060

Table of Contents

Tables & Figures

* Extracted from Armstrong's 1775 map of Ayrshire.

D. James Kennedy
A.B., M.Div., M.Th., D.D., D.Sac.Lit., Ph.D.,
Litt.D., D.Sac.Theol., D. Humane Let.

October 13, 1999

Mr. Edwin Nisbet Moore
3962 Wood Valley Drive
Aiken, SC 29803

Dear Mr. Moore:

As per your request, my original letter of endorsement follows,
with correction:

OUR COVENANT HERITAGE is a profound work, remarkable for
its primary-source material research. Theologically, doctrinally,
historically, and Scripturally, *OUR COVENANT HERITAGE*
contains many intriguing and revealing lessons for Presbyterians
concerned about their origins as a church, and for Christians of all
denominations who seek enlightenment and augmentation of their
knowledge of church history.

The story of the rise and fall of the Scottish Church is enriched by
the author's access to firsthand accounts written and preserved by
our Presbyterian forefathers during and after the years of
persecution stemming from the differences between the
Presbyterian and Anglican religions. Actual sermons delivered
during this eventful era of church conflict in the British Isles are
utilized to personalize history in a most dramatic way.

This is an excellent treatise for "Covenanters," whom Moore
considers to be all genuine Christians, to reaffirm to themselves the
fundamental tenets of their faith, and to renew, perhaps, their own
sense of commitment and conviction.

Dear Brother, you have completed an enormous task and are to be
commended for your scholarly work. Please feel free to use any of
the comments above as endorsements or for promotional purposes.
May God bless the production and the distribution of this worthy
undertaking. Thank you for sharing it with me.

Sincerely in Christ,

D. James Kennedy, Ph.D.

Preface

With the Norman Conquest in 1066 came English kings who sought headship over both church and state. One of these kings was King William II (1056–1100). Especially fond of consuming church revenues, William succeeded in subjugating Scotland as well as England. One day while hunting in the woodlands of his newly acquired land of Scotland a wild boar charged directly toward him. All fled except one man who saved the king's life by killing the charging boar. In appreciation, the king knighted the valiant warrior, naming him Sir Nisbet after observing the distinctive nosepiece (called a "ness-bit" in that day) on the man's helmet. As centuries passed under the control of foreign kings, the motto of this man's descendants became, "I Byde It."

When the Protestant Reformation swept the land, some of this man's descendants placed themselves in great peril for their new King, the Lord Jesus Christ. Many more of his descendants did likewise for earthly kings and goods. Although the main characters of this true account are Nisbets, this book is not about Nisbets. It is about the rise and fall of a Christian nation: pursuit of biblical truth and trust in God propelled its rise; neglect of church unity and trust in man precipitated its demise. The Nisbets and the land they loved, the Lowlands of Scotland, are merely the actors and the stage of a great drama.

The true drama depicted in this book took place in Scotland in the late seventeenth century when English kings conducted a twenty-eight-year reign of terror intended to destroy the Presbyterian faith, which challenged their headship of the church. Historians refer to those persecuted as Covenanters because they had sworn a covenant to preserve the Reformed religion in Scotland and to promote reformation of religion in England and Ireland. During this persecution, thousands chose to suffer persecution rather than to acknowledge the king as head of the church—a title the Bible reserves for Christ alone. Many awaited their execution singing one last psalm and speaking one last passage from Scripture. Their genuine Christian witness forever influences anyone who examines the lives of this cloud of witnesses for God's Word.

These Scottish martyrs gave up their lives defending the differences between Presbyterian and Anglican beliefs. The troubles of one such martyr, John Nisbet of Hardhill (1627–1685), began when he refused to have one of his children baptized by the Episcopalian curate, who occupied the pulpit of his beloved, banished Presbyterian minister. This decision and others like it led to the loss of all his earthly wealth, the death of his wife and young daughter, and ultimately his own execution.

What modern man would die for the rite of baptism? This paradox so deeply haunted my soul that I read everything I could find to understand what motivated these people. What inspired such intensity of belief? What preachers did they hear and what was their message? Why did a large proportion of those willing to lay down their lives reside within a twenty-five-mile radius of John Nisbet's hometown? Why has the modern church neglected their ideal of a united, truth-bearing church within a Christian nation? Only after I became more knowledgeable of the history and fundamentals of religion did I begin to understand. To see history through the eyes of John Nisbet required that I challenge many of my preconceived ideas about religion, Presbyterianism, and even the so-called "glorious American Dream" of religious liberty. It required an appreciation that the Presbyterianism of John Knox (1514–1572) was radically different from modern Presbyterianism.

John Nisbet's son James (1667–1728) survived to leave his memoir that chronicles the difficult choices that Christians must make during and after periods of persecution. Through the pages, one plainly sees the process of sanctification as Christ renews James in His image. Near the end of his memoir, James breaks forth with page after page of prayer and praise. In his memoir, he writes a letter to a friend in which he answers the question, "Who were the Covenanters?" He describes them as men primarily dedicated to the pursuit of God's covenant promises. Their true covenant was the Covenant of Grace, which is the central theme of the Bible. Their covenant pledge to promote reformation of religion was merely the logical act of a people dedicated to God's Covenant of Grace. After the persecution, James was forced to decide between joining the church, which no longer pursued the noblest covenant ever devised by man, or adhering to God's Covenant of Grace, which requires that Christians join with the true church even if imperfect. From his struggles, we learn the necessity for pursuing both unity and truth within the church.

During such struggles, Christ's saints stand out in sharp contrast from the world around them. This stark contrast between the vibrant faith of the Covenanters and the lukewarm faith of modern Christians compelled me to study the history and ways of the Covenanters. The concept of a people willing to lay down their lives for the smallest truth in the Bible is foreign to the modern mind. We would do well to heed one of the Covenanter's favorite sayings: "*Self Preservation* must stoop to *Truth Preservation.*" Perhaps the greatest truth lost by the modern church is the necessity of both truth and unity. A simple comparison of their culture with ours yields some surprising results: In contrast to their Christian culture, our modern Christian culture rejects the idea of a Christian nation wherein the citizens belong to a single church whose members share a common doctrine, strive to obey all of the Ten Commandments, and zealously combat false religion. Not only do we not possess these blessings, but we have lost the desire for them also. Where in Scripture do we obtain support for the modern maze of denominations and toleration of false religion?

Today, the church community, even in Scotland, views the Covenanters as "Radicals" who sought to blur the distinction between church and state. Nothing could be further from the truth. As you read this book and come to see how they gave their lives to protect the world from the horrible philosophy in which the state seeks to define right and wrong by its own standards and to control the hearts, minds, and consciences of its citizens, you will see that they were both patriots and saints. They only asked that church and state conform to their distinctive, God-given roles, without which there can be no spiritual or civil peace. Did some err in the process? Yes. Although this book attacks departures from the truth by various denominations, its harshest criticism is of departures from the truth within the mainline Presbyterian denominations..

This book documents the quest of a modern Presbyterian elder to understand his religious heritage and duty. It contains three main sections. The first section examines the rise and fall of the Scottish church, and the events leading up to the eviction of John Nisbet's family from their home. The middle section examines, through the eyes of history and James Nisbet, the struggle and testimony of the remnant of the Scottish church during a period of severe persecution. The last section explores what the modern church can learn from the Covenanters. To aid the reader, the extensive quotations used in this book are modernized (corrected spelling, capitalization, and punctuation), where appropriate.

I thank God and friends such as Rev. Jim Moss and his wife Dot for their encouragement in completing this book. Without the editing help from Nancy Parker and many friends, this book would not have been possible. I also thank my faithful wife—my God-given helpmate.

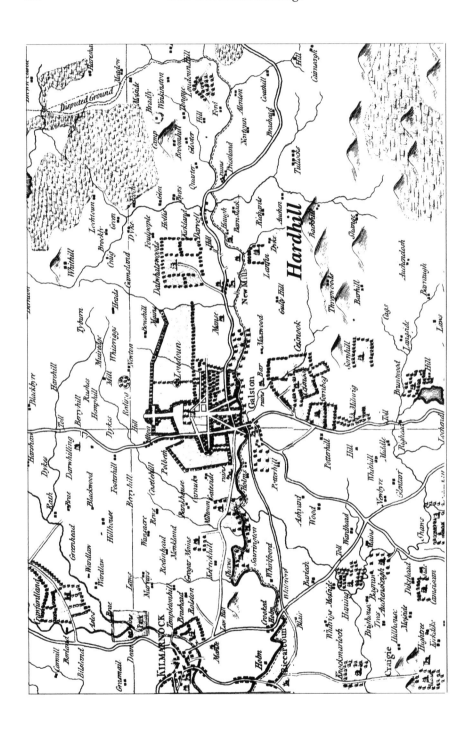

OUR COVENANT HERITAGE

Map of Scotland (above) & Loudoun Area (left)

Introduction

Self-preservation must stoop to truth preservation.
– Favorite saying of Scottish Covenanter martyrs

The Problem

Despite severe persecution, the early Christian church remained united in truth for several centuries. The church, as the woman in Revelation (Rev. 12), appeared clothed in radiant garments washed by Christ's blood, crowned with the truth of the apostles teachings, and victorious over the things of this world, depicted as the moon under her feet.[1] Despite Satan's efforts to devour new Christians as they were born, Christianity overcame the heathen world as evidenced by the conversion of the Roman Empire. Infuriated, Satan caused the woman to flee into the wilderness, where the great enemies of Christ's church sprouted forth. First, the rules and traditions of men gradually replaced Scripture as the rule of faith and practice. Second, the apostolic form of government, in which elders rule under the headship of Christ, gave way to a hierarchy of priests and prelates, who limited access to God and institutionalized false doctrine. Third, the church was invaded by the worldly as Christianity became the nominal religion of Rome. Fourth, divisions arose as schismatic Christians, such as the Donatists, refused to forgive those who had faltered during persecution. Fifth, the most heinous error of all, the error of Pelagius (late 4th and early 5th centuries), placed man, not God, in control of man's salvation. Pelagius was a monk who contended, in the words of Loraine Boettner (b. 1901), "that man could grow holy and spotless, that he could secure God's grace, and attain to salvation by an act of his own free will."[2]

Over the centuries, many Christians laid down their lives to defend the church from these and similar errors. Sometimes the state was the persecutor and sometimes the church. In either case, the persecution worked to the glory of God as observed by the theologian Charles Hodge (1797–1878): "The acts of the wicked in persecuting the early church were ordained of God as the means for the wider and more speedy proclamation of the gospel. The sufferings of the martyrs were the means not only for extending but also for purifying the church."[3]

Eventually, Reformation swept Europe following the courageous acts of reformers like Martin Luther (1483–1546) and John Calvin (1509–1564). Although there was remarkable doctrinal similarity among the various reformers, major differences separated Christians. These differences were so great that wars raged throughout Europe as church and state struggled for control of hearts and minds. This disunity among Christians is clearly not the ideal envisioned in the Bible and by the reformers who dreamed of a church united by the Word of God. Calvin remarked, "There could not be two or three churches unless Christ be torn asunder."[4] In a letter, Calvin expressed his desire for union:

> I wish it could be brought about that men of learning from the principal churches might have a meeting; and, after a careful discussion of the several points of faith, might hand down to posterity the doctrine of Scripture, settled by their common judgment. But amongst the greatest evils of our age, this also is to be reckoned, that our churches are so distracted one from another that human society scarcely flourishes amongst us; much less than holy communion of the members of Christ, which all profess in words, and few sincerely cultivate in fact. Thus, it happens that the body of the church, by the dissipation of its members, lies torn and mangled.[5]

Although the church as a whole never attained this hoped-for unity, the Church of Scotland achieved it for a time during the seventeenth century. The resultant light of this united, truth-bearing church shined so brightly that the people of Scotland covenanted together to sustain it. Many believed as Samuel Rutherford (1600–1661), "Now, O Scotland, God be thanked thy name is in the Bible."[6] In 1643, the three kingdoms of England, Scotland, and Ireland engaged themselves in a *Solemn League and Covenant* to share and spread this unity in true church doctrine, worship, and government. Learned men, as Calvin had envisioned, met at the Westminster Assembly to develop a shared, biblically based set of standards to guide church reformation.

Unfortunately, this grand reformation, called the Second Reformation, ended in persecution for the Covenanters for three fundamental reasons. First, the English independents esteemed religious toleration more than religious reformation and unity. The fast growing shoots of the sects of all conceivable beliefs choked any effort to seek ecclesiastical unity based on the Word of God. Second, in their haste for a king to oversee their beloved covenants, the Scots initiated actions that ultimately put Charles II (1630–1685) on the throne. Within a few years after taking power, he systematically reversed the Second Reformation and subjecting the Scots to a twenty-eight-year reign of terror and persecution. During this persecution, Daniel Defoe (1661–1731) estimated that authorities killed, impoverished, or banished over eighteen thousand people who refused to acknowledge England's king as head of the church.[7] Although many modern scholars dispute these figures, no better figures are available and not included are tens of thousands of Scots who fled to Ireland and Holland.[8] Presbyterianism never fully recovered. The destruction would have been complete had Holland's Prince of Orange not led a revolution in 1689, restoring the Presbyterian religion in Scotland. Third, the Scottish church split over internal disputes into two acrimonious factions. This division allowed Charles the opportunity to work one side against the other to bring down the entire church. The unity that once shown forth as a beacon from the Scottish church was never recovered. The church today will gain little by restoring the doctrines of Second Reformation unless it also restores the zeal for unity in truth that made the Second Reformation possible.

In today's parlance, one might say that the seventeenth-century Scots had a dream. They found the blueprint for the society of their dream in the Bible, as the nineteenth-century preacher and historian, Thomas McCrie (1772–1835) observed,

> They found in the Bible the character and the qualifications of rulers; and there they learned the duty of subjects. To fear God, and to keep all his commandments, they understood to include the whole duty of man, in every station in which providence may place him. This truth they fearlessly exemplified in their lives; and, without hesitation, demonstrated their belief in it to the world, by their suffering and their death.[9]

The three main parties, under God, in their mutual compact were the church, the state, and the individual. Each party sought to fulfill its obligations to obey and glorify God. Implicit in this conception is the premise that in each land there must be one civil government and one church—a church united in worship, doctrine, and government. Their compact was by no means a peace treaty between the church and state: it was a shared declaration of spiritual war on God's enemies.

These principles are exactly opposite to those of modern culture, which according to Robert Bork (b. 1927) has been sacked "by the barbarians of modern liberalism."[10] Bork identifies the two operating principles of the modern liberal culture; namely, the zeal for "radical egalitarianism [the equality of outcomes rather than equality of opportunities] and radical individualism [the drastic reduction of limits to personal gratification]."[11] Both of these principles are the natural fruits of a society whose primary focus is man. These themes dominate not only our culture, but our religious life as well. Radical individualism has led to a general minimization of the role of the church and the proliferation of sects representing the entire spectrum of beliefs. Radical egalitarianism has fostered the idea that all religions are equal—all leading to salvation, spiritual growth, and improved moral behavior. Recently, on the radio a woman described herself to a talk show host as a spiritual person. The woman described herself as interested in all religions because she believed that only narrow-minded people would adopt one religion. Yet when asked by the host about specific religious precepts, such as the Ten Commandments, the woman would not admit to owning any specific absolute precepts. In embracing all religions, she embraced none.

The reason our culture is defective is that the modern church has abandoned Christianity as taught in the Bible. For example, most professed Christians no longer believe that God is in control of all things, the Bible is completely true, Christians can agree on essential Bible truths, the church should be united, the Sabbath should be observed, etc. Is it possible to be a Christian and not believe the Bible is true? Can one overcome the world without absolute conviction that Jesus is the Son of God (1 John 5:5)? Although the Covenanters erred in many ways, they did not have these problems. Perhaps we can learn from them.

The Solution

In order to understand what can we learn from the Covenanters, this book examines their lives from several different perspectives and sources. A brief overview of the beliefs they treasured that are different from those many hold today follows:

God is in Control: Is it possible that we could learn from a culture that was the exact opposite of ours today? Unlike modern culture, the culture of the Covenanters did not tolerate beliefs and behaviors contrary to the Word of God. They considered God, not themselves, as the source of strength and truth. If there is such a thing as a "core" principle on which all the other principles of the Covenanters rested, it is that *the "rights of God" take precedent over the "rights of man."*[12] Such a perspective transforms a lowly man into an awesome fighting machine, willing to give up the things of this world for the smallest scriptural precept. One of the rights of God is that Christ is head of the church, and the Coven-anters were willing to lay down their lives to oppose any who usurped this prerogative. Those who deny Christ as king, even if they claim him as savior, are lost. In our modern culture, the concepts of absolute truth and obedience to God's laws are alien and disgusting concepts. We would rather follow the Jiminy Cricket axiom, "let your conscience be your guide," rather than "let the Word of God be your guide."[13]

Their high conception of God, called *Calvinism*, derives its strength from its reference point. According to the Calvinist perspective, men are "dead in sin," and thus incapable of choosing to follow God. In fact, men are at war with God. As a result, men must be "born again" or re-generated by God before they can choose to follow God: *"No man can come to me, except the Father which hath sent me draw him"* (John 6:44a). In this rebirth, God imparts Christ's righteousness to men and begins the proc-ess of sanctification to transform them into the image of Christ. Further, God chooses those whom he calls before the creation of the world—a be-lief called predestination. In contrast, most modern Christians hold to the teaching of Jacobus Arminius (1560–1609). Arminius taught that al-though God makes the offer of salvation, it is up to man to accept or re-ject it; therefore, it is man rather than God who is in charge. Of these two perspectives, the Calvinistic perspective is the only one with any power because it places total reliance on God.

The Calvinistic perspective is not derived from human reason, but from the inescapable evidence that God presents in his Word. According to Cornelius Van Til (1895–1987), the Calvinistic approach starts "with the absolute authority of Christ speaking in the Scripture"; thus ena-bling man "to see that the foolishness of God is wiser than men."[14] Reli-ance on Scripture rather than human wisdom is essential, according to Calvin, because "human curiosity renders the discussion of predestina-tion, already somewhat difficult in itself, very confusing and even dan-gerous," leading into a labyrinth from which there is no exit.[15] Van Til contended that this issue is not simply a minor theological or philoso-phical debate, but it is the root cause of division within the church.[16]

Until the nineteenth century, most Protestants were Calvinists. For example, Charles Spurgeon (1834–1892), the famous Baptist minister, proclaimed, "John Knox's gospel is my gospel. That which thundered through Scotland must thunder through England."[17] He remarked, "I as-cribe my change wholly to God," and acknowledged that he was "born, as all of us are by nature, as Arminian." Further, self-examination con-vinced him, "I am bound to the doctrine of the depravity of the human heart, because I find myself depraved in heart, and give daily proofs that in my flesh there dwelleth no good thing."[18] In one of his sermons, he extolled Calvinism and its cornerstone *predestination*:

> If anyone should ask me what I meant by a Calvinist, I should reply, "He is one who says, Salvation is of the Lord." I cannot find in Scripture any other doctrine than this. It is the essence of the Bible. "He only is my rock and my salvation." Tell me anything contrary to this truth, and it will be a heresy; tell me a heresy, and I shall find its essence here, that it has departed from this great, this fundamental, this rock-truth, "God is my rock and my salvation." What is the heresy of Rome, but the addition of something to the perfect merits of Jesus Christ—the bringing in of the works of the flesh, to assist in our justification? And what is the heresy of Arminianism but the addition of something to the work of the redeemer? Every heresy, if brought to the touchstone, will discover itself here. I have my own private opinion that there is no such thing as preaching Christ and him crucified, unless we preach what nowadays is called Calvinism. It is a nickname to call it Calvinism; Calvinism is the gospel, and nothing else.[19]

It is beyond doubt that "Calvinistic theology is the greatest subject that has ever exercised the mind of man."[20] This is because "the value of a religion depends on the truth and sufficiency of its idea of God. Its power to mold the individual is immense in that 'Calvinism leaves the individual man alone in the presence of God,' resulting in men whose first question is 'What would God have me do?'"[21]

It is possible to agree on Scripture truth: How did their beliefs differ from those held today? Fortunately for us, fifty-two sermons that John Nisbet's hometown minister John Nevay delivered shortly before the persecution survive. These sermons are entirely on God's Covenant of Grace and its precious promises to those who cling to Jesus Christ as their Savior. They provide a first hand look at the preaching and doctrine that inspired many to die to this earth for God's holy truths!

From examining these sermons, we learn the necessity to interpret Scripture in light of God's Covenant of Grace. Without this understanding, it is not possible for the church to preserve the truth. The woes of the modern church, and consequently society, are a direct result of a flawed understanding of these truths. If Christians really believed the Bible to be true, then they would agree on its truths. In fact, English-speaking people once agreed on these truths and documented them in the Westminster Standards. Unlike modern Christians, they believed without reserve, with full persuasion, assurance, and understanding (Luke 1:3; Rom. 8:39; 14:23; Col. 2:2; 2 Tim 1:12; 3:16–17).[22]

As evidenced by John Nisbet's choice of martyrdom, the difficult choices of this world are simple for those who sincerely believe God's promises are true. A witness to his execution makes this observation:

> After he wrote this his last speech, he was taken out immediately to the Council, and from that to the place of execution; all the way thither, he had his eyes lifted up to heaven, his face shined visibly, he seemed to rejoice, but spoke little till he came to the scaffold. When he came there, he jumped up on it and cried out, "My soul doth magnify the Lord, my soul doth magnify the Lord! I have longed these sixteen years to seal the precious cause and interest of precious Christ with my blood, and now, he hath answered and granted my request. [He] has left me no more ado but to come here and pour forth my last prayers, sing forth my last praise to him in time on this sweet and desirable scaffold, and mount that ladder. Then I shall quickly get home to my Father's house, see, enjoy, serve, and sing forth the praises of my glorious Redeemer forever more, world without end."[23]

Christians must pursue a holy life: What can we learn from their religious struggles? John Nisbet's son James left an eyewitness account of these struggles. James Nisbet's memoir, entitled *The Private Life of the Persecuted*, provides a simple, unvarnished, and "faithful exposition of the principles, practices, and way of life" of the Covenanters; it was written by one educated on the run as he and his family struggled to survive.[24] The book you are now reading contains his memoir, supplemented with additional information to provide an historical context so that you, too, can see these times through their eyes. Substantial portions of their testimony consist of prayers and meditations on Scripture. We can only speculate whether James's seemingly endless prayers were the result of persecution or the reason for his survival. Although these two Nisbets were saints, just as many with their name were not, as evidenced by seven other John Nisbets encountered in this book.

From their religious struggles, we learn the blessing of a holy life. Although God saves those chosen throughout eternity, he requires that they be his people. Because he is a Holy God, his people must be a holy people who obey him and seek his covenant promises. Without faith from God, however, it is not possible to lay hold of these promises or to obey him. It is through faith that God enables and equips his saints through the Holy Spirit to be his people. Many critics see this strong emphasis on meeting covenant obligations as contradictory to God's free grace, claiming that Covenant theologians taught this doctrine to sweeten the sour taste of predestination. This dynamic tension between two seemingly contradictory concepts is the heart of Calvinism. As G. K. Chesterton (1874–1936) put it, "Christianity got over the difficulty of combining furious opposites, by keeping them both furious."[25] As this book demonstrates, only the sound doctrine of Covenant Theology explains man's free will in light of God's sovereign grace.

Only truth can unite the church: What can we learn from their struggle to maintain both biblical truth and church unity? James Nisbet faced a more difficult struggle than did his father. Although the new government after the persecution re-established the Presbyterian religion in Scotland, it and the church tolerated other religions in violation of the covenants, for which his father had gladly suffered and died. Because the church and state had abandoned their covenant promises to maintain the purity of religion, a small surviving band of Covenanters refused to join the national church or pledge allegiance to the new government. James Nisbet's dilemma was that the government and the church no longer stood up in common defense against the forces of disunity and distortion. Yet, the national church displayed all the marks of a true church and remained strongly Calvinistic in doctrine, government, and worship. Should he join with the national church and fight to defend the new government, or should he stick with a small remnant that survived the persecution? Fortunately, able ministers influenced James to uphold both truth and unity. One such minister, Alexander Shields (1660–1700), was the leading proponent of joining with the imperfect Church of Scotland after the persecution, yet he was one of the most vocal in speaking out against ministers that were unfaithful during the persecution. He left a detailed treatise explaining why men, such as John Nisbet, were right in laying down his life during the persecution, and on the other hand, why men, such as James Nisbet, were right in joining the church after the persecution. Alexander's brother, Michael, also left a detailed account of *Faithful Contendings* for truth and unity during the period of greatest persecution.

From their struggles, we learn that the church must strive, at all cost, for *both* unity and truth. Christ has given his bride the church an engagement ring, which aptly symbolizes this necessity, as expressed by Robert McWard (d. 1681):

> Unity amongst brethren is a very desirable thing; (and the Lord will require it at his hand, who endeavors it not in his way) but there is a

Jewel, of infinitely more value, oneness with God, and oneness with and in the truth; and if our pursuing of the one be not minded, in its just subordination unto, and for the promoting of the other, it loses its intrinsic value, and becomes a plague; and thus, that which should have been our welfare, is made our trap. Let Union amongst brethren be accounted the ring, never to be broken; but let union in Truth, and with God, be counted the Ruby and Diamond.[26]

The great struggle of the Christian church through all ages is to wear the jeweled ring given to it by Christ. Although a diamond is of greater worth, the ring is necessary for its display unto the world and for its owner's enjoyment. Admittedly, there are times when one must take the stone and leave the ring. Nevertheless, in doing so, the stone bearer takes on himself an awesome responsibility, for he must stand before God on judgment day and explain why his brother is not standing with him. However, the taker of the ring without the stone faces a worse fate, for unity without truth is of no value before God. The sad reality of today's age is that the church has traded the gold ring of unity and the priceless stone of truth for trinkets of lesser worth. The achievement and maintenance of unity in truth requires churches and individuals willing to give up their trinkets and to place on their finger the true ring of Christ's church. A holy zeal to attain both truth and unity caused the Church of Scotland to shine brightly for more than one hundred years; departure from these essentials has led to the modern church, which values unity more than truth.

Religion extends to all aspects of life: What can we learn by examining the behavior and duty of each social class: nobility, clergy, and the common man? Although unknown today, the leading Covenanters were familiar figures in the homes of early American settlers, whose three most popular books were the *Bible, Pilgrim's Progress,* and *Scots Worthies.*[27] Today, this latter book, which contains an account of the martyred Scottish Covenanters, is not even in the Presbyterian College Library.

A particular stronghold of such saints was within the general vicinity of John Nisbet's hometown of Newmilns. Newmilns is nestled in the Irvine River valley—the homeland of Scotland's liberator William Wallace (1274–1305). Nearby sites include Fenwick Church where William Guthrie (1620–1665) wrote *The Trial of Saving Interest;* Loudoun Castle, the home of the Earl of Loudoun (John Campbell, d. 1663), a staunch Presbyterian who led Scotland through the Second Reformation; and Loudoun Hill, an historic battleground.

From examining their lives, we learn the necessity for Christian leaders, the church, and individuals to combat false religion and to make disciples of all nations. Modern man has forgotten how sweet the blessing is of dedicated Christian leaders in church and state. True Calvinism is quite different from the stereotype of Calvinism held by most modern adherents, as the Oxford historian James Froude (1818–1894) observed:

> This was not the religion of your fathers; this was not the Calvinism, which overthrew spiritual wickedness, and hurled kings from their thrones, and purged England and Scotland, for a time at least, of lies and charlatanry. Calvinism was the spirit which rises in revolt against untruth, the spirit which, as I have shown you, has appeared and reappeared, and in due time will appear again, unless God be a delusion and man be as the beasts that perish.[28]

Reformation requires covenant commitment: What can we learn from their covenanting? Although James rightly joined the church, the church wrongly abandoned zeal for the truth. A truth-bearing church without zeal is as useless as seawater to a thirsty man adrift on a raft. From their struggles and the sad state of the church since, we learn the necessity of a covenanted reformation, wherein Christians engage in covenant commitment to reform themselves, the church, and society.

In summary, John Nisbet had been on the front lines of a battle for truth, without which there can be no religious liberty. When truth fell, unity fell shortly thereafter, sweeping John's son James from the second row of trenches. Modern man is not even sure where the battle lines are. If Knox were alive today, would he recognize the modern Presbyterian Church? On one hand are several hyper-reformed groups that would make an ancient Donatist blush. On the other hand, the main Presbyterian bodies in Scotland and America have departed from the Word.

With God's Word as the focusing lens rather than the imaginations of man, Knox showed his generation the errors of the Roman church so clearly that within a few decades there was no longer a Roman church in Scotland. It is only through this lens that we can see seventeenth-century Scotland, as did those willing to die for what most today might view as small differences in religion. Rather than continue to pursue fruitless, halfway measures, let us journey into the Covenant Zone. There we find a society that actually tried to apply God's Word in every civil and ecclesiastical relationship. Perhaps there is a better way than our current path of unbounded human liberty. Take comfort for God promises victory.

RISE AND FALL OF THE SCOTTISH CHURCH

12

King James I

King Charles I

King Charles II

King James II

William and Mary

Oliver Cromwell

John Calvin

Lord Loudoun

John Knox

Some of the Characters

1

The Breaking of the Bronze Serpent

He [Hezekiah] removed the high places and broke the sacred pillars, cut down the wooden images and broke in pieces the bronze serpent that Moses had made; for until those days the children of Israel burned incense to it, and called it Nehustan.
–2 Kings 18:4 NKJ

The First Reformation (598–1559)

In A. D. 598, St. Columba, the missionary saint to Scotland, died after copying the tenth verse of Psalm 34, *"The young lions do lack and suffer hunger, but they that seek the Lord shall not want any good thing."*[1] A millennium would pass before the psalms he planted in the hearts of the Scots would fully blossom. In 664, the missionary-oriented Celtic Church that he founded united with the Catholic Church, which over time slipped away from Biblical truth. Accelerating its decline was the effectual subordination of the church to the English state under the Normans, and later the subordination of the state under the medieval Catholic Church.

"I Byde It" is an appropriate motto for the Lowland Scots, who suffered under the constant oppression of successive invaders.[2] The rolling nature of the mineral-deficient Lowland hills provided little in the way of wealth, natural defenses, and iron for armaments. Consequently, over the centuries the Lowlanders suffered under many conquerors, while the mountain-dwelling Highlanders remained relatively free. This constant oppression produced a distinctive personality described as dour, durable, serious, independent, and persevering. One author describes their personality as like the "quills upon the fretful porpentine."[3]

From these conditions sprang the covenant-keeping tradition of the Scots. This tradition is traceable to Robert the Bruce (1274–1329), who in 1307 defeated an English army many times the size of his own at a battle on Loudoun Hill. This victory was the first of many that eventually led to Scottish independence, at least during the Bruce's lifetime. Before this victory, three leading nobles provided the necessary unity by engaging in a covenant (or bond), in which they sought divine sanction and pledged to support the Bruce with their earthly goods and lives.[4]

Centuries later, this tradition took on a deeper meaning as the Protestant faith spread throughout the land. This more important tradition, which focuses on keeping God's covenant, began when the first Scottish Protestants, called Lollards, obtained copies of the New Testament translated by the English reformer John Wyclif (d. 1384). Several of these Scottish Lollards suffered martyrdom, with the first being James Resby in 1406.[5] In 1494, thirty Lollards from the Ayrshire area, known as the Lollards of Kyle, appeared before the king and his council on charges of heresy. One, named Adam Reid, skillfully defended himself from a bishop's query concerning whether God was in Heaven:

> I neither think nor believe, as thou thinks, that God is in heaven; but I am most assured that he is not only in Heaven, but also in the earth. But … ye think that there is no God at all, or else that he is so shut in the Heaven that he regards not what is done [on] earth; for if thou firmly believed that God were in Heaven, thou should not … altogether forget the charge that Jesus … gave to his apostles, which was to preach the Evangel.… And now, Sir (said he to the king) judge ye whether the bishop or I believe best that God is in Heaven.[6]

Many of the most noted Lollards were from the Newmilns area. One named Murdoch Nisbet (1470–1558), the great-grandfather of John Nisbet, translated Wyclif's Bible into the Scottish tongue around 1520. He used this translation to share the gospel with many from a secret cellar. Although Murdoch's translation was never mass-produced, it captures the Scottish tongue of that era.[7]

> *Our fader that art in heuenis, hallewit be thi name. Thi kingdom cum to. Thi wil be done in erde, as in heuen. Gefe to vs this day our breid ouer vthir substance. And forgif to vs our dettis as we forgef to our dettouris And leid vs nocht into temptatioun, bot deliuer vs fra evile. Amen.*[8]

In 1517, Martin Luther posted the *Ninety-five Theses* on the Wittenberg Church door, setting into motion the Protestant Reformation that would change the face of Europe. Luther grasped the essential idea of Scripture lost for centuries by the Catholic Church, which had replaced reliance on the Word of God with reliance on the traditions of man. Luther rediscovered that man is a sinner, incapable of salvation by his own volition, and that salvation is only possible by the grace of a sovereign God. God is a holy God, and his wrath requires the punishment of sin by death. As a monk, Luther vainly attempted to live a sinless life and to confess each of his sins. Luther's mentor told him he was making religion too difficult and suggested he simply try to love God. Luther, fully realizing the hopelessness of any attempt by man to save himself, reached an important conclusion, "Love God? I hated him!"[9] For a cure, Luther's mentor suggested that he study and teach the Bible. Luther started in Psalms and, after several years, finally found peace:

> Night and day I pondered until I saw the connection between the justice of God and the statement that *"the just shall live by his faith."* Then I grasped that the justice of God is that righteousness by which through grace and sheer mercy God justifies us through faith. Thereupon, I felt myself to be reborn and to have gone through open doors into paradise. The whole of Scripture took on a new meaning, and whereas before the "justice of God" had filled me with hate, now it became to me inexpressibly sweet in greater love. This passage of Paul became to me a gate to heaven....[10]

Through the eye of faith, Luther was finally able to "look upon his [God's] fatherly, friendly heart, in which there is no anger nor ungraciousness."[11] Luther discovered that faith alone enables man to stand, justified through the atoning work of Christ, before a holy God. True reformation of man or of society can only take place when men understand that they are sinners, incapable of salvation apart from God, who gives them the gift of faith.

Luther believed that "A simple layman armed with Scripture is to be believed above a pope or council without it." Yet, he did not limit the church's teachings and practices to Scripture alone. For example, he allowed forms of worship unless Scripture prohibited them. The Swiss Reformers, Ulrich Zwingli (1484–1531) and later John Calvin, carried the Reformation a step further by limiting church teachings and practices only to those found in Scripture. In 1536, Calvin completed the first version of his *Institutes of Christian Religion*, which along with his prodigious commentaries and the *Genevan Book of Church Order* deeply influenced the Scots. Calvin's beliefs were distinctive from Luther's in several important ways:[12] First, unlike many modern Lutherans, both Luther and Calvin believed in predestination. However, there is an important difference in emphasis as articulated by B. B. Warfield (1851–1921):

Lutheranism springs from the throes of a guilt-burdened soul seeking peace with God, finds this peace in faith and stops right there.... Calvinism asks with the same eagerness as Lutheranism the great question: "What must I do to be saved?" and answers it precisely as Lutheranism answers it. But it cannot stop there. The deeper question pressed upon it, "Whence this faith by which I am justified?" ...It has zeal, no doubt, for salvation, but its highest zeal is for the honor of God, and it is this question that quickens its emotions and vitalizes its efforts. It begins, it centers, and it ends with the vision of God in his glory; and it sets itself before all things to render to God his rights in every sphere of life activity.[13]

Second, unlike Luther, Calvin believed that a body of elders rather than an elder should govern each church. Likewise, bodies of elders, called presbyteries, rather than individuals (i.e., bishops) should settle matters among churches. Third, Calvin placed great emphasis on worship to which he applied the regulative principle, allowing only those forms of worship expressly allowed in the Bible. For example, Calvin stressed psalms of divine origin, whereas Luther allowed hymns of human origin. Fourth, Luther believed the elements of the Lord's Supper represented the physical body and blood of Christ, whereas Calvin stressed the spiritual presence of Christ.

Within a few years of Luther's awakening, the light of gospel spread throughout Scotland and England. Tyndale's (d. 1536) English translation of the New Testament in 1527 further fanned the flames by making the Bible more available to the common man. Tyndale once remarked to a priest, "If God spares my life, ere many years I shall cause the boy that drives the plough to know more of the Scriptures than you do."[14]

As soon as Calvinism spread to Scotland, so did the persecution as Catholics burned Protestants at the stake. Instead of suppressing the faith, the persecution had the opposite effect, fanning the flames of the Christian conscience. One example, illustrative of the growing faith in the land, is the execution of a Robert Lamb and his wife for refusing to acknowledge the saints and the Virgin Mary in their prayers. On the way to their respective executions, Robert's wife exhorted him, "Husband, be glad; we have lived together many joyful days; and this day on which we must die we ought to esteem the most joyful of all, because now we shall have joy forever. Therefore, I will not bid you good night, for we shall meet again in heaven." Just before her own execution by drowning, she implored her neighbors to be kind to her children as she handed away the child from her breast.[15]

Although there were pockets of faith, most people remained "vassals of the Romish church, priest-ridden, ignorant, wretched, degraded in body, mind, and morals." It was a time when "gross darkness covered the land and brooded like an eternal nightmare upon all the faculties of the people." Many like Murdoch Nisbet escaped persecution by fleeing abroad. When Murdoch returned, a few years later, he dug a vault under his house where he secretly shared the gospel with others until his death.[16]

Soon Scotland's own Calvin arrived on the scene to break the yoke of the Roman church. Strong and clear preaching of the Word of God by men such as John Knox and John Hooper (1500–1555), the founder of Puritanism, had converted many in Scotland and England to the Protestant cause. Knox saw no room for compromise with the Roman Catholic Church, which he considered as an unscriptural, false church:

> We must define the church, by the right notes given to us in God's Scripture. We must discern the Immaculate Spouse of Jesus Christ from the Mother of Confusion, Spiritual Babylon, lest we imprudently embrace a harlot instead of the chaste spouse—yea, to speak in plain words, lest we submit ourselves to Satan thinking that we submit ourselves to Jesus Christ.[17]

Knox considered the destruction of idolatry and false worship as a biblical mandate. In his view, the true church is engaged in spiritual warfare against false religion; therefore, he considered peaceful coexistence with a false religion inconceivable.

In England, reformation proceeded gradually for different reasons. In 1534, the king of England, Henry VIII, broke with the Roman church because the pope refused to grant him a divorce. To achieve his end, Henry had Parliament pass the *Act of Supremacy* that established the king as the head of the Church of England, also called the Anglican Church. The doctrine remained unchanged, however, and the persecution of Protestants continued. Nonetheless, Henry's vice-regent Thomas Cromwell (1485–1540) promoted the Protestant cause by facilitating the translation and distribution of the English Bible and overseeing the consolidation of the remaining monastic system under the king's control. Cromwell, a master administrator, saw in the Bible itself the most efficient means of edifying and educating the common man, eliminating the need for an atrophied and expensive ecclesiastical infrastructure.[18]

England gradually adopted Protestant ideas. During the short reign of Henry's son Edward VI, which ended in 1553, the Anglican Church took on a decided Protestant character with a revised creed, which Knox helped develop. The great English theologians of this era all believed in predestination, and the *Thirty-nine Articles*, their creed, embodied this concept.[19] Unfortunately, the revised prayer book, called the *Book of Common Prayer*, retained many elements of the Catholic worship service.

Regrettably, these reformations were largely undone during the five-year reign of Edward's sister Mary Tudor (1516–1558), who attempted to restore the Catholic faith in England. The persecution of Protestants was so intense during Mary's reign that historians call her "Bloody Mary," and many Protestants fled to Holland to escape persecution. In 1558, Elizabeth I (1533–1603) succeeded her sister Mary and re-established the Anglican Church; however, the church maintained many of the Catholic trappings and errors.[20]

In Ireland, reformation did not succeed. One barrier, often overlooked, is that the English, Scottish, and Irish languages of that era were as foreign to each other as Murdoch Nisbet's translation is to us today. Consequently, attempts in Ireland to replace the Latin mass with an English version failed. Not only did they fail, these attempts created within the Irish heart a sense of identity as a Catholic nation as well.[21]

First Scottish Reformation (1559–1572)

After spending several years in Geneva studying with Calvin, Knox returned to Scotland in May 1559. He returned at the request of the country's leading nobles who engaged in a covenant to support the cause of Christ. Calling themselves and those they represented the *Congregation*, they pledged (1) "to keep constant amity, unity, and fellowship together"; (2) to do "all things required of God in his Scripture ... to destroy and put away all things that dishonor his name, so that God may be truly and purely worshipped"; and (3) to spare no "labors, goods, substance, bodies and lives" in defense of any member of the Congregation.[22] Please observe how their pledges to uphold unity encased their pledge to uphold truth. Hence, the Scottish Reformation followed the Old Testament pattern of the days of Ezra and Nehemiah wherein the leaders of church and state, represented by men such as Lord James Stewart, the Campbells of the Newmilns area, and John Knox, renewed their covenant promise to be God's people. They saw themselves much like the nation Israel, specially chosen by God to be his people. In this spirit of joyous anticipation, people singing the 124th Psalm greeted Knox at his return.[23]

Had not the Lord been on our side—may Israel now say;
Had not the Lord been on our side—when men rose us to slay;
They had us swallow'd quick, when as—their wrath 'gainst us did flame:
Waters had cover'd us, our soul—had sunk beneath the stream.[24]

The collapse of the Catholic Church in Scotland shortly after Knox's return was phenomenal. After one of his sermons, a riot broke out in Perth where the rioters smashed the idols, icons, and paraphernalia of the church. The riot began after a priest infuriated a crowd by daring to conduct a Mass, which the people thought idolatrous. In anger, the priest struck a boy who in return threw a rock, which broke an image. After the uprising, Mary, Queen of Scots (1542–1587), threatened to "destroy the town, man, woman, and child," and she called her nobles and French allies to aid her cause.[25] The people rose in self-defense to form a Protestant army, augmented by twenty-five hundred men from Ayrshire, to save Perth from destruction. Similar scenes took place across southern Scotland, leaving no icons intact. In early 1560, with the assistance of an English army and the death of the queen, the Protestants finally succeeded in forcing the French to leave.[26]

Within two years of Knox's return, the reformed church had sixty ministers, largely converts from Catholicism. Concerning the unprecedented pace of this radical reformation, the historian James Kirkton (1620–1699) commented, "Within ten years after popery was discharged in Scotland, there were not ten persons of quality to be found who did not profess the true reformed religion." In the words of John Knox, "it appeared as if men had rained from the clouds." To establish the framework for the new religion, documents such as the *Confession of Faith, First Book of Discipline,* and *Book of Common Order* were prepared, all based solely on the Word of God. The *First Book of Discipline* established a church government elected by the people and consisting of elders, deacons, pastors, and superintendents. The office of superintendent, not to be confused with a bishop, was a temporary expedient to offset the paucity of trained pastors and was discontinued as the incumbents died. The superintendent, equal in rank to a pastor, served as a missionary and supply pastor to large districts. At no time was the temporary office of superintendent inconsistent with the foundational premise, "One is your master, and all ye are brethren."[27]

Another characteristic of these early Presbyterians was the use of covenants, an oath of allegiance or an agreement between parties. James Hewison (b. 1853) observed that the use of covenants was "an inevitable result of the movement for reform in the life, character, and faith of the people, and was the first fruit of the development of a spiritual life which quickened anew the sense of personal responsibility to God." In April 1560, the leading noblemen of the land signed the *Leith Covenant*. This covenant combined the traditional promise to strive for "reformation of religion according to God's Word" with the political obligation to unite with England to defend the two countries from France. It also affirmed that the people, not the king, are the "custodians of the Word of God."[28]

Six simple rules encapsulate Knox's attitude regarding church and state relations, the great shibboleth of the Scottish Presbyterians:

1. If God's law conflicts with civil law, follow God's law. Knox's preaching in violation of civil laws is proof of this point.
2. The state is obligated to protect the true religion as revealed in God's Word. Knox firmly believed that "God craves of kings that they be the foster-fathers to his church." For example, after the Protestant religion was established, law forbade the Catholic Mass with progressively severe penalties leading to death for those with multiple violations. Knox, in a sermon to Queen Mary said, "One mass is more fearful to me, than if ten thousand armed enemies were landed in any part of the realm, of purpose to suppress the whole religion."[29]
3. It is lawful to resist with the sword in self-defense, but the sword should not be the first weapon of choice for Christians. Knox approved of prisoners escaping if they not shed the blood of their guards, and he took pride that he was never the "malefactor and the shedder of blood." When asked by Queen Mary about the lawfulness of raising swords against rulers, Knox replied, "If their princes exceed their bounds, Madam, no doubt they can be resisted, even by power."[30]
4. Regarding owning the authority of the queen, Knox remarked at his trial for treason, "I never made myself an adversary to the queen's majesty, except in the head of religion." The court, convinced of his innocence, acquitted him. At another occasion, he advised the queen that he "shall be as well content to live under Your Grace as Paul was to live under Nero." Yet his allegiance was on the condition that she not defile her "hands with the blood of the Saints of God."[31]
5. Knox believed that the church and state must mutually strive to provide relief for the poor and to educate the masses by establishing schools in every parish. According to Knox, the kirk (church) must "provide for the poor within itself"; however, this responsibility does not apply to "stubborn and idle beggars." Further, the church and state are obligated to educate children in a Christian environment because the mind and soul are more important than the body. The *First Book of Discipline* requires that every group of several churches appoint a schoolmaster and

every larger city erect a college. Those that could afford this education must do so, but "the children of the poor must be supported and sustained on the charge of the church." To Knox, school was a place where "tender children shall be nourished and brought up in knowledge and virtue" rather than in "strange and unknown places." Nobles and bishops who siphoned off two-thirds of the revenues from the church lands, leaving only one-third for the support of the queen's court and the kirk, thwarted achievement of Knox's vision.[32]

6. The church is obligated to maintain spiritual discipline, and the state is obligated to punish evildoers. These obligations are closely related. Knox and the early Scottish church took their obligation to maintain discipline very seriously; consequently, the elders (a non-paying job) met weekly to enforce ecclesiastical discipline. Adulterers, Sabbath breakers, and backsliders were likely to appear before the session.[33] Knox believed that the state, not the church, should be the first to act in offenses such as "blasphemy, adultery, murder, perjury and other crimes capital, worthy of death." When the state fails in meeting its obligation, the church should excommunicate "open and manifest contemnors," until restored through public repentance. The reason given is that "no Commonwealth can flourish or long endure without good laws and sharp execution of the same, so neither can the kirk of God be brought to purity neither yet be retained in the same without ecclesiastical discipline." The state did pass laws that required the punishment of adulterers, but typically, did not act on them, leaving the discipline of such offences to the church.[34]

Knox's battles with the state were not academic; they were matters of life and death. The queen's (Mary, Queen of Scots) relatives in France were so determined to wipe out the Protestant faith that in 1572 on and following St. Bartholomew's day, they tricked and killed tens of thousands of French Protestants. Equally determined to re-establish the Catholic faith in Scotland was Mary, who would have succeeded if it had not been for Knox and the united stand that the Presbyterians took against her designs. These confrontations and widespread unpopularity forced her to abdicate in 1567, leaving the Scottish government to her infant son James I (1566–1625), under the control of the Regency of Moray (Lord James Stewart until 1570). At Mary's fall, more than one thousand Protestant churches existed in Scotland with more than 250 ordained ministers. That same year, Parliament* established the Church of

---

* The Scottish Parliament consisted of representatives of the three estates (nobility, population centers, and the church). Parliament convened only when summoned by the king. Another body referred to as the Convention (or Committee) of Estates, smaller in number and composed of representatives of the estates, acted between called sessions of Parliament.

Scotland, with the *Confession of Faith* as the unifying doctrine. To the detriment of the church, Parliament did not endorse a fixed form of church government.[35]

A few years later in 1572, John Knox died. The epitaph pronounced at his burial is appropriate: "There lies he who never feared the face of man!" Perhaps Knox's greatest contribution was not the delivery of the people from popery but his dedication to prayer for the church. His last request was that his wife read John 17:3: *"And this is eternal life, that they may know you, the only true God, and Jesus Christ whom you have sent."* Years earlier, this passage had inspired him to begin his journey of faith. In this chapter, Jesus prays for his disciples, *"They all may be one, as you, Father, are in me, and I in you; that they also may be one in us, that the world may believe that you sent me."*[36] Perhaps, the Lord will yet fulfill this promise and deliver his church from division.

The War over Church Government (1572–1617)

While the collapse of the Catholic Church was sudden and dramatic in Scotland, the Reformation in England proceeded along a different course, driven more by political rather than by religious motivations. Nowhere was this difference more evident than in the approach of the two countries regarding church government. In England, bishops ruled the church, whereas in Scotland, elders ruled in keeping with the apostolic model. Although many of the English Puritans acknowledged the scriptural warrant of the Presbyterian form of government, they reluctantly accepted the Anglican bishops and hoped to reform the church from within. This divergence, as we will later see, would have dire consequences on the Scottish church.

The same year that Knox died, the Scottish church restored the office of bishop at the urging of the young King James's Regent. Although subject to church assemblies, the bishops owed primary allegiance to the king rather than to the church. So odious to the Scottish people was the office of bishop that they called black dogs with white marks bishops.[37]

A new leader, Andrew Melville (1545–1622), soon rose to take Knox's place. Although Melville never took up arms against the king, he was the forerunner of the later Covenanters who rebelled against unlawful intrusions of the civil power in ecclesiastical matters. Melville was convinced, along with the Swiss church, that a bishop must be the pastor of one flock. He was instrumental in developing in 1578 the *Second Book of Discipline*, which clarified the responsibility and authority of the ecclesiastical and civil powers. It boldly declared Christ as head of the church and that both church and state are of God and have one purpose, "to advance the glory of God, and to have goodly and good subjects." In 1580, the General Assembly (governing body of the church) recommended abolishing the office of bishop; Parliament failed, however, to implement its recommendation.[38]

When King James came of age in 1581, he signed the *King's Covenant*, which declared his commitment to the Protestant cause. Adherents of this document confessed, subscribed, and affirmed the "true Christian Faith and Religion" as expressed in the *Confession of Faith* adopted in 1560. Adherents also promised to defend the king and the church, and agreed to "abhor and detest all contrary religion and doctrine; but chiefly all kind of papistrie in general." Contrary to the position of the church, the covenant was silent concerning the bishops.[39] The king would later use this fact to undermine the Presbyterians.

To save the young king from the influence of his popish advisers, some of the nobles kidnapped him. After his rescue from these nobles, he surrounded himself with advisors unsympathetic to the Presbyterian cause and had the *Act of Uniformity* passed in 1584. This act deprived the church of the right to call free assemblies, required ministers to acknowledge bishops as superiors, and declared any affront to the king's authority as treason.[40] The king wrote to the pope, "I have as yet deserved nothing at your hands, but it shall not always be thus." Excluding Melville who fled to save his life, the other ministers subscribed to the act, some appending the clause, "according to the Word of God."[41]

The failed attempt in 1588 of the Spanish Armada to invade England checked the downward trend and increased support for the Presbyterian cause. This change of events led the Scottish Parliament to repeal the *Act of Uniformity* and to restore the Presbyterian form of government.[42]

To counteract this trend, King James initiated a series of gradual actions that he termed as "Kingcraft." His purpose was nothing less than to restore his bishops to power and restore himself as head of the church. The king's favorite sayings included: "No bishop, no king," and "a Scottish Presbytery agreeth as well with monarchy as God and the devil." When James allowed the return of the popish exiles, Melville reminded him that he was just a member, not the head of the church. Yet, he pledged obedience to the king's civil authority.[43] Shortly thereafter, the king banished one minister for questioning his authority in ecclesiastical matters and issued warrants to arrest ministers with similar views. Using "Kingcraft," James defined the debate on his terms by approving the *Act of Linlithgow* in 1596, which required ministers to acknowledge the king's civil authority. He then called a General Assembly in the Catholic-leaning city of Perth. This assembly passed a number of resolutions favorable to the king (e.g., prohibiting the church from criticizing civil legislation, calling General Assemblies, or appointing pastors without the king's consent). He tightened his control over the church, by appointing commissioners to govern the church, and over the state, by having the commissioners included as voting members of Parliament.[44] Thus by small steps, King James succeeded in breaking down the Presbyterian system of church government.

The king did not limit persecution to Presbyterians. In England, he forced "non-conformists" who separated from the church to flee to Holland. These "Separatists," called "Brownists" because they followed the teachings of Robert Brown, emphasized the importance of pietistic, small-group fellowships and de-emphasized the importance of the church.[45]

In 1598, the king wrote a treatise concerning the law, duties, and rights of monarchs, in which he portrayed the office of king as an absolute ruler and father of the people, not bound by civil laws. In the first draft of this treatise, he encouraged his son to banish Presbyterians, hate Puritans, and restore the Episcopalians. This work was partly in response to a work written in 1579 by George Buchanan (1506–1582), James's childhood tutor, concerning the roles and responsibilities of monarchs and citizens. Buchanan wrote that kings are "created for the maintenance of civil society"; hence, it is their "duty to administer justice to every man according to the directions of the law." A king becomes a tyrant and enemy of the people if he undermines the law and is "guilty of acts tending to the dissolution of that society." When this happens, people are not obligated to obey him and have a "right to kill that enemy." Although Presbyterians in Melville's time stopped short of open rebellion against the king, the later Covenanters refused to acknowledge the authority of a king who was an avowed enemy of religion.[46]

Queen Elizabeth's death in 1603 strengthened James's hand by making him king of both England and Scotland.[†] Not fearing persecution because of James's Catholic wife, more than 150 Catholic priests came to England that same year.[47] James continued the slow process of erosion by appointing bishops as constant moderators of the synods, by bribing

---

[†] The children of Henry VIII (Edward, Mary, and Elizabeth) died without qualified heirs, leaving James, the great-great grandson of Henry VII, as king of both kingdoms. Although the sixth James of Scotland, he is generally referred to as James I, the first James of both England and Scotland.

the nobility, and by imprisoning or banishing any vocal Presbyterian leaders. In 1610, the king achieved total victory when the General Assembly in Glasgow restored full authority to the bishops and declared the king as head of the church. The king imprisoned or banished ministers that resisted, including Andrew Melville and John Welsh (1558–1622), the son-in-law of John Knox.

The War over Church Worship (1617–1637)

Now as head of the church, James sought next to rebuild the Scottish church in the image of the Anglican Church with all its liturgies. In 1617, the king, focusing first on the external, refurbished the Holyrood[‡] chapel with statues of apostles, portraits, and an organ. This greatly offended the Scottish people, for it reminded them of the Catholic images that their fathers had fought so hard to remove. The organ was an unwelcome intrusion because the Presbyterians believed that the musical instruments of the Old Testament temple worship were types or shadows pointing toward Christ, therefore, no longer necessary because Christ is now present with his church. Calvin considered any emphasis on the "shadows of a departed dispensation" as a means of burying the light of the gospel.[48] That same year, a group of fifty-four offended Presbyterians wrote to the king, protesting the presumption that he and the bishops could make laws for the church without free General Assemblies. This angered the king who summoned some of the leaders to appear before him to defend their protest. One of these leaders, David Calderwood (1575–1650), answered that he would give passive obedience, but he would "rather suffer than practice."[49]

The king developed five articles to impose Anglican worship practices on the Presbyterians. In 1621, a stacked convocation at Perth adopted these articles, called the *Five Articles of Perth*, and Parliament ratified them. These articles established practices such as kneeling at the Lord's Supper, performing the sacraments in private, and observing holidays, such as Easter and Christmas. Although seemingly innocent, these articles undermined essential points of religion. The Presbyterians argued that because the disciples sat in fellowship at the first Lord's Supper, they should do likewise. They considered kneeling before the altar a Catholic practice. Supporting their position is the book of Psalms

---

[‡] The scenic city of Edinburgh is built around a one-mile-long, sloping street that connects the Edinburgh Castle, at the top of the hill, to the Holyrood House, which served as the Royal Palace (James Howell, *Epistolae Ho-Elianae* [London: Thomas Guy, 1673], p. 261).

that commends a variety of worship postures, "kneeling" being mentioned only once. It is ironic that in the wilderness, Satan asked Christ first to fall down, then to worship him (Matt. 4:9). Satan works first on the external, whereas Christ works first on the internal. Further, they considered the observance of days inconsistent with the Apostle Paul's admonition: *"Ye observe days, and months, and times, and years. I am afraid of you, lest I have bestowed upon you labor in vain"* (Gal. 4:9–11).[50]

King James died in 1625, leaving his son Charles I (1600–1649) as the new king. The historian Bishop Gilbert Burnet (1643–1715) observed, "It is certain no king could die less lamented or less esteemed than he was." Today, James is known best for the King James Bible, prepared by the Puritans to whom James referred to as "brain-sick." At James's death, there was a great deal of spiritual apathy in the rural churches due to a general lack of education, funding, and trained pastors. The corrupt bishops compounded the situation by consuming the majority of available funds. Under James, the persecution was moderate. Typically, those persecuted fled to Ireland and frequently returned to hold outdoor prayer meetings called coventicles. Even though many ministers failed to stand against the king's tyranny, the church remained united. As we shall see, the later Covenanters suffered for not heeding this practice. Samuel Rutherford, one of the most vocal Protesters, referred to the church as his "harlot mother."[51]

The year of James's death corresponded with religious revivals in several rural parishes. The most notable revival was in the Stewarton River valley not far from Newmilns. Its origin is traceable to the preaching of David Dickson§ (1583–1662), minister of Irvine.[52] A "solid, serious, and practical piety that distinguished the converts" to such a remarkable degree that they were said to suffer from "Stewarton Sickness." Lord Loudoun, who resided a few miles from Newmilns, captured the mood of the people in a reply to the king's concern about the changing atmosphere: "Sire, the people of Scotland will obey you in everything with the utmost cheerfulness, provided you do not touch their religion and conscience." The historian McCrie refers to Loudoun as the "chief assertor both of civil and religious rights in the country." Samuel Rutherford praised Loudoun for his Christ-given courage "to come out into the streets, with Christ on [his] forehead."[53] Although the Second Reforma-

---

§ David Dickson's most noted work is his commentary on Psalms. It is one of the best devotionals ever written. He and several other notable Scottish preachers banded together to publish a set of Commentaries, many of which are available today through the Banner of Truth Trust.

tion did not officially begin for several years, God was already preparing his people.

It was in this year of revival, 1627, that the hero of our story, John Nisbet of Hardhill, was born near the town of Newmilns. John grew up under the ministry of James Greig, who "preached with such ardor and vehemence, that often striking two fingers of one hand on the palm of the other, the blood oozed from the tips of his fingers." Greig also left a lasting legacy in the Newmilns area when, in one winter, he taught forty people, all more than forty years of age, to read the Scripture.[54]

The Lord also blessed John Nisbet with godly parents dedicated to training their family in the practice of holiness and in the fear of God.[55] When John Nisbet's father died, John inherited Murdoch Nisbet's handwritten New Testament. James Nisbet, in his memoir, provides the following sketch of his father, John Nisbet of Hardhill, who put unity in truth into practice:

> From the days of his youth, he always wore a small pocket-bible upon him, full of marginal notes, which he made great use of in reading on all occasions. As also, from his youth, he often retired to secret prayer where he spent many hours of the day and sometimes whole nights. He was long under heavy soul exercise anent his own salvation, which made him keep at the utmost distance from all things he knew was sinful. He was a close walker with God and opposed much the sins of his heart and nature and the sins and backsliding of the times wherein he lived.... He could never endure the least thing that looked like a countenancing of the enemies of God, ...for which he met with temptations, afflictions, and reproaches, both from enemies and false friends.
>
> Notwithstanding that, he studied much the spirit of meekness and moderation, but as a flint set his face in the cause of God against all storms, because he had counted the cost and laid his account with the worst; from whence it did appear that he was endued of God with a particular gift of suffering for Christ and his cause (Phil. 1:29; Rev. 2:10,13,20; 3:8,10; Heb. 10:35). He was an exact observer of the Sabbath, keeping it holy unto the Lord, rising earlier on that day than any other. Although he was a man of strong affections to his children, yet he kept them under a strict discipline, as far as his suffering circumstances would allow, and took them often with him to secret prayer, for the discharge of which duty he carefully instructed them and was an example to them therein himself.... He was strong and healthy and of a bold undaunted spirit; yet if he was at any time touched with sickness, he was as meek as a lamb, saying, "It is the will of God that he should feel a little of that bitter which many are long afflicted with." He could not endure that any

persons should boast of their religion, still exhorting all not to be high minded but to pass the time of our sojourning here in fear; saying, "I love well to see people humbly live up to their profession, and be truly concerned about the life and power of godliness." These he loved dearly and encouraged all he could, but those who seemed to be nominal and formal in their religion, he much pitied, lamented, and often took occasion to warn them of their danger.[56]

He was very tender of God's glory: he could not endure to hear any of the truths of the Christian religion opposed. [...Yet], he could never endure to hear any religious person's name reproached or exclaimed against upon the account of weakness of parts; and as he was tender of truth in hair and hoof, so he was likewise very tender of the name of others in whom he saw the least of the image of God.[57]

Meanwhile in England, the Puritans enjoyed relative peace until William Laud (1573–1645) became Bishop of London in 1628 and then Archbishop of Canterbury in 1633. Laud, who desired reconciliation with the Catholic Church, was determined to crush the Puritans, causing a thousand to flee England for Massachusetts in 1630, followed by another twenty thousand by 1640.[58]

King Charles I, with the aid of Archbishop Laud and English prelates (Anglican priests), swept "away the remaining framework of a Presbyterian Church" by imposing the *Book of Canons and Constitutions* on the church in 1636. Not satisfied with destroying the framework, the king next sought to destroy the heart as well. In 1637, Laud directed the Scottish church to begin using a new service book known as *Laud's Liturgy*. The Presbyterians found *Laud's Liturgy* intolerable because parts of it resembled the Catholic Mass.[59]

For writing against Laud's innovations and Arminian leanings, the Court of High Commission in Edinburgh banished Samuel Rutherford to Aberdeen so that he could receive indoctrination at the hands of their Episcopal-leaning professors.[60] While there, Rutherford wrote letters of encouragement to the civil and religious leaders of his day. As illustrated in the following excerpt from one of these letters to John Nevay, Rutherford's writings provide a precious glimpse into the speaking and preaching language used by the Scottish ministers of that day.

> Suffering for Christ is the very element, wherein Christ's love lives, and exercises itself, in casting out flames of fire and sparks of heat, to warm such a frozen heart as I have: And if Christ's weeping in sackcloth be so sweet, I cannot find any imaginable thoughts to think what he will be, when we clay-bodies (having put off our mortality) shall come up to the

marriage-hall, and great palace, and behold the king clothed in his robes-royal, sitting on his throne. I would desire no more for my heaven, beneath the moon, while I am fighting in this house of clay, but daily renewing feasts of love with Christ, and liberty now and then to feed my hunger with a kiss of that fairest face, that is like the sun in his strength at noon-day.[61]

The origin of faith in the hometowns of Samuel Rutherford and John Nisbet share a common source. Interestingly, tradition records that the Lollards of Kyle had given a copy of Wyclif's bible to the Gordons of Earlston, who owned a castle near Rutherford's birthplace (the village of Nisbet) and who had been beacons of truth to that part of Scotland. Similar accounts tell of Lollards in covenanting strongholds (e.g., Fife and Stirling).[62] In an odd sort of way, the Covenanting Reformation is traceable to a few of Wyclif's bibles. What a difference a few bibles make.

The War over Church Doctrine (1617–1637)

In addition to Satan's assaults on the form of church government and worship, Satan launched a more insidious and harmful attack on the very heart of religious faith. The year after the death of Arminius in 1609, his followers codified his teaching in a Remonstrance to the Dutch government. Because the Arminian philosophy was totally in opposition to the accepted creeds of the European Protestant churches, a Dutch synod (the Synod of Dort) with representatives from other countries met in 1618–1619 to consider the Remonstrance. The synod vehemently rejected the Remonstrance and issued the Canons of Dort, which countered the five points of Arminianism with five points of Calvinism. Table 1.1 contrasts these two systems of doctrine. As evident, these two approaches to interpreting Scripture are two entirely different and irreconcilable systems of doctrine. Prove any one point false and the entire system fails. This is because all points in each system rest upon a foundational premise implicit in each system. Calvinism holds that salvation is entirely God's work; whereas, Arminianism teaches that salvation is the joint work of God and man, with the ultimate choice resting with man. Although the Arminian approach appeals to humanistic logic and sentiment, it is inconsistent with Scripture, as is proven throughout this book in more detail than space allows in this section. Every verse cited in defense of the Arminian position (e.g., John 3:16; 6:40; Acts 10:34; 1 Tim. 2:4–6; 1 John 2:2) can be explained within the context of the Calvinistic doctrine, yet it is impossible to explain the verses cited by the Calvinists (e.g., John 6:37–44; 10:28–29; Rom. 8:29–30) within the Arminian framework. The only logical outcome of accepting the Arminian approach is to reject Scripture. The choice is between the clear teaching of Scripture that God "works all things according to the counsel of his will" (Eph. 1:11) and the reasoning of man, to whom the gospel is foolishness (1 Cor. 1:18).[63]

Table 1.1
The Five Points of Calvinism and Arminianism

	Calvinism	Arminianism
T	*Total depravity*: Man is unable to save himself and to do, to understand, and to desire good. Man is free to choose good over evil, but by his own free choice, he rejects and rebels against God.	*Incomplete depravity*: Although injured by the fall, man is able to do good works and to choose salvation for himself with God's help.
U	*Unconditional election*: God chose from the foundation of the world to save a limited, but large, number of fallen mankind through his grace and mercy. The choice is founded on nothing within man but on God's sovereign will and for his good purpose.	*Conditional election*: God elected those he foresaw would choose salvation and would persevere in obtaining it. In essence, man not God makes the choice and is in control.
L	*Limited atonement*: Christ died for his elect sheep only. God's love for his sheep is effectual; Christ loses none given him by the Father.	*Universal Atonement*: Christ died to make salvation possible for all men.
I	*Irresistible grace*: God draws his elect to him; they cannot resist his call. He changes the heart of the elect; thus freed from the bondage of sin, the elect freely choose Christ and his way.	*Resistible grace*: Man in his natural condition is able to choose or to reject God's offer of salvation.
P	*Perseverance of the saints*: Once saved, always saved. The elect's perseverance does not rest within themselves but in God.	*Precarious salvation*: Although men may accept God's offer of salvation, they may fall and lose their salvation.

By 1637, the battle lines were well entrenched with the Calvinistic Puritans and Covenanters in close combat with the Arminian bishops.

2

The Rise and Fall of Truth
and Unity

*And the king stood by a pillar, and made a covenant before the LORD, to walk af-
ter the LORD, and to keep his commandments and his testimonies and his statutes
with all their heart and all their soul, to perform the words of this covenant that were
written in this book. And all the people stood to the covenant.*   −2 *Kings 23:3*

Second Reformation (1637–1643)

When the bishops attempted to institute Laud's new liturgy at St.
Giles Church in Edinburgh on July 23, 1637, the people rebelled.
As the prelate started to read the liturgy, the people began murmuring,
shouting, and clapping. An old woman, whom tradition names as Janet
Geddes, threw her stool in disgust at the prelate's head and shouted,
"Villain, dost thou say Mass at my lug [ear]!" Soon other stools were fly-
ing, forcing the poor prelate to flee for his life. When a bishop attempted
to restore order, the people responded with the cry, "A pope! A pope!"
Just as decades earlier when the actions of a boy ignited the First
Scottish Reformation, the actions of a woman ignited the Second Scottish Reformation.[1] Perhaps real reformation today will begin when
women and children shame men into action.

The entire nation rapidly united in active defiance−not one person
would publicly read the liturgy for any sum of money. The Lord also
blessed this reformation with a strong leader, Alexander Henderson.
Henderson's peers looked to him as "incomparably the ablest of them
all" and as if "he were all crystal glass." Yet, he was a humble man, looking always to the Lord to direct his steps. Henderson framed the legal
defense for not using the new liturgy. He argued that neither the General Assembly nor Parliament had approved the new liturgy for use, nor
is it necessary to obey orders inconsistent with God's law.[2]

To bind themselves and their fellow citizens to reformation of religion, the Scottish leaders drafted the *National Covenant*. It consisted of three parts: the *King's Covenant of 1581*, a summary of the acts of Parliament supportive of the Reformed cause, and the covenant promise. The covenant promise required all to faithfully promise "by their solemn oath" to defend the "true religion" and the "king's majesty, his person, and estate." Those who entered into this promise bound themselves and their heirs to "labor by all lawful means to recover the purity and liberty of the gospel"; to "endeavor to keep [them]selves within the bounds of Christian liberty"; to "be good examples to all others in godliness, soberness, righteousness; and to fulfill their duty to God and man." In addition, they pledged "most humbly [to] beseech the Lord to strengthen us by his Holy Spirit for this end." The covenant emphasized responsibility to *both* God and king, contending that these two obligations are "so straightly joined, as that they had the same friends, and common enemies, and did stand and fall together."[3]

This heavy emphasis on the obligation to obey civil authority was largely due to the influence of Robert Baillie (1599–1662). Baillie pleaded for forbearance of the imposed Anglican practices "till they be tried and allowed in free assemblies and parliaments."[4] As we will see, if the later Covenanters had diligently remained true to this principle, the Covenanting movement could have survived to this day.

The leading nobility and ministers of the land swore the *National Covenant* at Greyfriars Church in March 1638 with great sense of solemnity. After a sermon, Lord Loudoun addressed the "assembled multitude, dwelling on the importance of this bond of union in present circumstances, and exhorting all to zeal and perseverance in the cause of the Lord." After prayer by Henderson, all those present signed the covenant. Within a few weeks, the majority of the nation, except a few cities like Aberdeen and some of the moderately Catholic northern provinces, signed the covenant. This act bound them together, akin to the nation Israel, in a solemn oath to God. An extraordinary revival of religion accompanied its signing.[5]

In response, the king replied, "I would rather die than yield to their impertinent and damnable demands." "As long as this covenant is in force," he bemoaned, "I have no more power in Scotland than as a Duke of Venice." By July 1638, both sides were openly arming for war.[6] The king sent his commissioner, the Marquis of Hamilton, to meet with the Covenanters. On his way to Edinburgh, he had to pass by sixty thousand people lining the route by the sea and seven hundred ministers standing on a hill. Eventually, the king relented and called a free General Assembly to meet in Glasgow in November 1638. The Scottish people, standing together behind a united church, prevailed.[7]

The General Assembly of Glasgow was a "noble, grave, and competent body" consisting of ninety-eight ruling elders who were mostly landed gentry and nobles, Lord Hamilton the king's commissioner, and 140 ministers supportive of the covenant. From the world's perspective, as stated by Hamilton, the assembly was mostly constituted of men "totally void of learning" and under the control of ministers who were the "most rigid and seditious puritans that liveth." The purpose of the assembly was nothing less than to resolve the question, "Who is head of the Scottish church?"[8] To accomplish this task, the assembly had to draw a fine line of distinction between the roles of church and state. The able moderator Henderson set the stage:

> It hath been the glory of Reformed churches, and we account it our glory after a special manner, to give unto kings and Christian magistrates what belongs unto their place, and we know the fifth command of the law ... that next to piety towards God, we are obligated to loyalty and obedience to our king ... to spend our lives in his service.[9]

Henderson then pushed the assembly to pass judgment on the bishops. This action forced Hamilton, in the king's name, to declare the assembly dissolved and to walk out. Dissolution of the assembly at this point would have been equivalent to declaring Charles as head of the church. In response to Hamilton's action, a member read a prepared protest to the assembly: "In the name of the Lord Jesus Christ, the only head and monarch of His church ... we profess with sorrowful and heavy but loyal hearts, we cannot dissolve this assembly."[10] Henderson provided the needed leadership by reminding the assembly that Christ's authority was greater than the king's authority:

> [Christ] hath given divine warrants to convocate assemblies whether magistrates consent or not; therefore we perceive men [Hamilton] to be so zealous of their Master's commands, have we not as good a reason to be zealous toward our Lord, and to maintain the liberties and privileges of his kingdom?[11]

Echoing this appeal, the assembly united to such a degree that one of the few participants who had not yet sworn the covenants pleaded to do so. The assembly then proceeded to annul the acts of previous unlawful assemblies, censure and depose prelates, excommunicate the most offensive bishops, condemn the liturgical innovations, forbid ministers to hold civil positions, direct the erection of schools, declare prelacy dead, and restore the Presbyterian system of government.[12]

The Assembly passed these acts with only a few dissenting votes. One of these dissenters was Robert Baillie, whose voice of moderation cautioned against haste in condemning those who had given in to the innovations, the prelates, or the king's authority. "No clause might be put which might oblige us in conscience to count" the office of bishop as "wicked and unlawful in itself," Baillie pleaded. In his closing remarks, Henderson expressed his appreciation for godly nobles, such as Loudoun, who had provided rock-hard support for the cause. Henderson likened them to the "tops of mountains that were first discovered in the deluge" because the "Sun of Righteousness had been pleased to shine first upon these mountains" (2 Sam. 23:4). As a closing hymn, the assembly expressed their shared unity by joyfully singing Psalm 133: *"Behold, how good a thing it is, and how becoming well, Together such as brethren are in unity to dwell."*[13]

In response to the assembly's ostensible declaration of war, King Charles retorted, "I will either be a glorious king or a patient martyr."[14] He promptly planned a crushing blow with over forty-five thousand troops on all fronts. However, limited support from Parliament and united resistance from the Scottish people thwarted his plans. When Charles, falling in popularity, finally crossed into Scotland, only four thousand troops came with him. The main Covenanter force of twelve thousand men, assembled under blue banners stamped with *For Christ's Crown and Covenant* in golden letters, had built strong defenses on Dunse Law Hill in preparation for the anticipated English attack. They waited for the attack, feeding their hearts on Psalms such as Psalms 3, 27, and 72.[15] Baillie describes the spirit of the troops:

> They were clothed in olive and gray plaiden, with bonnets having knots of blue ribands.... The sight of the nobles and beloved pastors daily raised their hearts.... Had you lent your ear in the morning, and especially at even, and heard in the tents the sound of some singing psalms, some praying, some reading the Scripture, ye would have been refreshed.[16]

The king wisely did not attack, thus ending the First Bishop's War, named after the bishops and their allies who supported it. After several days of negotiations, the king refused to acknowledge the Glasgow General Assembly, but he agreed to the vague promise that "all matters ecclesiastical should be settled by assemblies of the kirk [church] and all civil matters by Parliament."[17] Although they had taken up arms to defend their Christian rights, the Covenanters still owned the civil authority of the king, to whom they pledged to "yield all civil and temporal obedience." In defense of the uprising, Loudoun told the king, "They only asked to enjoy their religion and liberties, according to the ecclesiastical and civil laws of the kingdom."[18]

The General Assembly met again in 1639, this time officially to repeat work of the Glasgow Assembly and to restore church discipline, weakened by years of Episcopal control. The assembly ended with a plea by the moderator, David Dickson, to love, not insult, those who had been of "discrepant judgment from us anent the matter of ceremonies and the government of the church." The Scottish Parliament then assembled and ratified the acts of the assembly, including an act excluding ministers and bishops from membership in Parliament. The exclusion of bishops from Parliament decimated the king's voting power.[19]

These acts were a direct affront to the king's authority, causing Charles to hasten his preparations for war. To this end, Charles imprisoned Loudoun, forcing him in exchange for his release "to promote an accord between the king and the Scots." In May 1640, Charles dissolved the English Parliament, known as the "Short Parliament" because it refused to fund his preparations for war with Scotland. This action infuriated the English people who were tired of merciless religious persecution, during which those who spoke out against prelacy had been branded, mutilated (ears cut off and noses split), or banished.[20]

The Scottish Parliament removed all traces of Episcopacy and authorized military preparations "for a just and lawful defense of their religion, laws, lives, liberty, and country." This defense included the subduing by military force of citizens, towns, and areas within Scotland that refused to accept the covenants. In August, the English welcomed Scottish troops as they preemptively invaded England. The Scottish army, outnumbering the king's troops by three to one, defeated the king's troops at Newburn, forcing Charles to call a new Parliament. This new Parliament, called the "Long Parliament," recognized that "the Scottish army was the best guardian of the English Liberties."[21]

In both England and Scotland, the people had awakened to the need for reform and for effective church government. So popular was the subject of church government that "between 1640 and 1660, no fewer than thirty thousand pamphlets" were published on this subject. The Scots took advantage of their position to educate England about the evils of bishops through lectures and tracts. The tracts condemned Episcopacy as inconsistent with early church practices and Scripture, claiming that it led to popery. Modern man scoffs at this domino theory of bishops, but to the Protestants of that era it was no laughing matter.[22]

Reinforcing the fear of popery was an uprising in 1641 in which Irish Catholics killed, without mercy, more than forty thousand Irish Protestants. This brutality further aroused the English Puritans, called "Roundheads" in reference to their short-cropped hair. The Roundheads blamed the bishops and their Catholic queen for the uprising. Charles, after a failed attempt in 1642 to arrest the leaders of Parliament, fled from London and raised his banner, "God save the King Charles and hang up the Roundheads."[23] Charles formed an army composed of nobles and Royalists, referred to as "Cavaliers" because of their daring horsemanship and their long flowing locks. The breach widened in 1643 after Charles signed a truce with the Irish Catholics promising them toleration and granting them rule over some districts. This action caused the English Parliament to form a military alliance with Scotland. To elicit the Scots' support, the English Parliament sent a declaration to the Scottish General Assembly in which they professed their desire for reformation according to the Word of God.[24]

Westminster Assembly (1643–1644)

The changes in Ireland and Scotland produced a profound effect on English public opinion. In 1643, the English Parliament, which two years earlier had totally supported prelacy, signed the *Solemn League and Covenant* with Scotland and Ireland, pledging to exterminate prelacy and popery.[25] To facilitate this change of religion, Parliament summoned an assembly of renowned theologians to meet at Westminster to develop standards for religious worship and practice.

Solemn League and Covenant: The *Solemn League and Covenant* was the natural outgrowth of an intense desire, characteristic of that era, for unity in religion. Well before the covenant materialized, the Scots were zealous in prayer for "one Confession, one Directory for Public Worship, one Catechism, and one form of Kirk Government" for both kingdoms.[26] The Scottish Commissioners to the Westminster Assembly believed that there was "nothing so powerful to divide hearts of the people as division in religion; nothing so strong to unite them as unity of religion."[27] The concept of *unity of religion* dominated seventeenth-century history. In contrast to modern thinking, the church leaders of that era sought unity, purity, and service rather than diversity, toleration, and liberty. All social actions were for the glory of God, not man. The American cry, "Give me liberty or give me death!" would translate in that era to, "Give God glory or give me death!"

When the English approached the Scots to form a civil alliance, the Scots suggested that they also form an ecclesiastical alliance. To facilitate this alliance, Henderson drafted the *Solemn League and Covenant* (paraphrased below), which the Scottish church, Westminster Assembly, and the civil governments in England and Scotland promptly adopted.[28] In the covenant, the people in all three lands solemnly pledged, with uplifted hand, to God that they would endeavor:

(1) ... the preservation of the Reformed religion in the Church of Scotland ... [and] the reformation of religion in the kingdoms of England and Ireland ... according to the Word of God and the example of the best Reformed churches: And shall endeavor to bring the churches of God in the three kingdoms, to the nearest conjunction and uniformity in religion....

(2) ... the extirpation of popery, prelacy,... superstition, heresy, schism, Profanity, and whatsoever shall be found to be contrary to sound doctrine and the power of godliness....

(3) ... [the] preservation and defense of the rights and privileges of the Parliaments,... the king's majesty's person and authority,... the true religion, and liberties of the kingdoms ...

(4) ... the discovery of all such as have been, or shall be incendiaries, malignants, or evil instruments, by hindering the reformation of religion, dividing the king from his people, or one of the kingdoms from another, or making any faction, or parties amongst the people contrary to this league and covenant ...

(5) ... [the conjoining] in a firm peace and union to all posterity ...

(6) ... [the assistance and defense of] all those that enter into this league and covenant.... And [we] shall not suffer ourselves ... to be divided and withdrawn from this blessed union....

And because these kingdoms are guilty of many sins, and provocations against God, and his Son Jesus Christ ... we profess and declare before God, and the world, our unfeigned desire to be humbled for our sins,... to amend our lives, and each to go before another in the example of a real reformation; that the Lord may turn away his wrath.... Most humbly beseeching the Lord, to strengthen us by his Holy Spirit ... to the

Glory of God, the enlargement of the kingdom of Jesus Christ, and the peace and tranquility of the Christian kingdoms and commonwealths.

The *Solemn League and Covenant* attempted to create a brave new world where nations embrace Reformed Christianity in much the same way as an individual. The fundamental premise underlying this covenant is that nations derive their power from God and are accountable to Christ for suppressing evil, promoting righteousness, and protecting religion. Likewise, the people, also subject to Christ, must pledge to uphold, support, and implement their obligation to live godly lives and encourage others to do likewise. These principles are in opposition to those in the *U.S. Constitution*, which mentions not God and recognizes not the essential role and obligation of government to honor Christ and to protect his church. It is also noteworthy that Henderson was perfectly willing to sacrifice the cherished Scottish doctrinal standards for the cause of biblical unity: "This [reformation and unity] must be brought to pass with common consent, and we are not to conceive that they [England and Ireland] will embrace our form; but a new form must be set down for us all."[29] He assumed, of course, that any new standard would be consistent with Scripture. All that the covenant required of England and Ireland was a commitment to reformation of religion.

Westminster Assembly: By order of the English Parliament in July 1643, an assembly of 121 ministers (called Divines) and thirty lay representatives convened in Westminster Abbey to deduce from Scripture "the Liturgy, Discipline and Government of the Church of England."[30] About thirty Anglican scholars failed to show up because the king proclaimed the assembly illegal. Several Scottish Commissioners (including Robert Baillie, Alexander Henderson, Samuel Rutherford, George Gillespie, and Lord Loudoun) participated as deliberative but non-voting members. The general aim of the Westminster Divines was to build on the Presbyterian model successfully demonstrated in Scotland. The divines were in almost unanimous agreement regarding matters of doctrine and worship, but they disagreed on the proper form and nature of church government.

Doctrine and Worship: The assembly prepared a set of standards that define the practices and beliefs of the Reformed faith regarding doctrine and worship. These standards include the *Directory of Public Worship of God*, *Confession of Faith*, and the *Larger* and *Shorter Catechisms*. The most important of these documents is the *Confession of Faith*. Although the Confession is not equivalent to Scripture, it is an "echo of that voice from souls that have heard its utterance [divine words], felt its power, and are answering to its call." Adherence to the Confession protects the church from errors, promotes a shared understanding of the truth, and provides "security that those who are to become their teachers in future generations shall continue to teach the same divine and saving truths."[31]

To standardize worship practices, the Westminster divines attempted to establish a shared Psalter, as true as possible to Scripture. The *Scottish Psalter*, with many competing versions, had been in common use for more than eighty years. In 1645, the Westminster Assembly endorsed with suggested alterations a new metrical version by Francis Rous (1579–1659), published in 1643.[32] In a metrical Psalter, all the psalms are phrased to match an 8-6-8-6 count called "Common Meter." This metrical construction matches many common, easy-to-learn melodies such as "Amazing Grace," enabling the singing of any psalm during personal or family devotionals or in public worship without the need for musical instruments. The Puritans and the Scottish Presbyterians adhered to Calvin's "regulative" principle of worship that precluded the use in worship of any form or device not expressly commanded in Scripture:

> Levites, under the law, were justified in making use of instrumental music in the worship of God; it having been his will to train his people, while they were yet tender and like children, by such rudiments until the coming of Christ. But now, when the clear light of the gospel has dissipated the shadows of the law, and taught us that God is to be served in a simpler form. It would be to act a foolish and mistaken part to imitate that which the prophets enjoined only upon those of his own time.[33]

After reviewing it for conformity to Scripture in 1647, the Scottish General Assembly decided that the Psalter needed substantial revisions. The assembly assigned the task of revising the Psalter to various committees, assigning John Nevay the task of revising the last thirty psalms. The assembly approved the resultant revised *Scottish Metrical Psalter* in 1650 for use in all congregations

Church Government: The majority of the Puritans favored the Presbyterian system and began implementing it when prelacy collapsed (early 1640s). Other factions represented at the assembly include the Independents, who believed that church government was a congregational matter, and the Erastians, who believed that discipline of the church was a civil matter. Both of these latter parties had strong supporters in Parliament, but they only accounted for a small fraction of the divines. Not represented were the numerous sects, called Sectarians, which had taken root under the bishops' lax biblical teaching and church discipline.[34]

Although the divines hotly debated the issue of church government, the political intrigues of the Independents and Erastian members prevented its settlement. Without agreement on church government, the Scots could never achieve the unity they so desperately sought. The civil authorities repeatedly urged the Westminster Assembly to settle this matter because the collapse of prelacy left no established system of church government. Consequently, no formal process for ordaining new ministers, disciplining members, or settling religious differences existed in England. Under these conditions, the sects proliferated like weeds.

The outnumbered Independents dragged out the debate by acknowledging no authority above the congregation to ordain ministers and settle matters of discipline. The Independents assumed that church members were all highly qualified Christians because they admitted only "true saints"; however, such purity is impossible to maintain without discipline. The Independents argued that periodic synods could perform the work of presbyteries, but they were unwilling to grant these synods any power or authority over congregations. They further ignored the weight of Scripture that clearly shows the presence of multiple elders in each particular church.[35] Without presbyteries, the form of government proposed by the Independents lacked a standing ecclesiastical government, essential for the maintenance of doctrinal purity and church unity. Rather than rely upon the organs of the church for discipline, the Independents relied upon the civil magistrate. They argued that all churches could be governed as well as Geneva "if the magistrate oversees them and keeps each to his duties."[36] Years later in New England, the weaknesses of this congregational system became evident as the civil authority assumed the role rightfully belonging to the church courts. Is it possible to trace the American distaste for Puritanism to the ungodly application of civil authority without a counterbalancing ecclesiastical authority? The real weakness of the approach of the Independents was the extraordinary emphasis on the individual member and congregation to the detriment of the church, the body of Christ.

The Erastians falsely believed "that the Jewish state and church were all one," and so they believed that England should follow this pattern. This position, the natural conclusion of a long English tradition where the king served as head of both church and state, had strong support in Parliament. The Erastians acknowledged that Christ was head of the church, but they believed that he "had delegated the power of jurisdiction to the Christian civil magistrate, defending that opinion by the analogy of the Jewish state and kings."[37] This view is in stark contrast to the Reformed view of the role of church and state. The reformers envisioned that the "two jurisdictions, civil and ecclesiastical, ought to be, and remain co-ordinate and distinct, mutually supporting and supported, but each abstaining from interference with the others intrinsic and inherent rights, privileges, and powers." George Gillespie masterfully proved that the Jewish church and state adhered to these principles.[38]

Despite pressure from an Erastian Parliament, the assembly concluded, "The Lord Jesus, as king and head of his church, hath therein appointed a government, in the hand of church Officers, distinct from the civil magistrate."[39] However, the assembly's resultant standard, the *Form of Presbyterian Church Government*, addressed only the broad principles of Presbyterianism and did not address discipline. This failure would hobble Presbyterian church government in England and later in America. Parliament reluctantly issued an ordinance to erect presbyteries in 1646, but they imposed substantial obstacles to retard implementation.

Toleration: In Knox's day, Christian liberty meant the freedom to hold beliefs consistent with the Word of God. Today, Christian liberty to many Christians means freedom from the Word. This unbounded toleration is the antithesis of unity and true Christian liberty. If modern man is ever to achieve true Christian unity, there must be some limit to toleration. Satan successfully used this unbounded toleration, demanded by the Sectarians of that era, as the tool to undermine the effectiveness of the Westminster Assembly. George Gillespie concluded his treatise on Christian Liberty with a plea for accommodation (to the extent allowed by the Word of God), not toleration. Gillespie earnestly desired a unified, biblically based church:

> Do not, O do not involve yourselves in the plea of toleration with the Separatist and the Anabaptist.... If you be the sons of peace, you shall be characterized by the shibboleth; you will call for accommodation, not for toleration.... Alas how shall our divisions and contentions hinder the preaching and learning of Christ, and the edifying one another in Love...! There is but one Christ, yea the head and the body make one Christ, so that you cannot divide the body without dividing Christ.... O brethren, we shall find one heaven, let us pack up our differences in this place of our pilgrimage, the best way we can. Nay, we will not despair of unity in this world. Hath not God promised to give us one heart and one way...? Hath not the Mediator prayed that all his may be one?

Brethren, it is not impossible, pray for it, press hard toward the mark of accommodation. How much better it that you be one with the other Reformed churches, though somewhat strained and bound up, then be divided through at full liberty and elbowroom.[40]

To Gillespie, the Word of God is the only rational basis for Christian liberty. This means that when a church, even the most reformed church, finds something in its doctrine or worship inconsistent with Scripture, it must conform to Scripture. John Knox actually wrote such a commitment into the *Scottish Confession of 1560.*[41] This commitment is implicit in the *Westminster Confession of Faith's* description of true Christian liberty: "God alone is Lord of the conscience, and hath left it free from the doctrines and commandments of men which are in any thing contrary to his Word, or beside it, in matters of faith or worship." Therefore, any creed or church confession based on Scripture should not be a threat to Christian liberty. William Hetherington (1803–1865) contended that Scripture requires the suppression of "certain forms of errors—as of idolatry and blasphemy; but gives no authority to man to punish errors of the mind, so far as these amount not to violations of known and equitable laws, and disturb not the peace of society."[42]

English Civil War (1644–1649)

There is no doubt that the presence of a Scottish army of twenty thousand men in northern England provided the courage that Parliament needed for the changes that led to the Westminster Assembly. However, at the zenith of the Presbyterian ascendancy, the forces of disunity began to appear. Some of the Scottish nobles, under the leadership of the Marquis of Montrose (1612–1650), secretly banded together to prevent the total usurpation of the king's authority by joining forces against the supporters of the covenant, which they considered "traitorous and damnable."[43] During September 1644, Montrose appeared at Perthshire "at the head of an army comprised of Highlanders and Irishmen, with a charge "to kill and pardon none." This army terrorized the countryside; visited Aberdeen with a "horrible scene of carnage, lust, and rapine"; massacred "six thousand trembling fugitives at the battle of Kilsyth"; and left in its wake the "threefold scourge of war, famine, and pestilence."[44]

Meanwhile in England, an army of Bible-carrying, psalm-singing Puritans called the "New Model" army defeated the king's forces at the Battle of Naseby in June 1645. The New Model army was under the leadership of Oliver Cromwell (1599–1658) and under the spiritual influence of Sectarian- and Independent-lay ministers. Cromwell was not a Covenanter, but he certainly was a Calvinist. A characteristic of his troops was an "austere morality and fear of God, which prevailed all ranks."[45] Cromwell's success made it possible for a portion of the Scottish army in England, under the command of General Alexander Leslie, to return to Scotland and defeat Montrose at the battle of Philiphaugh in September 1645. These battles destroyed Charles's hope for a military victory. After another lost battle the following year, Charles surrendered to the Scots and expressed his readiness "to be instructed concerning the Presbyterian government."[46]

After the battle of Philiphaugh, Scottish troops allegedly slaughtered three hundred Irish camp followers and fifty Irish soldiers that had been granted quarter. Parliament, meeting later that year, absolved the Scots of this crime by authorizing the death of all "Irish prisoners taken at and after Philiphaugh."[47] Parliament documents outline the reasoning for this action: "If this defense of quarter be sustained, then the whole nation, especially the Estates of Parliament, does violate the oath of the Covenant, and the oath of the Parliament anent the prosecuting and censuring of malignants, opposers of the covenant."[48]

In May 1647, Scottish troops killed 259 Irish soldiers, captured at an outpost called Dunavertie. Sir James Turner (1615–1686) accused John Nevay of urging the military leader, General Leslie, to slaughter the prisoners to avoid the "curses [that] befell Saul, for sparing the Amalekites."[49] However, before we pass judgment, let us consider the facts. First, the prisoners had not been granted quarter (in fact, they had refused an offer of quarter). Second, just five months earlier, in response to public outcry against Montrose's excesses, Parliament had ordained the killing of "Irish prisoners taken at or after Philiphaugh…, to be executed without any assize or process."[50] Third, the Irish invaders had been responsible for unspeakable horrors. In particular, the defenders were MacDonalds who had engaged in clan vengeance against their archenemy, the Campbells, and who had refused to disband as requested by the king after Montrose's defeat.[51] Fourth, Sir James Turner would later become an infamous, cold-hearted persecutor of Presbyterians (as we will soon see) and likely exaggerated the facts. Finally, I offer as evidence the Christian witness provided by Nevay's flock, recounted in the remainder of this book, as they faced decades of persecution during the reign of Charles II.

As in any civil war, families fought on both sides. For every Nisbet who defended the covenants, another opposed them. For example, Sir Alexander Nisbet, a distant relative of John Nisbet, opposed the Covenanters and suffered mightily in defense of the king. During the English civil wars, he lost three of his sons and his castle, which had been in his family for five centuries. One of his sons, also named John Nisbet (d. 1664), fled to England.[52]

With the king's power overthrown, the Independent-dominated army under the leadership of Cromwell struggled for ascendancy with the Presbyterian-dominated Parliament, which had enabled the Westminster Assembly. The army settled the matter by marching on London with the expressed intent of setting up a new government. It gained possession of King Charles, charged eleven of the Presbyterian leaders of Parliament with treason, causing them to flee, and overcame the determined but disorganized defense of the citizens of London. Although Charles later escaped to "virtual imprisonment" on the Isle of Wright and the Presbyterians still maintained a majority in Parliament, Cromwell's troops were in control.[53]

To regain power, the Scottish Royalists, under the command of the Duke of Hamilton, entered an "Engagement" with the king that led to an invasion of England by the Scottish Army. In this Engagement, the Scots agreed to restore Charles to the throne if he would establish the Presbyterian system in England for three years and "suppress the independent Christian sects whose influence was paramount in the Roundhead army."[54] The majority of the Scottish ministers and General Assembly were opposed to this Engagement because it did not require that Charles adhere to the covenants. Lord Loudoun originally supported the Engagement, but he withdrew his support when he learned that the church was against the Engagement. A force of two thousand Covenanters, including John Nevay (and possibly John Nisbet), from the Western Lowlands took up arms in defense of the covenants to stop the Engagers from entering England and assisting King Charles. These brave troops took communion with swords in hand before fighting the much larger army of Engagers. The Engagers easily routed Nevay and his hopelessly outnumbered associates. The Engagers then marched into England where Cromwell easily defeated them.[55]

Parliament exonerated Nevay and his associates and passed a law (the *Act of Classes*) precluding Engagers from holding office for several years. Since this act excluded many of the Scottish nobles from office for several years, the "kirk party," a group of lesser nobles and landowners, under the strong influence of the kirk, led Parliament. During this short period, Parliament abolished patronage (the right of nobles to select ministers) and passed measures to aid the poor. Consequently, the nobles increasingly dissociated themselves from the Presbyterian cause.[56]

Meanwhile, in England Cromwell consolidated his power by throwing forty Presbyterian members of Parliament into prison and excluding the other 160. The remaining sixty members of Parliament, known as the *Rump Parliament*, were strongly sectarian. Fearful that King Charles would regain power, the Sectarian-dominated army executed King Charles on January 30, 1649, for the crime of treason, leaving Oliver Cromwell and the Sectarian-dominated Parliament firmly in control.[57]

The People Want a King (1649–1651)

The Scottish Parliament, having no part in Charles's execution, considered the execution a mockery of the covenants and of Scotland's sovereignty. They declared Charles II, the Prince of Wales, the lawful successor on the condition that he subscribe and faithfully execute the covenants.[58] Both the Scottish government and the kirk sent commissioners to obtain Charles's assurance that he would fulfill the terms of the covenants, and that he would introduce neither prelates nor irreligious advisors into the affairs of Scotland. Charles, in an attempt to avoid these demands, authorized Montrose to invade Scotland; however, the Covenanters destroyed Montrose's small invasion force and executed Montrose. As a last resort, in a nefarious act of duplicity, Charles swore to uphold the covenant in order to use the Scottish people to his political advantage. The warning signs were evident—one of the commissioners observed, "In Charles Stuart, they carried the plague of God to Scotland."[59] As one of the commissioners put the pen in Charles's hand, he warned him to be "satisfied in his soul and conscience, beyond all hesitation, of the righteousness of the declaration" before signing the covenants. Charles assured him of his sincerity.

Shortly thereafter, Charles violated one of these promises by selecting many avowed enemies of the Presbyterian cause as advisors. The Scots referred to such men as *malignants*, defined by George Gillespie as "the seed of the serpent—enemies to piety and the Presbyterian government—a generation that have not set God before them."[60] Illustrative of such men is Thomas Hobbes (1588–1679), Charles's tutor. Hobbes, in his book the *Leviathan*, insisted that not only is the king the absolute sovereign in all civil matters, but also he is the "supreme pastor," the source of all ecclesiastical power. According to this theory, it is not proper to divide the king's powers or to subject the king to civil laws or to church censures. Hobbes taught that citizens may not hold private opinions on matters inconsistent with the civil law, disobey the civil law for reasons of conscience, depend on supernatural assistance for faith and sanctity, and may not insist on absolute propriety over their goods. Hobbes considered those who did as enemies of the state, the only judge of right and wrong. A covenant to Hobbes and to his pupil Charles was only binding on the people.[61] Is it any wonder that a deep rift developed within Scotland between those who supported Charles and most of the Lowland ministers who considered the malignants just that? It is astonishing, moreover, that Hobbes is lauded as one of the fathers of liberal thought while the Covenanters, who gave their lives to defend the church and society from such tyranny, are labeled as radicals and rarely mentioned in textbooks.

In response to the direct threat posed by Charles, Cromwell prepared to attack the Scots. In an attempt to avoid conflict, Cromwell questioned the Scots concerning their covenant with Charles: "Is it therefore infallibly agreeable to the Word of God, all that you say? I beseech you, in the bowels of Christ, think it possible you may be mistaken."[62]

The Scots, likewise, prepared for war, going to great lengths to purge their army of malignants. Although weakened by purges, the Scottish Army soon trapped Cromwell within a ring of hills surrounding Dunbar. Nevertheless, Cromwell routed the Scots in September 1650 when the Scots, in an act of impatience, moved down from the hills. After routing the Covenanters, Cromwell paused long enough for his troops to praise God for the victory. He chose Psalm 117, the shortest, for the occasion in order to resume the attack as soon as possible.

This setback was the cause for great alarm in Scotland. Rutherford and others warned the nation and King Charles to repent. The Covenanters of southwest Scotland increasingly dissociated themselves from Charles and many fell under Cromwell's control as he occupied this portion of the country in late 1650. Many perceived Cromwell and the Sectarians the lesser of two evils. Despite the military setbacks and the ample evidence of Charles's insincerity, the Scots not under Cromwell's control crowned Charles II as king in January 1651. The text selected for the ceremony expresses the expectation of the people:[63]

And he brought forth the king's son, and put the crown upon him, and gave him the testimony; and they made him king, and anointed him; and they clapped their hands, and said, God save the king ... And Jehoiada made a covenant between the LORD, the

king, and the people, that they should be the LORD'S people; between the king also and
the people (2 Kings 11:12, 17).

Before taking the oath, the minister again warned the king of the seriousness of the covenant obligations. Unaffected, Charles read the *National Covenant and the Solemn League* and swore, "By the Eternal and Almighty God, who liveth and reigneth for ever, I shall observe and keep all that is contained within this oath."[64] The Lord Argyle (1607–1661), much to his later regret, placed the crown on Charles's head. As proof of his fallibility, Lord Loudoun was there as well.

War of the Presbyteries (1651–1660)

On the verge of military defeat, the Scottish Parliament, at the urging of King Charles and Royalists removed restrictions that precluded the Engagers from civil and military service. Parliament also received resolutions form the Scottish General Assembly urging that any permitted to receive communion be permitted to hold military or government office. This left the doors open for many malignants and Engagers to obtain high posts in the government upon feigned repentance. For example, Sir James Turner confessed in his *Memoirs* that many, at the urging of the king, gained high office after disowning the Engagement by "deceitfully speaking against the dictates of our own consciences and judgments."[65]

Many of the Scots in the southern and western shires, including John Nisbet and his pastor John Nevay, protested these resolutions. These "Protestors," under the leadership of James Guthrie (d. 1661), were suspicious of Charles from the beginning. They believed that these resolutions were in violation of the fourth article of the *Solemn League and Covenant,* and that they would lead to an end of the Covenanted Reformation and to God's wrath as malignants gained power.[66] Those who supported the resolutions, called "Resolutioners," wanted to heal the split caused by the Engagement and to provide the necessary military leadership to thwart Cromwell's troops from overrunning their country. The public mood had swung in support of the Resolutioners because many blamed the purges of suspected malignants for the defeat at Dunbar. This change in national sentiment coupled with the partial enemy occupation led to a General Assembly meeting in 1651 with a strong Resolutioner majority. The Resolutioners took advantage of the situation by deposing Guthrie and several leading Protestors. The net result was the first schism within the ranks of the Presbyterians since the Reformation.

Even worse, the many malignants allowed to power would later aid Charles in persecuting the Presbyterian cause.[67]

In September 1651, Cromwell decisively defeated the Scots at Worchester, forcing Charles to flee to France. This was a crushing blow to the Covenanters. Their covenant with England and their hope for a universal covenanted reformation lay shattered. S. A. Burrell (b. 1912) summarizes the historical significance, "Thenceforth the Covenanting tradition would turn in upon itself, and become part of the heritage of a single nation, its claims to universality all but forgotten."[68] The Scots were defeated not only militarily but also spiritually insomuch as the root of bitterness had poisoned any hope of reconciliation between the Resolutioners and Protestors.

With their Scottish allies defeated, it was not long until the demise of the Presbyterian dominated Parliament in England. In 1653, Cromwell dissolved Parliament and declared himself Lord Protector. In Scotland, he promoted religious toleration for all but Catholics, allowed limited toleration for Episcopalians, and opened Scottish pulpits to Sectarian ministers. The Scottish Presbyterian split widened as the Protestors and Resolutioners met in separate General Assemblies. Cromwell eventually dissolved the Assemblies but allowed presbyteries to continue to meet. Although the cause for division no longer existed, all efforts to heal the breach failed. Unity would have required that the Protestors forbear venting some truths for the peace of church. For the Protestors, who considered it necessary to vent some truth for the peace of the church, this was not possible. On the surface, the truth in question was the validity of the *Solemn League and Covenant*, for which the Protestors still contended. However, the real issue was the Presbyterian form of government as evidenced by the Resolutioners' criticism, one of many, of the Protestors for allowing elders to pray in public meetings.[69] Presbyterian ministers such as James Durham (1622–1658), respected by both sides, made repeated attempts to reconcile differences to no avail. Durham was so distressed at his failure that, shortly before his death, he wrote *A Treatise Concerning Scandal* in which he addressed the age-old nemesis of the church, the conflict between truth and unity. Durham considered division a great evil: "Sure there is no evil doth more suddenly and inevitably overturn the church than this; which makes her fight against herself, and eat her own flesh, and tear her own bowels: for, that a kingdom divided against itself cannot stand."[70]

Despite division, reformation blossomed during Cromwell's reign, particularly in the south and west of Scotland, as Kirkton observed:

Every parish had a minister, every village had a school, every family almost had a Bible, yea, in most of the country all the children of age
could read the Scriptures.… Every minister was a very full professor of
the Reformed religion, according to the large confession of faith framed
at Westminster.… None of them might be scandalous in their conversation, or negligent in their office, so long as a presbytery stood.… I have
lived many years in a parish where I never heard an oath.… Also, you
could not, for a great part of the country, have lodged in a family where
the Lord was not worshipped by reading, singing, and public prayer.[71]

In September 1658, Oliver Cromwell died. When Cromwell's son
proved unable to fill his father's shoes, General Monk (1608–1670), who
had led Scotland under Cromwell's thumb, took command via military
force in early 1660. He established a Parliament favorable to the Presbyterian cause, which approved the *Westminster Confession of Faith*, and ordered the *Solemn League and Covenant* reprinted and read annually in all
churches.[72] Unfortunately, this success was short lived.

Restoration of Charles II (1660–1661)

On May 1660, the misguided efforts of the Resolutioners in Scotland,
the supporters of prelacy in England, and the nobles in both lands
restored Charles II to power. With Charles's restoration, the people
abandoned the Puritan dream of godly government as they joyously cast
aside what they considered to be the "pettiness and tyranny" of Puritanism. Puritanism ceased to exist as national influence. With Charles came
national leaders whom one observer of the king's court called "the most
profane, swearing fellows that ever I heard in my life."[73] Within eighteen
months of gaining power, Charles restored the Episcopacy, abolished for
over a decade in all three kingdoms, as the religion of the land. When
one of the Scottish leaders recommended the Presbyterian form of
church government, Charles replied, "Let that go, for it was not a religion for a gentleman." At Charles's urging, his Cavalier Parliament dis-
mantled all the constitutional reforms of the previous two decades and
ordered the public burning of the covenants.[74] Through a series of acts
known as the Clarendon Code, any worship other than that sanctioned
by the Church of England was prohibited with severe penalties.

In Scotland, Charles lulled Presbyterians into a false sense of security
by promising "to protect and preserve the government of the Church of
Scotland, as it is settled by law, without violation."[75] In early 1661, hopes
quickly vanished when the servile Scottish Parliament passed the *Act of*

Supremacy, which established the king as supreme judge in all matters civil and ecclesiastical, and passed the *Act Rescissory*, which made owning the covenants unlawful. These acts undid all the works of Reformation from 1638 to 1650 and made it high treason to acknowledge Jesus Christ as head of the church. The few faithful Presbyterians at the vote for the *Act of Supremacy* tried to add the word "civil" to qualify "supreme authority." So-called reasonable men assured them that this did not imply authority over the church. By gradual steps and Trojan words, the king subverted law and destroyed freedom.[76]

Charles's appointment of leading Resolutioners to positions of authority further divided the feuding Protestors and the Resolutioners. There is no doubt that a united church, such as that in 1638, would have persevered. Consequently, the blame for the persecution to come rests partly on those on both sides who refused to listen to Durham's warnings about schism and division. Nevertheless, the greater blame rests on the Resolutioners for choosing man's way over God's way.

After setting up a corrupt puppet government in Scotland, referred to as the "Drunken Parliament," Charles next had the leading opposition leaders executed. The Marquis of Argyle, the first executed, commented at his sentencing, "I had the honor to set the crown upon the king's head, and now he hastens me to a better crown than his own!" Before his execution, he warned those gathered that in the coming times they would have to choose between sin and suffering. He concluded his warning by pointing out that those who choose sin will face eternal suffering: "When I shall be singing, they shall be howling."[77]

Next executed was James Guthrie, a leading Protester who a decade earlier had warned Scotland about Charles II. The court condemned Guthrie's children to a life as beggars and reversed his coat of arms. Shortly before his execution, Guthrie lifted his son to his knee, saying, "Willie, the day will come when they cast up to you that your father was hanged, be not thou ashamed, lad. It is in a good cause."[78] Much of his testimony on the scaffold would apply today. He warned the country that they had "changed the glory of the incorruptible God into the image of a corruptible man, in whom they placed all their salvation." He then gave three reasons for God's wrath on Scotland, namely: (1) by that deluge of profanity that overflows all the land, (2) by that horrible treachery and perjury that are in the matters of the covenant and the cause of God; and (3) by our horrible ingratitude. Following his execution, they placed his head over one of the city gates where it, as he predicted during his trial, "would preach more ... than ever in the pulpit."[79]

In August 1661, Charles declared his intention to the Scottish Council: "We declare our firm resolution to interpose our royal authority for restoring the Church of Scotland to its right government by bishops, as it was before the late troubles." Shortly thereafter, Charles disbanded presbyteries and installed bishops. One of the first appointed to the office of bishop was James Sharp (1618–1679), a self-serving minister whose sole purpose was the pursuit of power. Sharp, a leading Resolutioner, had played an instrumental role in lulling Scotland into a false sense of security, enabling Charles to gain power. To veil his ambitions, Sharp offered the office of archbishop to the highly respected Presbyterian minister, Robert Douglas (1594–1674). Douglas refused and rebuked Sharp: "I perceive you are clear—I see you will engage—you will be Archbishop of St. Andrews: take it then—and the curse of God with it." During Sharp's installation to this office, the English bishops first degraded Sharp from his Presbyterian office.[80]

Before we return to the account of events in Scotland, it is illustrative to ponder, "Why did Presbyterianism never take hold in England?" The truth is that at the beginning of the English Civil War, according to the philosopher Thomas Hobbes, "almost all" of the citizens of London and "the greater part of all other cities and market towns of England" were devoted to Presbyterianism.[81] This devotion grew into ten presbyteries in London alone by the time Cromwell disbanded the Long Parliament, which was representative of the people and strongly Presbyterian. During his reign, however, Cromwell systematically replaced with Sectarians all the Presbyterian ministers who refused to take an oath of allegiance. The Sectarian Parliament further eroded the power of presbyteries in 1654 by establishing a council of ministers to ordain all ministers and by appointing commissioners with power to eject scandalous ministers, leaving no essential function in the control of presbyteries. King Charles II completed the destruction of Presbyterianism in England by forcing nearly two thousand Presbyterian and Puritan ministers out of office for refusing to embrace prelacy.[82] With this single stroke, Charles decapitated both Puritanism and Presbyterianism. Neither ever recovered. It is true, however, that a sinful England rejoiced at their demise. As we will see, the Scottish Presbyterians suffered a similar fate.

John Nisbet

Somewhere between 1648 and 1650, John Nisbet returned from military service on the continent and settled down to life as a farmer at

Hardhill, near Newmilns. It is likely that he served with Scottish troops who fought in the Thirty Years' War. This war, which ended in 1648, resulted in religious tolerance in Germany and enabled other European countries to select their own religion. During this thirty-year period, all Europe was engaged in a war of religion so severe that in Germany alone the war destroyed two-thirds of the population. Historians agree that many Scots like John Nisbet sought military service abroad during this era, but they disagree about the motives of these men. It is without doubt that many Scots sought fame and fortune abroad considering there were limited opportunities at home. Sir Walter Scott (1771–1832) attributes their motivation to "the national disposition [of Scots] to wandering and adventure."[83] Alternatively, because religion during these years was a matter of life or death, the Scots may simply have aided other Christians in defense of religion.

John Nisbet, "a close adherer" to the principles of the Protestors,[84] records, years later in his dying testimony, his great concern regarding the sinful courses of the Resolutioners. History proved him right.

> Now, my dear friends in Christ, I have always, since the public Resolutioners were for bringing in the malignants and their interest, thought it my duty to join with the Lord's people in witnessing against these sinful courses, and now we see clearly that it has ended in nothing less than making us captives that we may return to Egypt by the open doors that are made wide to bring in popery, and set up idolatry in the Lord's covenanted land, to defile it, and thereby to provoke him to pour down his fierce wrath upon it and the inhabitants thereof.[85]

These trying times profoundly influenced John Nisbet's life:

> John, after he was married, lived Christianly and comfortably with his wife and family, until the year 1661, when King Charles and his underlings overthrew the glorious and ever famous work of Reformation. [John] conceived such dislike of them and their wicked proceeding … [after] they burnt the covenant, he would neither cut his beard nor countenance them in the least, but witnessed against them on all occasions in his place and station.[86]

Today a few stones mark John's hilltop home. The living stones who once dwelled there and in the valley below were about to undergo the great fury of the antichrist's wrath. At stake in the coming battle was none other than the religious future of the English-speaking world.

3

The Burning Bush

Behold, the bush burned with fire, and the bush was not consumed.
–Motto of the Church of Scotland (Exod. 3:2b)

The Outing (1662)

In the middle of the harsh winter of 1662, the puppet Scottish government forced, at the urging of King Charles, all ministers who would not acknowledge the authority of bishops to resign. Consequently, approximately three hundred faithful Scottish Presbyterian ministers, over one-third of the ministers of Scotland, were forced from office. Each minister had to decide between standing for principles and staying with his flock to guard against greater corruption of the church. The majority of those who left were Protestors; thus, Charles and his allies swept the church clean of those who would take a stand at the boundary line of God's Word rather than the natural line of human expediency.[1] This was an immense loss for the church. Bishop Burnet, an opponent of Presbyterianism, described the able preaching of the Protestors as so effective that even servants were able to pray extemporaneously. To add insult to injury, the able and beloved Presbyterian ministers were replaced with Episcopal curates whom Bishop Burnet described as "the worst preachers [he] ever heard; they were ignorant to a reproach; and many of them were openly vicious."[2]

Especially hard hit was the town of Newmilns. Their faithful pastor John Nevay was banished for refusing to take the oath. He moved to Holland where he continued to support the cause and uphold the faithful in prayers and letters. Surviving to this day are some of his sermons, which are examined later in this book.

Other towns suffered similar fates. One sad parting occurred when John Knox's grandson John Welsh (d. 1681) bid farewell by a riverside to his congregation. As he rode away, his congregation followed him for a long distance "with bitter weeping and lamentation."[3] In another town, Reverend John Blackader (1622–1685) prepared his flock by contrasting the Presbyterian and the Episcopalian form of church government that would take its place. The approach of dragoons, intent on his arrest, interrupted his farewell address. He calmly closed the sermon and retired to the manse. The troops, thinking he had fled, took the names of those attending the church because it was a finable offense not to attend one's own church. After the soldiers left, he finished his sermon with the following charge to his sobbing congregation:

> Go and fend for yourselves: the hour is come when the shepherd is smitten, and the flock shall be scattered…. When the faithful pastors are removed, hirelings shall intrude, whom the Great Shepherd never sent, who will devour the flock, and tread down the residue with their feet. As for me, I have done my duty, and now there is no time to evade. I recommend you to Him who is able to keep you from falling, and am ready, through grace, to be disposed of as the Lord pleases.[4]

John Wilson (1804–1835) provides a graphic, handed-down, historical re-creation of the "Outing" of one prominent minister, Alexander Peden. The account describes how a large psalm-singing crowd had gathered to hear Peden's last message. After preaching from noon to dusk from a raised tent prepared for the occasion, Peden concluded his sermon with a warning by calling the congregation's attention to a hawk chasing a sparrow overhead:

> I'll tell ye what, my friends—the twosome did not drift down this way from that dark cloud and along that bleak heathery side of a hill for nothing. They were sent; they were commissioned; and if ye had arisen to your feet [as] they passed and cried, "Shue!" ye could not have frightened them out of their mission. They came to testify of a persecuted remnant and of a cruel pursuing foe—of a kirk which will soon have to betake herself like a bird to the mountains, and of an enemy which will not allow her to rest by night nor by day…. I have a request to make before we separate this night, never in this place to meet again. (Hereupon the sobbing and the bursting forth of hitherto suppressed sorrow were almost universal.) Ye men all stand upon your feet and lift up your hands and swear, before the great Head and Master of the Presbyterian Kirk of Scotland…, that till an independent Presbyterian minister ascend the pulpit, you will never enter the door of that kirk manse; and let this be the solemn league and covenant betwixt you and me, and betwixt my God and your God, in all time coming! Amen! —So let it be!

In this standing position, which we had thus almost insensibly assumed, the last prayer or benediction was heard, and the concluding
psalm was sung:

> For he in his pavilion shall—me hide in evil days;
> In secret of his tent me hide—and on a rock me raise. –Ps. 27:5[5]

I never listened to a sound or beheld a spectacle more overpowering.
The night-cloud had come down the hill above us—the sun had set. It
was twilight; and the united and full swing of the voice of praise ascended through the veil of evening, from the thousands of lips, even to
the gate of heaven.

As the singing concluded, Peden locked and sealed the church door
with the warning, "I attest thee in my Master's name that none ever enter by thee save those who enter by the door of presbytery."[6]

The Illegal Monster (1663–1666)

A lexander Shields accused Charles of having initiated the "greatest
revolt from, and rebellion against God, that ever could be recorded
in any age or generation." The scandalous moral example of King
Charles and his court coupled with the removal of the Presbyterian ministers in England and Scotland led to a general lowering of the moral
standards and a sense that God's judgment was at hand. The visitation
of the great plague in 1665 and the great London fire in 1666 height-
ened the sense of doom.[7] Yet, these horrors pale in comparison to the
evil monster let loose in Scotland to devour Presbyterians with dreadful
effectiveness.

In obedience to God's Word, the Covenanters refused to conform
and sought to worship under their "outed" ministers at every opportunity. In obedience to their call, the ministers opened their homes for
worship services or held services in open fields (coventicles). In obedience to civil laws, the civil magistrates punished those who attended
these services. Enraged by this visible affront to their authority, the prelates encouraged the magistrates to engage the full force of tyranny to
stop this practice. The tyranny took the form of a standing army under
the leadership of the penultimate mercenary James Turner to enforce
order at the expense of the citizenry. Turner, whom Defoe labeled as a
butcher, had fought for most of the powers in Europe, including the
Covenanters in earlier years.[8] The common people nicknamed him
"Byte-the-Sheep." Another equally vicious military persecutor of this period was Thomas Dalziel, described as "a strange looking man, with a

perfectly bald head, a long white beard, and (wearing) a single tight jerkin." To accelerate the persecution, Parliament established a Court of High Commission in 1664 with power to inflict any punishment short of death. Evidence indicates that no one ever escaped unscathed.[9]

Archbishop Sharp and his fellow bishops were guilty of this bloodshed inasmuch as they encouraged the excesses of Turner and Dalziel. The curates assisted by turning over names of those absent from church to the magistrate, the magistrate then quartering soldiers in the violator's home until they were impoverished. Those suspected of attending coventicles were required to take a "Jesuitically framed" oath that implied the king was head of the church. As these measures proved ineffective, the Scottish government imprisoned, banished, branded, or sold into slavery anyone caught at a coventicle or who assisted an "outed" minister.[10]

These excesses rendered Charles II universally unpopular in all three kingdoms. In a remark to a French ambassador, he professed his true religion: "No other creed matches so well with the absolute dignity of kings than Catholicism." Of these corrupt times it was alleged, "The bishops get all, the courtiers spend all, the citizens pay for all, the king neglects all, and the Devil takes all." To make matters worse, conflict with Holland resulted in great economic distress on Scotland since the Scots and the Dutch were strong trading partners. In fear of a Dutch and Scot alliance, Charles disarmed the Lowlands and taxed them to pay for their defense.[11] The disarming of citizens is tyranny's herald. A people without military power, according to Hobbes, have no legislative power.[12]

The field-preacher John Blackader frequently visited Newmilns to partake of the local mineral water, noted for its therapeutic value. Coventicles and baptisms would accompany each visit. John Nisbet and his family were active participants. When John Nisbet had one of his sons baptized by Blackader, the Episcopal curate of the area threatened to excommunicate him. Providentially, the curate died a few days before the planned excommunication.[13] The Covenanters considered no truth in Scripture unworthy of defense with their lives.

For his active role in coventicles, Blackader and his family found no peace. One night while he and his wife were away at a coventicle, soldiers found and pillaged their hideaway, greatly terrifying Blackader's children. One of Blackader's young sons managed to escape, but he found no neighbor willing to open his door during the night. The child finally found rest on top of the town cross. The next morning, a kind woman, noticing something white on top of the cross, discovered the sleeping child and exclaimed, "Jesus save us! What art thou?"[14]

These events forced Blackader's family to scatter, seeking shelter and food from any willing to risk imprisonment, for helping them was a crime. Wherever Blackader went, he found people hungry for the Word. In one town as he went for a walk, "he looked about to the fields, and saw the people gathered together from every [direction], in great multitudes—with which he was surprised and astonished, and saw the necessity laid upon him to make for the work."[15] Another account gives testimony to the evangelical character of his preaching:

> At one time, after having removed all impediments that might hinder sinners from embracing the terms of salvation offered in the gospel, he said at the conclusion, "I must enter my protestation in my Master's name against any here will not close with this offer, and give their consent." A woman cried out, "Hold your hand sir: do it not, for I give my consent."[16]

Located just a few miles across the river from Newmilns is the town of Fenwick. An able and world-renowned Presbyterian minister named William Guthrie, a cousin of James Guthrie, lived in Fenwick where he amazingly escaped eviction from his church for two years after the "Outing." It is almost certain that John Nisbet heard him preach on many occasions. Guthrie's book entitled *The Christian's Great Interest* was one of the most popular books in its day and is one of the classics of the Christian faith. John Owen (1616–1683) said of this book, "I have written several folios, but there is more divinity in it than in them all."[17] Only Guthrie's desire to reach the lost exceeded his great writing and preaching ability. Disguised as a traveler or a sportsman, Guthrie would visit those who did not attend church and invite them to church. On arrival at church, the families were surprised to find their newly found friend a preacher. So great was the general respect for Guthrie that he continued to preach until the archbishop suspended him in July 1664. Although Guthrie did not publicly preach in his church after his suspension, he continued his ministry until his death at age forty-five by leading his flock to hear a nearby minister.[18] We should all take a lesson from Guthrie's use of all legal means to bring sinners into the church and to look after the welfare of his flock. He did not rise up in arms or openly violate the civil law.

Another notable of this period bore the name John Nisbet, but this John Nisbet, called Lord Dirleton (1609–1687), served a different master. Dirleton's career started with great promise, in that he served as James Guthrie's lawyer in 1661. He soon found, however, that persecution of God's saints was more lucrative. Dirleton was such an able persecutor that he had acquired a large estate by 1663, and he acquired the position of lord-advocate by 1664. Burnet recorded that he was a man of great learning and integrity, but "he loved money too much."[19] Kirkton captured Dirleton's true motive, "For money might sometimes have hired Fletcher [Dirleton's predecessor] to spare blood, but Nisbet [Dirleton] was always so sore afraid of losing his own great estate." The Covenanter historian Robert Wodrow (1679–1734) captured the depth of Dirleton's depravity in the following account: On one occasion, Dirleton took the ring of a captured Covenanter who refused to reveal the hideouts of his fellow sufferers. Dirleton sent the ring to the man's wife with the message that her husband had cooperated with the prosecution and asked her to do likewise. The poor woman, taking the ring as proof of her husband's request, told the authorities everything they wanted to know. This resulted in great suffering among the brethren and the death of her husband, a short time thereafter.[20]

Satan was now in seemingly complete control of the earthly powers. A minister of that time, Hugh MacKail (1640–1666), referred to civil and ecclesiastical leaders of this era as a Pharaoh on the throne, a Haman in the state, and a Judas in the church. The publication *Naphtali* describes this combination as an "illegal monster" with Bishop Sharp as the head. *Naphtali*, written by Sir James Stewart (1635–1713) and Rev. James Stirling, provides a powerful indictment against the ungodly and unlawful persecution of the Covenanters.[21] In this publication and a later work, *Jus Populi Vindicatum*, Stewart argued that it is appropriate to rebel against unlawful, tyrannical authority, particularly when the actions of the tyrant are in violation of covenant commitments. Stewart contended that any rebellion would be a "rising for lawful authority" rather than "against lawful authority." In support of his position, Stewart cited Scripture and precedents from Scottish history where rebellion for these reasons (e.g., the uprising led by Knox in 1559, Henderson in 1638, and the Protestors in 1648) was later sanctioned by parliamentary bodies.[22]

Eventually the persecution became too great. To the honor of Christ, it was not until there was a complete collapse of the earthly institutions that Christian men rose up in arms, then only in self-defense.

In November 1666, four Covenanters captured four soldiers near Galloway to stop them from roasting an old man alive. Two hundred men promptly rose in defense of the Covenanters. They captured the local military leader, Sir James Turner, and marched toward Edinburgh to seek redress for the wrongs the government had committed against them. This act led to a popular uprising, and their ranks soon swelled to more than a thousand rebels, one being John Nisbet of Hardhill. They treated their prisoners well and elucidated them with a sermon in route, to which Turner jokingly replied, "It would be hard to turn a Turner." At Lanark, they re-swore the covenants and declared their rising as one of self-defense. On learning that Dalziel was approaching with an army to destroy them, they resolved to march all night in the cold and rain, hoping that others would come to their aid. The march was so severe that one half of their number dropped out along route. The next night near sunset, they reached the Pentland Hills where, as they set up their defense, they observed the approach of Dalziel's superior force. Although they repulsed several attacks, their outnumbered army was soon "enveloped in the embrace of a hideous boa-constrictor—tightening, closing, crushing every semblance of life from the victim enclosed in his coils." John Nisbet, having received seventeen wounds in this battle, managed to escape, but it took him a year to recover.[23]

James Nisbet begins his memoir with a description of the search for his father, John Nisbet:

> The first passage of divine providence that I record exercised towards me is, I was born in the month of February 1667, of parents both of them really and eminently religious. But the times were extremely unhappy, because of an illegal, tyrannical, prelatical persecution begun five years before, and keenly carried on by King Charles II, Middleton, and Lauderdale, and treacherous Bishop Sharp, and many other of their perfidious accomplices. Because of which, though my parents were persons of considerable worldly substance, yet they could not conveniently get the benefit of school education for their children; and so I got little or none, but what I acquired at my own hand when under my after hidings [during the persecution]. For, before I was born, my father and others, standing up in defense of the gospel, were attacked and routed by the enemy at Pentland Hills in 1666. Many were slain and my father received several wounds; but lying close among the dead till night, he, with great difficulty, got off with life. The enemy came to his house in search of him; but they missing him, they held a drawn sword to my mother's breast—who had me in her belly, threatening to run her through unless she would discover her husband. She, weeping, told them, that for anything she knew he was killed, for she had heard that it was so. They took what made for them in the house and went away for that time. But some days after, they, getting notice that he was still alive,

returned with greater fury than before, and threatened my mother with present death, first with a drawn sword at her breast, and also with a bended pistol. Contrary to all law divine and human, they dragged her alongst with them, with a burning candle in her hand, through all the rooms in the main house, and then through all the office-houses, they still raging at her, and threatening her with their drawn swords and bended pistols. But, after all their searchings they, missing my father, beat the servants to tell where my father was, and to strike the greater terror on my mother to tell where he was; but she neither would nor could. Then they took a young man, called David Findlay, away with them to where their chief commander was, called General Thomas Dalziel, who caused the said David Findlay to be shot to death. In less than half an hour's warning, [they carried] away all my father's stock of moveable effects, which was considerably great. For half a year after, there was seldom a day ever passed but they were at the house, either in the night or in the day, in search of my father; but the Lord still preserved him from their hands.[24]

The Burning Bush (1666–1678)

Persecution: After the battle of Pentland Hills, the persecution of the saints was severe. As earlier mentioned, one of the chief persecutors was John Nisbet of Dirleton. He, "determined that no one implicated in the ill-starred movement should escape the sorest penalties the law," tried and convicted many in their absence. Although it is illegal to do so, he, "appealing to Roman law, to the reason of the thing itself, to the practice of Parliament, and to the analogy found in those investigations into the conduct of a rebel which had followed the actual endurance of the death-penalty, browbeat the occupants of the bench into agreement."[25] Without God's law as society's foundation, liberty soon disappears.

One of the men captured after the battle of Pentland Hills was the minister Hugh MacKail, who soon learned firsthand the logic of Dirleton's reasoning. MacKail had marched with the Covenanters on the way to Pentland but had dropped out after falling ill. For refusing to confess to being at the battle, civil authorities tortured him with the boot, a device consisting of a metal frame and wedge to crush the victim's leg. At his trial, Dirleton would not accept MacKail's defense that he was not at the battle, arguing that simply keeping company with those in revolt for one-half hour was a capital crime. On hearing his death sentence, MacKail cheerfully praised God: "The Lord giveth life, and the Lord taketh, blessed be the name of the Lord." Upon return to his cell, a fellow prisoner asked Hugh about the condition of his leg. Hugh replied, "The fear of my neck now makes me forget my leg." The night before his execution, Hugh encouraged his fellow prisoners awaiting execution by advising them to overcome the gazing crowd and sight of the scaffold by "conceiving a deeper impression of a multitude of angels, always ready to serve and strengthen dying sinners." He urged them to focus on the representation of heaven as described in Revelation 21, and to hold forth their love to Christ, for in doing so was the only way to "apprehend the joys of heaven."[26] On the morning of his execution, he prayed:

> Now Lord, we come to thy throne, a place we have not been acquainted with. Earthly kings' thrones have advocates [e.g., Dirleton] against poor men, but thy throne has Jesus, an advocate for us. Our supplication this day is not to be free from death, but that we may witness before many witnesses a good confession.[27]

On the scaffold, he sang Psalm 31:1–5 and then read from Revelation 21. While awaiting his death, he spoke of seeing angels and melodiously prayed farewell to those in this life and a welcoming to God and Christ. He then left the tear-filled crowd behind as he swung on the rope.[28]

> Into thine hands I do commit–my sp'rit, for thou art he,
> O thou, Jehovah, God of truth–that hast redeemed me. –Ps. 31:5[29]

To punish those who refused to submit, General Dalziel and his soldiers descended on the western shires and committed numerous atrocities. These barbarities were so horrendous that even churches in the shire of Ayrshire began to fill.[30]

Coventicles: The Council established harsh penalties, including fines, banishment, or death to suppress coventicles in home or fields. Nevertheless, the coventicles flourished because the Covenanters conducted them in a peaceable and edifying manner. The participants "looked upon a coventicle much as the Israelites viewed the Tabernacle and Ark in the wilderness, as the presence of God." Evidencing the religious impact is the fact that "Covenanting districts were characteristically free from penal offences." Alexander Shields contended that once people tasted "the sweetness of the Lord's presence at their persecuted meetings," they "generally all reformed from their former immoralities … even robbers, thieves, and profane men." Shields contrasted the suffering encountered by the people with the unspeakable joy the coventicles provided: "I doubt if there ever were greater days of the Son of man upon the earth since the apostolic times.... [Or] ever a blacker night of darkness."[31]

The following is a first-hand account of one of these outdoor services, held at East Nisbet over a three-day period. The communion service took place in a grass-covered valley beside a waterway, and five ministers administered it: Welsh, Blackader, Dickson, Riddell, and Rae.

> We entered on the administration of the holy ordinance, committing it and ourselves to the invisible protection of the Lord of hosts, in whose name we were met together.... There was a solemnity in the place befitting the occasion, and elevating the whole soul to a pure and holy frame. The communion tables were spread on the green by the water, and around them the people had arranged themselves in decent order.... And truly the spectacle of so many grave, composed, and devout faces must have struck the adversaries with awe, and been more formidable than any outward ability of fierce looks and warlike array.... Though our vows were not offered within the courts of God's house, they wanted not sincerity of heart, which is better than the reverence of sanctuaries. Amidst the lonely mountains we remembered the words of our Lord, that true worship was not peculiar to Jerusalem or Samaria–that the beauty of holiness consisted not in consecrated buildings or material temples....
>
> The ordinance of the Last Supper, that memorial of his dying love till his second coming, was signally countenanced and backed with power and refreshing influence from above. Blessed be God, for he hath visited and confirmed his heritage when it was weary. In that day Zion put on the beauty of Sharon and Carmel, the mountains broke forth into singing, and the desert place was made to bud and blossom as the rose. Few such days were seen in the desolate Church of Scotland; and few will ever witness the like. There was a rich effusion of the Spirit shed abroad in many hearts; their souls, filled with heavenly transports, seemed to breathe in a diviner element, and to burn upwards as with the fire of a pure and holy devotion. The ministers were visibly assisted to speak home to the conscience of the hearers. It seemed as if God had touched their lips with a live coal from off his altar; for they who witnessed declared, they carried more like ambassadors from the court of heaven, than men cast in earthly mould.
>
> ...The communion was peaceably concluded, all the people heartily offering up their gratitude, and singing with a joyful voice to the Rock of their salvation. It was pleasant as the night fell to hear their melody swelling in full unison along the hill: the whole congregation joining with one accord, and praising God with the voice of Psalms.[32]

The Indulgence: The excessive cruelty proved too much for a civilized society to bear; consequently, the government sought new means of converting the Presbyterians into Anglicans. To lead this new strategy, the king appointed Lauderdale (1616–1682), a former Presbyterian described as a grotesque, vulgar, and fawning worldling, as the chief Commissioner in Scotland. Earlier, Lauderdale had been the leading noble in sponsoring the Engagement, which had been so destructive to Scottish unity. The keynote of the new strategy, devised by King Charles, was "to continue hunting down obdurate Covenanters while treating the mass of the people gently." The underlying intention was to divide and conquer. The first action was the passage of an act through Parliament that granted a pardon to participants of the Pentland uprising if they would promise not to rise in arms again, but the act excluded certain insurgents and those opposed to curates.[33]

In 1669, King Charles and Lauderdale initiated a strategy that proved ruinous to the Presbyterian cause. The Scottish Council passed an act granting a conditional Indulgence to Presbyterian ministers who would acknowledge the authority of bishops and the king over the church, agree to preach only within their bounds, and agree to be orderly (e.g., not to speak against the ecclesiastical and civil authorities). More than forty ministers, out of obligation to fulfill their commission to preach, accepted these conditions. Their acceptance created division within the ranks and weakened the position of the other ministers who opposed the Indulgence.[34] The purpose of these changes was not for "the sake of freedom of conscience itself but to separate the most moderate from the extremist in order to facilitate the destruction of the latter." Several attempts by the bishops to develop an amalgam of the Presbyterian and Episcopalian forms of government all ended in failure.[35]

In 1670, Charles entered a secret treaty with King Louis XIV of France, in which he affirmed "the truth of the Catholic religion and resolved to declare it and reconcile himself with the Church of Rome as soon as the welfare of his kingdom would permit." In addition, Charles promised to join with France in war against Holland in return for financial support for troops, which would reduce his dependence on Parliament. To cover up this deal, five members of his Privy Council, appropriately referred to as the Cabal (each letter represented one of the five— e.g., Lauderdale was "L"), signed a second secret (known only by a small inner circle) treaty implementing an Anglo-French alliance. Charles's wife, Louis's sister, referred to the conspiracy as "the design about R."[36]

The greatest hindrance to Charles's design was the determined faith of the Covenanters, whose destruction he sought with renewed zeal.

That same year, the Council pursued two major initiatives to drive the wedge deeper between the divided Presbyterians. One initiative was an attempt to convert the Presbyterians into Episcopalians. Burnet described the results when a group of six Episcopalian ministers journeyed into the countryside to appeal directly to the peasants:

> The people of the country came generally to hear us, though not in great crowds. We were indeed amazed to see a poor commonality so capable of arguing upon the points of government, and on the bounds to be set to the powers of princes, in matters of religion: Upon all these topics they had texts of Scripture at hand, and were ready with their answers to anything that was said to them. This measure of knowledge spread even among the meanest of them, their cottagers and their servants.[37]

The other initiative, the passage of a second Indulgence, allowed Indulged ministers freedom to form presbyteries but restricted their ministry to the narrow confines of their churches. The intent was to contain the Indulged much as one contains a fire in small pockets.[38] In general, the ministers in the northern and eastern shires universally accepted the Indulgence, but many in the southern and western shires refused to bend to the yoke of tyranny. In general, the Resolutioners accepted the Indulgence and the Protestors did not. Yet many Resolutioners (e.g., John Dickson) chose imprisonment instead.

Although the Indulgence resulted in divisions, the "zeal of the lovers of Christ was blazing" as long as they focused their attention on the true enemy. The more the true enemy tried to "extinguish it, the more it broke out and blazed into a flame." Their enemies did not extinguish the Covenanter's flame; they extinguished it themselves when they allowed defection and division to "divert their zeal [from] the enemies of God."[39] Conflicts grew into bitter divisions within the Presbyterian ranks, which remain unhealed to this day.

Defoe described how many ministers accepted the Indulgence "in order to preserve the privilege of exercising their ministry and preaching the gospel to the people." More telling is the people's response:

> But the persecuted people, whose zeal commanded them not to do the least evil to reap the greatest benefit, began to protest against this compliance of their brethren as wicked and detestable, declaring not only against the indulgence itself, but [also] against all those who submitted to

it, as guilty of yielding to the power of the prelate's homologating the supremacy, forsaking their principles, and breaking the covenant.[40]

From the viewpoint of the persecutors, rejection of the Indulgence was rejection of lawful government; hence, the persecutors felt justified in hunting down those who refused it as enemies of the state. Recalcitrant Presbyterians took on the derisive label of "Whigs."[*] To suppress coventicles, the government impoverished or evicted attendees, executed or intercommuned[†] ministers, and attempted to fine heritors [estate owners] whose tenants engaged in coventicles. The Earl of Loudoun[‡] and most of the heritors of Ayrshire refused to pay these penalties, but they did promise that they and their servants would not engage in coventicles. As a further repressive measure, the government imposed a tax called the cess to "levy and maintain forces for suppressing and dispersing meetings of the Lord's people."[41] This led to yet another source of division as people debated the legality of paying this tax or associating with those who did.

In 1677, public indignation over the government's excessive measures forced Dirleton to resign.[42] To suppress the ever-growing discontent, the next year the government garrisoned eight thousand Highlanders in the homes of Presbyterian Lowlanders where they remained until they ate the dissidents out of house and home.

After almost two decades of continuous strokes from the merciless hammer of persecution, fissures and cracks began to form in the Covenanter's rock-hard body. Eventually, sharp and ugly splinters began to fly. The escalating conflict finally resulted in men taking up arms in self-defense, which is a justifiable action, and a few taking justice into their own hands, which is not a justifiable action. The bitterness of eighteen years of persecution erupted when some of the persecuted men from Fife took the life of the Archbishop Sharp at Magus Moor in May 1679.[43] This resulted in increased persecution, leading to the deaths of many saints for years to come when interrogators asked them the question, "Was Archbishop Sharp's death murder?" One of the Sharp's murderers was a hot-tempered character named James Russel whom we will meet again as this story unfolds.

---

[*] According to Defoe (*Memoirs*, p. 220), the term refers to a mixture of water and sour milk the wanderers drank. The term Whig is also traceable to the derisive title "Whiggamore," given to Nevay and those who opposed the Engagement, possibly derived from the term "whiggam" used by the Covenanters to urge on their steeds (Ian Donnachie and George Hewitt, *A Companion to Scottish History*, p. 206). Another theory (Americana Encyclopedia) is that it means "We Hope in God."

[†] It was against the law to help those "intercommuned" in any way.

[‡] James, the second earl, succeeded his father in 1663.

A few weeks later at the town cross in Rutherglen, Sir Robert Hamilton (1650–1701) and eighty Covenanters burned all the acts that had rescinded the works of the Second Reformation, then posted a declaration, which protested the government's "sinful and unlawful acts."[44] In response to these acts of defiance, the government unleashed Claverhouse and his armed dragoons in the southwest Scotland with orders to suppress armed resistance with deadly force.

James Nisbet

James Nisbet (John's son) experienced these years as a child. He recounts how his sister saved him from drowning in 1670 at the age of three through the Lord's providential care, for which he offers praise: "O my soul! Bless and praise the Lord for his sparing and preventing mercy, for he is God, even the most high God, that performeth all things for me" (Ps. 57:2). From an early age, he felt the Lord's hand on him: "I was cast upon you from birth. From my mother's womb you have been my God" (Ps. 22:10). James's account of his early years follows:

> When I was five years of age, it pleased the Lord to give me some warm awakenings anent something that was more momentous, and of a greater concern, than only to live, to eat, drink, and sleep; and that there was something after time to be sought after to be enjoyed, though, alas! I knew little what the nature thereof was. The occasioning of my awakening was this. As I was returning from the churchyard (where they had been burying my mother's mother), [I observed] a good man, called George Woodburn, who all the way homeward was exercised with his hands and eyes often lifted up, and his lips often moving. [This] sight created a warmth upon my spirit, and [it] made me think that there was some better thing to be exercised with and earnestly sought after; and so I began to be a volunteer in prayer, and also to ask some questions at my mother and other friends. From this, I remark [concerning] the dreadful insensibility that sin has sunk me into; for though I had all the advantages of pious example and instruction that one of my years was capable of, yet I do not remember that ever I had before this one serious thought, or the least-engaging concern about the mystery of religion.... For through this warm awakening concern was such that I could never altogether forget it, yet I was never able to move one step in my spiritual progress, but when so influenced as aforesaid, either by providence or word and spirit of God. [A] great advantage ... is to be had by keeping with good company, for I have often reaped much advantage by it. [A] great loss and disadvantage ... is sustained by being with ill company,

which I have cause to lament: "But, O! Glory to God in Christ, and the riches of his free grace, who pities and plucks burning brands out of the midst of the fire, and manifests himself to be the Lord God, gracious and compassionate, by setting open the two-leafed gates of grace and redeeming love."

The sixth, seventh, and eighth years of my age, original indwelling sin bore very hard and violent upon me, to the actual commission of sin, yea every sin that that age could be capable of. For, alas, notwithstanding of my former wakenings, I was not acquainted with the secret distempers, inward windings, and turnings of my deceitful heart; [nor with] those wiles, depths, and devices of Satan; [nor with] my own light and carnal spirit. But blessed be the Lord forever, for restraining grace and paternal rebukes. Also, during these three years I had now and then many heart-meltings, at which times, after my ignorant manner, I essayed to give up myself to the Lord to be his servant. But, alas, often indwelling sin deadened my heart and cooled my affections very much; yet the Lord again and again put always new work in my hand: sometimes [by] convictions and impressions on my mind; sometimes by my parents counsels and reproofs; and sometimes by providences. From this I remark—the woeful bent and propensity of heart and nature to sin, so that now I was a very servant to sin. This I speak and write to my shame, and for my continual humiliation—"Glory to God, whoever denied me success in sin, but ever continued to be a reprover to me." If it had not been so, I would undoubtedly have been ruined, if I had been left to follow the cursed bent and sinful inclination of my own heart. Rich grace, how free and sovereign is it! Bless the Lord O my soul, because his mercy endureth forever. So far as I can remember the war and conflict betwixt the flesh and the spirit was now begun, which did and does continue to the making me cry out, "*O wretched man that I am! Who shall deliver me from the body of this death*" [Rom. 7:24], but I thank God for Jesus Christ.[45]

In the year 1678, when going in my ninth year of age, there was a great host of Highlanders came down in the middle of the winter to the western shires of Scotland. The shires of Ayr was the center of their encampment or cantooning, where they pillaged, plundered, thieved, and robbed night and day; even the Lord's day they regarded as little as any other. At their first coming, four of them came to my father's house, who was overseeing the making of his own malt. They told him they were come to make the Whig (so they termed the Presbyterians) to take with God and the king: this they repeated again and again, and pointing to his shoes, they said they would have the brogue off the Whig's foot and accordingly laid hands on him. But he being a very strong man, threw himself out of their grips, and turning to a pitchfork, which was used at the stacking of his corn and they having their broad swords drawn, cried, "Claymore!"§ and made at him. But he quickly drove them out of the kiln, and chased them all four away from the house, and knocked one of them to the ground.

The next day about twenty of them came to the house; but he not being at home, they told they were come to take the Whig and his arms. They plundered his house, as they did the house of every other man who would not conform to the then laws. Such was their thievish disposition, and so well acquainted were they with the second-sight, that let people hide their goods ever so well, yet these Athole and Broad-Albian men would go as right to where it was hid, whether beneath or above the ground, as if they had been at the putting of it there, dig it up, and away with it, rejoicing as through it had been their own. From this I remark that though four of us children were so cowed and terrified with their nightly searches, unruliness, and barbarous inhumanity, that we chose for two months time to lie all night in the open fields to shun them. Yet it pleased the Lord of his great mercy not one of us contracted any hurtful cold that we were sensible of, though it was the depth of winter. When they left that country they drove away many black cattle and sheep, as also many good horses, with household furniture and provisions....Yet before a twelvemonth was over, they were much poorer than when they came to the west country; for I saw some of them come a begging the next year, and heard them often say in their broken English, "You Lowland folk are better than our folk, for God hath cursed us and all that we had, because we took your gear from you." Upon which, I cannot but observe what is written: "God is known by the judgments which he executes (Ps. 9:16); the Lord is righteous in all his ways, and holy in all his works (Ps. 145:17); and the Lord is a God of judgment; blessed are all they that wait for him (Isa. 30:18)." O, that I could praise the Lord, for his right hand is ever exalted, and doeth valiantly. Amen.[46]

---

§ A claymore is a type of Scottish sword. The term means "On guard" in the sense used.

4

Drumclog and Bothwell Bridge

Despotism corrupts the man that submits to it much more than the man that imposes it.[1] *– Alexis De Tocqueville*

Battle of Drumclog (1679)

The inevitable battle took place a few miles from Newmilns at Loudoun Hill, where centuries earlier the great Bruce had defeated a superior British force and where Wallace avenged his father's death.[2] Wallace's sword, which rested at Loudoun Castle, would soon ring again. James Nisbet describes how the battle began:

> In the year 1679, and tenth of my age, upon the 1st of June, being Sabbath, there was a field-preaching by a Presbyterian minister called Mr. Douglas at a place called Drumclog. Upon which meeting came a squadron of the enemy, commanded by one Graham of Claverhouse, to seize upon the poor people of God met for his worship in the fields, because there was none in the churches in that place of the country but Episcopal curates. The enemy had taken many prisoners by the way of those that were coming to the sermons, amongst which, Mr. John King, a very worthy minister, was one, a man whom my father dearly loved. The people who were met to hear [a] sermon, seeing the enemy coming, sent for my father in all haste to come and help to oppose the common enemy.[3]

An account, extracted from an Appendix to *Scots Worthies*, of the battle of Drumclog follows. It is narrated by the Laird of Torfoot, who passed down an account of the battle through his descendants. Several generations later, one of his descendants, Thomas Brownlee, published this account.[4] The account begins as Torfoot describes the preparations for battle upon detection of the approaching enemy:

The officers collected their men, and placed themselves each at the head of those of his own district. Sir Robert Hamilton placed the foot in the center, in three ranks. A company of horses well armed and mounted was placed on the left, and a small squadron also on the left. These were drawn back and they occupied the more solid ground,... with a view to ... arrest any flanking party that might take them on the wings. A deep morass lay between the ... enemy and us. Our aged men, our females, and children retired ... slowly. They had the hearts and the courage of the females and children in those days of intense religious feeling, and of suffering. They manifested more concern for the fate of relatives, for the fate of the church, than for their own personal safety. As Claverhouse descended the opposite mountain, they retired to the rising ground in the rear of our host. The aged men walked with their bonnets in hand. Their long gray locks waved in the breeze. They sang a cheerier psalm. The music was that of the well-known tune of *Martyrs*; and the sentiment breathed defiance. The music floated down on the wind. Our men gave three cheers as they fell into their ranks. Never did I witness such animation in the looks of men. For me, my spouse and my little children were in the rear. My native plains, and the hails of my father, far below, in the dale of Aven, were full in view, from the heights [that] we occupied. My country seemed to raise her voice–the bleeding church seemed to wail aloud. "And these," I said, as Clavers [Claverhouse] and his troops winded slowly down the dark mountain's side, "these are the unworthy slaves, and bloody executioners, by which the tyrant completes our miseries."

Hamilton here displayed the hero. His portly figure was seen hastening from rank to rank. He inspired courage into our raw and undisciplined troops. The brave Hackston, and Hall of Haugh-head stood at the head of the foot soldiers and re-echoed the sentiments of their chief. Burley and Cleland had inflamed the minds of the horsemen on the left to a noble enthusiasm. My small troop on the right needed no exhortation; we were a band of brothers, resolved to conquer or fall.

The trumpet of Clavers sounded a loud note of defiance–the kettledrum mixed its tumultuous roll–they halted–They made a long pause. We could see an officer with four files conducting fifteen persons from the ranks to a knoll on their left. I could perceive one in black: it was my friend King.... "Let them be shot through the head," said Clavers, in his usual dry way, "if they should offer to run away." We could see him view our position with great care. His officers came around him. We soon learned that he wished to treat with us.

Claverhouse sent an officer, under the flag of truce, to request that the Covenanters lay down their arms and turn over their ringleaders. Hamilton refused to surrender, and the Covenanters echoed their support by singing part of Seventy-sixth Psalm. This response evoked Claverhouse's wrath:

> When the report was made to Claverhouse, he gave the word with a savage ferocity, "Their blood be on their own heads. Be '*No quarters*' the word this day." His fierce dragoons raised a yes, and "*No quarters*" re-echoed from rank to rank, while they galloped down the mountain's side. It is stated that Burley was heard to say, "Then be it so—even let there be *no quarters*—at least in my wing of the host. So God send me a meeting," cried he aloud, "with that chief under the white plume. My country would bless my memory, could my sword give his villainous carcass to the crows."

Claverhouse's troops attempted to outflank the Covenanters by repeated attacks across a swamp; however, the Covenanters repulsed each assault. Torfoot describes how, after repulsing the last assault, John Nisbet arrived to lead a successful counterattack:

> The firing of the platoons had long ago ceased, and the dreadful work of death was carried on by the sword. At this moment, a trumpet was heard in the rear of our army. There was an awful pause; all looked up. It was only the gallant Captain Nisbet and his guide, Woodburn of Mains: he had no reinforcements for us, but himself was a host. With a loud huzza and flourish of his sword, he placed himself by the side of Burley and cried, "Jump the ditch and charge the enemy." He and Burley struggled through the marsh. The men followed as they could. They formed and marched on the enemy's right flank.
>
> At this instant, Hamilton and Hackston brought forward the whole line of infantry in front. *"God and our Country"* re-echoed from all the ranks. *"No quarters,"* said the fierce squadrons of Clavers. Here commenced a bloody scene.

To protect Claverhouse, his troops surrounded him inside a hollow square. The Covenanters repeatedly assaulted the square, but they failed to break through. Torfoot remarks that Claverhouse moved so rapidly among his troops that "I could sooner shoot ten heather cocks on the wing, than one flying Clavers." Eventually, the Covenanters routed Claverhouse's troops and freed the captured ministers:

> We speedily regained our friends; what a spectacle presented itself. It seemed that I beheld an immense moving mass heaped up together in

the greatest confusion. Some shrieked, some groaned, some shouted, horses neighed and pranced, swords wrung on the steel helmets. I placed around me a few of my hardy men, and we rushed into the thickest of the enemy in search of Clavers; but it was in vain. At that instant, his trumpet sounded the loud notes of retreat; and we saw on a knoll Clavers borne away by his men. He threw himself on a horse, and without sword, without helmet, he fled in the first ranks of the retreating host. His troops galloped up the hill in the utmost confusion. My little line closed with that of Burley's, and [we] took a number of prisoners. Our main body pursued the enemy two miles and strewed the ground with men and horses. I could see the bareheaded Clavers in front of his men, kicking and struggling up the steep sides of Calder Hill. He halted only a moment on the top to look behind him, then plunged his rowels into his horse and darted forward; nor did he recover from his panic until he found himself in the city of Glasgow.[5]

Following their commander's orders and the rules of war of their day, John Nisbet and the Covenanters showed little mercy on the fleeing troops. As you recall, the order on both sides had been "No Quarter." Although there is no evidence that any prisoners granted quarter were executed, it greatly grieved both Robert Hamilton and John Nisbet to behold "some of them [dragoons] spared, after the Lord had delivered them into their hand."[6] John Nisbet explains why in his manuscript listing the causes for the God's wrath on Scotland.

> As there has been rash, envious, and carnal executing of justice on his and the church's enemies, so he has also been provoked to reject, cast off, and take the power out of his people's hand, for being sparing of them, when he brought forth and gave a commission to execute on them that vengeance due unto them (Ps. 149:9). For as justice ought to be executed in such and such a way and manner as aforesaid, so it ought to be fully executed without sparing, as is clear from Joshua 7:24. For sparing the life of the enemy and fleeing upon the spoil, 1 Samuel 15:19, Saul is sharply rebuked; and though he excused himself, yet for that very thing he is rejected from being king. Let the practice of Drumclog be remembered and mourned for. If there was not a deep ignorance, reason might teach this; for what master, having servants and putting them to do his work, would take such a slight at his servants' hands as to do a part of his work and … say to the master that it is not necessary to do the rest; when the not doing of it would be dishonorable to the master and hurtful to the whole family. Therefore was the wrath of God against his people.…[7]

Note that he equally condemns taking God's justice in one's hands unless commissioned to do so. From the perspective of our times, we may debate the legitimacy of his commission. In Hardhill's defense, James Nisbet records that his father "was very tender of the blood of his enemies. One instance whereof, amongst many, is this":

> Three of the enemy came upon him where he was writing; he quickly catched up his sword and a pair of pistols; then spoke to the enemy…, "Gentlemen, beware of what you do; for if any of you three offer to draw a sword or cock a pistol against me, I will send you all to eternity; and, poor souls, I am afraid that you are very ill prepared for it; but if you have a mind to lose your lives, you may fight, for I will not be taken with you." He spoke to them of the wrath of God, of the sin of their way of living, and of their danger of hell. He drew his sword and cocked both his pistols, at the sight of which they drew off. When they came to their garrison, as was afterwards told us, their officers threatened them for not killing him; they answered, "They were much afraid of his words but more when they saw his great broad-sword."[8]

The victorious leaders of the Covenanters were entertained at Loudoun castle after the battle. The Loudouns were willing to support the Covenanters privately but not publicly.[9]

The Battle between the Battles (1679)

There are really two battles of Bothwell Bridge: one between the Covenanters and the king's troops, the other within their own ranks. The Covenanters lost both battles.

After the battle of Drumclog, the people, fearful of separation, decided to stick together and protest their treatment. Under the leadership of Sir Robert Hamilton, they marched to Glasgow and set up camp outside the city. Loyalist forces barred them from entering the city.[10] Soon, after burying the heads and hands of martyrs, other bands of Covenanters joined them to the great joy of the populace, in each city they passed through. Over a period of several days, an untrained, poorly led, ill-equipped army of about six thousand men had assembled. As can be said of Christ's disciples, these men truly loved one another with bonds of love and affection strengthened through years of bitter struggle. Unfortunately, the harmony of the Covenanters was soon broken as they strove to develop a shared declaration of purpose. Shortly after the Covenanters began to assemble, they agreed upon a declaration that stated that their uprising was in defense of themselves and Reformed religion.

It also declared that they were "against popery, prelacy, Erastianism, and all things depending thereupon."[11] Their harmony was soon shattered as the men debated two contentious issues.

First, should one associate with and hear ministers who had accepted an Indulgence, and who were not repentant for doing so? The moderates were concerned that the original declaration was too condemnatory of the Indulgence, which many considered a matter of conscience not yet declared sinful by a lawful General Assembly.[12] Sir Robert Hamilton, two ministers (Donald Cargill [1619–1681] and Thomas Douglas), and the majority of the officers insisted that a statement condemning and excluding the Indulged ministers be included in the declaration. On the other hand, Rev. John Welsh and the majority of the ministers (sixteen out of eighteen) agreed that accepting the Indulgence was sinful but refused to exclude the Indulged from their cause.[13] When Hamilton attempted to declare a day of fasting and mourning for the sinful defections of the land, Welsh urged that they fast over the sinfulness of those who would divide the church over an issue that had not been declared unlawful by church judiciaries. When Hamilton demanded that the preachers preach against the Indulgence, one of them replied that he had fought against Erastianism all his life, and that he considered Hamilton's request the worst kind of Erastianism.[14]

The breach widened as they also began debating their rationale for taking up arms against the king. Hamilton and his followers proposed the adoption of the Rutherglen Declaration, which disowned the king's legal authority because the king was an avowed enemy of Christ, his church, and his people. John Welsh and his followers declared that the Bible requires that all must acknowledge the king's authority, and they cited the third article of the covenant in defense of their position. The Hamilton faction pointed out that the king had broken his promises to uphold the true religion as called for under the *Solemn League and Covenant*; hence, in their opinion, it was biblically lawful to take up arms against him. To counter this argument, John Welsh and his followers cited the precedent set in 1638 by the Scottish church when under similar attack it did not declare war on the king. The majority prevailed at the expense of unity and published the *Hamilton Declaration** on June 13.[15]

---

* The reasons cited in the Hamilton Declaration include (1) "the defending of the Protestant religion and Presbyterian government … and maintaining of the kingly authority of our Lord Jesus Christ over his church"; (2) "defending the king's majesty's person and authority in the preservation and defense of true religion and liberties …"; and (3) the obtaining of a free and unlimited parliament, and of a free general assembly.…"

The greatest failure of the Covenanted army was in allowing these internal debates to result in a mortal breach within the ranks. The true battle of Bothwell Bridge proved to be the above-mentioned debate, which was so intense that it continued until the king's forces over-whelmed the two feuding factions. Not only did they lose the battle over these two issues, but the church to this day also remains divided regarding Christians involvement in sinful associations and in civil matters. To understand this debate, it is necessary to understand the antagonists and the background of the dispute.

Cameronians: Historians label the faction led by Hamilton as the Cameronians because their most recognized leader was Rev. Richard Cameron, who at the time of Bothwell was in Holland.

Sir Robert Hamilton: Sir Hamilton was a vocal and natural leader who descended from a long line of staunch supporters of the Presbyterian faith. Two contrasting portraits best frame him. John Howie (1735–1793) stated that through the efficacious work of the Holy Spirit, Hamilton "came to espouse the true-covenanted testimony of the church of Christ in Scotland, for which he was, through divine grace, enabled to be a true and faithful witness to his life's end."[16] In contrast, Sir John Blackader, Reverend Blackader's son, described Hamilton as a young incompetent convener of meddlers and sticklers.[17] I leave the choice of "Which portrait is correct?" to the reader as the story unfolds.

Rev. John Welsh: John Welsh inherited "the piety, the zeal, and the indomitable fortitude" that distinguished his great-grandfather John Knox. An active preacher at field coventicles, Welsh was continually on the run eluding Claverhouse. On one occasion to escape capture, he sought refuge in the house of a man hostile to the Presbyterian cause. Not telling the man who he was, Welsh revealed that he was on a mission to apprehend rebels, and he knew where they would be preaching the next day. The day after this cordial visit, the man accompanied Welsh to the coventicle, where the assembled crowd made way for Welsh to preach, to the man's great surprise. After the sermon, the speechless man acknowledged, "You said you were to apprehend rebels, and I, a rebellious sinner, have been apprehended this day."[18] Although John Welsh refused the Indulgence, as did the other ministers at Bothwell, he empathized with the plight of the Indulged and sought reconciliation with them. After the defeat at Bothwell, the Cameronians reviled Welsh and blamed him for the defeat.

Other Ministers: The dying testimonies of John King and John Kid, two of the ministers who sided with Welsh, are illustrative of their posi-

tion. Shortly after the battle of Bothwell Bridge, these two men were
captured and charged with field preaching. Both confessed but refused
to acknowledge supporting rebellion against lawful authorities. On the
way to the scaffold, Kid remarked to King with a smile, "I have often
heard and read of a kid sacrificed, but I seldom or never heard of a king
sacrificed."[19] On the scaffold, King requested that the bystanders pray for
their persecutors and obey civil authorities in the Lord.[20] Although John
Blackader was not at Bothwell, he would have argued for an even more
spiritual approach: "The Lord called for a testimony by suffering rather
than by outward deliverance."[21] On another occasion, Blackader cautioned some that had stockpiled arms, "Trust rather in Jehovah and the
shield of omnipotence."[22] Later, when the appearance of these well-
armed men caused the enemy to flee, Blackader cautioned them, "My
friends, your part is chiefly to defend yourselves from hazard, and not to
pursue: your enemy has fled—let their flight sheath your weapons and
disarm your passions."[23]

The Indulged: The Covenanters had good cause to reject unrepentant
Indulged ministers. A few years later, in his dying testimony, John Nisbet reflected upon the great harm done by the Indulgence and by those
who accepted this sinful compliance:

> I die testifying against the woeful Indulgence, the fruits and conse-
> quences of which have so much strengthened the enemy, increased our
> divisions, widened our breaches, and deadened the spirits, and cooled
> the zeal of the Lord's people, and stumbled and offended the weak. In a
> great measure, [it] retarded the carrying on of a testimony for truth, by
> condemning the things contended for, and reproaching those that con-
> tend for truth.... Wherefore I leave my testimony against all the accep-
> tors thereof, and all ministers and professors who are any way guilty of
> any of the woeful defections and sinful compliances with the enemies of
> truth.... Let all such ministers and professors know that this their prac-
> tice at the best is a denying of Christ...; therefore, let them take warning
> and ponder these scriptures (Ps. 1:16–21; Prov. 1:10–15; 17:15; Isa. 8:9–15; 5:20–24;
> Amos 5:10; Matt. 10:32–33, 37–38; 16:24–26; Mark 8:34–37; Gal. 2:18).[24]

On the other hand, many who accepted the Indulgence were men
who viewed deserting their flock as a worse crime than deserting their
Presbyterian principles. Rather than flee the country or desert their ministry, they believed it was their obligation to continue to preach. One
such minister was Archibald Riddell (d. 1708). Because such men
walked a thin line between obedience to civil authorities and obedience
to Christ, the government kept them under close watch. In 1680, the

government arrested Riddell and falsely charged him with field preaching. Although he had been an active field preacher before the loss at Bothwell Bridge, after the battle he accepted indemnity. Yet, he had preached in his home without the required permission of a curate. In response to the charges against him, he replied, "If I do anything contrary to the laws, I am liable to the punishment due the law."[25] The prosecutor challenged Riddell's defense by declaring that one should "either conform to the law or go out of the land." The reply given by Riddell shows that many who complied with the government believed that their actions were consistent with God's Word:

> My lord, I doubt that argument would militate against Christ and his apostles as much as against us; for they both preached and acted otherwise against the laws of the land; and not only did not judge it their duty to go out of the land; but the apostles, on the contrary, reasoned with their rulers—Whether it is better to obey God or man, judge ye.[26]

Any compliance with a tyrannical state simply leads to further compliance. When asked by the judges to promise never to preach in the field, Riddell drew the line between compliance for a season and compliance forever; consequently, the civil authorities imprisoned him on the Bass Rock and, several years later, banished him to America.

The Battle Begins: As the Covenanters watched the king's army approach, their debates intensified. Hamilton's followers wanted to organize for battle; Welsh's followers wanted to submit a petition of grievances to the king. By the next day, the vehement debates had so impaired relations that neither party was willing to serve under officers from the opposing party; as a result, a motion was made for existing officers to step down to allow new elections. Although Hamilton and his followers were willing to entertain this proposal, they brought up the issue of Indulged ministers. Finding no satisfactory resolution, Hamilton and most of the officers walked out of the meeting. The remaining leaders could only agree on a petition to lay their grievances before the king and began prayer toward this end.[27] A petition was prepared, and Hamilton signed it thinking that Reverend Cargill has drafted it.

On June 22, 1679, the king's advance guard was within a few hundred yards of Bothwell Bridge. A delegation from the Covenanters submitted their petition to the Duke of Monmouth (1649–1685), the king's son and leader of the king's army. The duke listened patiently to the petitioners as they requested the right to exercise their religion, to establish a free Parliament and General Assembly, and to receive a pardon for gathering under arms. The duke refused to answer them until they laid down their arms, and he gave them thirty minutes to persuade the army of Covenanters. The duke's demand precipitated an unfruitful debate among the Covenanters; thus any hope of meeting the duke's conditions was lost.[28] Having lost the inner battle, it was not long before the Covenanters lost the outer battle as well.

Battle of Bothwell Bridge (1679)

With this background, let us return to Torfoot's account of the battle. The account describes how a single well-placed battery of cannon supported by Burley's infantry and Nisbet's dragoons defended the bridge against repeated assaults by the King's troops. Meanwhile, efforts to unite the main body of Covenanters to take up positions proved fruitless:

> Meantime, while we were thus warmly engaged, Hamilton was laboring to bring down the different divisions of our main body into action; but in vain he called on Colonel Cleland's troop—in vain he ordered Henderson's to fall in—in vain he called on Colonel Fleming's. Hackston flew from troop to troop—all was confusion; in vain he besought, he entreated, he threatened. Our disputes and fiery-misguided zeal, my brother, contracted a deep and deadly guilt that day. The Whig turned his arm in fierce hated that day against his own vitals. Our chaplains, Cargill, King, Kid, and Douglas, interposed again and again. Cargill mounted the pulpit; he preached concord; he called aloud for mutual forbearance. "Behold the banners of the enemy," cried he; "Hear ye not the fire of the foe, and of our own brethren? Our brothers and fathers are falling beneath their sword. Hasten to their aid. See the flag of the covenant. See the motto in letters of gold—CHRIST'S CROWN AND THE COVENANT. Hear the voice of your weeping country. Hear the wailings of the bleeding kirk. Banish discord. And let us, as a band of brothers, present a bold front to the foeman. Follow me, all ye who love your country and the covenant. I go to die in the forefront of the battle." All the ministers and officers followed him—amidst a flourish of trumpets—but the great body remained to listen to the harangues of the factious.

Unfortunately, the cannon fell silent when the Covenanters discovered that their remaining kegs of powder contained raisins. Once the enemy discovered the cannon's silence, they poured across the bridge. Torfoot describes the last valiant efforts to repulse the renewed attacks:

I sent a request to Captain Nisbet to join his troop to mine. He was in an instant with us. We charged the lifeguards. Our swords rang on their steel caps. Many of my brave lads fell on all sides of me. But we hewed down the foe. They began to reel. The whole column was kept stationary on the bridge. Clavers' dreadful voice was heard—more like the yell of a savage, than the commanding voice of a soldier. He pushed forward his men, and again we hewed them down. A third mass was pushed up. Our exhausted dragoons fled. Unsupported, I found myself by the brave Nisbet, Paton, and Hackston. We looked for a moment's space in silence on each other. We galloped in front of our retreating men. We rallied them. We pointed to the General almost alone. We pointed to the white and to the scarlet colors floating near him. We cried, *"God and our Country."* They faced about. We charged Clavers once more— "Torfoot," cried Nisbet, "I dare you to the forefront of the battle." We rushed up at full gallop. Our men seeing this followed also at full speed. We broke the enemy's line, bearing down those files that we encountered. We cut our way through their ranks. But they had now lengthened their front. Superior numbers drove us in. They had gained entire possession of the bridge. Livingstone and Dalziel were actually taking us on the flank. A band had got between Burley's infantry and us. "My friends," said Hackston to his officers, "We are last on the field. We can do no more. We must retreat. Let us attempt, at least, to bring aid to those men behind us. They have brought ruin on themselves and on us. Not Monmouth, but our own divisions have scattered us."

At this moment, one of the lifeguards aimed a blow at Hackston. My sword received it—and a stroke from Nisbet laid the foeman's hand and sword in the dust. He fainted and tumbled from his saddle. We reined our horses and galloped to our main body. But what a scene presents itself here! These misguided men had their eyes now fully opened on their fatal errors. The enemy was bringing up their whole force against them. I was not long a near spectator of it, for a ball grazed my courser. He plunged and reared—then shot off like an arrow. Several of our officers drew to the same place. On a knoll, we faced about—the battle raged below us.

Torfoot describes the scene of carnage as he and a few officers struggled to save their flag and their general:

Dalziel and Livingstone were riding over the field, like furies, cutting down all in their way. Monmouth was galloping from rank to rank and calling on his men to give quarter. Clavers, to wipe off the disgrace of Drumclog, was committing fearful havoc....

The standard bearer was down, but he was still fearlessly grasping the flagstaff while he was borne upright by the mass of men who had thrown themselves in fierce contest around it. Its well-known blue and scarlet colors and its motto, CHRIST'S CROWN AND COVENANT, in brilliant gold letters, inspired us with a sacred enthusiasm. We gave a loud cheer to the wounded ensign and rushed into the combat. The redemption of that flag cost the foe many a gallant man. They fell beneath our broad swords; and, with horrible execrations dying on their lips, they gave up their souls to their Judge …

While my gallant companions stemmed the tide of battle, the standard, rent to tatters, fell across my breast. I tore it from the staff, and wrapped it round my body. We cut our way through the enemy, and carried our general off the field.

Having gained a small knoll, we beheld once more the dreadful spectacle below. Thick volumes of smoke and dust rolled in a lazy cloud over the dark bands mingled in deadly fray. It was no longer a battle, but a massacre.

The small band of mounted Covenanters, under the leadership of Paton and Hamilton, attempted one last attack on Claverhouse:

We formed and made a furious onset. At our first charge his troops reeled. Clavers was dismounted. But, at that moment, Dalziel assailed us on the flank and rear. Our men fell around us like grass before the mower. The bugle man sounded a retreat. Once more in the *melee* I fell in with the General and Paton. We were covered with wounds. We directed our flight in the rear of our broken troops. By the direction of the General, I had unfurled the standard. It was borne off the field flying at the point of the sword.… That honor cost me much. I was assailed by three fierce dragoons; five followed close in the rear. I called to Paton—in a moment, he was by my side. I threw the standard to the General, and we rushed on the foe. They fell beneath our swords. But my faithful steed, which had carried me through all my dangers, was mortally wounded. He fell. I was thrown among the fallen enemy. I fainted. I opened my eyes on misery. I found myself in the presence of Monmouth—a prisoner—with other wretched creatures, awaiting in awful suspense, their ultimate destiny.[29]

Other accounts portray the actions of Hamilton less glamorously, contending that Hamilton and the cavalry fled once the bridge was lost.[30] Perhaps we will never know the truth.

RISE AND FALL OF THE REMNANT

Loudoun Castle (circa 1690) - Courtesy Alloway Publishing

Loudoun Kirk (circa 1850) - Courtesy Alloway Publishing

Loudoun Kirk and Castle

5

Truth Preservation

And for those who will not suffer for little truths when called thereunto, it may be feared that they shall never be honored to suffer for those called greater truths. — Alexander Shields[1]

None perish that trust in him. —Psalm 34:22 from Scottish Psalter

After the Battles (1679–1681)

After the battle, more than fifteen hundred captives were marched to Greyfriars Churchyard in Edinburgh where they, as prisoners exposed to the elements, languished for months and several hundred died from exposure. Worse, as they marched into Edinburgh, citizens taunted them with the rebuke, "Where is your God now?"[2]

The government offered an Indemnity (called the *Bond of Peace* or the *Black Bond*) to those who would acknowledge that the battle of Bothwell was rebellion, agree to never again take up arms against the king, and refrain from field coventicles. John Blackader wrote a letter urging the prisoners to refuse this bond; however, other ministers actively encouraged its acceptance. Many subscribed to the bond, but more refused, contending that Bothwell was not an act of rebellion but of self-defense. Many of the ringleaders, heritors, and ministers were banished as slaves. Sadly, many died in a shipwreck on the way to servitude. Before the ship went down, their captors sealed the hatch, keeping most from escaping. One of the few to escape the sinking vessel was Thomas Brownlee. The combination of events crushed the spirit of the captured Covenanters to such an extent that only thirty-three of the remaining prisoners refused the bond.[3]

The testimony of these holdouts provides insight into the reasoning of those who would rather hold on to their beliefs than to their freedom. One of these holdouts, Robert Garnock, contended that he was not in rebellion because he faithfully followed all legal laws. Garnock's jailer asked why he would not take the *Black Bond* considering that both Romans 13 and the *Solemn League and Covenant* commanded obedience to the government. Garnock replied, "No, they just bound me to the contrary. What if popery was to come into the land, should we bind ourselves never to defend true religion?"[4] The example set by these noble truth bearers eventually convinced more than a hundred of their fellow prisoners to join with them in refusing to bow to tyranny.

The execution of the five most recalcitrant holdouts took place on November 18, 1679, near the spot of Bishop Sharp's murder. Garnock was not one of those executed because none of his compatriots would bear witness that he was at Bothwell. One of those executed was James Wood of Newmilns, a relative of John Nisbet. In Wood's dying testimony, he expressed his desire that the Lord would let him die a martyr. The testimony of the others was just as inspiring. One sang the Thirty-fourth Psalm, containing the line, *"None perish that trust in him."* Another avowed, "If … every hair on his head were a man, and every drop of blood a life, he would cordially and heartily lay them down for Christ and this cause that he is now sentenced." Another left his weeping family at the foot of gallows as he cried, "Welcome, Lord Jesus." Another affirmed, while waiting his turn, that he was "not a whit discouraged to see [his] three brethren hanging before his eyes."[5]

After the battle, many of the nobles of southwest Scotland and those involved in the battle at Bothwell refused the Indemnity and fled to Holland. One of those who fled was Sir Robert Hamilton, for which he forfeited his large estate. In Europe, as the appointed commissioner of the Covenanting remnant (those who remained after the battle of Bothwell Bridge), he facilitated the training of ministers faithful to the covenants.

Suspected ringleaders and those who refused the Indemnity were either heavily fined or declared rebels—their names listed on portable rolls. Among those listed was John Nisbet. Soldiers scoured the countryside in search of these fugitives. Many supporters of the crown became wealthy by collecting rewards and feasting off the confiscated property. James Nisbet describes how these events forever changed his life:

> Accordingly, after the Lord's people were defeated at Bothwell Bridge [on] June 22, being a Sabbath, the next Sabbath, June 29, they came to my father's house to seek him; but he being got out of their way, they carried away about sixty bolls of malt and barley and as much meal and oats. On Monday, they came again and carried away all his horses, black cattle, sheep, household-furniture, and all the victual they had left the day before; and [they] beat my mother and my eldest

brother severely and turned us all out of doors. In the meantime, that forenoon, they denounced my father a rebel to the government at the market-cross of the next borough and offered three thousand merks for him, one hundred for my mother, and one hundred for each of their four children (of which I was one) to any person or persons that would apprehend him, my mother, or any of us. They threatened all the country under a great penalty not to harbor him, her, or any of us. Further, by the treachery of some wicked neighbors, they got the most of my father's papers and seized on all his money. Within three hours after we were thrust out, there came back a fresh party to apprehend any or all of us, but [they] missed their prey.... The kind and ever watchful providence of God was such towards us that before they returned we were all gone out of the way, some of us one [direction] and some of us another; though they searched the neighbor's houses carefully for us, yet they got not one of us.

What shall I render unto the Lord for all his benefits? Who gave me not up for a prey to the will of enemies, nor left me to fall a victim to the revenging fury of these men who were skilful to destroy, nor left me to be cut off for a religion, the sweet fruits and incomes of which I was a great stranger. Glory to him, for he made me to see that he sits on the floods of man's fury (Ps. 29:10), and that the wicked cannot destroy those whom he has appointed to live.... [So] this our preservation came forth from the Lord of Hosts alone, who is wonderful in counsel and excellent in working (Isa. 28:29). And further, it was some allay to our great affliction that those who were our enemies were God's enemies and enemies to his work and people. It was some comfort to us that their enmity and rage against us was for those things which was matter of conscience to my father and mother, both of whom were willing, as the Lord would enable them, to undergo any kind of suffering rather than sin against God, wound their own consciences, or offend the generation of the righteous. Though the wicked robbed them of all that they had in the world, yet they suffered joyfully the spoiling of their goods; notwithstanding of which, they never wanted food and raiment, for the Lord sustained them and theirs. Glory to him who is a present help in the time of trouble (Ps. 46:1, 5).

And here, to the lasting honor and fame of the Right Honorable Earl of Loudoun [James], who, when my father's house was plundered, sent his servants and laid claim to several things as his own. [He] sent for my father from his lurking place in the nighttime, paid him money for what his Lordship had laid claim to, and showed him much other kindness. And further, though all persons were forbidden, on the severest terms, not to harbor any of us, yet the Lord, in his kind providence, never shut one door upon us, but he quickly opened another for us, so that we evidently saw the earth is the Lord's and the fullness thereof (Ps. 24:1). Sometimes we were most befriended by those who professed little religion themselves: so that we could not but allude to Rev. 7:16, when the dragon did vomit forth floods of water, the earth helped the woman; and we all had it to remark that all those who were (at this time) the most violent persecutors of my father and who got the most part of his worldly substance did perish within a few years.... Yea, even those of his neighbors who did inform against him, for love to get a part, quickly came to nothing; they all, within two years, either died or came to begging poverty because of a visible blasting that seized everything they had. Upon which I heard my father say, Lord pity and spare these poor mortals and give them repentance if it be thy holy will; he added, with David, they that render me evil for good are my adversaries, because I follow the thing that good is (Ps. 38:20). Indeed, they could not get any occasion against him except in the matters of his God, as is said of Daniel in Daniel 6:4–5. Bless the Lord, O my soul, and all that is within me because his mercy endureth forever. O that men would praise the Lord for his goodness and for his wonderful works to the children of men. The Lord is good to them that wait for him and to the soul that seeketh him; he will not cast off forever, but though he cause grief, yet will he have compassion, according to the multitude of his tender mercies, for they are new every morning. Great and much to be adored is he who hath faithfulness for the girdle of his loins. Amen.[6]

To divide the populace, the government granted and then recalled another Indulgence. Many ministers took this so-called favor, the third Indulgence, which allowed a weak form of presbytery. The introduction to James Nisbet's memoir describes the resultant division:

About the same time, the indulged ministers were required to take a bond, obliging themselves to live peaceably, to refrain from preaching against the defections of the times, and to present themselves, when called before the privy-council, under a penalty of six thousand merks Scots, for which they were to find security—whence this last indulgence got the name of the Banded indulgence. As under the terms, living peaceably, was understood a disapproval of all field meetings and what the government chose to call irregularities, among which were comprised almost every essential of a free ministry. Those of the persecuted who had constantly contended for the supreme kingship of Christ in his church opposed this new imposition as sinful, scandalous, and inconvenient. At a meeting of a number of ministers those additional oaths were acceded to by many who had hitherto resisted all former obligations, but

who now, to avoid the imputation of rebellion, or worn out with pro-
tracted suffering, took advantage of the precarious freedom.... [This in-
dulgence], clogged as it was, was soon recalled, though not before it had
occasioned an irreparable breach between many of the best and purest
friends of presbytery and of the gospel.[7]

Let us now focus on the suffering and martyrdom of the small remnant that remained after Bothwell to contend for the cause of Christ. In
October 1679, Rev. Richard Cameron returned from Holland to serve
as one of the few ministers willing to support the Covenanting cause. He
and Cargill provided the needed anchor for the faithful remnant that
survived the Bothwell Bridge fiasco. At a sermon preached in May 1680,
Cameron declared that although the most part of Scotland acknowledges Charles as their king, "We will have no other king but Christ." On
the anniversary of Bothwell Bridge, Cameron posted a declaration of
independence on the Sanquhar Cross. The declaration threatened re-
taliation against the "enemies to our Lord Jesus Christ, his cause and
covenants." It was, in essence, a declaration of war against the king and
all his supporters. Shortly thereafter, the king's troops surrounded and
massacred Cameron and many of his supporters at Ayrsmoss. They affixed Cameron's head and hands to the Netherbow port, where is said,
"There's the head and hands of a man who lived praying and preaching,
and died praying and fighting." Cameron's lieutenant Hackston, a hero
of Drumclog and Bothwell, met a worse fate. On the scaffold, the execu-
tioner raised him with a rope to the top of the gallows and dropped him,
cut off his hands, again raised and dropped him, cut out his heart, then
disemboweled, decapitated, and quartered his body.[8]

At Torwood, in September 1680, Cargill excommunicated King
Charles and other persecutors. Cargill cited a number of reasons for the
excommunications: drunkenness, adultery, murder of God's people, perjury in renouncing the covenants, and mocking God. In response, the
government cracked down on staunch Covenanters by posting larger
rewards for their capture.

After Bothwell, most ministers accepted the Indulgence, but not all
who refused sided with Cameron and Cargill. For example, John Blackader, who baptized John Nisbet's children, continued to preach and to
encourage the remnant. Blackader's beliefs differed from those of Cameron and Cargill only in that he would not disown the king's authority
or avoid associations with Indulged ministers. Blackader was finally captured in April 1681 and imprisoned on Bass Rock, where he remained
until near his death.

The government fiercely went after the supporters of Cargill and executed all they found. Among them were two women, Isobel Alison and Marion Harvie, charged with supporting the declarations of war made by Cargill. In her defense Marion said, "They say I would murder—I could never take the life of a chicken, but my heart shrinked." When they appeared before the Council, they loudly sang the Twenty-third Psalm to drown out the voice of a bishop who attempted to force them to listen to a prayer. Marion contended that she was "a true Presbyterian in [her] judgment," accusing the court, comprised of many professed Presbyterians, "Ye are all gone blind."[9]

The court sent Archibald Riddell, an imprisoned minister, to convince the two women to change their minds, but he left with their rebuke of him. Riddell attempted to convince them that the Bible (citing the examples of Manasseh, Joash, and Nero) required obedience even to evil magistrates. Riddell also challenged the legality of a single minister (Cargill) excommunicating civil authorities because excommunication rightfully is a church function. Riddell asked Isabel, "Who is the church?" Isabel answered, "If there was a true church in the world, that little handful [the Covenanting remnant] was one, though never so insignificant, of which handful we own ourselves a part." As most martyrs of their day, they sang metrical psalms (Psalms 74 and 84) and read Scripture (Mark 16 and Malachi 3) while awaiting their execution. "Farewell, sweet Bible … Farewell, sweet Scripture," were their parting words.[10]

> They fired have thy sanctuary—and have defil'd the same,
> By casting down unto the ground—the place where dwelt thy name.
> Thus said they in their hearts, Let us—destroy them out of hand:
> They burnt up all the synagogues—of God within the land.
> Our signs we do not now behold—there is not us among
> A prophet more, nor any one—that knows the time how long.
> How long, Lord, shall the enemy—thus in reproach exclaim?
> And shall the adversary thus—always blaspheme thy name?
> Thy hand, ev'n thy right hand of might—why dost thou thus draw back?
> O from thy bosom pluck it out—for our deliv'rance sake.
> For certainly God is my King—ev'n from the times of old,
> Working in midst of all the earth—salvation manifold. –Ps. 74:7-12[11]

Meanwhile in England, parliament grew increasingly fearful of Popish plots to establish a catholic dynasty through King Charles's Catholic brother James, the Duke of York. To protect his brother from parliament, Charles sent him to Scotland as his Royal Commissioner in late 1680. Once in Scotland, the duke began remolding the Scottish High Commission in his image by forcing Lauderdale to resign, causing the

Earl of Argyle to flee for his life a year later, and craftily, as events allowed, replacing commissioners with men sympathetic to Catholicism and absolute monarchy. Lauderdale, who had sold his soul for power, died in 1682 a broken man without heirs. In parallel, Charles, with support from his French allies, tightened his grip on England by gaining possession, through coercive means, of numerous town charters, including the city of London, which he placed under Tory control.[12]

In the summer of 1681, the Duke of York reopened the Scottish Parliament, which had been inactive for nine years. For all practical purposes, it was a puppet government with no power to initiate legislation. In obedience to their master, the Scottish Parliament passed additional laws placing heavy fines on landowners who allowed field meetings, removing religious affiliation as a prerequisite for kingship, requiring ministers to report those absent from church, and compelling all property owners and officials to take an oath. This oath (called the Test) required subscribers to renounce the covenants, to acknowledge the king as the "only supreme Governor ... in all matters ecclesiastical as well as civil," and to profess the *Confession of Faith* adopted by King James (in 1567) rather than the *Confession of Faith* adopted by the Westminster Assembly. The test was contradictory considering that King James's *Confession of Faith* declares that "it is not lawful for man or angel to intrude" on Christ's office as head of the church.[13]

James Nisbet's memoir chronicles how the persecution during his pre-teen years shaped his Christian character. To avoid detection, his parents placed their children under the care of others in separate homes. In this environment, James found "the Word made good, *"Trust in the Lord and do good, so shalt thou dwell in the land, and verily thou shall be fed"* (Ps. 37:3). No longer under his parents protective care and good example, however, he soon found himself "captive to sin and Satan" and discovered that he "was a monster of sin, yea a mass of sin and sinful corruption." He laments how in this environment he picked up the sinful habits of other children, disregarded the Sabbath, devised half-truths to hide his identity, and ignored the hardship of others.[14] In all these matters, the Holy Spirit convicted his conscience of the need for a Savior, leading James to seek sweet communion with God:

> These are some of the ways whereby the great mystery of iniquity was further laid open, to my great shame and confusion, because of which I had many melancholy struggles with a body of sin and death. Upon the account of which I gave up, in a measure, with my foolish and wicked companions and restricted myself to as narrow a compass of re-

tiredness as my circumstances would admit of. I plied close to the reading of my catechism and the Holy Bible, sought a lesson from anybody
that would give me one, frequently set time apart for prayer, and took
on vows against my sins to give up with all my iniquities. But, alas!
They proved like Samson's withs,* through the strength of my unruly
corruptions, because of which I could not escape drawing this inference,
that the more near that any are engaged to God by duties and privileges,
and yet not thoroughly reconciled to him by faith in the blood of Christ,
the more closely are they exposed to the wrathful shot of his fiery indignation.

Sometime after this, I met with great Mr. Guthrie's *Trial of Saving Interest* and Mr. Richard Alleine's *Vindication of Godliness*,[†] and [I] read them
closely. [I found] in them the scheme of personal covenanting, the which
duty, after several times set apart to seek the Lord for light and assistance, I attempted, and, as the Lord helped me, attained much melting
enlargement of heart and soul therein. I had not peace to make use of
their express words, because I thought it was too formal, but I held close
by their scope; only I was often more large in lamenting my lost condition and in essaying a thorough closure with Christ on gospel terms.
Which covenant I, in process of time, drew out in writ, and often renewed upon the back of the more treacherous slips that my perfidious
heart played me. But, after all, when I found the treacherous deceivings
of my heart to continue, I quickly ran into a fatal mistake, judging all
my attainments to have been mere delusions, because that sin was not
totally subdued. For, I certainly thought it was so with every one who
was effectually called and instated in covenant with God in Christ, that
they had surely gotten complete victory over sin. O! Gross and childish
ignorance! Upon examining the case of the Scripture saints, ups and
downs, and betters and worse of the temper of my heart, I at length
found, like Rebecca, I had two contrary parties within me, the law of my
members warring against the law of my mind, or the flesh lusting
against the spirit and the spirit lusting against the flesh. Having conversed with some of the godly and experienced Christians on this point,

---

* See Judges 16:7 -*And Samson said unto her, "If they bind me with seven green withs that were never dried, then
shall I be weak, and be as another man."*
† Richard Alleine in his book *A Vindication of Godliness* (London, 1663), on pages 72–80, identifies
five treasures possessed by those with the truth: the *pearl of great price* symbolic that Christ is now
theirs (Song of Sol. 2:6; Matt. 13:46); the *white stone* symbolic of Christ's atoning work (Rev. 2:17);
the *white robe* symbolic of holiness made possible from a renewed heart (Matt. 12:35; Heb. 12:10;
Rev. 6:11); the *adoption* symbolic of our transformation into sons of God (Luke 15:22, 31; John
1:12; Rom. 8:15–16; 1 John 3:1); and the *kingdom* with all its blessings bestowed upon the flock
(Luke 12:32). To the world, these blessings are invisible; to the saint, knowledge of them is his life.

by them I understood that this was a warfare that I was to lay my account to be exercised with as long as I was in the body.

The sight and sense of my sinful wretchedness and unworthiness in playing fast and loose with God continuing, I became weary of my formal personal covenanting, and [I] retired myself as much as possible … from all wicked company, both old and young, and also from the company of all professors who were given to disputation and did not live up to their pretences of religion. In some measure, I loved the company of the truly and tenderly godly, although I was ashamed because of my sins to use any freedom with them, except to my mother, or when much urged to it by others, for I affected retiredness very much from a sense of my great unworthiness. I spent some of my time in the search of that hidden manna which carries the poor soul above all sublunary things, so that I might have Christ to be my light, my life, my lawgiver, […and my savior]; and so that I might be directed with his unerring counsel to know where, and upon what grounds, to state my sufferings if the Lord should deliver me up into the hands of the enemy; and so that I might not be left altogether to take up with other men's light. Although the suffering party, with whom I most part conversed, were greatly harmonious in judgment, as to what was sin and what was duty, yet there were some amongst them who differed much on both hands; some saying this and some saying that, some being for one thing and some for another; from which I learned, I was to make no man's light my standard.

Now while I was thus exercised, when my frame was any way suitable…, I took the advantage of it for prayer in private, and also ejaculatory prayer; and when my heart was dead and carnal, and I every way unframed, then I essayed the same duty either mental or vocal. Thus, I spent sometimes a great part of the day and sometimes a great part of the night crying to the Lord to remove and heal the many woeful plagues of my heart, [to] reveal himself savingly in me and to me, and [to] grant me ever much of his divine aid and assistance. [I prayed] that he would ever give me a holy and humble heart, and help me ever to be exercised in embracing a whole Christ for justification, sanctification, and final perseverance in grace unto the end.[15]

In his prayers, James was forever thankful for the "rich and unspeakable gift, Christ Jesus the Lamb of God, who taketh away the sins of the world" and for the "covenant of free grace, which is the blessed ark of safety, in which is embarked all the heirs of grace until they swim up to be possessed of glory." His prayer was to be "always swallowed up" in God's unfathomable love and to avoid "Time's vanities" until "eternity takes place of time."[16]

Although most Covenanters were in great peril, James lived in relative safety during these years (1679–1681):

> [My] dear father was in great danger because he went on contending, on the one hand, against prelacy and Erastian supremacy and, on the other hand, against the erroneous schismatical extravagances of one John Gibb*, a very lewd and wicked man, and his party who affected a nonsensical singularity. [My father] adhered to the truths of God, as revealed in the Scriptures of the Old and New Testament and summed up in our *Westminster Confession of Faith* and *Catechisms Larger and Shorter*; all which truths were sworn to in our covenants, *National* and *Solemn League*, which, alas, were broken a long time before that time and lie buried yet to this day in the ashes of our dreadful apostasies. Thus, I say, he went on contending for and against these things deliberately and resolvedly, cost what it would, and in hearing the gospel preached by that eminently faithful servant of God, Mr. Donald Cargill. They, with some others, spent much of their time in fasting and prayer to and before the Lord for aid, light, and counsel anent what was duty, and what was sin, in that dark, critical and suffering dispensation that was befallen them.[17]

Soldiers captured Cargill in July 1681. On his way to jail, another John Nisbet, referred to as a bishop's factor*, taunted Cargill to say "one more word." Apparently, Cargill had used these words in some of his sermons. Cargill replied, "Wicked poor man, why do you mock? Ere you die you will desire one more word and not get it." Shortly thereafter, the poor man (John Nisbet the bishop's factor) died with a swollen tongue. At his trial, Cargill responded to the threats from Lord Rothes, one of those he excommunicated at Torwood, by prophesying that Rothes would not see his death. Rothes soon became violently ill and called for some of his wife's beloved Presbyterian ministers because, as Patrick Walker (1666–1745) recorded, "his ministers were good to live with but not to die with." After hearing their words, Rothes said, "We all thought little of what that man [Cargill] did, in excommunicating us; but I find that sentence binding upon me now, and will bind to eternity." Concerning this, the Duke of Hamilton said, "We banish these men from us, and yet when dying we call on them." Even the Duke of York

---

* Extreme times give rise to extreme men. One of these was John Gibb, the leader of the sweet-singers. He and his cult of followers renounced everything except bread, water, and the pure text of the Bible. They exhibited strange and bizarre behavior characteristic of a cult such as tearing up Bibles containing human-added chapter names. Eventually, authorities exiled them to America where Gibb impressed the Indians with his fanatical behavior.

* A factor (or factotum) is one who acts for another or manages one's estate. As an aside, yet another John Nisbet of this era was an unpopular curate, serving at Crawfordjohn.

concluded, "That all of Scotland was either Presbyterian through their life or at their death, profess what they would."[18]

Upon hearing the sound of a trumpet that announced the indictment against him, Cargill remarked, "That's a weary sound, but the sound of the last trumpet will be a joyful sound to me, and all that will be found having on Christ's righteousness." At the foot of the gallows to the roll of drums, Cargill declared his execution as the most joyful day of his life, exclaiming that his "joy is now began." He then sang the last half of the Psalm 118, sang by Christ and his disciples after the Last Supper. This psalm contains a comforting promise to Christians: "I shall not die, but live, and the works of God discover." As he mounted the ladder, Cargill stated, "The Lord knows I go up this ladder with less fear and perturbation of mind than ever I entered a pulpit to preach."[19]

Another important event happened that day. A young man named James Renwick (1662–1688), a recent graduate from the University of Edinburgh, witnessed the execution. The dying testimony of Cargill had such a "powerful influence on the mind of young Renwick" that Renwick made up his mind to study the ministry. Two years later after completing his studies, he would take up the "banner that fell from the hand of the dying Cargill."[20]

In October 1681, the government tried and executed another five staunch Covenanters. One of these, Robert Garnock, warned the judges of the danger in passing judgment on men who in good conscience chose to obey the laws of God rather than the laws of men. Garnock accused the government of being the real breakers of God's law. The night following their execution, James Renwick and his friends retrieved the heads of Garnock and his associates from public display and buried them in a nearby rose garden.[21]

Society People (1682)

The death of Cargill left the remnant broken in spirit and devoid of ministers willing to preach in the field. Throughout the persecution, small groups of Christians banded together to form *societies* for mutual defense and for edification through prayer and spiritual conference. These societies encouraged the Covenanters to uphold their testimony "for the prerogatives of Christ, the privileges of his church, and the liberties of mankind; and against not only tyranny upon the one hand but also defection upon the other."[22]

Walter Smith, executed the same day as Cargill, wrote guidelines for conducting these society meetings. Scripture (Ps. 137; Mal. 3:16; Acts; Col. 3:15; 1 Thess. 5:11; Heb. 10:24–25) evidences the practice by God's people to form societies, particularly during time of exile or persecution, Smith contended. Each society typically contained fewer than twelve members and maintained communication with other societies via correspondence. Psalm singing typically opened and closed each meeting. During the meeting, members prayed and freely shared Scripture for their mutual edification; however, they avoided contentious issues (unless ministers were present). The proper exercise of secret prayer, family devotion, and the leading of an exemplary Christian life were not simply encouraged; they were required! Members held one another accountable for their Christian walk and sought to stir one another up to good works.[23] John Howie remarked that "the decay and thriving of religion goes hand in hand" with meetings such as these throughout the history of the church. Howie contended that such meetings are an important supplement to formal worship because formal worship does not provide the opportunity to exhort one another to duty or for women to join in prayer and exhortation (See Acts 1:14). Forty years earlier, to avoid the spread of error and the potential for division that could arise from the societies, the Scottish Assembly had developed guidelines to ensure that such societies were subject to the control of church sessions.[24]

For mutual defense, the societies banded together to form a General Correspondence (also called General Society), holding their first convention in December 1681 and meeting quarterly thereafter. This body did not consider itself a civil court or an ecclesiastical judiciary, but simply an assembly of representatives of the various praying societies, which had bound themselves to share a united testimony. To this end, they pledged, "Nothing [involving their common testimony] should be done by any particular person without the consent of the society whereof he was a member."[25] In general, the societies were comprised of those who had sided with Hamilton at Bothwell. They, like Hamilton, rejected all preachers who had yielded to tyranny or refused to speak out against the Indulgence. In the absence of church courts to pursue complaints, the only means of protest available to the faithful remnant was withdrawal. Typically, the General Society met in remote and desolate areas such as Auchengilloch, a few miles from Newmilns. Auchengilloch is a depression in the moor large enough to hide five hundred people, yet not visible until "the traveler comes immediately upon it." A nearby hill provides a view for miles, and the rough terrain is "inaccessible to cavalry." By 1683, there were about eighty society groups with a total membership of about seven thousand.[26]

On January 12, 1682, sixty Covenanters, including James Renwick, posted a declaration on the Lanark Cross. This declaration, approved at the first convention, outlined their position and grievances. The Scottish Council countered by burning the *Solemn League and Covenant* and the Covenanter's declarations at the same cross a week later. Later in 1682, the Society sent its most able lad, James Renwick, to Holland for ministerial training.

At the second convention, the Society commissioned Alexander Gordon, Sir Robert Hamilton's brother-in-law, to visit the Reformed churches on the continent to plead their case. A young man named John Nisbet (yet another John Nisbet) accompanied Gordon to London.[27] This John Nisbet was one of four Society members commissioned to study for the ministry. While Gordon visited abroad, this John Nisbet maintained correspondence between Gordon and the societies. As a cover, Nisbet served as tutor for the children of the Rev. Matthew Meade (1630–1699).[28] A few years later, the government would charge this John Nisbet (the tutor), along with Gordon and Meade, with involvement in a plot to overthrow the king.

It was the custom at the beginning of each General Society meeting to query each representative to verify that he and those he represented were free of public scandal and clear in their testimony. Unfortunately, some went too far by adding undue burdens on their brethren. One question concerning the rightfulness of paying customs at ports and bridges caused a split within the ranks that never healed. Considering these taxes were of ancient origin and not for the purpose of persecution, the General Society concluded it was a Christian's duty to pay them. One troublemaker, James Russel, and his followers refused fellowship with the General Society over the tax issue. Russel considered any participation with the state an evil. Russel was a hot-tempered man who caused much "discouragement and grief" by misrepresenting the societies "by word and writing, at home and abroad."[29]

Much of the division, however, resulted from disowning the government of King Charles by the societies. The General Society rejected and rebuked many godly Presbyterian ministers because they would not disown the king although they shared the same views concerning church doctrine, worship, and government. To make matters worse, the societies broke fellowship with those who listened to such ministers, causing further divisions.[30]

During the year 1682, persecution intensified. Many land, pulpit, and office holders chose to give up their property and positions rather than to take the Test. As you recall, the Test required all holding positions of public trust to acknowledge King Charles as head of the church. The dreaded dragoons were active throughout the southern and western shires looking for fugitives and suppressing coventicles. The list grew with new names weekly as many refused to take the oath or to attend church. During this period, Claverhouse, who was a sheriff in one of the regions, pushed the limits of law in persecuting the Covenanters. Those caught in his net ended up injured, impoverished, homeless, banished, or dead. The account given by James Nisbet of children being beaten and tortured was commonplace.[31] In some areas, these tactics proved successful and church attendance increased as people chose to hear curates rather than to suffer. Not even Claverhouse, who had had success in suppressing coventicles in some areas, was able to suppress the Covenanters in the shires of Ayr (where Newmilns is located) and Lanark.[32] It was during this period, according to Defoe, that Claverhouse began the practice of executing obdurate Covenanters; however, he did so only to the extent of his legal authority.[33]

The government increasingly resorted to hanging for the slightest offense. They hanged Robert Gray for writing a letter to a prisoner advising him not to take the Black Oath. As Gray awaited his execution, he warned his fellow prisoners not to listen to those who encouraged peace with the enemies of God: "My soul trembles to think of that peace; to seek peace with the enemies of God and say they have peace in it." He advised them to follow God, not man: "Follow no man further than he follows the Word of God." For his gallows song, Gray selected Psalm 84, which contains the verse, *"O thou almighty Lord of host, who art my God and king."* The government hanged Alexander Hume for attending two coventicles. On the gallows, he sang Psalm 17, which contains the verse, *"But as for me, I thine own face in righteousness will see; and with thy likeness when I wake I satisfied will be."* A woman named Christian Fyfe avoided the noose when the court declared her mad for proclaiming, "There was not an honest minister left in Scotland."[34]

It was during this year, through several close escapes, that James Nisbet learned how he stood "in absolute need of a Savior" to 'redeem, convert, strengthen, direct, and comfort him.' As he saw his friends "daily dropping into eternity," he learned how "fully and safely" he was "compassed about with the garments of salvation," and how the Lord was preparing his heart to "sing through all eternity." In his memoir, he describes the events of 1682:

In the year 1682, when in the thirteenth year of my age, in the conduct of divine providence, things in my father's family began to take a turn, in order to our being further tried, after the following manner. It was designed by my friends that I should go and stay with a kinsman of my father's; but, upon second thoughts, without any foreseen reason it was judged more proper to send my younger brother, which was a kind providence to me that I could never enough admire and wonder at; for shortly after he went, there was a party of the enemy came to that man's house to search for some of the persecuted party. When the people of the house saw the enemy coming, they fled out of the way; but the cruel enemy got my dear brother into their hands. They examined him concerning the persecuted people, where they haunted, or if he knew where any of them were; but he would not open his mouth to speak one word to them. They flattered him: they offered him money to tell where the Whigs were; but he would not speak. They held the point of a drawn sword to his naked breast: they fired a pistol over his head: they sat him on horseback, behind one of themselves, to be taken away and hanged; they tied a cloth on his face and set him on his knees to be shot to death; they beat him with their swords and with their fists; and they kicked him several times to the ground with their feet. Yet, after they had used all the cruelty they could, he would not open his mouth to speak one word to them. Although he was a very comely proper child, going in ten years of age, yet they called him a vile ugly dumb devil and beat him very sore; then [they] went their way, leaving him lying on the ground, sore, bleeding, and in the open fields. Hereby the Lord fulfilled his Word, *"Surely the wrath of man shall praise thee, and the remainder of wrath thou wilt restrain"* (Ps. 76:10). From this passage of providence I remark, "The kind over-ruling power and providence of God"; for if the enemy had gotten knowledge whose son he was, they would have put him to death upon his father's account. How might my dear brother sing with David, *"I will render praise unto thee, O God, for thou hast delivered my soul from death"* (Ps. 56:12-13). I could never enough reverence the good hand of God in considering my frame and preventing my going to that house, for I was always more easy in my temper, and sooner wrought upon, than my brother. O! What shall I render unto the Lord for his sparing and preventing mercy, in that he did not lead me into this temptation, but delivered me from that evil; but what shall I say, himself did it, whose is the kingdom, the power, and the glory forever. Therefore, be thou exhaulted, O God, above the heavens, and let thy glory be above all the earth (Ps. 57:2,5,11), because thou art God, even the Most High God, who performeth all things for me. Amen.

At this time I was obliged to [move] several times from one place to another because of the vigilance that the enemy used to get notice of us; yet, through the mercy and kind providence of God, we were all still preserved. But, the last half of this year came to be very trying to all of us; for the enemy swore that if we were out of hell, they should have some of us, if not all of us. For that end they disguised one of themselves, a fair well-favored young man, in women's clothes, like a gentlewoman, giving out that she was a cousin of our own come from Ireland to invite us over to our friends there, because they had heard of our troubles in Scotland. This gained credit amongst our friends who knew where we were; especially seeing the metamorphosed, she was so like our family, and because of the other probabilities of his discourse. And so he got exact notice where we were; and returning back to his garrison, gave them an account; and so the next morning the whole troop came all out on horseback to the place where we were, which was about ten miles distant.

But behold the kind providence of God, who always shows himself a wonder-working God for me, even for poor me, who was always most unfit for the trial. Therefore, he always for the most part kept me farthest from it: for, half an hour before the enemy came to the house where we stayed, my mother sent me about some business to my father who was two miles farther off on the other side of a moss. I was but a little way gone from my mother when I found myself pressed with a strong desire to pray; and, accordingly, I fell down in the moss and prayed. Then rising and running a little way I was again, through fervency of spirit, forced to fall down flat upon the ground to pray, and a third time; but finding my vehement desire to pray, and yet to run, increase upon me, I resolved to run bareheaded. And, accordingly, I ran and cried with all the strength of my voice, and yet I thought the cries of my heart and vehemence of my spirit far exceeded that of my voice; and I would take no denial, but mercy, mercy, pity, and compassion from the Lord I would have for myself and father's family. After I had near run the two miles, I was led out to mix my prayers with praises. I knew not what the matter meant until I came where my father was met with some other Christians for prayer at the outmost edge of the moss, amongst whom I found my mother and the rest of her children; and they were all on alarm. But nothing could make me afraid at that time; only I thought it strange to see them alarmed, and to find my mother there, she having no thought of it when I left her. She told me that, about a quarter of an hour after I left her, she saw the enemy coming, and had not above six or seven minutes to shift herself and her children into the moss, the house being on the edge of the moss, and she thought surely they had gotten me. I told her I had not seen them or any other body since I left her; but I did not at that time tell her how I was employed.[35]

James's family's joy in their escape was tempered by the knowledge that the owner of the house they had resided in was imprisoned, tortured, and released only after "taking the abominable oath called the Test and paying a fine." From these narrow escapes, James observes that the Lord was training him "to live by faith, and not by sight and sense" (2 Cor. 5:7; John 20:29) and calling him to a "praying work." Looking back at the impact of these times on his family, he sees how the Lord "was disengaging our hearts from all creature refuges, that we might seek to him to be our alone refuge" (Ps. 142:4–5; 3:8). He concludes his meditation with praise for the Most High God, "the possessor of heaven and earth" (Ps. 103:20–22; Gen. 14:19–20), who exercises providential care over all things (Ps. 24:1).[36]

The Test (1683)

By early 1683, the government rewarded Claverhouse, the mortal enemy of the Covenanters, with a promotion and a seat on the Privy Council. Claverhouse used his newly won position to persuade the Duke of York to execute the laws against the Covenanters. To veil its true intent, the government promised to grant a pardon to anyone who would take the Test before August 1, 1683, later extended to March 1, 1684. As each of these deadlines passed, Claverhouse and his henchmen pursued the Covenanters with increased vigor and with increased clarity of conscience. Furthermore, they sifted the Indulged ministers with oaths and summons, causing many to flee to avoid imprisonment.[37]

The government hanged John Nisbet's nephew, also named John Nisbet (1657–1683) in Kilmarnock on April 4, 1683.[38] His replies to the interrogators' questions are insightful:

Q. When saw ye John Nisbet [of Hardhill]? A. I did not see him this good while. Q. But when did you see him, and where did you see him? A. Although I could, I would answer, to discover my neighbors. The Major said he would make me tell, or he would make me sit three hours in hell. I answered, that was not in his power ...

Q. Then said they, say "God save the king." A. I answered, it was not in my power to save, or condemn him. Q. Would you not say, "God save your beast, if it were fallen into a hole?" A. No, because it is a taking of his name in vain...

Q. Was Bothwell rebellion? I answered, it was self-defense, which was lawful. Q. How prove ye that? A. By that Confession which ye build your Test upon. Then they said jeeringly, I was a grammarian.

Q. Own ye a law? A. Yes. Q. Own ye the law as it is now established? A. Since ye make your questions matters of life and death, ye ought to give time to consider upon them.

Q. Own ye the king in all matters, civil and ecclesiastic, and to be head of the church? A. I will acknowledge none to be head of the church but Christ. Q. Who is lawgiver? A. Christ. Q. Is the king the king, or not? A. He was once a covenanted king. Q. Is he the king now? A. I refer it to his obligations in his coronation oath, to be considered. Q. Is he your king, or not? I told them, I would not answer any more such questions at this time. This is all that passed for the most part, except a number of senseless questions. No more at present, but have my love remembered to all friends in Christ. I am very well borne through blessed be the Lord for it.[39]

While on the scaffold, John Nisbet the Younger sang "with a great deal of affection and joy" from the Sixteenth Psalm; his song starting at verse five, *"God is mine inheritance and cup of portion,"* and ending in the verse, *"Before thy face; at thy right hand are pleasures evermore."* For his parting Scripture, John selected Romans 8, which includes the famous promise, *"Who shall separate us from the love of God?"* His last act was to commend the necessity of godliness to the crowd: "Death is before you all, and if it were staring you in the face as nearly as it is to me at present, I doubt not there would be many awakened consciences among you."[40] The poem on his tombstone begins:

> Come, reader, see, here pleasant Nisbet lies;
> His death doth pierce the high and lofty skies;[41]

A month later, the government executed John Wilson along with several others. Wilson, in his "Last Speech and Testimony," remarked, "I have read of some single ones dying for opinion (not truth), yet could I never read of a track of men, such as have been in Scotland these twenty-two years, laying down their lives for naked opinion, so calmly, so solidly and composedly, with so much peace and serenity."[42] Others executed that year gave similar testimony. Another martyr, John Dick, sang the Second Psalm and read Ezekiel 9 before his hanging. These texts reveal the attitude of the Covenanters toward government. The Covenanters believed that kings derive their power from God and are obligated to serve Christ in fear and trembling, or perish. They believed that a government that does not seek to serve Christ would perish: *"Kiss ye the Son, lest in his ire ye perish from the way"* (Ps. 2:12). The passage from Ezekiel (Ezek. 9:3–6) clearly conveys the duty of the people to grieve and cry out against the sins of their nation. Ezekiel speaks of God pouring out his wrath on those that do not speak out, starting with the church leaders because of their obligation to do so, and then the church.

During 1683, James Nisbet learned that God "has the reigns and government of all hearts and hands at his beck," as God miraculously delivered him from several narrow escapes with death. As he reflects on the following narrow escapes, he concludes: "What can I say to all these things, but what Moses the man of God said upon a great deliverance at the Red Sea: *Who is like unto thee, O Lord! Who is glorious in holiness, fearful in praises, and doing wonders* (Exod. 15:11)? *O blessed be his glorious name for ever; and let the whole earth be filled with his glory* (Ps. 72:19). Bless the Lord, O my soul, for his mercy endureth forever. Amen."[43]

The year 1683, being the fourteenth year of my age, was a year of heavy trials, wherein I met with many singular proofs of the Lord's providential care and kindness to me, in that he was pleased graciously to interpose himself betwixt death and me. For, in the month of March, I escaped very narrowly being drowned in the river Clyde. In the month of May, I was with two other men taken prisoners; the manner was thus. The enemy came in the midst of the night to the house where I stayed and searched the house. [They] took [the] other two men and me out of our bed, handled us roughly, and [then] made us stand in the remote corner of the house until they filled their bellies with the best of such victuals as the house afforded, whereof there was plenty. The people with whom I stayed had five daughters, all young women. Although one of the other two men was their brother, and the other was their uncle, yet the Lord inclined the hearts of two of the daughters, while the enemy was busy at meat, to put forth their hand and draw me behind them, close to the wall. They stood close before me all the while the enemy was busy at meat; who, when they had done, they took the two men out of the corner where they had set us. One of the enemy said there were three; another said there but two. After some debate about the number of their prisoners, they went away with the two without any further search. But how much is the goodness of God to be admired in this my delivery? For the commanding officer, to whom they were taken to be examined, would have known me, for he was particularly acquainted with all my father's family. Although my surname was changed [so] that none in that place of the country could tell my right name, yet it would have been to no purpose if I had been brought before him. This was a singular instance of the ever watchful and overruling providence of God, who always waits that he may be gracious.

Further, in July, one morning, at six o'clock, I went out to a wood a little distant from the house; and within a little [time], I heard the sound of people among the trees drawing near me. When I looked up, [I] saw men clothed in red; and as I got to my feet, one of them bade me stand dog and be shot. I said to him, "What good will my blood do you?" and when he cocked his pistol, another of them said, "Hold man, do not shoot the bonny lad." The man with the pistol said I was a Whig. They asked my name, and I told them my new name. They said one to another [that] they had none of that name in their lists. He that commanded them said, "Since we have none of that name, let him alone." The first man that came unto me swore again, that he would have me shot; but two of them would not let him. So they went off and left me. I stayed about five or six hours in that place, considering what lessons I was to learn from that merciful deliverance, whereby, in a manner, I was miraculously preserved from this and the foregoing danger, when the two sisters concealed me behind them. From both which I remark, "The Lord is infinite in wisdom to contrive, and infinite in power, faithfulness, and goodness to bring about deliverance, to and for them whom he has appointed to live."[44]

In August 1683, a small ship, which had barely survived a storm at sea, landed in Rye on the coast of England. On this ship was the recently ordained minister, James Renwick, on his way to Scotland to pick up the fallen banner of preaching to the Covenanting remnant. The city was up in arms because a plot to kill the king, called the Rye House Plot, had just been discovered, ultimately leading to the death of several nobles and leaders in England and Scotland. Because of this plot, the king renewed the persecution of the Covenanters with increased intensity. The small party quickly put again to sea and landed in Dublin. Renwick arrived in Scotland in September, and held his first public service in November. He preached from the same text as Cargill's last sermon, *"Comfort ye, comfort ye, my people"* (Isa. 26:20). With great joy and hopefulness, many flocked to hear him preach. One of the attendees was James Nisbet, who left a vivid portrait of the character and impact of this man James Renwick. Renwick, likewise, left a vivid portrait of an even greater presence in Scotland:

The Lord is wonderfully to be seen in every thing and assists in what he calls unto; for, in coming through the country, we had two field meetings, which made me think, that if the Lord could be tied to any place, it is to the mosses and moors of Scotland.[45]

One of Renwick's famous sayings was "Let us be lions in God's cause and lambs in our own." He was a bold, poetic, dashing spirit who always had a fleet horse saddled and ready for escape if the dragoons discovered the site where he was preaching in the fields. Although not a large man, Renwick possessed great character, knowledge, and spirit. Unfortunately, a faction persistently refused to hear Renwick for a variety of hair-splitting reasons, including Renwick's ordination by those who used musical instruments in worship services. Even Reverend Peden initially warned people against Renwick.

To compound their worries at home, public sentiment abroad turned against the Society People. Many abroad were concerned with the remnant's controversial views on several subjects: namely, their refusal to acknowledge the king's authority, their overly restrictive requirements for fellowship, and their lack of ecclesiastical capability to call and oversee ministers. These concerns made it almost impossible to ordain additional ministers abroad.[46] The following questions posed to attendees to the General Society meetings are illustrative of the extent to which they went to remain free of the defections of the day:

(1) Do ye know the principles and practices of these societies from whom ye have your commission? (2) Do ye and they own our covenants and engagements, our faithful Declarations and Testimonies? (3) Are ye and they free of giving any manner of bond to the enemies? (4) Are ye and they free of paying cess, locality, and any militia money? (5) Are ye and they free of paying stipends to the curates or to the Indulged? (6) Are ye and they free of taking the enemies pass or protection? (7) Are ye and they free of answering unto enemies their courts? (8) Are ye and they free of capitulation any manner or way with the enemies, or furnishing them with commodities? (9) Are ye and they free of counseling and consenting to any in their compliance, any of their foresaid ways, for you, in your name? (10) Are ye and they free of joining with the curates or indulged, by hearing them preach, accepting the administration of the sacraments at their hands, subjecting unto their discipline, or being married by them? (11) Are ye and they free of joining any of the foresaid ways of complying, unfaithful, and silent ministers of the time?

The severity of life on the run combined with the endless criticism from home and abroad bore hard on the Society People. Even nature seemed to turn against them because the winter of 1683 was one of the coldest on record, compounded by the reality that many of the Society People were without shelter. It was during this harsh winter (one of the worst on record) that James Nisbet lost his dear mother and sister. Concerning James's account of this sad event, the historian Alexander Smellie (1857–1923) remarked, "It is difficult to believe that, in all literature, one will encounter any story more bitter-sweet."[47]

[In] the latter part of this year 1683, the bloody persecution being still very hot, my father's family had much difficulty to escape the fury thereof; yet the Lord was very kind and provided them still with one pekah [an opening] after another. The last of which to my mother and sister was a poor cottage, where they ended their earthly pilgrimage. The manner was as follows: In the month of December, my father took me alongst with him, on a Saturday night, four miles distant from the place where my mother with her children was. I stayed with him all Sabbath day, which was spent in the worship of God. At night, when he and those with him were going away from the house where we had stayed all day, I could not get him parted with, neither could I well speak for weeping: upon which I knew well, from former experience, that such violent emotions of grief and heart meltings were a presage of some ensuring sore trial. My father asked what the matter was? I said I knew not; but I feared we would get sad news of one another. Some of those who were with him began to boast me to silence; but he desired them to let me alone, telling them, that sorrow was twice sorrow to me; and so he comforted and exhorted me. I desired, since he could not stay with us, that he would cry to the Lord on our behalf; [this] he promised, and spoke kindly to me, and so parted.

On Monday morning, I returned to go to my mother; but all the way I could do nothing but weep, groan, and lie down and sleep; for, though I had but four miles to go, yet I was seven or eight hours in making it out. When I came to my mother, I found my younger brother fallen in the fever, and my sister near death of a consumption that she had contracted about twelve-months before. When I had delivered my errand to my mother, which I went along with my father for, and [had] done some other necessary business according to my mother's command, she shut the door of the cottage. [She] says to me, "You have been as dutiful a son as a woman could expect, for which I give you my hearty blessing; and I am going to pray to the Lord, that he may abundantly bless you, my husband, and the rest of my children." [She] went about family worship with much enlargement of heart in prayer, recommending herself, soul and body, her husband, her children, and the work and people of God to the Lord's kind care and infinitely wise disposal. After prayer, taking a piece of money in her hand, she says, "This is all the money which your father has, dig a hole in this place (pointing to the ground) and hide it there, and the first time you see your father give it him"; for, says she, "My days are near at an end." If any person had been witness to us, they should have seen as much sorrow, and yet, as much quietness and composure of mind as two persons in such circumstances could be capable of. But, behold, he, who appointed me from everlasting to have such a pious sweet well-disposed mother, knew that I could not well bear to part with her. Therefore, he wisely thought fit to hide sorrow from me in a way of his own blessed contrivance. For the heavy sorrow I was under the two former days sunk me this night, before the morrow, into a high fever, in which fever I lost my senses, which continued so with me for fifteen days; all which time, I had no knowledge, nor remembrance of anything, and spoke but little, except when calling for drink. On the second day of my fever, my mother turned sick. We were all four lying like persons deadly wounded in the field of battle; but the Lord, who is a present help in the time of need, inclined a gentlewoman to come and see my mother. The gentlewoman, seeing none of us able to give another a drink, … provided us with a servant; and after that another, who both proved good friends to us.

My mother died on the seventh day of her sickness. Word was sent to my father, who hastened back to us, and [he] came just [in] time [for] my sister's burial, who died the sixth day after my mother. He, finding his wife dead and buried, he said with Job, "*Naked came I into the world, and naked must I go out of it again.* The Lord is now lopping my roots, like that of a tree, that I may fall the more easily." Indeed, the loss of my mother was a stroke that touched him to the quick and humbled him much; and it could not be otherwise, considering that he was a man of a strong affection, and she a woman many ways very endearing, especially in piety, sweetness, and easiness of temper.[‡]

A few instances of her piety and religious disposition are as follows: [My] aunt, my father's sister, … told me that as soon as my mother found herself with child, she always gifted the fruit of her womb to the Lord; and after they were born, she always took some of them with her

---

[‡] In the *True Relation of the Life and Suffering of John Nisbet of Hardhill*, James provides additional details concerning his father's response to these events: As "friends were putting his dead daughter in her coffin, he stepped and kissed the corpse, saying, 'Religion doth not make void natural affection, but we should be sure it run in the natural channel of sanctified submission to the will of God, of whom we have our being.'" After checking on his sons, one of those with him said, "Sir, I hope you know who hath done this?" He answered, "I know that he hath done it that makes all work together for the good of them who love him and keep his way…." "At eleven o'clock in the night, they carried away his daughter; and had two miles to Stanhouse Churchyard, where her mother was buried…." He held her head all the way.

to secret prayer, and my father [took the] other some of them with him. Further, my aunt told me, she had never seen anybody go beyond my mother in subduedness of spirit; closet and family piety was her constant care and study; but never pretended to any great knowledge of public matters of a religious concern. Before their family keeping was broken up in the year 1679, she was ever learning of her husband. When any trial came to them in point of compliance with the sins of the time, he was ever telling her, from such and such places of Scripture, the unlawfulness of such compliance. For instance, when the cess and locality came to be imposed by the then authority to bear down the rendezvous of rebellion, a term of ignominy that the enemy gave to the religious meetings of the Lord's people, he said to her, "See the narrative of their act is in express terms to bear down the worship of God and persecute his cause and people; and if I should cast in my lot with the wicked and give them of my worldly substance, wherewith to support them in their wicked courses, I become guilty of their persecution; and, therefore, I dare not give them anything." She answered him meekly, and said, "God forbid; see that you do nothing that may wound your conscience, or wrong the Lord's work and people, come of me and my children what will; and if you, they, and I, get safe to Emanuel's land, we shall be more than sufficiently made up of all our worldly losses." "I must say," said my aunt, "I never knew a person bear their crosses with more quietness of mind, patience, and evenness of temper, than your mother did, notwithstanding of her vast worldly losses, and notwithstanding of the innumerable straits and dangers that she and hers were made to undergo." Yet, after all, I must say (as she often said herself) with Paul, "What had she to lose?" Or what had she to bear up under her losses with but what was given her? For as she found all her springs were from the Lord's all-sufficiency, by whom, and through whom, she could do all things, he strengthening her, so I found her always willing and ready to give him the glory of all (Rom. 11:36; 1 Cor. 4:7; 2 Cor. 3:5; James 1:17).

O that I could bless and magnify him for his kind providence to me, in my having such a mother, who concerned herself with the inward and serious part of religion, and constantly pressed the study of it upon her children and servants. She urged us always to give all diligence to make sure of a personal interest in the free favor of God, through the Mediator Christ Jesus, the virtue of whose blood and merits we were to seek, to have effectually applied to us by the Holy Spirit, in his saving and powerful efficacy and operations. She likewise pressed us much to take cross dispensations in good part out of the Lord's hand, and entirely resign ourselves to his disposing will.[48]

A short time after his sister's burial, James recovers from his fever. Deeply impacted by the loss of mother's "good counsel and sweet company," he, nevertheless, thanks God for taking away his "mother and sister to a land where the weary are at rest,... where the wicked cease from troubling the just," and where his "loss was undoubtedly [their] unspeakable gain." He also ponders on how the Lord shortened the lives and hastened the ruin of those who got his family's worldly substance and those who would later betray his father.[49] He learns much from these reflections:

> O how much is God to be had in reverence, who is righteous in all his ways and holy in all his works, for the whole earth is full of his glory! From hence, I may see the brevity and uncertainty of this human life (Job 14:1-5; Ps. 39:4-5; 90:3-6:). From hence, I may always see that all these things come forth from the right hand of the Lord, and are performed by him to whom belongeth all the issues from death (Ps. 68:20). From hence, I do see that now the Lord is in a special way remarkably upon his mighty acts, both of mercy and judgment, with respect to my father's family (Ps. 65:5). From hence, I may learn that the Lord doth often tryst his own people with the dark and wrath-like side of the cloud of his providences first, and afterwards with the light warm and friendly side next (Ps. 29::3,10; Heb. 12:11). From hence, I may learn, when the Lord is exercising me with judgments, it is not for me, a poor blind ignorant creature, to arraign his holy and spotless procedure at the bar of my blind and vitiated reason; but rather put a blank in his hand, and let him fill up my lot with what he pleases (Lev. 10:3; Job 34:29; Ps. 39:9; Dan. 4:35). From, hence, I see that no creature comfort or enjoyment is to be taken up with, neither any foundation sought to rest upon, but wise and kind Omnipotence (Isa. 1:10). From hence, I learn that all rational beings are set on the stage of time to act for an eternity; and then, when their day comes, to take flight to the world of spirits, never more to return to their friends on earth, but they must go to them and make way for others. So death breaks all bonds of union and relations, betwixt friend and friend, husband and wife, parent and child, even though loving to one another beyond expression; the thoughts of which makes me cry out, "O vanity of vanities! All Time's things are vanity and vexation of spirit" (Eccl. 1:4; 3:1-2,19; 8:6-8; 9:5-6,10). From hence, I learn,... while on this stage of time, God hath put a great work in my hand, which is to glorify him all the days of my life, and to work out my own salvation (Ps. 13:2,4; Rom. 11:36; 1 Cor. 10:31). From hence, I see the great need there is of making sure a personal interest in the free favor of God through Christ, and to have this daily intimated to my soul, by the inward testimony of his Spirit, accord-

ing to the outward testimony of his Word. I cannot but adore the sovereign wisdom of God, in that he preserved my life, and yet hid the sorrow of my mother's death from me, by throwing me into a fever, which death I could not otherwise well have borne. O glory to God, for he is wonderful in counsel and excellent in working. From hence, I learn the great need I have of making daily use of Christ, as for justification, so also of his fullness for growth and suitable advances in sanctification, and to be kept by the power of God through faith unto salvation, till his time come: that I must remove after my friends from this region of sins, calamities, and vexations of spirit, and get home unto the uninterrupted enjoyment of God and of my godly relations (Col. 1:12–14; Heb. 12:23–24; 1 Pet. 1:5). O Lord, bear up in mercy to that, and in that day. Amen.[50]

Truth Preservation (1684)

Increasingly, church and state united to tighten the noose around the neck of the Covenanting Remnant. The Privy Council passed several acts during 1684 that granted Claverhouse and his allies the right to search, seize, examine, evict, banish, or apprehend any who refused the oath or who did not carry passes. One of these acts established commissions, comprised of the leading persecutors such as Claverhouse, to oversee execution of the laws.[51] Another act required the apprehension of nearly two thousand known fugitives if they would not take the Test by August 1. These new powers in the hands of the military led to a period of persecution called the "Killing Times." After completing a ring of stocked outposts in April, Claverhouse boasted that he was in a position to subdue the country.

The civil authorities tormented Indulged ministers for the slightest reasons. For example, they arrested Anthony Shaw, an elderly, Indulged minister from Newmilns, for holding a communion service outdoors because the crowd overflowed the church. The court deemed this violation an illegal field coventicle, for which they imprisoned Shaw, then liberated him, revoked his Indulgence, then imprisoned him again for refusing to post a bond (covering future preaching), then finally released him when friends posted the bond. By accepting the terms of this bond, Shaw agreed not to exercise any ministerial function. Evidencing Shaw's civil obedience was a remark made by John Nisbet the Younger in his own trial that Shaw thought that those who "would not pray for the king in his person and government" should be punished.[52] Other Indulged ministers were banished or jailed for similar infractions.

All social ranks were subject to the persecution. The Commissioners initiated legal proceedings against more than sixty nobles, heritors, and tradesmen for involvement in the battle of Bothwell Bridge. Among those persecuted from the Newmilns' area were the Campbells, whose ancestors numbered among the early Scottish Protestants (Lollards). To avoid persecution, James Campbell (d. 1684), the Earl of Loudoun, fled to Holland. Unwilling to flee, Sir Hugh Campbell of Cessnoch (d. 1686) faced trial for treason. Fortunately, the Commissioner's case against him fell apart when one of their witnesses testified that he had never seen Cessnoch before and the other retracted his testimony.[53]

The civil authorities persisted; in a later trial for involvement in the Rye House Plot to kill the king, they imprisoned Hugh on the Bass Rock.[54] Many of the leading nobles in Ayrshire were involved in this plot, including Sir James Stewart, the co-author of *Naphtali*. As previously mentioned, John Nisbet (the tutor) and Alexander Gordon were also arrested for involvement in this plot. The incriminating evidence against Nisbet (the tutor) was a coded letter that he had sent to Gordon while abroad. Other nobles involved in England and Scotland included the Duke of Monmouth, the Earl of Essex, and the Earl of Argyle. The plotters planned to ambush and to kill King Charles and the Duke of York, and, at the same time, lead an uprising in arms to take power. There is evidence that John Owen and many of the London non-conformist ministers were aware of the plot. Owen defended a limited right of Christian rebellion when the enemies of religion endeavored to "destroy the rights, liberties, and privileges" of Christians. However, Owen denied knowledge of the plot on his deathbed.[55]

In March 1684, civil authorities hanged five Covenanters. They charged one of these men, John Richmond, with being in the company of John Nisbet and for not acknowledging the battle of Bothwell as rebellion. The prosecution attempted to prove his presence at Bothwell, but the witness, when asked under cross-examination, responded to the question, "How far away was John Richmond when he saw him?" with the answer, "about half a mile." On the scaffold, Richmond stated, "O if ye knew what I have met with since I came to prison … what matchless love for my sweet and lovely Lord, ye would long to be with him and would count it naught to go through a sea of blood for him."[56]

At John Richmond's funeral, John Nisbet's cousin, Lieutenant Robert Nisbet, recognized and apprehended James Nisbet of Darvel (1625–1684), a close relative of John Nisbet. This same Lieutenant Nisbet would capture John Nisbet of Hardhill the following year. James, hanged in June 1684, was an ardent supporter of Cargill and Cameron, and he disowned the authority of the king "in so far as he made the work of reformation and the covenants treason." His judges offered to free him if he would acknowledge the king's headship over the church. He refused all such offers with a notable quote from that era: "*Self-preservation must stoop to truth preservation.*" He argued, "It is true that none can merit heaven by their suffering, but it is as true that he has said, '*He that will not forsake all and take up his cross and follow me, he cannot be my disciple.*" With a clear conscience, he wrote in his testimony, "Now I am brought hither this day, to lay down my life for the testimony of Jesus Christ, and for asserting him to be head and king in his own house, and for no matter of fact that they have against me." Today, an inscription on a monument in Glasgow honors James Nisbet of Darvel and his fellow martyrs: "The dead yet speaketh."[57] The words of William Wilberforce (1759–1833), concerning how persecution influences Christians, apply to men such as James Nisbet:

> Christianity especially has always thrived under persecution. For at such times it has no lukewarm professors. The Christian is then reminded that his Master's kingdom is not of this world. When all on earth looks back, he looks to heaven for consolation. Then he sees himself as a pilgrim and a stranger. For it is then as in the hour of death that he will examine well his foundations and cleave to the fundamentals.[58]

That same year, civil authorities captured and executed another one of John Nisbet's dear friends, the aging Captain John Paton. Alexander Smellie, in his book *Men of the Covenant*, referred to Paton as "Mr. Valiant" and to John Nisbet as "Mr. Valiant's brother." Paton, like John Nisbet, had served abroad on the continent during the Thirty Years' War. Paton, like John Nisbet, was a Presbyterian elder. Paton, like John Nisbet, commanded front line cavalry troops at the battle of Bothwell Bridge. In his last testimony, Paton affirmed, "He hates bloodshed, directly and indirectly." When asked if he acknowledged authority, he said, "All authority according to the Word of God."[59]

As the year progressed, persecution intensified. Many of those persecuted during 1684 included children. The prisons, such as the dreaded Dunnottar Castle, soon swelled as magistrates imprisoned more than a thousand men and women for refusing the oath. To relieve overcrowded conditions, the civil authorities offered the more penitent prisoners a nineteen-week journey into slavery in the Carolinas. Michael Shields, the secretary of the General Society, described the severe persecution in letters to supporters in Holland:

> Assuredly, if ever a poor church was battered at by Satan and his instruments, we are that church; if ever a poor people were beset round with right and left hand opposites, we are that people: if ever a poor remnant were the objects of Antichrist's cruelty and apostatical malice, we are that remnant.... Many of us are daily led as lambs to the slaughter.... Some are shut up in prison houses, laid in irons.... Others are sent away to foreign plantations to be sold as slaves; and all of us, we may say, put to wander with our lives in our hands, and to eat our bread in the peril of our lives, many of our residency being in the wild mountains, dens, and caves of the earth, the enraged adversary still searching and pursuing after us, and many still permitted to fall into their hands.[60]

In response to the relentless persecution, the General Society in November 1684 affixed a declaration called the *Apologetical Declaration* on church doors and at city crosses. Renwick signed the declaration against his better judgment. The declaration refers to those issuing it as "a people by holy covenants dedicated unto the Lord ... for defending and promoting this glorious work of Reformation." It disowned the authority of King Charles and all authority descending from him as not being of God's institution. It threatens that all enemies to God and the Covenanted Work of Reformation would be subject to punishment if they "obstinately and habitually, with malice ... proceed against us." It declares abhorrence of private acts of vengeance without deliberation and proper judicial process and the "hellish principle of killing all who differ in judgment or persuasion from us; it having no bottom in the Word of God or right reasons."[61] It was not a call for private citizens to take justice into their own hands; the Society disassociated with those few members who did so. Was their response the appropriate Christian response to tyranny? The legitimacy of their actions is examined in more detail later in this book.

In response to the *Apologetical Declaration*, the council authorized Claverhouse to search out and to kill without trial all suspected people who refused to take the oath or answer questions. In reality, this act merely formalized the practice already in place. On November 25, 1684, the council devised the *Abjuration Oath*. This oath required renunciation of the *Apologetical Declaration* and the "villainous authors thereof."[62] The council also established a bounty for the discovery of Society members and required all to obtain certificates vouching for their loyalty. Destruction of the remnant became a national priority. Increasingly, the military, rather than the courts, decided matters. In early December, Claverhouse with a force of one thousand infantry and four troops of cavalry set out to force the Covenanters into submission.

Although 1684 was a dangerous year for Presbyterians, James Nisbet passed the year in relative safety in "a gentleman's house, in which all things were thriving except real religion." He spent the year reading, meditating, and recording his private devotions. One book, *Popery Anatomized* by John Welsh, equipped him to reject false doctrines from false teachers "with their own weapons." He also "read much of the great Mr. James Durham's writings, which helped [him] to see more distinctly into the spirituality of the divine law of God, and also to understand more distinctly the doctrine of grace, and God's method of salvation, as held forth to [him] in the gospel." Through this period of reflection, he learned that God had blessed him with "the rich jewel of a rational and mortal soul." With this mortal soul he was to level "all the actions of [his] life to the glory of God, and to look beyond time to a future state, and prepare for the same." He was not to rest until his "noble capacities be renewed in Christ" and "framed for the service of God." He learned the necessity of relying on the "revealed will of God in his Word," making it his "only rule in all matters of faith and practice." He committed to himself, "If I get no light, I am to remain unclear in circumstantial [matters], rather than be the instrument of division. O God, send forth thy light, and lead me in thy everlasting way." During this year, he avoided capture by refusing to appear when the magistrate summoned all within a four-mile area to take an oath. He defended this act of self-defense by stating that he "could not in his conscience own these judges as legal."[63]

6

Killing Times

By faith Moses, when he became of age, refused to be called the son of Pharaoh's daughter, choosing rather to suffer affliction with the people of God than to enjoy the passing pleasures of sin. —Heb. 11:24–25 NKJ

Since there is no way for us to escape, but in the Lord, come, let us sing the praises of God, and let him work his own work. —John Nisbet of Hardhill

Killing Times (1685)

The sanguine year of 1685 referred to by its survivors as the Killing Times. New acts made owning the covenants and participation at field-coventicles punishable by death. In January 1685, the council instructed magistrates to have all within their bounds subscribe to the *Oath*.[1] James Nisbet tells how dragoons scoured the countryside with instructions to kill any that refused to submit:

> ...Every one that swore this oath was obliged to have a [certificate] from the judge that administered the oath to them, as an evidence of their loyalty and conformity to the laws of the then government. All of the military were empowered to examine every person they met with and [to] shoot to death every one that [lacked] this pass and mark of sinful compliance. So eager were they in putting their orders in execution that they shot several to death who had that pass (lest they should come short in their measure of cruelty).... The young gentleman with whom I stayed did not take this oath, he, or any of his family, whose names with the names of all others who refused it were taken up by the enemy, and my name amongst the rest, as an enemy to their government.[2]

On his deathbed, King Charles professed his wish to die a Catholic, as was his brother James, the Duke of York, who succeeded him on the throne on February 6, 1685. Although the subservient Scottish Parliament never required the new king James II (1633–1701) to take the coronation oath, he took power and increased persecution.

Alexander Shields, who would later become a leading minister for the Covenanters, enters the stage during this period. After interning under the famous Puritan John Owen, Shields was ordained as a minister of the gospel in 1684. In January 1685, he was arrested in London for preaching a sermon entitled *"Naphtali is a hind [doe] let loose"* (Gen. 49:21).[3] He equated those suffering in southwestern Scotland to the tribe of Naphtali—born with great wrestling, blessed with God's favor and beautiful Word, promised lands south and west of the Sea of Galilee, and connected to Judah at the Jordan towards the rising sun.[4]

To save his life, he took the *Oath of Abjuration* with some liberty in wording: "I do abhor, renounce, and disown in the presence of God, that *pretended* declaration [*Apologetical Declaration*], in so far as it declared war against the king, and asserts, that it's lawful to kill all employed by him in church, state, army, and country." As soon as he returned to his cell, grief overcame him for this defection: "I cannot find words to express, nor groans to bemoan it…. [It] leaves such a stain upon my profession, as a sufferer of Christ, that I cannot wipe it off, and such a sting upon my conscience, that I shall never weep it out."[5] He recanted at the first opportunity: "For I durst not disown these covenants they declare an adherence to, nor the declarations there insinuated, or the principle of defensive arms, the whole is founded upon." He lamented, "It is very low with the interest of Christ, when it hath no better Patrons that such a pitiful creature as I am, to own it in the Supreme Judiciaries of the Nation." When challenged to explain why he refused to follow the Apostle Paul's directions concerning obedience to civil authorities as contained in Romans 13:1, 2, and 5, Shields replied, "I would pick my answer out of the verses you left out." When pressed to acknowledge the king's authority, he remarked, "I cannot own all authority simply" but only as directed in the Word. When demanded to swear allegiance to the king, he explained the distinction between subjection, which he gave as required by the Word, and allegiance, not required by the Word.[6]

> I told them I was a subject, and content to be one, in subjection to any government, which providence sets over us. But for owning the present constitution of it, as God's appointment, and according to law, I durst not give an active acknowledgement of it, nor own any as my lawful sovereign, but in terms of the covenant so far as it may consist with the security of religion and liberty.[7]

After repeated interrogations by the court, Shields signed a statement: "I should own King James II, his authority, and disown that declaration, if so be, such things were contained in it."[8] For this compliance, the court spared his life but imprisoned him on Bass Rock. He escaped by dressing as a woman. On returning to the remnant, he confessed his error with great sorrow, and the Society People granted him forgiveness. The restoration of one that had been unfaithful but repentant is the best proof of the genuine Christian spirit of the Covenanting remnant. After restoration, Shields preached concerning the importance of speaking out against one's own and others' sins, citing 2 Corinthians 5:11, *"Knowing therefore the terrors of the Lord, we persuade men."*[9]

The following accounts convey the intensity of the persecution in the small town of Newmilns during the month of April alone. During this period, a troop of dragoons led by Captain Peter Inglis terrorized the town and surrounding countryside. In one instance, dragoons dressed as fugitives visited the home of one of the Covenanters. As the Covenanter fed them, the soldiers coaxed him into incriminating prayers that served as warrant for his execution. In another instance, the dragoons cut off the head of a captured Covenanter and played football with it. They then rounded up several Covenanters and locked them in the Newmilns Tower. Later that night, armed Covenanters freed the prisoners. Guards shot John Nisbet's brother-in-law, John Law, as he helped free the prisoners. The next day dragoons took revenge by killing a man for simply providing refreshments to the rescuers.

In May 1685, Claverhouse captured John Brown of Priesthill (located about a dozen miles from Newmilns) and shot him in front of his wife and children. As Brown's wife Isabel gathered her husband's bloody head in her lap, Claverhouse asked her, "What thinkest thou of thy husband now, woman?" She boldly answered, "I thought ever so much good of him, and as much now as ever!" Claverhouse threatened to lay her beside him, to which she replied, "If you were permitted, I doubt not but your cruelty would go to that length." To this he declared, "To man I am answerable; and for God, I will take him in my own hand." Later that afternoon, a neighbor comforted Isabel by finishing the morning worship at the point where John Brown had left off in the Twenty-seventh Psalm. As was the custom, they sang the next few lines:[10]

> For he in his pavilion shall—me hide in evil days;
> In secret of his tent me hide—and on a rock me raise.
> And now ev'n at this present time—mine head shall lifted be
> Above all those that are my foes—and round encompass me. —Ps. 27:5–6

Defenders of Claverhouse deny that he was a cold-blooded murderer, yet Claverhouse himself recorded that he had John Brown executed after finding bullets, matches, and treasonable papers in his home. His report also mentions capturing John Brown's nephew at the same time. In an attempt to avoid his uncle's fate, the younger Brown (or Browning) confessed involvement in the April jailbreak in Newmilns and gave Claverhouse the names of other Covenanters. Claverhouse's defenders argue that this act of mercy vindicates their hero, yet they fail to take into account the fact that Claverhouse turned the young man over to military authorities who executed the younger Brown a few days later. His defenders also contend unconvincingly that the testimony of Brown's widow is false because she did not mention the younger Brown.[11] More likely, with her dead husband's head in her lap, she noticed little else.

Men were not the only martyrs during this period. In Wigtown, civil authorities drowned two female Covenanters by tying them down on the beach and waiting for the incoming tide. The curate turned in their names because they had stopped going to church—a sure sign of affiliation with societies and coventicles. The older woman, staked farther out, wrestled to free herself as the waves overcame her. As the older women drowned, a soldier mockingly questioned the younger woman, Margaret Wilson, about what she thought of her friend now. Margaret replied, "What do I see but Christ wresting there? Think ye that we are the sufferers." Before her death, Margaret sang from the Twenty-fifth Psalm, including this appropriate verse: *"Let not the errors of my youth, nor sins, remember'd be: In mercy, for thy goodness' sake, O Lord, remember me"* (Ps. 25:7). Margaret's killers vainly tried to offer her the *Oath* before she drowned, but her reply was, "No, no sinful oaths for me."[12]

On May 28, 1685, the Covenanters posted a protestation on the Sanquhar Cross. This protestation reaffirmed their intention to abide by the covenants and declared James disqualified as king, because he was a murderer of God's saints, an idolater, and an enemy of the church. It also renounced the authority of Parliament and encouraged a Christian response to any aggression against God's people.

Much strife arose when the Lord Argyle landed with an expedition to overthrow the government. Protestants in Holland and Europe sponsored the expedition to avoid a Catholic dynasty in England. Sponsors included James Campbell, the Earl of Loudoun, who died abroad in 1684. James Renwick and the General Society refused to assist Argyle because he would not promise to support the covenants; consequently, the expedition failed and Argyle lost his life. Although John Nisbet opposed supporting Argyle, James Nisbet did not take sides. Nevertheless, many Presbyterians in Scotland aided Argyle because they desperately sought to rid themselves of the intolerable government of King James. The resultant strife did much to break down their unity of spirit.[13]

After the defeat, two of the ministers who came over with Argyle's party sought to join with the Society. The Society rejected them because they had left the country during a time of need, joined with Indulged ministers in worship, spoken out against the Society, associated with Argyle's expedition, and had not supported Cargill and Cameron. In their defense, the two ministers compared their associations abroad with Renwick's foreign ordination and expressed concerns regarding the Society's testimonies and declarations. The two ministers would not abstain from fellowship with the Indulged, but "declared their willingness to lay things in present controversy aside, until they should be determined by a competent judicatory."[14] The Society members, finding these terms unacceptable, decided not to join with these two ministers. Some left with the two ministers resulting in yet another painful division.[15] Walker recorded that one man who wrote harsh accusations against Mr. Renwick later told him that he regretted doing so: "I dipped my pen in gall to him, and he dipped his in honey to me." Walker also listed James Nisbet as one who could attest to the conflicts that took place among the Society members during this time.

James's memoir describes how he saw first hand the divisions that resulted from the Argyle affair:

> But, alas! I got my comforts a little lowered this day upon the reason following: There came to that meeting some of the worthy gentlemen who came home this year with the Earl of Argyle on his expedition; they and some other of our Christian friends looked shy and cold upon one another upon the account of some difference in judgment and opinion that was among them. [This] was matter of sorrow of heart to me now, but much more so afterwards, when I saw the woeful consequences thereof; for I quickly observed that these differences of opinion occasioned much alienation of affection, even among those who were otherwise truly religious. Likewise, it served much to eat out the vitals of religion in the waste of much precious time, which was spent in debating and contending, which might otherwise have been very usefully spent in seeking after and in pursuit of the one thing needful, the better part, which could not have been taken from them.[16]

Life on the Run (1685)

Of 1685, his sixteenth year, James remarks, "It is impossible for me to narrate all that I met with this year, only I take notice of some of the more remarkable occurrences of providence, wherein I was brought many times to the very jaws of destruction, and then wonderfully delivered by him who waits that he may be gracious. So, I have good cause to sing of mercy and of judgment through the whole of this year." Reflecting on his experiences, he urges all of God's children in need (Ps. 9:18; 12:5; 140:12) to trust always "in the Lord, for in the Lord Jehovah is everlasting strength" (Isa. 26:4).[17]

During April, May, and June, James Nisbet narrowly escaped death on several occasions:

> On April 26, 1685, it pleased God in his good providence to send that great man Mr. Alexander Peden to the gentleman's house where I was. On April 27, he preached on John 10, from which he spoke long and well with application to the present times. After he ended, he paused awhile as if he had been meditating. Then with great emotion of spirit, [he] broke silence and said with a loud voice, "Cursed be those in the name of the Lord that speak of my being come to Scotland" (for he was but come from Ireland a few weeks before). [We learned] afterwards that a wicked, malicious woman did, at the very same hour that he pronounced the curse upon her, go and inform the enemy ... where he was. However, notwithstanding of what God had warned him, and he us of, yet we all went to bed securely where I dreamed the whole night on what befell us the next day.
>
> In the morning, the servants and I went to work in the fields; where, before nine o'clock in the morning, we saw a troop of dragoons coming at the full gallop. Mr. Peden and those that were with him in the house fled, which we at work knew nothing of, but we ran everyone as providence directed. The watchful providence of God, which was ever kind to me, led me as by the hand to a moss two miles distant from where we were working to which those with Mr. Peden were fled for shelter; which I knew nothing of till I came hither. The way to it was very steep and ascending ground. Two of the dragoons pursued me very hard; but spying another man [following] me, him they pursued off at the right hand of my way. They fired at him, but it pleased the Lord he escaped at that time. Other two of them came in chase of me, and I was sore put to it for my life. The day was very hot, the sun bright in my face, and the way mountainous; yet the Lord was very kind to me and enabled me to run. I had sometimes thoughts of turning to this hand, and sometimes to

the other, and I often had thoughts to dive into the moss-water pits [with] my head [hidden] in the rush-bushes....

Yet, I was overpowered beyond my inclination to keep on in my way to that moss where the rest were; at the edge of which there was a bog or morass about ten or twelve yards broad to which my good guardian, kind providence, brought me at last. Here the Lord was a present help in the time of need to me. Just as I was got through the bog and drawing myself out of it by the heather of the moss, the two dragoons came to the other side. Seeing they could not get through to me with their horses, they bade me stand dog and be shot. They fired upon me, but God directed the ball by my left ear. Finding that I had escaped the shot, I ran farther into the moss. Kind providence led me just where my persecuted friends were lurking in a moss-hag, about twenty in number; at meeting with whom I was gladly surprised; but being so run out of breath, it was sometime before I could speak any.*

We stayed there for some time until a second troop joined the first troop ... to take the moss on their foot to search us out. After some firing on both sides without any execution done, we drew off and traveled the midst of the moss. They seeing this, horsed again, and pursued us by the edges of the moss; but we always kept ourselves on such ground where horses could not come. We ran that day hither and thither, forward and backward, about thirty miles. We got no manner of refreshment all that day but moss-water to drink, until night, that each of us got a drink of milk. Mr. Peden left those that were with him and went one way; I left them and went another. I lay all night far from any house amongst heather.

The next day when I wakened after the sun rose, I saw about two hundred foot and horse searching all the country far and near. Seeing no way of escape unobserved by the enemy, I clapped close among the heather. So kind and condescending was the Lord to me that not one of the enemy came near the place where I lay: so tender was he of me that he pitied my weak mind and fatigued body and laid no more on me than I was able to bear. All glory and praise to him forever! But still all this time, I was strongly impressed with apprehensions of more trouble to follow; so that I must say, although it has pleased the Lord many times to exercise me with unforeseen and surprising dispensations of providence, yet at other times, I have often had frequent presages of approaching troubles and trials; and it was so just now.

---

* Patrick Walker, in a parallel account, adds that Peden, noticing that one of James's hair knots was shot away, removed the remaining knot with a knife, remarking, "Oh, Jamie, Jamie, I am glad your head is safe. For I knew it would be in danger" (Walker, *Six Saints*, vol. 1, p. 82).

Accordingly, within three or four days, Graham of Claverhouse, a violent persecutor, came for a general search with a hundred horse and three hundred Highland men.[18] They sighted seven of us about the middle of the day and pursued us hard until near midnight, but the Lord preserved us from these bloodthirsty men. We got no refreshment all that day except a few mouthfuls of bread and cheese and moss-water. The horse getting before us and the foot being behind us and we very much fatigued, we were brought to a great strait what to resolve upon for our safety. But at last, finding my comrades resolving still to run, I told them that the Lord had preserved me these days past by running; but now, if he preserved me not some other way, I must fall in the enemy's hand, for I could run no more. So, my friends and I parted before the sun rose. Then I went to as obscure a place as I could think on, clapped as close as I could, and cried out, "Now, O Lord, the great and omnipotent God, thou alone has the long and strong arms of infinite wisdom, infinite power, and infinite mercy. Employ them now for me and [ever] be my sure hiding place from my cruel foes; they are thy enemies, and my enemies for thy sake. O hide me from them or strengthen me to suffer cheerfully for thy cause! O let me not shrink in the hour of death! Neither let me sin against thee by seeking to save my life on sinful terms."

Here I lay in great composure and quietness of mind beholding the wonderful works of God in the conduct of his divine providence, for the enemy, like sons of their father Lucifer, passed by on both sides of the place where I lay. But, he who made them held their eyes that they saw me not, although they passed by within pistol-shot of me. Seeing this, I silently said, "O but this is like God, this is the finger of God, and this is the work of God who is now making bare his holy and outstretched arm for me." Surely, he is in this place though I see him not; yet, he sees me and makes me to see the fruitful effects and glorious operations of his infinite wisdom, of his infinite power, and of his infinite mercy.

Now I get a sight of the wisdom of God in contriving ways and means for my escape. Here I get a sight of the power of God in restraining his and my enemies. Here I get a sight of the mercy of God in hiding me under the covert of his divine encampment. Here I get a sight of the condescendency of God in removing all my fears, doubts, and disquietedness, for now he gives me more peace and serenity of mind, yea much more than at some other times when in no danger at all. Here I get a sight of the enmity that is betwixt the seed of the serpent and the seed of the woman. Here, once more, I get a new sight of my great need of peace and reconciliation with God through Christ, to be savingly and effectually applied to me and witnessed to my soul by the inward testimony of his Spirit and by the outward testimony of his Word. Here I get once more a new sight of my great need to be so far advanced in mortification, as to be denied to myself and all Time's things, yea to natural life itself.

In this place, I stayed some hours after the enemy passed me. About half an hour [later], they shot a man in the open fields; about one hour after that, as I understood afterwards, they came up to my friends that left me who were lain down in the open fields to sleep. They got [one of them] into their hands and beat him cruelly, but for haste they carried him away prisoner that they might overtake the rest, whom they pursued thirty-three miles that day but got no more of them. All praise and glory be to him who often cuts bloody enemies short of finding the enterprises of their hands! Yet, one of these, my friend called William Reid languished a few weeks and died.

After this, I languished some days and then was seized with a high and violent fever. I got into a poor man's house [where] his wife made me a bed in the byre [barn] beside the cows, because her husband might not see me so that he might be free to give his oath that he harbored no Whigs. The next day, one Colonel Buchan, another of the persecutors, came with two troops of dragoons to search that country. He, with some more dishorsed, came into the poor cottage where I was lying, and asked the poor woman what men were in this den? She answered, "There was no man but a young lad of her own lying sick at the point of death." Then they came where I was; [Buchan] lifted up my head by the hair with a bended pistol in his right hand, looked me broad in the face, and said to those who were with him, "There is nothing here but a young creature dying," and so let my head fall out of his hand and went away. I was then so sick that I was not capable of fear at the danger or of joy at the escape. The poor woman conceived such fear lest she came to trouble on my account, as she would not for any persuasion, let me stay any longer; so, I was carried a great way to another poor woman's house, [where] on the ninth day, I got a cool and continued languishing for seven days.[19]

It took another month for James to recover, during which time he suffered two life-threatening relapses. These close encounters with death made him realize that he "would be squeezed through one trouble to another while in this world, as water from one vessel to another." This notwithstanding, he willingly acquiesced to God's "disposing will," finding "these Scriptures ... subservient thereunto: Job 23:13–16; 38:39–41; Dan. 4:35; Acts 17:24–28; Matt. 10:29–31."[20] He found comfort only in the Word and hearing it preached:

After this, I went sixteen miles with some of those good people, to hear a sermon preached by the great Mr. James Renwick, a faithful servant of Christ Jesus, who was a young man endued with a great piety, prudence, and moderation. The meeting was held in a very large desolate moor, and the minister appeared to be accompanied with much of his master's presence. He prefaced on the Seventh Psalm and lectured on the 2 Chronicles 19, from which he raised a sad applicatory regret that the rulers of our day were as great enemies to religion as those of that day were friends to it. He preached from Mark 12:34 in the forenoon; after explaining the words, he gave thirteen marks of a hypocrite backed with pertinent and suitable applications. In the afternoon, he gave two marks of a sound believer backed with a large, full, and free offer of Christ to all sorts of perishing sinners [who] would come and accept of him for their Lord and Savior, and for their Lord and Lawgiver. His method was both plain and well digested, suiting the substance and simplicity of the gospel. This was a great day of the Son of man to many serious souls who got a Pisgah view of the Prince of Life and of that pleasant land that lies beyond the banks of death, Jordan.[21]

After the sermon, dragoons captured several Covenanters. James, ill with fever, narrowly escaped capture through the Lord's deliverance:

All friends left me and went to shift for themselves because I was not able to travel so swiftly as they, except only a godly woman, whose name was Mary Wilson. Her I desired also to leave me and shift for her own safety, telling her, "I was in a good hand where I could not miscarry—come life or death"; but she would not part with me. So we traveled about four miles, as I was able to walk, discoursing to one another upon the nature and suitableness of the subject that was preached to us. [We discussed] what reach of experience we had anent those marks which he laid before us in time of sermon and what part of them were borne home upon our souls for conviction, for confirmation, and for consolation. And all the way that we traveled, the Lord was remarkably kind to us; for, although we were last in the moor, yet there was not one of the enemy came near us, because they were gone in pursuit of those who were first out of the moor. And thus, after we had traveled four miles slowly, my friend brought me to a house where I lay twenty days in a very sore and heavy fever; yet, as at the first three times when in the fever so at this time, I got nothing to drink but whiged sour milk all the time of my sickness.[22]

In August, shortly after his recovery, the Lord delivered him again:

Then, as a friend and I were going into a house to get some meat, immediately there came a troop of the enemy to the house. As they dismounted their horses at the one door, my friend and I had just as much time as run out at another door, without getting the thing we went for, and into a wood we went where was a little cave, which my friend and I entered. We surely thought the enemy had seen us and still expected that they would come upon us. But here, as many times formerly, the Lord was very kind and gracious to me, for they had not seen us; and so we escaped this danger also, by the kind care of him who is mighty to save. In this cave, we stayed until near midnight, which time was spent in prayer and preparation for death, as the Lord helped us. Then we ventured out to seek some meat; [we went] to the back-window of a gentleman's house and knocked softly; out at which a gentlewoman whispered softly and told us there were sixteen or eighteen of the enemy in the house. She desired us quickly to go a back where we were, and she followed us with some meat, of which we were very glad for we had fasted long.

Thus he, who feeds the young ravens, fed us in his own season. Upon which I called to mind that he dealt with us as with Israel in the wilderness, whom he tried, proved, and humbled, by suffering them to hunger and thirst that he might let them see what was in their hearts; then fed them to the full. Thus the Lord brought me often to the brink of perishing; then interposed himself by his kind and watchful providence so that the enemy could bring nothing to pass against me, but what his holy hand had determined to be done. Therefore, good ground I have to say, "Hitherto hath the Lord helped me. Glory, glory, to his name, because he said to my proud enemies as he says to the raging waves of the sea, 'Hitherto shall ye come and no farther.'" Therefore, not withstanding of all the troubles that I met with, which were many and great, for I was never sooner out of one trouble, but I was presently overtaken with another; so that I can say of a truth, I was born to trouble, as the sparks fly upwards. Yet in the midst of all, I had still matter of praise given me, for the Lord always graciously nicked my extremity, making it his opportunity to work my deliverance, for my time of danger was still his time of salvation. Although I had always matter of sorrow, when I looked to the world and seeing all doors shut, yet, when I looked to the Lord of Hosts, I saw always ground to rejoice. As I have often occasion given me to think, that never poor creature was so much squeezed with affliction, and oftener cast in death's jaws than I was, yet I am often made to think, that never any were so quickly rescued, raised up, and wonderfully delivered than I have been. For from often-repeated experiences of the Lord's goodness to me and kind care of me,... I always have good cause to say and sing, "The mercy of the Lord endureth forever."[23]

James Nisbet vividly recalled his father's last few months of life as they, having made Moses' choice, struggled to survive during the Killing Times. In the following two anecdotes, James shows how the Lord's strengthening and comforting presence was visible in his father's every action, leading his friends to conclude that "he could not live, nor be long out of heaven":

> One instance is—On a Sabbath morning when some were met for the worship of God privately, while he was seeking a blessing on the portion of Scripture to be read and sung, for much of the Lord's manifested presence to be with them, and for fitting them for the duty of the day; there was such a shining luster in his countenance and such powerful weight in the words and arguments that he used with the Lord, as made all present weep and some of them in danger of fainting under their frame. [This] frame continued with him and them through all the parts of the duty with a great gale of soul enlargement; then he retired to secret prayer, as [was] his manner. After he was gone out from the rest, some of them said, "We never saw the like of this; the Lord is fitting this worthy man for some great trial in that he gives him so much of himself."[24]
>
> …At another time when in company with my father and some suffering friends on a Sabbath day, which was spent in the worship of God, a little before sunset unexpectedly there came a troop of the enemy to the house next to where we were. This, at first, put some of our company to fear, who said, "What shall we do?" My father answered, "Since there is no way for us to escape but in the Lord, come, let us sing the praises of God and let him work his own work," to which the rest consented; and, accordingly, the most part after calling upon the name of God, the Ninety-first Psalm was sung:
>
> > He that doth in the secret place—of the Most High reside,
> > Under the shade of him that I–th' Almighty shall abide.
> > I of the Lord my God will say—He is my refuge still,
> > He is my fortress, and my God—and in him trust I will.
> > Assuredly he shall thee save—and give deliverance
> > From subtle fowler's snare, and from—the noisome pestilence.
> > His feathers shall thee hide; thy trust—under his wings shall be:
> > His faithfulness shall be a shield—and buckler unto thee. –Ps. 91:1-4[25]

All the time of the singing, there was little or no fear observed to be amongst us. Upon the contrary, they were impressed with great cheerfulness, both of heart and of countenance. Although we still expected …

the enemy would come amongst us with their slaughter-weapons; for, they never spared any from present death whom they found in the immediate act of worship. It is not ordinary to sing the triumph before the victory, yet here it was sung with much soul-satisfaction and inward sensation of consolation. But, behold the kind care and restraining power of our infinitely gracious God who interposed himself betwixt all danger and us. Though there was no way of escape for us, being in a plain country far from any wood or moss, yet the Lord wonderfully provided us with safety. When the enemy had searched the three next houses to that house which we were in, they rode quite off and did not so much as speak where we were. The remembrance of this wonderful deliverance and of this Sabbath's frame, especially in singing the Ninety-first Psalm, has been strengthening, reviving, and refreshing afterwards to me times out of number. O praise and O praise for evermore be to him alone who is the object of all adoration! O angels, praise ye him! O sun, moon, stars, and all ye pieces of the creation, praise him! And, O my soul bless thou the Lord.[26]

Shortly before his father's capture, James spent three whole days alone with his father in an old-waste house, where they spent most of the time in prayer. In these prayers, James records that his father "insisted much that the Lord would glorify himself in us, by us, and upon us; and that he would make us entirely his own and set us wholly apart for himself by a distinguishing act and work of his sovereign grace and mercy." Shortly thereafter, his father "had [at least two] presages of his approaching death and martyrdom":

First, one morning, as he retired to the fields for secret duty, there fell two drops of blood on his Bible when he was reading; looking if he could perceive from whence the blood came, he saw the appearance of a dragoon mounted on a black horse with a drawn sword in his hand. My father, supposing it was a real dragoon, drew his sword, and asked him what he was for? Or whom he would have? Whether the apparition answered him or not, he would not tell, but after a little it vanished out of his sight, and he continued long at secret prayer.

Second, the Sabbath night seven nights before he was taken, as he, I, and three more were traveling, it being exceeding dark, no wind, but a thick small rain, and no moon, for that was not her season, behold! Suddenly the clouds clave asunder above our heads from the south-west to north-east, and there sprung forth a light as bright as that of the sun, when shining at noon-day; yea, it was much more pleasant though very amazing and astonishing, which light continued about the space of two minutes. We all heard a noise and were much surprised, saying one to another, "What may that mean?" But he spoke none; only he uttered three deep and heavy groans. William Woodburn, his friend, asked him what it might mean? He said, "We know not well at present, but within a little we shall know better; yet we have a more sure word of prophecy to which we would do well to take heed." Then he groaned and said, "As for me, I am ready to live or die for him, as he in his providence shall call me to it and bear me through in it. Although I have suffered much from prelates and false friends these twenty-one years, yet now I would not for a thousand worlds I had done otherwise. If the Lord spare me, I will be more zealous for his precious truths; but if not, I am ready to seal his cause with my blood, for I have longed for it these sixteen years, and it may be ere long I will it to do. Welcome be his will; if he help me through with it, I shall praise him to all eternity."[27]

John Nisbet's Last Days (1685)

In November 1685, John Nisbet attended a society meeting near Fenwick in a hiding house called Midland. He met with three of his brethren, Peter Gemmel, George Woodburn, and John Fergushill, to settle some points of contention. The next morning, a nearby party of forty dragoons under the leadership of Lieutenant Robert Nisbet captured Peter Gemmel's brother, John Gemmel, and two of his employees, William Wyhe and his son. These captives refused to take the Oath; consequently, the court sentenced them into slavery in the Barbados.[28]

Also that morning, John Nisbet and his associates, being advised that troops were searching for them, attempted to leave the house, but the ill health of the elderly Fergushill forced them to return. That afternoon, they narrowly escaped detection by a party of dragoons that searched the house. On the road back to town, the dragoons met two individuals who teased them with the comment, "You are good seekers, but ill finders," causing the troops to decide to return to the house.[29] The troops returned to the house where they captured John Nisbet of Hardhill, who left the following account of his capture:

> [When discovered by the soldiers] according to our former resolution, we did resist them, having only three shot and one of them misgiving. Upon this they fired above twenty-four shot at us; when we had nothing else, we clubbed our guns till two of them were quite broken and then went them; when they saw they could not prevail, they cried, to go out and fire the house. Upon this we went out after them, I received six wounds in the going out. After [noticing who] I was, some of them cried out to spare my life, for the Council had offered three thou-

sand merks for me. So, they brought me towards the end of the yard and tied my hands behind my back, having shot the other three to death. He that commanded them scoffingly asked me, "What I thought of myself now?" I smiled and said, "I had full contentment with my lot; but thought I was at a loss, that I was in time, and my brethren in eternity." At this he swore, and said he had reserved my life for a further judgment to me.[30]

James Nisbet, in his memoir, describes how he learned of his father's capture:

The night before [my father's capture], I went to the Earl of Loudoun's house. Being concealed all night in one of the office-houses, in my sleep, I dreamed of all the passages of the trouble that my father was in. I awoke with much sorrow on my spirit. I immediately arose and essayed prayer; but alas, alas, I was both dead, lifeless, and overwhelmed with such a flood of sinking sorrow, that I could do nothing all that day but sigh, to the breaking of my heart. At night, I was taken into the hind's house where two of the young ladies, namely, Lady Mary and Lady Jean, came and sat down by me. Seeing me in much sorrow, [they] asked if had got any meat. It was told them I could eat none all that day; upon which they opened their skirts, wherein they had meat; and very kindly and affectionately, they both urged me to eat; but I could not. They asked [what] was the matter with me. I told their ladyships I knew not, but I was waiting until the Lord in his providence should send me an interpreter. At which, the young ladies burst forth in tears, and one of them says, "Then I must be that sorrowful interpreter"; for, says she, "early this morning, forty of the enemy came upon your father, George Woodburn, John Ferguson [or Fergushill], and Peter Gemuel [or Gemmel] near Fenwick Kirk. They have killed the other three, and your father has received seven wounds and [has been] taken prisoner. He is this night in Kilmarnock tollbooth." At the hearing of which sad news, I was struck to the heart, but the honorable and worthy ladies were hearty sympathizers to me and did all they could to comfort me, but I could not take any notice of what they said or did, for such was my sorrow, that words could have no weight with me.

I arose immediately and went out to the fields, but kind providence ordered the matter so, that though very dark, yet I met with an eminent Christian, William Woodburn, my father's much honored friend who counseled, "Submit to and acquiesce in the will of God who will be a father to the fatherless. Although your father and my brother be our near and dear friends, yet they are not too dear to suffer for Christ and seal his noble and honorable cause with their blood; therefore, we are to be still and know that he is God who hath done this thing." Upon this blessed advice and seasonable counsel, the weight of my burden was much taken off, my sorrow alleviated, and all fretting at the sad dispensation prevented.[31]

Shortly after John Nisbet's arrival at the Tollbooth of Ayr, when asked if he owned the king's authority, he replied, "While the king owned the way and work of God, I thought myself bound, both to own and fight for him; but when he quitted the way of God, I thought I was obliged to quit him." When asked if he would own the Duke of York, as king, he replied, "I would not, for it was both against my principles and the laws of the nation." He was then transported to Edinburgh, where the second night after his arrival he was taken to the King's Privy Council for trial. When the council asked him what "might conduce to the peace and security of the nation," he replied, "When I came to particulars, I should speak nothing but truth, for I was more afraid to lie than to die." A series of questions and answers followed:

Q. What did ye in your meetings? A. I told them, we sung part of a psalm, read part of the Scripture, and prayed time about. Q. Why call ye them fellowship and society meetings? A. I wonder why you ask such questions, for these meetings were called so when our church was in her power. Q. Were there any such meetings, at that time? A. There were in some places of the land. Q. Did the ministers of the place meet with them in these? A. Sometimes they did, and sometimes they did not. Q. What mean you by your general meetings, and what do you do at them? While I was thinking what to answer, one of them … jeeringly said, looking to me, "When they have done, then they distribute their collections." I held my peace all the time. Where keep ye these meetings? A. In the wildest moors we can think of.

Q. Will you own the king's authority? A. No. Q. What is your reason? You own the Scriptures and you own the *Confession of Faith*? A. That I do with all my heart. Q. Why do you not own the king's authority (naming several passages of Scripture, and that in the 23rd chapter of the confession)? A. There is a vast difference; for he being a Roman Catholic, and I being not only brought up in the Presbyterian principles from my youth but also sworn against popery. Q. What is that to you, though he be popish, he is not bidding you be a Papist, nor hindering you to live, in your own religion? A. The contrary does appear; for we have not liberty to hear a gospel preaching, but we are taken, killed, and put to the hardest of sufferings. They said, it was not so, for we might have the gospel, if our wild principles would suffer us to hear it. I said, they might say so, but the contrary was well known through the land; for ye banished away our faithful ministers, and thrust in such as live rather like profligates than like ministers, go that poor things neither can nor dare join with them.

Q. Are ye clear to join with Argyle? A. No. Q. Then one of them said, "Ye will have no king but Mr. James Renwick"; and asked, if I conversed with any other minister upon the field than Mr. Renwick: I told them I conversed with no other. And a number of other things passed that were to little purpose.[32]

After hearing his answers, the judges sentenced him to death. Hardhill received his sentence with thankfulness, praising God for the opportunity to suffer for Christ's sake. During the twenty-seven days that he awaited his execution, chains bound his body but not his soul. In various letters to his dear friends and acquaintances, he asked them to pray that he not wrong the truth. He exhorted them to "be more diligent in savoring Christian duties," regretting that he "was not more sincere, zealous, and forward for [Christ's] work and cause."[33]

Before his execution, John Nisbet gave a friend his "Last and Dying Testimony" for safekeeping. This testimony is a treasure chest of Covenanted Reformation principles, with Scripture references to support every aspect. In it, he warns those who depart from the truths of the Covenanting Reformation, and he encourages the surviving sufferers to continue their faithful witness. He confirms all the remnant's declarations and testimonies "so far as they agree with God's Holy Word." He owns all their appearances in arms in defense of the gospel, and he prophesies that God will cut off the name of the Stuarts (i.e., King Charles II, King James II, and their heirs). As we will see, God did remove them from power. He faced his death with the "full assurance of being a member of his Church Triumphant, which is the New Jerusalem and city of the living God!" He closes his testimony by praising God and looking forward to eternal dwelling with Christ.[34]

[Be not scared] at his sweet, lovely, and desirable cross. Although I have not been able because of my wounds, which I received at my taking, to lift up or lay down my head, but as I was helped, yet I was never in better case all my life. He has not given me one challenge since I came to prison for any thing less or more. On the contrary, he has so wonderfully shined on me with the sense of his redeeming, strengthening, assisting, supporting, through-bearing, pardoning, and reconciling love, grace, and mercy, that my soul doth long to be freed of bodily infirmities and earthly organs, that so I may flee to his royal palace, even

the heavenly habitation of my God. [There] I am sure of a crown put on
my head, a palm put in my hand, and a new song put in my mouth,
even the song of Moses and the Lamb, so that I may bless, praise, magnify, and extol him for what he hath done to me and for me. Wherefore,
I bid farewell to all my dear fellow-sufferers for the testimony of Jesus
who are wandering in dens and caves. Farewell my children; study holiness in all your ways, praise the Lord for what he hath done for me, and
tell all my Christian friends to praise him on my account. Farewell sweet
Bible, and wanderings and contendings for truth; welcome death; welcome the city of my God where I shall see him and be able to serve him
eternally with full freedom; and welcome blessed company, the angels
and spirits of just men made perfect. Above all, welcome, welcome, welcome, one glorious and alone God, Father, Son, and Holy Ghost: into
thy hands, I commit my soul, for thou art worthy. Amen.[35]

John Nisbet's execution took place on December 4, 1685, in the
Grassmarket at Edinburgh. He was fifty-eight years old, and he left behind three sons: Hugh, James, and Alexander.[36] Before his execution, he
sent the Countess of Loudoun an enigmatic letter, warning her to repent.[†] He mounted the scaffold with much boldness, as described in the
Introduction to this book; after which, he concluded his testimony as
described by eyewitnesses of his martyrdom:

> Then he resumed the heads of his last testimony to the truth and
> enlarged upon what he owned and what he disowned. But, drums were
> always caused be beat when he spoke to the people, which you are sure
> deprived us much of the satisfaction that otherwise we might have had.
> Yet over this difficulty we heard him say, "The covenanted God of Scot-
> land hath a dreadful storm of wrath provided, which he will surely pour
> out suddenly and unexpectedly like a thunder-bolt upon these cove-
> nanted lands, for their perfidy, treachery, and woeful apostasy; and then
> men shall say, 'They have won well away that got a scaffold for Christ.'"
> He exhorted all to make much use of Christ for a hiding-place, for
> blood, blood, blood, shall be the judgment of these lands. He sang the
> first six verses of the Thirty-fourth Psalm and read the eighth to the
> Romans.[37]

[†] John Nisbet's note (Wodrow Archives-Oct xxviii, National Library of Scotland) to the countess
warned her that if she did not amend her ways that the "house of Loudoun would become as void
of the name of Campbell as Hardhill was now of Nisbet." In the letter, he forgave her for cruelty
(specifics not given) to him and his family, and he warned her to repent to avoid the curse of her
children, whom he considered godly. Her husband, James, had fled to Holland to avoid persecution, where he died in 1684. The historian Kirkton recounts how the countess would ingratiate herself with both parties when necessary. On the other hand, their acts of Christian mercy, often performed behind the scenes, stand witness to their Christian commitment (Kirkton, pp. 377–378).

God will I bless all times; his praise—my mouth shall still express.
My soul shall boast in God: the meek—shall hear with joyfulness.
Extol the Lord with me, let us—exalt his name together.
I sought the Lord, he heard, and did—me from all fears deliver.
They look'd to him, and lighten'd were—not shamed were their faces.
This poor man cry'd, God heard, and sav'd—him from all his distresses.
—Ps. 34:1–6[38]

He prayed divinely with great presence of mind and very loudly; but for noise of drums, as hath been said, we could not distinctly hear what he either spoke or prayed, except when his face was toward the place where we stood, so that in such disturbing circumstances this is all his scaffold speech that we could safely gather. He went up the ladder rejoicing and praising the Lord, which we all evidently saw.[39]

Another martyr executed that day was Edward Marshall. When asked at his trail if he owned the king's authority, Marshall replied, "He owned him as far as he [the king] owned God, his cause, and people." To which the judge replied, "That was not to own the king at all."[40]

Reflections on the Killing Times (1685)

James Nisbet, reflecting on the loss of his dear relatives and on his numerous narrow escapes, praises God for his miraculous deliverance from the jaws of death:

There were nine of his nearest relations [who] did all seal the same cause with their blood, betwixt 1679 and 1685, inclusive—namely, Thomas Nisbet, James Nisbet, Joseph Nisbet, John Brown, elder, John Brown, younger, James Wood, Joseph Gibson, Joseph Law, elder, and Joseph Law, younger. [They] all walked in the fear of God and were true lovers of his covenanted work of reformation. My father was the tenth of my nearest relations that suffered death within the compass of seven years to seal that noble cause with their blood. So, my dear youngest brother and I were stripped naked of our relations and left as orphans, destitute of all paternal or relative care, to the care of him in whom the fatherless find mercy, who has always been to us a present help in the time of need. Because of which, we have good cause to say, "Though friends die and leave us, yet God abides forever, in whom are all our springs and from whose all-sufficiency proceeds every good thing that our needy condition requires." Therefore, let us sing that the mercy of the Lord endureth forever: to whom be glory and praise. Amen.[41]

O my soul! Bless and praise the Lord for his kind and watchful providence over me, in that he visibly prevented my losing my life at all the places following—namely, when amongst the hurry of the enemy's cruel searches at my father's house, at the Bennel-hill, at Gelt-hill, at Garclagh-hill, at the Castle of Kyle, at Dornes, at Corseon-hill, at Greenock-mains, at Gargilloch, at Wallaceton, at Cubb's-craig, at Barlonochie, at the Heilish-wood, at Hairstocks, at Garnduff-hill, at Frier-Midden moor at Spangna-glen, Hoggan-burn, at Caims-camb, at Lead-loch, at Crossford, at Middton, at Burn-house, and at Louden wood. At all which places, I was in imminent and visible danger, yea, within an inch of loosing my life by the bloody enemy. Yet, watchful and kind providence was at all these times and places conspicuously on work for my protection and preservation....[42]

To him, the "whole year was one continued lash, then a kiss, now a frown, then a smile, now a trial, and then a deliverance, conveyed to [him] by the kind and skillful hand of wise and unerring providence."

Through the whole of this year, I was so frequently borne up, supported, and mercifully rescued out of the devouring jaws of death and deadly enemies, that every one of these attributes, in their turn, and often the whole of them together, did conspire my safety, and remarkably shed abroad their benign influences upon me and for me. I, with much cheerfulness, do confess [that] I was ever under the influence of infinite wisdom, which contrived ways and means for my escape (Isa. 29:29). I was ever under the influence of his infinite power, which was ever [at] work to deliver me, and set me in safety; upon which I must cry out, *"O Lord God! Who is a strong and faithful God, who is like unto thee?"* (Ps. 89:8). And I do confess that I was ever well secured under the influence of infinite goodness and mercy (Ps. 106:44; Isa. 30:18; 43:1–2; 57:16; Lam. 3:32–33).[43]

Because of these wonderful deliverances, James pledges to be ever thankfully acknowledging God's glory, goodness, and mercy; earnestly seeking Christ as the only source of happiness, salvation, and sanctification; zealously mourning for Zion's desolation, wickedness, and divisions. He pledges to make the Word his "only rule of faith and practice," to keep his "conscience void of offense towards God and towards man," and to exercise "faith, patience, humility, and submission." He promises "to prepare for that endless eternity of tranquility, perfect peace, and felicity" and "to shun all the sinful ways that lead to an eternity of endless torment."[44]

7

Nowhere to Look but Up

Since God will have us leave father and mother for his sake, certainly he will have us leave lords for his sake. – Martin Luther[1]

Persecution of One Another (1685–1686)

James Nisbet records the bitter divisions that arose during the Killing Times:

> My bitter lamentations [resulted from] the dissensions and divisions that arose this year among the suffering remnant. These divisions were begun, industriously augmented, and handed about on the one side by secret enemies and self-seeking temporizers and, on the other side, too much opposed and unwisely resented, by some hot and inconsiderate persons of rash tempers whom I many times addressed as follows:
>
> O! My dear Christian friends, far, far be it from me to blame or condemn any of you for walking up to your light; yea, I should rather rejoice to see everyone occupying the talent that the Lord hath given them to trade with until he come again. Because years should speak and teach wisdom, therefore I should hold my peace, being a child.... The grief of my soul wants a vent to you, my dear friends, while my heart is surcharged with sorrow to see some of you differing much in judgment from one another. In that which one calls light, another calls darkness; what one calls truth, another calls error; and what one calls duty, another calls sin; in the meanwhile, carrying frowns in your angry brows at one another, and by sharp words spout fire at one another. O! Alas! My friends, this ought not to be so. Where is the spirit of meekness, self-denial, mutual forbearance, and lowliness of mind that all should be exercised with, each one preferring another before themselves, and each one loving another as themselves? Is not the unity of the spirit in the bond of peace a pleasant field, large enough for every one of you to act your part to the glory of God..., loving your neighbor as yourself, without dividing one from another and without condemning one another?

Alas! Are not our breaches already wide as the sea? Why, then, should we be such great fools as to add more fuel to our flame?

[Instead, we should] suspect our own opinion of things, and bring them to the standard of God, the law, and the testimony to see if they be of the right stamp or not; and whether we ourselves are acting in all we do and say from a right principle, in a right manner, and to a right end, rather than suspect and censure our friend. Not that I am for denying any the use of a discretive judgment, but I would first have everyone to begin with themselves. Why do we not look twice into our own bosoms, when but once to our neighbors? Why are we not often eyeing our own monstrous corruptions and the frequent misgivings of our own treacherous hearts? Why are we not striving to take the bulky beam of foolish miscarriages out of our own eye before we seek to take the mote out of our brother's eye? For, alas! Are there not, even with the best of us, sins, great and many, against the Lord our God? O! Then, why will not every one take with their own faults? And let that time which is spent in reproaching one another and [in] debating and contending with one another be spent in searching out every one his own sins. Confess and mourn over them; before the Lord, speedily forsake them. Cry mightily unto the Lord that he would return and bless us abundantly with much power, light, life, and unity amongst ourselves, and that he would be unto us a healer of breaches.

O! My dear Christian friends, let us look back to the practice of the Lord's people in all ages of the church; we shall see that they never stated separation from their brethren upon the account of differences of judgment and practice, except where the sins of error, defection, and backsliding from the Lord and his way were willfully persisted in contrary to clear truth and an express command. But rather, the strong bore with the weak, pitied their infirmities, and dealt with them in the gospel spirit of meekness. [They knew] that everyone's light, gifts, capacities, and graces ... were never all one size, but some more, some less, according to the measure given them of the Lord for the edifying and completing of his mystical body, the church, which, in some sense, resembles that of a human body where there are fingers and toes as well as legs, arms, head, and heart. Therefore, all you self-seeking temporizers, as ye would not be found to fight against God, cease, cease, and meddle no more to the scorn and reproach of those worthies who are for a strict way of witnessing for Christ's precious truth. [They would] not lose hair nor hoof if God honor them to resist unto blood, striving against sin, he making them to overcome by the blood of the Lamb. I would not, yea, I durst not, for many worlds, be found to think, speak, or act against them, lest innocent blood were laid to my charge, and lest they rose up in judgment against me at the great day. How terrible a thing will it be for any to be found with the blood of the saints in their skirts when God comes to make inquisition for the blood of his faithful martyrs? And O! How wicked a thing is it to be found guilty of condemning those who are approven of God? And, on the other side, O, all ye hot, inconsiderate, and unadvised persons, cease, cease. Why should the fire of your blind zeal lead you to condemn those who are for a more enlarged way of contending for truth and are willing to venture and lose their all while standing up for liberty and property in particular, or the Protestant interest in general? For, indeed, God hath this year highly honored some eminent persons this way. Should we sit and speak against our mother's sons and deny them the honor of martyrdom ... because they could not come up to the light and length of others in point of judgment? This is to make our measure the rule, and not God's measuring line of his sanctuary. This is to dishonor those whom God hath highly honored. This is to set up ourselves for judges of what is matter of conscience to others; this be far from us. But, let us rather turn our prejudices at others to self-judging and close examining of ourselves and our own ways. In the meanwhile, use the mantle of charity and spirit of meekness to those who cannot come our length on either hand, knowing that this is our state of imperfection wherein some are strong men in Christ, some are young men, and some are babes.

Those united with the worthy Mr. Renwick in a general correspondence are many of them great and good men, eminently godly and highly favored of the Lord to witness a good confession for Christ's persecuted cause and interest; therefore, [they] ought to be highly respected of by us. Likewise, the Right Honorable the Earl of Argyle and many of those worthy patriots that joined with him in that unsuccessful expedition were also highly favored and much honored of God to seal their declared adherence to the Protestant interest with their dearest blood.... O! How unbecoming a thing it is for any of the professors of religion to be throwing dirt upon any of those noble cloud of witnesses, noble patriots, and worthy confessors. Though differing a little in their judgment as to the state of their testimony,... all of them are right in the main fundamentals of the Christian religion! O! Tell not our divisions in Gath, neither publish them in the streets of Askelon! Let every one of us strive to go before another, as examples to one another of faith, love, humility, zeal, and condescendence; seeking by all means to be reconciled to God in Christ, reconciled to his truth, reconciled to his cross, and reconciled to one another in the strongest bonds of Christian love; loving all in whom we see any thing of the image of God with the tenderest of love, counting them the excellent ones of the earth, in whom we much delight. O! My dear friends whom I love much, allow me the freedom to tell you, with a sore heart and a weeping soul upon the account of our divisions, that I am more than convinced that the offered mercy of God in Christ, held forth in the gospel, is loudly calling upon us to love and concord among ourselves. I am more [than] convinced that the wrath and anger of a jealous God … is now poured forth against us for our great and manifold sins and provocations [that] are crying aloud upon all of us to love, [maintaining] harmony among ourselves.

Is not the cruel rage and fury that our persecuting enemies are exercising upon us crying aloud that we be united in the Lord and at peace one with another? Doth not our afflicted, low, and bleeding condition cry aloud upon us to be united in the Lord and at peace amongst ourselves? Doth not the Scripture clearly and abundantly warn us not to divide and bite one another, lest we be consumed one of another? Doth not the blood of martyrs on scaffolds, fields, and seas cry aloud on us to be at peace and love with one another? And O my soul! Cry aloud unto the Lord that all that name the name of Christ Jesus may be helped, through grace, to depart from this iniquity of reproaching and speaking evil of one another, and of becoming stumbling-blocks to one another. Alas! How lamentable a matter is it to see one saint allowing himself to be a scourge to another saint! And that this, my complaint and humble request, may be the better understood, let these scriptures be seriously considered and suitably applied: 2 Chron. 30:1–21; Ps. 133:1–2; Rom. 12:17–18; 14:1–4, 19, 22; 16:17; 1 Cor. 1:10; 3:4; Eph. 4:3–6, 29–31: Phil. 3:18; Col. 3:12–16; Heb. 12:14. O Lord, make thy people as one stick in thy hand, turn all our heart-burnings at others to heart breaking for our own sins, and quench the fire of our divisions by the flames of brotherly love. Help us to consider that grace doth not fire the heart with passions but with love and compassion. Help thou us, by grace, to keep the word of thy patience, and keep thou all of us in the hour of temptation wherewith now we are sharply tried. Send forth thy light and thy truth to lead and guide us in thy way everlasting, thou enabling us to steer a straight course betwixt right and left hand extremes. All-sufficient God! Be unto us the strength of our heart and our portion forever: Even so come, O Lord Jesus Christ, come quickly, and abide with us. Amen.[2]

A Hundred Poor, Daft, Silly Bodies (1686)

Persecution abated in the year 1686. The most notable martyr that year, David Steel, was shot in front of his wife. As she bound her dead husband's head, a neighbor heard her say, "The archers have shot at thee, my husband, but they could not reach thy soul; it has escaped like a dove, and is at rest far away. Lord, give strength to thy handmaid that will prove that she has waited for Thee, even in the strength of Thy judgments."[3]

James Nisbet spent much of the year in prayer and Bible study as he sought the Lord's guidance in steering clear of the subtle hazards that face Christians in the absence of an organized church:

> 1686, when in the seventeenth year of my age, now, as the former year, left me with one trouble and trial trampling upon the heels of another, leaving me no [way] to look to but upward to unseen All-sufficiency; so did this year meet with me. Near the beginning of it, as I was joining in worship one day with six of the suffering remnant, some of whom had offensive arms, and two of our number did act therewith so rashly and inconsiderately. Henceforward I had no more peace nor satisfaction to stay any longer in that part of the country, but removed a great way off where I remained a long time and grappled with many difficulties. In this place, I was much solicited to join with a Christian society of the persecuted remnant, which met once a week in the nighttime for the worship of God, to which at last I was persuaded to yield. We who met at that occasion, for fear of the enemy, were obliged to come and go from the place of our meeting under cloud of night, and one of us ordinarily prayed by the way, turnabout. One night, as I was at prayer, we were suddenly surprised with a great light: the rest saw it and the time of its continuance; but when I saw it, I closed my eyes and cried to the Lord thus, or to this purpose, "O! Give us much saving illumination and gracious manifestations of thyself, but no vision or delusion." At the mentioning of which, it quickly disappeared as those of our company told me; and I was ever of the mind that it was Satanical. As formerly, at many other times, so here, I was much carried out in prayer that the strong and mighty God of Jacob would hasten on his way, break the yoke of the bloody persecutors, and grant a reviving to his work and people. In this I would not, yea, I could not, take any nay-say. And from this, by the bye, I have often observed that when the Lord gives a heart to pray, he gives an ear to hear and a hand to help and deliver; but he is not to be limited to times because he hath all times and seasons in his own hand.[4]

King James's Catholic tendencies soon became evident as he obtained exemptions for Catholic landlords from the Test, equipped Holyrood Chapel for Catholic services, and took advantage of every opportunity to place Catholics into positions of power. When Parliament refused to allow Catholics the liberty of private worship, James dissolved

the Parliament. James gained strength as high-ranking sycophant Episcopalians and Royalists defected to Catholicism. The disingenuous government, under the guise of expanding religious freedom, imposed the
Bond of Regulation that required tenants to "live regularly, keep the kirk,
and refrain from coventicles," to which many yielded.[5]

To compound the persecution from the state, the remnant faced increased persecution from fellow Presbyterians who shared their doctrine
but disagreed with their rejection of the king's authority. These antagonists actively campaigned to discredit Renwick and the societies. The
root of bitterness had grown into a suffocating vine. The results were so
devastating that their enemies reported, "All had now left Mr. Renwick
but about a hundred poor, silly, daft bodies, that were running through
with him and robbing the country." The remnant's opponents entered
the prisons and persuaded many of the respected imprisoned ministers,
such as John Dickson, through misrepresentations to write a general
warning to the people concerning the societies. Opponents contended
that the societies arrogated to themselves the roles of both church (rejecting ministers) and state (rejecting the king and annulling laws made
during his reign), and were for "killing all that were not of their own
judgment."[6] They sent similar misrepresentations to Ireland and Holland, turning essentially all the Society's old allies against them. They
also threatened to bring Renwick and Hamilton to justice if General Assemblies were ever re-established. Robert Hamilton, the remnant's agent
in Holland, informed the remnant of the bleak outlook for ordaining
additional ministers abroad considering that all their allies had deserted
them. In March 1687, Alexander Shields published the Society's response in a document entitled the *Informatory Vindication*. In this document, the remnant clarified that they "positively disown, as horrid murder, the killing of any because of a different persuasion or opinion from
us."[7]

Although division increased, there was also reconciliation. On his
deathbed, Peden mended his relationship with Renwick. When first seeing Renwick, Peden exclaimed, "I think your legs too small, and your
shoulders too narrow, to take on the whole Church of Scotland on your
back." Before Renwick left, Peden drew him near him and said, "You
have answered me to my soul's satisfaction and I am very sorry that I
should have believed such ill reports about you.... Sir, I find you a faithful servant to your Master; go on in the single dependence upon the
Lord, and you will win honestly and cleanly off the stage ..." Walker
listed James Nisbet as one who could attest to these statements.[8]

James Nisbet provides a colorful portrait of Peden's background, preaching style, and impact on the suffering remnant:

> Now, as it is said of men, who are in frequent converse and intimate correspondence with one another, that they love one another dearly, exchange secrets with one another, and share with one another in grief and joy. This was eminently exemplified in David and a Jonathan, who made a covenant of brotherhood and league of entire friendship because they loved one another as their own souls. Yet all this is but a faint and shallow resemblance of these clear and sweet interviews, and rich communications that the Lord Jehovah entertains his beloved Jehohadahs with, when he is declaring, even to bystanders, that he loves them and manifests himself unto them: ... such as Moses whom he knew face to face and conversed with as a man doth with his friend; such as Daniel, O man greatly beloved; such as Paul who was wrapped up to the third heavens; and many others recorded in Scripture and ecclesiastical history who were highly privileged with being admitted to know the secrets of the covenant of their God (Ps. 25:15) and also the secrets of his providences (Gen. 18:17). Hence, what is written [in] John 15:15 is fulfilled to these in great measure; amongst the number of whom, this great man Mr. Peden was one. [He] seemed to be eminently honored of God with many of those secret whispers, sweet glances, and clear interviews that passes betwixt God and his people, which carry such evidences and assurance alongst with them that they are of God, and from him, that there is no room left to doubt of their being of a divine extract, or thus saith the Lord. From which, for instruction's sake, I touch at three particulars concerning him.
>
> When he was a young man, [he was] preceptor and session-clerk in the parish of Tarbolton [where a base woman falsely charged him of fathering her child.] So, Mr. Peden was pursued at the kirk-session; but standing to his innocence, he was tried before the presbytery; but there he refuted the charge also. During the time of which process laid against him, there was a whole year spent; all, which time Mr. Peden, cried to the Lord (who is a prayer-hearing God) that he would graciously make a way of escape for him.... Just as Mr. Guthrie ended [his] sermon and was entering on the action against Mr. Peden, the child's father stood up and ... made a full and free confession of the whole fact, concluding with telling the congregation that the Lord obliged him to this confession by the heat and torment of his own conscience. And the wretched woman went to the ... ditch, where Mr. Peden had prayed so long and so often, and drowned herself. And in this, these scriptures were fulfilled: Ps. 9:16, 18; 12:5; 34:4–6.

Although every act of worship that Mr. Peden was engaged in was full of sublime flights and useful digressions, yet they carried amongst with them a divine stamp. Every opening of his mouth seemed for [the] most part to be dictated by the Spirit of God; and such was the weighty and convincing majesty that accompanied what he spoke that it obliged his hearers to both love and fear him. I observed that every time he spoke, whether conversing, reading, praying, or preaching, betwixt every sentence he paused a little, as if he had been hearkening what the Lord would say to him or listening to some secret whisper. Then sometimes he would start, as if he had seen some surprising sight; at which he would break silence and cry out to the commendation of God in Christ, to the commendation of his redeeming love, and to the commendation of his grace in the souls of his people in their conviction, conversion, up building in Christ Jesus by the power of his Holy Spirit, and how that work ebbed and flowed according to the sovereign will pleasure of their sweet Lord and Savior and according as their walk was tender or untender, watchful or unwatchful. He spoke often to the commendation of those who had really closed with Christ Jesus by the power of his Holy Spirit on gospel terms, and was willing to take up his cross and venture their all for him.

He often foretold many sad things to befall this sinful land, in a way of judgment, to be executed by the hands of the French and Spaniards; and he also foretold many things that [were] to befall particular persons and families. He [also] foretold many things antecedent thereunto; the most of which I have lived to see fulfilled. The Lord in mercy, prevent the last and worst of what he foretold.[9]

During this year, James Nisbet renewed his personal covenant. He took comfort in the "unparalleled love of God" evidenced in the covenant blessings that God provides his children during trials and tribulations.[10] Scripture-filled books and preaching watered his spiritual growth:

The last half of this year I read Mr. Guthrie's *Trial of Saving Interest* and very many of his sermons in manuscript, as also all Mr. Gray's* sermons [*Works of Andrew Gray*[11]] that are in print, and many of the last speeches of crying martyrs, with all which I was much edified and refreshed. I had occasion to hear Mr. Renwick from these words, Hab. 2:3, *"For the vision is yet for an appointed time, but, at the end, it shall speak, and not lie: though it tarry, wait for it; because it will surely come, it will not tarry."* Which words he explained, improved, applied, and vindicated the sovereignty

---

* Andrew Gray (1630–1654) was a Scottish preacher who emphasized the necessity to close with Christ as the beginning, middle, and end of all his sermons.

of God, notwithstanding of his long delay to come with deliverance to his church and people. Likewise, he pressed the great necessity of faith, patience, and humility, under the Lord's delay. Towards the close of his sermon, he, with a great asseveration, assured us that for these sins, whereby the Lord was provoked to withhold deliverance from his church and people, Scotland should be laid as desolate as a barren mountain. [He cautioned all] who are helped, through grace, to follow Christ in the regeneration to take … for their comfort that the stroke, when it came, should be the deepest Jordan that ever his people wadded in, so it should be the narrowest. Upon which he exhorted all to make sure of a personal interest in the Lord Jesus Christ and to walk closely with him in newness of life; for that trial, when it came, would be both sore and heavy. But on the back of that sad cloud there should be as glorious days in Scotland again, as ever was any where since the Apostles' days, at which time the nation should be married to the Lord covenant-wise. The place of this meeting might be called Bochim, for both minister and people wept much.

I meditated much on the thoughts of the wonderful attributes and shining perfections of God, of which I had seen, felt, and enjoyed so much of since I came to the world, especially the last year, when I was so often mercifully rescued from many great and imminent dangers. Therefore, [I] cannot but admire [God], adore him, and reverence him, who is a spirit, eternal, unchangeable, and incomprehensible, whose center is everywhere, and his circumference nowhere.…[12]

From these reflections, sermons, and Scripture (e.g., Ps. 24:12; 130:5–6), he learned to "acknowledge God alone as the creator of all things"; as "supreme and sole governor of all his creatures and their actions"; and as chooser, ransomer, caller, and sanctifier of "a certain number of fallen man's sons and daughters." He also learned that "whosoever will not hear and be obedient" to the Word "shall be left inexcusable," and he learned that God has appointed both the ends and the means of salvation. From this he saw the absolute necessity for believers to "heartily, fully, wholly, and cordially" embrace Christ: "Thus Christ, and he alone, and the virtue of this purchase, must be entirely gone into, closed with, and forever rested on …"[13] He discusses the duties incumbent on those that close with Christ:

I am to read the Word of God that I may know what is sin and what is duty, what to choose and what to refuse. I am to read often systems of sound divinity. I am to hear the gospel preached by Christ's faithful ambassadors. I am to pray often in secret and private. I am to sing the praises of God. I am to exercise myself in frequent meditations on the works of creation, works of providence, work of redemption, and on the Covenant of Works made with man in innocence, and how it was transgressed by Adam's fall; on the Covenant of Redemption, agreed on betwixt God the Father and God the Son, in favors of the elect; and on the Covenant of Grace, established with believers in Christ, and how it is clearly made known and gloriously displayed, with all its properties and privileges, in the Word of God and a preached gospel. I am to be much in self-examination inquiring narrowly into the temper, frame, disposition, and inclination of my heart and soul. I am to endeavor to live peaceably with all men, in the study of holiness, dearly loving all those who bear anything of the image of God. [For all these] duties of my general calling, I am to cry to the Lord for the help of his Holy Spirit that I may perform these things in his strength, humbly believing in him, without fainting.

Also, there are Christian duties extraordinary, which may, and often do, fall in my way: such as, how to take up the cross for Christ's cause, [when to join] in Christian society with those who meet for the worship of God, [how] to state separation in case of error in judgment or practice, [and whether to] carry defensive arms in opposition against tyrannical and bloody men.[14]

He also learned the necessity of not rushing to perform duties at the calling of good men or from the calling of his own spirit, but only "by the direction of the Spirit of God, according to his Word." This requires that Christians carefully search 'the mind of God in his Word, plead for the direction of the Holy Spirit, wait for the opportunity provided by the Lord through providence, and guide their actions in fulfilling their duty by the Word alone.' He took great comfort in the Scripture examples of Moses' forty-year wait, Gideon's and David's diligence in seeking God's will before any action, Boaz's adherence to biblical obligations in obtaining the right to marry Ruth, and Abraham's servant's prayerful dependence on God in seeking Isaac's bride. James prayed, "Lord, leave me not to act unadvisedly out of blind zeal, nor yet from example of others, but according to thy Holy Word; and grant that thy statues may ever be the men of my counsels that I am to be guided by, and afterwards receive me to glory. Amen."[15]

In addition, he learned that nothing had befallen him and his "suffering friends, but had befallen the Lord's people from the beginning of the world."[16] These devotionals led him to pray:

Bring and keep me under the verge of thy protecting power, and bring and keep me under the influences of all thy mediatory offices. Forgive all my sins, subdue all my iniquities, and wash away all my filthiness. The more unframed and indisposed I am for holy duties; help me to run the faster to thee, who is a quickening spirit. The more thou frowns, help me to creep the lower before thee, and the nearer unto thee, and cause thy face to shine upon me. Break the yoke of our bloody oppresses, rebuke Satan and all his instruments. Revive thy work, as in former years; and restore to thy church and people all their ancient privileges; and grant that we, who have long hung our harps as on the willows, may now have cause to rejoice in the Lord, and sing the songs of Zion. Amen.[17]

Toleration vs. Scripture (1687)

King James's Looking Glass Called Toleration: King James, now in complete control, influenced the Scottish Council in February 1687 to issue a proclamation concerning religious toleration. This proclamation allowed Presbyterians the right to hear licensed (Indulged) ministers in churches and private homes, Quakers the right to meet in licensed buildings, and Catholics the right to worship in homes or chapels. It also restored the political rights of Catholics. In July, the council extended these rights to permit worship in any licensed building and annulled penal acts against dissenters. Those who refused the Oath could preach as long as they were orderly. On this news, many of the exiled ministers returned home to resume their ministry. In spite of the fact that the majority of the ministers who returned from abroad preached against Renwick and the wandering remnant, the Society increased in size. One of the reasons for their growth was that all Protestants shared a deep suspicion of King James's motives in granting the toleration because James was a practicing Catholic. The societies, determined to hold out until a king supporting the covenants was in power, issued a Testimony against King James's Toleration.[18]

James Nisbet's Looking Glass Called Scripture: James spent most of 1687 in a "remote part of the country" where he observed "the abounding wickedness and profanity" of the world, which caused him to reflect on his own sinful condition:

...Also taking a look of myself by meditation and examination, I found the violent workings of indwelling sin accompanied with the poisonous bullets of Satan's fiery injections and the power of strong unbelief. Upon which sight of my sinful self and of a blind world, I plainly perceived myself in great hazard and danger of departing from the Lord and his way, sometimes on the one hand and sometimes on the other. Both of which ways of sinning lead down to the chambers of death and tend much to overthrow the ends of creation and redemption, whereby God is greatly dishonored, Satan greatly gratified, and myself in great danger of being ruined for time and eternity.

This observation led him to "set up the following Scripture perspective glass" to enable him "to steer a straight course, betwixt all right and left hand extremes, towards Emanuel's land."

1. I am to seek with all earnestness to be implanted in Christ, the Prince of Life, that from him, as my living head, I may obtain new and fresh supplies of all Grace to guard against and avoid all vicious sensuality of heart and conversation. [Thus,] I have my rational being and other valuable privileges to a far other end than [the] sinful pursuit of satisfaction to the lusts of the flesh and pride of life (Ps. 73:24; Rom. 11:36; 1 Cor. 10:31; 2 Cor. 7:1).

2. More particularly, I am ever to take a humbling view of the falls of many of the Scripture saints, which are recorded as so many warnings for me not to be high minded, but fear, lest I split on those rocks where they shipwrecked the peace of a good conscience and stained their integrity through a sinful unwatchfulness. [For example], did Noah sin through excess of wine after a great deliverance (Gen. 9:21)? Then I am to watch carefully against that vice, and walk with God in uprightness of life and sincerity of heart as he did (Gen. 6:9). Did Abraham sin twice, by a distrustfulness of God's power and all sufficiency, in denying his wife (Gen. 12:12; 20:2)? Then I am to watch against the sin of lying and ... be strong in the faith as he was (Gen. 15:6; Rom. 4:3, 18, 20).... Did David fall into the abominable sins of murder and adultery (2 Sam. 12:9)? Then I am to watch against both these sins and [to] cry to the Lord for restraining strengthening, renewing, and sanctifying grace as he did (Ps. 18:23; 19:13). Did Solomon glut and surfeit himself with sinful sensual pleasures and forsake the Lord and his way (1 Kings 11:1–12; Eccl. 2:1–11)? Then I am to watch my heart with all diligence and believing application to the Lord for strength (Prov. 4:23).... Did Jehosaphat sin in joining with the ungodly (2 Chron. 19:2)? Then I am to watch and guard against all wicked company and sinful association (Ezra 9:14; Prov. 13:20). Did Hezekiah sin through pride and vain ostentation (Isa. 39:2)? Then I am to watch, be humble, and walk softly before the Lord as he did (2 Chron. 32:26; Ps. 119:36–37). Did Josiah sin in going unadvisedly against the king of Egypt? Then I am not to lean to my own understanding, but watchfully to acknowledge

the Lord in all my ways (Prov. 3:5-7; Jer. 10:23). Did Peter and the rest of the disciples sin by ... being vainly confident (Matt. 26:33-34)? Then I am not to be high minded, but fear, watching unto prayer, that I enter not into temptation (Matt. 26:41; 1 Cor. 10:12; Eph. 6:11,18). Were there contentions between Paul and Barnabas (Acts 15:39) and much carnal clashing against one another amongst the believing Corinthians (1 Cor. 1:11; 3:3-4)? Then I am to watch and strive against all strife and division, and [I am to] condescend as far as possible to live peaceably with all in the study of holiness (Rom. 12:9-10,16,18; 14:19; 15:1-3; Eph. 4:12-17; Phil. 2:1-3; Heb. 12:14; 1 John 4:7, 11). Did Peter dissemble in Judaizing (Gal. 2:10,14)? Then I am to contend earnestly for the faith, studying to know nothing but Christ and him crucified (Acts 4:12; 1 Cor. 1:2; 3:11; John 10:15; 14:6).

3. I am continually to search the scriptures, confession of faith, catechisms, and Mr. Durham's exposition of the ten commands. From these [I am] to learn through grace to know what is sin and what is duty, what is to be believed and practiced, following no man farther than they follow the Lord and speaking truth from his Word (Isa. 8:20; Luke 16:29; Gal. 1:18; 2 Tim. 3:16-17; Titus 1:9; 2:12-14).

4. ...When [the Lord] deserts me and hides himself and exercises me with many cross providences; yet,... I am to be far from finding fault with him, or with the conduct of his spotless providence. Neither am I to draw any wrong conclusion anent God's eternal purpose and anent my future state; neither am I to sit down, dejected and discouraged, forgetting God, my maker, who giveth songs in the night. No! That be far from me: but my duty is to ascribe righteousness to him (Job 36:3) and abhor myself in dust and ashes (Job 13:6) [for my sins against him] until he arise and plead my cause and execute judgment for me (Ps. 39:9; Lam. 1:18; Micah 3:8). [Pending deliverance], I am to do as Israel, in Exodus 2:23-24, sighing and groaning heavenward, Godward, and Christward until my cry come up into his holy ear, and he remember for me his covenant of promise.

5. [May he enable me] to rejoice in the God of my salvation; [to make] much use of Christ at all times; [to be] more and more quickened to prayer, praise, and other pieces of Christian exercise; [to enjoy] communion with God, Father, Son, and Holy Spirit (John 17:21; 1 Cor. 7:4-6; Eph. 2:18; 1 John 5:7); [and to make me whole as] he did for the man at the pool (John 5:8; 7:23). [While waiting on the Lord, I am] ... to bend the whole powers of heart and soul to live by faith upon unseen all-sufficiency (Isa. 1:10; John 20:29) [and to grip fast to Christ and] the virtue of his blood ... as the criminal under the law to the horns of the altar. Though he long refuse to help and though Satan and a deceiving heart tempt and incline me to let go my hold of him, yet, O my soul, yield not, consent not to

these enemies of my salvation; but cry out, "No, no!" If I must die, I will die here; for this is the place of my safety; this is the horn of the golden altar, where never any perished; this is the firm anchor-hold where never any were shipwrecked. He is the blessed venture for eternal life, in whose hands never any miscarried, neither came short of their salvation. He is the life-giving fountain where never any were killed with thirst. He is the glorious granary of heaven and the true Joseph affords his people the bread of life. He is the great anti-type of the brazen serpent,... the strong and mighty Redeemer,... the blessed anti-type shadowed forth by all the slain beasts under the law,... the fountain opened up and shadowed forth by the Levitical ceremonial washings,... the city of refuge and chamber of divine encampment,... [and] the king of nations and king of saints. This is he who hath established a blessed connection betwixt his love and his rod and betwixt the crown and the cross, each of which he hath lined with love in that he makes all things work together for his glory and their good. This is he who hath made peace and reconciliation between an angry God and perishing sinners,... who hath been proposed in all ages to those that are in desertion and affliction as the only sure ground of their strong consolation,... who sits at the helm of all affairs while his poor passengers are sailing through the world's storms,... [and] who married our nature, and became bone of our bone and flesh of our flesh, that he might be real man, sin excepted, as well as real God. [He did so] that he might consecrate and path out a new and living way through the veil of his flesh, whereby everlasting redeeming love might find a free passage to expatiate itself forth unto and for all his peculiar chosen ones, to effectuate all those great and glorious things for them. O then, my soul! Be no more bewitched with the perishing pleasures of this transitory life, neither do thou any more sink and despond under desertions and afflictions; but up and fly, fly fast in unto the warm bosom and outstretched-redeeming arms of this dear Redeemer, the Lord Jesus Christ. Amen.[19]

Darkness Before the Dawn (1688)

Despite the surface-deep acts of religious toleration, the government pursued the societies and their leaders with increased zeal. In 1687 alone, "the royal troops, thirteen times, made the strictest search for" Renwick.[20] James Nisbet shares his precious memories of Renwick's sermons, given during this period of great trial.

The latter end of this year, I heard that great man of God Mr. James Renwick preach. [He preached] on the Song of Solomon 3:9–10, where he treated sweetly on the Covenant of Redemption agreed on betwixt God the Father and God the Son, his equal in favors of the elect, and on the Covenant of Grace established with believers in Christ. This was a great and sweet day of the gospel, for he handled and pressed the privileges of the Covenant of Grace with seraphic-like enlargement to the great edification of the hearers. Sweet and charming were the offers that he made of Christ to all sorts of sinners. There was one thing this day that was very remarkable to me. Though it was rain from morning until night and we as wet as if drenched in water, yet not one fell sick. Though there was a tent fixed for him, he would not go into it but stood without in the rain and preached. [This] example had great influence on the people to patience when they saw his sympathy with them. Though he was the only minister that kept closest to his text and had the best method for the judgment and memory of any that ever I heard, yet now, when he perceived the people crowding close together because of the rain, he digressed a little and cried with a pleasant melting voice, "My dear friends, be not disturbed because of the rain; for to have a covenant interest in Christ, the true Solomon, and in the benefits of his blessed purchase are well worth the enduring of all temporal elementary storms that can fall on us. This Solomon who is here pointed at endured a far other kind of storm for his people, even a storm of unmixed wrath. And what would the poor-damned reprobates in hell give for this day's offer of sweet and lovely Christ to be their redeemer! How welcome would our suffering friends in prison and banishment make this day's offer of Christ! I, for my own part, as the Lord will help me shall bear my equal share of this rain in sympathy with you." And then, he returned to his sweet subject again and offered us peace and reconciliation with God through Christ by his Spirit.

Words fail me to express my own frame and the frame of many others; only this, we would have been glad to endure any kind of death to have been home at the uninterrupted enjoyment of that glorious Redeemer, who was as so lively and clearly offered to us that day. O my soul, behold and wonder! What shall I render to the Lord for all his benefits! For here, he was remarkably present with us by inward consolation and outward preservation.[21]

In 1688, the "whole country, for the most part, enjoyed peace and quietness; nevertheless, the Society was" troubled and discouraged "as they could not join in the toleration, or any other of the enemies' pretended favors."[22] To add to their woes, the government captured their beloved Renwick in February and sentenced him to death. When Renwick heard the drums sounding to take him to the gallows, he remarked to his mother: "Yonder is the welcome warning to my marriage; the Bride-groom is coming. I am ready. I am ready." On the scaffold, to the roll of drums, he sang part of Psalm 103 and read Revelation 20. Psalm 103 starts with the line, *"O thou my soul, bless God the Lord—and all that in me is."* His selected psalm witnesses to the fulfillment of the chief end of man as specified in the *Shorter Catechism*: "To glorify God and enjoy him forever." In this psalm, David lists the six things that all believers should be thankful for, namely that God has forgiven, healed, redeemed, crowned, satisfied, and renewed them (Ps. 103:2–5). Unless men understand they are mortally sinful, ill, lost, poor, thirsty, and corrupt, the gospel is of little value to them. After praying and addressing the audience, he declared that he was laying down his life for three things: (1) for disowning the usurpation and tyranny of King James, (2) for preaching against paying the cess, and (3) for teaching that it is lawful for Christians to bear arms in defense of their meetings to hear the persecuted gospel. He closed by declaring, "I think, a testimony for those is worth many lives; and if I had ten thousand I would think it little enough to lay them all down for the same."[23]

James Nisbet grieved over the loss of Renwick, whom he considered a man of "unstained integrity" and one of the great Scottish divines:

> …When I speak of him as a man, [there were] none more comely in features, none more prudent, none more brave and heroic in spirit, yet none more meek, none more humane and condescending. He was every way so rational as well as religious that there was ground to think that the powers of his reason were as much strengthened and sanctified as those of any mere man I ever heard of. When I speak of him as a Chris-tian, [there were] none more meek, yet none more prudently bold against those who were bold to sin. [There were] none more prudently condescending, none more frequent and fervent in religious duties, such as prayer, conversation, ejaculation, meditation, self-examination, preach-ing, prefacing, lecturing, baptizing, and catechizing. [There were] none more methodical in teaching and instructing, [none more] accomplished with a sweet charming eloquence in holding forth Christ as the only remedy for lost sinners, none more hated of the world…. [Although he] was liable to natural and sinful infirmaries, as all mere men are while in this life, yet he was as little guilty this way as any I ever knew or read of. He was the liveliest and [most engaging] preacher to close with Christ of any ever I heard. His converse was as pious, prudent, and meek; his rea-soning and debating were the same, carrying along with them a full evi-dence of the truth of what he asserted. For steadfastness in the way of the Lord, few came his length: he learned the truth, counted the cost,

and so sealed it with his blood.... O my soul! Bless the Lord that ever I heard this great man preach the un-searchable riches of Christ to poor lost sinners, of whom I am the chief....[24]

[The loss of Renwick] was ... an unspeakable loss, for now I wanted him who preached the word of life and taught me the way of salvation faithfully, fervently, meekly, and without all bitter reflection like a faithful servant of Christ Jesus, the want of which made my bowels to roll within me. It is true I had occasion to hear others, but their way of preaching was not so agreeable to my taste. Some of them, though great and good men..., for the most part insisted in describing and testifying against the public sins, apostasies, and defections of that day, seldom pointing out the sins of our hearts and natures, as the procuring cause of our ruin, and seldom pointing out Christ Jesus as our only remedy.... Likewise, there were others [who] preached piously and to good purpose, insisting on the doctrine of free grace, but not witnessing against the sins and defections of the day by setting the Lord's trumpet to their mouth to give us faithful warning of our danger. Instead, [they] winked at and by practice homologated the ungodly proceedings of our wicked rulers, which practice of theirs did very much stumble me and marred the success of the gospel, which otherwise through the Lord's blessing it might have had.[25]

During this difficult year, James struggled "to steer betwixt both parties of these suffering Presbyterians, some of whom were for owning that wickedly designed toleration and some not for owning it":

I neither inclining much to the one nor to the other; my light not serving me to go up with the foremost nor to stay aback with the hindmost, but [I] used charity to both. [I] studied moderation in speaking little, but when obliged to give my opinion, [considering] my young years, I used caution ... to be very ingenuous, declaring my cordial adherence to all Protestant Presbyterian principles as far as consistent to and agreeable with God's will revealed in his Word, summed up in our confession of faith and catechisms, and sworn to in our covenants. I also accordially owned the dying speeches of all that died on scaffolds, sealing their declared adherence to the Protestant Presbyterian principles with their blood, as far as they are agreeable to God's Holy Word. I still allowing all of them the honor of martyrdom though differing in their judgment about some things, such as owning the civil part of the then authority, which some eminent men never had clearness to disown. On the other hand, I freely disown and testify against the exercise of all illegal arbitrary power and supremacy in matters ecclesiastic in the state, all diocesan episcopacy, and all lording it over the house of God contrary to his

Word and contrary to the sworn principles of the Presbyterian Church of Scotland. I disown the wicked toleration granted the last year to open a door to popery and all false religion, which will prove to the utter subversion of all true religion if the Lord interposes not with his preventing mercy. I approve of defensive arms to be made use of by those who have light for it, but I witness against all shedding of blood except strictly in self-defense, by a just war, and by the civil magistrate according to God's Word. I would humbly desire all Christ's sent ambassadors to be faithful, plain, and positive against the sins and backslidings of the day, but chiefly to insist in showing people their lost state and the great necessity of their recovery there from, in, through, and by a glorious Mediator, Christ Jesus. [Ministers should] plainly hold forth to perishing sinners what [Christ] is; what he has done and suffered for elect sinners; how he is to be sought after, closed with, and embraced, as their only up making portion, on gospel terms by the power of his saving grace; and what great need there is for both ministers and people to adorn the gospel of Christ Jesus by a holy life and conversation.[26]

Although Renwick was the last martyr hanged, others fell for the cause after his death. The persecution intensified after the remnant attacked a body of soldiers to free a captured Irish minister sympathetic to their cause. In response, the government declared all Covenanter literature illegal, and soldiers asked all they met on the street, "Do you own the Covenants?" Such questions caused many to commit perjury to save their lives. Perhaps the last martyr was a sixteen-year-old boy named George Wood, whom a trooper shot without warning. The trooper's defense was, "He knew him to be one of the Whigs, and they ought to be shot wherever they were found."[27]

Just as "the night goes before the day and the last hour of the night darkest," James feared the imminent "threat of universal ruin" during the melancholy year 1688. His concern grew when the "enemy came through ... and searched very narrowly for arms, a thing they had often done before: upon which [he] conceived a heavy apprehension of a designed massacre, which apprehension was strengthened by the enemy's loud brags and other presumptions." These events caused him to "cry earnestly to the Lord" to "remember mercy in the midst of deserved wrath" and to "spare a remnant to be a seed to serve him." Little known to James, "Scotland's wonder-working and covenanted God" would soon impose "himself betwixt poor Britain's neck and the block."[28] The dark night of persecution was soon to end.

8

The Revolution Settlement

For we got not the land in possession by our own sword, neither did our own arm save us, but thy right hand, O Lord, and thine arm, and the light of thy countenance.
—*Psalms 44:3*

Revolution Settlement (1688–1689)

The birth of King James's son awakened many Protestants to the threat of a Catholic dynasty. This fear caused the Protestant supporters in England, Scotland, and Holland to join forces in overthrowing King James. The end of the persecution finally came when the Dutch leader, William, the Prince of Orange, and his wife Mary, daughter of James II and heiress to the English Crown, invaded England with a Protestant army. The popular support for King James was so low that within weeks of landing in late 1688, William's army of fourteen thousand defeated King James's army of thirty thousand without fighting a single full-scaled battle.[1] Facilitating William's successful victory were many English officers and soldiers who deserted en masse over fears that King James was determined to establish Catholicism. This coup was orchestrated by John Churchill (ancestor of Winston Churchill), one of James's leading generals, who had secretly pledged his support to William and Mary (1662–1694) a year earlier.[2] These events eventually forced King James to flee the country. Before leaving, he raised Claverhouse to the position of Viscount of Dundee to encourage continued resistance.

For this miraculous delivery from persecution, James Nisbet gives God all the credit:

> ...This was the Lord's doings, and it was marvelous in our eyes [Ps. 118:23]: O that it may be marvelous in the eyes of all following generations, because God's ways with us were all wonder, like himself! For now, in a remarkable manner was he on his mighty acts of mercy for us,

as he was for those in Psalm 106:44–45. Thus, the Lord repeated and reacted over again his merciful deliverances for us, which he wrought many a time for his people in the days of old. And O that there were such a heart in us to improve all continually to his glory, and ever to cry out with the psalmist: *"Not unto us, not unto us, but unto thy name be the glory"* [Ps. 115:1]; *"For the right hand of the Lord is exalted, and the right hand of the Lord doth valiantly"* [Ps. 118:15–16]; *"For we got not the land in possession by our own sword, neither did our own arm save us, but thy right hand, O Lord, and thine arm, and the light of thy countenance"* [Ps. 44:3] did drive out the heathen. *O Lord God of Hosts, who is a strong Lord like unto thee, or to thy faithfulness round about thee* [Ps. 89:8]? *For thou art a God full of compassion, and gracious, long-suffering, and plenteous in mercy and truth* [Ps. 86:15], because thou hast helped us and comforted us after twenty-eight years of bloody persecution and heavy oppression. All which time, every year, every day, and every hour, grew still darker and darker with us, until at last, when all hopes were gone, the Lord, the Lord God merciful and gracious, did awake as a mighty man for these poor lands, made Britain's sky to clear once more, and overwhelmed his and our enemies with confusion. Even so arise, O Lord, and let all thy enemies be ever scattered, and let thy own people be delivered that they may serve thee without fear.[3]

Released from their fetters, mobs evicted the curates and demanded that the evicted curates promise to cease preaching. The anger of the mobs was not satiated until they expelled all curates from the five western shires. Although unpleasant, this persecution was not equal to the death and destruction wrought on them.[4]

Radical changes also took place within the covenanting societies. Thomas Linning, ordained in Holland, succeeded Renwick. Joining him were two other ministers, Alexander Shields and William Boyd. The General Society decried the defections of their Presbyterian brethren and refused to meet with previously Indulged ministers unless they repented. The members of the societies re-swore the covenants in March 1689 with minor corrections, referring to the civil magistrate rather than the king. At this ceremony, Shields preached on Deut. 29:25, concerning the hazard of forsaking covenant obligations.[5] Following the sermon, the members of the societies confessed their own transgressions, as well as those of their fellow Presbyterians during the persecution.

Near this time, the Convention of Estates restored lawful government and "declared King James to have forfeited his rights to the crown, [listing] the same reasons for it, that the United Societies formerly had given."[6] However, the new government was in great danger because

Claverhouse was raising an army to restore King James to the throne by force. The new government called on the Society People to raise a regiment because they were the "only body that both possessed the power and the inclination to protect their country's liberties, and might be trusted in this hour of peril."[7] In May, after a two-month-long heated debate, the societies raised a regiment (called the Cameronian Regiment) to assist in defending the throne rights of William and Mary. Their internal debate centered on the lawfulness of association with an army that did not exclude malignants and with a government that had not sworn to uphold the covenants.[8] The General Society agreed to support the regiment only if the government accepted a long list of qualifications. These qualifications included provisions to serve under officers of their choosing and demands that the government redress their grievances. Because it was impossible for the government to grant some of these qualifications and because the country was in great peril, the troops agreed to serve on the following terms:

> To declare that you engage in this service, of purpose to resist popery, and prelacy, and arbitrary power; and to recover and establish the work of reformation in Scotland, in opposition to popery, prelacy, and arbitrary power in all the branches and steps thereof, till the government in church and state, be brought to the luster and integrity which it had in the best of times.[9]

Although the majority concurred with this declaration, the extreme members, such as Robert Hamilton, protested the action.[10]

Parliament met and offered the crown to William and Mary as joint sovereigns. In their coronation oath, they promised to secure the "true religion" but made no promise to support the confession of faith or the covenants. William refused to commit to "root out all heresies and the enemies of the true worship of God" because he feared that doing so would make him a persecutor. The Calvinism of King William was certainly a different type than that of the Covenanters. During the seventeenth century, reformation in Holland had become increasing pietistic, focusing on private and family devotions, rather than reformation of church and society. Although the Dutch confession required the government to exterminate false religion, the Dutch rulers "preferred to allow the continued existence of diverse religious cultures," which served as the breeding grounds for the sects and independents.[11]

Further complicating the situation was the fact that King William sought a balance between offending the Anglican leaders in England

and the Presbyterian leaders in Scotland. He achieved this balance by letting each country choose its religion. William instructed the Scottish Parliament to establish church government in a way most agreeable to the glory of God and agreeable to the inclination of the people. In Scotland, Parliament rescinded the acts used to suppress the Presbyterians, abolished prelacy, adopted the *Westminster Confession of Faith,* but ignored the *Form of Presbyterian Church Government* to avoid offending the Anglicans. Unfortunately, they left the acts that had undone the work of the Second Reformation on the books; consequently, the *Solemn League and Covenant* remained an illegal oath. Defoe stated that "not a dog wagged its tongue against the Presbyterian Establishment, not a mouth gave a vote for Episcopacy."[12] However, the full truth is that many in the northern and eastern areas of Scotland strongly supported prelacy and Catholicism. In England, the Episcopal majority ensured the establishment of the Church of England. The net result was an abandonment of the pledge contained in the *Solemn League and Covenant* for the preservation and reformation of religion.

By July 1689, Claverhouse assembled a force of Highlanders, Irish, and Loyalist supporters of the deposed King James to overthrow the new government. The awaited battle between the armies of Claverhouse and King William took place at Killiecrankie, where Claverhouse's army of Highlanders ambushed and defeated William's larger army under the leadership of General Hugh McKay. The onslaught of a horde of broadsword-wielding Highlanders, naked from the waist down, was too much for the inexperienced troops of McKay's army to withstand. This onslaught left eighteen hundred of McKay's troops dead and five hundred taken prisoner. Claverhouse's troops suffered few casualties; however, one of these was Claverhouse, whose leadership was irreplaceable.[13] Yet, another John Nisbet, a young lieutenant in McKay's defeated army, got in the history books that day. The Loyalists captured Lieutenant Nisbet and imprisoned him in the Castle of Blair where one of the victors, a man named Johnson, told Nisbet how he had caught the wounded Claverhouse as he fell from his horse. Johnson claimed that before Claverhouse died he asked how the day went. Johnson replied that the day went well for the king (James) and that he was sorry for his lordship (Claverhouse). Claverhouse responded, "It was the less matter for me, seeing the day went well for my master [the king]." After Claverhouse fell, an unknown party stripped and left him naked on the field–a fitting end for the life of the "Bloody" Clavers.[14]

Although the Cameronian regiment under the command of Lt. Col. Cleland arrived too late for the battle, they soon found themselves surrounded in the town of Dunkeld by the Highlanders and Irish who outnumbered them six to one. This small force of Covenanters, consisting of a few hundred men, was now the only creditable fighting force that could deprive King James of victory. Dunkeld was the perfect place for this epic battle: "A primitive town girded by menacing hills, with its hoary Cathedral, laird's house, narrow streets, walled enclosures … quite the place consecrated for the last stand in a religious cause." To solidify their resolve to fight to the death, Cleland had his men shoot their horses. The Cameronian regiment consisted of many of the surviving hard-core Covenanters and their sons, including men like Patrick Walker, Alexander Shields, and likely James Nisbet. This regiment shared many similarities to a mobile, fighting church with twenty elders to "superintend the moral and religious behavior of the corps."[15] When finding themselves surrounded, this regiment chose to entrench themselves around the town rather than surrender. From the entrenchment and houses, the psalm-singing Covenanters repelled repeated assaults. To replenish their dwindling ammunition, they melted down lead torn from the houses. The Highlanders drove the Cameronians back to the Cathedral, but the Cameronians turned the tables on the Highlanders by setting fire to the surrounding houses. The Highlanders eventually gave up, declaring, "They could fight against men, but it was not fit to fight any more against devils." Unknown to the Highlanders, the Cameronians were down to their last charge of powder.[16]

After another battle, the Highlanders and Irish simply melted away, eliminating any hope of restoring King James to power. Thus, James Nisbet recorded his vote on the obligation of Christians to bear arms in defense of their government, even if the government is imperfect. If Robert Hamilton had his way, this regiment would not have existed, and it is likely that the dominant religion of English-speaking people today would be Catholicism. Hamilton considered the joining of this regiment as a "sinful association with malignants" and demanded that the General Society not admit the soldiers who joined this regiment.[17]

Revolution Aftermath (shortly after 1689)

The Church of Scotland that arose from the Revolution Settlement was not the same church that swore the covenants. Hundreds of Episcopal curates remained in the nine hundred parishes of Scotland. In contrast, only sixty ministers remained of those forced out of the church in 1661. Of these sixty ministers, most had either accepted an Indulgence or wasted away in prisons during the twenty-eight years of persecution.[18] Although ministers were required to subscribe to the Presbyterian form of government, they were not required to declare the Episcopalian form of government unscriptural because it was the adopted form of church government of England. The Presbyterianism that had forged an ideal blend of doctrinal purity, evangelical spirit, and cultural involvement during the Second Reformation ceased to exist.

The Society People, eager to seek redress and to re-establish the covenants, submitted to Parliament a petition listing nine grievances. This petition, however, never reached the Parliament because a committee established to review grievances did not want to offend the king. The government's refusal to hear their petition, to adopt the covenants, and to take positive action to root out false religions infuriated the Society People. James Nisbet discusses these grievances in his memoir:

> Raise thou up the fallen tabernacle of David in these lands that thy great name may be made known and exalted to the ends of the earth. [May] all who have been sorrowful for the solemn assemblies ... again have cause to be glad in the Lord and [to] rejoice in the God of their salvation, to whom all the issues from death doth belong; for to him, and him alone, we owe lasting praise for this remarkable deliverance. But now, alas! Alas! After I had solaced myself with some of the first fruits of the happy, happy, but ill-improven Revolution—namely, in seeing the yoke of our oppressors broken so that we might serve the Lord without fear, yet I quickly saw my expectation defeated [in nine ways]. [Sadly,] our recovery and reformation from our defections, sins, and backslidings was not according to the pains the Lord had been at with us, nor according to our best times, [nor] in having our holy religion established on her own basis. First, when the Parliament sat down in 1689, they voted presbytery into the church because it was most agreeable to the inclinations of the people, as is to be seen in the claim of right, and, not because it was according to the Word of God and his own platform of church government plainly set down in the New Testament. Second, when the Assembly met the same year, instead of fixing on any thing done betwixt 1638 and 1649, they went back and fixed on an act made in the year 1592, thereby excluding part of the best times of our reformation. Third, all the nation's deep defections and dreadful backsliding were all atoned for by one day's fasting and humiliation; then there were converts enough from prelacy to presbytery. Fourth, alas, it was not a returning to the Most High. There was no engaging to the Lord against

sin and for duty, covenant ways, as was greatly expected and earnestly desired by many. Fifth, there was no pursuing of criminals guilty of the blood of the Lord's people, as they deserved, and was by us earnestly expected. Sixth, [there was] the pardoning and employing many of these guilty of innocent blood as elders in church judicatories. Seventh, [many] were employed in state and army who had been avowed enemies to the work and people of God. Eighth, if there was any reparation made for losses sustained in the time of persecution, it was as very partially distributed. Ninth, all those who had been most exposed to the brunt of persecution were most slighted and neglected.

All these things were very weighty and discouraging grievances to me; so that I was again brought to go with a pain at the heart and a bowed down back, and [I] knew not well what to do. I had sometimes served heartily a volunteer in the military to suppress the mad attempts of the enemies to the Revolution, headed and commanded by one Graham of Claverhouse, who sought to overthrow the Revolution footing and restore the abdicated King James. I was a hearty revolutioner and a great adorer of God's goodness to these lands in sending that great man, King William, to overthrow our enemies and redeem us from slavery. Yet, the aforesaid nine grievances stuck close with me and stumbled me greatly, whereupon I had thoughts to go off the country. But alas, alas! Before that project was ripe, I met with some who otherwise were good men, but they had stated a separation from church and state after the Revolution because of the aforesaid nine grievances, to which they added many more. I at last was overcome with their arguments and joined with them in the inadvertent simplicity of my heart, being influenced with zeal not altogether according to knowledge. I continued … in communion with them for some time, which laid a foundation for a train of many after trials to me. I quickly found that I was out of the frying pan into the heart of the fire: for, though I saw great reason for these grievances on the government side, yet, amongst the dissenters, I found many grievances some which were intolerable unto me.[19]

Fortunately, James Nisbet and the majority of the Society People eventually perceived the true course of Christian duty–much to the credit of their three ministers. Despite its warts, the Revolution Settlement church was the church. The Society's three remaining, young ministers recognized this truth and pleaded with Society members to join this wounded body of Christ, the Church of Scotland. Michael Shields recorded how earlier to no avail, these three ministers had attempted to persuade the Society members to unite with ministers that had defected during the persecution because the persecution was over.

For albeit we had sufficient grounds to withdraw from these ministers [those that defected] in time of persecution, which was a broken and unsettled time, yet now, when the same was removed and the church growing up in reformation, the case was altered. As there was one way of contending then, which was by withdrawing, so there was another was now, which is by joining with a protest against defection.[20]

The majority was only willing to do so if the ministers who had defected would confess and repent of their sins. The three ministers proposed that Society members leave justice to the church courts, rather than take it in their own hands. The ministers argued that each could avoid sinful associations by joining the Church of Scotland under written protest. Although the General Society initially rejected the proposal, over time the majority of the Society People joined the Church of Scotland. Those who joined received little satisfaction inasmuch as the Church of Scotland, which dared not offend the king, largely ignored their pleas for action. The three ministers, following their own advice, submitted a letter outlining their grievances to the Church of Scotland, but the letter never got past a review committee. The reviewing committee claimed that the letter contained errors such as, "The Church of Scotland could not own a league with the Church of England." The only satisfaction the ministers received from the church was the listing of several of their complaints as reasons for a day of fasting. The lack of repentance on the part of the church simply reinforced the concerns of many Society People, who were vehemently opposed to the compromised church and the abandonment of the covenants.

Although the overwhelming majority of the Society People followed their ministers and joined with the Church of Scotland, a large number of holdouts, led by Robert Hamilton, continued to rail against church and state. The last official record (in *Faithful Contendings*) of the General Society was a blank letter of protest for individual Society members to use when they resumed membership in the Church of Scotland. This protest concludes with these lines, "Thus having given in our testimony against these sins and all other defections and corruptions in this church; we protest that our present joining may not be interpreted an approving of any of these sins, nor a condemning of, or receding from our former or present testimony."[21] James Nisbet's friend Patrick Walker left the following account of how most dealt with this dilemma:

All know that it was the fewest number of the United Societies, that was led off with Robert Hamilton to the disowning of King William as king of Britain and his Government; the greater part reckoned it their duty to

take a legal united way of witnessing by humble pleadings, representa-
tions, and protestations, pleading for and with their mother to put away
her whoredoms.[22]

James Nisbet agonized over this difficult choice. Should he stick with
those Society People who claimed to remain faithful to the principles for
which his father died, or should he join the clearly imperfect Church of
Scotland? Based on the following account from his memoir, it is likely
that he parted from the Society shortly after the Revolution Settlement
because of the dangerous errors and behaviors of its members:

> Their criticizing upon and censuring of all others who are not exactly
> of their judgment in every punctilio, grievously aggravating their faults
> and often fixing some where there is none; yea, seldom sparing one an-
> other even where they are one in judgment, [they made] the terms of
> their communion straighter than what God allows in his Word. They
> will allow no masters of families to be of their communion who pay any
> taxes to the present government, making no difference betwixt this legal
> and the former illegal and tyrannical government. They will allow no
> children or servants to be in their communion who obey their parents
> and masters in doing any service to those in public trust in the govern-
> ment. They will allow none to hear any of the present ministry, even
> though transiently, to be in their communion. They spend the most part
> of their precious time in arguing and praying against the sins and defec-
> tions of the public, neglecting to watch the heart; and here, to my
> shame, I was greatly guilty of this, among others. We spent much of our
> precious time in framing arguments to debate with others, greatly ne-
> glecting to be distinctly acquainted with the principles of the Christian
> religion and to be savingly acquainted with the inward and serious part
> of real godliness. They would publish a declaration disowning the au-
> thority of the great King William and against the validity of the present
> church communion.
>
> When I earnestly besought, with much entreaty, that every article of
> that declaration might be reasoned, they would not allow it: upon
> which; I protested against it for myself and for all that would adhere
> unto me. I thought and said, "Since God, of his infinite goodness, had so
> wonderfully, graciously, and mercifully wrought such a great deliverance
> for us and redressed so many of our former intolerable grievances, by
> sending in that great and famous instrument King William, it was a de-
> spising of many valuable mercies, because we got not all we would and
> should have had." It was a reflecting dishonor on God and on his wor-
> thy instrument. [It] was a sign of great ingratitude and unthankfulness in
> us to refuse allegiance and obedience to King William and his govern-

ment, he ruling under God in the execution of the ancient law of this kingdom, for the preservation of our privileges sacred and civil. I alleged what was wrong in the administration of our laws either in church or state is more through the default of some of the administrators than either to the laws now in being, or yet to the supreme magistrate. From which I see I cannot state my sufferings upon anything amiss, although they are still grievous; neither can I have peace to refuse obedience to the civil magistrate in all things according to the Word of God.

Thus my protesting, and refusing, to join with them, enraged them exceedingly against me. As their scourge of tongues was grievously bent against others, so now was it against myself in a most grievous, unjust, and unreasonable manner. [They] very hypocritically gave it out far and near that I was going to turn Quaker, which is what I ever hated, name and thing; for I ever looked upon the abominable Quakers to be of a religion composed of all sorts of error. My former friends the dissenters very hypocritically and industriously spread that false report far and near; but my good and gracious God remarkably pleaded my cause against the author of that lie. And although it had not been so, yet, where the glory of God and the peace of my own conscience are so nearly concerned, I am to let name and all go for the sake thereof. Thus, I left that party of the dissenters who now commonly go under the name of Mr. McMillan's people. I had never any thing to do with the Quakers, Gibb's faction, the Harlaw's faction, and episcopacy by bishops in matters of religion, neither directly nor indirectly; yea, my soul abhors all their evil ways. [Instead,] I lived retired by myself; all which time, the Lord, pitied me and restored me to some measure of communion with himself. Praise, praise. Amen.[23]

In the final analysis, it was preaching of the gospel that convinced him to join the church:

But, after some interval of time, two of my dear friends prevailed with me to go and be a hearer at a sacrament where four ministers were helpers; three of which I heard to no purpose although they were very able men in preaching the gospel. O hard heart of mine! O the strength of prejudice! {These} two evils [are] ever to be much lamented by me. O my soul, behold and wonder at the long-suffering patience of a good God who waits that he may be gracious. Just as I was resolving to come away without any satisfaction, there came up a fourth minister, whom, for the honor of God and of that great day's work, I record his name, which was Mr. John Anderson [1668–1721], minister of the gospel at West-Calder in West-Lothian. He preached on Rev. 22:14, *"Blessed are they that do his commandments, for they have right to the tree of life and shall enter in through the gate into the city."* He spoke from this portion of Scripture as if he had been immediately sent of God to carry a message of good tidings to me, a forlorn wretch, and as if he had been sent out to seek a strayed lost sheep; and, indeed, I was the person. He spoke with such power and demonstration of the spirit as not only melted down my hard heart to contrition and quite removed all my prejudices, but also fully persuaded me that it was the gospel of Christ Jesus and Word of eternal life which he preached. He sung and prayed in the midst of his sermon. [He] then proceeded wonderfully, holding forth to us our lost state, inability and unwillingness to help ourselves and keep the commandments, and also how Christ is the tree of life and true trysting-place betwixt a holy God and perishing sinners, and how that through him, and the virtue of his purchase, there is an entrance of access to the bosom of God's favor, heaven and eternal life.[24]

Other than from his memoir, we know little concerning the later portions of James Nisbet's life. We do know from other sources that he married Agnes Woodburn and served as a sergeant and later a lieutenant at Edinburgh Castle, which overlooks the spot of his father's execution. Although some family histories, including that of my own family, claim that James Nisbet sired two sons who moved to America in the early 1700s, it is more likely that he had no children. Wodrow recounted that shortly before his death, James Nisbet told an acquaintance that "he was the last of his old family (and had no children)," and that he planned to leave his papers to his nephew. As further proof, Murdoch Nisbet's Bible passed into the hands of others.[25] It is possible, but unlikely, that he lost contact with his alleged two sons who would have been in Ireland on their way to America at the time of his death. Hence, only God knows which of the John Nisbets examined in this book is my ancestor.

During his later years, James laments the declining condition of the church and learns to rest solely upon Christ to preserve the church.

> Now, as formerly, I durst not but yield all true allegiance to the civil magistrate: so after this I durst not refuse any longer to hear the ministers of the present Presbyterian establishment. [These ministers] preach precious Christ, our dear Redeemer, to be the way, the truth, and the life, and adorn their doctrine with a gospel-becoming conversation. All who do not so will have much to count for, both with respect to themselves and with respect to those whose souls they have the charge of: for woe will be to the idle and idol shepherds: but great will be the reward of Christ's faithful servants that will have it to say at the last day, "Lo!

Here am I and the children which thou, O Lord and righteous judge, hath given me." But that the gospel preached by the present ministry has not the wished-for success in power and life is a charge inferring guilt that comes home to every person's door, people as well as ministers. Yet it is to be observed that where ministers are and have been most straight in their judgment to the received principles of the covenanted Church of Scotland in doctrine, worship, discipline, and government, and are most godly and exemplary in their lives and conversations, there the gospel has had most flourishing success.

Under the ministry of some of which worthy ministers I lived many years; and though, alas, I did not profit according to the means of grace clearly dispensed in gospel ordinances. Yet, as I grew in years and understanding, I was enabled by the help of what I heard to reflect with some comfort upon some past experiences of my life since my childhood, and also to increase more and more in the knowledge and experience of my great need and necessity of living by faith and humble dependence upon a God in Christ. [Thus, I learned] to derive the strength of all grace out of his mediatory fullness to die to all sin, to die to all self, to die to all inordinate affections to all of time's enjoyment, and to live in him ... and live for his glory, holding communion with God, Father, Son, and Holy Spirit, which Trinity of persons is the alone center and sure foundation of all the safety, comfort, and consolation of every heaven-born soul. Though there was with me sad pieces of decay and intermittings of a work of grace now and then and much to be lamented unwatchfulness and untender walking with and before the Lord on my part; yet he waited to be gracious to me and pitied me, long preserving me from all overwhelming damps and down castings of spirit.

[This continued] till a while before the much to be lamented death of the eminently religious, brave, and valiant William, Prince of Orange, king of Great Britain, our never to be forgotten kind and compassionate deliverer, who died, March 1702. At which time, I was much borne down with great exercise of spirit and heavy presages of approaching sorrow, but [I] could draw no conclusion from what quarter till the sad news of his death came. [These] bitter tidings to me filled me with so much grief and sorrow that it very near broke my heart, sunk my spirit, and greatly impaired my health. If the Lord had not comforted me from his Word, I could not have borne nor stood up under that much to be lamented public and universal loss: but the Lord pitied me and encouraged me, under my continual grief, with what is written (Ezra 21:27; Ps. 90:1; 97:1-2; 99:1; Isa. 30:18). The Lord, by these scriptures, taught me to see that I am not to place my trust in princes, nor in any of the children of men; that whatever piece of work the Lord has to work, he will not

[lack] instruments to carry it on. It is to be observed through all ages that the Lord carries on his work, one piece of it by one instrument and another piece of it by another instrument.... We may all read our sin in our punishment; for we all sadly abused the mercy of God, who gave us such a king, yet [we] did not act for his glory under the verge of such a noble instrument. We were neither thankful to God, nor to our worthy king; therefore, the Lord justly took him away from us, an ungrateful people. The Lord of Hosts is King of Nations and King of Zion; therefore, though all instruments were removed, yet he would make his ark and work plead its own quarrel to the confusion of all its opposers; truth is strong and will overcome. O glorious and kind Omnipotence, powerfully determine my soul ever to be on truth's side, to fall and stand therewith! The death of this great man and worthy protector of the Protestant interest sent me many errands to the Lord and [to] the throne of his grace, lamentingly to bewail our loss and [to plead] that he would sanctify the dispensation to all of the Protestant persuasion,... defend and preserve his own work, and raise up carpenters to hew the horns of the beast. The Lord, in some measure, answered [this request] in the successful conduct of the great Duke of Marlborough and Prince Eugene of Savoy. In March 1708 when the Pretender came with the French fleet to land in Scotland, whom Admiral Byng pursued, this caused great thought of heart to me for a short time; but the Lord comforted me with and sent quick deliverance, by fulfilling for us what is recorded, *"When the enemy cometh in as an overflowing flood, the Spirit of the Lord will lift up a standard against them"* (Isa. 59:19).

Thus, from the time I left the dissenters, I wrestled through all the reign of great King William and Queen Anne, enjoying the gospel clearly and faithfully preached by several worthy ministers to the great edification and comfort of my soul, meditating frequently on the scriptures, and repeating weekly the *Shorter Catechism* to myself. All which I found much sweetness and satisfaction in.

Now and then, [I] meditated on the following subjects, namely–How much delight and satisfaction so ever I take in the enjoyment of friends and relations, so much and sometimes more sorrow and grief shall the parting with them occasion to me, unless I use them with much self-denial and kindly submission to the disposing will of God. No creature can move any way of themselves to my satisfaction or dissatisfaction, neither can they smile or frown upon me, hurt me, or do me good, but as a wise God sees fit to order it. Success in sin is of all things most dangerous; therefore, it is a great mercy when the Lord continues to be a reprover. To be left of God to consult with flesh and blood and follow the counsels of a corrupt heart and perverse spirit, is a great sign of wrath. Discovered wants is a great mercy when sanctified. Discovered wants is ... given for a ground ... to humble the soul under a sense of its wretchedness and inability to help itself, and to make it run to the Lord and wait patiently and diligently about his hand for suitable supply to all its wants. Be still to know that he is God. I find it a great difficulty to get Christ, the fair Plant of Renown, loved entirely for himself, but rather for his benefits. Yet, O praise, praise to him, for I find him sometimes now and then causing me to ascend from a sense of my need to a sense of his mercy, from a sense of his mercy to a sense of his redeeming love, and from a sense of his redeeming love to a vehement desire to be ever with himself; and it is for matter of lamentation to my soul that it is not always so.[26]

The poor misguided soul named Lieutenant Robert Nisbet, who for earthly fame and reward money captured and turned in two of his own cousins, received just reward for his deeds. If you remember, he captured three other men the same day he captured John Nisbet. These three captured men, sold into slavery in the Barbados for refusing to take the oath, returned to Scotland as free men after the Revolution Settlement. As fate would have it, the first person they saw when they stepped off the ship onto Scottish soil was the former Lieutenant Robert Nisbet. Their first thoughts were of revenge, but they decided to heed Scripture: *"Vengeance is mine; I will repay, saith the Lord"* (Rom. 12:19).[27] John Howie, in *Scots Worthies,* records Robert Nisbet's fate:

> After the Revolution, he [Robert Nisbet] soon came to beg his bread as old soldiers oft-times do; and it was said that coming to a certain poor woman's house in the east country, he got quarters, and for a bed she made him what we call a shakedown, before a mow of peats, being all her small convenience could afford on which he lay down. She going out on some necessary errand a little after, when she returned, she found the wall of peats fallen upon him, which had smothered him to death; a very mean end for such a courageous soldier.[28]

Alexander Shields served several years as a minister in St. Andrews; he then, motivated by missionary zeal, participated in the Darien expedition, a failed attempt to establish a Scottish Settlement in the Americas. For his missionary effort, he justly deserves the title of Scotland's first missionary.[29] Also resting on this expedition were Scotland's hopes to free its economy from England's New-World-trade monopoly. In this failed expedition, thirteen hundred Scots in four ships set out to establish a colony near Panama. They anticipated that they would supplement an already established settlement, but they found the settlement abandoned. Things got worse: fire destroyed their food; disease destroyed their health; inept leadership destroyed their morale; and irreligious Scots and quarreling ministers destroyed their spirit. Obviously, the Scottish religious unity that existed before the persecution no longer existed after the Revolution Settlement. To make matters worse, nearby Spanish troops and ships threatened the colony's safety. When the leader refused to engage in war with the Spaniards, Shields advised him that it was lawful for Christians to engage in war. The leader rebuked Shields by accusing him of "nonsense, contradicting the gospel, and tempting men to atheism."[30] Eventually, the colonists, at the urging of Shields, decided to attack and destroy a nearby Spanish fort. When news reached Edinburgh of their victory, it was cause for national celebration. The victory celebration ceased when eleven Spanish warships attacked the colony, forcing it to surrender. In addition to the material loss, the poor Protestant Scots realized the spiritual loss when the victorious Spanish used their largest building to celebrate Mass. The defeated colonists barely made it back to Jamaica, where Shields died—a man crushed by the "divisions, impiety, and unrighteousness" that characterized this ill-fated expedition. His last sermon was based on Hosea 14:9, *"The ways of the Lord are right."* Of the remaining 360 men, few made it back to Scotland. Some ended up in Charleston, South Carolina.[31] Descendants of Alexander's brother, Michael, live in Jamaica today.

It seems that many of those who suffered during the persecution ably served both Christ and their earthly king after the persecution. Sir James Stewart, the man who had advocated the overthrow of kings that violated their covenant obligations, served as the King's Advocate, the highest law official in the land.[32] Sir Hugh Campbell, the third Earl of Loudoun, served on the Privy Council and was later keeper of the Great Seal of Scotland. Many who had been banished found their way back home after the persecution. Archibald Riddell, after preaching in America, returned home upon word of the Restoration Settlement; however, within sight of the English coast, a French ship took him captive. Several years later, after servitude, imprisonment, and unspeakable hardships, he finally returned to useful service as a minister in Scotland.[33] Sir Robert Hamilton, forever a thorn in the side of the new government, served an eight-month-long jail sentence for posting a seditious proclamation at Sanquhar in 1692. A good test of his character and dedication to principles came when he refused to take title to his brother's large estate because acceptance necessitated that he pledge allegiance to the king. Hamilton refused to swear allegiance because the king did not restore the *Solemn League and Covenant* as the foundation of government.[34]

Claverhouse's widow met her fate in a house fire in Rotterdam. She had once jokingly commented that if she ever heard a Presbyterian minister her house would fall on her. Wodrow contends that she heard a Presbyterian minister the night before her death.[35]

Their Struggle: Although James Nisbet chose to part with the Society People and to join the Church of Scotland, many who still adhere to the *Solemn League and Covenant* to this very day would criticize his choice. The remnant rejected the Revolution Settlement church because some of its ministers and elders had taken unlawful oaths and indulgences during the persecution. They rejected the Scottish government because it had abandoned the covenants and had established Presbyterian doctrine for popular rather than scriptural reasons. There are two sides to these arguments as presented by Thomas Houston (1803–1882).

> One side, outlined in Dodd's *Fifty Years' Struggle of the Scottish Covenanters,* presents Renwick as "Like the shepherd overwhelmed in the snow storm, he perished within sight of the door" that was opened by the revolution. In this conception, "the Revolution Settlement—in the main adopting what was universal and rejecting what was exclusive, or over-grasping in their [the strict Covenanters] views...."[36]

> Presenting the other side, Houston contends that the Revolution Settlement was a "deliberate abandonment" of the principles that the Covenanters died for; namely, that the covenants were a perpetually binding "marriage tie" with God wherein "the authority of Scripture was supreme in constituting the national society, in enacting and administering laws, and in regulating the lives and official acts of the rulers."[37]

According to Houston's view, James Nisbet could not have been a true Covenanter because he broke with the remnant. Which of these positions is correct? Or else, is there a deeper question? Were not the struggles of the Covenanters to honor God's authority in church and state simply part of a deeper and more pervasive struggle, one in which Satan seeks to overthrow God's authority in all things? The next chapter examines this larger, ongoing struggle.

9

The Ongoing Struggle

Then the anger of the LORD was hot against Israel; and he said, "Because this nation has transgressed my covenant which I commanded their fathers, and has not heeded my voice, I also will not henceforth drive out the nations ..."
—*Judges 2:20–21*

Satan's Attack

The Revolution Settlement marks the end of an era where each nation went forward into battle under one church banner. Taking advantage of this opportunity, Satan intensified his assault on the very foundations of the Christian faith. The almost complete destruction of the Reformed faith under the reign of the Stuarts, coupled with the onslaught of Arminianism, toleration, enlightenment, and the scientific revolution substantially affected the church. Arminianism removed God's government from man's soul, toleration removed God from man's social relationships, the enlightenment removed God's authority over man's mind, and the scientific revolution removed God's influence altogether from the world since it seemingly ran perfectly well without him.

Satan's main point of attack has always been against the God's authority, without which there is no hope. To this end, Satan launches his insatiable fury in an unrelenting, three-pronged attack on the agents of God's authority—namely, godly institutions (church, state, and family), the souls of God's covenant children, and the foundation of both—Scripture. As John Nevay observed, these are the only three objects of hope mentioned in Psalms: *hope in the Lord* (Ps. 33:22), *hope in his mercy* (Ps. 147:11), and *hope in his Word* (Ps. 130:5). All three rest in *hope in Jesus Christ and his Gospel* (Col. 1:5; 1 Tim. 1:1), as revealed in the New Testament.[1] They also correspond to the three offices of Christ and the three commands of the Great Commission. Upon reflection, every woe that faces us today is attributable to the deformation of these objects of hope. Undoubtedly, Satan's chief points of attack are Christ's lordship, mercy, and Word.

His Word: Satan's attack against God's Word is also multi-pronged. First, Satan seeks to establish human reason and philosophy in place of Scripture as the source of knowledge concerning God. The Bible as the primary source of knowledge of God was assaulted by empiricists such as John Locke (1631–1704), who contended that the experience of the senses was the true foundation of knowledge. Locke is deservedly called the father of modern Christianity because he held that the only essential belief was that Jesus was the Messiah.[2] Locke's new breed of Christianity denied the supernatural and promoted the individual to the position of knowledge perceiver. Thomas Hobbes, the father of moral relativism, took a more narrow view, which limited the source of empirical knowledge to material things (materialism). George Berkeley (1685–1753) took the opposite view, which denied the reality of the material world (idealism). David Hume (1711–1776) challenged all *a priori* facts, which underpin religious beliefs, by contending that cause and effect relations were simply products of the mind unless empirically demonstrated. Because these philosophies did not provide a coherent framework to understand cause and effect relationships, their adherents turned to more-virulent world views, such as Marxism and Evolution.

Second, Satan seeks to convince us that Christians cannot agree on the teachings of Scripture. The Latitudinarian movement, which began in the late seventeenth century, "attempted to draw a definitional line separating fundamental from non-fundamental elements of Protestant theology."[3] This attempt to escape from the whole counsel of God is the root problem. The modern ecumenical mantra to identify a few fundamental principles to serve as the basis of unity is doomed to failure.

Third, a movement in the nineteenth century, initiated by German scholars, attacked the authenticity of Scripture texts. According to this movement, Moses did not write the Pentateuch. Since Jesus said he did, the teaching of this untruth at most modern colleges (including many Christian colleges) teaches by inference that Jesus was a liar.

Fourth, Satan is exhaulted when he convinces men that the Old Testament and moral law no longer apply. Those so convinced are called Neonomians. In contrast, the Covenanters viewed salvation and sanctification as inseparable. To them, being a Christian meant taking up Christ's cross daily and eagerly seeking God in his Word. If asked why modern evangelical Christians are so ignorant of the Bible, they would conclude that such might not be Christians.

His Lordship: Satan also loves to attack the agents of God's authority here on this earth. In the last half of the seventeenth century, Puritan Congregationalists such as John Owen and philosophers such as John Locke disallowed almost all authority of the church or state "over human souls and consciences."[4] Nevertheless, Owen and Locke disallowed toleration of Catholics, fearing their allegiance to foreign powers (i.e., the pope), and of atheists, believing that the oath of a man without religion could not be trusted. Although complete toleration is the underpinning of the modern pluralistic society, it stands in stark contrast to the dream of a united church and a Christian state shared by the Reformers, who considered Scripture as the basis for their authority. The modern refusal to acknowledge God's authority in church and state has resulted in the following adverse consequences:

First, Christians no longer feel obligated to combat false religion, as commanded by Scripture. Satan would have us all be moderates, who eschew all forms of enthusiasm and honest talk about the true doctrines of the church and the true destiny of men without Christ. As we shall see, in America, this hemlock tree grew from the soil of unbiblical personal liberty; in Scotland, it grew from the soil of unbiblical state intervention. Nevay and the Covenanters would see no difference between the Indulged ministers of their era and most ministers of our era who fail to preach against false religion. In the final analysis, according to Nevay, ministers who refuse to testify "against the evils and errors of the times" fail to "preach Christ, and the whole Christ." It is not possible for men to "be faithful unless they contend as much for his [Christ's] crown interests, as for the interests of his person and other offices."[5]

Second, modern Christians disallow any church influence over their lives or within society. Owen and Locke viewed the church as a voluntary association, comprised of churches, each voluntarily associated with other churches, rather than as a united church. This philosophy has led to an ineffective church that watches interdenominational agencies, boards, and mission societies do the work God assigned to the church. Iain Murray observes that the Puritan's view of the church is in stark contrast with the "what's in it for me" attitude of the modern Christian:

> The whole orientation of the Puritan spiritual character was different at this point. The church and her visible biblical structure, seen in her ordinances, her unity, her preaching and her discipline, was in the forefront of their thinking. Her strength and purity must take precedence over all other considerations because she is the church of Christ. Her welfare is bound up with the honor of her Head in whose name, and ac-

cording to whose will, all her work is to be performed.… The church is focal in God's eternal design to bring glory to his Son. This concept inspired the passion with which the Puritans and Covenanters threw themselves into the work of church reformation, and it also lay behind international concern for the unity of the church in doctrine and discipline. Their piety had a strong corporate emphasis; for the individualistic type of evangelical living they had no sympathy whatsoever.[6]

Third, modern Christians refuse to allow the state any religious or moral function. Not only did Locke reject a united church, but also he maintained, "There is absolutely no such thing, under the gospel, as a Christian Commonwealth." The modern Christian emphasis on salvation of individuals to the total neglect of the spiritual welfare of nations evidences abandonment of the Great Commission. The Covenanters took the Great Commission literally: *"Go therefore and make disciples of all the nations"* (Matt. 28:19 NKJ). The Covenanters hoped for the fulfillment of Christ's Great Commission and the Second Coming as two inter-related but separate events. They were not content with the expectation that Christ would save some few persons; they expected Christ to save nations (i.e., many in every land): *"All nations whom thou hast made shall come and worship before thee, O Lord; and shall glorify thy name"* (Ps. 86:9; see also Ps. 22:27; Isa. 2:1–4; 60:2–4; 66:8; Jer. 31:34; Ezek. 47:1–5; Dan. 2:44; 12:4; Micah 4:1–5; Zech. 8:20–22). It covered not simply citizens, but national leaders: *"Yes, all kings shall fall down before Him."* (Ps. 72:11a). In these passages, the references to Israel and Jerusalem now refer to Christ's church. These prophetic passages speak of a future state where the gospel will not simply permeate men's souls, but it will become the very fabric of society resulting in great peace on earth.

Fourth, emboldened by their successful assault on the earthly agents of the Lord's authority, Satan and his agents now openly assault the Lord's name, as evidenced by the rampant profanity of modern times.

His Mercy: Having thus impeded the water supply and breached the outer walls, Satan assails the inhabitants of the City of God, seeking to convince them that they, not God, are the source of their salvation and good works. He accomplishes this latter assault, on God's Covenant of Grace, by way of subtle departures from truth, which poison the human soul. His most effective assaults use scriptures rather than Scripture, e.g., "Did God not say?" Questions best reveal these hemlock seeds:

First, are men by nature spiritually dead or simply spiritually sick? Calvinism teaches the utter inability of man to save himself because of Adam's fall. In contrast, most modern Christians deny that natural man is spiritually dead due to Adam's fall; instead, they perceive him only in need of medicine. They see Adam not as "the federal head or representative of his posterity, but only their natural parent."[7] Consequently, they allege that Calvinism "puts an exaggerated emphasis" and "undue stress on sin." To them, sin is "an incident or an accident in the nature and history of man" rather than "the essence of man."[8] They, like the Neonomians, cry out, "Back to Christ," decrying Calvinism as sincentric. The nineteenth-century minister Samuel Smith answers, "Calvinistic theology; however, strictly speaking, is neither sincentric nor yet Christcentric; it is Theocentric."[9] God not man gives life. This is why modern evangelical preaching, which accentuates the role of man rather than God in repentance and conversion is the ultimate distortion of God's mercy.[10] Salvation requires rebirth, which must precede faith. It requires more than a renewed mind, will, or heart; it requires a renewed person. This is why modern evangelical preaching, which appeals to either the mind, heart, or will by its different methods will never fully succeed.

Second, did Christ die for all men or only for the elect? The post-Revolution Settlement church was awash with ministers whom the bishops had infected with the Arminian philosophy, which teaches that Christ died for all men. This error replaces the "personal union" of God with each of his children with a faceless union, governed not by God's will but by man's will, with the human race.[11] All the passages of Scripture that seemingly support universal salvation (e.g., John 3:16, Gal. 3:26) are properly understood as referring to God's promises to save some from all peoples and do not contradict the ocean of promises regarding God's elect, chosen from all peoples. In fact, as we shall see in the next chapter, the central theme of Scripture is the progressive revelation of God's redemption of his chosen people. Hence, the concept of universal salvation is inconsistent with Scripture. The real question should be, "Why does God save any at all since we all deserve his wrath?"

In modern times, many who call themselves Calvinists claim they accept God's election of some but hold open God's choosing of others; this is merely a more virulent form of the same error. This error was popularized by the Huguenot minister Moses Amyraut (1596–1664) in the mid seventeenth century, and it is built on three plausible but false premises, namely—God equally loves all men, Christ died equally for all men, and God gives all men sufficient grace to believe.[12] Its adherents refuse to accept that a God of love would limit his saving mercy to some. John Murray clarifies this complex topic by distinguishing the love of God to his elect and to mankind in general. God's love for mankind is beyond question. All men benefit from God's providential mercies, which rain equally on the just and the unjust. Christ's love and prayer for his enemies further evidences God's love for all men, which he commands his disciples to emulate. In conformity to God's character, believers evidence that they are "sons of the most high" when they love their enemies (Matt. 5:44, 45; Luke 6:27, 35). Nevertheless, Scripture boldly declares God's special gospel love wherein Christ gave his life for his sheep (John 10:10–29) and his church (Eph. 5:25–27) to gather a sanctified and holy people unto himself. Further, the certainty of the promise in John 3:16–17 demands that it be applied only to those to which it is effectual (i.e., true believers). In essence, this verse defines what God's love of the world really means. God's gospel love transforms men into those who believe in him, love him, and keep his commandments (John 14:23). In summary, although "the non-elect enjoy many benefits from the atonement," they "do not participate in the benefits of the atonement."[13]

However, as Spurgeon observes, this gospel love extends to the vilest of sinners that God renews and draws unto himself. The elect and the lost that Christ came to save are one. In this sense, God's gospel love extends to the world.[14] Men come to Christ knowing they are lost rather than elect.[15] As Calvin observes, that "God's love requires righteousness; that we may then be persuaded that we are loved, we must necessarily come to Christ, in whom alone righteousness is to be found."[16]

Many refer to Amyraut's error as Modified Calvinism, yet it is an entirely different doctrine than Calvinism. Real Calvinists grasp, as did Calvin, the crucial nature of the doctrine of election:

> There is no consideration more apt for the building up of faith than that we should listen to this election, which the Spirit of God testifies in our hearts to stand in the eternal and inflexible goodwill of God, invulnerable to all storms of the world, all assaults of Satan, and all vacillation of the flesh. For then indeed our salvation is assured to us, since we find its cause in the breast of God.[17]

Third, given the truth of God's eternal decrees regarding election, is it proper to ask unregenerate men, who cannot possibly accept Christ unless God regenerates them, to accept Christ? Those who would restrict the bold and free proclamation of the gospel for this reason are called Hyper-Calvinists. In contrast, true Calvinists evangelically proclaim the whole gospel to all, for all men are accountable for the sin of unbelief just as they are for the outward sin. Evidencing the Covenanters commitment to hold forth the gospel to the unregenerate are the words of Rutherford's last letter, "If ye exclude all non-converts from the visible city of God ... shall they not be left to the lions and the wild beast of the forest.... Nor can it be approven by the Lord in Scripture ... to shut the gates of the Lord's gracious calling upon all these (because they are not in your judgment chosen to salvation)...."[18] This teaching is consistent with the Larger Catechism (Question 63), which declares that Christ "excludes none that will come unto him."

Calvin, seeing no contradiction in Paul's declaration that God *"will have all men to be saved"* (1 Tim. 2:4), offered the following reasons why it is consistent to preach the gospel to all, yet maintain that God saves only his elect:

1. In 1 Timothy 2:4, "the Apostle simply means that there is no people and no rank in the world that is excluded from salvation."[19] On similar verses Calvin remarked that "so wonderful is God's love towards mankind that he would have all to be saved." He "stretches forth his hand without a difference to all."[20] The "whole blame of the evil is laid on the people for rejecting the amazing kindness of God."[21]
2. Although "God invites all to hear his Word," Scripture teaches that he converts none but the elect (e.g., John 6:37, 44, 64; Rom. 9; 11:2, 5, 7; Eph. 1:3, 8, 11; 2 Tim. 2:19; 1 Pet. 1:2). God, not man, is the one who is the "author of conversion" (2 Tim. 2:25), gives the increase (1 Cor. 3:6), makes men new creatures (2 Cor. 5:17; Eph. 2:10), and renews hearts (Deut. 30:6; Jer. 31:33; Ezek. 36:26). The promise is only to the spiritual seed (Rom. 9:8, 11).[22]
3. Men freely reject God's call "according to the hardness and impenitence of their hearts," thus they justly deserve of God's wrath. Hence, there is no contradiction in God's willing the preaching of the gospel to all and his willing the salvation of some.[23] In condemning some, God "wills not iniquity" (Ps. 5:5). Instead, our consciences condemn us, as did David's, *"I was as a beast before thee"* (Ps. 73:22).[24]
4. The apostles preached to many in Acts, yet only those "ordained to eternal life believed" (Acts 13:48). In response to the prophet's question, *"Lord, who hath believed our report?"* (Isa. 53:1; Rom. 10:16), Paul answers, *"the election hath obtained it, and the rest were blinded"* (Rom. 11:5-7). Natural man does not receive the things of God because he does not will to do so; these things must be spiritually discerned (1 Cor. 2:14).[25] Unless God opens ears and renews hearts, the message goes unheeded as evidenced by the Jew's rejection of the sermons of the prophets (Ps. 40:6-7; Isa. 6:9), by the apostles (Acts 28:25; Rom. 11:8), and even by Christ in person, accompanied by miracles (John 12:37; see also Matt. 13:9, 14; Luke 8:8, 10; John 12:40).[26]
5. Calvin clarifies this complex topic by distinguishing between proximate and remote causes. God's will is indeed the remote cause of our salva-

tion or damnation; man's will is the proximate cause. Adam did not fall against God's will, yet by his own will he fell.[27] To those who would ask why God would will such, Calvin replies, "You ask on something greater and higher than the will of God itself, and this cannot be found."[28] We should heed Paul's warning not to impute unrighteousness unto God, *"O man, who art thou"* (Rom. 9:20), for as Paul declares, *"So then it is not of him that willeth, nor of him that runneth, but of God that showeth mercy"* (Rom. 9:16).[29]

Fourth, must men depart from sin before they can accept Christ? This is somewhat a trick question. An overemphasis on man's decisions and works, with the presumption that man has the "ability do all that God requires of him without divine aid," ultimately leads to an diminished emphasis on the regenerating work of the Holy Spirit and on "the duty of embracing [Christ] as Savior."[30] On the other hand, although faith must precede repentance in the gospel order, they are inseparable; Scripture instructs Christians to repent and believe (Mark 1:15). Indeed, sincere, heart-felt sorrow for our sins is required for salvation, but it is God's work in us rather than our own. The *Confession of Faith* calls it repentance unto life.[31] Herein lies the distinction: every man is under obligation to repent (i.e., legal repentance), but repentance unto life requires faith. Its motivation is not so much the fear of God's wrath, but remorse over the violation wrought by sin of God's authority, glory, and honor. In the final analysis, accepting Christ means more than departing from sin. It means the death of our sinful self—an act that natural man finds unconscionable unless reborn from above. In the words of John Murray (1898–1975), "those for whom Christ died are those who die to sin and live to righteousness" (Rom. 6:4–5; 2 Cor. 5:14–15; Col. 3:3).[32]

Fifth, is assurance of salvation the essence of faith? William Young, who edited and published Nevay's sermons in 1748, conceded, "assurance of salvation is attainable in this life, as these scriptures plainly show" (2 Sam. 23:5; Job. 19:25; Ps. 22:1; Song. of Sol. 2:16; 6:3; Gal. 2:20), and "it is every persons duty to give all diligence to make their calling and election sure" (2 Pet. 1:10). Yet, he "positively denied that assurance is of the essence of faith" because there are many instances in Scripture where those saved "had faith but no assurance" (2 Kings 7:3–4; Ester 4:16; Job. 13:15; Ps. 77:1–12; 88; Isa. 35:3; 50:10; 54:11; Matt. 8:2; Mark 9:24; Heb. 2:15). Illustrative of these verses is *"Lord, I believe; help thou mine unbelief"* (Mark 9:24).[33] The danger of the belief that assurance is of the essence of faith is that it leads men to presume their salvation upon the mere intellectual acceptance of Christ. Sadly, most who answer the altar call, insisted upon by the modern evangelical method, never come to a saving knowledge of Christ. Yet, the question remains, "How does one know that they are elect?" Calvin answers, "I answer that Christ is more than a thousand testimonies to me. For when we find ourselves in his body, our salvation rests in a secure and tranquil place, as though already located in Heaven."[34] The doctrine of election and assurance find meaning only when we rightly apprehend Christ and his eternal love (Eph. 1:4–5).[35]

Admittedly, Calvin and the early Reformers, in reaction to the Roman Catholic teaching that assurance in this life is unattainable, emphasized the close relation between assurance and faith.[36] However, Calvin did not speak "of an assurance which is never affected by doubt."[37] The Westminster divines clarified that assurance was not the essence of faith.[38] Was Calvin wrong? John Knox's teachings provide insight to this riddle: he argued that we are assured of our salvation "when we hear and undoubtedly believe that our election … consists not in ourselves, but in the eternal and immutable good pleasure of God."[39] For this reason, neither Knox nor Calvin could conceive of a mature Christian who did not grasp the doctrine of election. The Westminster divine's definition of faith clarifies this issue and guards against a legion of errors: "Faith in Jesus Christ is a saving grace, whereby we receive and rest upon him alone for salvation as he is offered to us in the gospel."[40] Unless one's faith rests in God, there are no grounds for assurance. The divines defined assurance as founded on the "divine truth of the promises of salvation, the inward evidence of those graces unto which the promises are made," and the "testimony of the Spirit of adoption." Divine truth is infallible, yet internal evidence may be "shaken, diminished, and intermitted."[41]

Sixth, is faith the condition for entry in God's Covenant of Grace? The Covenanters, Puritans, and Westminster divines insisted that faith is a necessary condition; whereas, most modern Reformed authors refuse to use the word "condition" associated with salvation for fear of implying that salvation in any way depends upon man. Although this is excellent reason, it is an inadequate reason, as demonstrated in the next chapter. The real question is whether faith is something wrought by God or something wrought by man within himself in response to the gospel offer. The former is clearly a condition for salvation; the latter is neither a condition nor grounds for salvation. Over the last several hundred years, the latter definition of faith has replaced the former in evangelical thought, but Scripture still holds the former.

God's Covenant: All of the above-mentioned errors, as shown in the following review of history since the Revolution Settlement, are traceable to departure from God's authority and from a proper understanding of his Covenant of Grace, first in an almost unrecognizable seed form, then later in full bloom. Most masquerade under the banner of new theology or Modified Calvinism; however, all are inconsistent with the Calvinistic system of doctrine, as perfected in the Westminster Standards. The remaining chapters of this book examine how the Covenanters resisted these errors through a proper understanding of God's Covenant of Grace. The following illustration is helpful on this journey.[42]

Figure 9.1
Scottish and American Presbyterian Churches

1750   1850   1950

Church of Scotland   1929

Society People   1733   1761   1839   1843
1733   Reformed Presbyterian Church   Free Presbyterian Church   APC
Relief Church   Free Church   1863   1893   1989
Secession Church   Free Church
1747   Burghers   Old Light / New Light   1799   1817   1900   United Free Church
1820   1827   United Presbyterian Church
Anti-Burghers   New   1806   Old   1842   1852   Synod of United Original Seceders   1956
Scotland

America   Seceders   1782   Associate Synod of NA   Associate Presbyterian Synod   1965
From Scotland and Ireland   1753   Associate Reformed Synod   1858   United Presbyterian Church   RPC
Covenanters   1822   Associate Reformed Presbyterian Church
1774   Old Lights   1965   1969 1982
1833   Reformed Presbyterian Church of NA   1956   1973   PCA
New Lights
From Scotland, Ireland, England, France, Holland, etc.   Presbyterian Church in the U. S.   Bible PC
Old Side   (Southern)   1861   1938   1958   PCUSA
1741   Presbyterian Church in the U. S. A.   Old School   1869   EPC
1706   1758   1857   (Northern)   1936   Orthodox Presbyterian Church
New Side   1837   New School
Cumberland Presbyterian Church   1906
PCA Presbyterian Church in America   1810
EPC Evangelical Presbyterian Church   Second Cumberland Presbyterian Church
RPC Reformed Presbyterian Church   1869
APC Associated Presbyterian Churches

A Former Covenanted Land

British/Scottish Church History: The effects of this onslaught on England and Scotland were devastating. In England, Puritanism faded away. In Scotland, the national church became a shell of its former glory, no longer focused on fighting a common enemy. Even the Scottish national zeal had waned, enabling the *Act of Union* in 1707, which merged the governments of England and Scotland. In theory, the Church of Scotland remained intact and independent.[43]

It did not take long for the Erastian policies of England to permeate throughout Scotland. In 1703, the queen's commissioner dissolved a Scottish General Assembly when it attempted to draft an act asserting the supremacy of Christ and the divine right of Presbyterian government. All accepted without protest the queen's Erastian action, evidencing their abandonment of the kingship of Christ, the truth for which their fathers had died.[44] In 1712, Parliament passed the *Act of Patronage*, which allowed authorities outside the church to appoint ministers, and the *Toleration Act*, which allowed the use of the Anglican liturgy in Scotland.[45] On his deathbed that same year, Thomas Halyburton (1674–1712), who like James Nisbet lost his father during the persecution, commented on the sad state of religion:

> O Sirs, I dread mightily, that a rational sort of religion is coming in among us; I mean by it, a religion that consist in a bare attendance on outward duties and ordinances, without the power of godliness; and by this means people shall fall into a way of serving God, which is mere deism, having no relation to Christ Jesus and the Spirit of God.[46]

Herbert Skeats (d. 1881) described the tragic scene in England around 1720 where "breadth of thought and charity of sentiment" became the "mental habit of the nation." It reached such an extreme that even the London non-conformists abandoned subscription of belief in the Trinity.[47] This failure is traceable to the adoption by many English Presbyterians of Modified Calvinism, opening the door for other heresies.[48] The "zeal of Puritanism" ceased to exist and "the doctrines of the great founders of Presbyterianism could scarcely be heard from any Presbyterian pulpit in England."[49]

In the early eighteenth century, in both Britain and America, the concept of a static God who had left the world to run by natural laws replaced the concept of a dynamic, covenant-keeping God. Christians still believed religion was important, but they believed that God governed through natural laws. For example, they believed that American prosperity was a natural result of a religious society rather than an "un-merited gift of a generous God." Taken to its logical conclusion, one religion was as good as the next.[50] Such thinking led to the "fatal habit of considering Christian morals as distinct from Christian doctrines." William Wilberforce predicted that the failure to correct this fatal error would lead to the destruction of the British Empire.[51]

In Scotland, a series of events slowly drained away the strength of the Scottish church. The blame rests in two root causes:

First, the church, over time, swallowed many of the previously mentioned errors. After the Revolution Settlement, the church increasingly drifted towards legalism and Hyper-Calvinism, perhaps as an overreaction to the onslaught of Arminianism brought in by the curates who had joined the church. In response to the resultant sterile presentation of the gospel, several ministers, inspired by a book, *The Marrow of Modern Divinity*, sought to preach the gospel in a more evangelical manner. In 1720, the Church of Scotland condemned this book for seemingly endorsing through veiled and ambiguous language a number of errors, including that "believers are not under the law as a rule of life" and that Christ died for all men.[52] Although the book itself is ambiguous and perhaps worthy of censure, the writings of the ministers who supported it, e.g., Thomas Boston, are generally orthodox. Boston's writings depart, however, from the understanding of the Covenant of Grace held by the Puritans and the Covenanters in several subtle ways. For instance, Boston, contrary to his Covenanter forefathers, refused to refer to faith as a condition of the covenant. As demonstrated in the next chapter, Boston's approach undermines the strength of Covenant theology.

Second, the evil of *patronage,* through which the state manipulated the appointment of ministers for political purposes, resulted in a moderate church with diminished focus on the Lord's work. Concerning the great hazard of patronage, Hugh Miller (1802–1856), in his book *The Headship of Christ*, contended that not only does patronage have "a direct tendency to destroy the church, but … it has also a tendency equally direct to render it worthy of being destroyed."[53] In 1733, the Secession Church split from the main church over the issues of patronage (opposed by Secession Church) and adherence to the covenants (supported by Secession Church). By 1766, the Secession Church contained 120 churches. It subsequently spit into groups favoring and opposing the Burgess Oath–requiring allegiance to "the true religion presently professed within the realm." Each of the groups split yet again over the innovations arising from the Great Awakening, which resulted in an increased emphasis on evangelism and personal piety. In 1761, the Relief Church broke away from the Church of Scotland in defiance of patronage and state church establishment. Each departure left the church more moderate. By the end of the eighteenth century, Moderatism reigned in the established church.[54] Moderatism, Hugh Miller wrote, "had most certainly no intention of bringing down the establishment; it is well aware how miserably it would fare without it."[55] The established church was beholden to the state, which exercised control over the church through patronage, management of church properties, and limitations on the jurisdiction of the church. Although the moderates retained the Westminster Confession as the recognized standard, many did not consider its Calvinistic doctrine as suitable material for the pulpit. Instead, they esteemed peace and unity above truth, toleration above zeal for truth, morality above true religion, and reason above doctrine.[56]

In 1843, more than four hundred ministers broke away from the Church of Scotland over the issue of patronage to form the Free Church. The new church, however, remained committed to the principle of an established church. This new church excelled in missions and grew rapidly, building five hundred churches in its first year.[57] Unfortunately, within a few decades, liberal theology and its biblical criticism infected this new church through the universities.[58] By the time patronage was abolished in 1874, the majority of the original Seceders and Reformed Presbyterians had joined the Free Church, which had won a strong following in the Highlands. In 1900, the United Presbyterian Church (UPC), which had formed in 1847 from a union of the Relief Church and New Light Seceders, joined with the majority of the Free Church to form the United Free Church, which was a body larger than the Church of Scotland.[59] Declaratory Statements adopted by the UPC and the Free Church in the last decades of the nineteenth century made this union possible. These statements opened the door for the teaching of Modified Calvinism and related errors, took a neutral position on the Christian duty of the state, and allowed ministers liberty of opinion "not entering into the substance of faith." Toleration was no longer a vice but a religious duty.[60] The majority of the United Free Church and the Church of Scotland members united in 1929, jointly casting off the last traces of state control. Of course, in many of these unions, minorities remained to carry on the church name. Representative of these smaller churches are the Free Church, the Free Presbyterian Church, and the Reformed Presbyterian Church, which all adhere to Reformed principles. For instance, the Free Presbyterian's discipline of church officers for attending Catholic services led in 1989 to the formation of the Associated Presbyterian Churches, who thought such discipline too severe.

By the end of the nineteenth century, the larger Scottish churches had ceased to depose ministers with views inconsistent with the *Westminster Confession of Faith*, such as the universal view of the atonement.[61] By the late nineteenth century, the scriptural, Calvinistic view of God's mercy was almost extinct in England and fading away in Scotland. The so-called evangelical view, which emphasizes man's role in salvation more than God's, had taken its place. Opposing this trend in Scotland was the Free Church minister John Kennedy of Dingwall (1819–1884), who labeled the new mode of evangelism as Hyper-Evangelism. Kennedy argued that this new false faith teaches men that mere belief saves them, ignoring the necessity for self-condemnation, sincere repentance, and conversion. It emphasizes Christ as our substitute who disposes of our sins rather than Christ himself. It teaches a man "to think of his sin as a great calamity, rather than a heinous crime." Such a man "is not likely either to reverence God or respect His law." In contrast, "True faith is the act of a soul who, up to that hour, was a lover of sin and an enemy of holiness, but who now cordially receives the Savior in order to the destruction of what he loved, and the attainment of what he hated before." True faith requires conversion, which is an act of God.[62]

One of England's last holdouts for the scriptural view was the Baptist minister Charles Spurgeon. Remarking on the large scale defection from the belief in election, Spurgeon observed that for the same reason men left Christ: When Christ proclaimed *"...that no man can come unto me, except it were given unto him of my Father... many of his disciples went back, and walked no more with him"* (John 6:65–66).[63] Eventually, Spurgeon chose to break fellowship with the Baptist Union because the Baptists refused to adopt a creed that boldly declared scriptural truth, choosing instead to hide disagreements with ambiguous word. Standing in opposition to the trend to give up truth for unity, Spurgeon was unbending, even rejecting a declaration of faith by the Baptists that had been approved by two thousand votes to seven. In one of his sermons, Spurgeon remarked, "Truth is usually in the minority in this evil world."[64] Spurgeon did not consider loyalty to a denomination more important than loyalty to Christ and the words of his apostles, who declared that *"he that knoweth God heareth us; he that is not of God heareth not us"* (1 John 4:6).[65]

The modern Church of Scotland is but a shadow of its former self. Although it is the country's dominant Protestant religion (seven members for every one from other Protestant denominations), it has drifted from doctrinal purity. Declaratory Statements have reduced the status of the *Westminster Confession of Faith*, by allowing ministers liberty of opinion "not entering into the substance of faith."[66] Having no definition of the substance of the faith, the standards ceased to serve any unifying value. Further, the church removed specific clauses offensive to Catholics from the standard because there are now almost as many Catholics in Scotland as Protestants. John Knox would not be happy with these concessions or with the fact that the church allows women ministers and enjoys membership in the World Council of Churches.[67]

What happened to the Society People? The Society People who did not join the Revolution Settlement church remained without a pastor until 1706. Not only did they refuse the Revolution Settlement church, they also refused to acknowledge the authority of the civil magistrate because the government did not acknowledge the covenants. Even after obtaining a pastor, they remained organized in small society groups. They were so strict in their interpretation of doctrine that they refused to ordain other candidates for the ministry because they did not have a presbytery. One applicant remained a licentiate until his death in 1732.[68] Another licentiate, Andrew Clarkson, wrote a detailed defense of the Society People's position entitled *Plain Reasons for Presbyterians Dissenting from the Revolution Church in Scotland*. However, after years as a licentiate, he also gave up and recanted.[69] The Society People finally got a second minister in 1743 and formed the Reformed Presbytery. A decade later, this small presbytery split apart when several of its ministers adopted the unscriptural view of universal atonement.[70] Fortunately, the main body renounced this heresy. Their modern descendents, the Reformed Presbyterian Church of Scotland, still maintain that the *Solemn League and Covenant* is perpetually binding on the people of Scotland.[71]

The pattern in Ireland was similar except that the Irish Society People remained without a minister until 1758.[72] Although the establishment of the Anglican Church in Ireland led to persecution of Presbyterians, religion flourished. Despite persecution, tens of thousands of Scots migrated to Ireland to obtain better land and to flee from a seven-year famine, which Peden had predicted for the nation's apostasy.[73] Many of the Scotch-Irish settlers later migrated to America in the 1700s to avoid persecution and poor economic conditions.

Scotch and Scotch-Irish immigrants who remained faithful to the covenanting tradition formed three church bodies in America by the end of the eighteenth century: the Associate Synod consisting of mostly Seceders; the Reformed Presbyterian Church consisting of mostly Covenanters; and the Associated Reformed Synod consisting of both. Their modern descendants are the Reformed Presbyterian Church, which staunchly adheres to Covenanting principles, and the Associate Reformed Presbyterian Church, which retained exclusive psalmody until 1946. Many other Scotch Irish immigrants, generally staunchly adherent to the Westminster Standards, joined the mainline Presbyterian denominations. In English speaking countries today, a few small denominations and congregations remain faithful to the covenants; some even refuse allegiance to civil constitutions that do not acknowledge Christ as King.

The Supposed City on the Hill

The Reformed tradition in America traces its roots back to multiple sources. In general, the Reformed-faith groups in American can be classified by the degree of emphasis on doctrine, culture, or evangelical piety.[74] The doctrinal influence emphasizes strict adherence to the confessional standards; the pietistic influence emphasizes practical Christianity, evangelism, revivals, personal commitment, and conversion; and the cultural influence covers a wide range of incompatible approaches such as the "social gospel" on one extreme and Theonomy on the other. Until recently, these three approaches shared a common emphasis on "doctrinal orthodoxy." Regrettably, in this century, the crosscutting influences of modernism, dispensationalism, fundamentalism, and the neo-orthodoxy have frayed this fragile thread.[75]

The vision of the early America settlers to create in the New World a City on the Hill, which would be a beacon of light to all nations, slowly faded away. The cultural flavor of American Presbyterianism is traceable to the tolerant spirit of the city, Philadelphia, and state where the first presbytery was organized around 1705. The tolerant law of Pennsylvania promised that no one would be "molested or prejudiced for their religious persuasion" and required that citizens only believe in God and live "peaceably and justly."[76] In this environment, the early American Presbyterians abandoned the "Reformed impulse to establish a Christian commonwealth" for several non-biblical reasons.[77] First, they were fearful of predilection of their British rulers to establish Episcopacy. Second, two-thirds of the colonies had established state churches (typically Congregational or Anglican), making Presbyterian establishment unlikely.

Although the early American Presbyterians were strongly Calvinistic, it was not until 1729 that the church adopted the *Westminster Confession of*

Faith and *Catechisms*. This act, called the Adopting Act, allowed ministers to take exception to "those articles in any such sense as to suppose the civil magistrate hath a controlling power over Synods with respect to the exercise of ministerial authority; or power to persecute any for their religion."[78] Adoption of this act culminated an extended debate among the Scotch-Irish Presbyterians who supported strict subscription of church officers to the standards and those Presbyterians of English or Dutch descent who opposed strict subscription.[79] The final compromise required ministers to subscribe to the Confession in all articles except those judged as "not essential and necessary in doctrine, worship, and practice." The church granted few exceptions, chiefly those related to the role of the civil magistrate.[80]

The Great Awakening, which began in Germany, reached America in 1734 through the preaching of men like Jonathan Edwards (1703–1758), who spoke against the rising tide of Arminianism.[81] People no longer accepted religion based on authority and demanded rational explanations, which Edwards provided in his work, *Freedom of the Will*. Edwards contended that man is following his free will in rejecting God unless God supernaturally transforms his will. He asserted, "God's Spirit operates in conjunction with his Word, opening the hearts of sinners to receive Truth."[82] Although a true and useful explanation, substituting philosophy for covenant theology led many to over-intellectualize the Christianity with fatal results. In response to a question regarding his effectiveness from Jonathan Edwards's son, a minister responded: "The reason is that you present the gospel as a proposition to be proved, and go on to prove it, whereas I endeavor to exhibit it as something already admitted and to impress it upon the heart and conscience."[83]

The Great Awakening "terminated the Puritan and inaugurated the Pietist, or Methodist, age of American church history."[84] The Great Awakening split the Puritans into evangelical New Lights who required evidence of one's salvation for church membership, and the Old Lights who emphasized morality and distrusted the new evangelical methods that emphasized man's role more than God's.[85] As they divided into Arminian and Antinomian factions, the New England theologians increasingly abandoned the Covenant of Grace's perfect balance between God's sovereignty and man's free will. By the mid-1700s, the New Lights had ascended to power in New England legislatures and seminaries.

The Great Awakening also caused the Presbyterians to split in 1741 into the New and Old Sides, analogous to the New and Old Lights in New England. The Old Side, a stronghold for the Scotch Irish, emphasized strict adherence to doctrine and confessional standards. In contrast, the New Side challenged men's presumptions concerning salvation and emphasized evangelism and personal piety.[86] Illustrative of the New Side ministers was Gilbert Tennent, whose father had founded the Log College to supply much-needed ministers for the expanding colonies. Influenced by Dutch pietism, Tennent contended that belief in doctrine or Scripture was insufficient; instead, he required "a spiritual conversion that included three stages: a conviction of sin under the divine law; an experience of spiritual rebirth; and a reformed life that gave evidence of the work of the spirit in practical piety."[87] The field preaching of George Whitefield, an Anglican Calvinist, further fueled the revival. The excesses of revivalism, however, fueled the Old Side concerns.

The breach gradually healed, leading to the reunion of the two sides in 1758 for a number of reasons. The daunting challenge of an ever-expanding frontier, a large influx of Scotch-Irish immigrants (favoring the Old Side), a shortage of Old Side ministers, and a growing supply of New Side ministers caused both sides to seek union.[88] The theological gap narrowed as both sides (including Tennent) recognized the Great Awakening as an act of God but also acknowledged its excesses. The orthodox doctrine and warm evangelical piety of John Witherspoon (1723–1794), a respected Scottish minister who accepted the leadership of Princeton, provided the medicine needed to heal the breach.[89] To combat liberalism, he taught his students Scottish Common Sense, the philosophy of Thomas Reid, which contended that common sense enabled man to discern the divine influence in the world.[90] Finally, a shared and increased emphasis on morality contributed to their unity: "The assumption was that society was in some measure Christian, and the function of the church was to make it more so."[91]

The Separatists and the Baptists greatly benefited from the Great Awakening and quickly grew to fill the gaps created by the splits within the Puritan and Presbyterian ranks. The Methodists, who rejected Calvinism, also appeared on the scene and quickly grew over fourteen hundred percent during the period from 1774 to 1784.[92] This rapid growth was due largely to aggressive field preaching.[93] The emerging congregations marked the beginnings of a pluralistic society and the end of denominational dominance within regions.[94]

By the Revolutionary War, religion was at low ebb due to the growing influence of French Skepticism, English Deism, and the hard life and endless opportunity facing the colonists.[95] The moral character of the nation was "marked by skepticism and widespread immorality," especially "on the frontier."[96] This presents a paradox when one considers that approximately two-thirds of the American population at this time was associated in some manner with Calvinistic faiths.

> It is estimated that of the 3,000,000 Americans at the time of the American Revolution, 900,000 were of Scotch or Scotch-Irish origin, 600,000 were Puritan English, and 400,000 were German or Dutch Reformed. In addition to this, the Episcopalians had a Calvinistic confession in their Thirty-nine Articles; and many French Huguenots also had come to the western world.[97]

The reality is that the American brand of Calvinism had lost its moorings. A few decades before the revolution, a noted minister lamented the hesitancy in which the doctrine of predestination was defended even though the doctrine was "such a fundamental of my faith, that I know not what any other article would avail" without it.[98] By the turn of the century, "Massachusetts was on the brink of Unitarian schism, and Connecticut's establishment was besieged by dissenters."[99]

Presbyterians significantly contributed to the American Revolution. In fact, the British called it the "Presbyterian Rebellion" and referred to the patriots as Whigs. One of the reasons for this contribution was the extensive communication network, inherent in the Presbyterian system of government, which facilitated focus on important issues.[100] Leading Presbyterians such as John Witherspoon taught that people had the right to resist unjust governments and that the rulers derived their powers through the consent of the governed.[101] Nevertheless, they cautioned that one must submit until "corruption becomes intolerable,"[102] yet, equally insisted that it was one's duty to "resist their king when he rages with cruelty beyond measure, or subverts the laws of the state, and to defend their liberty."[103] Witherspoon, the only minister to sign the Declaration of Independence, exhorted its hesitant signers, "To hesitate is to consent to our own slavery."[104] Illustrative of their political involvement is the warning of Presbyterian minister William Tennent III (1740–1777) to South Carolina women to avoid the tea tax: "Every ounce of tea you buy, I will fear be paid for by the blood of your sons."[105] They opposed such taxation without representation as robbery. In addition to political opposition, the Presbyterians significantly contributed to the war effort. For example, at the defeat of Cornwallis (1738–1805), "all the colonels of the Colonial Army but one were Presbyterian elders."[106]

After the war, the Presbyterians joined with other non-established denominations to end establishment of religion by the states. In overtures to legislatures, synods and ministers pleaded the absurdity of the state choosing among the multitudes of denominations and giving any one denomination legal status or privilege at the expense of the others. For example, William Tennent pleaded before the South Carolina Assembly for "Equality or Nothing."[107] Consistent with their demand for reform of the church and state relationship, the Presbyterian Church in the U.S.A. made significant modifications to *the Westminster Confession of Faith* in 1789, essentially eliminating any responsibility of the civil magistrate over moral or religious issues. In addition, it also deleted from the *Larger Catechism* the admonition against toleration of false religion (Question 109).[108]

The Second Great Awakening began in the early 1800s with some of its first fruits being the students of Timothy Dwight (1752–1817), the president of Yale. These students went forth throughout the land to ignite American interest in joining forces to combat liberalism and to restore faith in the Puritan covenant. Dwight's efforts were successful, but his watering down of Calvinism and his encouragement of mission societies to perform the work of the church proved to be dragon seeds.[109]

Iain Murray (b. 1931) traces the awakening to Kentucky where it began among Presbyterians at outdoor-communion camp meetings and quickly spread to the Methodists and Baptists.[110] This revival left a lasting imprint of evangelical Christianity as it explosively spread throughout the southern states.[111] With this explosive growth came more divisions within denominations and a proliferation of new sects.[112] The Kentucky "Presbyterians were virtually shattered by divisions."[113] It also left in its wake a reduced emphasis on the necessity of educated ministers, a renewed emphasis on miraculous gifts, a fragmentation of church structures, and a general rejection of "the Calvinistic understanding of the gospel that had hitherto prevailed among all evangelical Christians."[114] The Arminian emphasis on the individual's decision had replaced the biblical emphasis on God's eternal decrees. A number of innovations such as the altar call emphasized that the faith choice comes first, followed by regeneration, in contradiction to Scripture. The entire emphasis was on the external rather than the internal act and on saving people from the punishment rather than the power of sin.[115]

To address the needs of a growing population and westward expansion, the Presbyterian Church adopted a Plan of Union in 1801 to join forces with historically Calvinistic Congregational churches. The net result was (1) the spread of the increasing "prevalence of lax and unsound theology" that characterized the New England churches of this era, and

(2) the introduction of Congregational practices in the Presbyterian Church. This in turn led to a general falling away from a strict adherence to the Westminster Standards and a general weakening of church discipline.[116] In response to these changes in 1837, the Presbyterian Church terminated the Plan of Union, and it split into the conservative "Old School" and the more evangelical "New School" camps. The "Old School" group held to the philosophy that "where the Bible was silent, the church should be silent"; and that "the church of Christ is a spiritual body whose jurisdiction extends only to the religious faith and moral conduct of her members."[117] This philosophy precluded speaking out against slavery–a popular position for Presbyterians in the South. However, on the positive side, the Presbyterian Church C.S.A. declared its evangelical focus and set about to accomplish its purpose through the organs of the church rather than through mission societies:[118]

> We wish to develop the idea of the congregation of believers, as visibly organized, is the very society or corporation, which is divinely called to do the work of the Lord. We shall therefore endeavor to do what has never yet been adequately done–bring out the energies of our Presbyterian system of government.[119]

One of the most devastating consequences of the increased emphasis on the individual was the de-emphasis of the church. Louis Berkhof (1873–1957) observed, "It seems rather peculiar that practically all the outstanding Presbyterian dogmaticians of our country, such as the two Hodges, H.B. Smith, Shedd, and Dabney, have no separate locus on the church in their dogmatical works and, in fact, devote very little attention to it."[120]

Shortly after the Civil War, union of the northern Old School and the New School Presbyterian elements was achieved "not by resolving differences, but by ignoring and absorbing them." Without the southern, more-conservative Old School, this northern Presbyterian body (Presbyterian Church in the United States of America) slowly drifted away from the historic Calvinism. Accelerating this drift were new theories in science (e.g., evolution), which dethroned God as creator; in psychology, which unseated ministers as counselors; and in textual criticism, which undermined the Bible as a source of authority. Modern liberalism arose out of well-intentioned efforts to adapt doctrine to these new theories.[121]

Influenced by liberal seminaries, the northern Presbyterians softened their confessional standard in 1903. They adopted a Declaratory Statement that urged interpretation of the doctrine of God's eternal decree (i.e., election) in harmony with the doctrine of God's "love to all mankind" and "the doctrine that God desires not the death of any sinner." Through amendments, the good deeds of unregenerate men were no longer sinful, and the pope was no longer the antichrist. New chapters expanded on the Holy Spirit and God's love.[122] This trend to seek unity at the expense of truth would have dire consequences.

In 1910, to combat the open disregard by many liberal ministers regarding unquestionable fundamentals of faith, the church issued a declaration that identified five articles of faith (e.g., inerrancy of Scripture, virgin birth) as "essential and necessary" doctrine but also declared that "others are equally so." The sad truth was that the grand, systematic creed of the Westminster divines had ceased to have practical application as a standard of orthodoxy. Worse, more than a thousand Presbyterian ministers signed the *Auburn Declaration*, a liberal manifesto that refused to acknowledge even these five fundamental truths.[123] By 1925, General Assembly, in response to a growing liberal consensus, decided that it had no power to rule in creedal maters (i.e., decide essentials) unless it obtained concurrence from the presbyteries to change the church's constitution. In truth, the real authority in American Presbyterianism had always resided in the presbyteries. Having achieved control, within a few years the liberals took action to undermine the church's conservative seminaries.[124] Although the church was unwilling to act against defamers of truth, it willing pursued the conservatives in the church judiciaries as defilers of unity. In the late 1930s, many conservatives broke away to form the Orthodox Presbyterian Church.[125]

The struggle in the southern Presbyterian Church, more properly known as the Presbyterian Church in the United States (PCUS), followed along similar lines but more slowly. Around 1942, the PCUS irreversibly began the shift from a conservative to a liberal denomination. Evidencing its conservative nature was a letter that year from its General Assembly to the President of the United States insisting on observance of the Sabbath in the conduct of the war, with appropriate allowances for acts of mercy or necessity.[126] Evidencing its new liberal direction was the addition that year to the confession of essentially the same two chapters the northern church had adopted a few decades earlier.[127] Just five years earlier, the PCUS had declared such changes unnecessary because the *Westminster Confession of Faith* already contained forty-five references to the work of the Holy Spirit, fourteen references to God's general love, and twelve references to God's special love for his people.[128] These new chapters declared God's "love for the world and his desire that all men should be saved" without even mentioning election. The God of this Modified Calvinism pleads with men to accept the gospel offer rather than draws men to himself.[129] These changes undermined the Calvinism of the original confession, which emphasized, as does Scripture, "God's special love for his own" more than "his general love for mankind."[130]

Although a more extensive revision of the confession failed in the late 1950s, the PCUS adopted broadening statements inconsistent with the Westminster Standards. In 1972, the PCUS rejected the Bible as the "only authority to govern Christian belief," replacing it with a multitude of authorities "including the Bible, the church, human reason and experience," subject of course to the guiding of the Holy Spirit. In essence, the new position established the Holy Spirit alone to guide men's consciences in place of the "Holy Spirit speaking in the Scripture," as specified in the Westminster Standards.[131] These rejections of the sovereignty of God and the authority of Scripture left conservatives no choice but in 1973–1974 to withdraw and form a new denomination, the Presbyterian Church in America. Freed from the Whigs, the main southern body united with the northern church in 1983 to form the Presbyterian Church (U.S.A.).

Sadly, in 1959 the Associate Reformed Presbyterian Church also adopted two similar new chapters and the Modified Calvinism implicit therein.[132] The Marrow theology and the original Seceder's love for it is cited as basis for this change, which proves the inherent hazard of ambiguity in religious writings. A year earlier, the largest American body of Seceder and Covenanter descendants, the United Presbyterian Church, completed its century long slide from conservative principles by joining the liberal northern Presbyterian Church.

The above-mentioned struggles within the Presbyterian churches mirrored the rise and fall of a national movement titled "Fundamentalism," which arose early in the twentieth century to combat liberalism. The *Concise Oxford Dictionary* defines fundamentalism as "maintenance, in opposition to modernism, of traditional orthodox beliefs such as the inerrancy of Scripture and literal acceptance of the creeds as fundamentals of Protestant Christianity."[133] Although the goals of the movement were noble, the reality is that in today's common vernacular the term is associated with "distrust of reason, shoddy apologetics, cultural barrenness, eccentric individualism, [and] indifference to churchmanship."[134] Unfortunately, as J. I. Packer observes, Fundamentalism deserves many of these barbs: "It grew intellectually barren. Culture became suspect. The responsibilities of the Christian social witness were left to the purveyors of the 'social gospel,' and Fundamentalism turned upon itself limiting its interest to evangelical and the cultivation of personal religion."

Although sparks of reformation were evident, most attempts in the twentieth century to combat liberalism failed. For example, the neo-orthodox theologian Karl Barth (1886–1968) replaced the Calvinistic concept of election with the concept that only Christ was elect, with mankind being elect through him. Such innovations demonstrate the mutant nature of Modified Calvinism.

Alas, the great offensives of the twentieth century against modernism lie scattered on the battlefield in a hand-to-hand combat. On this battle-field, one finds few effectively organized battle units with almost all lines of communication cut. Our Christian heritage and the mighty artillery of the Word are unused weapons. Even if the guns would fire, the shells are made of rubber inasmuch as we dare not offend one another's con-science. The great resources and spirit of our nation lie dormant—or worse—in the hands of an enemy who knows how to use them. The ecumenical movement pleads that we leave our trenches and unite hold-ing hands under the enemy's barrage. Others plead that we form more rear support organizations. We desperately need to reduce our toleration and increase our thinking. We need to follow the advice of J. G. Machen (1881–1937) who ably responded to the liberal criticism that the evan-gelically orthodox do not think:

> Liberal thinking, he maintained, is really superficial, and can be shown to be so; and the true remedy against Liberalism is for men to think, not less (as some Fundamentalists seem to suppose) but more—more deeply, more vigorously, more clearly and more critically.[135]

So, let us accept Machen's challenge and do some serious thinking. What can we learn from the Covenanters? Before we can answer this question, we must accept a premise. The premise is that the objective of the Covenanters—namely, to build their lives, their church, and their state in the image of Christ—is indeed the proper objective for Christians today. This premise allows that in some specific actions they fell short, but their objective should be our objective. An essential corollary to this premise is that there are clearly defined landmarks discernable from the Scriptures to guide the Christian, the church, and the state.

Assuming this premise and its corollaries are valid, how can we apply the lessons learned from the Covenanters? The following analysis at-tempts to accomplish this purpose, with the end goal of a reformed Christian, church, and state. Reformation knows no earthly bounds!

LESSONS FROM THE COVENANTERS

(1) *All true Christians are Covenanters. The central theme of the Bible is God's Covenant of Grace.*

(2) *The church must re-establish unity in truth as attained during the Second Reformation and the apostolic era.*

(3) *Christians must put their covenant obligations and duty to be God's people first. This requires closing with Christ and improving the relationship daily.*

(4) *Christians must fulfill thier biblical obligation to make disciples of all nations and to be the light and salt of the world.*

(5) *Christians must covenant with God and should covenant with one another to seek reformation of their lives, churches, and society in accordance with the Word of God.*

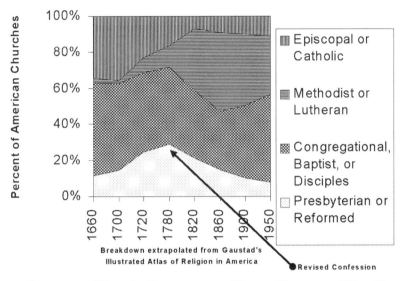

American Church Government Types (Percent of Total)

Martyrs

Wallace's Sword versus Drumclog Dragoon's Sword

Courtesy of Alloway Publishing

Statistics, Songs, and Swords

10

Lessons from the Covenant

Obey my voice, and I will be your God, and you shall be my people. –*Jer. 7:23 NKJ*

*L*esson #1: All true Christians are Covenanters. The central theme of the Bible is God's Covenant of Grace.* The principal idea of the gospel is not salvation of lost individuals; it is the progressive revelation of the kingdom of God to his covenant people. Stuart Robinson (1814–1881), in his book *The Church of God,* boldly declared the central revelation of Scripture: "It is the history of the administration of one king–Jesus Christ, the same yesterday, today, and forever–one community, having essentially one Lord, one faith, one baptism, throughout the series of ages."[1] Robinson expounded on this principle by comparing the progress of Protestant thought with man's evolving concept of the solar system:

> The Zwinglian, taking as the central principle of its structure the truth that the Word of God alone can be any authoritative rule to the conscience, developed from that point a true, in opposition to a counterfeit gospel; yet a gospel too easily perverted by reason of its tendency to exalt the rational man of earth into the center of the spiritual system, or at least, from its narrowness of view, to obscure the higher truths of the scheme of redemption. The Lutheran theory, taking as its central principle the justification of the sinner by grace alone through faith, after the fashion of Copernicus, exhibited Jesus Christ, the sun of righteousness, as the real center, to whom the rational man of earth, with all that concerns him, is attracted, and around whom he revolves. Calvin, whilst perceiving that the central truths of both Zwingli and Luther were indeed great truths, yet, with the still wider vision of La Place and the moderns, beheld not only the rational man revolving around the mediatorial sun of righteousness as his true center, but also the man and his central sun revolved again around a still profounder center, even the eternal purpose of God, fixed in the counsels of eternity before the world began.[2]

It is this understanding of God's covenant that John Nevay preached, and it is this understanding that led those in the Newmilns area to lay down their lives for God's truth. Nevay's sermons provide the only satisfying explanation of why the Covenanters, particularly those near the town of Newmilns, were willing to lay down their lives. Although Nevay was banished to Holland at the beginning of the persecution, he sent back to his home parish a series of fifty-two sermons on the Covenant of Grace, which he had preached while in their midst. Nevay selected David's last words, 2 Sam. 23:1–7, as the keynote for these sermons, with particular emphasis on 2 Samuel 23:5–the central text for forty-nine of these sermons. This verse, as translated in the King James Version, captures the realization that David, despite his own personal failures, had full confidence in God's everlasting covenant blessings.

After examining these sermons and James Nisbet's reflections on the Covenanters, I became convinced that the name *Covenanters* applies to adherents of God's covenant promises. Both Nevay and Nisbet speak on the topics of covenants and Covenanters, yet they rarely mention the *Solemn League and Covenant*. Their entire focus is on God's Covenant of Grace. Only after we understand the message in Nevay's sermons can we understand what motivated the Covenanters to sacrifice all for God's truth. I am confident that after you read the summaries of Nevay's sermons, included in this and subsequent chapters, that you, too, will reach the same conclusion. I am confident that you, too, will agree with the premise that all true Christians are Covenanters. Before reading the following summaries of Nevay's sermons, please be advised that they will change your life and worldview. Maybe you, too, will become a Covenanter. A warning is in order, however. Serious examination of Scripture, reflection, and prayer along with the guidance and renewing of the Holy Spirit are required to discover the deep theological treasures of God's Covenant of Grace, but the rewards are literally out of this world.

The Covenant – What is it?

God's Covenant of Grace is the central theme of the Bible. It was made initially with Adam when he failed to keep the Covenant of Works. The Old and New Testaments are but different dispensations of the same covenant.

Covenant in General: It is a sad state when a man or a society has no foundation (Ps. 11:3; 72:5; Jer. 17:3–4). In difficult times, it is "the great advantage of the people of God to make one thing certain." This one thing is that Christ is the only *"sure foundation"* (Isa. 28:16), given by the Father *"for a covenant to the people"* (Isa. 13:6). Be assured that God will over-turn any foundation other than Christ (Ezek. 21:27). Nevay defines a *cove-nant* as "an agreement between parties, by promise and engagement, on certain conditions and articles." The Hebrew word for covenant, *berith*, means "to choose or cut in pieces; for in making covenants they used to cut the sacrifice in twain, and to pass between the pieces, which did ex-press a curse on the covenant breaker" (Gen. 15:10,18; Ps. 89:3; Jer. 34:18; Luke 12:46). The New Testament word for a covenant, *testament* (Heb. 7:22; 9:16), signifies a "disposition or legacy; it holds forth a agreement between God and Man, wherein the riches of Christ, and the great things of sal-vation and eternal life, are disponed [conveyed] to man upon condition of believing and receiving Christ for righteousness." Both words refer to a covenant made by sacrifice (Ps. 50:5; Luke 22:20).[3]

God has "made two covenants with man." The first, called the *Cove-nant of Works* or the Law, he made with Adam. It bound man to perfect obedience "under pain of a curse and eternal death" (Gen. 2:16–17; Deut. 5:29; Ezek. 18:4; Rom. 2:5; 6:14; 10:5; Gal. 3:12).[4] Although the law is *"holy, just, and good"* (Rom. 7:12), it leads to death (Rom. 4:15; 7:10). The other covenant, called the *Covenant of Grace,* or the gospel, is made possible by the blood of Christ (Luke 22:20). It brings salvation, eternal life (Titus 2:11), peace (Isa. 54:10; Ezek. 37:26), and reconciliation (2 Cor. 5:9) with God. The first covenant leads to bondage, whereas the second leads to liberty (Gal. 4:22–24). The two covenants differ as shown in Table 10.1.

Table 10.1
Comparison between Covenants of Works and Grace

Covenant of Works	Covenant of Grace
Requires doing (Gal. 3:12)	Requires believing (Acts 16:31)
Yet, faith also commanded	Yet, works required as evidence (Matt. 5:16; Phil. 4:13; Titus 2:12)
Works precede the promise	Works follow believing (Rom. 16:26; Titus 3:8)
No mediator	Jesus is mediator (Heb. 9:15; 12:24)
Depends upon man's strength and inherent righteousness	Depends upon God's strength (Ps. 89:19) and imputed righteousness from Christ
Rewards based upon works	Rewards based upon God's grace (Rom. 4:4)
Sure to be broken; leads to death	Made to stand forever and leads to life
Under curse of the law (under the law)	No longer under curse because Christ was made a curse for those within the covenant

They are alike in that both covenants have the same author (God), the same parties (God and man), the same end (glorifying of God), and the same offered reward (eternal blessedness). Both are conditional and unchangeable (Jer. 33:20; Matt. 5:17), "require perfect righteousness" (Rom. 3:31;

1 Cor. 6:9), and "bind under a curse" (Deut. 27:26; 1 Cor. 16:22).[5] In summary, the entire Bible addresses the Covenant of Grace: "The covenant published on Mount Sinai was not a Covenant of Works but a Covenant of Grace, dispensed in types and legal terrors." The law is simply "a schoolmaster to lead us to Christ" (Exod. 24:6–7; Gal. 3:24; Heb. 8:7–8).[6]

No one can be under them both. Believers under the Covenant of Grace are no longer *"under the law but under grace"* (Rom. 6:14), because the *"ordinance against them"* has been *"nailed to the cross of Christ"* (Col. 2:14). Although believers are no longer under the curse of the law, they are *"still under the law to Christ"* (1 Cor. 9:21) and "under him as king and lawgiver" (James 4:12). This is true because Christ *"came not to destroy the law, but to fulfill it"* (Matt. 5:17). Christ kept the law and "prescribed it to others." The "same mind should be in believers as was in Christ" (Phil. 2:5). Paul *"delights in the law of God after the inward man"* (Rom. 7:22) and "calls the law spiritual, good, holy, and just" (Rom. 7:14). In the New Testament, duties "are pressed from the authority of the law" (1 Cor. 9:8–9); those that resist the law resist the kingship of Christ (Luke 19:14) and declare their "enmity against God." Against those who claim that they must only obey the law written in their hearts, Nevay counters, "What is upon the heart can be no perfect rule" because the heart is deceitful (Jer. 17:9). One must check their heart against the touchstone of the written Word.[7]

To apply this knowledge, "follow after holiness; knowing that the law now is the law of Christ, so fulfill it" (Gal. 6:2; James 1:25). Those who enter covenant with God do so by choice and under penalty, as in the days of Nehemiah: *"They clave to their brethren, their nobles, and entered into a curse, and into an oath, to walk in God's law, which was given by Moses the servant of God, and to observe and do all the commandments of the LORD our Lord, and his judgments and his statutes"* (Neh. 10:29). Covenant keepers (i.e., those who are in Christ—who kept the covenant and paid the penalty) will receive great things (1 Cor. 1:30); covenant breakers will be cut to pieces (Luke 12:46).[8]

Old and New Testaments: The Old and New Testaments are different dispensations of the Covenant of Grace. The Covenant of Grace "was made with Christ in eternity" and progressively revealed through Scripture promises. Although both dispensations have many things in common, there are differences. These similarities and differences are shown in Table 10.2.[9] Although the Old and New Testament refer to a "new covenant," the New Testament "is only a new covenant in the manner of administration." Although the old is a veiled, shadow form of the new, they "are one and the same in substance" (Isa. 42:6; Acts 26:22; Eph. 2:12–13,20; 1 John 1:1). Nevay rejects the premise that the old dispensation was a mixture of the works of law and grace: "Abraham's faith was imputed for righteousness" (Rom. 4:9–11). Where the Bible speaks of breaking the old covenant, it is "broken by unbelief." The promises of temporal blessings in the old covenant do not make it a different covenant because the "land of promise" is a "type of that rest prepared for the people of God." In short, they "did eat the same spiritual meat and did drink the same spiritual drink with us" (Matt. 8:11; 1 Cor. 10:1–4).[10] Rutherford adds, Christ is the rock of both (Deut. 32:4; 1 Cor. 10:1–6): "For they [those with Moses] drank of that spiritual Rock that followed them, and that Rock was Christ."[11] Calvin concurs: "The covenant made with all the fathers in so far a differing from ours in reality and substance, that it is altogether one and the same; still the administration differs."[12]

Table 10.2
Comparison between Old and New Dispensation

Common to Old Dispensation and New Dispensation	
Both flow from God's free love and choice (Deut. 7:7–8; Eph. 1:5).	
Both have the same great promises and blessings such as communion with God (Lev. 26:12; 2 Cor. 6:16), forgiveness of sins (Ps. 32:1–5; Rom. 4:6), and adoption as children of God (Jer. 3:19; Gal. 4:5).	
Both require faith as a condition (Hab. 2:4; Rom. 4:11; 11:20).	
Both have the same spirit of faith (John 7:39; 2 Cor. 4:13).	
Both have the same rule of life and reward (Isa. 33:2; James 4:12). Both offer eternal life and salvation (Isa. 45:17; Matt. 22:32; Luke 2:30,32).	
Both have the same church (1 Cor. 10:1–4; Gal. 3:7; 6:16).	
Both have the same gospel preached (Rom. 1:2) and same covenant (Acts 3:21).	

Nature of Old Dispensation	Nature of New Dispensation
The old was dispensed by God the Father, or by the Son not incarnate, and mediated by Moses (Deut. 5:27; Heb. 3:5).	The new was published by the Lord Jesus Christ coming in the flesh and mediated by Christ (Heb. 9:15; 12:24; 3:6).
The old was burdensome and dark (Acts 15:10; Gal. 4:2–3).	In the new, the yoke is easy and the burden light.
The old was more dark, as shadows of events to come: eternal life (Ps. 16:11; 17:15; 95:11; Dan. 12:2), Christ (Gen. 14:18; Deut. 18:18; Isa. 9:6), the kingdom (Luke 1:31–33), and justification (Exod. 24:7–8).	The new is more clear: *"The earth shall be full of the knowledge of the Lord"* (Isa. 11:9); *"The light of the moon shall be as the light of the sun"* (Isa. 30:26); *"They shall all know me, from the least of them unto the greatest of them"* (Jer. 31:34).
The old made nothing perfect (Heb. 7:18–19), and it had less effectual spirit (John 7:39; Gal. 3:23; 4:6–7).	The new has a more effectual spirit, characterized by spirit, faith, and joy: the light of world (John 1:9). Christ, the standard, is clearly revealed (Eph. 4:13).
The old was given only to one people for a time (Heb. 9:10).	The new is given unto all peoples (Rom. 3:29). It is everlasting (Rev. 14:6).

These truths have important implications: First, "if the old covenant
and the new be the same, then the Scriptures of the Old Testament are
not to be rejected" (Rom. 15:4; Eph. 2:20; 2 Tim. 3:15–16). Second, we should rejoice to live in new covenant times and not *"neglect so great a salvation"*
(Heb. 2:3). Third, since the heavy yoke is removed, we "should be a more
free-hearted and willing people in offering up spiritual sacrifices" (1 Pet.
2:5, 16). Fourth, having a much clearer light than Abraham, we should rejoice (John 8:56), "walk as children of light" (Rom. 13:13; 1 Thess. 5:5–6), be
"filled with the Spirit" (Eph. 5:18; 2 Tim. 1:7), and be "abundantly fruitful"
(Luke 12:48). If we open our mouths wide, God promises to fill it (Ps. 81:10).[13]

The Covenant – Its Origin and Maker

*The triune God established a covenant of everlasting mercy and infinite goodness. He re-
vealed it to man through a series of covenant promises that contain all the good that believers
do receive.*

Its **Author**: In a most divine mystery, the triune God established this
covenant as an outworking of triune love:

> They all held the counsel in eternity, in eternal wisdom, did draw up the
> agreement in the draughts of everlasting love, and did design the flowing
> forth of everlasting mercy and infinite goodness: The Father so loved the
> world, that he decreed to send the Son: The Son so loved the Father and
> lost man, that he agreed to be sent: The love of the eternal Spirit was
> such, that he engaged to anoint and abundantly to furnish him that was
> sent: the Father prepared a body for the Son; the son put on the body,
> and took it in, into the unity of his person, the same person with his
> Godhead; and the Spirit did pour unto him the oil of gladness above his
> fellows.[14]

In his memoir, James Nisbet reflects on this great mystery:

> In reading the four Evangelists, I observed something of the wonder-
> ful contrivance of the infinite wisdom and unparalleled love of God, in
> sending his Son to be a day's-man for making peace and reconciliation
> betwixt a holy and righteous God and unholy [and] sinful sinners. As
> formerly, in the promises, so now, this wise, mysterious contrivance was
> wonderfully displayed in the incarnation and tragic sufferings that the
> Son of God underwent from his conception in the virgin's womb to his
> resurrection and ascension to glory…. And O my soul! Methinks I stand
> at the cross of Christ on Mount Calvary beholding a wonderful convo-
> cation of contrary parties, each one acting their part. There is infinite
> justice and righteousness demanding satisfaction of the Lamb of God for

the sins of the elect! And there is the infinite love of God engaging him to give full and complete satisfaction! And there is the infinite power of God supporting his humanity in that nonesuch undertaking! And there are all the sins of the elect presenting themselves as the crime to be satisfied for! And there is the devils and wicked men raging furiously to help forward the execution, and as they designed to frustrate the great work of man's redemption! And there is the infinite wisdom and unaccountable sovereignty of God ordering the whole matter, in a sinless way, to his own everlasting glory! And that the crown might be set on free grace's head for evermore, to the endless and unconceivable consolation of all his elect sons and daughters; and to the endless confusion of the devils, and all willful rejecters of this dear-bought salvation.[15]

God revealed the covenant to man through a progressive series of covenant promises made with Adam (Gen. 3:15), Noah (Gen. 6:18), Abraham (Gen. 17:1), Isaac (Gen. 17:21), Jacob (Gen. 25:10), Moses (Exod. 19:5; Deut. 7:6), David (Ps. 89:3), Solomon (Ps. 89:36), and Israel (Jer. 31:31; Ezek. 37:26). Only God with his infinite majesty, love, wisdom, skill, and power could have been author of the covenant because man is unable even to understand (Matt. 16:17; Col. 1:21) the depth of its riches.[16]

It is Already Made: Nevay declares, "All the good which believers do receive, it is all conveyed to them by covenant" (Luke 1:72). We must expect all good only from this covenant way. God chose to deal with man in this way for several reasons. He did so to reveal, *"He is God, the faithful God, who keeps covenant"* (Deut. 7:9). He did so "to separate a people for himself" (Exod. 19:5; Lev. 20:24; Ps. 4:3), placing them under a bond of obedience (Ezek. 20:37). He did so to prove he cannot lie (Heb. 6:17–18) and to disengage us from other covenants and lovers (Hos. 2:5, 19–20). He did so to honor his people (Deut. 26:18–19), to honor Christ, and for his glory: *"For all the promises of God in him are yea, and in him [Christ] Amen, unto the glory of God by us"* (2 Cor. 1:20).[17]

It is an everlasting and unalterable covenant: "It is a covenant already made, agreed upon, concluded and ended in eternity in the well-ordered decree" (2 Sam. 23:5; Ps. 103:17; 119:89; Prov. 8:22–23; John 19:30). From eternity, the Father gave Christ "for a covenant" (Isa. 42:6; Micah 5:2). It "is not now to be made, but to be declared, remembered, and kept" (Neh. 1:5; Ps. 2:7; 3:7).[18]

It is essential that we apply these doctrines. First, to partake of this covenant, we must "consent to the bargain, wherein the Lord becomes our God; he gives Christ, and then, with him, all things freely" (Rom. 8:32). Second, to receive its good, we must be in it, for the Lord reveals his secrets and paths only to those who fear him and keep his covenant

(Ps. 25:10, 14). Third, take comfort that the covenant is already established and unchangeable: worry not, for the Lord will "heal our distempers" (Ps. 89:33) and "our backsliding" (Hos. 14:4). Fourth, this fact notwithstanding, the covenant is made void to us if we "do not willingly receive it," or if we reject, undervalue, or "do not rest satisfied with" it (Luke 7:30; John 1:12). Fifth, Christians should take comfort that admittance to God's covenant is not based on man's merits; instead, an unchangeable God, who can "stay the heart of doubting Christians," foreordains it.[19]

The Covenant – Its Parties

The Father and the Son established the covenant, wherein the Son would redeem those, the elect, given to him by the Father by paying the price for their sins. Thus, the elect are also a party and are irrevocably bound to believe in him and pursue the covenant promises.

Father and Son: It began "without beginning, betwixt the Father and him," and all that the covenant requires "is to be found betwixt the Father and the Son" (See Isa. 42:6; 53:10–11).[20] Christ "is the principal seed, with whom the father enters covenant" (Gal. 3:16; Heb. 1:5); through him, "we are made alive" (1 Cor. 15:22). All the promises are made "first to him, and then to us, according to our measure." For example, "The *Mother Promise* that God will be his God was first made to him (Ps. 89:26: John 20:17) and so to us" (Jer. 32:38).[21] The Father and Son work in close agreement to fulfill the promises:

> The Father gives so many to the Son, and draws them that they may come, and the Son makes them welcome, and in no wise will cast them out (John 6:37, 44). The Father gives them to the Son, and the Son gives to them his Words (John 17:6, 8). The Son never parts with them until he raise them up at the last day (John 6:39–40).[22]

To fulfill the covenant promise to redeem his people, Christ has "a special commission from God to execute and bear a threefold office," wherein he serves as prophet (John 12:49), priest (John 10:18), and king (Psalm 2:6). For this purpose, the Father made great promises to the Son: God promises him the Spirit (Isa. 11:1–2), help (Isa. 42:4, 6), success (Isa. 55:5), kingship (Ps. 110:1–2), and glory (John 17:5, 24). The Son, *"being found in fashion as a man, he humbled himself, and became obedient unto death, even the death on the cross"* (Phil. 2:8). Hence, Christ "stands for God to man, and for man to God, as umpire betwixt both." He is the messenger (Mal. 3:1), the witness (Isa. 55:4), and the surety (Heb. 7:22) of the covenant. Likewise, he "is the surety for us to the Father." He paid the price for our sins "to give us new hearts, to write his law in them (Jer. 31:33; Ezek. 36:26), to cause us to walk in the Lord's statutes (Ezek. 36:27), and to put his fear in our hearts that we may not depart from him" (Jer. 32:40).[23] For his people, he serves as mediator (Heb. 12:24), testator (Heb. 9:16–17; 10:4; 13:20), representative (Heb. 2:13), and leader (Isa. 55:4) in a multi-faceted covenant relationship with the Father. Considering this great work, his people should honor this treaty of peace by engaging themselves with the help of the great mediator to perform the "eternal business" of the covenant.[24]

The Elect: Because "Christ is a testator in the covenant, there must be a party in the covenant, to which the legacy which he does bequeath by his death is left" (Heb. 9:16). This party consists of those chosen from the beginning of time (2 Tim. 1:9) to believe in him—each "bound to keep the covenant" (Ps. 25:10). Those who do not believe are "broken off" (Lev. 26:15; Rom. 11:20).[25] The children of the promise are the spiritual seed promised to Abraham (Rom. 9:6–8; Heb. 2:13). They are the fruit of an unfathomable covenant love, exemplified in the love between David and Jonathan (1 Sam. 20:17; 2 Sam. 1:26). The richness of God's condescending love humbles us. Although we are most vile, Christ makes us heirs, kings, and priests unto God (Rom. 8:17; Rev. 1:5–6), and spreads "the skirt of his covenant over us" to "cover our nakedness"; in so doing, "we become his and he ours" (Ezek. 16:8). At the realization of the magnitude of God's covenant love, the great saints of the Scripture were smitten with wondering astonishment, self-abasement, great thankfulness, submission and yielding to the Lord's disposal. Consider how Abraham *"fell on his face"* (Gen. 17:3) and David cried out, *"Who am I, O Lord God, and what is my house that thou hast brought me hitherto?"* (2 Sam. 7:18).[26]

Those who "have not yet come under the bond of the covenant, let them hasten to do it" and "give themselves up to God in a covenant." To enter this covenant, believers must consider themselves unworthy (Luke 15:19), "break covenant with old lust and lovers" (Matt. 6:24), and "yield to the terms of the covenant" (Luke 9:23). They must recognize Christ's sacrifice (Ps. 50:5; Heb. 9:26). They must "enter cheerfully … and never go out again; for it is a marriage covenant, and the betrothing is forever" (Hos. 2:19). Those who keep it are a peculiar treasure to God, and they consider breaches of the covenant as worse than adultery. To aid in keeping it, "know it well" and make use of it when in trials and spiritual troubles.[27]

Only the Elect: David knew he was one of those chosen by God: The Lord *"has made with **me** an everlasting covenant"* (2 Sam. 23:5). There are some whom the Father loved from eternity, whose names are in the

Lamb's Book of Life. The Father gave these, the seed promised to Abraham, to Christ who "calls his own sheep by name" (Gen. 17:7; Isa. 43:1; Luke 10:20; John 10:2; Rom. 9:13; Rev. 13:8).[28]

Unfortunately, the majority of modern evangelical churches do not believe this biblical truth; instead, they hold an Arminian view, which contends "that all have sufficient means and power to reject or accept Christ offered in the gospel." They argue that Christ's death was sufficient for all but effectual only to believers. According to this view, God made his covenant with all, has a "universal and like goodwill to all," and purchased "a possible salvation" for all. Such possible salvation for all in theory would allow all to perish if none chose to believe.[29]

In contrast, the Reformed view holds that Christ died for particular persons, whom the Lord chose to save and "to show some special love."[30] Nevay offers the following proofs for the Reformed view called predestination: First, the Father gave and trusted Christ with particular sheep, who keep God's word (John 17:6,8) and for whom Christ died (John 10:11). For these and not all Christ prays: *"I pray for them: I pray not for the world, but for them which thou hast given me; for they are thine"* (John 17:9,24). The reason men do not believe is that they are not his sheep (John 10:26). Second, it is not possible for Christ to lose any of those given to him by the Father (John 6:37,39; 10:11,14; 13:1). Likewise, he must cast out those who are not his sheep (Matt. 7:23; 25:32; Rom. 9:11–12). Third, it is inconsistent with the "wisdom and justice of God to purchase redemption for all, yet to suffer many [who never heard the Word] to die ignorant of it." Fourth, the Arminian philosophy fastens "upon Christ a blind bargain" which makes covenant relations impossible. How is it possible for shepherd not to know his sheep, a husband not to know his wife, an advocate not to know those for whom he advocates? Fifth, the Arminian is "against all reason and justice, that ransom should be paid, and the captive not loosed; it is against both law and gospel." According to Isaiah, *"The ransomed of the LORD shall return, and come to Zion with songs and everlasting joy upon their heads..."* (Isa. 35:10; also Exod. 21:30; 1 Pet. 1:18,19,21). Sixth, Christ did not simply purchase a potential redemption but a "complete redemption": Christ *"gave himself for us, that he might redeem us from all iniquity, and purify unto himself a peculiar people, zealous of good works"* (Titus 2:14; also 1 Cor. 1:30; Eph. 5:25–27; Col. 1:14). In addition, "the very words, reconciliation, redemption, and surety" speak against the Arminian view. Christ only redeemed those who enter his kingdom *"with singing and everlasting joy"* (Isa. 51:11) and *"being dead to sin, should live unto righteousness"* (1 Pet. 2:24; also Gal. 1:4; 1 Pet. 1:18). None of those redeemed can perish. Finally, all dispensations of grace (e.g., election, adoption, sanctification) spoken of in the New Testament are to "particular and definite persons" rather than "to general and indefinite persons."[31]

Nevay contends that the Arminian error "is grounded upon the misinterpretation of the words *All* and *World*," and he demolishes this misconception:

> This participle, *All*, and the word, *World*, are taken divers ways in Scripture. The world is gone after him (John 12:19) is meant of none but the generality of the people of Judea. In Luke 17:27, *destroyed them all*, is not meant of all and every one, for eight persons were saved; the world and the whole world is sometimes put for the gentiles only (1 John 2:2), sometimes, for the wicked only (Rom. 12:2 and 1 John 5:19), sometimes, for the Messiah his world (John 3:16). And *all* does signify all sorts of men (John 1:16).[32]

Nevay refutes the Arminian interpretation given to many verses: First, to those who take the word *world* in John 3:16 to mean every person, Nevay remarks, "There is no love of Christ in Scripture, but that which is effectual: It betroths forever (Hos. 2:19); it is a love that makes those he loves more than conquerors (Rom. 8:37). It is a love that washes and cleanses his church (Eph. 5:25–27). It gives everlasting consolation and good hope through grace (2 Thess. 2:16). It makes those he loves kings and priests (Rev. 1:5–6)." Christ did not lay down his life for all men but only his *friends*, who do what he commands (John 15:13–14).[33] Second, regarding the passage, *"The free gift came upon all men to justification of life"* (Rom. 5:18), Nevay points out that the verse following it refers to *many* and the preceding verse qualifies those to whom verse 18 refers. Third, in the passage, *"As in Adam all die, so in Christ shall all be made alive"* (1 Cor. 15:22), the first *all* refers to every man, but the second *all* is indirectly qualified by verses 17 and 18 to mean believers in Christ's resurrection. Fourth, passages such as 1 John 2:2, which offer salvation to the whole world, must be interpreted in light of passages such as Hebrew 7:25, which clearly limit the saved to those for whom Christ intercedes. Fifth, where 1 Timothy 4:10 refers to God as *"the Savior of all men, specially of those that believe,"* it "is not meant of Christ the Mediator, but of God in external providences and salvations." In summary, in Scripture *all* is often put for *many*; so sometimes many is put for all the elect (e.g., Matt. 20:28).[34]

Because it is a covenant with particular people, "we should try whether our names be particularly within it"; for *"Happy is that people whose God is the Lord"* (Ps. 144:15). If so, we have *"a nail in a sure place"* (Isa.

22:23) to hang all our vessels. Nevay lists five marks of those with a nail in a sure place:[35]

1. They rest on Christ alone for salvation; they know that Jesus Christ is in them (Rom. 10:3; 2 Cor. 13:5).
2. They take care to keep covenant with God (Ps. 103:17–18; 119:106).
3. They break their covenant with sin and divorce all idolatry and dishonesty (Hos. 2:19–20; 2 Cor. 4:2).
4. They choose him as Lord and as the one whom their soul loves above all things (Ps. 119:106; Song of Sol. 1:7; Phil. 3:8).
5. They "make much use of Christ as a mediator, asking and pleading for that which we want in his name."

Those within this covenant should give thanks, as did Christ for his disciples: "I thank thee, O Father, Lord of heaven and earth, because thou hast hid these things from the wise and prudent, and hast revealed them unto babes. Even so, Father: for so it seemed good in thy sight" (Mat 11:25–26).[36]

Covenant Children: The children of believing parents are a party in the covenant, at least the external visible covenant: "Infants at least some of them, not only may be, but are within the Covenant of Grace and Redemption; they, as such, are among those that were from all eternity given to Christ." Nevay's arguments in support of this proposition are as follows: First, it is beyond doubt that some specific infants are among the elect (Jer. 1:5; Luke 1:15; Rom. 9:11,13), and that their election does not depend on the sins of their parents, as in the case of Jeroboam's child (1 Kings 14:13). Second, God promises mercy to many children (Exod. 20:6), and he comforts believing parents not to mourn but to hope that they will see their children again (Jer. 31:15–16; Matt. 2:17; 1 Thess. 4:13). They have good grounds for hope because "the seed of the righteous are pronounced blessed" (Ps. 37:26). Third, Christ equates them to the kingdom of God (Mark 10:14). Although clearly in the visible kingdom, the love Christ showed them "gives good ground to think they did belong to the invisible kingdom also." Fourth, the "Lord compares his love often to that love which parents bear children" (Ps. 103:13; Isa. 66:12–13; Matt. 23:37). Fifth, he directs that we receive children in his name (Compare Matt. 18:5 with Mark 9:41). Sixth, just as promises in the Old Testament applied to Abraham and his household, in the New Testament "there are promises of salvation made to whole households" (Luke 19:9; Acts 16:34). Nevay argues, "there is no reason why children should be excluded from these promises, when often they are the larger parts of households." Seventh, since God enters covenant with "man and his seed" (Gen. 3:15; 17:7), "it is irrational to exclude little children from being part of that seed."[37]

Nevay proposes two applications of this knowledge: First, "there is ground of comfort to believing parents concerning their children dying as infants." Second, because some children are members of the invisible church, "it would be a sin" to exclude them from the visible church. Nevay contends that it is just as difficult to know the state of infants as it is to know with certainty the state of adults. Further, some children, particularly those near death, have exhibited the signs of grace at an early age.[38] Nevay considers this subject so important that he devotes another whole sermon, covered later in this book, to this topic.

The Covenant – Its Condition

The Covenant of Grace is a free gift from God, but it requires that the elect come to Jesus in faith and partake of his fullness. Faith is the lone thing required to enter into the Covenant of Grace. It is in no way earned or merited by man.

Conditional Covenant: Nevay declares, "The Covenant of Grace is conditional, so as no good promised in it can be expected, unless the conditions be performed." It is important to qualify immediately such a bold proposition:

> While we call the Covenant of Grace conditional, we may not understand it in the most strict sense, condition, as of parties alike able to perform the conditions each for their own parts; but as conditional so as the bargain cannot stand, unless the conditions be performed. It is as if a parent made the covenant with the child, upon the doing of such a thing, to give him such a reward, yet the father performs the condition in and by the child; yet the bargain holds not unless the condition be performed: Yet since the father does perform the condition, no ground of pleading merit; all is free. So that is true. First, that the Lord saves us, not without ourselves; we are to work out our salvation in fear and trembling (Phil. 2:12). And yet, second, we are so saved, as all boasting is excluded (Rom. 3:27). The Lord does both work faith and all our other works in us; [it is] he that ordains the peace (Isa. 26:12).[39]

Hence, the fact that it is conditional "does not hinder it from being a Covenant of Grace, that is, a free covenant: all is given in it most freely; Christ, and with him all things" (Rom. 8:32; Rev. 22:17).[40] Nevay clarifies, "The absolute promises do hold forth the cause of salvation," and they "give good ground for closing and adherence and for constant dependence." But, "the conditional promises, when the condition is found, do beget and strengthen assurance: when the Lord says, I will do it for my own sake, that is absolute; believe and thou shall be saved, that is conditional."[41]

In the Gospel offer, *"Come unto me, all ye that labor and are heavy laden, and I will give you rest"* (Matt. 11:28), "coming to Christ is the condition, and so coming sensible of our need for him." In this coming, "there must not only be a listening to the bargain, but [also] a coming to Jesus, the buying up of his wares, the receiving, eating, drinking, and so partaking of his fullness" (Isa. 55:1,3; Rev. 22:17). In short, "there is both coming and taking called for and men must be willing to the bargain, and thirsting after it."[42]

Nevay offers six proofs of the conditional aspect of the covenant.

1. The "Lord did never promise life absolutely to any creature." Even those that sound absolute (e.g., Isa. 43:25; Ezek. 35:21–22) have "both Christ and faith included."
2. The "very name and nature of the covenant does signify an agreement upon conditions" (Gen. 21:23–24, 31–32; 31:48–54).
3. Scripture promises the covenant on condition of obedience to commandments (e.g., Deut. 7:11–12).
4. The Lord promises to bring his people "into the bond of the covenant" (Jer. 13:11; Ezek. 20:37).
5. When Scripture refers to keeping or breaking the covenant (Ps. 25:10; Isa. 24:5), "it is meant of the conditions of the covenant."
6. The word *covenant* not only means "that which God promises" but also "that which God requires" (Gen. 17:7,9); specifically, God requires our assent to the terms of the covenant (Exod. 24:3,7).[43]

Why did the Lord make it conditional? First, transforming creatures of darkness into creatures of light (i.e., evidencing the condition) displays the Lord's glory, worthy of our praise (1 Pet. 2:9). Second, although grace is free, "to stop the mouth of murmurers … it is so dispensed, as God may reckon with men upon the point of keeping or breaking condition[s]; so that the Lord may demonstrate his justice and fairness" (Ezek. 18:25; Matt. 20:13). Third, "the condition wrought in the saints is the better and stronger ground of consolation, concerning the certainty of the bargain."[44]

Therefore, it is essential that believers "labor to keep the condition, as they desire to take assuredly of the blessing" and to receive the "crown of righteousness." This requires that you *"fight the good fight"* (2 Tim. 4:7–8), *"give diligence to make your calling and election sure"* (2 Pet. 1:10), pursue every last promise through faith (Heb. 3:19–4:1), and remember, *"The*

Lord is with you while ye be with him" (2 Chron. 15:2).[45] Nevay addresses several common objections to a conditional covenant as shown in Table 10.3.[46]

Hence, believers should "seek out the conditional promises, and be still examining whether you have the condition": *"Examine yourselves, whether ye be in the faith"* (2 Cor. 13:5; see also 1 John 3:18–19). Peter, in 2 Peter 1:5–9, commands us to try ourselves in this manner.[47]

Table 10.3
Nevay's Defense of Conditional Covenant

Objections	Nevay's Rebuttal
Heb. 9:15–17 refers to the covenant as a testament, thus without conditions.	It "is a testament," but "in verse 15 the condition is expressed, the promise of the inheritance, as a means of death; so there must be receiving of the redemption of the transgressions." His testament is clearly for believers of the Word (John 17:20, 24).
There "are absolute promises made to us in this covenant," such as Ezek. 11:19 and 36:25, which promise a new heart.	Nevay answers, "even these, as they are made to us, are made in Christ; *all promises are yea and Amen in Christ Jesus"* (2 Cor. 1:20). Many Scripture promises are expressly conditional (e.g., Matt. 5:3–10; Rom. 8:23; 10:10, 13). Nevay adds, "The condition is the Lord's work; it is rather properly in the Covenanter, than in the covenant; the Lord does first fit the party, and then engage them."
According to Ezek. 36:25–27 and Heb. 8:10, God gives us a new heart and causes us to *"walk in his statutes."* Hence, God does it all, "leaving us nothing to do."	Nevay gives three answers: First, "the condition is not antecedent to God's making of the covenant, but to the believers being actually within it." Second, the "Lord does undertake all, as he will both have us doing our part, and cause us to do it (e.g., Jer. 4:4; Ezek. 18:31; Eph. 4:23). Third, although God does the work, we still are accountable because "sinful inability does not take away moral obligations; believers are under gospel ties to obedience."
To make the Covenant of Grace conditional is to confuse it with the Covenant of Works and "to bring the free spirit of Jesus under bonds."	The conditions are different (i.e., works versus faith). Fulfilling the "evangelical commandments," such as *"repent and believe"* (Mark 1:15) and *"let not sin reign in your mortal body"* (Rom. 6:12), requires God's Grace (Rom. 6:14). Although we are required to act, e.g., *"Work out your own salvation with fear and trembling"* (Phil. 2:12), it is God's work, i.e., *"the Lord works in you to both will and to do his good pleasure"* (Phil. 2:13). The Lord performs this work not under bonds to us but by his free promise.
Conditions preclude an everlasting covenant.	"Christ's faithfulness is surety for our being faithful; so the covenant will not fail."

The conditional aspect of the covenant is not a contradiction to the free grace offered in the covenant. It is "by grace are ye saved through faith; and that not of yourselves: it is the gift of God: Not of works, lest any man should boast" (Eph. 2:8–9). We are saved by grace through faith, as further expounded by these truths: First, the "Lord did purpose to give faith first and then life": "The words of faith give life, they are spirit and life" (John 6:63). Second, "all the conditional promises are promises of the gospel, so of grace." They are not of the law because "the law is not of faith, so not of grace" (Gal. 3:12). Third, "faith, which is the condition" receives "all from grace most freely and without price; both justification, sanctification, and glorification." Fourth, "this condition is not, nor ever was, a cause influencing God to give either grace or glory"; nor is it a reason for boasting because works are by God's grace. Last, "it is an act of grace, that pleased him to make the covenant conditional, and upon so easy a condition; and then another act of grace, that he himself should work the condition."[48] This condition is faith. Understanding this truth enables Christians to refute doctrinal errors and to understand their daily need for Grace.[49]

Faith is the Condition: John Nisbet was a Calvinist and a firm believer in predestination; his faith was fully in God and not in himself. Nevay considers this type of faith, provided by God, a condition of the Covenant of Grace. Modern Reformed writers avoid the term *condition*, using instead the term *instrumental cause* to avoid any implication that man rather than God is the originating agent. Nevay acknowledges that the term *condition* is subject to misinterpretation, and he even uses the word *instrument*:

> This is against these who make faith so a condition, as not an instrument; as it is a habit within the man, and not acting upon Christ: They turn the covenant legal, who make anything within the man, or anything proceeding from the man or performed by him: Faith does neither justify as a habit, or as any act or work of ours, but as an instrument apprehending Christ and his righteousness.[50]

The modern phobia of the term "condition" is unfortunate, in my opinion, for several reasons: First, Scripture clearly defines faith as the condition of the covenant (John 3:16; Rom. 4:16; 10:9–10). Second, the term "condition" better communicates to men's minds than the term "instrument" the necessity for closing with Christ using the faith that God has provided them. It better communicates the fact that the undeniably conditional promises of the Old Testament were of the Covenant of Grace, and the real condition required of the Hebrews was faith (see Heb. 3:19). Third, Nevay's use of the term condition is consistent with the *Westminster Confession of Faith* and the *Larger Catechism*. Although the *Westminster* standards clearly state that no condition within men motivates God to grant faith unto them; however, they equally state that faith is required [i.e., an implicit condition] for justification, salvation, and "as the condition to interest [men] in [Christ]."[51] It is, however, not the "grace of faith or any act thereof" that justifies someone, "but only as it is an instrument which [one] receives and applies Christ and His righteousness."[52] Fourth, in Nevay's era, almost all the Scottish theologians (e.g., Rutherford, Gillespie, Guthrie, Durham, Dickson) referred to faith as the conditional aspect of the Covenant of Grace, and all qualified this as a condition performed by God.[53] Likewise, the same is true of the English theologians (e.g., Flavel, Owen, Watson, Perkins).[54] I trust them more than I do modern theologians.

Illustrative of the English divines is John Flavel (1630–1691). Flavel argued that just because the covenant union is made possible by God's strength, "does not make it cease to be our work" (1 John 3:23; Phil. 2:12–13). Although this is not a meritorious work, the benefits are suspended until performed. If the "covenant of grace be altogether absolute and unconditional," then "it cannot be man's duty in entering covenant with God, to deliberate the terms, count the cost, or give his consent by word or writing, to the terms of the covenant. There must be consent of the will, but the will must first be made whole by the redeeming, unmerited work of Christ."[55] Those thus engaged, according to Thomas Watson (d. 1686), are a humble (1 Pet. 5:5), willing (Ps. 110:3), and consecrated (Deut. 7:6) people.[56]

Illustrative of the Scottish divines are Andrew Gray and Samuel Rutherford. Gray states, "Faith is the condition of the promises; and it is certain, that Christ giveth a believer that condition, as well as he giveth him the promise": "To you it is given to believe" (Phil. 1:29).[57] According to Rutherford, the problem is that people "ignorantly confound the promise, and the thing promised; the covenant, and the benefits covenanted."[58] He contended,

> "The promise is made to them absolutely, whether they believe or not. But the blessing of the promise and the Covenant of Grace is given and bestowed only conditionally, if they believe. The promise is absolutely made: it is called conditional from the things conditionally given."[59]

Louis Berkhof, a modern theologian, referred to the covenant as both conditional and unconditional, depending upon the point of view. He contends that it is acceptable to refer to it as conditional because (1) the Bibles does so, (2) the Bible warns those who ignore the condition, and (3) a bond requires two parties.[60]

Nevay, in lockstep with his contemporaries, boldly declared that faith is the only "thing required as the condition of the covenant." Clearly, belief and confession are required for eternal life (John 3:15; Rom. 10:9–10). Faith is central to the gospel: God's grace is its origin (Rom. 4:16); preaching opens its door (Acts 14:27); obedience is its result (Rom. 16:26); and salvation of our souls is its end (1 Pet. 1:9).[61] Scripture clearly makes faith the condition. First, "the blessings promised in this covenant are not attainable in ourselves" (1 John 5:12). Second, no human work can save (Rom. 8:3; Gal. 3:21). Third, faith is a gift of God's free grace for which God alone deserves praise and honor (Rom. 4:16; 11:6; 1 Cor. 1:29,31; Eph. 1:6). Fourth, through faith believers receive "all the great things of the covenant" (2 Chron. 20:20; Rom. 4:16); consequently, believers must make use of faith to enjoy the benefits of the covenant (Acts 10:43; Rom. 3:29–30; 4:13; 8:32; 2 Cor. 1:24; Gal. 3:14).[62]

Recognition that faith is the condition is of great use. First, through faith believers discover "the happy estate of those that are in the covenant" (Ps. 144:15) and, on the other hand, "the misery of those that are not in the covenant with him, without Christ" (Eph. 2:12). Second, faith allows Christians "to break their covenant with sin, Satan, and self." Third, faith "breeds earnest desires … the soul's desire will be working by night and day in seeking God" (Isa. 26:8–9). Fourth, faith reveals "the Lord's willingness to enter in covenant with self-lost sinners" (Prov. 1:22–23; Isa. 55:1; Jer. 3:4; Ezek. 33:11; Matt. 11:28). Fifth, faith enables believers to be reconciled with God (2 Cor. 5:20). Sixth, it "puts the soul to a most serious consideration of the invitations and encouragements," such as our "marriage with the king's son," wherein he brings "all things which may give satisfaction, solace, and security." The bridegroom promises, *I will betroth thee unto me forever, yea, I will betroth thee unto me in righteousness, and in judgment, and in loving kindness, and in mercies; I will even betroth thee unto me in faithfulness"* (Hos. 2:19–20). Seventh, faith "reveals how believing is all that is required"; it allows the believer to find Christ's "yoke easy, his dominion sweet, and his service reasonable" (Matt. 11:29; Rom. 12:1; 1 John 5:3). Eighth, for those who come to him in faith, he *"will in no wise cast out"* (John 6:37).[63]

We must "make use of this faith in improving" our covenant relationship with God. First, we must assure that our closing with Christ has been right and full (Heb. 10:22; 1 John 3:19). Second, faith "improves this blessed bargain by taking the soul to the throne of grace that it may get grace for help in time of need" (Heb. 4:16). Third, after faith has engaged souls to God, "it will teach men that great lesson, how to walk to God." Faith shows us our duty; it enables us to seek his strength (Isa. 11:2; Luke 11:3; 2 Cor. 12:9), rule (Ps. 119:66), and glory (1 Cor. 10:31); protects us as a shield (Eph. 6:16); and encourages us in God's ways (Ps. 119:32; Heb. 11:25). Fourth, we must make use of faith when we sin (1 John 2:1), lack grace (Gal. 3:14), fear falling away (2 Tim. 4:18), and face any duty (Ezek. 36:27). Fifth, faith teaches us to recognize God's great work and to honor him: *"He has formed us for himself that we might show forth his praise"* (Isa. 43:21). To honor God, we must praise (Neh. 9:5), serve (Ps. 116:16), esteem (Neh. 6:3), and trust in (Ps. 56:3) him. We must also submit to his authority (Isa. 66:2), "stand for him in declining times" (Ezek. 44:15–16), keep our covenant vows (Ezek. 16:59), and "live always sensible of [our] unworthiness" (1 Chron. 29:14).[64]

Nevay considered it an antinomian error not to consider faith as a condition of our salvation. Our faith is "antecedent to our actually engaging in covenant with God" (Heb. 11:5–6; see also Rom. 3:22, 25; Gal. 2:16; Phil. 3:9), to our justification (Rom. 8:30), to our salvation (Num. 21:9 with John 3:14–15; Isa. 45:22), and to the imputation of the righteousness of Christ to us (Rom. 4:3; Gal. 3:6). In essence, all of these blessings are dependent upon and cannot be "separated from that act of [God's] grace, which works faith in us and draws forth faith to act." Hence, those "who desire to have their interest secured, must not rest in the covenant as made with Christ in eternity, but labor once to have faith, and then to act[*] it; or else they can never be actually possessed of and in the covenant, and the great things that are in it."[65]

On the other hand, Nevay contended, "no qualification within ourselves is the condition," such as the human habit, act, or work. The condition of the covenant is not faith as a human habit, but "it is faith, as acting, and as an instrument apprehending Christ." Such faith is best expressed by Paul, *"I am crucified with Christ: nevertheless I live; yet not I, but Christ liveth in me: and the life which I now live in the flesh I live by the faith of the Son of God, who loved me, and gave himself for me"* (Gal. 2:12). Hence, through faith we live as sons of God, who walk by faith (2 Cor. 5:7) and perform the work of faith (1 Thess. 1:3), "because faith by acting does receive [and embrace] the promise and the privileges in it" (John 1:12; Heb. 11:13). There-

---

[*] Regarding the acts of saving faith, the *Westminster Confession of Faith*, in Section XIV.2, states, "By this faith, a Christian believes to be true whatever is revealed in the Word … yielding obedience to the commands, trembling at the threatenings, and embracing the promises of God for this life, and that which is to come. But the principle acts of saving faith are accepting, receiving, and resting upon Christ alone for justification, sanctification, and eternal life, by virtue of the Covenant of Grace."

fore, abiding in the covenant is not an isolated act, but daily acting in faith, "for life is in these actings."[66]

The Covenant – Its Properties

The covenant is free, uniting, everlasting, well-ordered, sure, holy, and full.

Nevay identified, from 2 Samuel 23:5 and other scriptures, seven properties of the covenant: free, most-uniting, everlasting, well-ordered, most sure, holy, and most full. He devoted a sermon to each, expounding on its excellency and usefulness. The Newmilns' Covenanters, who sacrificed all, understood these properties. So should we.

Free Covenant: The "covenant the Lord makes with his people is most free": *"Ho, everyone that thirsts, come ye to the waters, and he that hath no money; come ye, buy, and eat; yea, come, buy wine and milk without money and without price"* (Isa. 55:1; see also Rev. 22:17). His offer is without conditions (Gen. 17:2; Deut. 7:7–8; 1 Sam. 12:22; Job 22:2; Isa. 42:6). Consider the following proofs of its freeness. First, all aspects of it are freely dispensed: election (Eph. 1:4), effectual calling[†] (1 Cor. 1:26–28), justification (Rom. 3:24), sanctification (Rev. 21:6), adoption (Rom. 9:25; Eph. 2:19), and all things (Rom. 8:32; 1 Cor. 2:12). Second, Scripture reveals that God takes some people, families, cities, and nations into covenant and not others. Frequently, he chooses the blind, lame, harlots, and sinners. In fact, none deserve it (Rom. 3:23). Third, "this covenant is free, in respect of its fountain and cause; it does not rise from either worth or will in us, but from the good pleasure and free love of God." Fourth, he first chose us: *"Ye have not chosen me, but I have chosen you"* (John 15:16). Fifth, the Father first freely gave our gift to the Son (Ps. 2:7–8). Sixth, "the condition is such that hinders not the freeness; yea, there is a clause put in, whereby the breach on the believer's part is made a trespass, and not a forfeiture" (Ps. 89:28–38).[67]

He made it free for these reasons: (1) to give hope to those in despair, (2) to glorify his name, (3) to make it sure to his seed, and (4) to give no excuse to those who reject it. We must recognize, *"By the grace of God I am what I am"* (1 Cor. 15:10). All is freely given: "It is like good news from a far country to a sick and sinking soul." In response, we must humbly fall at the feet of Jesus with praise: *"Not unto us, O Lord, not unto us, but unto thy name give glory, for thy mercy, and for thy truth's sake"* (Ps. 115:1). Such free love cannot but make us love him and "those who cannot recompense us"

[†] Effectual calling is the act wherein God calls the elect out of their state of sin and misery and enables them, through the work of the Holy Spirit, to embrace the gospel offer.

(Luke 14:12–14). Nevay closes, "Ah! This must be a cold world that cannot be won with the fresh and free and warm love of Jesus."[68]

Most-Straight and Uniting Covenant: It "is so straightly bound and compact, one piece of it with another, that nothing can come between, nothing can separate or loose the knot": *"Who [or What] shall separate us from the Love of Christ"* (Rom. 8:35)? Although covenant relations between men fail, God's covenant is unbreakable. In this relationship, Christ is like a friend (Song of Sol. 5:16), kinsman (Job 19:25; a kinsman is a redeemer), father (Isa. 9:6), brother (Heb. 2:11), and bridegroom (Eph. 5:25; Rev. 21:9). In this covenant union, we are "joined to the Lord in one spirit" (1 Cor. 6:17) so closely that we "come to have but one name." In short, we are the body of Christ, and he is our head (1 Cor. 12:12). Scripture speaks of this relationship using similitudes: the "foundation and the building" (1 Pet. 2:4–5), the "tree and graft" (Rom. 11:17), and the "vine and the branch" (John 15:1). Regarding this union, Christ commands, *"Abide in me, and I in you. As the branch cannot bear fruit of itself, except it abide in the vine; no more can ye, except ye abide in me ... for without me ye can do nothing"* (John 15:4–5). It is a spiritual union, wherein the two parties are one spirit. Its nearness is like a marriage covenant (Hos. 2:19–20): "It is such a love, as will be satisfied with nothing but love again: *'Let him kiss me with the kisses of his mouth'"* (Song of Sol. 1:2). In it, "there is mutual delight" (Song of Sol. 2:3–5), "heart ravishing" (Song of Sol. 4:9), "holy wondering" (Ps. 36:7), and "satisfaction as with marrow and fatness" (Ps. 63:5).[69]

Nevay ponders the implications of such a union with God: First, since we are joined in a spiritual marriage covenant with God, "every willful sin is spiritual adultery, by which the Lord's Holy Spirit is vexed" (Isa. 63:10). Likewise, bodily sins violate the temple of the Holy Spirit (1 Cor. 6:15,16,19). Second, considering how the covenant "makes a people near God, and God near them," we should "be ambitious to be within it." Third, we should "read and consider the duties" of our relationship with Christ. Fourth, persecuting those in covenant with God is a great sin: *"Precious in the sight of the LORD is the death of his saints"* (Ps. 116:15). Consider God's wrath against those who would "harm the apple of his eye" (Zech. 2:8), "pluck the lamb from his bosom" (Isa. 40:11), "pull the crown from his head" (Isa. 62:3), and "rent the seal from his heart" (Song of Sol. 8:6). Fifth, no power in this world can break our bond with Christ. Sixth, think often on the duties of the many relationships wherein we stand with God; believers "must break all relations, before they break these." Seventh, remember, *"Draw near to God,"* for those far from him will perish (Ps. 73:27–28).[70]

Eternal Covenant: We, like David, rejoice because the Lord *"has made with me an everlasting covenant"* (2 Sam. 23:5). It is a covenant of life and mercy: *"Incline your ear, and come unto me: hear, and your soul shall live; and I will make an everlasting covenant with you, even the sure mercies of David"* (Isa. 55:3). Scripture frequently attests to its eternal nature (Jer. 32:40; 33:20; Ezek. 37:26; Heb. 13:20). It is called everlasting regarding its decrees (Ps. 103:17–18; Isa. 54:9–10; Titus 1:2); its fountain (i.e., the mercy, Isa. 54:10, and love, Jer. 31:3, of God); its seed (Gen. 17:7; Isa. 59:21); and its continuance, *"Lord thou has been our dwelling place in all generations"* (Ps. 90:1). Consider the following reasons why the covenant must be everlasting. First, God is unchangeable (Mal. 3:6; Rom. 9:16). Second, Christ purchased eternal redemption for us (Heb. 9:12). Third, Christ eternally intercedes for us (Heb. 5:6; 7:25). Fourth, the Spirit daily renews us by repentance. Fifth, the things covenanted are everlasting (e.g., forgiveness, Jer. 31:34; joy, John 16:22). It must be "everlasting on our part": *"Come, and let us join ourselves unto the Lord in a perpetual covenant, which shall not be forgotten"* (Jer. 50:5).[71]

An eternal covenant is a great comfort to believers: *"The mercy of the Lord is from everlasting to everlasting upon them that fear him, and his righteousness unto children's children"* (Ps. 103:17–18). From such a covenant, we can draw "exceeding joy" from deep "wells of consolation [and] salvation." One cannot measure the goodness of such a covenant from a time-bound perspective (Isa. 55:8–9). Considering the enduring nature of God's covenant, it is a great sin to break covenant with others: "We would learn after his example to be constant and perpetual in our covenants, both with God and man,"[‡] Nevay advises. "There is a matter of fear and trembling to all who engage in this covenant: The bargain is not of time things, but of things everlasting; the matter is of everlasting concernment; it is either of everlasting life, or everlasting death" (Isa. 33:14; 54:8; Rom. 6:22). Those who enter it take comfort that it, unlike our earthly life, is lasting (Ps. 102:11–12), and it cures fear of men, *"I, even I am he that comforts you, who art thou that should be afraid of a man that shall die"* (Isa. 51:12).[72]

Well-Ordered Covenant: We, like David, rejoice in the well-ordered covenant: *"Yet he hath made with me an everlasting covenant, well-ordered and sure"* (2 Sam. 23:5). Consider how its decrees (Ps. 31:19; Isa. 64:4), parties, blessings (Rom. 8:32), manner of revelation (Jer. 3:15; 2 Cor. 4:7; 5:19; Eph. 4:30), ends (John 5:23; Eph. 1:6), security (Num. 23:19; Isa. 41:10; 42:4; Heb. 6:13–19), and rewards

---

‡ Nevay refers to the *Solemn League and Covenant* in only this one paragraph in his entire book. He argues that since they "have been honored above many nations, to be engaged solemnly with God, they should "see to the keeping" of their covenants. He contends that no earthly authority can loose these bonds.

(Prov. 11:18; Rom. 4:4–5; Heb. 10:35) are well-ordered in every respect. The reason it is well-ordered is obvious when we consider the unchangeableness (Job 23:13; James 1:17) and infinite wisdom, power (Isa. 28:29), love (1 Pet. 4:8; 1 John 4:16), mercy, knowledge (Acts 15:18), and tranquility of God.[73] Nevay offers some uses for this knowledge:

> *The depths of the riches, both of the wisdom and knowledge of God!* (Rom. 11:33).

> If it be thus ordered in all things, then is it high presumption in any to change its order; especially in the great things of the counsel and decrees of it, which they do, who make election to hang upon foreseen faith and works.

> Seek all to be within this well-ordered covenant; and then seek the things, which are promised, in the right order, and by using the means, which are commanded therein.

> The covenant is so ordered, that all the articles are linked together; so, who ever hath one of them, hath all of them.[74]

Sureness of the Covenant: Attesting its surety is that it does not depend upon man, cannot be altered because God cannot lie, and is the "result of infinite wisdom upon eternal deliberation" (Ps. 33:11). It is sure because it depends on the Lord's righteousness, justice, mercy, power, goodwill, and truth (Gen. 17:1; Ps. 31:1; 40:11; 85:9–10; Luke 2:14; 1 Cor. 1:9; 10:13; Rev. 19:11). For example, *"If we confess our sins, he is just and faithful to forgive us our sins, and to cleanse us from all unrighteousness"* (1 John 1:9). Not only has God said it (Ps. 89:34), but also he has written it down (Hos. 8:12), sworn unto it (Ps. 89:35; Heb. 6:13, 17), sealed it with sacraments (Rom. 4:11), and put the Holy Spirit in our heart as an earnest payment (2 Cor. 1:22). It is sure because *"he works all our works in us"* (Isa. 26:12). Further, if his children break covenant, he will *"visit their transgressions with the rod, and their iniquities with stripes; nevertheless, his loving kindness he will not utterly take away, nor suffer his faithfulness to fail"* (Ps. 89:28–38). It is certain. Not only will he correct us, but he will heal our backsliding also (Hos. 14:4). In short, he makes our part sure: *"I will put my fear in their hearts, that they shall not depart from me"* (Jer. 32:40; see also John 6:39–40, 44, 54; 1 Thess. 4:17).[75]

The sureness of the covenant is a "sweet comfort and strong consolation to believers." It helps us "not to judge God's purpose, by present dispensations, but by his promises": *"My flesh and my heart faileth: but God is the strength of my heart, and my portion forever"* (Ps. 73:26). Since it is sure, "We should set the things of the covenant above all the uncertain vanities of a deceitful world" (1 Tim. 6:17): "Nothing is sure but that which is ensured by the covenant." He who makes it sure, Christ, is a "nail in a sure place" (Isa. 22:23). A sure covenant "condemns the Skeptic seekers, and the Arminian indifferency, and all who turn religion into an uncertainty, and make this covenant loose and uncertain." Consider the "assurance the Lord hath given, even for the outward establishment and prosperity of the church" (Isa. 62:8–9; Jer. 32:41–42; Micah 2:12–13). In summary, the promises are sure: "Weary not in waiting for them."[76]

Holiness of the Covenant: The Covenant of Grace is a holy covenant (Dan. 11:28,30; Luke 1:72–73). Its author is holy: those near the throne "rest not day nor night, saying holy, holy, holy" (Rev. 4:8). Its parties are holy: Christ sanctifies those in him (1 Cor. 1:30); thus, his people are holy (Deut. 7:6; 28:9; Jer. 2:3). Its condition, faith, is holy (Jude vs. 20). Its promises are holy: *"He remembered his holy promises"* (Ps. 105:42). Its commandments are holy (Lev. 20:7; 1 Pet. 1:15; 2 Pet. 2:21). Its calling, by which "we must separate and touch no unclean thing" (1 Thess. 4:7; 2 Tim. 1:9), is holy. Its effect is to make a people holy (Isa. 63:18; Ezek. 36:25; 2 Cor. 7:1). Its ends, which are to let us "partake in holy things" and have fellowship with God and his church, are holy (Matt. 22:12; 1 John 1:3).[77]

Nevay offers some uses for this knowledge. First, "it is strange that men should fear so much at holiness: If the beauties of it were seen, and the blessedness to which it leads were believed, men would think a man blind and mad, that would not run after it … none ever shall taste of the better blessing of it, who come not under the condition and bond of it." Second, love of holiness is a certain mark of those in the covenant. This holiness requires that a man "set himself apart for God" (Ps. 4:3; 2 Cor. 6:17), give himself to the Lord's service (2 Chron. 30:8; Ps. 119:38), plant the "habits of grace" in his soul (John 1:16; 2 Cor. 1:21; 1 John 2:27), and practice holiness (Ps. 119:1; Isa. 35:8; Gal. 5:22–23; 1 Pet. 1:15). True holiness must be "joined with the truth," patterned after God's holiness (1 Pet. 1:16), exhibited in observance of both tables of the law (1 Thess. 2:10; Titus 2:11–12), focused towards the glory of God (1 Cor. 10:31), and evidenced by a hatred of sin (Rom. 7:24). Third, there cannot be holiness and communion with God "without conformity with God" (1 John 1:3). Fourth, of those who reject holiness in life, Christ says, "None of these men will taste my supper" (Luke 14:24). Fifth, be assured that the Lord will not break his covenant. Sixth, "holiness is and was the end for which we were taken into covenant"(Isa. 43:21; 1 Pet. 2:9) and "our evidence that we are the children of God."[78]

Fullness of the Covenant: It is a fullness that "satisfies the soul" (Jer. 31:14), which David viewed as "all my desire" (2 Sam. 23:5). All other "things are empty nothings in comparison" (Ps. 39:5) to the "unsearchable riches of Christ" (Eph. 3:8) and his covenant: "In it is that treasure hid in the field, for joy whereof a man sells all that which he has" (Matt. 13:44). How can it not be full when we consider its origin: "for it did spring from an eternal and infinite love, which neither hath brim nor bottom" (Rom. 11:33–36; Eph. 3:18–19)? How can it not be full when God engages himself "to be the believer's full reward" (Gen. 15:1)? All fullness dwells in Christ (Col. 2:9), and *"he is able to save to the uttermost all that come to God by him"* (Heb. 7:25). All his promises are abundant: pardon (Isa. 55:7), knowledge (Isa. 11:9), grace (Rom. 5:17), peace (Isa. 48:18), and joy (John 16:24). It is a light in darkness (Isa. 50:10). It is full in faith (Heb. 10:22), obedience (Rom. 16:26), and heart satisfaction. It is a fullness that lacks no good thing (Ps. 84:11): it is full of reward "given in good measure, pressed down, shaken together, and running over." It is fullness wherein our mouth cannot be opened so wide, but there is in this covenant to fill it" (Ps. 81:10).[79]

Nevay identifies several uses of this knowledge. First, if men "knew what fullness and satisfaction were in this bargain, they would quit all other bargains and engage in this" (Isa. 55:2). Second, "ministers of the letter, and not the spirit; and people resting in the letter, and not seeking to know that fullness which is in Christ and his gospel covenant, make a sad village of the visible church." Third, "if this covenant be so full, and all fullness be in it, what a sin and madness must there be in those who care not for it" (1 Cor. 4:8). Fourth, we should labor to be *"filled with all the fullness of God"* (Eph. 3:19; 4:13). Fifth, "is this covenant every way so full? Then it is worthy to be suffered for, even to the loss of all things; for, all losses are abundantly made up in its fullness" (Phil. 3:7–8). Sixth, seek its abundant fullness: *"They that seek the Lord shall not want any good thing"* (Ps. 34:9–10).[80]

Nevay also examined David's estimation of the fullness of the covenant: *"For this is all my salvation and all my desire"* (2 Sam. 23:5). Those "who desire either to enter or to abide in this covenant" must "take a full view, as David …, of all the great things in it." In doing so, they are better able "to draw in the sons of strangers to build up the walls of Jerusalem, and their kings to minister to her" (Isa. 60:10). Doing so makes your yoke easy and soul humble, and it is a "great encouragement to duty." If one took a "serious look at the great things of the covenant," it would not be possible to stand aloof from it. Nevay offers the following suggestions:

> Weakness is not from any defect in the covenant, but from the not acting faith fully on it.

We would do with the Covenant of Promises, as Abraham did with the Land of Promise, in Gen. 13:17, walk through it in the length, and in the breadth of it; we should not satisfy ourselves with the far off sights, like that which Moses had of the Land from the top of Pisgah, Deut. 34:1–2, but labor to have near hand sights, deep and narrow, most earnestly prying and searching looks; so shall we be able to know it ourselves, and to give a right verdict of it to others; for commending it to them, as David doth in this.

Learn to make this covenant all your desires; for there are in it all desirable things: Christ is in it, and he is altogether lovely, Song of Sol. 5:16, it may be expounded as well, "He is all desires."[81]

The Covenant – Its Blessings

All the blessings of the new covenant do lie in, and are conveyed unto us by promises, the chief being–I will be your God. The promises depend not upon men; they transform men into the image of Christ. The promised covenant blessings are repentance, forgiveness of sins, sanctification, adoption, perseverance, everlasting life, and temporal blessings.

God's covenant is a *Covenant of Promise* because all its blessings come to us by promises (Rom. 9:4,8; Acts 3:25; Eph. 2:12). These promises are exceedingly great and precious (2 Pet. 1:4): "One of the Lord's promises is of more worth, and much more precious, than [the] whole heaven and earth" (Matt. 5:18). Scripture also calls the covenant promises good (1 Kings 8:56; Isa. 39:8), holy (Ps. 12:6; 105:42), gracious (Ps. 45:2; Isa. 61:1,2; Luke 4:22), free (Rom. 5:15–16; Gal. 4:23,26), sure (Isa. 55:3; Rom. 4:16), rich (Rom. 9:23; Eph. 1:7; Phil. 4:19; James 2:5), and faithful and true (Jer. 10:10; 1 Cor. 1:20; Rev. 3:14).[82] God delivers blessings via promises (1) to engage fallen man to come before him with faith, patience, and humility; and (2) to manifest "his wisdom, power, goodness, and truth." This method of conveyance is of great advantage to believers: the promises that believers receive in this life are but down payments; they fully furnish them for good works; they endear them to the Lord; they provide access to his throne; and they "make man a partaker of the divine nature and to escape the pollution of the world."

Even the first promise will "make a man conqueror of hell, death, and the devil"; and even "one promise rightly apprehended, may take a man to heaven."[83] Believers should be thankful that such promises "do not depend on things to be done in time or to be performed by man": "Such doctrine as makes covenant blessings hang upon any thing in the creature, would rob the Christian of all the fair advantage, which the believer has by the promises and blessing coming in their way." Believers should treasure up the Bible's general promises (e.g., Gen. 15:1; Rom. 8:28), salvation promises (e.g., Jer. 31:31–38; 32:37–42; Ezek. 36:24–31), particular promises for times of affliction and temptation, and lastly, promises of temporal blessings.[84]

There is one promise that summarizes all the blessings of the covenant: *I will be your God.*[85] The other part of the promise, *and ye shall be my people* summarizes all the duties of Christians. It is "the great promise, the mother promise, which has all other blessings, as it were, in its womb." To Nevay, no other thing compares to this promise. First, "there is much in that of Exodus 33:19, *'I will make all my goodness pass before thee.'* O! But there is much more in this, the Father is ours (2 Cor. 6:18), the Son is ours (Hos. 2:19–20), the Spirit is ours (1 John 3:24), all things are ours (1 Cor. 3:21)." Second, there "is no rock like him" (1 Sam. 2:2), who is matchless in keeping covenant (1 Kings 8:23). Third, "He satisfies the soul with fatness, and his people with goodness" (Jer. 31:14). Fourth, to those in covenant with him, "he gives grace and mercy, and withholds no good thing" (Ps. 84:11). Fifth, to "the poor and needy who seek water and there is none," he promises, *"I will make the wilderness a pool of water"* (Isa. 41:17–18). Sixth, he will deliver us even when we go astray as sheep (Ps. 119:176). Seventh, "His betrothing is forever" (Hos. 2:20–21), and his vineyard, the church, is ours (Song of Sol. 8:12; Isa. 27:2). In short, "They are the happy people indeed, whose God is the Lord" (Ps. 33:12; 73:25).[86]

In fact, the mother promise is the unifying thread of the covenant: it is the same covenant promise made to the saints in both the Old and New Testament (Gen. 17:8–9; Lev. 26:12; Jer. 31:33; 32:36–40; Ezek. 11:19–20; 34:23–31; Zech. 13:9; 2 Cor. 6:16).[87] John Murray correctly observed that this "constant refrain," the central revelation of Scripture, depicts our "relationship with God" as "the crown and goal of religion, namely, union and communion with God." This communion is satisfied with nothing less than the promise of Revelation 21:3, *"Behold, the Tabernacle of God is with men, and he will dwell with them, and they shall be his people, and God himself shall be with them."*[88]

Nevay next addresses each of the covenant blessings, describing their precious worth and the right of believers unto them. These blessings are repentance, forgiveness of sins, sanctification, adoption, perseverance, everlasting life, and temporal blessings. It is no wonder that the Newmilns' Covenanters sought these blessings through Christ.

Repentance: The first blessing of the covenant is repentance. It "is the first thing called for in the gospel call (Mark 1:15), and it is the first gospel blessing which the exalted Prince gives (Acts 5:31)." John [the Baptist] preached it (Matt. 3:1–2), and the apostles first took notice of it in the conversion of the gentiles (Acts 11:18).

It is an excellent blessing: *"Blessed are they that mourn"* (Matt. 5:4). The following Scripture truths evidence its excellency. First, it "brings a man from a state of darkness into a state of light" (Col. 1:13; 1 Pet. 2:9). Second, the "whole blessed Trinity" works to comfort the broken hearted (Isa. 40:1–2; 61:1,3; 2 Cor. 7:5). Third, the Lord promises to dwell with and revive those *"with a contrite and humble spirit"* (Isa. 57:15). Fourth, Scripture promises the repentant great blessings. It promises joy (Ps. 126:5–6; Isa. 35:10; Luke 6:21): *"Their sorrow shall be turned to joy"* and *"their joy shall be full"* (John 16:20,24). It promises delivery from troubles (Ps. 34:17–18) and knowledge (Ps. 35:9). It promises healing: *"If my people, which are called by my name, shall humble themselves, and pray, and seek my face, and turn from their wicked ways; then will I hear from heaven, and will forgive their sin, and will heal their land"* (2 Chron. 7:14). Fifth, its alternative, impenitence, leads to a hardened heart and God's wrath. Sixth, its rarity and its opposition by Satan, who teaches men to "feign and counterfeit it," demonstrate its excellency. Seventh, it has excellent fruits: softness and tenderness of heart," "precious communion with God" (1 John 1:5–6), "burden bearing with others," and "watchfulness against sin."[89]

It is "prophesied and promised" (Jer. 50:4–5; Ezek. 20:43; 36:26; Zech. 12:10). Repentance must come through God's grace. It "is not only that which advances the work of conversion, but the whole almost of it; at least, it ends in it, 'Repent and be converted'" (see Acts 3:19). Scripture promises conversion (Isa. 1:27), sorrow for our sins (2 Cor. 7:9), contrite hearts (Ps. 51:17), abundant pardon (Isa. 55:7), and comfort (Isa. 57:18); these require repentance. In summary, gospel repentance is a promised blessing: *"To appoint unto them that mourn in Zion, to give unto them beauty for ashes, the oil of joy for mourning, the garment of praise for the spirit of heaviness; that they might be called trees of righteousness, the planting of the LORD, that he might be glorified"* (Isa. 61:3).[90]

True gospel repentance is most sorrowful of the fact that our sins have wronged and dishonored God and Christ's precious blood, person, and interest; and it produces in us "not only a dislike, but a perfect hatred of sin" and a departing from it. When Satan tells us that our sins are too great for repentance, remind him that Christ died "to give repentance to such an one as I am." Remember, "repentance is a gift, so it should be taken when it is offered."[91]

Any distortion of the biblical model of faith and repentance presents a great hazard to the church. For example, the practice of the Covenanters of listing the sins and defections of the day is admirable, yet there is a danger in any approach taken to excess. Calvin expresses the real hazard:

> For, while they are wholly occupied with the enumeration of their sins, they lose sight of that lurking hydra, their secret iniquities, and internal defilements, the knowledge of which would have made them sensible of their misery. But the surest rule of confession is, to acknowledge and confess our sins to be an abyss so great as to exceed our comprehension. On this rule we see the confession of the publican was formed, "God be merciful to me, a sinner" (Luke 18:13). [92]

Forgiveness of Sin: The second blessing of the covenant is forgiveness of sins. Its biblical name means taking off a heavy burden (Hebrew) or letting a guilty man go free (Greek). In forgiveness, God covers over (Ps. 32:1), blots out (Isa. 43:25), and pardons (Ps. 32:2) our sins, casting them behind his back (Isa. 38:17) into the depths of the sea (Micah 7:19), to be no longer seen (Num. 23:21) or found (Jer. 50:20), even upon diligent search. Nevay depicts the state of the unrepentant, "Sin un-repented covers and darkens the soul, like a thick cloud (Isa. 44:22), and covers, as it were, God with a cloud, that prayer cannot pass through (Lam. 3:44), but sin, when it is once pardoned, the cloud is dissipated."[93]

It is an excellent blessing, which Scripture refers to as *blessedness* (Rom. 4:6–8). From it all the other blessings spring: "All the good that Christians do get by believing is put down under that one word, *remission of sins*" (Acts 10:43). Its excellency is seen in its author, Jesus, and its fountain, grace (Exod. 34:6; Rom. 8:32; Eph. 1:7; Titus 2:12). Its excellency is also seen in the free (Isa. 48:9, 11; Rom. 5:16), full (Ps. 86:5, 15; 103:3), and unmerited nature of remission of sins, which is a wondrous blessing, considering the depravity and great evil of sin against God. Sin defiles, debases, and separates us from God (Isa. 59:1-2); it turns blessing into curses (Mal. 2:2) and deprives us of all good things (Jer. 5:25). Yet, God pardons and heals even backsliders (Ps. 145:14; Jer. 3:22; Ezek. 34:16; Hos. 14:4). [94]

It is a promised covenant blessing. In fact, it is among the chief articles of the covenant (Jer. 31:34; 33:8; Ezek. 36:25, 29), wherein he *"pardons the iniquity and passes by the transgression of the remnant of his heritage"* (Micah 7:18). Its promised nature is evident when we consider how God, the *Father of mercies* (2 Cor. 1:3), pardons sinners because Christ paid the price. In short, "there is no way to save sinners, but by forgiveness of sin." It is Christ's office to pardon freely (Isa. 55:1; John 7:37), wherein *"the Son quickens whom he will*; and the first quickening is a pardoning mercy"* (John 5:21). Evidencing the unlimited nature of his pardoning mercy is his command "to forgive one another, even *until seventy times seven"* (Matt. 18:22).

The right understanding of forgiveness has several uses. First, "it speaks against the Papists who assert a forgiveness of the fault and not the punishment." Second, it is a "comfort to doubting Christians: free forgiveness does take away sin, so as if it had never been." Third, "without reconciliation, there can be no blessing, and without remission [of sin] there can be no reconciliation." Fourth, given that all blessing depend upon it, we must possess it. Although Christ purchased it, it requires repentance, and it does not free us from the consequences of our sins in this life. It is also helpful to acquire a fresh sense of forgiveness when old sins "rise up on us like ghosts of dead men." Fifth, we rest assured that sins are pardoned when we (1) walk in his covenant (Ps. 103:17–18), (2) esteem him highly (Luke 7:47), (3) die to sin (Rom. 8:13), (4) "mourn for Christ pierced" (Zech. 12:10), (5) forgive others willingly (Matt. 6:14), (6) confess our sins freely and fully (1 John 1:9), and (7) possess a holy fear of God (2 Cor. 7:1). Sixth, those who think their sins too great for forgiveness should take comfort from Scripture: *"Come now, and let us reason together, saith the LORD: though your sins be as scarlet, they shall be as white as snow; though they be red like crimson, they shall be as wool"* (Isa. 1:18). Seventh, it is a gift from God, without which there is neither peace nor blessedness. God sees all our sins. Hence, we must search, acknowledge, and confess our sins, "bringing Christ as the undertaker, and the price of redemption, to the Father. Eighth, the promise requires duty: *"Walk before Me and be thou perfect"* (Gen. 17:1).[95]

Imputed Righteousness: The third blessing of the covenant is the imputed righteousness of Christ. As an act of mercy, "God made Christ, who knew no sin, to be sin for us" (2 Cor. 5:21); hence, "his righteousness is by covenant made over unto us and so imputed unto us" (1 Cor. 1:30). This process takes place in the following steps: First, we are by nature sinners, deserving of God's wrath. Coming to understand this, we judge ourselves condemned, with no ordinary possibility of saving ourselves from "a sin-revenging God." Our best acts of self-justification are "but glittering sins" that are an "abomination in the sight of God" (Luke 16:15b) and are but filthy rags, which we use to cover our nakedness before God, as Adam and Eve did with fig leaves. Second, from the offer of the gospel, we learn that the "sins of self-lost sinners are all charged upon Christ, as many as shall believe in his name," because he sacrificed himself for our sins, paying the penalty due for our sins in full. Third, we learn that by the covenant made between Christ and the Father it was "agreed that when [Christ] should offer up his soul for sin (and in contemplation thereof) he should see his seed, and travail of his soul, and be satisfied" (Isa. 53:10,11). Fourth, we learn "that whosoever by faith should consent to this bargain, [Christ's] payment should be counted theirs, and his purchased righteousness made over to them." Fifth, "the poor sinner, taking notice of all this and of the well-ordered covenant, in all the articles thereof, and of Christ in the heart of it, as mediator and surety, he takes hold on it by faith and casts himself on Christ for righteousness ... [giving] up himself to Christ, not only as Jesus but as Lord also." Sixth, then imputation of righteousness occurs:[96]

> When it is, the Father as judge pronounces the sinner free, seeing no iniquity in him, for he has pardoned it, and accepted him in the beloved (Eph. 1:6) for he finds him in him, wholly and completely covered with his elder brother's garment ... He is now found of God in Christ, *not having his own righteousness, which is of the law, but that which is through the faith of Christ, the righteousness which is of God by faith* (Phil. 3:9). And so, the righteousness of God, so called in Romans 3:5, 21, 22, does become the righteousness of the saints (Rev. 19:8), thus Christ's righteousness imputed, making us in the covenant sense, the righteousness of God.[97]

Imputed righteousness is an excellent blessing: First, it is the righteousness of Christ, the lamb without spots (1 Pet. 1:19), rather than the righteousness of man, which is like filthy rags. Second, consider its qualities: it heals (Mal. 4:2); it is as pure as fine linen; it is beyond measure; and it protects like armor (2 Cor. 6:7). Third, consider its excellent effects: it makes us at peace with God, breeding "peace and quietness within us": *"the work of righteousness shall be peace; and the effect of righteousness quietness and assurance for ever"* (Isa. 32:17). Where there is righteousness and peace, joy follows (Rom. 14:17). Christ promises those who possess it a crown of righteousness (2 Tim. 4:8). Fourth, "the excellency of this righteousness appears in Satan's malice against it: there is no point of truth more contradicted than this, of free justification by the imputed righteousness of Christ." Fifth, it is "the whole substance of the Gospel[98]Righteousness is a promised covenant blessing and a great comfort to the church. When the Bible speaks of the "gift of God," it speaks of his righteousness (John 4:10), which is like living water. Jeremiah promises that the church will call on the *"Lord Our Righteousness"* (Jer. 23:6), which is Christ's name: "He spreads it as his banner, and she wears it as her crown" (see Song of Sol. 2:4; 3:11). Daniel prophesies an everlasting righteousness, which will *"make an end of sin and make a reconciliation for iniquity"* (Dan. 9:24). Christ's righteousness is made the righteousness of his people by covenant (Isa. 49:8; 1 Cor. 1:30; 2 Cor. 5:21); this righteousness is by faith.[99]

Those without it will be "found naked in that day of their appearing before God." Those with it need not fear man's judgment, for they look to the Lord as their judge. The blessing is only to those who desire it greatly: *"Blessed are they who hunger and thirst after this righteousness, for they shall be filled"* (Matt. 5:6 NKJ). Such righteousness is truly a covenanted blessing that provides a "strong defense against temptation" and allows "bold access to God": "When they have put on Christ and his righteousness, how boldly may they step forward? For, there is nothing that can be laid to their charge, for God hath justified them (Rom. 8:33). If there be any after failings, they have an advocate with the Father (1 John 2:1)."[100]

Sanctification: The fourth blessing of the covenant is sanctification. According to Scripture, faith and works are inseparably related. True faith leads to a new creature transformed by the renewing of his mind unto delight in obedience to the law written in his heart (Rom. 7:22; Eph. 4:23; Col. 1:13; 3:10):

> By this work of sanctification, there is a disposition and inclination in the heart, mind, and will to do what is commanded; and the heart thus stamped, doth sway and turn about the whole man to the work and ways of obedience and sanctification; so as all who see the man, may clearly discern him to be a changed man, by his life and conversation.[101]

It is an excellent blessing. It "will make a holy man not only blessed in himself but [also] a blessing to others" (Gen. 12:2). It "makes not only promises but [also] commandments the sinner's delight" (Ps. 119:92, 143), and it breeds peace (1 Thess. 5:23). It conforms us to the image of God, and it "makes our souls live the life of God." Sanctification produces holiness, which "is the most excellent blessing because all promises, which have all the blessings in them, are annexed to it." Those with it receive "showers of blessing," whereas the throats of those without it are like "open sepulchers" (Ps. 5:9). The holiness derived from sanctification "is profitable to all things" (1 Tim. 4:8), and it makes all things pure and clean to those that possess it (Titus 1:15).[102] Evidencing its excellence, the standard of holiness is perfection (Matt. 5:48; 1 Pet. 1:16).

Holiness, resulting from sanctification, is a promised covenant blessing from God: "neither the herb of grace nor of holiness grows in man's garden but comes from above" (James 1:17). God promises to sanctify (Lev. 20:7-8) and establish unto himself a holy people (Deut. 28:9)—*"a kingdom of priests, a holy nation"* (Exod. 19:6). He promises to put his Spirit within them, giving them a new heart, which has the law and the fear of God within it (Jer. 31:33; 32:40; Heb. 8:10; 10:16; Ezek. 36:25–27). The promise is for corporate as well as individual sanctification: *"For then will I turn to the people a pure language, that they may all call upon the name of the LORD, to serve him with one consent"* (Zeph. 3:9). The promise is for a people who will walk in his statutes (Ezek. 36:27) and speak no lies (Zeph. 3:13). Regarding this promise, consider how God has chosen (Eph. 1:4) and redeemed (Luke 1:75) us, providing all things necessary for godliness (2 Pet. 1:3). Consider how essential holiness is for God's honor (Ezek. 36:20–21) and communion with him. Consider how God has sworn it, Christ suffered and prayed for it, and the Holy Spirit works to produce it within us. Since it is the work of God, be assured that he will not neglect it. Recognize that "by the covenant, we shall be a people made ready for God (Luke 1:17) and a bride, adorned for our husband Christ (Rev. 21:2), and none of these can be without holiness; so, if the one be promised, the other is also promised."[103]

Nevay proposes several uses for this knowledge. First, since sanctification "is no easy work," we should "make it our business to have it and to increase it." Second, as believers increase in holiness and perfection, sin becomes more apparent: "O! But sin has an ill-favored face to a spiritual and rightly discerning eye; purity brings peace, but there is no peace to the wicked; they are like the troubled sea, when it cannot rest, whose waters cast up mire and dirt." Third, even if believers lose all earthly possessions, they should take comfort knowing, "They are well clothed with humility and holiness; and they are well fed, who have it their meat and drink to do the will of their heavenly father." Fourth, be confident that God will not neglect his covenant promise to make the desolate wilderness of our souls to "blossom abundantly" (Isa. 35:2). Fifth, if we wonder "why we have so little holiness, we are too little in fetching it from the promise; we pump dry cisterns."[104]

The significance of sanctification is evident when we consider that Nevay preached almost one-half of the fifty-two sermons, covered in a later chapter, on this topic. The hallmark of the Puritans was an emphasis on Christ's transforming work of sanctification. "If it does not grow, it is because it does not live," they contended.[105]

Adoption: By nature, "we are born under the curse" and are "children of the flesh." Fortunately, the state of believers changes when they "receive the spirit of adoption," and become "heirs of God and joint heirs of Christ" (Rom. 8:17). The word *adoption* is a legal word that "signifies the taking of one from one family, and planting him in another."

Once believers accept "the righteousness of Christ, they are instantly adopted and owned by the Lord as dear children," who cry "Abba Father" (Rom. 8:15). They, as David, stand in amazement at adoption: "Who am I, or what is my life, or my father's family in Israel, that I should be son-in-law to the king" (2 Sam. 7:18)?[106]

It is an excellent grace when "we consider it in the low state from which the believer is taken, or the high state to which he is raised." The excellency of this high state is evidenced by its (1) dignity, (2) liberty, and (3) privileges:

> Through adoption, we acquire the **dignity** of kings, priests, conquerors (Rom. 8:37), sons of God (John 1:12; 2 Cor. 6:18), and bride of the king's son (Matt. 22:2). We enter into "fellowship with the Father and the Son, and with all the royal company of believers (1 John 1:3), and with all the holy prophets, apostles, and martyrs." What greater dignity is there than to have the Holy Spirit dwell within you and to dwell in God (1 John 4:13)?[107]

> Adoption "sets us **free** of the basest captivity and slavery that ever was; it brings us from under the captivity of sin and Satan." It frees us from *"that spirit of bondage, which is unto fear"* (Rom. 8:14, 15), and from bondage to men (1 Cor. 7:23). It upholds us with God's free spirit, for "which David did beg" (Ps. 51:12). Those free in Christ are *"free indeed"* (1 John 1:3).

> Through it, we receive the high **privilege** of becoming "children of the most high," and we become "partakers of the divine nature" (2 Pet. 1:4). These privileges include taking on Christ's name (Isa. 63:19), bold access to the throne of God through prayer (Eph. 3:12), loving correction from the Father (Lam. 3:31; Heb. 12:6), admission to church ordinances, and the "protection of our heavenly father." God "gathers his own, as the hen does her chickens, under his wings" (Matt. 23:37). In short, it is an excellent privilege to be "heirs of all the promises."[108]

As evidenced by the above-mentioned Scripture, adoption is a promised covenant blessing. For further proof, consider the many promises he makes to his people: to be their father (Jer. 31:9), to give them a spirit of grace and supplication (Zech. 12:10), and to give them heaven as an inheritance (1 Pet. 1:4). Given our nature as "children of wrath," the gift of adoption must be a promised blessing.[109]

Reflection upon adoption helps Christians to "settle their hope, banish their fear, quicken their love, and found their patience and perseverance." Those who possess the grace of adoption have three marks: (1) a spirit of grace and supplication, (2) a spirit of faith and repentance that manifests itself in prayer, and (3) an honoring of God as the Father (Mal.

1:6). Those with these marks should seek to preserve the dignity, "improve the liberty," and use the privileges of adopted children of God.[110]

Perseverance: Perseverance is the "crowning blessing" because "it is only they that endure to the end that shall be saved." Scripture expresses perseverance in a variety of ways: "abiding in Christ" (John 15:4); "dwelling in God" (1 John 4:13); "fighting out the good fight of faith" (2 Tim. 4:7); "working out our salvation in fear and trembling" (Phil. 2:12); "having our work abiding" (1 Cor. 3:14); and "being confirmed to the end" (1 Cor. 1:8). Scripture also expresses it as continuing "in his Word" (John 8:31), "in the faith and profession of the same" (Acts 14:22), "in the grace of God" (Acts 13:43), "with Christ in his temptation" (Luke 22:28), and "in the hope of the gospel" (Col. 1:23). Christ only abides in those who abide in him and continue in his word; only those that do so are his disciples; only they will bear fruit.[111]

It is an excellent blessing. Those who "dwell in the courts of God are blessed": *"[Wisdom] is a tree of life to them that lay hold on her, and happy is every one that retains her"* (Prov. 3:18). Those without it can have no other blessing or happiness; they are "like the dog turning to his own vomit" (2 Pet. 2:22). It is the essence of the Christian trial (1 Pet. 1:7) and the means by which our strength is renewed and Satan is bruised (Rom. 16:20). Perseverance "is every grace acting to the uttermost." In it, we make "the hope of glory lively" and "our souls the bride adorned for the lamb." To those who overcome, it is promised that they will *"eat of the tree of life"* and *"hidden manna"*; will have the *white stone, white raiment,* and the *new name*; will *"overcome the second death,"* will not have *"their name blotted out"*; and will *"sit with Christ on his throne"* (Rev. 2:1–3:21).[112] Its excellent reward is salvation (Matt. 10:22). The best mark of salvation is perseverance, wherein we are "made partakers of Christ" (Heb. 3:14).[113]

Scripture, from its very beginning, presents perseverance as a covenanted and promised blessing: *"The seed of woman shall bruise the serpent's head"* (Gen. 3:15). This treatment continues throughout Scripture: those *"planted in the house of the Lord shall flourish in the courts of God"* (Ps. 92:13–14); they are as *"a tree planted by the river of water"* (Ps. 1:3) and a *"house built upon a rock"* (Matt. 7:24). Believers *"are kept by the power of God though faith unto salvation"* (1 Pet. 1:5); *"he is able to keep them from falling"* (Jude 1:24). For further proof, consider God's plan of election (Rom. 8:28,30), Christ's intercession on our behalf (Rom. 8:34–35), his promises not to forsake us (1 Sam. 12:22), his sealing of us in the spirit (Eph. 4:30), and his promise of a crown to those that persevere (Rev. 2:10). Because "there is no steadfastness in man," Christians should take comfort in their "inseparable union with Christ"

(Hos. 2:19), God's unchangeable nature and love (Mal. 1:6; John 13:1), his ever-lasting covenant promises (Isa. 54:9–10), and his pledge that nothing can separate us from his love (Rom. 8:35).[114]

Nevay identified several uses of these doctrines. First, perseverance requires "not only beginning well, but a running to the end, notwith-standing all the storms that blow." However, it is "not of ourselves; it is of God, and Christ dwelling in us." Hence, "we must move, being moved," as if in a race to obtain the incorruptible, triple crown of right-eousness, life, and glory (1 Cor. 9:24–25; 2 Tim. 4:8; James 1:12; 1 Pet. 5:4). Second, if we are not in a state of grace, nothing will abide (1 Cor. 3:15). Third, if perseverance is blessed, then consider "how cursed a thing it is to perse-vere in evil" (Ps. 68:21). Fourth, the chief cause why people do not perse-vere is that "they do not know how excellent a thing perseverance is" (Job 17:9). Fifth, those without it are unstable in all their ways (James 1:8). Sixth, those who desire it "must hold it by rooted principles of real grace, such as faith, love, etc., and maintain it by daily begging influence of assisting grace (Eph. 6:10) and supply of the spirit of Christ" (Phil. 1:19). They must "keep good watch over the heart" (Prov. 4:23), "be much in prayer" (Eph. 6:18), maintain good purposes and zeal (Gal. 4:18), beware of insincere repentance (2 Cor. 7:10), practice self-denial, keep an "eye on the Lord's coming" (James 5:9), and "be ever pressing forward" (Phil. 3:13–14). Seventh, it is not possible for the saints to fall away: "the seed remains" (1 John 3:9).

Eighth, the marks of perseverance are "an earnest endeavor to perse-vere," an "acting and walking by inward principles of rooted grace," a conscientious use of the "means of perseverance," a "heart hatred and real abhorrence" of the works of those "who turn aside" (Ps. 101:3), a "holy fear" made "captain of the watch," a daily progress, a resolution against temptation and for dependence on God, a "forgetting of things that are behind," and a crucifixion of self to the world (Gal. 6:14).[115]

Everlasting Life: It is "pleasures evermore" (Ps. 16:11). It is "that blessed estate wherein perfect knowledge and full enjoyment of God is attained, when we shall see face to face, and know as we are known" (1 Cor. 13:12). It is called the "blessed hope" (Titus 2:13) and can only be known through Scripture because "*the eye has not seen, nor ear heard, neither has it en-tered into the heart of man, the things which God has prepared for them that love him*" (Isa. 64:4; 1 Cor. 2:9).[116]

It is an excellent blessing. Scripture refers to it as an excellent glory (2 Cor. 4:17; 2 Pet. 1:17), beyond our understanding. In eternal life, we are "freed of all evil" (Gal. 1:4) and "personally united to the Son of God"; we have the nearest union, fellowship, and marriage communion with him (John 17:21; 1 Cor. 1:9; Heb. 2:16; Rev. 21:9). No longer will "we be hindered by the body in its actings." Our "vile bodies shall then conform to Christ's glorious body" (Phil. 3:21). The Son shall introduce us to the Father: *"Behold I and the children whom thou has given me"* (Heb. 2:13). We shall see with our own eyes "the sight of God in Christ" (Job 19:27; Isa. 33:17) and forever have delightful "communion with an ever present God" (Prov. 8:31). We will have eternal fellowship without weariness with the "company of angels and saints" (Heb. 12:23), which we "will meet in perfect love, never to be scattered or parted."[117]

It is a promised covenant blessing: *"Thou wilt show me the path of life: in thy presence is fullness of joy; at thy right hand there are pleasures for evermore"* (Ps. 16:11). The covenant is a covenant of life (Mal. 2:5), which is the end of Christ's redemption (2 Tim. 1:10). Eternal life is the end of our calling and justification, and it is the aim of holiness, sanctification, repentance, and faith (Acts 11:18; Rom. 6:22; Titus 3:7; 1 Pet. 1:1,3–5). Christ is its author (1 John 5:20); the Holy Spirit is its worker (John 4:14); and God is its reward. To Christ is promised an "everlasting kingdom and priesthood" (Ps. 110:4; Dan. 7:13–14), and "everlasting righteousness" is promised to us through him (Dan. 9:24; Rom. 5:20). The "God of the living" promises through his grace to reward some with eternal life, wherein death is no more (Ps. 31:15; Hos. 13:14; Matt. 22:32; Rev. 21:3).[118]

Nevay suggest we put this knowledge to use. First, we should highly prize eternal life, and the ways and means thereunto, being "accurate, exact, and zealous" in its pursuit. Second, all those who have not forsaken sin and closed with Christ will be outside this estate: *"Without are dogs"* (Rev. 22:15). The sad truth is that many "take great pains to go to Hell." Third, the marks of those with eternal life are (1) a willingness to make Moses' choice (Heb. 11:25–26); the possession of a lively and purifying hope (1 Pet. 1:3; 1 John 3:3); a heart that seeks Heaven and rests on free justification; a conversation evidencing "the kingdom within"; and spiritual works done for God's glory.

Fourth, we should live and die as heirs of grace, seeking "not great things here, but the things of eternity" (Jer. 45:5). Fifth, we should "pity those who have great portions of the world, and want [lack] this." Sixth, Nevay ponders, "how many are they, who, though they be and abide within the pale of the visible church, live as without it." Seventh, those who desire eternal life and who understand their great distance from Heaven should look to Christ (Acts 5:31), pleading themselves "heirs of that righteousness which is by faith" (1 Tim. 6:12; Heb. 11:7). Then, by walking in Christ (John 14:6) and daily studying to loose themselves from the world, they should seek his guiding counsel (Ps. 139:24; 143:10), "be willing to endure much for it" (Rom. 8:18), labor to keep a good conscience (Acts 24:15-16), and "exercise their graces on the things of eternity, faith, hope, love, patience, etc."[119]

Nevay's teachings on the blessing of eternal life were not in vain as evidenced by the dying testimony of John Nisbet, who considered it his greatest treasure:

> Now, being in such a case of communion with him, I am pained till I be freed of the remains of a body of sin and death, till I be freed of the world and all things therein, and also of this natural life, and be possessed of himself and with himself in his eternal inheritance, which is incorruptible, undefiled, and that fadeth not away.... O to be there where I shall sin no more, where I shall be tempted no more, neither feel any more of his hidings, the withdrawings of the Spirit's presence, and light of his glorious countenance, but shall be ever with him, see him as he is, and serve him for ever and ever![120]

Temporal Blessings: Temporal blessings "are common favors, which the Lord dispenses unto all": *"The Lord is good to all: and his tender mercies are over all his works"* (Ps. 145:9). Covenant seekers have the added blessings of "freedom from external evils" (Ps. 34:4, 19) and "enjoyment of all good things" (1 Tim. 6:17).[121]

Temporal blessings "are good blessings in themselves, but more excellent when given out of the Father's hand." Such "treasures ... cannot be exhausted." They are part of Christ's purchase and are "bands of love" (Hos. 11:4), which hold forth God's glory. They are given to "lead us to repentance, life, and health" (Rom. 2:4); as "helps to cheerfulness of service" (2 Cor. 9:7); and "treasures out of which charity may dispense." Although God gives temporal blessings to all mankind, to believers they are covenant blessings, from which believers extract more sweetness and use to nobler ends than do non-believers.[122]

God promises them as part of the covenant to those who keep his covenant (Lev. 26:3-11; Deut. 7:12-13; 8:18; Ps. 111:5; Ezek. 34:25, 27; Hos. 2:18, 21-22). God promises to free us from evil (Ps. 91:10; 121:5-7) and preserve us when afflicted (Jer. 30:17; 2 Cor. 1:5). Temporal blessings are dispensed according to our need (1 Pet. 1:6), ordered to our manifold good (Deut. 8:2-3; Rom. 8:28; Heb. 12:9-10), and measured to our strength (Jer. 46:28; 1 Cor. 10:13). As our Father, he knows our needs; he gave us Christ and all things (Matt. 6:32; Rom. 8:32). He "made his covenant with the whole man" (Matt. 22:32; 1 Cor. 6:20). Take comfort that he considers it a great sin to neglect one's dependents (1 Tim.

5:8). The Lord is good: *"He is good and does good"* (Ps. 119:68). Consider his temporal blessings as a down payment for better things.[123]

Nevay suggests we put this knowledge to use. First, Christians should not measure their blessings by common blessings. Second, those, particularly those outside the covenant, who do not use their blessings to God's glory may find them a curse rather than a blessing (Mal. 2:2). Third, those who vow to maintain poverty mock God's blessings. Fourth, *"For thou shalt eat the labor of thine hands: happy shalt thou be, and it shall be well with thee"* (Ps. 128:2). Fifth, learn to consider them as "a fountain opened for us in the blessed heart and side of Jesus." Sixth, take comfort that God promises temporal blessing (Ps. 37:25). However, if we lack these things, we may find the reason in the breach of God's covenant (Jer. 5:25). Seventh, those "who would have temporal blessings, especially those who would have them blessings indeed, must go in to the Covenant, and fetch them from it," following Christ's example in prayer (Matt. 6:11; see also Jer. 31:12; Luke 15:17). In doing so, we come to understand the necessity to "obey and serve God, keep covenant with him, and depend upon him" (Ps. 37:3; Isa. 1:19) for everything. Remember that he best knows our needs and only promises "that which is necessary and suitable" (1 Tim. 6:8). Eighth, "we must think of serving God, not with the inward man only, but with the outward man also, because we hold both of God."[124]

Many modern Christians dismiss dependence on God for temporal blessings as unspiritual. This is unfortunate, as Andrew Gray observes: "It is easier to trust Christ for eternal life [i.e., spiritual promises], than to trust him for our daily food [i.e., temporal promises]."[125]

The Fruits and Means of Sanctification: The fruits of sanctification are peace, assurance, joy, comfort, and communion with God. The means of sanctification are hearing the Word, observing the sacraments, prayer, and praise. Brief summaries of Nevay's sermons on these subjects are included in subsequent sections of this book.

The Covenant – Its Means

All the great things of the covenant are conveyed through Christ, the only mediator between God and man. As mediator, he fulfills the threefold office of prophet, priest, and king.

Christ "is the one and only mediator betwixt God and man" (1 Tim. 2:5); through him are conveyed all the "great things of the covenant." Nevay discusses this topic under five heads.

First, all covenant transactions are by a mediator who performs a four-fold work of redemption: (1) enabling man to enter into covenant

with God, (2) molding "his heart to accept it" (Gen. 9:9; Acts 11:21), (3) enabling him "to perform the duties of the covenant" (Ezek. 36:26-27), and (4)
bringing him to "glory, and to be where Christ is" (Heb. 2:10). It is only
possible to go to God "in the hand of a mediator" who is united with
both parties.[126]

Second, a mediator is "a middle person dealing between two parties
who are at odds." Hence, "reconciliation by a mediator" requires an ini-
tial fellowship, a breach, a struggle for unity, and mutual reconciliation.

Third, Christ is the mediator because only Christ, as "both God and
man," can "deal betwixt God and man." The mediator is fully God (1)
to bear the burden of wrath (Rom. 1:4), (2) to pay the price (Acts 20:28), (3) to
give his Spirit (Gal. 4:6), (4) to conquer Satan (Luke 1:68-69), and (5) to give
salvation and rest (Heb. 4:8-9). The mediator is fully man (1) "to undergo
the law" (Gal. 4:4), (2) to intercede in our name (Heb. 1:3), (3) to be a merciful high priest (Heb. 4:15), and (4) to "make way for our adoption" (Gal. 4:5).
Only Christ, a completely innocent person, is pleasing to God, and so
enables our acceptance. He, like Moses, "went up alone into the mount."
He is the Word made flesh, "and so, our God and our kinsman." Only
he is able "to save to the uttermost" (Heb. 7:25). Hence, "we should never
go to God without him," asking all things in his name (John 16:23-24). This
doctrine rebukes those who would call on God in any other name: it is
futile to call on God in the name of Mary, saints, or angels; for the dead
are ignorant of us and can not redeem us (see Isa. 63:16).[127]

Fourth, only Christ the mediator can perform the duties of his three
offices. As prophet, he "reveals his Father's will"; he "alone knows the
mind of the Lord, and we must have it from him" (Deut. 18:15; John 1:18; 3:2,
13; Acts 3:22; 1 Cor. 1:24; 2:16; Heb. 3:1). As priest, he "reconciles us who were
alienated, and enemies in our mind, in the body of his flesh and death,
to present us holy" and blameless to the Father (2 Cor. 5:19; Col. 1:20-22; Heb.
7:16-19). As king, he governs us and deals with all matters concerning our
salvation. He "not only rules in the kingdom of men for his church (Dan.
4:17), but [also] he rules in his church and sits upon the throne of his father David" (Luke 1:32). His universal kingdom extends through all ages,
is over all men, and is "over all things to his church" (Dan. 7:14; Matt. 22:42-
44; Eph. 1:21-22). His eternal kingdom "is to be considered as more special
and inward, over souls and consciences," and it "brings eternal happiness and peace to all that are in it" (Dan. 2:44; Rom. 14:17; Rev. 1:18). When we
accept his Lordship and "employ him in all things," it is like having "the
mind of God concerning the way of salvation."[128]

Fifth, from before time (Rev. 13:8), the Father appointed (Heb. 3:2), furnished, solemnly invested (Isa. 61:1), and sent forth (Heb. 10:5) Christ to serve as mediator. Christ carries out this work by serving as judge (John 5:22), messenger (Mal. 3:1), surety (Heb. 7:22), "king, head, and husband; and appearing still as king and advocate." Hence, we can put our trust in a covenant drawn up by such a friend.[129]

The Covenant – Its Duties

God requires that we be his people. This requires that there be a real and cordial divorce from sin, an actual closing with Christ, a yielding of ourselves to and dependence on God, and making full use of the covenant promises for our sanctification and the glory of God.

Just as the "blessings of the covenant are comprised in one [promise], *I will be your God*; so, all the duties of the covenant are summarily comprehended in that one [promise], *You shall be a people unto me*" (Jer. 31:33). This requires nothing short of being perfect in our walk before God (Gen. 17:1); "serving God without fear in holiness and righteousness"; and living in a "soberly, righteously, and godly" manner.[130]

The first great duty: Our duty under the covenant is to "enter into it, every one personally, and churches as churches." Consider how "Israel solemnly enter[ed] this covenant" (Deut. 29:10–12), and how "the good kings of Judah renew[ed] it often after a breach." Scripture promises and commands us to enter into a covenant relation with God: *Thou shall call me, My Father, and shall not turn away from me* (Jer. 3:19). *They shall call upon my name, and I will hear them: I will say, "It is my people"; and they shall say, "The Lord is my God"* (Zech. 13:9). *I entered into a covenant with thee, says the Lord God, and thou became mine* (Ezek. 16:8). Therefore, the Lord's people must "particularly and personally enter into covenant with him and own him." The "end of the covenant is to make us a special people" (Lev. 20:6; Deut. 7:6), and he commands us to be so: *"You shall be my people."* This "mutual and nearest union and communion" requires an "actual closing with him [Christ] in Covenant": "He must be in us, and we in him" (John 17:21). For this purpose, "He is given for a covenant to the people" (Isa. 42:6). To not close with him in covenant is rebellion: *"For it is his commandment, That we should believe on the name of his Son Jesus Christ"* (1 John 3:23).

Nevay expounds the what, how, and why of this duty to close with Christ, for which there is no substitute.[131] He first explains *what* it means to enter into covenant with God.

234 Lessons from the Covenant

1. There "must be a real and cordial divorce from all these things that hinder closing." In short, we must give a "bill of divorce ... to the world and to sin." This is a "comfort to those who have been so humbled, as to see their desperate condition in following their old lovers." Although "this divorce will not be so full and formal, until we be brought to Christ," it must be "desired, resolved, and endeavored," leading us to divorce "all other husbands" (2 Cor. 11:2).[132]

2. There "must be an actual closing," evidenced by four acts of faith: (1) There must be "assent to the truth of the promise: *whosoever believes in Christ shall not perish, but have eternal life*" (John 3:16). This assent includes *"believing all things which are written in the Law and the Prophets"* (Acts 24:14). (2) We must not simply believe; we must also "receive Christ's power" and "become children of God" (John 1:12). This requires that we embrace "the promise and Christ in it" by "an opening of the heart" (Acts 16:14), a "reaching forth of the hand, a laying hold on eternal life" (1 Tim. 6:12), and "a hungering and thirsting after righteousness" (Matt. 5:6). (3) We must rest on the promise and trust in the Lord as commanded in Psalms 2:12 and 37:5. We should "adventure, like drowning men, on the cord of the promise, when we are like to perish in the deep." (4) We must act in full assurance because "not closing fully is as good as not closing at all." Without full closure, we "utterly disable ourselves from doing duty; like a member out of joint; acting without life and strength." We must not hold back in thinking our sins are too great because "the greater the sinner be, the Lord has the greater advantage of glory" (Ps. 25:11; 34:6).[133]

3. There must be "resignation, a yielding of ourselves to God." We must give "ourselves to the Lord," offer "ourselves a living sacrifice to God" (2 Chron. 30:8; Rom. 12:1; 2 Cor. 8:5), and recognize that *"My beloved is mine and I am his"* (Song of Sol. 2:16).[134] This is a terror and a curse to those who are deceivers (Mal. 1:14).

4. There must be "dependence on God" in "faith, hope, love, and patience." There must be "a forgetting of our father's house (Ps. 45:10–11): All our vessels must hang on Christ (Isa. 22:24), and we must abide by" him (Hos. 3:3). Those "who desire to maintain and keep themselves within the Covenant ... must maintain a dependence upon him as Lord."[135]

How: Entering must be "done with knowledge" (Jer. 31:34; Hos. 2:20) because God rejects "blind and lame sacrifices" (Deut. 15:21). Do it willingly with the whole heart (2 Chron. 15:15); "clearly, expressly, distinctly" (Ps. 16:2); and "with good advice and upon mature deliberations, as in the building of a house, or the making of war" (Luke 14:28, 31). Do it irrevocably (Heb. 10:38), completely, and with the "whole soul, body, and spirit." Nevay contends that the reason for "lifelessness and backsliding" in our Chris-

tian walk is due to "some crack or unsoundness in our manner of closing." Therefore, those "who have it yet to do" should "go about it in the
right manner, with fasting and prayer."[136]

Why: There are many advantages in entering God's covenant. It sets
our soul "free of sin's dominion" (Rom. 6:14) and brings us into "near union and communion with God" (John 14:23). It provides us with help (Ps.
89:19, 26), sure deliverance (Ps. 91:14–16), comfort (Ps. 91:12), freedom from
anxiety (Phil. 4:6), freedom from fear and doubting (Matt. 14:31), guarding
against temptation, all the blessings of God's covenantal care, and simply all things (1 Cor. 3:21–23). The best cure for doubting is an "acting
faith." Those that do not close with Christ are "under the power of corruption," thus subject "to every temptation." They are "full of anxiety
and fears," living "in estrangement from God" and without "the least
part or interest in Christ and promises." Worse, "delay does daily disable
them more and more." Do not wait; follow Eliphaz's advice to Job: *"Ac-
quaint thyself now with him, and be at peace; thereby shall good come to thee"* (Job
22:21).[137]

The second great duty: Those who enter God's covenant are obligated to make full use of the promises contained in the covenant. Nevay
proposes three ways to improve or to make use of the covenant.

First, *make use of the promises, Christ, and God.* It is a Covenant of Promise (Eph. 2:12) made to "children of the promise." First, we must "study to
know them." Table 10.4 provides examples of covenant promises.[138] Second, "we must [also] mind and remember them: promises are our fundamental rights; [it is] as good not to know them at all, as to not remember them" (Heb. 12:5). Right remembering requires that we esteem,
lay up (Job 22:22), and live by these promises: "Practice is the best art of
memory." Third, not only must we remember them, but we must also
apply them, as did the apostles and the patriarchs. Application "involves
receiving (John 1:12), eating and drinking (John 6:53–54), opening (Song of Sol.
5:2)," and "reaching forth and pressing toward the mark (Phil. 3:13–14)." In
application, our soul pursues the Lord (Ps. 63:8), determined to bring
"home Christ to our mother's house" and "to not let him go" (Song of Sol.
3:4). Fourth, right application requires "serious thoughts on the Word,
prayer to have it revealed, comparing it with our case, resting upon it…,
and an eye both to the condition and the duty." It also requires that we
"apply general promises particularly (1 Kings 8:37, 40; 2 Chron. 20:8, 10) and particular promises generally," where appropriate (Josh. 1:5–6; Heb. 13:5). It requires that we "look upon promises to be performed in their due order
and subordination" (Jer. 29:10, 12; Ezek. 36:37; Matt. 6:33) and "make promises

both the ground and rule of prayer" (Gen. 32:9,12). In prayer, "temporal things are only to be sought conditionally" (Mark 10:30).[139]

Table 10.4
Types of Promises

Types of Promises	Illustrative References
Original Promises to the Son	Ps. 2:6–10; 110; Isa. 42:1–9
Mother Promise	Ezek. 36:28
Promises of Son	Isa. 9:6
Promises of Spirit	Luke 11:13
Great Gospel Promises	John 3:16
General Promises	Ps. 84:11; Rom. 8:28
Absolute Promises	Jer. 31:31–35; 32:38–41; Ezek. 11:19–20; 36:25–29
Conditional Promises	Isa. 45:25; 55:1–6
Particular Promises	Many for particular cases (e.g., Prov. 3:9–10)

Make use of Christ, for "he is given for a covenant to us" (Isa. 49:8). We must make use of him "in his names and titles" (Isa. 9:6), natures (Titus 2:13; Heb. 2:17), covenant relations (1 Cor. 1:30), offices (Isa. 55:4; Micah 4:2; Eph. 5:25; Heb. 2:11), and his resurrection (Rom. 8:34). Remember, Christ is "not only as the object of our faith" (1 John 3:23) but also "as author and finisher of it" (Heb. 12:2); hence, we must "make use of him for all the promises; for they are yea and amen in him" (2 Cor. 1:20). In particular, we must make use of promises for entering (John 10:7), abiding (John 15:7), and obtaining all spiritual (Eph. 1:3), temporal (Prov. 3:16), and eternal (John 10:28) "blessings of the covenant."[140]

Make use of the Father. This requires that we "make use of the mother promise to the full" as God reconciles (2 Cor. 5:19), draws (John 6:44), justifies (Rom. 8:33), adopts (2 Cor. 6:18), sanctifies, and glorifies us (Rom. 8:30). Make use of all of his attributes and "all the works and ways, in and by which he manifests himself" (e.g., word, Ps. 119:58; worship, 138:2; works, 145:17). In short, "make use of God": *For that which is impossible with man is possible with God"* (Luke 18:27). This must be done "boldly, yet with humble fear" (Isa. 25:9; Eph. 3:12; Rev. 14:7). Pray Augustine's prayer, "Give, Lord, what thou craves, and crave what thou will."[141]

Second, *formally engage in the covenant.* We must formally make use of the covenant "as a mutual stipulation and engagement; remembering how by it the Most High stands engaged to us, and we to him." Strive to use the covenant in all its properties (e.g., it is free, so quit self-righteousness; it is sure, so keep hope in all situations). All "God's promises call for our duties, and our duties are first his promises" (Ezek. 36:27).[142]

Third, *make use of its ends.* We must make use of the covenant for "all salvation," spiritual and temporal (Ps. 27:1-2, 9), and for all our desires (Ps. 38:9). First, our chief desire should be the glorification of God, which requires full use of the covenant: *"Having therefore these promises, dearly beloved, let us cleanse ourselves from all filthiness of the flesh and spirit, perfecting holiness in the fear of God"* (2 Cor. 7:1). Second, our focus should be the "enjoying of God, union and communion with him." Third, it is necessary to "fetch contentment from the covenant" to obtain a "contented estate" (Phil. 4:11). Fourth, grateful should we be for "how highly he esteems his people, as a peculiar treasure" (Exod. 19:5; Song of Sol. 7:6; Isa. 62:3; Lam. 3:24; Ezek. 7:20; Zech. 9:16; Mal. 3:7; Rom. 8:17). Consider the great end of the covenant:

> Consider how the great end of the covenant is to make God ours, and all in him for us; his love, for our comfort; his truth, for our assurance; his power, for our protection; wisdom, for direction; holiness, for sanctification; and to make Christ ours, all in him, his mercy, merits, and his all sureness; and all the Spirit ours, his workings, sealings, and fellowship.[143]

Nevay reproves those who pretend an interest in the covenant, yet do not seek to improve their covenant relationship with God. For example, to those who plead, "It is worse with me than with others," Nevay counters, "Every saint must choose his own, rather than another's cross, for another's cross would not fit him so well." To those who consider their service useless to God, Nevay replies, "Remember how there is a reward for being faithful in little" (Luke 19:17). To those who would wait until they are in a more settled state, Nevay answers, "Men in the most settled estate in this world are but vanity" (Ps. 36:5). To those who plead that the Lord does not hear them, Nevay advises, "Even the silent workings of the heart are loud murmurings before the Lord." In short, we are without excuse.[144]

In summary, we must "learn to improve the Covenant," especially in three areas: (1) "as a bridle to restrain and keep us from sin, and as a bond unto duty" (Lev. 18:4; Josh. 24:17-18; Ezra 9:13); (2) "for the aggravating of sin" (Amos 3:2; Rom. 2:4); and (3) "for the praises of God" (Isa. 60:6; 1 Pet. 2:9).[145]

The Covenanters referred to this duty as "closing with Christ," upon which topic Andrew Gray preached many sermons. Gray warned that once we close with Christ, we must not let go of (Song of Sol. 3:4), disturb (Song of Sol. 3:5), or limit (Song of Sol. 2:7) him. Instead, we must make use of him (Job 23:3), keep nothing from him (Job 23:4), enjoy him (Song of Sol. 8:1), and walk humbly with him (Micah 6:8).[146] Those within the covenant should take comfort knowing, "There is not a duty that is required of a Christian, but is converted into a promise."[147]

Interestingly, Gray preached only two years before his premature death. Any who read his sermons will never use a short time available as a reason for not obeying God's call.

The Covenant – Those outside It

In 2 Samuel 23:6–7, David calls those outside the covenant the "sons of Belial" and describes how they live in a "dangerous and desperate estate." Whoever *"shall touch them must be fenced with iron, and with the staff of a spear; they shall be as thorns thrust away, and utterly burnt in the same place."* The covenant promises are a "terror to all Sons of Belial, who are kings in their will, and slaves to their will, both at once."[148] They are aptly called "thorns" because they are cursed (Gen. 3:18; like Idumea, the people of the Lord's curse in Isa. 34:5); "they are forever pricks and thorns to the people of God" (Josh. 23:13); "they stop and choke every good motion, and motion for good"; and "their ground bears nothing but thorns."[149] They "are men with whom is no dealing"; "there is no taking them with hands."[150]

Covenant keepers have nothing to fear from the sons of Belial, because Satan's power is nothing compared to that of God. Although these thorns "cannot be taken with man's hands, yet the Lord can grip and handle them to purpose."[151] The focus of believers should be on the covenant promises and not on the thorns: "The word of promise is good company, and the breast of the everlasting covenant are so full, as we may milk out abundantly from them, and be delighted with the abundance of glory" (see Isa. 66:11).

James Nisbet, in his memoir, ponders the destiny of those in this desperate estate:

> O! How much more shall it be so in hell, where the furious rebukes of a holy and sin-revenging God shall set the gnawing edge of their own consciences ever awake, to be a never-dying worm within them, through that eternity which shall never have an end! Upon all which considerations, how great and manifold are the obligations that the poor lost sons and daughters of Adam lie under, who win to any measure of a well-grounded hope of enjoying union and communion with God through Christ ...[152]

11

Lessons for the Church

Let my tongue cleave to the roof of my mouth, if I remember thee not; if I prefer not Jerusalem above my chief joy. –Ps. 137:6

L esson #2: *The church must re-establish unity in truth as attained during the Second Reformation and the apostolic era.* The Scottish Confession of Faith identifies three marks of the true church: (1) true preaching of the Word of God, (2) right administration of the sacraments, and (3) ecclesiastical discipline uprightly administered.[1] Unity in truth requires a church possessing these marks. The following sections examine how the Scottish church treasured and distinctly displayed these marks.

The Word – Marks of the Church

T hese marks share a common foundation, the Word of God, and a common purpose, the preservation of unity in truth. They roughly correspond to the three offices of Christ: prophet, priest, and king. They represent the most foundational aspects of doctrine, worship, and government. They reflect the three imperatives of the Great Commission: making disciples, baptizing believers, and teaching all that Christ has commanded (Matt. 28:19-20). Unfortunately, the various confessions and creeds of the Reformed churches differ concerning these marks. Calvin and the modern *Book of Church Order* for the Presbyterian Church in America identify only the first two of these marks; nevertheless, the absolute necessity for discipline is implicit.[2] The *Westminster Confession of Faith* and *Catechisms* list only one mark embodied within the definition of the visible church, which "consists of all those throughout the world that profess the true religion, together with their children."[3] The "profession of the true religion," in the words of James Bannerman (1807–1868), "is the one essential mark of the true church."[4] Despite the apparent contradiction, these declarations concerning the marks of the church agree.

The application of the marks depends on the sense in which they are applied and on the meaning of the terms.

First, application depends upon the sense in which the word *church* is used. Scripture uses the term *church* to mean either (1) all those that profess belief and their children (visible church), (2) the elect (invisible church), (3) particular churches, (4) associations of particular churches, or (5) church officers representing church members.[5] James Bannerman, a nineteenth century Scottish minister, correctly insisted that Scripture applies the term *church* in all these senses; however, the Presbyterian system is the only one true to all five. The Congregational churches speak only of the church using the second and third senses, whereas Catholics speak only of the church using the first, third, and fifth senses.[6]

The modern use of the word church to refer to *denominations* has no scriptural warrant. In Scripture, an association of particular churches *under a common government* existed in each major city. Collectively, these churches, united in the profession of the true faith, constitute one true church, the bride (not the brides) of Christ. Hence, the right question is whether a particular church is part of the true church. Although a particular church or denomination may not be part of the true church, many of its members may be part of the invisible church.

Second, "what is essential to its existence as a church is something very different from what is essential to its perfection as a church."[7] No church is perfectly true. James Bannerman applied the test for a true church in a two-step fashion. One must first acknowledge all that profess the true religion, which would have excluded the Catholic Church in his day and many Protestant churches in our time.

He applied a more rigorous test for joining in "union or cooperation" with other churches. For Bannerman, union was not possible with any church if it would require the adherence to or the practice of something unlawful in doctrine, worship, or government. For example, he could not join with either the Congregational churches or the Church of England because it would require him to serve under a church government not sanctioned in Scripture. The lax doctrine, "a creed that is wide enough to cover both Romanism and Rationalism," of the English church posed yet another barrier. The question of whether his church, the Free Church of Scotland, should unite with the Church of Scotland was more complex. Both churches shared sound practices in doctrine, worship, and government; they differed on the question of patronage (state financial support of the church). The Confession is silent on patronage, but Bannerman considered it an evil. Although he would agree to church union under protest, he would refuse to be an officer in a church that endorsed patronage.

Third, although "inner" spiritual matters are more important, the "outer" ordinances are important. In general, *ordinances* are the "outward and ordinary means whereby Christ communicates to his church the benefits of his mediation" and his covenant. Examples include preaching of the Word, observance of sacraments, prayer, thanksgiving, church government and discipline, religious fasting, oaths and vows, psalm singing, catechizing, collecting money for the poor, dismissing people with a blessing, and ordaining church officers.[8] The Scottish Covenanters, as evidenced by the last testimony of James Wood, were willing to lay down their lives for any of the ordinances: "That however there be some more precious ordinances [than church government], yet that is so precious that a true Christian is obligated to lay down his life for the profession thereof."[9] All are necessary for the church to achieve its purpose, "the gathering and perfecting of the saints."[10]

Although necessary, none of these outward ordinances has any value apart from Christ and his Word. Thus embodied within the one mark, *true faith*, are all the ordinances. Since perfect observance will not be upon this earth, one must not judge a church that does not practice all of these ordinances as apostate. The *Westminster Confession of Faith* asserts, "Particular churches ... are more or less pure, according as the doctrine of the gospel is taught and embraced, ordinances administered, and public worship performed more or less purely in them."[11]

Fourth, more than outward observance is required in a true church; Christ must be present. James Ramsey (1814–1871), an American minister, deduced two marks of the true church from the two symbols (candlesticks and stars) associated with the seven churches in the Book of Revelation. He derived the first mark from the candlesticks: "The golden candlesticks and their *lights* represent the church as holding forth by her organizations, ordinances and holy example, the word of life in a dark world."[12] The light can continue to shine only as the church depends upon an external source of light, Jesus Christ. If it merely possesses the outer form of a candlestick, it is not a true church. It shines brightest when the church bases its every utterance and practice, particularly its worship, solely upon Scripture, and when its members live "a holy life exemplifying the truth."[13] Although many of the seven churches evidenced numerous visible defects, the presence of Christ's light marked them all as true churches.

Ramsey derived the second mark from the stars held in Christ's right hand: "The stars ... represent, not the light the church gives or the influence she exerts, but that which the Lord gives to her." He has vested "that *authority* ... in messengers raised up and sustained by His right hand, as walking in her midst He cherishes and brightens the flame of her example and teaching." The light of the stars is in no way derived from or dependent upon the church or its members; it derives its "light and influence from Christ alone." Each church has one messenger, representative of its officers and ministers who derive their authority from Christ alone: "Surely that society can have no claim to be part of the visible kingdom of Christ, which does not acknowledge Him as head, by submission to His sole authority." Church officers must "act as deputies of the King, teaching and enforcing nothing but what He commands, and all that He commands." Christ upholds them in His right hand. Church members are accountable to elect officers who evidence the gifts and qualifications outlined in Scripture. The emphasis is on the function rather than on the officeholder.[14]

Last, compliance with the Word is the only useful measure for each of these marks. The evidence of Christ's presence is the Word dwelling among us. The terms (e.g., *sacraments*) have no meaning apart from the Word. The greatest desire of the true church is to mold itself in consistency with the Word. The true church forever presses *"until we all come in the unity of the faith, and of the knowledge of the Son of God, unto a perfect man, unto the measure of the stature of the fullness of Christ"* (Eph. 4:13).

The Word – Preaching Commanded

True preaching involves conveying the whole counsel of God with zeal, sincerity, and knowledge to expose man's sinful condition, to communicate the only cure (i.e., Christ), and to explain the duty required of Christians. It must be within the context of public worship.

James Nisbet remarked that his desire to hear the true Word preached by faithful servants of the Lord made his "bowels to roll within" him.[15] It was this true preaching of the Word that persuaded James Nisbet to return to the established church. This fact notwithstanding, he observed in the established church a decline, which has continued to this day, in the true preaching of Word and purity of doctrine. He noted that "where ministers are and have been most straight in their judgment to the received principles of the covenanted Church of Scotland, in doctrine, worship, discipline, and government, and are most godly and exemplary in their lives and conversations, there the gospel had the most flourishing success." Nevertheless, James's decision to join a church that lacked perfect purity is consistent with that of the great reformers and principles of the Second Reformation. Although the established church had rejected the *Solemn League and Covenant* and many of the attainments of the Second Reformation, James had no choice but to join with it because it bore the marks of the true church. In doing so, James did not reject the fundamental principles of the Second Reformation. What he did reject was any attempt to place the *Solemn League and Covenant* on the same level as Scripture.

However, there is no doubt that most of the ills of the modern church are traceable to the departure from the ideals of the Second Reformation. The writings and sermons of Covenanting ministers such as Nevay, Gray, and Durham provide many lessons regarding preaching that would greatly benefit the modern church. Nevay emphasized that not only must the Word be preached, but it must also be spoken, sung, and heard.[16] James Durham, a contemporary of Nevay, in his *Commentary Upon the Book of Revelation* identified "some general observations concerning preaching," which are summarized in the following sections. Andrew Gray, who preached only two years before his death at age twenty-four, left a lasting legacy of sermons that emphasize the necessity to close with Christ. In examining these sermons, we readily observe six principal marks of the Covenanting Preachers.

The Scope–The Whole Counsel of God: The sermons of the Covenanting ministers were true to the Word.

First, the Word was their guide. John Knox in his paraphrase of Deuteronomy 4, boldly declared that the church must use the Word as its foundational guide: "Not that thing which appears good in thy eyes, shalt thou do to the Lord thy God, but what the Lord thy God has commanded thee, that do thou: add nothing to it; diminish nothing from it."[17] Illustrative of the application of this principle is their attitude toward idolatry. To Knox, idolatry was any "worshipping of the mind or brain of man in the religion of God." This includes any belief that "our own inventions" are "righteous in the sight of God, because we think them good, laudable, and pleasant." It also includes any "honor and service of God not commanded by the express Word of God."[18] He based this belief on God's displeasure with Saul's sacrifice at Mount Gilgal (1 Sam. 13:8-14), Saul's refusal to destroy the sheep and oxen of the Amalekites (1 Sam. 15:13-23), and Nadab's and Abihu's offering of strange fire (Lev. 10:1-7). In all cases, the offenders offered sacrifices to God based on their own judgment rather than on God's Word. Knox reminds us to heed the admonition given to Joshua not to "alter one jot, ceremony, or statute, in all the law of God, nor yet to add thereunto, but diligently to observe that which was commanded."[19]

Second, the covenanting ministers held forth the entire gospel message in every sermon. Durham observed that this was the pattern of Christ: "We see that our Lord Jesus puts together an entire mold of the whole doctrine and practice of godliness, giving as at one view, a sight of our natural sinfulness and hazard, and of the way these may be remedied." Likewise, in the sermons of the apostles, "the sum of the gospel is usually comprehended."[20] The framework of Covenant Theology, as discussed in the previous chapter, relates all aspects of the gospel message.

Third, they preached both the Old and New Testament. According to Durham, "the Law and the Gospel should be preached and pressed together."[21] One of the important differences between historic and modern Reformed preaching is the modern neglect of the Old Testament and Covenant Theology. Many think it enough to be New Testament Christians! As evidenced by Nevay's sermons, the Covenanters believed that the Covenant of Grace is the gospel and is the same covenant in both the Old and New Testaments.[22] To them, a "proof out of the Old Testament is as much gospel if rightly applied, as any in the New Testament."[23] This emphasis on the Old Testament is consistent with Christ's teaching (see Matt. 5:17–18). Many Christians argue that the final authority is Christ rather than Scripture, and so judging to receive "only what is in harmony with his life and teachings." J. I. Packer rightfully argues that this position is flawed: "If we reject his [Christ's] attitude to the Old Testament, we are saying in effect that he founded Christianity on a fallacy."[24] Calvin emphasizes the necessity to base doctrine on both testaments more directly: "Let this then be a sure axiom—that there is no word of God to which place should be given in the church save that which is contained, first, in the Law and the Prophets; and Second, in the writings of the Apostles."[25]

Fourth, they preached sound doctrine. To Gillespie and "all Protestant orthodox writers," the maintenance of the true doctrine and faith was "made one, yea, the principal mark of the true visible church." Preaching without sound doctrine is futile. Forsaking the way of truth will cause us to "wander from mountain to hill, and forget our resting place" because "one error breeds a hundred, and a hundred will breed ten thousand." We must "prove all things" by searching Scripture and by being "vigilant"; for once we turn aside from truth, we are like a man in quicksand: "The more he wrestles out the more he sinks." Gillespie warned: "Men are sooner drawn from truth than from error." He echoes Paul's warning that those heresies *"which are approved may be made manifest among you"* (1 Cor. 11:19). According to Gillespie, "Heresy is a gross and dangerous error, voluntarily held and factiously maintained by some person or persons within the visible church, in opposition to some chief or substantial truth or truths grounded on and drawn from the Holy Scripture by necessary consequence."[26] Gillespie defined fundamental truths as "all such truths as are commonly put in the confessions of faith, and in the more full and large catechisms of the Reformed churches." Although Gillespie did not consider all who err from the truth to be heretics, he thought that the "most damnable heretic" is one who claims to subscribe to no confession other than Scripture, but "who yet will not subscribe to all truths which necessarily follow from the words of Scripture."[27]

In a letter to his old congregation in Berwick,[28] Knox admonishes that "if in any of the chief and principal points any man vary from that doctrine which ye have professed, let him be accursed." Specifically, he lists—

If any man teaches any other cause moving God to elect and choose us than his own infinite goodness and mere mercy;

If any other name in heaven or under heaven wherein salvation stands but only the name of Jesus Christ;

If any other means whereby we are justified and absolved from wrath and damnation that our sins deserve, than by faith only;

If any other cause or end of good works than that first we are made good trees, and thereafter bring forth fruits accordingly;

If any teach prayers to be made to others than to God alone;

If any mediator betwixt God and man but only our Lord Jesus;

If more or other Sacraments be affirmed or required to be used than … Baptism and the Lord's Table or Mystical Supper;

If any deny remission of sins, resurrection of the flesh, and life everlasting to appertain to us in Christ's blood, which, sprinkled in our hearts by faith, doth purge us from all sin, so that we need no more nor other sacrifices than that oblation once offered for all, by which God's elect be fully sanctified and made perfect. If any, I say, require any other sacrifice to be made for sins than Christ's death, which once he suffered, or any other manner whereby Christ's death may be applied to man than by faith only, which is the gift of God, so that man hath no cause to glory in works; and yet if any deny good works to be profitable as not necessary to a true Christian profession, let the affirmers, teachers, or maintainers of such doctrine be accursed of you, as they are of God, unless they repent.

Regrettably, many modern Protestant denominations have abandoned even these essential doctrines. Without these principles, the modern ecumenical movement is doomed. Attempts to water down these principles, such as basing salvation on "faith" rather than "faith alone," are likewise doomed. Rutherford defined fundamentals not simply by creeds, which express the object of our faith, but also by the objects of our hope (e.g., according to the Lord's Prayer), and by the objects of our "love to God and our brethren" contained in the Decalogue.[29]

Fifth, they were committed to continual reformation. A church that thinks it has attained perfection in doctrine deceives itself; a church that does not uphold its doctrine deceives others. Until this century, the Church of Scotland required officers to own, believe, assert, maintain, practice, and defend the "whole doctrine."[30] In contrast, the Presbyterian Church in America (PCA) requires officers to receive and adopt the "system of doctrine." Neither approach is perfect. The proper approach should combine the adoption of the whole standard with the demand that it be continually subject to scriptural validation. In such an approach, one must list any exception, promise not to teach it, and work diligently to resolve any conflicts through study of the Word and the church courts. The church must confess "only what is jointly declared or approved."[31] True reformation requires continual comparison of practices and doctrines with the Scripture. We should put into practice the pledge of the six Johns who drafted the *Scottish Confession of Faith* to revise our confessions if ever proven inconsistent with the Scripture. To settle on any one standard with no possibility of revision is to place that standard on the same level as Scripture. On the other hand, the Westminster Standard has proven itself over several centuries, and history has proven that any revision of it, no matter how seemingly well-intended, leads to the neglect of important aspects of God's truth.

In summary, the sermons of the Covenanters were true to the Word. Many martyrs, like John Nisbet, confirm these principles in their dying testimony: "I die adhering to the Scriptures of the Old and New Testament as the undoubted Word of God, an unerring rule of faith and manners, and a firm foundation for principle and practice in the ways of godliness and true holiness." He also declared his belief that the West-minster standards embody the doctrine contained therein.[32]

The Method – with Zeal, Sincerity, and Knowledge: The preaching style of the Covenanting ministers, especially the Protestors, provides a pattern that modern ministers should examine. Alexander Smellie ably described the stark contrast between the preaching style of the Protestors and the Resolutioners:

> But formerly [Smellie refers to the bland and precise preaching of the Resolutioners] there was a dissonance in uttering it which grated on the ear, and almost made the gospel harsh. Now the speaker [a Protester] feels no down-dragging influences of Calvinism; he does not measure his syllables lest he should render the grace of God too large and too accessible; he soars away and aloft, like a lark … or like the angel of Bethlehem, throbbing with uncontrollable gladness as he publishes his message, 'Behold, I bring you good tidings of great joy, which shall be to all people.'[33]

Durham provides several recommendations regarding the method of preaching:

> Sermons should follow the pattern of the Epistles where all has the "divine stamp," presented in "an orderly method," and with a "style of speaking [that] is sweet and heavenly, yet plain and familiar."[34]

> A minister should be "zealous to get his message received; and, in sum to get them saved; therefore weightily does he follow it, inviting, exhorting, pressing and protesting as unwilling to be refused." He should have "a single serious desire to have them gathered and espoused to Christ."[35]

> Sermons should be delivered "boldly and authoritatively" as the "Lord's message." They "should be undertaken and begun with an eye on God" and "the weight should be still left upon the Lord." Only the Holy Ghost "can make it effectual."[36]

Sincerity, zeal, and knowledge were trademarks of the Puritan and Covenanter preachers. Knowledge is the language of the mind; sincerity is the language of the conscience and heart; and zeal is language of the will. James Melville (1535–1617) observed that even near the end of Knox's life his preaching "was so active and vigorous that he was likely to beat the pulpit in pieces, and fly out of it."[37] In contrast, James Durham and Jonathan Edwards calmly delivered their sermons to equal effect. What do these approaches have in common? *The messenger in all the cases believed the message with all his heart and with no apologies. They* preached Christianity on the offensive with sincerity as in the sight of God (2 Cor. 2:17).[38] They aimed the arrows from their bows right at the heart of Satan–laying their shield aside to pull back the string with more force.

Such vital preaching requires a knowledgeable and an educated clergy. One of the causes for the failure of English Presbyterianism was the fact that non-conformists were deprived of university education for decades following the Restoration.[39] Iain Murray stresses the important role of educated ministers in the Reformation:

> It was the authority of true doctrine which shook the whole structure of the Papacy in the sixteenth century and emptied the Roman church of multitudes of adherents; it was from the prayerful study of such doctrine at the Colleges of Edinburgh, Glasgow, and Cambridge that the men who preached in the revivals of the seventeenth century came.[40]

The Problem – Man's Sinful Condition: It was James Nisbet's humble desire that ministers "insist on showing people their lost state, and the great necessity of their recovery there from."[41] Luther encourages ministers to follow the pattern established by Paul who began his Epistle to the Romans by "rebuking the gross sins and unbelief that are plainly evident."[42] To Luther, the first duty of a preacher is "to rebuke and to constitute as sin everything that is not the living fruit of the Spirit and of faith in Christ, in order that men should be led to know themselves and their own wretchedness, and to become humble and ask for help."[43]

James Durham encouraged ministers to follow the example of Christ by tailoring their message to the particular needs of the hearers. For example, the Church of Laodicea, which was free (since not charged) of "errors in doctrine or gross scandal in practice," most needed the medicine concerning "the nature of the covenant and justification by Christ":

> The beating down of error and the banishing of gross profanity are but, as it were, the taking in of the outworks of the devil's kingdom; therefore, when these are gained, the main batteries are to be directed against self-righteousness, hypocrisy, presumption, self-confidence, etc. that the soul may be brought to receive Christ in earnest, and zealously and seriously to study holiness without which a formal profession will be but a stone of stumbling.[44]

Durham offered other recommendations (abridged) to preachers concerning the focus of their sermons:

Ministers "ought to conform themselves to the case of the church and persons to whom they preach." It "is more difficult … to reprove one that is godly, or to withstand one Peter, than to threaten or contend with many that are profane."[45]

Sermons should be "leveled at hearers, so as to make them know that it is they who are reached."[46]

Ministers should strike at errors that are gross in nature, have hurtful consequences, and are "presently troubling the church."[47]

"If we look to our Lord's practice while in the flesh, we do not find him more frequent on any subject than this, viz. That the way to heaven is narrow, that many were first that shall be last, that hypocrisy should be guarded against."[48]

"The Lord does not insist upon the most high, sublime, and obscure things.… He presses the most plain, obvious, and incontrovertible duties of religion, viz. repentance, self-examination, faith, zeal."[49]

Ministers should follow the example of Christ's preaching to Laodicea where he "opens their sinful, dangerous and hypocritical case"; "batters down the ignorant self-confidence"; "proposes the right remedy"; clears up the "terms upon which the gold and white raiment is obtained"; and "most sweetly, and yet vehemently presses it."[50]

The Remedy – Closing with Christ: Ministers must communicate the necessity for sinners to close with Christ.[51] To communicate the gospel effectively, it is essential that the message extend beyond the mere communication of doctrine by trained ministers. It is essential that both the desperate reality of man's condition and the incomparable excellency of Christ be communicated and contrasted. Few were better at this than Andrew Gray. According to William Tweedie, all of Gray's sermons led to Christ: Gray "does not preach about Christ, but preaches Christ himself." Likewise, Jonathan Edwards, who contended that the hearer must "see the proper foundation of faith and trust with his own eyes," echoed this emphasis on the incomparable value of Christ. This is essential because "It is the sight of the divine beauty of Christ that captivates the wills and draws the hearts of men," and "is the beginning of true saving faith in the life of a true convert."[52]

The sermons of most Puritans express this view of Christ's beauty. John Flavel asserted, "Jesus Christ is the loveliest person souls can set their eyes on."[53] John Owen proposed, "No man shall ever behold the glory of Christ by sight hereafter, who doth not in some measure behold it by faith here in this world."[54] This view of Christ's beauty is what James Nisbet saw when he heard James Renwick in the rain and John Anderson in the pulpit. Moreover, it has captivated my attention as I gaze at the work of Christ visible in the cloud of witnesses who occupied Scotland in the sixteenth and seventeenth centuries.

The Result – Application of the Word: The richness of the Covenanters was not only in doctrine preached but also in doctrine applied. To them, sanctification was as important as salvation because one does not exist without the other. Because of their great emphasis on sanctification, the entire next chapter is devoted to this topic. James Melville remarked concerning Knox's preaching: "When he came to application, he made me so thrill and tremble, I could not hold a pen to write."[55] Calvin stressed the importance of application: "To doctrine in which our religion is contained we have given the first place, since by it our salvation commences; but it must be transfused into the breast, and pass into the conduct, and so transform us into itself, as not to prove unfruitful."[56] Nevay closed each of his sermons by listing several specific ways for believers to apply the sermon. Durham provides several recommendations (abridged) to preachers concerning application:

> The main qualifications of a minister are rightly to divide the Word and to manage any universal applications thereof with "spiritual wisdom and prudence." The minister must intermix reprobation and approbation to strike at the hypocrite, yet avoid injuring the tender soul or hardening the secure.[57]

> The "application should be pathetic, pungent and weighty, according to the matter pressed, so it may have weight upon the conscience of the hearers." This requires that it "should not rest in the general; for the Lord is particular in all the Epistles" by specifically mentioning and giving evidences of sins, particularly inward sins.[58]

> Ministers should square their application "to the edification of the hearer" and "should not be addicted to, nor always dwell upon one thing."[59]

The Context–Worship: Preaching is most effective within the context of public worship, followed by private worship and meditation. To the Puritans and Covenanters, preaching was the central element of worship. There is no substitute for vital preaching, public worship, and proper observance of the Sabbath: "The welfare of the entire nation would stand or fall with the use or abuse of this holy time."[60] Such worship requires speaking, singing, and hearing of the Word.

First, they spoke and meditated on the Word. It is hard to find a better example of speaking the Word than to read the words of James and John Nisbet, or any other Covenanter for that matter. John Nisbet makes no apology for citing a seemingly endless list of proof text for every proposition in his dying testimony:

> Let none reflect upon me for citing so much, for the Scripture hath been to me from my youth the living oracle of his divine and sacred lips. When I was crying, "What shall I do to be saved?" and when I was saying, "How shall I know the way of the Lord, that I may walk therein?" then his Word was "a light to my feet, and a lamp to my path," exhorting me as it is in these Scriptures (Isa. 55:1–8; Jer. 3:13–14, 22–23; 31:18; Hos. 14:1; John 6:35; Rev. 3:20; 22:17).... When I was grappling with sin, Satan, and the world, and my own wicked and deceitful heart, the grand enemies of my salvation, His Word was as props and pillars to me.[61]

The Word was constantly on the lips of these Christians. Their language is reflective of the love relationship portrayed in the Song of Solomon, which was the source of many sermons from this era. For example, Andrew Gray contended that "the Christian must endeavor to kiss and embrace—the mouth of Christ, the hand of Christ, and the feet of Christ: the kissing of the feet importing the exercise of love, the kissing of his hands the exercise of subjection, and the kissing of his mouth the exercise of communion and fellowship with him."[62] To the Covenanters, this book allegorically depicts the love relationship between Christ and his bride, the church. Modern commentaries avoid or misinterpret the book as a glorification of sexual love. For evidence of this shift in interpretation, please see the radical difference between the footnotes in the original *Geneva Bible* and the *New Geneva Bible*. Those who doubt the allegorical interpretation should read James Durham's or Matthew Henry's (1662–1714) commentaries on this book; then read Psalm 45, rich in the symbols of the Canticle, and Psalm 46, a song labeled for "virgins," used by Luther for his most famous hymn. It will remove all doubts. Is it possible that one of the reasons for the failings of modern Christianity is that it either misreads or ignores one book in the Bible?

Further, they meditated upon the Word. The Puritan Thomas Watson, citing the example that "the beasts under the law which did not chew their cud were unclean," reasons that those who do "not chew their cud by holy meditation are to be reckoned among the unclean." He argued, "Meditation is like a soaking rain that goes to the root of the

tree and makes it bring forth fruit." The "holy fire of meditation" is the
means by which we warm our souls and by which the impression of divine truths is stamped upon our heart. It produces reformation: *"I
thought on my ways and turned my feet unto thy testimonies"* (Ps. 119:59).[63]

Second, in addition to speaking and meditating on the Word, they
sang the Word. In 2 Samuel 23:1, David is referred to as the "Sweet
Psalmist of Israel."[64] The book of Psalms was a great comfort and joy to
the Scottish martyrs, and study of the Covenanting martyrs inevitably
leads the student to a cherished enjoyment of Psalms. The French martyrs of this era were so devoted to singing psalms that their executors slit
their tongues to keep them from singing on the way to their death. In
fact, "the singing of Psalms is a practice of the purest times of the
church; it is recorded in Acts.... And in all times of persecution under
heathen emperors, their great and frequent exercise was singing of
Psalms."[65] William Binnie observed that the "Psalter was the one book
the people had in their hands" throughout church history.[66] There are
"more testimonies cited out of Psalms in the New Testament, than almost out of any other book," and they contain much "sweet matter" for
contemplation and for use in the "public edification of the church."[67] According to Luther, in Psalms we find "not what one or two saints only
have done, but what the head of all saints has done, and what all saints
still do."[68]

Nevay considered Scripture the only suitable source for preaching or
singing in worship. Hence, he considered psalm singing a gospel ordinance, and he ably refuted the arguments of those who oppose exclusive
psalm singing. To those who argue that Ephesians and Colossians call
for use of psalms, hymns, and spiritual songs, Nevay replied that these
same titles are used for classification within the book of Psalms. To those
who argue that the songs used in the Revelation are different from those
in Psalms, Nevay countered, "much of them are taken from Psalms."
Further, the new song spoken of in Revelation 14:3 refers not to the
words but to "new heart and the new creature" that will sing the new
song.[69] Augustine, like Nevay, was an exclusive psalm singer, and he
noted that the North African churches "sing with sobriety the divine
songs of the prophets, whereas they [the Donatists] inflame the intoxica-
tion of their minds by singing psalms of human composition."[70]

Concerning the other side of the argument, many modern, Reformed
writers zealously defend with biblical arguments singing other than the
Psalms. On the one hand, the demand for exclusive psalm singing is an
issue that has caused great divisions within the church; on the other

hand, any worship song must be scriptural. I bring it to your attention because in modern times we almost exclusively do not sing psalms. For example, I recently scanned a modern church hymnal for the psalms the Covenanters died singing, and I found most absent. Their most popular tune, *Martyrs*, is missing altogether. Just as prayer is more edifying when based on Scripture, so is singing. The ability to sing God's Word to simple, common-meter tunes is a great blessing and comfort both in private and public devotions. In family devotions in our home, we have reclaimed common-meter tunes such as *Little Town of Bethlehem, Amazing Grace, Halls of Montezuma, and America the Beautiful* for use with the *Psalms of David* and urge others to do the same.

Those that speak and sing psalms renew their covenant vows with every psalm they sing because the book of Psalms contains over three dozen different "I will" promises. The two most frequent promises, with dozens of occurrences, are for praising God and for singing psalms. It is not surprising that these two promises are so repeated because the chief end of man is to glorify God and enjoy him forever. Further, it is not possible for a church to know Christ fully without knowing Psalms because Christ is so abundantly displayed within them, "particularly in Psalms 2, 16, 22, 45, 72, and 110."[71] Luther equated the psalms to manna by expressing how Christians are like the Jews in the wilderness who cried, "Our soul loathes this light bread." Luther further warned that the Jews who despised manna were plagued and died.[72]

Third, the Covenanter and Puritans rightly heard the Word, considering this practice to be a matter of life and death. They claimed that the reason we do not remember what we hear is that "God punishes those that are careless in hearing with forgetfulness."[73] To Nevay, the right hearing of the Word was "both an ordinance of God, in which we wait on him for spiritual good, and a grace whereby we are enabled so to depend." Right hearing, which leads to a daily learning of "our own unworthiness and Christ's excellency and usefulness," requires the following:[74]

1. We must prepare our hearts (Acts 10:33), acknowledge our ignorance (Isa. 2:3), desire to hear (1 Pet. 2:2), and engage with prayer (Ps. 119:18).
2. We must listen with a hearing ear to what is said (Deut. 32:46; Acts 16:14) and hear as if it were spoken directly to us (Prov. 2:1–2, 10). This requires that we not "hear lightly, as if it were the word of man; but hear it as the Word of God, and let it sink down into our ears" (Luke 9:44; 1 Thess. 2:4). There must be a humble, earnest, greedy, and discerning hearing (Job 34:3) that treasures the sweet taste of the Word (Ps. 119:103).

3. We must receive the message with faith (Heb. 4:3), meekness (James 1:21), fear (Isa. 66:1-2), and love (2 Thess. 2:10-11). The "hearing must not be on our strength," but with a trembling at the "most comfortable word."

4. We must receive it with an honest heart (Luke 8:15) with sincere intent on putting it into practice (Ps. 119:11; James 1:22). This requires that we "engage ourselves by oath to perform it" (Ps. 119:106), *"not turn from that which is commanded, to the right or left"* (Deut. 5:32-33), and hold fast to instruction as if it were life itself (Prov. 4:13; 8:33).

Right hearing is an excellent thing because "there are more excellencies in the Word than in any other manifestation of God," and because there are "many great promises made to this hearing" (Ps. 138:2; Prov. 1:8-9; 4:10; Isa. 55:3; John 5:24, 25). It is a "converting ordinance" (Ps. 19:7), a means "of increase of spiritual strength" (Acts 20:32), a source of eternal life (Ps. 119:9, 30; Isa. 57:19; John 6:68; Acts 5:20; 13:26), a comfort in "the time of affliction" (Ps. 119:50), and "all things are sanctified by it" (1 Tim. 4:5). It is a "sign of hardness of heart" to miss opportunities to hear the Word (Matt. 13:13; Luke 16:31; John 3:19; 2 Cor. 4:3; Heb. 6:7-8).[75]

It is a promised and a covenanted blessing: *"I will make them hear my words, that they may learn to fear me"* (Deut. 4:10), and *"the ears of them that hear shall hearken"* (Isa. 32:3). It is a free gift through which faith, obedience, learning, success, right worship, salvation, and sanctification are promised (Isa. 29:24; 55:10-11; Mal. 1:10; Rom. 10:17). "If right hearing be a covenanting blessing," Nevay concludes, "then the preaching of the gospel is a covenanting blessing; for we cannot hear without a preacher (Rom. 10:4), so, they who are enemies to both or either of these, are enemies to the Covenant of Grace."[76]

The Sermon – Putting it All Together: We can learn a lot from Nevay's sermons. In each, he applies the above-mentioned principles. He tests all statements against the Word and quotes dozens of verses in defense of essential points. His sermons are truly multi-dimensional in content—providing gall for the sinner, honey for the hungry, milk for the novice, and meat for the saints. Individually, each sermon focuses the heart of the hearer on digestible, divine truths. Collectively, they provide the hearer with a complete grasp of the whole counsel of God and provide practical advice concerning how to apply Scripture to their lives. More importantly, they always hold forth the stark contrast between man's condition and Christ's excellency. Both sanctification and salvation depend on faith; both require that men grasp the contrast between their plight if they do not close with Christ and their rich estate if they close with their beloved, Christ, and forever enjoy his covenant blessing and true beauty.

Nevay's sermons on the last verses of David's last words are illustrative of this plight. The fifth verse (2 Sam. 23:5), in the King James Version, is a capsule summary of the gospel: *"Although my house be not so with God; yet he hath made with me an everlasting covenant, ordered in all things, and sure: for this is all my salvation, and all my desire, although he make it not to grow."* In this verse, David bewails the condition of his earthly house, but he takes great comfort from God's everlasting covenant.

From David's "search of his condition and case," in the first part of 2 Samuel 23:5, Nevay derives four principles.

1. Believers, "in their search of their state and condition, should compare their present case and condition, with their former receipt." A believer should "remember all his good providences, and above all, his covenant mercies, and all the spiritual blessings, wherewith he has blessed us in Christ Jesus." We should also be mindful that even the sins of believers are subject to judgment: *"You only have I known of all the families of the earth; therefore I will punish you for all your iniquities"* (Amos 3:2).

2. Believers, "in their search, would bring their hearts and lives to the rule" and conform their lives to the Word (See James 1:23–25). This requires that we "examine strictly all our ways according to the strict rule, considering seriously whether our life does exactly quadrate and agree with the same."

3. The right estimate of our estate is not as it is before man but before God. This is important because we are accountable to God, not man. Only God knows our hearts and our secret sins: "If we be right with and before God, we cannot readily be wrong before men." "Our eternal estate is measured according to that which is here." We must not trust our hearts in the search, but we must guide our search by Scripture and these three questions: (1) "What of Christ is in it? (2) What and how much there is in it for God? (3) How it is with us as to prayer?"

4. We "ought to search how it is with our house." We should follow the example of Joshua who "did look to and engage his house to the Lord." Remember to *"be diligent to know the state of thy flocks, and [to] look well to thy herds"* (Prov. 27:23). This is essential because "if the work and worship of God be not looked to in families, how can it go well with the church?"[77]

Nevay derives the following principles concerning the verdict David passes on his house:[78]

1. Most "perfect men, upon serious search, will find that matters are not so right betwixt them and God as they ought to be."

2. Even "in best-ordered families many things may be amiss" because "Satan is a great enemy of godly societies." Consequently, it is necessary to "pray much for godly families, especially the head of them." We should ever be mindful that "albeit education may curb and restrain sin, it cannot cure it; it is only grace that can do that."

3. There "must be sound and clear conviction of wrongs done, or of that which is wrong, before we can well take hold on the Covenant." This sincere humiliation requires that sins are "loathed and left," the "absolute need for Christ" is seen, and "Christ is highly esteemed and the soul is made willing to receive him." Men "must find themselves prisoners in the pit, where there is no water, before they have benefit by the blood of the covenant" (Matt. 11:28). Nevay expounds,

> There is no coming to Christ, until man is weary of self.... There is no coming to the Covenant, without a coming to Jesus; and there can be no coming to him, until he be prized; and there will be no prizing of him, until the soul be humbled (Prov. 27:7).... There can be no closing with Christ in a Covenant, until there be a willingness to give a bill of divorce to every sin; and sin must be made bitter to the soul, before it part with it.... It is natural for men to ... dream of self-sufficiency ... but sound conviction of their wrongs will beat them through those vain confidences, and make them glad to turn in to the covenant.

4. As with David, "sin ought not to hinder self-lost creatures from taking hold of the Covenant": *"For the LORD will not forsake his people for his great name's sake: because it hath pleased the LORD to make you his people"* (1 Sam. 12:20,22). We take comfort that "the covenant was not made to shut out but to take hold of sinners." There are "two great articles or clauses in the Covenant": (1) *Come, buy wine and milk without money and without price ... for he will abundantly pardon* (from Isa. 55:1,7); (2) *I will heal their backsliding; I will love them freely* (Hos. 14:4).

Nevay closes with the exhortation, "Hearts fixed on Christ will find virtue from Christ both to kill corruption and to quicken holiness."[79]

The Word – Sacraments Commanded

Sacraments are a sealing ordinance and a means of sanctification in which Christ is spiritually present with his church. The Lord's Supper symbolizes God's promise to redeem and to maintain communion with his people. Baptism symbolizes the right of disciples to the Covenant of Grace. Parents are obligated to train children in their covenant duty, but God alone saves.

Sacraments: Stuart Robinson expressed the essential nature of the sacraments: "As the one sacrament is thus made the instrument of a perpetual process of creating the visible church itself, so the other sacrament is a perpetual attestation of the great promise to redeem his elect covenant people."[80] Thus, the sacraments present the covenant "promises of God as in a picture" or a "visible word."[81]

Nevay considers the sacraments a means of sanctification. The sacraments are "the dishes, in which the great things of the covenant are set before us." In each sacrament there is an "external thing, which is the sign; and there is an internal and spiritual thing, which is signified." These things "represent Christ, and the great benefits which are in him"; "confirm the Covenant, and assure our interest in him"; serve as "public and distinguishing marks" to set apart his people; and "are ordinances, whereby Christians come to be solemnly engaged to Christ and his service" (Rom. 6:3-4; 1 Cor. 10:16).[82] In essence, the chief distinctive of the Reformed view of the sacraments is the emphasis on the spiritual presence of Christ in the midst of his church. Because Christ is spiritually present, perversions of the sacraments especially dishonor Christ. For these reasons, we must approach the sacraments with the right attitude:

> We are to take the candle of God's Word and Spirit into the house of our souls, and to search our mind, will, affections, etc., and because Christ is to come in, in the Sacrament, we must put out all his enemies, our sins, to the door. –Rutherford[83]

> Each individual should descend into himself, and consider, first, whether, with inner confidence of heart, he leans on the salvation obtained by Christ, and with confession of mouth, acknowledge it; and, Second, whether with zeal for purity and holiness he aspires to imitate Christ; whether, after his example, he is prepared to give himself to his brethren, and to hold himself in common with those whom he has Christ in common; whether, as he himself is regarded by Christ, he in his turn regards all his brethren as members of his body, or, like his members, desires to cherish, defend, and assist them .... –Calvin[84]

> Make use of sacraments, not as bare seals, but as appointed of God to represent Christ, and to confirm your interest in him, yea, and as means to convey spiritual blessings to you, not by reason of any virtue in themselves, but by virtue of an ordinance, and working of the Spirit (Matt. 26:26, 28; John 6:63; 1 Cor. 11:24–25). –Nevay[85]

Lord's Supper: Nevay defines this sacrament as "the remembrance of his death" through which the spiritual blessings to believers are assured, their spiritual growth advanced, their engagement deepened, and in which they pledge their "bond of near communion betwixt them and

Christ." Needless to say, the benefits of the sacraments do not immediately appear, as evidenced by the experience of first disciples.[86]

To the Scottish Presbyterians, the Lord's Supper was not a converting ordinance, but it was an ordinance shared among professed Christians in communion with their Lord. One of the great debates at the Westminster Assembly was over whether Judas was present during the Lord's Supper.* Gillespie and the Scottish Presbyterians of his era contended he was not.[87] They believed that exclusion of those not capable of self-examination, such as children and the unregenerate, is necessary for their own good.[88] Likewise, they excluded the openly profane: "That the admitting of the scandalous and profane to the Sacraments gives the lie to the Word preached, and looses those whom the Word binds."[89] They also believed that communing with such people brought sin on the church. The Society People cited this reason for not communing with the unfaithful ministers during the persecution. However, Gillespie was careful to clarify that the scandalous persons spoken of are those who "have given no evidence of true repentance."[90] He described, moreover, how Christians remain free from the guilt of such scandalous people:

> If private Christians have interposed, by admonition given to the offender, and by petitions put up to those that have authority and power for restraining the scandalous from the Lord's Table, they have discharged their consciences, and may without sin communicate, though some scandalous members be admitted: for such persons sin in taking the Sacrament, but worthy communicants are not partakers of their sin.[91]

The guilt of admitting such individuals to the Sacrament rests on the church officers for failing to exercise church discipline.[92] The responsibility of church members is not to separate but to persevere and to hold church officers accountable. Gillespie, in his usual careful style, added an important qualification:

> I mean in a reformed and well-constituted church, where the thing is feasible. But where it cannot be done, because of persecution, or because of invincible opposition either of authority, or of a prevalent profane multitude, in that case we have only this comfort left us, *"Blessed are those who hunger and thirst after righteousness"* (Matt. 5:6 NKJ).[93]

The Covenanters emphasized observance of the sacraments as taught in God's Word. Although the "external form of the ordinance" is "of no

---

* All the gospel accounts of the Last Supper except Luke's agree there was a common supper before the Lord's Supper, and John 13:30 states that Judas left after taking the sop (i.e., the common supper). Choosing an orderly over a chronological account, Luke presents the Lord's Supper first.

consequence,"[94] it must be based on Scripture. Christ clearly used wine, the apostles used wine, and the *Westminster Confession of Faith* specifically calls for the use of wine in this sacrament. This practice continued until the rise of Fundamentalism that led to the Prohibition laws in America during the early part of the twentieth century. In the prior century, as evidenced by *Hodge's Systematic Theology*, the use of grape juice as a substitute for wine was unthinkable: "It has never been questioned in the church, if we exclude a few Christians of the present day.... Those in the early church whose zeal for tolerance led them to exclude wine from the Lord's Table were consistent enough to substitute water."[95] Hence, the almost exclusive use of grape juice among Presbyterians is a relatively recent change. Why should modern culture and misconceptions determine church practices? If the use of wine is sinful, then Christ sinned at Cana. Further, the use of other than wine violates the Reformed doctrine of only allowing those things that Scripture requires in Worship.

Further, the modern Protestant practice of bringing the elements to the communicants is actually a practice inherited from the early Independents. The early Presbyterians in Scotland believed communicants should sit around a table. The minister sat with them, as Christ sat with the disciples. The communicants broke real (common) bread and drank real wine with their fellow Christians. Regarding the differences between the Catholic and Reformed observance of the Lord Supper, Knox wrote:

> They differ in use, for in the Lord's Supper the minister and the congregation sat both at one table, no difference between them in pre-eminence nor habit as witnesseth Jesus Christ with his disciples, and the practice of the Apostles after his death. But in the papistical Mass the priests are placed by themselves at one altar. It will not excuse them to say, Paul commanded all to be done with order and decently. Dare they be so bold as to affirm that the Supper of Jesus Christ was done without order and [with] indecently?[96]

This was the practice of the early English Puritans and the Scottish Presbyterians. Thomas Becon (1512–1567) recorded the impact:

> O how oft have I seen, here in England, at the ministration of the Holy Communion, people sitting at the Lord's Table after they have heard the sermon ... bitterly weep, heartily repent, and sorrowfully lament their too much unkindness and unthankfulness towards the Lord God for the death of his Son, Christ, and for his other benefit.... What godliness also in life have I seen afterwards practiced by them that were communicants! What alteration of manners![97]

Knox did not make an issue over differences in a ceremony where there was agreement in all other matters concerning "the chief points of religion" with the Church of England and "hope of further reformation at a future time."[98] Notwithstanding Knox's strong belief concerning the necessity of sitting versus kneeling during communion, he advised his old Congregation in Berwick to obey the magistrate and kneel during communion when it became unlawful not to kneel.

> I am not minded, for maintenance of that one thing [sitting versus kneel-ing during the Lord's Supper], to gainstand the magistrate in all other and chief points of religion agreeing with Christ and his true doctrine; nor yet to break nor trouble common order thought meet to keep to be kept for unity and peace in the congregation for a time…[99]

Thus, he set the example for those seeking reform to bear with simi-lar imperfections in the church where there is hope for reform. Reform-ing the church from within became a hallmark of the Puritans. Knox in-sisted on this position a few years later when the magistrate jailed some of his followers in London for more than a year for refusing to kneel during communion. In a letter, he reminded them of the example of Paul who submitted to ceremonial purification in Jerusalem and who did not require others to stop listening to Peter when Peter mistreated gen-tiles. He admonished them: "God forbid that we should damn all for false prophets and heretics that agree not with us in apparel and other opinions, who yet preach the substance of doctrine and salvation in Christ Jesus."[100] Nevertheless, Knox set bounds on this reconciling spirit. He would not have supported compliance without hope of reformation.

Baptism: Nevay considered baptism "an ordinance for our solemn entry and admission into the church; by one spirit we are all baptized into one body" (1 Cor. 12:13). He also considered it "a seal of the Covenant of Grace, confirming unto us our right in all the Covenant of Grace" (Mark 1:4; Rom. 4:11; 6:3–4; Gal. 3:27; Col. 2:11–12; Titus 3:5).[101] To the Covenanters, baptism was the "Laver of Regeneration; it is the seal of sanctification, as well as justification."[102] Consistent with the philosophy, Nevay in-cluded it as a "means of sanctification." Because these graces are insepa-rable, there is much need to restore this emphasis today. Regrettably, the post-Revolution Settlement remnant took this truth to a dangerous ex-treme by over-emphasizing the private covenant instead of the act of Christ during observance of the sacraments.[103] Patrick Walker recounted that one of the first ministers to the Society People, more than a decade after the Revolution settlement, refused to baptize those children whose parents did not hold his extreme views in all matters.[104] James Nisbet expressed similar complaints. Nowhere in the Old or New Testament does God require perfection in doctrine for baptism or circumcision.

As you recall, John Nisbet's suffering began when he insisted on having his child baptized. Would we make the sacrifice that John Nisbet made for his belief in the covenantal aspects of this sacrament? If not, then we need to study the basis of our faith and practice. Perhaps we are leaving the Old Testament out of our lives. God's covenant with Abraham was not just with Abraham but also with his descendants and his household (see Genesis 17). In Exodus 12, each household, not each person, offered a lamb. In the New Testament (Acts 16), when asked, *"What must I do to be saved?"* The reply was *"believe in the Lord Jesus and you will be saved— you and your household."* In fact, each of the covenant promises to Adam, Noah, Moses, and David affected not just the recipient but also their households, their descendants, and society. This is a promise from God: *"I will pour my spirit upon thine seed, and my blessing upon thine offspring. And they shall spring up as among the grass, as willows by the water courses"* (Isa. 44:3-4). To sum up, the "infant-seed" of both the Old and New Testaments must share the same benefits because they share the same covenant.[105] However, as Calvin observed, the covenant sign of baptism is no guarantee of salvation: "While God promises that he will be merciful to the children of the saints through all generations, this gives no support to the vain confidence of hypocrites."[106] Evidencing Calvin's statement is Psalms 103:17–18, where in verse 17 the promise is offered to children, while in verse 18 the fulfillment is limited *"to such as keep his covenant, and to those that remember his commandments to do them."*

Basis for Infant Baptism: Nevay contends that "Infants, if any look impartially, and search diligently into the Scriptures, will be found undoubtedly to be under the external and visible Gospel Covenant, so a party therein; they will clearly be found members of the visible church." Just as the promise to the patriarchs applied to their seed (Isa. 59:21), it also applies now to the gentiles because "there is no difference now betwixt Jews and gentiles" (Rom. 10:11-12; Col. 3:11). In brief, "the blessings of Abraham are clearly ours" (Gen. 17:7,19; Gal. 3:14,17). Nevay offers the following reasons why infants are within the external covenant: First, children "cannot be excluded from being part of the visible kingdom" because "they are subjects too" (Lev. 25:41-42). Second, the "little ones [of Israel] are numbered amongst the party covenanting with God." If members then, they are members now (Deut. 29:10-12; 1 Cor. 10:1-3). Third, in the old dispensation "the child of eight-days old was reckoned within the covenant" (Gen. 17:12–13). Fourth, "to be without the pale of the church, is a most dreadful case: It is to be without God, and without hope" (Matt. 15:26; Eph. 2:11–12). Fifth, it "was the same covenant then and now" (Deut. 30:6,11–14; Rom. 5:5–10), and "circumcision is a seal of the same righteousness by faith, which is now preached in the gospel" (Rom. 4:11). Sixth, *"The generation of the upright shall be blessed"* (Psalm 112:2). Seventh, "either it must be said that infants belong to the world, and to Satan's visible kingdom, or to Christ's kingdom; there is not a third state." Eighth, "the Old and New Covenants are essentially the same, so the essential privileges must be the same." Ninth, the exclusion of infants would "put a stumbling block in the way of the Jews." Tenth, Scripture promises, *"The promise is unto you and to your children"* (Acts 2:39). As previously mentioned, however, this is no guarantee for individual children. Eleventh, believing members in a family sanctify others within the family (1 Cor. 7:13–14). Twelfth, "Christ was angry at those who kept back little ones from him" (Matt. 19:14).[107] Thirteenth, "Christ was head of his church in the Old Dispensation, as well as the new," and he "never took a privilege from his church …unless he put some better in the place." Fourteenth, the "visible church is the same in all ages" (1 Cor. 12:13). Fifteenth, education of children is a binding obligation throughout Scripture, which promises much to those who submit to the commandment (Gen. 18:19; Eph. 6:4). Last, narrowing church privileges is "contrary to the nature of the Gospel."[108]

Nevay answers the common objections to infant baptism. To those who object that baptism should not be for children of the flesh but for children of God, Nevay replies, "It is not by nature that infants are church members, but as children of the promise." To the objections that children are not capable of repentance or performing the required duties, Nevay replies that "the parent may lawfully engage his child to God" because it is promised in the covenant (Deut. 29:10–13). To the objection that it is inconsistent to preclude baptized children from the Lord's Table, Nevay replies that Scripture requires self-examination to take the cup (1 Cor. 11:28). To those who claim that Scripture is not clear concerning infant baptism, Nevay reminds them that many other spiritual truths, such as the Trinity, are just as hard to understand, and he sees no harm in being "in Christ's School even from infancy." Scripture requires baptism as soon as men become disciples, and children are disciples.[109]

Nevay believed there is no scriptural warrant for the Anabaptist practice of restricting baptism to those whose confession is convincing to all the church. For this same reason, he considered dipping unnecessary. The arguments for sprinkling, pouring, and washing have greater scriptural weight than those for dipping, i.e., *"I will sprinkle clean water upon you"* (Ezek. 36:25; see also Isa. 44:3; 1 Cor. 6:11; Tit. 3:5; Heb. 10:22; 1 Pet. 1:2). Statements such as "they went down both into the water" do not necessary imply submersion; there was little water in these desert areas. Scripture no more "appoints the measure of water in baptism" than it does the measure of bread or wine in the Lord's Supper.[110] In fairness, the *Westminster Confession of Faith* allows dipping, but it maintains that baptism is rightly administered by pouring or sprinkling water."[111]

Parental Obligations: Parents have an obligation, signified in baptism, to raise their child in the covenant. Nevay equates the importance of parents in the education of their children to that of rain in the growth of plants: "Doctrines should be dropped on them, as the rain upon the tender grass" (Deut. 32:4). However, parents must recognize that "planting and watering will not do it, if God give not the increase; yet in doing the duty the blessing is to be expected." Imagine the torment on Judgment Day "to hear [your] children cursing [you] for their bad education? Contrast this with the joy of saying, *"Behold, I and the children whom the Lord hast given me"* (Isa. 8:18).[112] Implicit in the Reformed tradition, with its covenantal understanding of Scripture, is the necessity of godly training of children within a household, following the pattern recommended by David:

> We will not hide them from their children, showing to the generation to come the praises of the LORD, and his strength, and his wonderful works that he hath done. For he … commanded our fathers, that they should make them known to their children: That the generation to come might know them, even the children which should be born; who should arise and declare them to their children (Psalm 78:4–6).

In addition to devoting Sunday afternoon at church for catechizing the youth, the *First Book of Discipline* required, "Every master of household must be commanded either to instruct, or cause to be instructed his children, servants, and family, in the principles of the Christian religion; without the knowledge whereof ought none be admitted to the table of the Lord Jesus."[113] This requirement applied as well to the adults, who could be refused admission to the Lord's Table for lack of knowledge or for failing to teach their children. There is evidence that the Scottish practice was still in effect in early American Presbyterian churches:

> On the Lord's Day, in the church, as part of the public religious services, the minister asked questions from the Catechism. The elders of the church and the heads of families were always questioned first, then the

younger members and servants. The exercise was never brief but always thorough.[114]

James Nisbet records that he recited them to himself weekly. If adults followed his example, the problem of catechizing children would be solved! He thanks God that he "was born of godly parents who did their utmost to instruct [him] in the fear and service of God, and were examples to [him] therein by cleaving to the Lord and his way with full purpose of heart."[115] Regarding his father's example, James records, "As for family worship, he never omitted it but when persecution cut him short. I often heard him say, that he had observed from his youth, that a family never prospered with the blessing of God who omitted his worship evening and morning."[116]

The Word – Church Discipline Commanded

The church is accountable to exercise biblical discipline that addresses the need to separate from sin, yet forgive and restore repentant sinners. The biblical form of government is with elders, never an elder. Only it enables peace, unity, and discipline within the church.

Discipline: Although Calvin did not mention discipline as the third mark of the church, Knox and the Scottish church insisted on it. Although it is not essential for the being, it is essential for the ends of the church.[117] Calvin rightfully would object to any mark that measures itself in human terms, even in terms of human purity.[118] Nevertheless, Calvin considered discipline vital to the church: "As the saving message of Christ is the soul of the church, so its discipline is like the sinews by which the members of the body each in its place are held together."[119] Concerning church government, Calvin remarked, "Whoever, therefore, studies to abolish this order and kind of government of which we speak, or disparages it as of minor importance, plots the devastation, or rather the ruin and destruction, of the church."[120] Both Calvin and the Apostle Paul would urge us to flee any church wherein Christ is not Shepherd and King: His children "know not the voice of strangers."[121] Hence, to this extent, discipline is a mark. A church that denies the ordinance of discipline undermines the other ordinances as well.[122]

The church needs to restore scriptural discipline as instituted by the apostolic church. Table 11.1 depicts in summary form the classification of offenses and associated punishments promulgated by the early Scottish church in *The First Book of Discipline* and *The Order of Excommunication and of Public Repentance*. These guidelines provide a careful balance between "Old" and "New" Testament practices, and they clearly underscore the need to separate from sin, as well as the need to forgive and restore repentant sinners to the church. Although overly severe by modern standards, they encapsulate biblical teachings on church discipline.

Table 11.1
Overview of Early Presbyterian Church Discipline

Subjects and Sources	Private or Public Offenses	Public Offenses	Capital Public Offenses
Examples of type of sin listed in *The Order of Excommunication and of Public Repentance* (1569) and *The First Book of Discipline* (1560)	Examples are wanton and vain words, uncomely gestures, negligence in hearing and preaching, abstaining from the Lord's Table, avarice and pride, superfluity or riotousness in cheer or raiment.	Examples are fornication, drunkenness, swearing, cursing, chiding, fighting, brawling, common contempt of church order, breaking of the Sabbath, oppressing and deceiving of the poor, open slandering or infaming of a neighbor, factiousness, or sowing of discord.	Capital offenders are willful murderers, adulterers (lawfully convicted), sorcerers, witches, conjurers, charmers, givers of drinks to destroy children (abortionists), and open blasphemers. Also included are apostates to papistry and perjurers. For ministers, add heresy and sins of perpetual infamy.
Punishment for church members	If secret and known to a few, then privately admonish. If sinner is not repentant, a minister should admonish or visit with 2–3 others; then tell congregation if needed (see Matthew 18). If public, then appear before session. If public repentance is required, then profess repentance to church. If unrepentant, then allow time to repent. If impenitent, then admonish church to pray that he repent and request his friends to help. If impenitent, then call him before session. If contumacious (unwilling to submit to church authority), then excommunicate.		Excommunicate until civil punishment is complete or until offender is reconciled through public repentance: (1) Satisfy reasonable demands of victim's kin; (2) Examine by session; (3) After time, sinner, in humbling attire, confesses at church door for three weeks. If all indicate satisfaction, then restore to fellowship. (The church "may not justly deny.")
Punishment for church officers	Admonish. Censure for family member's sins.	Depose for a time (suspend) if repentant. Church may call another after 20 days.	Depose perpetually.
Actions Required by Civil Authority	Offences are not punishable by civil sword (death) but are scandalous and offensive to the church. The church should act first.		Punishable by sword. State should act first. Otherwise, the church must exercise discipline.

A comparison of these guidelines with those contained in the modern *Book of Church Order* (BCO) for the PCA yields a number of salient differences. For instance, the BCO blurs the distinction among the categories of sins, leaving the church with washed-out landmarks on which to base discipline. In contrast, Knox sought a scriptural foundation for applying discipline where possible. For example, Knox's approach seems to apply the analogy that offences deserving capital punishment in the "Old Testament" deserve excommunication in the "New Testament" church if the sin is defiantly committed and until the sinner is restored by public repentance. The modern church can learn a great deal from John Knox's guidelines for church discipline based on God's Word.

Sinful Neglect of Discipline: Although discipline was the hallmark of the Scottish church, in 1651 when Cromwell rose to power, the Scottish General Assembly identified the neglect of proper discipline as one of the chief causes for God's wrath. Specifically, the Assembly cited the following causes: (1) lack of control over the ordination of ministers and elders, (2) "the gross slighting and mocking of kirk censures and of public repentance," (3) failure to exclude "scandalous and ignorant persons" from the Lord's Supper, and (4) the "keeping in of many continually and openly profane in the fellowship of the kirk."[123] If these were causes of the Lord's wrath in 1651, they most certainly are today.

Typical of the Scottish reformation in discipline is the example set by John Blackader. When John Blackader began his ministry in 1653, he first started by restoring discipline. He began by restoring the office of *elder*, which had fallen into misuse. Under his direction and their own mutual consent, the session reduced the number of elders to twelve though a process of examination. He then focused on the congregation. Through sermons, twice on Sunday and once mid-week, coupled with individual and family discipleship, the church soon blossomed. He also "instituted societies and meeting for family prayer and Christian fellowship." Discipline was maintained though frequent family visits, biannual training in the catechisms, and an active church court.[124]

Church Government: The effective implementation of discipline goes hand in hand with biblical church government. A church without proper church government is as a city without a magistrate.[125] According to the Bible, only the Presbyterian form of government will suffice for this purpose, because it was the form established by the Apostle Paul in the early church. Although the early Christian cities had bishops, the office was one of equality with the elders. In the words of Jerome, "a bishop is the same as a Presbyter."[126] Throughout the Bible, "elders" and never an "elder" alone exercise ecclesiastical power.[127] Unfortunately, over time the apostolic form of government degenerated as described by Ambrose: "The ancient synagogue, and afterwards the church, had elders, without whose advice nothing was done: this has grown obsolete, by whose fault I know not, unless it be by sloth, or rather pride, of teachers…."[128] Lack of this scriptural church government doomed the New England Congregationalists, and it threatens the modern church. James Thornwell (1812–1862), a Southern Presbyterian theologian of the nineteenth century, contended that the central question of Presbyterianism is the organization of the church itself: "God gave us church government, as truly as he gave us doctrines; and we have no more right to add to the church government, than to add to the doctrine."[129]

The reason for a plurality of elders is clear when we consider how often "Christ and his apostles foretell that the greatest danger with which the church was threatened would come from pastors."[130] Accordingly, one important under-girding of church government is the careful selection of elders. To ensure doctrinal soundness, Calvin established the practice of "insisting that everyone who rules in the church shall also teach."[131] Knox's early Scottish church elected elders annually so that none would take the office for granted.

However, too narrow an application of a sound principle can cause error. One of the reasons Presbyterians failed to compete in early American history was the shortage of trained ministers. Allowing the temporary office of Superintendents, such as those in the early Scottish church to cover and nurture several churches until sufficient ministers were available, would have circumvented this problem. Knox was not opposed to the office of bishop or superintendent; he was opposed to the abuse of office where one elder places himself above another.

On the other hand, failure to fully apply the Presbyterian form of government proved ruinous to English Presbyterianism. The Erastian impositions from the time of Cromwell forward certainly precluded the proper operation of Presbyterian government. Nevertheless, the lack of commitment to the true biblical concept was the real culprit. The English Presbyterian lack of emphasis on discipline within the church and the doctrinal purity of ministers led to the adoption of Modified Calvinism, which led to Arminianism, which led to Arianism (belief that Christ and the Holy Spirit are subordinate to the Father), which led to Unitarianism by the middle of the eighteenth century. Presbyterian ministers rather than Independent ministers were responsible for the failure of the

London non-conformists in 1719 to require ministers to adhere to confessional standards, even over matters as foundational as the Trinity. The de-emphasis of the office of elder by the English Presbyterians was certainly a contributing cause.[132] A church that is Presbyterian or Reformed in name only is a sad sight. Fortunately, recovery is underway.

Although modern Christians dismiss the importance of church government, John Nisbet considered it worthy of defense with one's life: "I die protesting against, and disowning popery in all its superstitious bigotry and bloody cruelty; and prelacy, the mother of popery, and all that depends upon that hierarchy." Without discipline and church government, unity in truth is not possible.[133]

The Word – Results in Unity in Truth

*Division, schism, and contention within the church are great evils, and every Christian and church must strive to achieve **unity in truth**, not just truth alone.*

Unity in Truth: James Thornwell declared unity as the first principle of Presbyterianism.[134] Likewise, the Apostle Paul highly valued unity. Regarding unity Gillespie declared, "To separate from, or gather new churches out of true reformed or reforming churches, has not the least warrant from the Word of God."[135] Calvin, likewise denounced "anathema against all who would in any way violate" the unity of the church.[136] However, his warning applies only to those who separate from the true church.[137] In other words, unity based on anything other than Scripture is false unity.

The greatest challenge of the church is to hold on to the truth and, at the same time, maintain unity. From the illustration of the candlesticks in the first two chapters of Revelation, we can derive three general principles regarding unity in truth. First, each church represented by a candlestick actually consisted of numerous particular congregations united in a common witness under a common government. Second, the multiple city-state churches (each represented by a candlestick) are united only by Christ in their midst. The active agents that Christ uses to achieve unity are (1) the presence of his Spirit, (2) the truth of his Word (double edges sword in his mouth), and (3) the authority of his messengers (stars in his right hand). Third, the churches differed in outward form and purity–ingredients not essential to unity in truth.

We can learn a lot from the covenanting remnant's struggle for unity in truth. Specifically, in our case, the question is "Did James Nisbet make the right choice by joining a church led by ministers who had been unfaithful to the principles that his father and others gave their lives to defend?" Although James's memoir offers significant insights, we can also learn from others who faced this same dilemma. One such person was Alexander Shields who left a detailed treatise on the subject entitled *Church Communion Inquired Into*. Shields was the most vocal defender of the remnant's position during the persecution, yet the most vocal proponent for reuniting the church after the persecution. He, like James Nisbet, testified for both truth and unity. Shields presented many of the same arguments used by James Durham in his attempt to heal the breach between the Protestors and the Resolutioners decades earlier. The advice of Shields is as applicable today as it was in James's time.

First, Scripture expressly commands believers "to endeavor to keep the unity of the Spirit in the bond of peace" (Eph. 4:3).

> The endeavors for union and concord among the lovers of truth are absolutely necessary, so that it cannot fall under debate, whether union should be endeavored; no more than it can be disputed, whether there should be preaching, praying, or keeping of the Sabbath, seeing it is so much commanded, commended, and pressed in the Scripture, as none can be found that is more frequently or clearly urged.[138]

> If the church be one, divisions and divided communions in her midst either infer that this one church is many, made up of heterogeneous parts, or that the church divided from is not a part of that one church, and hath broken off from that which compacts the body together.

> It is promised as a choice blessing of the well-ordered covenant.... *I will give them one heart and one way* (Jer. 32:39).... Yea, it is prayed for by our Lord Jesus Christ in his intercessory prayer, which is a specimen of his continued intercession to this day (John 17:11, 21, 23).

Shields lists three duties that "if conscientiously observed, could not miss speedily to produce" unity.

> If there were more love, there would be more union and communion, notwithstanding of differences.

> Reconciliation, agreement and receiving one another, is much pressed and inculcated in Scripture.... And if this reconciliation cannot be obtained any other way, there must be mutual forgiveness.... It is commended as a part or proof of the new man of grace (Col. 3:13) *to forbear one another, and forgive one another, if any have quarrel against any man*: Even as Christ forgave us, so also should we do.... *Receive you one another, as Christ also received us to the glory of God* (Rom. 15:6). How did Christ receive us?

Never until we were perfectly informed and reformed? Did he never receive us till we confessed all our particular sins, and such as we did ignorantly? No; then we had never been received, except he had pleased to take us with many faults and much ignorance. In many cases then, the way to *endeavor the unity of the spirit in the bond of peace* (Eph. 4:2–3) is with *lowliness and meekness, and longsuffering, to forbear one another in love*.

The study of seeking, pursuing, entertaining peace and peaceableness is much pressed and praised.... The want of peaceableness, as well as the want of truth, will make our salt to lose its savor.[139]

Second, Shields contended, with the Reformers and the Apostles, that "division, contention, and schism in the church are great evils."[140] James Durham aptly described the sin of division:

There is nothing that doth more tend to the reproach of the blessed name of our Lord Jesus Christ, that makes Christianity more hateful, that renders the gospel more unfruitful, and more mars the progress and interest of the kingdom of out Lord Jesus; and, in a word, doth more shut out all good, and let in by an open door every thing that is evil into the church, that the woeful evil of division does.[141]

Division is typically a judgment from God caused by "defection from the right ways of the Lord, to the right and or to the left, which is always the mother of division." It results in a vicious cycle of hurtful errors and further divisions as men attempt to defend the various causes. Divisions are aggravated by ignorance, facetiousness, selfishness, personal attacks, casting things in an odious light, suspecting the integrity of others, and putting the worst construction on the infirmities, words, or actions of others. On the other hand, not all unity is biblically sound. Shields sought no union "with sin, but with sinners now returned to duty." He does not propose "union that may obstruct us from duty, or obstruct the maintaining of testimony, or involve us in sin, or oblige us to palliate sin, or approve condemned sins, or condemn approved duties." He pleads not for "union in deformation, but in reformation."[142]

Third, Shields derived many of his arguments from Durham's *Treatise Concerning Scandal*. Durham insisted that union is attainable except in differences concerning fundamentals. The commonly allowed grounds for separation include heresy in doctrine, idolatry in worship, and intrusion, tyranny, or division in government. In attaining union, both sides must mutually condescend provided condescension does not involve sin or approbation of sin. Further, the party that has the most right or authority ought to follow Paul's example and "be the most condescending." For instance, Augustine was willing to yield to the Donatists "all particulars that do not involve consent unto, or approbation of what is wrong."[143]

Illustrative of non-doctrinal issues that cause divisions is the case where one party refuses to repent of a wrongdoing. Although "confession is the best way of removing offences," it is not always essential for union. Scripture does not require "confessing all, past offences" as a condition for joining or remaining in a church. Further, it may take years for those in error to become convinced of their sin, and "there is more access to engage them into a confession of them in an united way, than a divided way." Moreover, the proper forum for resolving issues in an established church is in the church courts, as emphasized by Calvin and Augustine: "Private individuals must not, when they see vices less carefully corrected by the Council of elders, immediately separate themselves from the church."[144]

The grounds for separation vary according to circumstances, Shields argued. For example, greater toleration is required in a reforming church than in a Reformed church. A Reformed church is one whose doctrines and practices are consistent with the principles of the Second Reformation, but it is ever reforming. In situations where the courts are inoperable, it may be necessary to withdraw from unrepentant sinners and ministers. Shields postulated that withdrawing from church communion with unfaithful ministers during the persecution was warranted on a conditional basis until the sins were forsaken and confessed. All the reasons for withdrawing from ministers during the persecution cited by Shields in the *Informatory Vindication* contain the phrase, "In a broken state of the church, in a declining, backsliding and troubled state of the church." The reasons for withdrawing no longer applied in the Revolution Settlement church, which had established church courts.[145]

Fourth, according to Shields, if one applies biblical guidelines for separation to the ministers of the post-Revolution Settlement Church of Scotland, "the scandal lies not in joining with them … but the offense lies in withdrawing." The "hinge of the controversy," is whether it is acceptable to join with ministers who were unfaithful during a period of persecution and unwilling to confess their sinfulness in this regard, yet who adhere to the true principles of church doctrine, worship, discipline, and government.[146] His arguments for joining with the Revolution Settlement ministers are as follows:

1. The grounds for separation, commonly allowed by the Reformers as previously discussed, no longer applied to the post-Revolution Settlement ministers. Hence, joining with these ministers cannot be consid-

ered as a "sign of approbation of them in their sin, directly or indirectly."
Nothing precludes the "owning and uniting with Presbyterian ministers
who have a commission from Christ, and an orderly call, by ordination
from the presbytery, and election of the people."[147]

2. Differences in judgment and practice are not grounds for separation,
even when the guilty do not admit error. Paul and Barnabus still supported each other's ministry although they differed over John Mark.
The Council of Jerusalem urged forbearance and condescension rather
than separation on the account of non-fundamental differences. Aquila
encouraged and corrected Appolos despite his doctrinal errors.[148] Scripture commends continued communion and condescension despite differences: *Him that is weak in the faith receive ye, but not to doubtful disputations*
(Rom. 14:1; see also 15:1,7). *Whereto we have already attained, let us walk in the
same rule, let us mind the same thing* (Phil. 3:16).

3. Shields concurred with Durham and Rutherford that the "sins of fellow
worshippers, whether they be officers or private Christians," are not sufficient grounds for separation from worship and communion even when
the sins are not confessed. Further, Shields contended, "There may be
union and communion with ministers and professors in a church where
many corruptions [excluding those previously identified as grounds for
separation] in doctrine, worship, discipline and government are tolerated
and entertained, neither confessed or reformed." He cites Old Testament
examples: Hannah continued worship despite the corruptions of Eli's
sons; the congregation did not separate despite Aaron's corruptions; and
the people did not break communion when priests took foreign wives
during Ezra's days. Consider the corruption within the Corinthian
church in doctrine (denying the resurrection of the dead), worship (eating in idol temples, debasing the Lord's Table, speaking in divers
tongues), and in discipline and government (tolerating defections and
murdering "weak souls for whom Christ died"). Nevertheless, Paul still
entertained communion in ordinances with them despite the fact that
these scandals were "not removed by censure or confession." In Galatia,
the corruption in doctrine, worship, discipline, and government "went
for some time maintained without confession." Despite many faults, the
seven Asian churches in the book of Revelation were commanded to
overcome, not to separate. Consider the corruption of the Jewish church
at the time of Christ, yet "Christ and his disciples attended their feast
and went to the temple ... He commands the leper to go to the priest ...
and commends the poor widow casting in her two mites into the Temple
treasury." Likewise, consider the example of righteous Simeon and
Anna, who "departed not from the temple, but served God with fasting
and prayers night and day." Shields concludes that "these joining of the

godly were not sin, because they did not join with these corruptions, but mourned over them and testified against them."[149]

4. From reason, Shields deduced that if men's sins were grounds for separation, then we could not have fellowship with ourselves or with family members. Further, "in withdrawing from one we withdraw from all: for the church is but one. And if we communicate with any one congregation, we have communion with the whole body" (1 Cor. 10:17; 12:13).[150]

Fifth, Shields answers the objections offered by the Society People for refusing to join the Revolution Settlement church. In refuting these objections, Shields does so only with respect to the conditions after the Revolution Settlement, for he used many of these arguments himself to justify separation during the persecution. There are legitimate grounds for separation; however, as Shields demonstrates, there are also legitimate grounds for striving to maintain church fellowship–a lesson much needed in the modern church. Where appropriate, James Durham's comments on the same topic are included.

a. The remnant claimed they were following the advice of Jeremiah: "Let them return unto thee, but return not unto them" (Jer. 15:19). *Answer:* The defections of the Indulged ceased with the persecution, Shields contends. Regarding this passage, Jeremiah continued to preach and to participate in sacrifices, feasts, and temple ordinances (Jer. 28) without even the hint of withdrawing.[151]

b. The remnant feared God's wrath against a church that does not confess its sins (see Prov. 28:13; Jer. 23:22–23). *Answer:* First, confession of sin is essential to communion with God, but it is not essential to church membership. Second, "the hearers may have communion with God when the minister hath it not." Third, those gathered in his name, "may have the expectation of his presence." Further, unity is a great blessing (Ps. 133).[152]

c. The remnant, citing Ezekiel 44:13, 15, believed that ministers who had accepted indulgences and similar entrapments had dishonored Christ's prerogatives so severely that they were no longer fit for the ministry. Citing James Durham, they maintained that ministers who depart from the truth are "no more to be accounted Ambassadors of Christ, or watchmen of his flock." *Answer:* This may apply to some ministers guilty of the grossest defections, but not to all ministers. In this passage, the errant priest were degraded in office but not deposed. Until deposed by a judiciary, ministers should not be looked upon as degraded. Durham's concern only applies "while they continued in that defection."[153] We should remember that Paul sometimes refrained from exercising censure (e.g., Gal. 5:12 and 2 Cor. 10:4, 6) for "respect to the union of the church." When we refrain from censure for the good of the church (i.e., what is edifying, as in 2

Cor. 12:19), Durham cautions, "Christian prudence" and Christ's honor, rather than what is pleasing to man, must guide edifying acts.[154]

d. The remnant argued that they should withdraw from ministers that perverted doctrine (e.g., Prov. 19:27). *Answer:* Shields agrees that one should avoid false teachers, particularly those unwilling to speak out against "popery, prelacy, Erastianism, and tyranny." However, the Revolution Settlement ministers were against these errors.[155]

e. *"We must come out from among them, and be separate, and touch no unclean thing"* (2 Cor. 6:14, 17), the remnant exclaimed. *Answer:* Shields concedes these verses prove "we should not join in any unclean things; however, we may join in gospel ordinances … which are not unclean things."[156] To avoid divisions over the sins or failings of ministers, Durham suggests that it is sometimes, necessary for a judiciary "to remove the minister from a particular place for the good of church unity."[157] The best solution is "zeal against such as are justly censurable," which "next to division in a church, is the greatest plague of a church." The same spirit that causes zeal to depose unworthy ministers is the same spirit that fosters "meekness and moderation" toward those worthy.[158]

f. Citing Scripture (Jer. 23:14–16 and Ezek. 13:10–14, 18, 22; 22:25, 28), the remnant refused to hearken unto those who defended, whitewashed, or justified their defections. *Answer:* Those who "whitewash defections are in hazard of being consumed in the punishment of the sins they defend." Further, there is no evidence in the book of Ezekiel "that the godly did withdraw from these builders and daubers" in worship, or in the book of Ezra for refusing to work with sinful priests in rebuilding.[159]

g. Scripture (Jer. 14:14–16) promises punishment to the hearers of false prophets. Consequently, one should withdraw from the unfaithful ministers to avoid God's wrath. *Answer:* Although "this unfaithfulness is a ground of separation, in a broken and declining church," Shields answers that the ministers in question are not now unfaithful. What Scripture really says is that the Lord "will not fulfill their false prophecies, but rather hasten the threatening judgment to a sinful people." He further asserts, "If it allows any withdrawing at all, it must be from those that prophesized" falsely. Hosea 2:2 requires that we protest against these defections. Our protest is "sufficient exoneration of guilt."[160]

h. The remnant viewed the ministers who deserted their ministerial duties during the persecution as "hirelings and strangers," from whom Christ tells his sheep to flee (John 10:5, 12). In 2 Thessalonians 3:14, Paul warns Christians not to associate with those who do not stand firm. *Answer:* Christ warns his sheep not to hear those who enter not by the door (false commission) and those with a strange voice (false doctrine). Further, "all that flee and leave the sheep are not [necessarily] hirelings and strangers." Thus, when shepherds who flee return, it is our duty to hear them, even those who "will not confess their fault, which is their duty to do." Evidencing this principle is Paul's treatment of John Mark. Shields insists that we can not withdraw from ministers who lawfully preach.[161]

i. The remnant argued that in Romans 16:17 Paul advises Christians to shun those who cause divisions. *Answer:* Shields concedes that both sides were guilty of schismatic behavior during the persecution, but Scripture (Romans 14 and 15) directs Christians to make every effort toward peace, especially when conflicts arise from the actions of a weaker brother. Where warranted, withdrawal must be from the offending individual—not from "church communion."[162]

j. The remnant considered "scandalous disorders a sufficient ground for withdrawing" because Paul warns us to shun disobedient Christians (1 Cor. 5:11; 2 Thess. 3:6, 14). *Answer:* Paul does require that we avoid civil and personal communion with unrepentant sinners, but ecclesiastical withdrawing "must be after the church's sentence in a constitute state of the church." Thus, ecclesiastical separation is permissible if there are no judiciaries (i.e., broken state of church), but it is not permissible before the action of the church courts.[163] Durham adds, dissatisfaction with persons is no grounds for division (e.g., Judas was one of the twelve). Failures of church government (e.g., "sparing of some corrupt officers and members") are not faults that "make a church to be no church."[164]

k. The remnant held that the pollution of the unfaithful ministers was such that "every work of their hand and that which they offer is unclean" (Hag. 2:12-14); hence, they inferred that communion with them was "participation of their sin" because "partakers of the bread" are one body (1 Cor. 10:16-17). They also cited Ephesians 5:7–11, which instructs believers to avoid partnership and fellowship with immoral people. *Answer:* Shields counters, "it is very consonant to the practices of the Lord's servants in all ages to have communion in ordinances with protestation against the corruptions of officers." In Haggai 2, "uncleanness of officers does pollute everything they handle," but "to the pure all things are pure" (Titus 1:15). In Ezra 3:5-6, the "prophet himself joined in ordinances with these same priests." In 1 Corinthians 10, Paul commands believers to withdraw from idolatry, not "the Church of Corinth." In Ephesians 5, Paul teaches us to "partake with none in sin, but we may partake with sinners in duty, especially when" they have forsaken their sins. In short, "the uncleanness of officers does not pollute the ordinances to others." Augustine answered the Donatists, who argued for separation from those who gave up their Bibles during persecution, in a similar manner: "He is sinfully joined with them, whoso commits any evil with them, or favors and connives with them that do commit it; but if he do neither, he is no way sinfully joined."[165]

l. The remnant held that those who "do not confess and forsake their sin" are subject to God's wrath. The Israelites did indeed suffer punishment for the sins of members (Josh. 7; Isa. 9:16; 43:27-28; Jer. 14; 15; 16; Lam. 4:13; Ezek. 13:10-11, 14; 22:25-31). *Answer:* Communion with sinful ministers and members is sinful if there is participation in their sin in any of the following ways: helping commit it; counseling or encouraging it; approving and applauding it; consenting or submitting to it; conniving at it, and not rebuking it; or not restraining or resisting it. On the other hand, guilt but not separation is warranted when we do not warn others of sin, mourn for their sin, or repress any desire to participate in their sin. The degree of guilt and associated punishment varies with the nature of the participation. For example, it is sinful to have communion with those involved in sins such as heresy, idolatry, corruption of others, or bloodshed; however, it is not sinful to have communion in the case of personal scandal or non-foundational church corruption. Otherwise, "the prophet would have commanded them to withdraw."[166]

m. The remnant feared that the church was beyond repair and that the church would bury their former testimony against sinful defections. *Answer:* Shields contends they can continue their testimony via communion under protest because the reasons for separation no longer apply. Their testimony against defection should not impede their testimony against schism. He begs them to consider "whether the inconveniences of division would be greater." To Shields, it was not possible for a Christian to live a private life without church communion (Ps. 26:8; 27:4; 42:1-2, 4; 43:3-4; 63:1-2; 84:1-4, 10; 89:15; and 122:1-4). He implores them to consider how long would a church last if "every scandal, defection and corruption not confessed" led to "rupture, division, and separation."[167]

n. Shields also answers objections regarding the "constitution and practice of this church," such as allowing the civil government to dissolve General Assemblies and to impose an Oath of Allegiance. *Answer:* Shields replies that they are "required to submit to nothing, but what our fathers, and all the Reformed churches would have gladly yielded unto." He acknowledges the "sinful weakness in ceding" to "encroachments upon some of the church privileges and freedom," but he does not consider these ground for separation. For separation, the Reformed divines require heresy in doctrine, idolatry in worship, or tyranny in government (e.g., imposing sinful terms of communion, intrusion in the ministry).[168]

In summary, the best defense against hurtful divisions is the "sustaining of the government and order of the church." The advice is simple:

(1) Restore respect for church government, which "division makes to appear contemptible." (2) Consider the ills that follow division, for generations to come, and condescend in all matters except in fundamentals to prevent it.[169] Nonetheless, there are legitimate grounds for separation, as evidenced by Shields' own separation during the persecution. Further, in cases where the majority departs from fundamental truth, the minority that separates is free of guilt.[170] From the false church Scripture commands, *"Come out of her, my people, lest you share in her sins, and lest you receive her plagues"* (Rev. 18:4–NKJ).

Opinions of Other Covenanters: Unlike the remnant after the Revolution Settlement, many Covenanting martyrs properly understood the necessity of maintaining Christian charity and unity as well as Christian truths. One such martyr, John Wilson, reminds us that "we can do no greater injury to the true church of Christ" than "cleaving to her adversary." Yet, this same man advises treating the Indulged charitably: "I wish all seriously godly to be tender towards such whose eyes are not enlightened to behold the evil of it."[171] John Nisbet describes in one of his manuscripts how he balanced truth and unity:

> Now, as for misreports, that were so much spread of me, I declare, as a dying person going out of time to eternity, that the Lord never suffered me in the least to incline to follow any one of those persons who were drawn away to follow erroneous principles. Only I thought it still my duty to be tender of them, as they had souls, wondering always wherefore I was right in any measure, and they got leave to fall in such a manner. I could never endure to hear one creature rail and cry out against another, knowing we are all alike by nature.
>
> Let all beware of refusing to join with ministers or professors upon account of personal infirmities…. But it shall be found a walking contrary to the Word of God, and so contrary to God himself, to join either with ministers or professors, that hold it lawful to meddle with sinful things; for the Holy Scriptures allow of no such thing. He is a holy God: and all that name the name of God must depart from evil.[172]

In his dying testimony, John Nisbet urges unity, but he also insists that we uphold truth in a manner deserving of Christ:

> My dear friends, forbear your contentions and censuring one of another; sympathize with and love one another, for this is his commandment. Keep up your sweet fellowship-meetings, and desirable general meetings, with which my soul has been often refreshed. What is agitate in them for carrying on of a testimony for truth and against defections,

let it be managed with Scripture light for direction, with zeal temperate
with knowledge, and with the spirit of meekness accompanied with patience and humility. Be always ready to give a reason of your faith, and
be much denied to the world, to yourselves, and to your natural life.
When God in his providence calls you to lay it down for him, do it
cheerfully, and embrace the cross of our sweet Lord Jesus with open
arms, for he will not send any a warfare on their own charges. Take for
your rule and encouragement these Scriptures (Isa. 3:9; 8:17,20; Mal. 3:16–18;
4:2; Gal. 5:19–26; 6:7–10; Eph. 6:10–17; Phil. 1:27–29; Heb. 3:10–11; 10:21–39; 12:11–15;
Jude vs. 3; Rev. 10:11; 14:1–5), with others, that I leave to your own search.[173]

These excerpts prove conclusively that John and James were of the same
opinion after all. Both truth and unity are necessary.

The Proper View of the Church: The Puritans and Covenanters
considered the church, the body of Christ, as a "divine institution,"
which the individual Christian is obligated to honor, promote, and support. They, like Abraham, held a high view of the church: *"For he looked
for a city which hath foundations, whose builder and maker is God"* (Heb. 11:10).
This high view is different from the modern view in at least eight ways.

First, their high view involves a church united in Christ. The "central
bond of union between members of the apostolic church" was not their
individual communion with Christ, but that "they were and felt themselves to be one in Christ." Evidencing this conclusion is the exclusive
reference to the church in the first twelve chapters of Acts as the *church*
rather than the *churches*.[174] Concerning this issue, James Bannerman contended, "A solitary Christian is worse than a contradiction, he is an
anomaly, standing out against the express institution of God, which has
appointed the fellowship of believers in one church."[175] Furthermore,
"The idea of a merely voluntary association of Christians, brought together by the common belief of the same doctrines and the common
practices of the same precepts, is totally opposed to the notion of a Divine institution."[176] James Durham argued that it is a strange doctrine to
hold that the Christ dissolved the unity of the church because it was
united in Old Testament and apostolic times. Durham contended, "Particular churches cannot be considered as parts of the whole, but the
whole must be supposed first." Particular churches are merely "diverse
branches [that] spring from one root."[177]

Second, their high view of the invisible church required that commitment to it take precedence over commitment to a particular congregation. Although the Covenanters encouraged covenant commitment
among those engaged in church fellowship, they required only that

church members profess their covenant with Christ. Their Covenant of Grace with Christ, not any covenant among members, is the only moral ground for any member's duty.[178] However, they considered it "lawful for a church to swear and by oath subscribe an Orthodox confession," which contains all fundamental points consistent with God's Covenant of Grace as revealed in Scripture. Rutherford considered such a covenant oath as required of church officers to maintain wholesome doctrine and prevent backsliding. He saw no reasons for members not to do likewise, for Christ calls his sheep "to suffer even death for the true religion" (Luke 21:15–16; Acts 7:57–58; Phil. 1:20–21; Rev. 12:11).[179] It is not the visible church but the invisible church that has "the rights to the sacraments," is "the spouse of Christ and his mystical body," has "Christ as its head," and is "the temple of the Holy Spirit." Only the invisible church is rightly in covenant with God and "is the subject of all the privileges of Christians and all the promises of the covenant." They viewed as erroneous the Congregationalist belief that the heirs of the covenant include all who profess Christianity (i.e., the visible church).[180]

Third, their high view emphasized the role of the visible church, for which Christ gives the ordinances and the keys of the kingdom.[181] The visible church, not the individual or any particular congregation, is the primary agent charged with accomplishing the Great Commission. Those who take up the work of the church without the church cannot presume Christ's blessing because Christ works through his church. To the Scottish Presbyterians, the rights of Christ's church were a cause worthy of martyrdom. Likewise, the Westminster divines believed that outside the visible church there "is no ordinary possibility of salvation" (see Acts 2:47).[182] The church, not the individual Christian, is the "pillar and foundation of the truth," the agent empowered to accomplish the Great Commission, and the holder of the "keys to kingdom."[183] Ecclesiastical power rests in Christ and his bride, not in individual Christians.

On the other hand, the church is not a substitute for Christ, nor does it stand between Christ and man. Although the Holy Spirit is a gift to every Christian, the Holy Spirit is one Spirit, who is one with Christ and the Father. Only the Presbyterian form of government properly balances both the role of the individual with that of the church by allowing individuals to elect officers who corporately exercise church power. Given the modern neglect of the biblical role and government of the church, is it any wonder that the trend for the last two centuries to accomplish God's work through boards, interdenominational agencies, and mission societies has fallen far short of the great needs?

At its inception, the Presbyterian Church in America (PCA) seemed to grasp the proper vision as evidenced by the opening speech to the First General Assembly.

> It is our purpose to rely upon the regular organs of our government, and executive agencies directly and immediately responsible to them. We wish to make the church, not merely a superintendent, but an agent. We wish to develop the idea that the congregation of believers, as visibly organized, is the very society or corporation which is divinely called to do the work of the Lord.[184]

The Presbyterian Church-CSA used these same words at its inception. Regrettably, since the War Between the States, the Presbyterian Church has adopted an increasingly spiritual focus, predominantly within the church itself. The church increasingly accepts the humanist perspective that views the church "as nothing more than a collection of individuals having no greater rights that the aggregate liberties of its members."[185] Unlike the Puritans and the Covenanters who viewed the church as their society, modern Christians no longer see the church as the ideal society. Our fathers considered the church more than an *assembly* because it still exists when it is dismissed; more than a *congregation* since it is more than a collection of people in one place; more than a *collection of saints* since many tares are members; and above all, more than a collection of volunteers.[186] To them, only the word *society* adequately applied to all the different senses in which Scripture refers to the church.[187]

The issue of *incorporation* is a good example of how far the church has slipped. Many modern churches have incorporated to avoid the assault of a litigious society. To incorporate in America, churches must agree to limit their *powers* to those of a tax-exempt corporation "organized *exclusively* for religious, educational, and charitable purposes *within* the meaning of Section 501(c)(3)" in sub-chapter F of Title 26 of the Uniform Code of law.[188] Such corporations are not allowed to transfer any funds to members, substantially influence legislation, or participate in any manner (including making statements) in the political process.[189] Further, churches must agree to limit their powers to those within any future change–sight unseen–to 501(c)(3) guidelines. Worse, the church allows itself to be defined using the state's vocabulary–a chief trick of liberalism. For example, the church becomes subject to federal rules and restrictions concerning tax-exempt educational institutions. Although these restrictions may be applicable to a tax-exempt corporation, they bind the witness of the church. Taken literally, they severely limit the diaconal work, societal influence, and the prophetic witness of the church. Although any violation may not cause the church to lose its tax-exempt status, any violation becomes a lie and a broken promise. Most churches rationalize the loss of church rights to speak out about societal ills by contending that they can maintain their witness through each member acting alone. Thus, one by one, churches in America have become corporations under the headship of their creator, the state. This is how far America's view of the role of the church has fallen! Please note that if one substitutes numbers for letters (i.e., f=6, c=3), the tax code reference becomes $(26 \times 6) + 501 + (3 \times 3) = 666$. Although the Internal Revenue Service guidelines imply that these restrictions apply to all churches, there is no clearly stated legal requirement to do so since the Constitution forbids Congress from limiting the free exercise of religion. Rather than fight to maintain their God-given tax-exempt status, honored even by heathen emperors for more than nineteen centuries, most churches have chosen to cede these rights to the state. A better solution would be to fight this Erastian attempt to limit the influence of the church.

Fourth, their high view is an optimistic, militant view. It considers that the best days of the church are ahead rather than behind. It views the mandate of the Great Commission not simply to save souls but to save nations. When the bible speaks of making disciples of all nations it means to convert the majority in every nation into members of Christ's kingdom (i.e., members of his church). Our Presbyterian forefathers militantly pursued this goal, contending, based on David's seizure of Mt. Zion from the Jebusites, that "Christ has no church but what he gets by spiritual conquest."[190] To them, abandonment of hope for the church is abandonment of his kingdom. Walter Chantry (b. 1938) contends that the terms "kingdom" and "church" are "inextricably woven together in Biblical usage": Christ "wed the ideas of church and kingdom."[191]

Fifth, their high view is a balanced view. Stuart Robinson, a Presbyterian preacher during the Civil War, contended that the "two great extreme tendencies of the Protestant Reformation has been either to magnify the importance of the church as the essential element of Christianity, to the exclusion of the great doctrinal truths of Christianity, or to magnify the doctrinal truths to the exclusion of the church."[192] The continued under-emphasis on the church is as fatal as the ecumenical movement's under-emphasis on doctrine. In either case, a distorted view of *church* and *doctrine* impedes the church in accomplishing its mission. Robinson further contends:

That every revelation ever communicated, every ordinance ever appointed, every promise and covenant made with God, has been, not to and with men as men, or as constituting nations, but to and with the church, as such—a body organized or contemplated as the elements of an organization.[193]

Sixth, their high view rests in Scripture, particularly in Psalms. Perhaps one reason for the modern lack of concern for the church is the modern lack of emphasis on Psalms. William Binnie, in his book, *The Psalms*, points out that "a consuming zeal for the house of God is common to all psalms." He lamented that Christians of his day [late nineteenth century] sang "that half the Psalter which expresses the various exercises of personal piety; but the other half, which summons them to remember Zion, calls forth little sympathy from their hearts." He observed that half the petitions in the Lord's Prayer, which Jesus begins with "Our Father," are personal, and one half concern "the general interest of God's glory on the earth; and the three public petitions are set down first." This perfect pattern for prayer in private and public worship requires that Christians consider the interest of God's kingdom first: *"Let my tongue cleave to the roof of my mouth, if I remember thee not; if I prefer not Jerusalem above my chief joy"* (Ps. 137:6).[194]

Seventh, their high view results in purity of worship. Illustrative of the Nevay's commitment to purity in worship was his refusal to include even the Lord's Prayer as a routine part of worship. Some of the early American Presbyterians (e.g., those of my home church originally in Old Waxhaw, South Carolina) continued this practice for some time.[195] The departure from pure worship, even in my lifetime, is heart breaking. Regarding Sabbath purity, until recent times the Scottish Church considered "a well spent Sabbath … to be a day of heaven upon earth." They would question whether those who did not delight in the entire Lord's Day were children of God.[196]

Eighth, their high view holds Christ as King. Stuart Robinson posited that the church's objective creed, "we preach Christ crucified"; its subjective experience, a "church in the wilderness"; and its government, "the Messiah as King ruling over an organized community through a tribunal of elders," remain constant throughout Scripture. Of these three, the latter is most prominent, Robinson argued. Christ's prophetic and redeeming functions make his kingship a reality. Earthly kingdoms and their citizens ferociously assault the proper form of church government because it leads men to view Christ, rather than man, as king. It is for Christ's government of his church that the Covenanters fought.[197]

12

Lessons for Christians

Without faith it is impossible to please Him, for he who cometh to God must believe that he is, and that he is a rewarder of them that diligently seek him. –Heb. 11:6 NKJ

*L*esson #3: Christians must put their covenant obligations and duty to be God's people first. The three great Christian virtues of faith, hope, and love appear together frequently in Scripture (Rom. 5:2–5; 1 Cor. 13:13; Gal. 5:5–6; Eph. 4:2–5; Col. 1:4–5; 1 Thess. 1:3; 5:8; Heb. 6:10–12; 10:22–24; 1 Peter 1:3–8; 21–22).[1] Concerning these three gifts, Calvin comments, "For what purpose does the whole ministry serve, but that we may be trained in these three gifts."[2] In his *Handbook of Faith, Hope, and Love*, Augustine describes the importance of seeking these three blessings:

> What is to be sought after above all else? What in view of the divers heresies is to be avoided above all else? How far does reason support religion; or what happens to reason when the issues involved concern faith alone; what is the beginning and end of our endeavor? What is the most comprehensive explanation of all explanations? What is the certain and distinctive foundation of our catholic [universal] faith? You would have the answers to all these questions if you really understood what a man should believe, what he should hope for, and what he ought to love. For these are the chief things—indeed, the only things—to seek for in religion. He who turns away from them is either a complete stranger to the name of Christ or else a heretic.[3]

Covenanter ministers, such as Andrew Gray, spoke of the important interrelationship among these graces: "Faith will be content with the promise, and hope will be content with the thing that is promised, but the ambitious grace of love will only be content with the promiser: love claspeth his arms about that precious and noble object, Jesus Christ."[4]

With these gifts as a measure and guide, the Covenanters shined as the sun. Their Reformed faith was not simply an intellectual creed but a vital and balanced religion. Reformation that does not focus on all three gifts is not true reformation. In the broader context, these three graces are part of the process of sanctification that God uses to mold Christians into his image. Although each grace is examined separately, the "gifts of the spotless lamb are so sweetly linked together, that they were like his own coat that was on his body, which was without seam, that could not be divided; and so except the whole gifts of Jesus Christ fall on us by divine lot, we can have no part or portion therein."[5]

This chapter explores what we can learn regarding sanctification from the sermons of Nevay* and others. Nevay's sermons all follow the same outline: (1) the definition, (2) the excellency, (3) the promise, and (4) the use of the grace. The lesson to learn in examining their intense desire to apply God's grace is that Christianity is more than a living expectation of eternal life; we must grasp the necessity and wonder of God's mercy, which underlies grace and its blessings. The pursuit of sanctification brings this truth home to us daily.

Sanctification – Its Two Parts

The covenant blessing of sanctification, which conforms us to the image of Christ, should be our great study, work, and ambition.

The Covenanters viewed sanctification as essential. Nevay refers to its two parts as "Mortification" and "New Obedience."

Mortification: Nevay emphasizes that conversion is a change "of the whole man" and all his "parts and powers." Yet, "there remains in every part and power of man an unrenewed part." In believers "there arises daily a strife and combat betwixt the unrenewed and the renewed part, which are called flesh and spirit." Mortification is the daily destruction of the "old man and his deeds," whereby we gain victory over the "law and dominion of sin" (Rom. 8:2) and "begin to cease from sin" (1 Pet. 4:1).[6] Mortification is the "pruning knife to the vine, which causes the greater fruitfulness" and forces us to mould "our desires to our estates." It results in "Christian contentment, which is a rare and rich jewel of the Christian."[7] There is joy in victory over Satan: "In mortification we fight the Lord's battles; so, are with him, and stand for him; and the promise is, if we be with him, he will be with us" (2 Chron. 15:2).[8] God promises victory, *"Sin shall not have dominion over you"* (Rom. 6:14): "Victory over sin is promised by the Father, undertaken by the Son, and wrought by the Spirit."[9] Although Nevay's sermon on this topic is excellent, Andrew Gray's is unsurpassed. Gray considered mortification essential because "unless

---

* Some liberty is taken in consolidating and reordering arguments in the abridgment process.

one dies with Christ, one cannot reign with him."[10] It is only through aggressive spiritual warfare that Christians can overcome the dominion of their lust, discover the deceitfulness of their own heart, see the deceiver face-to-face, grow in faith, attain intimate fellowship and communion with God, exercise and mature all the spiritual graces, develop an antipathy for and hatred against sin, and receive the hidden manna (sweetness of Christ) promised in Rev. 2:17.[11] It is only "in pursuit of His enemies" that a Christian is "admitted to put out his finger, and taste the honey, that his eyes may be enlightened."[12] The natural man fails in this warfare because he engages the outer rather than the inner sins, fights to avoid God's judgment rather than to display God's holiness, attempts to restrain rather than mortify sins, responds only when under affliction, and wrestles using his own strength rather than resting on God's.[13] The root cause of failure in overcoming sin is disbelief.[14]

Gray identifies three insights that each Christian must grasp to be an overcomer. First, "it is easier to mortify your lust than to satisfy them" as declared in Psalm 78:29–30: "They got their hearts' desire," yet *they were not estranged from their lust.* Second, "it is better to fight with your lust, than to fight with a living and eternal God." Third, "ye that are tasting the sweetness of sin cannot taste the sweetness of heaven." It is necessary "to have our souls constantly under the impression of the sinfulness of sin" and to mortify sin through self-examination, study, and secret prayer: "Sin goes not out but by fasting and prayer."[15] Satan, through subtle deception, sifts us as wheat by tempting us to respond to our predominate lust: "The hook wherewith he studies to take us, is varnished over with bait of imaginary divinity, with transient pleasures, and passing vanities." Gray insists, "Except ye be the ruin of your iniquities, iniquity shall certainly be your ruin."[16] Victory requires that Christians mortify their original sin (the flesh), their predominate sins (affections), and the first motions unto sins (lusts).[17]

Gray advises, "Christians hath the same power communicable unto him, for overcoming of temptations, which Christ had in the overcoming of principalities and power" (see Eph. 1:19–20). Gray offers several suggestions to use this power to overcome sin: First, Christians should use this power through the exercise of secret prayer and watchfulness: *"Watch and pray, that ye enter not into temptation"* (Matt. 26:41). Second, they must "be much in the meditation on the suffering, death, and love of Jesus Christ": *"For Thy lovingkindness is before my eyes"* (Ps. 26:3a). Third, they must exercise faith: *"Who is he that overcometh the world, but he that believeth that Jesus is the Son of God?"* (1 John 5:5). Faith "discovereth unto a Christian, that supereminent and precious excellency of Jesus Christ, at the appearance of which, the glory and luster of our idols do disappear." Fourth, Christians must mortify their lust with tenderness and with "the expectation of appearing before the judgment seat of Christ" at any moment.[18] Fifth, Christians must mortify the first evidence of lust and avoid all appearances of evil.[19] Sixth, mortification must be a "constant and daily exercise" with determination to mortify our love of the world. This is greatly aided if we "be much taken up in holy contemplation and spiritual beholding of the unsearchable excellencies that are in God. If once the soul of the creature were elevated to behold him, there should not be much difficulty to be mortified to the world."[20] Gray speaks against the antinomian misconception that "one should be dead to the sense and conviction of sin": "It is a killing of the new man within a Christian."[21]

New Obedience: The other part of sanctification is new obedience, which requires that *"if any man be in Christ, he is a new creature"* (2 Cor. 5:17). Nevay contends that this new creature fears and obeys God with his whole heart.[22] This new obedience requires "a fresh and daily supply of the spirit" (Phil. 1:19) and "a serious endeavor" to strive for perfect obedience, purity, and holiness.[23] We must "make sanctification (1) our great study, that we may know it; (2) our great work, to practice it; and (3) our greatest ambition, to reach perfection in it.'"[24] New Obedience is an excellent and promised blessing that is the source of much happiness.

> The man is pronounced blessed that fears the Lord, and delights greatly in his commandments (Ps. 112:1).

> O! Walking with God is a most excellent thing; to bear the image and impressions of God, and Christ, and to walk in the Spirit (Rom. 7:6), it cannot be told what happiness there is in it.[25]

> The happiness is not in knowing, but in doing the will of God.[26]

> All then, that desire not snares and judgments to be rained down upon them, but manifold blessings, let them choose the way wherein blessings do fall; it is in the gracious street of obedience, the beautiful ways of holiness: All who love excellency, love holiness.[27]

> It is promised to the believer that the Lord shall guide him continually—and that he shall be like a watered garden, and like a spring of water, whose waters fail not.... And, in Ezek. 11:19–20, it is promised; that he will put his spirit within them, and cause them to walk in his statutes, and they shall keep his judgments and do them.[28]

Nevay points out that "Christ gives this as sure evidence that men are his disciples, if they love him, and keep his commandments" (John 14:15). New Obedience seeks a clear conscience; strives against sins, particularly secret sins; performs works for the glory of God; desires fellowship with God and fellow Christians; chooses affliction over sin; puts Christ first; and brings the soul to frequent examinations.[29]

Sanctification – Its Grace of Faith

Faith is a saving and a sanctifying grace with which we fetch all the other covenant blessings and promises. It transforms believers into the image of Christ and serves as the uniting band for the church.

In their dying testimonies, the martyr's foremost praise to God was for saving them by his grace. John Nisbet had no doubt that God "determined his heart" and enabled his obedience.

> As for myself, it hath pleased the Lord Jehovah, of his superabundant goodness and infinite mercy, powerfully to determine my heart to close with, and embrace the Lord Jesus Christ, as he is made offer of in the everlasting gospel, for my king, priest, and prophet. That this conquest and captivating of me to his obedience … is the fruit of electing love, according as it is manifested in the covenant of free, free, free grace, will evidently appear from these scriptures {see note]….[†] Which he, by the power and concurrence of his Holy Spirit, hath made effectual to the convincing, converting, strengthening, and enabling of me to be his, and to be for him through well and through woe, through good report and through bad report, and they are so many sweet cordials to my soul when stepping out of time into eternity…. It is by him [Christ] that *I have fought the good fight, that I have finished my course, and that I have kept the faith* (1 Cor. 1:30; 2 Tim. 4:7).[30]

Not only is faith the essential "condition of the Covenant," but it is also a "gift of grace, exercised and showing itself mightily in the work of sanctification, and shining therein as a star of the first magnitude."[31] It is not simply "a piece of sanctification"; it is the very foundation.

Faith is an excellent grace; "it is the root, as it were, of our excellent mercies and of all other good things," as evidenced by the following

---

[†] Exod. 33:19; Ps. 45:1–9; 55:22; 57:2; 59:16–17; 68:18–20; 89:33–34; 110:3; Prov. 4:18; 8:30, 32–36; 28:13; Isa. 53; Matt. 11:29; John 1:1–15; 6:36, 39; 18; Rom. 1:16; 3:24–25; 4:6; 5:1–2, 17; 8:17, 29–30, 35–36; 9:11, 15–16; 8:1; 14:17; 1 Cor. 1:9; 2 Cor. 5:1, 19; 10:4; Gal. 2:16; Eph. 1:13–14; 3:17; 4:23; Phil. 1:6; 3:9–10; Col. 1:27; 2 Thess. 2:13; 2 Tim. 1:9; Titus 3:5–6; Heb. 9:14; 12:23; 1 Pet. 1:5; 1 John 5:13; with many more.

proofs. First, "by it we are brought into and kept in favor with God"; by it we are justified and "become the children of God" (Rom. 5:1; Gal. 3:26). Second, *"By faith Christ comes to dwell in the heart, exercising his office, and rooting and grounding the soul in love"* (Eph. 3:17).[32] Third, it "purifies the heart" (Acts 15:9) and "draws life and virtue from the promises" (2 Cor. 7:1). Fourth, it is the means by which we stand (Rom. 11:20), live (Heb. 10:38), grow (2 Cor. 5:7), and are kept (1 Pet. 1:5) in our Christian walk. Fifth, "it fights all our battles, until we have a complete victory, not only over the world but [also] against all enemies" (1 John 5:4). Sixth, it "is the common cistern to all grace; it is filled from the fountain, and from it all the rest come to be supplied." Seventh, although we are not worthy of the least of God's mercies (Gen. 32:10), "faith works wonders, making impossible things possible." Eighth, "all the precious and excellent promises are made to faith" (Gal. 3:14, 16). From faith, we derive forgiveness of sin (Acts 13:39), assurance in prayer (Matt. 21:22), peace and safety (Isa. 26:3), joy and comfort (Rom. 15:13), prosperity and establishment (2 Chron. 20:20), mercy on earth (Ps. 32:10), and "eternal life hereafter" (John 3:16, 36).[33]

Faith is a promised covenant blessing. First, "Scripture promises it" (Isa. 10:20; 17:7; 51:5; Jer. 3:19; Zeph. 3:12; Matt. 12:21; John 6:37). Second, "Scripture speaks of it as a gift" (Eph. 2:8; 2 Pet. 1:1). Faith comes from preaching, and preaching is a free gift (Rom. 10:14). Third, "believing is through grace" (Acts 18:27; John 1:16), and *"Christ is the author and finisher of our faith"* (Heb. 12:2). Fourth, it must be promised because it is God's work, not ours: *"No man can come to [Jesus] except the Father ... draws him"* (John 6:44); "none can believe but they be born again" (John 1:13); "the Spirit by whom we believe is a free Spirit" (John 3:8). Fifth, the apostles looked not to themselves, but to God to increase their faith (Luke 17:5). Sixth, faith is not only the foundation for the believer, but it is also the "uniting band" for the church. Seventh, it is indisputably a covenant blessing because it "is the root, as it were, on which other graces do grow."[34]

Nevay proposes the following uses for these doctrines: First, those without this faith are doomed to Hell (Luke 12:46; Rev. 21:8). Second, considering the excellency of faith, it is a terrible thing to pervert its doctrine or to "not earnestly contend for it" (Jude vs. 3). Third, faith is of great use in spiritual warfare as a shield *"to quench all the fiery darts of the devil"* (Eph. 6:16). Fourth, "seek to have this faith." Consider its necessity and great promises. Consider its excellent object, Christ, and its supporting role in the other graces. Fifth, be thankful for whatever faith you have, for it has the promise for more: *"To him that hath, it shall be given even to have more abundance"* (Matt. 13:12). Sixth, search to see if your faith is sound. The marks of sound faith include "purifying the heart from the love of sin," loving God (Gal. 5:6), loving "saints as saints" (Eph. 1:15), seeking to please God in everything that we do (Col. 1:10), making use of "every means of holiness" (Prov. 8:34), and studying to bring forth fruit suitable to the pains taken (Heb. 6:7–8). More particularly, evidences include "denying all things for him," "preferring to do God's will to the rewards of well doing," examining ourselves daily, increasing in humility as works increase, rejoicing in the spread of the gospel, praying with earnest, and avoiding self seeking. Seventh, having found this faith, "it should be our next work to most carefully maintain" and exercise it in sanctifying works.[35] Eighth, *"Without faith it is impossible to please him: for he that cometh to God must believe that he is, and that he is a rewarder of them that diligently seek him"* (Heb. 11:6). Ninth, it "shows the vanity and the wickedness of that error, which puts it in the power of man's will, to choose or refuse Christ." The "changeable will" of man is a sad "foundation for faith." Tenth, a reproof is in order to those who view faith "more as a work than a gift"; instead, they should view it as a "covenant blessing" and as the "work of the Holy Spirit." Eleventh, to Christians, faith is "their greatest jewel, and most useful tool in the spiritual building." With it, we can fetch all the other covenant promises. Twelfth, seek to increase this faith by going to the promises with humility, hunger, and thirst, seeking to plead for it as a free gift for use in God's service.[36]

Nevay and the Covenanters viewed faith, Christ, and the promises as inseparably interrelated; they are the only things called *precious* in the Bible. To the Covenanter Andrew Gray, "faith, as it were, has two blessed eyes; by one of these it beholds Christ, and by another of these it beholds the promises, and fixes itself on them."[37] Gray contends, "Let once your soul closes with Christ by faith and love, and then you may with boldness close with the promises."[38] Through the promises, "we are made partakers of the divine nature" for they are the "star that leads us unto the house where Christ doth lie, and there is no access to Christ, but by a promise." These promises are "the pencils that draw the … image of Christ on the soul."[39] Focusing on the promises helps us see and close with Christ, who is the *Pearl of Great Price* and the primary object of faith.[40] Without Christ, "faith is but an empty thing."[41] Christ is a divine, excellent, and precious being: "There is soul-conquering virtue in the face of Christ, and there is heart-captivating and overcoming power in the beauty of Jesus Christ."[42] However, Christ crucified, not Christ considered for his beauty, is the immediate object of our faith.[43]

The richness of the Covenanters' understanding of faith exposes the shallow understanding of modern Christians. Unlike many modern Christians, whose faith only looks to the promise of eternal life, the Covenanters viewed faith as perpetually contemplating and viewing all of God's promises, all commanded duties, and that "immortal crown of blessedness" reserved for those that persevere to the end.[44]

Sanctification – Its Grace of Love

A holy life is an absolute necessity because God gives us a new heart that desires to please and obey him above all things. Christ's unspeakable and undeserved love for us is reflected in our love of others, which reaches its highest expression in forgiveness.

Augustine observes, *"The faith that saves … is … the faith that works through love"* (Gal. 5:6b): "When we ask whether someone is a good man, we are not asking what he believes, or hopes, but what he loves."[45] God's gift of love enables us to love God and others. No matter how diligently we seek to obey or understand doctrine, unless we have the love of God in us, all is in vain (see John 5:37–42). Scripture sometimes refers to the grace of love as *charity*. Calvin calls charity God's gift for the edification of his church: "All other gifts, how excellent so ever they may be in themselves, are of no value unless they are subservient to charity."[46]

According to Nevay, love "is the affection of the soul, by which it goes after and cleaves unto some desirable and suitable good." It is not "a natural love by which man loves himself and the things good to nature"; it is "a spiritual love, which does bound and regulate that which is natural, giving to it a higher rise, and making it run in the right channel, to the right object and end."[47] The ultimate end of spiritual love is "union and communion with God," and it has a fivefold nature:

(1) A love of choice or dependence, whereby we settle and depend upon the one thing good: this is only due to God. (2) A love of delight and complacency, such as that of God in Christ (Matt. 3:17), and of a believer in God (Ps. 37:4) and in his Word (Ps. 119:92, 143). (3) A love of fellowship, mutual love, such as that between God and a believer (1 John 4:19) and between a man and his friend (Prov. 27:9, 17). (4) There is a love of benefice or a bountiful love; such also is God's love of man, and such ought our love be to one another. (5) There is a love of pity; such is God's love to sinners (Ps. 103:13). And this one sinner ought to bear to another, especially in distress (Job 6:14) we ought with this love our enemies.[48]

Love is an excellent thing. First, consider the excellency of its author, God who "is a God of love" (1 John 4:7–8, 16); its object, the "lovely Jesus";

its result, grace is with *"them that love the Lord Jesus in sincerity"* (Eph. 6:24); and its nature, it forever endures (1 Cor. 13:13). Although faith and hope are of great value, "only love abides when we shall have no more use of faith and hope." Second, Scripture makes many excellent promises concerning it: treasures (Prov. 8:21), safety and preservation (Ps. 145:20), assured deliverance (Ps. 91:14), eternal life and the kingdom (James 1:12; 2:5), and Christ's presence (John 12:26). Christ promises, *"He that loves me shall be loved of my father, and I will love him, and manifest myself unto him"* (John 14:21). Third, its excellency is evident in God's love to those who love him and the misery of those who do not: *"He is God, the faithful God, which keeps covenant and mercy with them that love him and keep his commandments to a thousand generations"* (Deut. 7:9); *"All things work together for the good to them that love God"* (Rom. 8:28); *"If any man love not the Lord Jesus Christ, let him be"* cursed (1 Cor. 16:22). Fourth, "it is one of the most necessary things to a soul; it is life of a soul and the soul's rest; without it the soul cannot be happy." Fifth, it is "throughout all eternity, the most full enjoyment of God." Consider how Christ makes believers dwell in the light, makes them alive, dwells with them, and perfects his love within them (1 John 2:10; 3:14; 4:12, 16). Even his love of enemies is excellent: he provides rain and sunshine to the just and unjust; he requires that we forgive them as he forgave us; and he requires that we love and help them.[49]

Love is a promised covenant blessing, as illustrated by these proofs:

(1) A new heart is promised; therefore a heart to love the Lord is promised; for, naturally we are haters of God (Rom. 1:30). (2) Faith is promised, as we have proved; now faith works by love (Gal. 5:6). (3) Obedience is promised, and love is the fountain thereof, the sweet constraint of love (2 Cor. 5:14), it is joined with service (Jer. 8:2). (4) Even betrothing in love is promised (Hos. 2:16, 19–20), and marriage love on Christ's side will ever ensure our love to him. (5) He has promised that he will rest in his love (Zeph. 3:17), and sure that love will begat love. (6) Knowledge of God and Christ is promised; and who can know them but will love them? (7) Grace and glory, and every good thing, is promised (Ps. 84:11), and all spiritual blessings (Eph. 1:3), and must not love be among them? (8) The pouring forth of Christ's name like ointment is promised; will not then the virgins love him (Song. of Sol. 1:3–4)? (9) Mortification is promised, so the purging out of self-love, and by consequence, the giving of sound love. (10) It is promised that the Lord will be the portion of his people (Jer. 10:16), [and] they cannot but love their portion. (11) The Spirit is promised (Hag. 2:5), and love is one of the fruit of the Spirit, and the first

that is reckoned (Gal. 5:22). (12) Heaven is so promised [to] those that love God (1 Cor. 2:9).[50]

Nevay lists several uses for these doctrines. Illustrations that show how the Puritans, Covenanters, and James Nisbet applied this knowledge are included, where appropriate. The fivefold nature of spiritual love serves as a guide to organize the discussion of these uses.

First, the love of God causes us to choose and depend upon him. God's "love is wages unto itself." Christians must "learn to know what true Christian love is, to distinguish between it and lust, yea, and between it and natural affection, and to fix it on the right and principal object of it, God." To quicken us to his love, consider "how all excellencies and desirable things are in him," how he has suffered and done great things for us (Gal. 2:20), and "how by covenant we are engaged to love him." In particular, consider "how he has first loved us."[51] John Owen contended that the foundation of our love is Christ's love for us: "We are never nearer Christ than when we find ourselves lost in holy amazement at his unspeakable love."[52] James Nisbet's memoir is replete with seemingly endless reflections on the infinite love of a sin-revenging God and the obligations of those who know this love.

> Who is a God like unto thee, that pardons iniquity, and passes by the sins and transgressions of his people, and retains not his anger forever, because he delights in mercy? O my soul! How vastly and infinitely extensive must the kind compassions of redeeming love be that incline the everlasting Jehovah to enter upon such a wonderful undertaking.... This was love that hath neither brim nor bottom! Here is matter of everlasting wonder and admiration for angels and men, through all eternity.... O thou my soul, and all that is within me behold him, embrace him, and wonder, love, and admire him! Amen.
>
> O infinite love…! All ye angels in heaven, and all ye inhabitants of this lower world, behold the man Christ Jesus swimming into the sea of wrath, and then swimming forth again, with all the elect embosomed within the circle of his redeeming arms, leading captives in triumph gloriously! And must not sin be forever abominable and hateful beyond comparison that no less than the blood of God-man could purchase and procure a pardon for it…? And must there not be a great depth of atheism, rebellion, with many other spiritual plagues, in the hearts of the children of men, that they should stand it out so long against innumerable kind invitations, against so many knockings of the spirit, against so many rods, afflictions, and persecutions, which are as so many iron whips to drive home straying sheep? Infinite love, wonderful in pains,…

expenses,… patience,… height,… breadth,… and unsearchable depth! O Lord, thou the God of infinite love, seek thy poor servant, and save the son of thine handmaid. Let me not turn aside to folly, neither grieve thy Holy Spirit, but keep me ever in the exercise of thy love, faith, fear, humility, self-denial, and all the other graces, though always enabling me to put in my claim for a share of this glorious Redeemer, and his dear-bought redemption. Amen.[53]

Nevay considered knowledge of the grace of love a "reproof and terror to those who have nothing of this true love." What a shame it is that "they know nothing of the law or the gospel; love is the fulfilling of the one and the perfection of the other." The sum of the law is expressed in Mark 12:30, and summed up in one word, *love.* Hence, what a loss it is to "know nothing of God; for he is love." Although all things work together for them that love him, all things work against those who do not.[54]

Second, the love of God leads us to love, to desire, and to delight in him. Nevay advises, "let all who love true excellency labor to attain it, and work up your heart to an earnest coveting of it as the best gift, and the more excellent way" (1 Cor. 12:31). Our love "should be such a tender love, as the least wrong done to it may go very near our hearts: such as David's that rivers of water did run down his eyes when men kept not God's law" (Ps. 119:136).[55]

The Puritan John Flavel wrote a great sermon, similar to many preached by the Covenanters, on the loveliness of Christ, *"Yes, he is altogether lovely"* (Song of Sol. 5:16). Flavel contended that Christ "is the loveliest person souls can set their eyes on" and contrasted Christ's loveliness with that of man. All other loveliness apart from Christ is secondary, relative, fading, perishing, ensnaring, confining, and unsatisfying.[56] Gray remarked, "A Christian being united unto precious Christ, by that golden and invisible chain of his beauty, and transcendent excellency, can with patience endure the loss of all things besides Christ."[57] Renwick said, "Indeed they that love not Christ, it is because they do not know him." Renwick describes the depth of Christian love by citing the Shulamite's request to her beloved (Christ): *"Set me as a seal upon your heart, as a seal upon your arm; for love is as strong as death, jealousy as cruel as the grave; its flames are flames of fire, a most vehement flame. Many waters cannot quench love, nor can the floods drown it. If a man would give for love all the wealth of his house, it would be utterly despised"* (Song of Sol. 8:6–7 NKJ).[58] The covenanting ministers filled their sermons with references to the Song of Solomon. Unfortunately, modern Reformed leaders ignore this book, which "in a continued parable does hold forth the promises of Love."[59]

James Nisbet describes how the apprehension of Christ's love overwhelmed the Covenanters:

It was surprisingly wonderful to see … how he made them glad to rejoice in the light of his countenance; and how he made them delight in himself, as their only up-making portion.[60]

How wonderfully did their dear, kind, and compassionate Lord own and assist them with the ravishing, transporting, and overcoming discoveries of the knowledge and glory of himself in the face of Christ, and of the beauty and sweetness of his cross, that they were often quite nonplussed! So that they made no more reckoning of death, nor of what men could say of them, or do to them, than the scratch of a pin; but, on the contrary, they, with much wonder and admiration, cried out thus, or to this purpose…. Our wonderfully good God makes us now to see such a beauty in his redeeming love … that we are no more afraid nor disturbed with enemies threatenings, or with the gazings of multitudes upon us, than we were with and speaking to our own children and meanest of our inferiors. O the reality of religion! The good will of God! The sweet outlettings of Christ! The supporting and comforting power of the Spirit of Grace! For the more we are gazed on, the more doth the holy courage of our hearts and souls increase: the more we are threatened, the less we are afraid of what man can do unto us. We fear not death in its most formidable attacks: we have learned of thrice and forever lovely Christ to die any kind of death for him, that we may get home to the uninterrupted enjoyment of him, whose ravishing beauty, infinite worth and excellency, has so overcome us that we can not endure to be absent from him any longer…. Come … quickly, Lord Jesus! …O for the sweet, for the warm, for the naked embraces of thee, thou glorious King of Saints, and highly-exhaulted King of Nations! O thou supereminently, matchlessly, excellent Jesus! O lovely, lovely, lovely, Jesus Christ of Nazareth, the Father's eternal, equal, and everlasting delight! O, our souls adore … admire … [and] delight in thee! Our souls long vehemently to be at the full enjoyment of one adorable God, Father, Son, and Holy Ghost, one, in three, and three in one!

O, who is like unto thee, who pardons iniquity, and passes by the transgressions of thy people, and retains not thine anger forever, because thou delightest in mercy!…[He] said unto us, live, live! Even us, who were enemies [and] rebels against him…. Yet, O us, even us, hath he abundantly pardoned and graciously forgiven, and brought us near himself, even very near, by the blood of his covenant. O Lord, is this the manner of man? No, no. That cannot be; it is not the manner of man nor angels; but it is the way and manner of a wonder-working God, and that our souls knows right well... O redeemed of the Lord, wonder at this, and praise him...! Who hath done all these unspeakably good things for us, and now hath singled us out to be cross-bearing, confessing, bleeding, dying, and triumphing witnesses for him and his despised truths? For in him, and by the power of his right hand, we fight, we die, we overcome. O sweet,... lovely,... light, and desirable cross of Christ...! Then all you who will venture honestly to take up his cross, in his strength he will bear you and it both, and will pay you the wages as if ye had done all the work. He hath done so to us, and he will deal no worse with those that come after us.... O, our souls are ravished... with the beauty of our fair, incomparably fair, Lord Jesus Christ, God-man, and his sweet cross! ...Our souls are ravished, and leap for joy, that we are got safe in under the refreshful shadow of this tree of life; Christ, and only Christ and his cross, is a rich portion, a sweet portion, and an excellent portion. O that every hair of our head were a man to die for him...! For all lives that are interested in his covenant ways, and lost for him, are found in him, saved of him, and redeemed by him to wear a crown of immortal life. Sweet scaffolds...! You are the way to the warm and endless embraces of the thrice and forever well-beloved of our souls! O that every faculty of our souls were as wide as the heavens and as broad as the earth, to receive much, to enjoy much, of sweet and lovely Christ, who fills heaven and earth! O praise him! O our souls praise; praise, for it is comely! Death, come do thy worst! Time and space flee out of the way. Come sweet, sweet Jesus Christ! Come lovely Christ! Why are the chariot wheels so long a coming? Come quickly! Make no tarrying, for we die willingly for thee, that we may live forever in and with thee![61]

Third, the love of God leads us to desire fellowship and communion with him (discussed later) and his saints. Love for one another is the chief mark of Jesus' disciples: *"By this shall all men know that ye are my disciples, if ye have love one to another"* (John 13:35 NKJ). This love is not just for others individually, but also for them corporately. According to Nevay, love of the saints has several marks: it is to all the saints; it manifests a high esteem and delight to none but the saints (Ps. 16:3); it increases the more they conform to Christ's image; it evidences the fruit of the Spirit within us (1 Cor. 13:4–5); and it is bountiful.[62] James Nisbet's description of the Covenanters provides an excellent picture of true brotherly love:

It was surprisingly wonderful to see how much they were taken up in provoking one another to love and good works, by being free to one another in their Christian counsel and holy advice, and by being exemplary to one another in all holy circumspection and upright walking before the Lord, before whom all things appear as naked and bare. [They did this by] setting him always before them, living under the awful impressions of him, and acknowledging him in all their ways, and by a free communicating to one another their experiences of the Lord's goodness to their souls.... In the midst of all dangers and deepest distresses, they could say ... for the comfort and encouragement of one another, (1) that the ways of the Lord are all pleasantness; (2) that all his paths are peace; (3) that his cross [is] a sweet, easy, light, and [honorable]; and (4) that the [embellishments] of their dear and sweet Lord of himself to their souls did more, by far, than defray all the charges and expenses that they were put to in bearing the cross. Upon which account, they cried out to one another, with the great Apostle Paul, (1) we are troubled on every side, yet not distressed; (2) we are perplexed, yet not in despair; (3) we are persecuted, but not forsaken; and (4) we are cast down, but not destroyed. For this cause we faint not, though our outward man perish, yet the inward man is renewed day by day. For our light afflictions, which are but for a moment, they work for us a far more exceeding and eternal weight of glory, while we look not at the things which are seen, which are temporal, but at those things which are spiritual and eternal, and now seen and enjoyed by faith.

Thus, those noble sufferers were burden-bearers and hearty sympathizers with one another; while, David-like, they said one to another, "Come here all ye that fear God, and I will tell you what he hath done for my soul." And it was observed, that those cross-bearers, if any of them were, at anytime, under a damp on their spirits, they acquainted their suffering companions with their case. Every one of whom would run there alone and cry to the Lord for light, counsel, and comfort to that person, and would seldom give over till the complainer's case was the best of all the company. So that through the goodness of the Lord their mouths were much oftener filled with his praises for his condescendency to them, than with complaints. Yea, it was a rare thing to hear any of them complain, notwithstanding of their straitened suffering circumstances; but rather, Caleb-like, followed the Lord fully, doing every thing to commend him, and bring a good report upon his honorable way; saying often with David, "Behold! Here am I, let him do with me what seems good in his sight, so being he may be glorified." O my soul! Bless thou the Lord, that ever I was embarked with such a wrestling and cross-bearing company, who had the mighty God of Jacob for the sword and shield of their excellency![63]

Unfortunately, after the Revolution Settlement, the Society People failed to exhibit this love. Instead, they spent most of their time "framing arguments to debate," neglecting the "principles of the Christian religion" and "real godliness." By emphasizing abstract principles and personal piety above love for fellow Christians and Christ's church, the hyper-reformed neglect the church, dooming it to a spiral of lower holiness and less adherence to principles. Although we are required to speak out against the sins of our brethren, it must be done with recognition that all have sinned and fallen short of the glory of God. John Knox, who spoke out boldly against sin, could do so because he openly confessed his own sinful nature. Knox leaves proof of this attitude in a letter to his mother-in-law:

> Albeit I never lack the presence and plain image of my own wretched infirmity, yet, seeing sin so manifestly abound in all estates, I am compelled to thunder out the threatenings of God against obstinate rebellers; in doing whereof (albeit as God knoweth I am no malicious or obstinate sinner) I sometimes am wounded, knowing myself criminal and guilty in many, yea in all things (malicious obstinacy laid aside) that in others I reprehend. Judge not, mother, that I write these things debasing myself otherwise than I am. No! I am worse than my pen can express. In body ye think I am no adulterer—let so be; but the heart is infected with foul lust.... Externally I commit no idolatry, but my wicked heart loveth the self.... I am no man killer with my hands, but I help not my needy brother so liberally as I may and ought.... And thus, in conclusion there is no vice repugnant to God's holy will expressed in his law wherewith my heart is not infected.[64]

Knox loved and was loved by those that knew him because they perceived him as a "common brother" who "trembled for [his] own sins before the face of God."[65] This deep appreciation for God's mercy and justice is the basis for the love bond among Christians. Christians are commanded to *"Forebear one another in love with all lowliness, meekness, and longsuffering"* (Eph. 4:2). Those who separate from the true church for reasons of piety do not possess it. Concerning this false piety, Spiros Zodhiates remarked, "When men judge themselves by the standards of their fellow men, they appear bright and wise, but when they compare their wisdom with God's, they see how worthless it is."[66]

Our love should extend to all, for love breeds a giving and forgiving spirit. In addition to meeting the need of the poor, Christians have an even more important duty to their fellow man. According to Augustine, "none of these alms is greater than the forgiveness from the heart of sin committed against us by someone else." In addition to forgiveness, Augustine contends that Scripture demands that we correct, pray for, rebuke, constrain, and administer discipline as appropriate, particularly to those under our command.[67] In particular, Christ rebuked the Pharisees for being conscientious in their financial tithing but neglecting "justice and the love of God," advising them to "give the kind of alms which shall make all things clean to you."[68]

Fourth, the bountiful nature of God's love produces within us a goodwill for God's glory, the good of his people, and a zeal for obedience.[69] Those who have true Christian love obey God. According to Nevay, the three marks of Christian love are a "holy care to please God," a "delight in doing his will," and a "zeal and jealousy against all these things which may hinder sweet intercourse betwixt the soul and God."[70] Scripture makes it clear that there is only one way to demonstrate our love for God: *"If you love me, keep my commandments"* (John 14:15). All the law can be "fulfilled and summed up in this one word, *Love*, and that *'love is the fulfilling of the law'"* (Rom. 13:10).[71] This required obedience is not simply obedience to the letter of the law, but it is obedience arising from our heart as we reflect on God's love for us. Such obedience is the parent, guardian, and source of all virtues.[72] Many modern Christians neglect the commandments because they foolishly conceive that Christ abolished the necessity of obedience to God's Law. It is only by obeying his commandments that we come to know God, have the love of God perfected in us, and come to know that we are his (1 John 2:3–6). Consequently, the Covenanters and the Puritans believed that a holy life was an absolute necessity. We should do likewise. Unlike modern Christians, who take a relativistic approach towards obedience, they were motivated through love and obedience to achieve the *Shorter Catechism*'s definition of chief end of man: "To glorify God and to enjoy him forever." We must perceive that "God's eye is what counts."[73]

The Covenanter and Puritans, along with the Apostle Paul, rejected the extremes of legalism (doctrine of salvation through good works) and Antinomianism (doctrine that the law no longer applies to believers).[74] Ernest Kevan speaks of the Puritan's view of the relationship of the law to salvation.

> They [Puritans] recognized that the law was the standard by which God would judge the world and condemn the ungodly, but they also perceived its saving use as it slew men's self-confidence, revealed their guilt and pollution, and drove them to Christ.... They were occupied with obedience to the law as the way of the believing man and with the ful-

fillment of the law as the end for which he was saved. The law of God thus connoted for the Puritan nothing but blessedness and delight: it belonged to the doctrine of salvation.[75]

When James Nisbet attempts to describe the Covenanters, he begins by depicting them as men that the Lord blessed with a genuine spirit of obedience to his Word, in all their thoughts and deeds.

> My opinion of them is that they, a few excepted, were persons highly favored of the Lord for these reasons: In that they were helped through grace to espouse, with heart and soul, all the attained-unto pieces of reformation, from anti-Christian darkness, error, and superstition, to presbytery covenant ways, in soundness and gospel simplicity, of principles and practices, according to the whole Word of God. [They] were so staunch therein, that they would not lose nor part with neither hair nor hoof for the pleasure of no man. Neither would they stain their consciences by denying their dear Lord and his righteous cause with the least of sinful compliances. Neither [would they] stain their life and conversation the least of immoral practices, but [they] lived straightly up to their light in the Lord. They were solid and serious, and conscientiously deliberated what to choose and what to refuse, never consulting with flesh and blood, but with God in his Word, and the judgment of sound divines; particularly the *Westminster Confession of Faith*, concerning what was duty and what was sin. They were much in the exercise of mortification, and abstemious from all inordinate and unnecessary use of the creature, both in meat, drink, and apparel. They were very hospitable and compassionate towards those in want, having all things, for most part, in common, resembling the primitive Christians; and this liberality they extended often, even to those who were not of their own judgment, yea, even sometimes to avowed enemies. Thus, their light of principles and honesty of practice did so shine before all, as made every thinking unprejudiced person praise God in their behalf; and very often struck even their worst enemies with a strong conviction, which occasioned even the bitterest of them sometimes to commend that people and their way which they most persecuted.[76]

Attempted obedience draws us to love God. The required obedience is in no way a human work; it is Christ's work in us. The Puritans were violently opposed to outer conformity or morality separate from the saving grace of Jesus Christ. They believed "obedience performed to God, must proceed from within, and come from the heart, else it shall be no whit acceptable to him."[77] Without saving faith, the law is of no value, and even helps to "augment sin, by reason of the flesh."[78] Morality without faith is as a "soft pillow from whence many slide insensibly into destruction," resulting in no lasting earthly change—"water heated to the highest pitch is but water still."[79] The concept that morality exists apart from the gospel is a fatal error of our society. It is the chief heresy of humanism and will lead to the destruction of our nation if not corrected.

Fifth, the love of God leads us to pity and to desire the salvation of sinners. Since God's truth is the only cure, not tolerating beliefs contrary to the Word of God best evidences our love. James Nisbet clearly predicts the outcome of toleration: "I disown the wicked toleration granted the last year, to open a door to popery and all false religion, which will prove to the utter subversion of all true religion, if the Lord interpose not with his preventing mercy."

One Sunday during my college years when visiting my home church, I learned this lesson firsthand. In response to the Sunday school message on the judgment of God, I remarked, "But God is a God of love!" The teacher, Glenn Alexander, quickly countered with Scripture verses that hushed my misguided platitudes, showing me that God's love and judgment are inseparable. It was the testimony and living witness of such men, whose love was manifest by sharing of the truth rather than the embracing of a half-truth, that led me to join the church in my late twenties. The church needs this type of love rather than the ecumenical embracing of half-truths that leads to death. The cold reality of "tough love," in the words of Cornelius Van Til, is that "a true ecumenism requires the exclusion from the church of Christ of those who have not the faith of Abraham."[80] Thomas Watson once remarked, "Love to God is armor of proof against error. For want of hearts full of love, men have heads full of error; unholy opinions are for want of holy affections."[81]

James Nisbet describes how the Covenanters acquired and exhibited love for God's truth:

> These noble adventurers and faithful cloud of witnesses for truth [were] strongly and sweetly determined by grace to count the cost, deny themselves, embrace their dear Lord and Savior, set apart themselves, surrender ... themselves to him, and take up their cross for his sake, and for his precious truth's sake, which was then much denied and despised.... He and his providences led them through many wants, weariness, bad report, and good report, yea, innumerable winding circuits of tribulations, while passing their pilgrimage through this world.... He ... humbled them, proved them, tried them, and ripened them by grace, for their greatest and utmost trials, in leaving them to fall into the hands of

their bloody enemies..., before rulers and great men who threatened them with death in all its ghastly and terrible shapes.

But, O then, to the glory of his great name, to the honor of his righteous cause, to the no small comfort and consolation of their souls, and to the shame and confusion of all his and their enemies; how wonderfully, graciously, and remarkably did the Lord, their kind and compassionate God, stand by them, own, and assist them! That so with much freedom and boldness in the face of their enemies, and with much quietness of mind, and composure of spirit, did they, on all hazards, declare their cordial and constant adherence to all the parts of his despised and trampled upon truths, counting the least part thereof worth many lives and much blood. And, indeed, it was very observable, that those of them that dallied and dipped least with the enemy, but stood closest to the received principles of the reformed-covenanted Church of Scotland, were the persons that were most singularly owned of God. How wonderfully did their dear Lord own and assist them with suffering grace, or grace to outface all dangers! For such was the strength of their love to him and his cause, that their affections could not be bribed with love of natural life, [relatives, or land] to deny him and [to] lay a confederacy with his enemies; but much rather would they forego, and lose all for his name's sake.

How wonderfully did their dear and compassionate Lord own and assist them, with a holy, filial, and reverential fear of himself, ruling in their hearts at all times, but especially when their trials and temptations were strongest, and their dangers greatest! So that they trembled to think of dipping in the least with God's enemies, or dally with a temptation..., to the dishonor of his great name, to the wounding of their own consciences, to the stumbling of the generation of the righteous, and to the hardening of enemies in their wicked courses. [They] often said to themselves and one to another: (1) "He that will not be faithful in that which is little, will not be faithful in that which is much"; (2) "If they cast down what they once built, they make themselves transgressors"; (3) "Those that will not confess him and his truths before men, them will not Christ, their dear Lord, confess before his father and the holy angels"; and (4) "They that love life, or any thing better than him, are not worthy of him." Therefore, when sinning and suffering came in competition, they wisely judged it was their incumbent duty earnestly to contend for the faith once delivered to the saints; they wisely judged it was better to obey God than man; and they wisely judged it was better to lose temporal perishing things, than lose those things which are spiritual and eternal.[82]

Finally, Nevay contends it is the Christian's duty to seek love from the promises using the following means: (1) We must pray because prayer "makes the soul bold and familiar with God," and "prayer does stir up and kindle the dying spark of love." (2) We must maintain a "fresh sense of sinfulness." (3) We "must learn to know the Lord; the more we know him, the better we love him." (4) We "must labor to have assurance of his love to us."[83] It is a great folly to think that God receives well the love of our own making: "The love that will please God, is that which he gives."[84]

God's promised love to his children is always effectual. Both Nevay (see page 203) and James Nisbet, evidenced in the following reflection, observed how God's promised love for his chosen people never fails to transform them:

> It was surprisingly wonderful to see ... how much he helped them to a victory over sin, to a victory over all heart-plagues, to a victory over Satan, to a victory over all temptations of losing the world, in that they suffered joyfully the spoiling of their goods, rather than save them on sinful terms. How he helped them to a victory over the frowns of parents and other relations, who were extremely angry with them for being Moses-like, in choosing to suffer affliction with the people of God in bearing testimony for him and his honorable way, rather than enjoy the pleasures of sin for a season.... Yet all these noble, self-denied, and cross-bearing venturers overcame in the strength of the Lord, by the power of his might. By his help, they overcame the threatening rage of their bloody enemies and the fears of death itself.[85]
>
> How wonderfully did their dear and compassionate Lord own and assist them with sanctifying, renewing, and strengthening grace and mercy! So that he mightily helped them with a victory over a body of sin and death. He sweetly loosed their bonds of sin, speedily knocked off their fetters of iniquity, and quickly made his reconciled face shine refreshfully on them; not but they had their own toilsome struggles with indwelling sin, damps of spirit, and clouds of desertion; but free ... grace and rich mercy made speedy and large advances for their relief and out gate. In regard that a wise God had other work cut out for them, which was to witness a good confession for him, against the sacrilegious encroachments made by wicked men upon Christ's incommunicable prerogatives, who is king and head in and over his own church; which through grace they were helped to do, with much, cheerfulness and constancy.
>
> How wonderfully did their dear, kind, compassionate Lord accompany them with such a sweet and soul-satisfying sense of his pardoning

grace and mercy, and of his distinguishing and redeeming love in Christ extended to them. [Consequently,] much of their little time, when amongst their enemies hands, and under the greatest trials, from the reproaches, scoffs, jeers, and bloody threatenings of their wrathful enemies was spent in admiring, blessing, and praising their God for the remission of all their sins.... For this thing, they often invited their Christian friends and religious companions to praise, and again to praise him, who had done so much for them in a way of grace and gracious condescending. [They,] who could do so little for him in a way of true obedience and in asserting and vindicating his declarative glory, often [said] to one another, "O that we had as many lives as there are hairs on our head! We would freely give them all up in his service, to seal his precious truths with our dearest blood, to bear witness for him, and to bear witness against the sinful encroachment of enemies."[86]

Sanctification – Its Grace of Hope

Hope breeds joy and delight in God, and reliance on the Lord. Our hope should not be limited to eternal life. It should also be for the fulfilling of the Great Commission, the salvation of the Jews, and the glorification of his church.

James Nisbet aptly expresses the Covenanters' view of the grace of hope:

> It is God's unchangeable all-sufficiency, through the blood of the Lamb, effectually applied to my soul by the Holy Spirit, which is my only foundation and hope of glory.... He is the only adequate object of a spiritualized mind; for there is no created thing that can fill and satisfy the heart of man and woman.[87]

Nevay, citing Romans 8:24, defines hope as "a certain and patient expectation of things not seen, from God, as he has promised them." Hope, like faith, looks to the promise, and these two graces are interrelated: *"For we through the Spirit wait for the hope of righteousness by faith"* (Gal. 5:5). Hope is also a great source of comfort when we face storms: "Hope does ride them all out; it is the anchor of the soul, both sure and steadfast." Its object is *God in Christ* (1 Tim. 1:1); its means are the *promise* (Acts 26:6) and *Christ* (Col. 1:27); its effects are *quieting the soul* (Ps. 42:5, 11) and *purifying the heart* (1 John 3:3).[88]

Hope is an excellent and useful grace. First, Scripture commends hope as good (2 Thess. 2:16), better (Heb. 7:19), blessed (Titus 2:13), lively (1 Pet. 1:3), sure, and steadfast (Heb. 6:19). Second, consider the excellency of the three objects of hope held forth in Psalms (i.e., hope in Christ's Word,

Lordship, and mercy) as previously discussed. These objects point to *hope in Jesus Christ and his Gospel* (Col. 1:5; 1 Tim. 1:1), with the ultimate object of hope being eternal dwelling with Christ.[89] Third, consider the nature of hope, for it is *"as an anchor of the soul, both sure and steadfast, and which entereth into that within the veil"* (Heb. 6:19). Fourth, consider its many excellent uses: "It is of use when no other grace is in the fight at all; yea, when God has withdrawn himself" (Ps. 43:5). It "breeds joy and delight in God" (Rom. 12:12; Heb. 3:6). It "makes a man not ashamed" (Rom. 5:5). It gives much encouragement in the Lord's work: *"Therefore, my beloved brethren, be ye steadfast, unmovable, always abounding in the work of the Lord, forasmuch as ye know that your labor is not in vain in the Lord"* (1 Cor. 15:58). Fifth, consider its excellent companion patience, which makes us rest in God and wait on Christ (Ps. 37:7; 2 Thess. 3:5). Sixth, consider how, as the helmet of salvation, it protects our head for eternity (Eph. 6:17). Seventh, consider the many excellent Scripture promises associated with it: *"Happy is he whose hope is the Lord"* (Ps. 146:5). Eighth, consider the excellency of eternal life with Christ (Col. 1:5; Titus 3:7). Ninth, consider "the misery of those who live and die without it."[90]

Hope is a promised covenant blessing. First, David credits God for his hope: *"Thou didst make me to hope when I was upon my mother's breast"* (Ps. 22:9). Second, hope is a covenant promise through grace from a God of Hope (Rom. 15:13). Third, the gospel is said "to bring a better hope" (Heb. 7:19). Fourth, "Christ is both raised from the dead and exalted for this very end, that we might have hope" (1 Pet. 1:21). Fifth, Scripture promises grace, faith, assurance, regeneration, eternal life, strength, all sufficiency, joy, and every good thing; these things are inseparable from hope (Ps. 84:11; Isa. 40:31; Lam. 3:24; Rom. 4:16; 7:24; 1 Thess. 5:8; 2 Thess. 2:16; Heb. 12:2; 1 Pet. 1:3). In short, God, who cannot lie, promised, before the world began, this hope in eternal life (Titus 1:2).[91]

Nevay proposes the following uses for these doctrines. First, there is no hope for those who "have not the promises, nor Christ for their hope." Their hope is "like a spider's web" (Job 8:14); it leads to destruction. Further, it is a "terror to those who live without the covenant," for they are in a sad estate, "they are both without God and without hope." When asked, *"To whom will you fly for help?"* they answer, *"There is no hope, but we will walk after our own devices, and we will every one do the imagination of his evil heart"* (Jer. 18:12). Second, we must study to have the right hope—that is hope in Christ and his promises: "If you shall have this hope of the great things which are to come, these things of eternity, hopes of ex-

ternal and perishing things will look but as lean things."[92] Third, test to
see if your hope is true:

(1) It only eyes God as the portion (Lam. 3:24). (2) It has nothing of confidence in the flesh, but rejoices in Christ Jesus ... (Phil. 3:3). (3) It has a special and firm certainty, leaning on the undoubted truths of Scripture ...
(Rom. 15:4). It is true; the believer's hope may be shaken, [as one does to
set an anchor], yet the upshot will be more sure fastening. (4) It will
keep and hold the soul close to truth, in the case of great opposition
made by men ... (Ps. 119:23, 81–82, 161; Isa. 8:17). (5) It is of sanctification, as
well as of salvation; it is of a purifying nature ... (1 John 3:3). (6) It breeds
quietness in the soul, and much contentment and joy of the spirit; so,
there is patience and rejoicing in hope (1 Thess. 1:3; Heb. 3:6). (7) It presents
things hoped for, so great, as it makes all other hopes vain and empty
things: it purges the heart of all love to them, or desire after them. (8) It
does revive the soul, and recruit it with fresh and new strength when
other things do fail (Ps. 73:26). (9) Where it is true, it will be joined with
sobriety ... (1 Pet. 1:13). (10) Rooted and well-grounded hope is the daughter of much and manifold experiences (Rom. 5:4).[93]

Fourth, it is essential that you "possess yourself by it; for it is as necessary as breath; we cannot live or work without it." When you have
gotten it, "labor to feed and maintain" it. Fifth, it is a "matter of solid
comfort to those who live and die within the Covenant of Grace"; for
no matter how dreadful their case, "all things in a covenanted God do
hold forth ground and matter of good hope." Consider the freeness and
abundance of his grace and mercy (Isa. 43:25; Eph. 2:4). Consider his "infi-
niteness of power" (Rom. 4:21), "infallibility of truth" (2 Tim. 2:13), and "infinite understanding and mercy." Only he knows "how to manage all our
matters to the best advantage" (2 Pet. 2:9). Sixth, how "horrible a sin must
it be" for those who have fled to Jesus for refuge "to harbor within them
thoughts of despair!" Such flight "charges God foolishly" and "makes
sin and Satan stronger than God." Note that Job is not guilty of this (Job
1:22). Those who despair cannot properly prepare their hearts to receive
the means of grace (e.g., hearing the Word). Seventh, those who "hope
in themselves and in their own strength" are in great danger. Rest assured, "God will reject all their confidences." The words of Isaiah rebuke
those who argue, "The Lord cannot but be good to the works of his
hands": *"It is a people of no understanding, therefore he that made them will have
no mercy on them"* (Isa. 27:11). Likewise, Scripture offers nothing but Hell to
those who falsely place their hope in church privileges (Jer. 7:4; Rom. 2:28) or
a false understanding of God's mercy (Luke 16:25). In short, there "is no

mercy to those who reject the offers" of God's mercy: *"For I say unto you, that none of those men which were bidden shall taste of my supper"* (Luke 14:24).[94]

Hope in the Gospel: As previously discussed, the Covenanters and Puritans held an optimistic outlook regarding the progress of the gospel. Shortly before his death, Richard Cameron expressed this hope for progress in making disciples of all nations in a sermon on Psalm 46:10:

> You that are in hazard for the truth be not troubled: our Lord will be exhaulted among the heathen. But many will say, "We know he will be exhaulted at the last and great day when he shall have all the wicked on his left hand." Yes; but says he, *"I will be exhaulted in the earth"* (Ps. 46:10). He has been exhaulted on the earth; but the most wonderfully exalting of his works we have not yet seen. The people of God have been right high already.... Yea, the Church of Scotland has been very high.... But, all this exalting that we have seen is nothing to what is to come.[95]

This optimistic view of the future of Christianity is called *postmillennialism.* Postmillennialists hold that there will be a millennial (but not necessarily 1,000 years) age before the return of Christ during which many Scripture prophesies will be fulfilled. It is beyond doubt that the Westminster divines, Puritans, and the Covenanters were postmillennialists, who believed in the salvation of the Jews and the fullness of the Gentiles promised in Scripture. Nevay remarks, "That there shall be a more glorious kingdom of Christ, in the preaching of the gospel, at the bringing in of the Jews, and the fullness of the gentiles, none acquainted with Scripture will much doubt."[96] James Durham, in his *Commentary Upon the Book of Revelation,* competently presents the post-millennial perspective.[97] Durham asserts that the success of the Protestant Reformation marks the beginning of the millennial age, in which those who bear the testimony of the martyred witnesses will reign.[‡] This golden age will arise

---

[‡] The postmillennial view holds that the seals, trumpets, and vials in Revelation represent three distinct periods. Durham views the death and resurrection of the witnesses and the seventh trumpet in Revelation chapter 11, the opening of the temple in chapter 15, and the binding of the Satan in chapter 20 to be concurrent events that inaugurate the millennial age. The seals depict the spread of the gospel throughout the Roman Empire and the associated persecution. The trumpets (chapters 8–11) and the persecution of the woman (chapters 12–13) represent the antichrist's persecutions of the true church for a period of 1260 years before the millennium. Durham, consistent with the *Westminster Confession of Faith,* holds that the false religion typified by the Catholic pope is the antichrist. Given this assumption, he contends that the resurrection of the witnesses represents the victory of the Protestant Reformation. He views the millennial reign as a period in which Christians uphold the testimony of the Protestant martyrs. Christ reigns not in person but through his saints. Durham speculates that the beginning of the 1260-year period corresponds to the beginning of the antichrist's rise to power, which he postulates to be after the year 300 (Rome established Christianity in 313). Hence, he postulates the millennial reign began around 1560 with the restoration of true

gradually, with vicissitudes, as the seven bowls of wrath are dispensed to complete the destruction of the antichrist. Other postmillennial interpretations propose different dates that vary widely. Perhaps, all that holds back the promised golden age is the modern lack of prayer and hope.

Is it any wonder that Satan desires to lower our expectations? The antithesis of the optimism of the Puritans and the Covenanters is the pessimism of the pre-millennial philosophy so prevalent in modern times. According to the pre-millenarian, J. N. Darby, there is no reason for hope for the triumph of the gospel in this world: "instead of permitting ourselves to hope for a continued progress of good, we must expect a progress of evil."[98] Ian Murray labels the pre-millennial concept the eclipse of hope because it assumes that the church has no future until the Second Coming of Christ to establish a millennium reign of Christ (after physically returning to earth with the resurrected saints) on earth led from Jerusalem. One text alone, Hebrews 9:27, is sufficient to refute it. The pre-millennial concept is based solely on an overly literal interpretation of the Bible text that was foreign to the Covenanters and the Puritans. Nevay remarked, "I say in that, Rev. 20:4, on which the Millenaries build so much, it is said, that the saints shall reign with Christ, but not that they shall reign on earth with him."[99]

Other views hold that the millennial age began with Christ's resurrection or that prophecy was fulfilled at the fall of Jerusalem. Although Christians may differ regarding their view on prophesy, any interpretation that does not acknowledge that Christ reigns in the hearts of his saints is in error. Even a thousand glorious years on this earth are but a drop in the great sea of eternal life; hence, Christians should never lose sight of their true hope of eternal dwelling with the Lord. Nevertheless, Christ commands that we pray that God's kingdom come, his will be done, *on earth as it is in heaven* (Mark 6:10). This should be our prayer.

---

church states, such as in Scotland. Durham also contends that the golden age will rise over the millennium period as the antichrist and his followers are further weakened by the seven vials (chapters 15–17) of God's wrath released after the seventh trumpet. Although the current apostasy seems to contradict this conclusion, there is no promise of instant or continually rising success. As Elijah learned, we must not judge the state of God's kingdom by the temporal evidence. At best during the millennial era, the church is but a camp—a camp (Rev. 18:4) that overcomes the world. Strength is measured not by numbers but by purity of truth. We win not by swords but by the one sword, the Word. The destroyed wicked are plenteous (Rev. 14). As the true gospel spreads, expect great resistance. Durham interprets the vials as destructive to the Church of Rome and false religion in general. Were not First and Second Protestant Reformations the first vials poured out on the antichrist's earth (i.e., false doctrine), sea (i.e., ordinances), and water sources (i.e., false gospel)? Is not the Jew's salvation (sixth vial) in progress as evidenced by the new nation Israel? Further evidencing the millennial era are the three unclean spirits (Rev. 16) from the dragon, the beast, and the false prophet. Could not these be Satan's assaults on the Lord's authority, mercy, and word?

Sanctification – Its Other Graces

Other sanctifying graces include knowledge to govern our mind, sincerity to bind our heart, zeal to inflame our will, temperance to guide self-denial, holy fear to enable communion with God, righteousness to enable proper relationships, humility to properly channel all graces, meekness to conform us to Christ, and patience to enable perseverance.

Nevay devotes a sermon to each of nine other sanctifying and saving graces.

Knowledge Governs our Mind: According to Scripture, "saving knowledge is a rare and inestimable blessing" that "lays the foundation for faith" (2 Cor. 4:13–14). It is one with wisdom.[100] Its foundation is the *truth*, which is Christ's principal mission: *"To this end was I born, and for this cause came I into the world, that I should bear witness unto the truth"* (John 18:37a). Truth is found in His Word: *"If ye continue in my word, then are ye my disciples indeed; and ye shall know the truth, and truth shall make you free"* (John 8:31–32). Christ promises, *"Every one that is of the truth heareth my voice"* (John 18:37b).

As can be seen in the dying testimony of John Nisbet and in the memoir of James Nisbet, the Word was their constant preoccupation. The Covenanters pursued truth as did David, *"Oh, how I love your law! It is my meditation all the day"* (Ps. 119:97). They defended the slightest of God's truths with their lives. The Puritan William Gurnall reminds us that the chief end of Satan is to rob us of the truth. To this end, Satan "comes as a serpent in the persons of false teachers" and "as a lion in the persons of bloody persecution." Hence, Christians must gird themselves with truth, laboring "to get a heart inflamed with a sincere love to the truth."[101] The Puritans and the Covenanters believed that truth cannot fail to sanctify believers (Josh. 23:14; Ezek. 36:25–27; John 8:32; 17:17; Eph. 4:21–23).[102]

Scripture holds knowledge "out as a most desirable and excellent thing: Satan knew no greater temptation for man, than to be as God, knowing good and evil" (Gen. 3:5). It is an excellent covenant blessing: First, the highest knowledge is knowledge of God. It seeks "to know God and ourselves, to know him, so as we may admire and adore him; and to know ourselves, so as we may abhor ourselves" (1 Cor. 2:10–12). Second, it alone provides believers the template for renewal in the image of God (Col. 3:10). Third, it "is indeed the eye of the soul and the light of the body." Fourth, what knowledge can compare with the knowledge that gives eternal life? Fifth, without knowledge of truth, "there is nothing but misery" because "the man that has not this light, cannot but stumble" (John 11:10). Sixth, it is the only knowledge that satisfies: all other *"knowledge increases sorrow"* (Eccl. 1:18). Seventh, the truth of Jesus is "the most inward penetrating knowledge" (Eph. 4:21). Eighth, "knowledge lays the foundation for faith" (2 Cor. 4:13-14). Ninth, "great things are promised of this knowledge": temporal blessing such as length of days (Prov. 3:13, 16; 24:14); spiritual blessing such as the multiplication of grace and peace (2 Pet. 1:2); and eternal life and happiness. Knowledge *"is a tree of life to them that lay hold on her, and happy is every one that retaineth her"* (Prov. 3:18).[103]

Knowledge is promised in great measure: *"The earth shall be full of the knowledge of the Lord, as the waters cover the sea"* (Isa. 11:9; Hab. 2:14), and every man shall know the Lord (Jer. 31:34).[104] This is evident from the following: First, the Lord promises to teach sinners, the meek (Ps. 25:8-9), and the simple (Prov. 9:4). Second, he promises to teach them his covenant (Ps. 25:12, 14), his fear (Jer. 32:39), all things (1 John 5:20), and the Scriptures (John 10:4). Third, he promises to write the law in their heart (Jer. 31:33), pouring forth his Spirit (Prov. 1:23), abiding in the Spirit (1 John 2:27), and bringing all things to remembrance (John 14:26). Fourth, knowledge of the truth is a promised covenant blessing from God to those who ask:

(1) It is a part of God's image that we lost, unto which we must be renewed, if God would have us (Eph. 4:23; Col. 3:10). (2) If it comes not from the promise, we cannot have it at all, being not only in our understanding darkened but darkness itself (Eph. 5:8). (3) By covenant we are children of light, so light must be given to us. (4) The covenant is a marriage covenant; and so, there will be a revealing of secrets betwixt Christ and his bride (John 15:15). [Wherein Christ says to his disciples] all things that I have heard of my father I have made known unto you. (5) Knowledge is the food of the soul, and pastors are promised to distribute this so necessary food; it was to Job more so (Job 23:12). (6) Heaven is promised; and this knowledge is one of the necessary keys by which it is opened (Luke 11:52). (7) Sanctification cannot be without it, for it is by truth (John 17:17). Without it, the heart cannot be good (Prov. 19:2). The want of it makes great boldness of sin, even to the crucifying of the Lord of Glory (1 Cor. 2:8). Even zeal without knowledge is naught (Rom. 10:2). (8) Christ was anointed a prophet for this end, that he might teach his people knowledge (Deut. 18:15; Isa. 61:1).[105]

Nevay proposes the following uses of these doctrines: First, we must realize the miserable condition of those who lack this knowledge. Without this knowledge, one is doomed to a life of misery and darkness, under the power of Satan and the curse of eternal fire (Ps. 14:1-4; Acts 26:18; Eph. 4:18; 2 Thess. 1:7-8). The lack "of this knowledge is a special ground of God's controversy, especially in a land where the light shines" (Ps. 76:1; Hos. 4:1). Second, "if this knowledge be so excellent a thing, how great must their sin be, who make it their work to deprive people of the means of knowledge?" Third, "we should cry after knowledge and lift up our voice for understanding, seek her as silver, and search for her as for hid treasures. O! Seek this knowledge, which only does put the true difference betwixt men and beast; the want of it makes men more brutish that the unreasonable creatures" (Ps. 32:9; Prov. 2:3–4; Isa. 1:3).

To acquire this knowledge, we must (1) study holiness (Prov. 8:9; 14:6), (2) deny carnal wisdom (Prov. 26:12), (3) seek God in prayer (2 Tim. 3:16), (4) study under the wise (Prov. 15:12; Mal. 2:7), (5) study humility and sobriety (Rom. 12:3), and, most importantly, (6) practice what we know (John 7:17). The evidences of saving knowledge are (1) desiring to increase knowledge through the means of grace (Ps. 1:2; Prov. 1:5), (2) determining to bring the Word home to our heart (Heb. 10:24), (3) practicing of duties as the will of God (John 13:17; 1 Thess. 4:3), (4) increasing in humility as knowledge increases (Prov. 30:2), (5) clinging to the words of Jesus and of the doctrine according to godliness (1 Tim. 6:3, 20), and (6) transforming of us into the image of God (2 Cor. 3:18).[106]

Fourth, these teachings are a "reproof and terror to those who have the means of knowledge, but have none of the knowledge." In particular, it should concern those who seek book rather than heart knowledge: "all knowledge which is not directed to the practice of holiness is naught" (Eccl. 12:12). Fifth, although we should seek after the mysteries of the Bible, we must seek that knowledge which "works up man unto conformity with God and his son Jesus Christ." The only source of this knowledge is Christ: "All the treasures of wisdom and knowledge are laid up in Christ, for them that believe" (Col. 2:3). Sixth, to acquire this knowledge we "must first be within the covenant, and in a covenant relationship to God." We must look upon Christ as the "first gift; yea, and received as such; then may other gifts assuredly be expected" (Rom. 8:32). Asking in his name, we must "fetch it from the promise; for, all in the covenant comes from the promise"; and we must "come empty, neither having it, nor the price in your hand to buy it up; it must be received as a free gift" (1 Cor. 8:2). Lastly, for those who live outside the covenant, Nevay asks, "What then will all knowledge avail them without this?" It is sad fate to die without wisdom (Job 36:12).[107]

Holy Fear Enables Communion with God: To understand holy fear, it is important to understand what it is not. It is not "natural fear, which may be without sin" (Heb. 5:7). It is not sinful fear that flees the yoke of Christ or the ways of God. It is not "fear of wrath and punishment, only being the effect and fruit of the spirit of bondage" (Rom. 8:15), as the devils have (James 2:19). It is not a fear "that makes man fly from God" (Rev. 6:16–17). It is not the "fear of man more than God," which brings a snare (Prov. 29:25). It is "a holy fear of God, which is both commanded and highly commended of God in Scriptures, so as other fear is forbidden" (Exod. 20:20; Isa. 8:12–13).

Holy fear has the following properties. First, "it is from a deep impression of the majesty, power, and perfection of God" (Gen. 28:16–19; 31:42, 53). "It fears not only the greatness but also the goodness of God" (Hos. 3:5). Second, it is most in the exercise of worship (Ps. 89:7; Mal. 3:16), the execution of judgment (Rev. 14:7), and the "doing of some rare work." Third, "this fear is most of sin, and offending God" (Prov. 13:13). Fourth, "it fears the Lord's displeasure, and so his wrath" (Ps. 90:11). It "is chiefly a fear that we be separated from God and his love," making "us more cautious and circumspect in our walk" and diligent in our duty. Consider his wrath, *"For our God is a consuming fire"* (Heb. 12:29). However, its purpose is not primarily to make us consider our just punishment, guilt, and misery, but to make us look to his mercy.[108]

Nevay contends holy fear is an excellent and useful covenant blessing: *"Blessed is the man that fears the Lord and delights greatly in his commandments"* (Ps. 112:1; 115:13; 128:1). God accepts only those that possess it (Acts 10:35). The following passages evidence its excellency:

> First, it is the *beginning of knowledge and wisdom* (Ps. 111:10; Prov. 1:7). Second, it is *clean and endureth forever* (Ps. 119:9). Third, it *is the whole duty of man* (Eccl. 12:13). Fourth, in it *is strong confidence, so as the children of those that have it shall have a place of refuge* (Prov. 14:26). Fifth, it is a fountain of life, to depart from the snares of death. Sixth, it makes a little to be more than a great treasure without it (Prov. 15:16). Seventh, he that has it shall abide satisfied, and shall not be visited with evil (Prov. 19:23). Eighth, by this are other graces well ordered in their exercise, and kept within the channel. Ninth, by it the heart is both fixed, that it cannot depart from God (Jer. 32:40), and it is enlarged in the worship of God (Isa. 60:5). *Yet further*, the excellency of this grace doth appear by the many fair promises which are made unto it … (Ps. 33:18–19; 34:7, 9–10; 103:11, 17; 111:10; 145:19; 147:11; Prov. 10:27; Mal. 2:5; 3:16; Acts 10:35). *Add*, in the last place, all the miseries and woes, which are threatened against ungodly men, who are void of this fear.[109]

Holy fear is a promised covenant blessing: *"They shall fear thee as long as the sun and moon endure, throughout all generations"* (Ps. 72:5). It is expressed more fully in Jeremiah 32:39–40:

> *And I will give them one heart, and one way, that they may fear me for ever, for the good of them, and of their children after them: And I will make an everlasting covenant*

*with them, that I will not turn away from them, to do them good; but I will put my fear
in their hearts, that they shall not depart from me.*

Imagine approaching God without the promised blessing of holy
fear: it is the very name of God (Gen. 31:42, 53), the whole duty of man (Eccl.
12:13), the sole means of perseverance (John 8:35), and the very beginning
of knowledge (Prov. 1:7). It is that which keeps our heart from fear (Ps.
112:7-8), and it enables us to lift our face up without spot to God (Job 11:15).
Without it, man is a proud and raging fool (Prov. 14:16). In short, there can
be "no worship nor communion with God without it" (Deut. 6:13; Mal. 1:6,
11; Acts 10:35). Holy fear is the very law of the kingdom (Heb. 12:28); hence, it
must be promised.[110] Angels surround those that possess it (Ps. 34:7), and
God shows them the secrets of the covenant (Ps. 25:14).[111]

Nevay proposes the following uses for these doctrines: First, do not
confuse natural fear with holy fear. Second, Christians should distinguish between "the fear of sons, and the fear of slaves; choose the one
and refuse the other." Further, fear not man: *"Fear not them which kill the
body, and are not able to kill the soul: but rather fear him which is able to destroy the
soul and the body in hell"* (Matt. 10:28). Third, Christians should "study not
only to have, but [also] to maintain this holy fear always in their heart
by bringing it daily to the Lord to get new impressions of his [highness,
holiness, greatness, and goodness.] O! This fear is a good companion
and noble guard for the heart."[112] Fourth, to those without it, God promises, *"Terrors shall take hold on [them] as waters"* (Job 27:20). Fifth, those that
possess holy fear must daily take great pains to guard and to protect it
as a precious treasure (Prov. 23:17; Isa. 33:6), "being ever thankful for it."
Sixth, those that lack this holy fear have reason to fear (Ps. 53:5); for "in
their prosperity, the destroyer will come upon them." On the other hand,
possession of this fear delivers men from all other fears (1 John 4:18). Seventh, unless you "study to fear God as God, else you cannot glorify him
as God." We must learn to fear God in "his power" (Job 37:23; Ps. 76:7; Jer.
5:22), "for his dominion" (Job 25:3; Ps. 99:1; Jer. 10:7), "in his glorious workings" (Hab. 3:16), "in his judgments" (Ps. 119:118-120), and "for all his goodness and mercies bestowed" (Ps. 130:4; Jer. 5:23-24).[113]

Eighth, those with holy fear bear these marks: First, they "shun everything evil in God's sight" (Prov. 3:7; 16:6). Second, they depart from, abstain from, and hate sin, especially secret sin (Gen. 39:9; Job 31:23, 27; Ps. 139:21;
Prov. 8:13; Jer. 2:11-13). Third, they rest not on their attainments, choosing
instead to seek perfection in obedience and to *work out their salvation in
fear and trembling* (Phil. 2:12; see also 2 Cor. 7:1). Fourth, "they fear not man"
(Matt. 10:28). Fifth, they revere and honor God's Word in public and pri-

vate worship (Ezra 9:4). Sixth, they deeply revere God's holy name (1 Kings 8:43; Mal. 1:14). Seventh, they keep good watch over their "heart, eyes, and ways" (Prov. 4:23–27).[114]

Zeal Inflames our Will: Augustine hypothesized that it is difficult to apply the graces of love, hope, and faith unless "a great zeal be kindled in the heart."[115] In this light, Nevay defines zeal:

> It is a holy fire; it is from heaven, and moves heavenward; it is that which makes a man a lion in God's matters, and a lamb in his own.... It is a grace which, by direction of holy and heavenly wisdom, quickens and inflames all within a man, and puts an edge on a man's endeavors, in the obedience and worship of God. It ... is especially in the preserving, promoting, and vindicating of God's honor, by all lawful means within the reach of a man's calling, [as did] Moses (Exod. 32:19–20) and Phinehas (Num. 25:7–8).[116]

It is an excellent blessing, and God rewards those who possess it (Num. 25:11–13; 2 Kings 10:30). First, "it is the Lord's royal apparel, his bright and shining garment. In Isa. 59:17, he clothed himself with zeal as a cloak." Second, "it is meat to Christ one way, even while it eats him up another" (Cf. John 2:17 with 4:34). Third, Paul advises, "it is good to be zealously affected always in a good thing." Scripture commands that we exercise fervent zeal (1) "in and about the Word" (Ps. 119:97; Luke 24:32; Acts 16:14; 18:25), (2) in obediently serving the Lord (Rom. 12:11), in prayer (James 5:16), in repentance (Jer. 31:19), in charity—loving another with a pure heart fervently (1 Pet. 1:22)—and especially "in most earnest contending for the truth" (Jude vs. 3). Fourth, "what is most for God is most excellent, be it man or thing:

> Zeal is in a special way for God: for his honor (Num. 25:13), for his house (Ps. 69:9), for his people (2 Cor. 11:2), for his kingdom (Luke 13:24), for his worship, the purging and restoring of it (1 Kings 19:10), and for the glorifying of him in good works (Titus 2:14). [It is] for Him against all the wicked in general; such was David (Ps. 26:5; 119:138–139); and in particular against hypocrites (Matt. 23:33), false teachers (Zech. 13:3; Phil. 3:18), against idolaters (Deut. 13:6, 8; 1 Kings 18:40), against superstition (Acts 17:16),... against profaners of the Sabbath (Neh. 13:17, 21),... against those who will not punish such (Judg. 21:5, 10), and against all the enemies of God's people (1 Sam. 11:1, 2, 6; 17:10, 48).

Fifth, "the excellency of this grace appears from the woe which is in the want of it," as in Laodicea (1 Sam. 2:12, 29–30; 2 Thess. 2:10–11; Rev. 3:16). Sixth, "it makes our service acceptable" (James 5:16). Seventh, "it is that grace which, in a manner, storms heaven; it makes the *kingdom of heaven to suffer violence, and the holy violent to take it by force*" (Matt. 11:12). Eighth, "there are many fair promises made to it" (Rev. 3:19–21).[117]

It is a promised covenant blessing, as evidenced by these proofs: First, it must come by promise since natural man has no zeal for godly things. Second, "zeal is no other thing almost but the intense act of" promised love and obedience. Third, "we have the Lord's zeal engaged by covenant," and his zeal "will kindle the zeal of the people" (Isa. 9:6–7; 37:31–32). Fourth, "true religion will not attain its end without it; there will be no entering the straight gate without striving; and striving is no other thing but the exercise of zeal" (Luke 13:24). Fifth, "godly sorrow is promised, and a special ingredient in it is zeal" (2 Cor. 7:11). Sixth, "it is promised that we shall glorify God" in times of severe persecution (Isa. 24:14–15). Seventh, "perseverance is promised and it cannot be without zeal." Eighth, "it was Christ's great design in the work of redemption, to purchase a people to himself, zealous of good works" (Titus 2:14). Ninth, incense on the altar foreshadowed gospel zeal (Exod. 40:5). Tenth, Scripture and the gospel zealously promise and command it (Isa. 2:2–3; Rom. 10:19; Rev. 3:19).[118]

Nevay proposes the following uses of these doctrines: First, lament the lack of zeal in our times compared to the zeal of reformers in Judah. We should mourn over our cold hearts. Second, seek zeal and beware of counterfeit zeal. True zeal "springs from love" with a focus on the "great and good things of God" rather than the "brats of man's own brain" and "great things for man's self" (Jer. 45:5).[119] Third, it is impossible to be a Christian without zeal: "Grace is asleep or dead where zeal is not." Fourth, examine yourself to see if you have the marks of zeal. True zeal must be (1) according to knowledge (Rom. 10:2); (2) with all our might (Eccl. 9:10); (3) with diligence (Acts 18:25); (4) meek in our own matters but hot in God's matters (Cf. Exod. 32:19 with Num. 12:3); (5) in deed as well as in word; (6) equal against all sin and for every duty (Matt. 7:4; 23:23); (7) intolerant of wickedness, error, and blasphemy (Rev. 2:2,4); (8) constant; (9) exercised consistent with other graces (e.g., humility as in 2 Cor. 12:20–21). Fifth, these facts are a terror to those with "wicked and blind zeal."[120]

Sixth, Scripture promises zeal to those who ask. Further, mighty times of greater zeal are ahead for God's church. Seventh, "all who desire to have it would go to Christ in the covenant, Christ in the promise, to have it; there is no other way to have it; it is a precious jewel, worth the seeking." Eighth, those who seek zeal should (1) "study to avoid all that which is contrary to zeal" (e.g., indulging our corruptions); (2)

"think much and often upon the Lord's goodness"; and (3) "be ashamed of [their] shortcoming." Further, to cultivate zeal we must use all the means of grace (e.g., attending the word, keeping company with zealous people [iron sharpens iron], and living under a lively ministry).[121]

Thomas Watson, one of the many Puritan ministers outed in 1662, emphasized the necessity for Christians to take the kingdom of heaven by storm (Matt. 11:12). To do so requires that Christians pursue *truth* and *salvation* with a holy violence. Watson considered truth "the best militia in the kingdom" and salvation "a matter of life or death." Taking heaven by storm requires Christians to perform all their duties (e.g., prayer, meditation, self-examination, Sabbath observance, reading and hearing the Word) zealously with a holy violence.[122] Such holy violence requires (1) *resolution of the will* (Ps. 119:106), (2) *vigor of affection* (Ps. 42:4), and (3) *strength of endeavor*. To the Puritans, there was no difference between the slothful and the wicked: *"Thou wicked and slothful servant"* (Matt. 25:26).[123] Modern society has long neglected the Puritan ideals, which viewed truth and the work ethic as the bulwarks of society.

Temperance Teaches Self-Denial: Temperance "is no small grace; if it be rightly exercised, it comprises a great part of man's duty, in right government of himself" (Titus 2:11–12). Temperance "puts restraint on a man, binds him up from lusting after unlawful things, and moderates his appetite in things lawful." Temperance moderates affections and "makes men think soberly, as well as live soberly."

It is "an excellent grace and ornament of the Christian" that subdues the spirit of man and "puts a man in good frame and case for spiritual exercise." Scripture assigns it noble companions: "It has before it Vigilance, and behind it Good Behavior; Sobriety has a good influence on both" (1 Tim. 3:2, 11). Consider the temperance exhibited by the saints (e.g., Daniel denied himself polluted food (Dan. 1:8)). Consider how the lack of temperance turns men into dogs and swine. Consider how temperance "puts a man in capacity of striving for the crown" (1 Cor. 9:25) and "in a right posture waiting for Christ's coming" (Luke 21:34–36).[124]

Temperance is a promised covenant blessing. It is part of promised mortification and "one of the chief ends of the gospel" (Titus 2:11–12). Scripture commands it (1 Thess. 5:6; 1 Pet. 1:13); whatever is commanded is promised. Without temperance, other promised blessings such as health, life, a new heart, and all things would not be possible.[125]

Nevay proposes the following uses of these doctrines. First, we must be wary that pleasant things may turn into snares. Second, we must be wary since "more perish by the abuse of things lawful" than unlawful.

The lack of temperance has brought down many strong men (Prov. 7:26).[126] Third, true temperance is found only within the covenant. Those outside may learn to be temperate in some things, but "they will prove intemperate in others." Fourth, test to see if you have the marks of true temperance, which include denial of "ungodliness and worldly lust" (Titus 2:12), living to "the will of God" rather than to the flesh (1 Pet. 4:2-4), rooting out of the "deeds of the body" (Rom. 8:13), and using delectable things as "if they had them not" (1 Cor. 7:29-31). Temperate men behave as Gideon's soldiers "that bowed not down to drink the water" (Judg. 7:6).[127] Fifth, learn the marks of intemperance: it is overindulgent, curious, unseemly, and too frequent in following of delights.[128] Sixth, the reason there is so little temperance is that so few are within the covenant. Seventh, those that desire it "must turn in to the covenant of Grace, and fetch it from Christ in the promise." To obtain it, men must "mortify their love for the world" (1 John 2:15), "watch well over the eye" (Gen. 3:6), weigh the emptiness and vanity of things (Eccl. 1:1-2). Those who desire it must "learn to look on pleasures, and carnal delights, as they go, and not as they come" (Rom. 6:21); beware of letting corruptions take them captive (Rom. 7:23); and realize that "wise men are temperate" and fools are not. We must learn to focus our appetite "after the pursuit of the best things."[129]

Righteousness Promotes Proper Relationships: Nevay distinguishes the righteousness that is "betwixt man and man" from the imputed righteousness of Christ. The former in Christians is the mirror of the latter. The righteousness that he speaks of here is also called justice and equity in Scripture, and it is exemplified by Abraham in his dealings with his "partners in war" (Gen. 14:24) and by Jacob in his dealing with Laban (Gen. 30:33). This righteousness is the grace "by which men are enabled to pay that which is due one another" (Rom. 13:7). This righteousness acts by "distributive justice by which every one has his due distributed unto him."[130]

Righteousness is an excellent grace in which *"judgment runs down as water, and righteousness as a mighty stream"* (Amos 5:24). Correspondingly, "it is a woeful plague to a land when judgment is turned to gall and the fruit of righteousness to hemlock" (Amos 6:12). Scripture promises that a righteous land will flourish (Ps. 72:2-3, 7); a righteous man will be blessed (Prov. 10:6; 20:7); and a righteous prince will achieve well-being (Jer. 22:15). Christ loves righteousness (Ps. 45:7), considers justice more acceptable than sacrifice (Prov. 21:3), and promises that "judgment shall dwell in the wilderness," making it a "fruitful field" (Isa. 32:15-16).[131]

Righteousness is a promised covenant blessing. Christ promises to establish a reign of righteousness in which *"they will not hurt nor destroy in all [his] holy mountain"* (Isa. 11:4,9; see also 32:1; 60:17-18). First, it must be by promise for man is naturally unjust (Zeph. 3:5). Second, external peace is promised: *"neither shall they learn war anymore. But they shall sit every man under his vine and under his fig tree"* (Micah 4:3-4). Third, glorious brightness in religious exercise is promised: *"Thy people also shall be all righteous: they shall inherit the land forever"* (Isa. 60:20-21). Fourth, "removing of oppression is promised" (Isa. 54:14). Fifth, "Christ the king of saints is just (Zech. 9:9), and so, by Covenant, he will make his people such." Sixth, "love is promised; and where it is, it will make all duties to be done betwixt man and man."[132]

Nevay proposes the following uses of these doctrines. First, the unrighteous "are enemies to society, and so to mankind, so they are an abomination to the Lord" (Deut. 25:16). It is miserable to live outside the covenant, for outside the covenant there is no righteousness. Second, righteousness is obtained "not as a virtue, but as a grace; not taught by the precepts of men, but infused by the Spirit." Righteousness is the "doing of that which is just and equal in every thing, to every person; not only because the Lord commands so ... but from love to Jesus, and with an eye to the glory of God." Third, those without righteousness have no excellency in public or private dealings. Fourth, "let us endeavor to have a right disposition as to justice in ourselves." To do so, we must deny self, crucify ourselves to the world, and "let no sin reign in us." Fifth, we must "be just to men at all times; and so just to men, as not unjust to God." Sixth, there is only one reason why there is so little righteousness: the reason is that "there is but little going in to the promise to fetch it from thence." Seventh, "let us beg this grace from the Lord in the covenant" and study to practice righteousness. This requires that we act justly, be honest, observe the Golden Rule (Matt. 7:12), do not take advantage of others, and be strict in observing covenants and bargains.[133]

Although Christians mirror Christ, we must heed the warning of Andrew Gray not to "mix our own righteousness with Christ's as the object of our believing."[134]

Sincerity Binds our Heart: Sincerity "is as the salt to other graces, both to make them sound and lasting."[135] It has many names: truth (Ps. 51:6), integrity (Ps. 78:72), soundness (Ps. 119:80), singleness (Acts 2:46), simplicity (2 Cor. 1:12), uprightness (Prov. 15:21), straightness (Prov. 4:25), perfection (Col. 4:12), and honesty (Luke 8:15).[136]

It "is an excellent and blessed thing": *"Blessed are the pure in heart; for they shall see God"* (Matt. 5:8). First, it "makes a man after God's heart" (1 Sam. 13:13-14) to have "holiness in truth" (Eph. 4:24). Second, "they that have it are the Lord's delight" (1 Chron. 29:17; Ps. 11:7; Prov. 11:20; 12:22). Third, it is the covenant mandate God gave to Abraham: *"walk before me and be thou perfect"* (Gen. 17:1). The standard is perfection. Fourth, it is the true measure of the value of man's service and offerings (1 Cor. 13:3). Compare the acceptance of the widow's mite (Luke 21:3) with the rejection of great offerings in Micah 6:6–8. The great proof of sincerity is love. Fifth, without it, no service is acceptable (Isa. 66:2-3). Sixth, "there are large temporal blessings" (2 Chron. 16:9; Ps. 37:18-20, 37; 112:2; Prov. 2:7; 14:11; 22:11) and "large spiritual blessing promised to it" (Ps. 15:1-2; 49:14; 112:6; 2 Chron. 16:9). Lastly, its excellency is best seen when contrasted to the "vileness of hypocrisy," which "is very abominable in God's sight" (Isa. 65:5).[137]

Sincerity is a promised covenant blessing. God promises to circumcise men's hearts so that they shall *"love the Lord with all the heart, and with all the soul"* (Deut. 30:6).[138] To this end, the Lord promises "to direct the work of his people in truth" (Isa. 61:8), to give them a whole heart to know and seek him (Jer. 24:7), to write his law in their inward parts (Jer. 31:33), and to refine and purify them (Mal. 3:3). The whole Trinity is engaged in fulfilling this promise: the Holy Spirit works truth in our inward parts; Christ betroths himself to us in truth and faithfulness; and the Father promises to dwell in and with us in holy communion. God enables and requires us to serve and obey him with sincerity and truth, singleness of heart, soundness in faith, and sincerity in love. Only those who are perfect, as he is perfect, and upright in their walk with the Lord will "ascend his holy hill" (Ps. 15:2; 24:3). It is good that these things are promised because fallen man is "desperately wicked," with a heart "like a deceitful bow" (Jer. 17:9; Hos. 7:16). Without sincerity, "all our spiritual armor would hang loose on us, for sincerity is the girdle of truth, which binds and holds all fast together" (Eph. 6:14).[139]

Nevay proposes the following uses for these doctrines. First, a sincere man must be a Jew inwardly, with a circumcised heart, *"in the spirit, and not in the letter; whose praise is not of men, but of God"* (Rom. 2:29). Second, "it is our duty to sit down and mourn and bewail the paucity of sincere and perfect men." Third, nothing said or done by those without it is acceptable. It is a woeful case to have vile hypocrisy in its place. Fourth, those that seek sincerity, delight in God and are God's delight; for in doing all duties, they look to God, not to men. The marks of this sincerity include having "our way and work good before the Lord" as "our great and chief design" (Col. 3:23); doing all things as we would be found at the last reckoning (Luke 12:43); loving and walking in the light (John 3:21); performing our duty "in secret as well as before men" (Matt. 6:6); being diligent in the "day of prosperity as of adversity" (Job 1:5,8); waiting on the Lord even when he hides his face (Isa. 8:17); abstaining from the "appearance of evil" (1 Thess. 5:22); confessing and forsaking sin rather than excusing and covering it (Prov. 28:13); conscientiously preparing for worship (Cf. 2 Chron. 12:14 with 19:3); keeping self from being the end of our duty (Isa. 58:3); searching ourselves for hypocrisy and hidden sins; and observing the least as well as the greater commandments (Matt. 5:19).[140]

Fifth, "if upon search you find little or nothing of this heart uprightness and integrity, you have reason to mourn over your dangerous estate; yet, readily one would not miss sincerity without sincerity." Take comfort; it is promised. Sixth, the prayers and cries of those without sincerity are to no purpose, and only serve to provoke God (Isa. 1:11–16).[141] Even if we do right, without sincerity it is to naught: contrast the acceptability of the imperfect works of Asa, whose heart was perfect (1 Kings 15:14) with the good works of Amaziah, whose heart was imperfect (2 Chron. 25:2).[142] Seventh, it is folly to think one can work sincerity into his heart because sincerity comes only from God. Eighth, acquire sincerity from God by the promise that he will give you the sincerity and truth that he requires of you. We should be ever mindful of how God delights in sincerity (Ps. 51:6), and how he "looks to the heart, and searches it" (Rev. 2:23).[143]

James Durham, in his book *Heaven Upon Earth*, describes how God's deputy, whom we know as our conscience, is charged to monitor all our actions, warning us if we stray from sincerely following the truth. God considers truth so important that he provides it three witnesses: *"I say the truth in Christ, I lie not, my conscience also bearing me witness in the Holy Ghost"* (Rom. 9:1).[144] A man's conscience is illuminated by the Holy Spirit and directly subject to God; therefore, a man is to obey his conscience, as far as it is consistent with the Word. It is our duty, and "an excellent means of advancing holiness," to always keep our *"conscience void of offense toward God and toward man"* (Acts 24:16).[145] Durham advises us to frequently reflect upon our ways: *"For our rejoicing is this, the testimony of our conscience, that in simplicity and godly sincerity, not in fleshly wisdom, but by the grace of God, we have our conversation in the world, and more abundantly to you-ward"* (2 Cor. 1:12). The conscience is like the beast with eyes before, behind, and within (Rev. 4:6). By conversing with it, we can say with David, *"I thought on my ways, and turned my feet unto thy testimonies"* (Ps. 119:59). Not only must we plant spiritual seeds in the garden of our heart, but we must also pluck up the weeds.[146]

Humility Enables other Graces: "Straight is the way and narrow is the gate, which lead to life: men big with self cannot enter." Humility "in some sort may be called the foundation to other graces, least seen, but not the least used." It is not the false humility of Absalom (2 Sam. 15:2-7). It "is humbleness of mind (Col. 3:12), and it is that poverty of spirit in Matt. 5:3." A humble man sees himself as "nothing before God" and others (Gen. 18:27; Job 42:6; Prov. 30:2-3; Eph. 3:8). It makes a man "renounce confidence in the flesh," cast "himself wholly upon free mercy," maintain a proper bearing in worshipping and conversing with God, and submit absolutely to any cross or yoke that the Lord lays upon him.[147]

It is an excellent grace. First, God highly esteems humility and a contrite heart (Ps. 138:6; Isa. 66:2). Second, Jesus excelled in this grace, and it is required of any who bear his yoke (Matt. 11:29). Third, it serves as a foundation to other graces because "it is the first stone that is laid in the spiritual building, and the Lord that gives more grace, gives grace to the humble" (James 4:6; 1 Pet. 5:5). Fourth, "no grace is sincere without it; it is the true character of every grace." Fifth, "it is necessary for seeking God and turning away his wrath" (2 Chron. 12:7). It produces meekness, which "is most like to a hiding place in the Day of Wrath." Sixth, humility protects us from the torment of envy of others. Seventh, many precious promises are made to the humble (2 Chron. 7:14; Job 5:11; Ps. 25:9; Prov. 3:34; 18:12; 22:4; Matt. 11:25). Eighth, humility leads to contentment. Ninth, it prepares a man to enter the straight gate. Tenth, it befits a Christian, "he being a debtor to God." Eleventh, "he who has it is edified by every means." Twelfth, the excellency is obvious when contrasted to the "evils and naughtiness of pride."[148]

It is a promised covenant blessing in that all men, as *"every mountain and hill, shall be made low"* (Isa. 40:4; Luke 3:5). In addition, *"every knee shall bow"* (Isa. 45:23). The following proofs substantiate that it is promised. First, men, by nature, cannot be humble "unless it is given to them" (Mal. 3:15). Second, Scripture says, "God gives grace to the humble" (1 Pet. 5:5). Third, God promises to dwell eternally with those of *"a contrite and humble spirit"* (Isa. 57:15). Fourth, "mortification is promised, and humility is the proper effect thereof, and the evidence of the same." Fifth, those who accept Christ receive honor; honor comes by humility (Prov. 4:8; 22:4). Sixth, "the great point of conformity to him is in humility" (Rom. 8:29; 1 Cor. 15:19). Consider the humility of Christ (Phil. 2:7-8). Seventh, faith is a humbling grace and makes a sinner loathe himself (Ezek. 16:60-63; 36:31; Rom. 3:27).

Eighth, Christ was humbled before he was exalted. Ninth, repentance brings men low. Tenth, the promise of salvation is to the humble (Job 22:29).[149]

Nevay proposed the following uses for the doctrine of humility. First, humility is a rare thing because, by nature, man holds God in low esteem while seeking to exalt himself above others. Second, "pride is a great enemy of grace and holiness; humility is a friend unto, and advances both; it teaches man to walk humbly with God and be no striver with man." Third, humility is tested best when we are prosperous, powerful, or provoked: "Even the sea will be calm when there is no wind." Fourth, a proud man is "an abomination in the sight of God," for a proud man "has no other grace." Nevay accurately describes the great hazard of pride: "It robs God of all that which is due him, it robs men of God, and all that which is due to him. It is against God, and God is against it."[150] Fifth, although the Lord esteems the humble, men despise them, as they did the apostles (1 Cor. 4:13). Sixth, without humility, "no other grace can be or thrive, for they all grow in a low ground, though they spring from on high, and with their top do reach above the clouds." Seventh, be joyous and thankful if you have humility, "for ordinarily men will seek to excel in any grace but this."[151]

Eighth, search to see if you have this grace. The marks of humility towards God include (1) acknowledging our nothingness (Isa. 40:17; 46:6); (2) submitting to strokes (1 Sam. 3:18; Ps. 39:9); (3) magnifying God's mercy (Gen. 32:10; 1 Chron. 29:14); (4) "holy wondering at the ways and works of God" (Job 42:3; Rom. 11:33-34); (5) grasping God's majesty and throwing our crowns at his feet (Rev. 4:10); (6) reverencing God in worship (Eccl. 5:1-3); and (7) undertaking the "meanest services for God," following the example of Christ (John 13:14). Humility towards men proceeds from humility towards God; hence, it has similar marks (e.g., bearing the reproach and contempt of others).[152] Ninth, God "resists the proud: Heaven's gate is straight, and they cannot stoop." Tenth, humility is promised to "those who turn in to the covenant promises." Eleventh, "pray upon the promises and it shall be given." These promises teach us to keep our "thoughts on the highness, majesty, and power of God" (1 Pet. 5:5); to ponder the dreadful state of those with proud hearts; to look "often upon [our] own sinfulness, weakness, and worthlessness"; to recognize that all we have is from his mercy (1 Cor. 4:7); to consider the humility of the saints; and to "look upon the irrational creatures," realizing "how we come short even of them in duty."[153]

Andrew Gray reminds us that Christians should have the humility of Moses whose "face did shine, and he knew it not."[154]

Meekness Conforms us to Christ: Meekness is a grace "of the Spirit of Christ, by which the spirit of man, is quieted, and his whole carriage is made sweet and temperate: it is called, as it is in the heart, tenderness; as in the mind, clearness; in the affections, moderation and calmness; in the disposition, good temper; and in the whole carriage, sweetness." It responds to any irregular uprising of the soul with David's words, in Psalm 42:11, *"Why art thou disquieted within me?"* Believers exhibit meekness toward God "in the receiving of his Word" (James 1:21), "in taking on his yoke"(Matt. 11:29–30), and in keeping "silent under the rod" (Job 40:4). In fact, these passages identify meekness as a requirement for receiving his Word and bearing his yoke. Believers exhibit meekness toward man by following "the perfect pattern of meekness" found in Christ, to which we are predestined to conform. Christ exhibited meekness as a king (Matt. 11:29), as a disciplinarian (Zech. 9:9), and as a lamb judging the wicked (Rev. 6:15–16). He displayed meekness "in speaking" (John 8:48–49) as well as "in silence" (Isa. 53:7). Instead of revenge (Luke 9:54–55), Christ chose to weep for his persecutors (Luke 19:41) and to answer his accusers meekly (John 18:22–23; 1 Pet. 2:23).[155]

It is an excellent covenant blessing because "by Christ the meek are pronounced blessed" (Matt. 5:5) and because God highly prizes meekness (1 Pet. 3:4). Meekness "is the very best portrait of Christ, both in life and death." Christ "teaches meekness, and then teaches the meek" (Ps. 25:9). Hence, it is the "mark of those that are the elect of God" (Col. 3:12). It "makes a man master of himself." Other Scripture promises for the meek include–the gospel (Isa. 61:1), mercy (Ps. 76:8–9; Isa. 11:4), safety (Zeph. 2:3), beautification (Ps. 149:4), and joyous communion with God (Isa. 29:18–19; 57:15). Its excellency is best seen when compared to the contrary vices of anger, bitterness, and clamor. The apostle James advises, *"Wherefore lay apart all filthiness and superfluity of naughtiness, and receive with meekness the engrafted word, which is able to save your souls"* (James 1:21).[156]

Meekness is a promised, covenant blessing. Scripture promises "the new heart and the new spirit," such *"that the wolf shall dwell with the lamb"* (Isa. 11:6–9). The elect are "predestined to conform to Christ," who is meek (Matt. 11:29; Rom. 8:29). It is a promised fruit of the Spirit (Gal. 5:23). Because our natural condition is unmerciful and fiercely opposed to good (Rom. 1:31; 2 Tim. 3:3), it must be received by promise.

Nevay proposes the following uses for these doctrines. First, meekness is not found in the soft manner in which Eli treated his sinful sons, the civil courteous carriage of Absalom at the city gates, or the oppressed and despondent spirit in Psalm 107:12. Meekness "is a gracious quiet frame, wrought by the Spirit of grace." Second, seek it from Heaven and the example of Jesus. "The meek spirit is the only great spirit; it commands both itself and other things" (Prov. 16:32). Third, those without it "can be neither masters of themselves, nor can they be useful unto others." Fourth, meekness should be "sought after more than gold." Following the example of the heavenly original, we should develop a longsuffering (Exod. 34:6), forbearing (Col. 3:13), reconciling (Titus 3:3), and edifying spirit towards others (2 Tim. 2:25). We should study to control our wrath (James 1:19), to bear the burdens of others (Gal. 6:2), to use gentle means (1 Cor. 4:21), to sweeten sharp dealings (Rev. 2:3), and to bear pleasantly Christ's yoke, cross, and reproof. Fifth, we should examine ourselves for the marks of meekness. It "yields much of man's rights, but nothing of God's." Although, in his own matters, Moses was the "meekest man on earth" (Num. 12:3); in God's matters, he would not yield (Exod. 10:26). Meekness "will stoutly oppose itself to sin," yet "it is not for shaming, but restoring of our brother" (Gal. 6:1). It does not neglect duty for fear of disturbing man's peace. It "is joined with truth, with gentleness, faith, and temperance, and with holy fear" (Ps. 45:4; Gal. 5:22–23; 1 Pet. 3:15). Sixth, if natural men could "see how wild their natures are," they would desire meekness; but being blind, they will have none of it. Seventh, it is folly to think that men could acquire meekness except by the promise. Men are "taught to counterfeit Christian meekness"; hence, be wary that they "may prove wolves when they are let loose." Eighth, it is a "comfort to those Christians who have rough natures, and are striving to have them subdued." They need not be discouraged; it is promised "if it be seriously sought." Ninth, those who desire meekness can find it only within the Covenant of Grace, by seeking the promises therein. Observe that "faith in the promises does subdue the soul unto silent meekness" (Ps. 62:1, 5; Isa. 39:8). It makes us respond as David, *"I was dumb, I opened not my mouth, because thou didst it"* (Ps. 39:9); and Eli, *"It is the Lord, let him do what seemeth him good"* (1 Sam. 3:18). It teaches us that "conformity to Christ is necessary" (1 John 4:17).[157]

Patience Leads to Perseverance: Patience is the "companion and bosom friend" of hope.[158] It "is a grace, springing from knowledge of God and ourselves, as also from faith, hope, and love; by which we are enabled to bear crosses, and to persevere in difficult duties, quietly, cheerfully, and constantly."[159] Patience is sometimes called long suffering or enduring, and "in it is perfected the work of the other graces" (Rom.

5:3–4). It "teaches men to bear well" as we look "on all that which befalls us as coming from God" (Acts 14:22), and as we comprehend "that the Lord is the potter, and we are the clay." Springing from the truth of faith, the expectation of hope, and the consolation of love, patience bears cheerfully (Col. 1:11–12) and constantly (Luke 9:23; James 1:4). Patience looks to a threefold object: it causes the Christian (1) to look to God, at whose disposal are all things (Job 1:20–21); (2) to look at the things and "the parties that vex him, as a rod and a staff in God's hand" (Isa. 10:5); and (3) to look at all duties that arise from affliction as "doing of the will of God" (Heb. 10:36). Correspondingly, it does not murmur (1 Cor. 10:10), seek revenge (Rom. 12:17, 19), or avoid duties (Heb. 10:38).[160]

It is an excellent grace: "The excellency of the Grace is in this, it is man's victory over himself and all things; by it a man possesses his own soul" (Luke 21:19). It is "the perfection of Christ's obedience" (1 Pet. 2:21, 23); hence, it is the perfection of the saints' and the prophets' obedience as well (James 5:10; Rev. 1:9). Those who have it "want nothing" (James 1:4), endure any hardship (2 Tim. 2:3), suffer all things (1 Pet. 4:19), suffer the loss of all things (Phil. 3:8), find it "useful in every way," and have all its companion graces as well (1 Tim. 6:11; 2 Tim. 3:10; 2 Pet. 1:6). Those who *"endure to the end shall be saved"* (Matt. 10:22). To understand its excellency, examine the evils of impatience.[161]

Patience is a promised covenant blessing (Isa. 40:29–31; 43:2; Rom. 15:5; Phil. 1:29; James 1:4–5). Considering the condition of natural man (Rom. 1:29), "patience must be given, or we cannot have it."[162] Patience is a promised fruit of the other promised blessings (e.g., faith in James 1:3), of God's correcting hand (Jer. 30:11), of manifold tribulations that Christians face (Acts 14:22), of seed planted in an honest heart (Hos. 14:8), and of the Spirit (Gal. 5:22).

Nevay proposes the following uses for these doctrines. First, "by what we have said of patience, it may be easily known as a very necessary grace." However, "it is not every suffering that is patience." Second, "let everyone of us try our patience, whether it be of the right stamp." It must "have God as the great party … and duties as our great business." Third, those that lack patience are at a great loss, for they also lack faith because faith and patience are linked together (Rev. 13:10). Fourth, "esteem highly of this grace, and seek carefully after it…; for better is the patient in spirit than the proud in spirit" (Eccl. 7:8).

Fifth, test to see if you have this patience. The marks of patience are a despising not of the rod (Heb. 12:5), "a readiness of mind to endure the worst things for the name of Jesus Christ" (Acts 21:13), a determination not to "desert our duty" (Heb. 12:12-13), a bearing of troubles "willingly and cheerfully" (Heb. 10:34), and a constancy when "there is no sign of favor from God" (Job 13:26; Hab. 3:17–18).[163]

Sixth, it is a "terror to those who live without the covenant; they can have none of this most needful grace patience." Seventh, it is obtained from the promise through perseverance: "This patience does not rest in bosom resolutions, or self afflictings, but in patient enduring of hard times, as good soldiers of Christ" (2 Tim. 2:3). Eighth, without patience, "man cannot be the master of himself, he cannot possess his own soul"; nor can his heart "be settled in any good thing."[164] Those who hold unto the good seed of the Word with patience will bear the promised fruit (Luke 8:15).[165] Believers grow in patience through prayer (Matt. 26:41; James 5:13) and meditation on the causes of our trouble (Isa. 10:5-6; Ps. 107:11, 12, 17, 34; Heb. 12:5-6). Such reflection helps us to see God's providential hand in action, to grasp the consequences of our sinful rebellion, "to mortify sin," and "to increase grace and knowledge, both of God and ourselves."[166]

Exhorting Christians to patience during suffering, Andrew Gray adds, "O! But a Christian when he sitteth down on mount Pisgah, to behold that Promised Land, might with patience bear the rod."[167]

Sanctification – Its Fruits

Peace and assurance enable men to hold truth preservation above self-preservation. Joy and comfort are the fruit of the sanctifying graces and communion with God.

Peace: The peace Nevay speaks of here is not the temporal or the eternal blessing of peace; instead, it is the spiritual blessing of peace. It is "called the peace of God, because it is from him, as a gift, and with him, as a party" (Rom. 5:1). Christ calls it his peace because he purchased it: in the words of Paul, *"he is our peace"* (Eph. 2:14). It is "commonly called peace of conscience." It has a twofold nature: (1) the peace of justification arises from "closing with and quietly resting on Christ"; (2) the peace of sanctification arises from the feeling of pardon that comes from "victory over sin."[168]

Peace is such an excellent blessing that God claims it as his name, the *God of Peace* (Heb. 13:20), and Christ claims it as his legacy, *"Peace I leave with you"* (John 14:27). Regarding its excellency, consider both its measure and its purpose: *"And the peace of God, which passes all understanding, shall keep your hearts and minds through Christ Jesus"* (Phil. 4:7). Consider how during suffering "it is the bird, as it were, in the bosom sweetly singing." Consider the contrast between a clear conscience, "which is the image of

Heaven," and "a self-condemning and tormenting conscience, which is the image of Hell." Consider the contrast between true peace, which is at peace with all things (Job 5:23), and "the evils that are the want of it": *"There is no peace, saith my God, to the wicked"* (Isa. 57:21).[169]

It is a covenant blessing, abundantly promised in Scripture (Ps. 29:11; 85:8; Isa. 54:10,13; 57:19; Zech. 9:10) to His people, the church: *"Behold, I will extend peace to her like a river, and the glory of the Gentiles like a flowing stream: then shall ye suck, ye shall be borne upon her sides, and be dandled upon her knees"* (Isa. 66:12). The gospel is a Gospel of Peace (Rom. 10:15), and peace is a promised "effect of Christ's death" (Isa. 53:5; Eph. 2:13–14). Adoption, holiness, joy, a heart sprinkled to cleanse us from an evil conscience (Heb. 10:22), righteousness by faith are all promised; these cannot be without peace. Just as "a wounded conscience knows no physician but God" (Ps. 147:3; Hos. 6:1), "a good conscience is peace" (1 Pet. 3:21).[170]

Nevay identifies several uses for these doctrines. First, we must "learn to esteem this peace above every peace, and love no peace that" lacks it. Those who would settle for peace with their lusts and with God's enemies know not this peace. Second, sound peace is (1) "attained by faith of that blood of atonement" (Exod. 30:10; Lev. 17:11; Rom. 5:11), and (2) "maintained by the spirit of holiness," which is "the fruit of righteousness" (Heb. 12:11). In these two, "we have both the fountain and the river of the true and most delightful peace." Third, those without this peace find terrors on every side (Job 18:11): *"There is no peace to the wicked, saith the Lord"* (Isa. 48:22). Those living outside the covenant cannot find peace with God or with man. For these reasons, we should pity those within the covenant "when they are under temptation and lack this sweet peace."

Fourth, examine yourself for marks of true peace: (1) It "does not spring up from any thing in us; it is not self-grown, but of a heavenly original." (2) It "is the effect of faith" (Rom. 5:1). (3) It "cannot bear with sin." Purity must precede peace (James 3:17). (4) It "sleeps in its armor, believing there is happiness in a holy fear." (5) It is under constant assault from Satan. (6) It "will not tolerate sin in others" (Lev. 19:17).[171] Fifth, "sorely troubled and shaken consciences" should take comfort, "The Lord both can and will speak peace to his people." Sixth, seek peace through the covenant: do this (1) "by seeking righteousness first" (Isa. 32:17); (2) by keeping "near Christ, the Prince of Peace"; (3) by avoiding "every sin which may mar peace"; (4) by speedily reconciling breaches of the peace; and (5) by keeping "company with the Sons of Peace."[172]

Assurance: Peace and assurance are "great blessings of the covenant." They are joined together "because the first makes the soul ride safe at anchor, and the last makes the anchor sure and steadfast."[173] Assurance is the grace whereby "we have our hearts assured before God" (1 John 3:19) on the foundation rock of faith. This "assurance is not faith but a fruit of it":

> Faith has one act, whereby it discovers Christ, and flies to him, as an eagle to the prey, and rests on him; and it has another act, whereby it comes to know assuredly, that it has closed with Christ; the one is a direct act, it goes straight toward its object Christ; the other does reflect on that which is done, and searches whether all be found sure work; and finding it sure, it has great boldness and confidence (Eph. 3:12).[174]

Assurance is an excellent blessing that "puts the soul beyond doubting" (Rom. 8:33–35), and it "breeds true Christian fortitude, whereby the soul is steeled against trouble, and stirred up and strengthened unto duty." When "one knows whom he has trusted" (2 Tim. 1:12), he wants to please and obey God (1 John 3:19, 22).

Assurance is a promised covenant blessing. God promises that his people will *"go from strength to strength"* (Ps. 84:7), and that righteousness will produce *"quietness and assurance"* (Isa. 32:17). The Scripture saints like David and Paul possessed this promised assurance.[175]

Nevay proposes several uses for these doctrines. First, right assurance "must be from clear understanding, sound hope, and unfeigned faith." Second, one should not be satisfied to simply know Jesus; one "must know assuredly and experimentally … that they are in him." Third, it is terror to those without faith (2 Thess. 3:2): "They live doubting, and … die despairing." Fourth, seek assurance because "it shall make us not only live but [also] live abundantly" (John 10:10). Fifth, assurance must be sought "in this covenant and by the promise" because it only comes "by faith of the promise."[176]

Such assurance enabled the Covenanters, whose last words were "self preservation must stoop to truth preservation," to die willingly for the truth.[177] Augustine stressed the importance of positively affirming our beliefs: "Now, if you take away positive affirmation, you take away faith, for without positive affirmation nothing is believed."[178] "Nothing makes a man so virtuous as belief of the truth," argued Charles Spurgeon. Moreover, he contended, "A man cannot have an erroneous belief without by-and-by having an erroneous life."[179]

Assurance is a great blessing, but false assurance based on delusion, presumption, or carnal confidence is a curse. According to Andrew Gray, many delude themselves by resting their assurance on one of the following ten false foundations: flashes of light and joy, numerous Christian duties, observance of the law, hatred of a particular sin, freedom from gross sins, gifts of prayer or knowledge, peace of conscience, approbation from others, observance of the ordinances, and external happiness.[180] In contrast, Gray identifies the marks of those with real assurance: They earnestly pursue "communion and fellowship with God" (Ps. 63:1; Song of Sol. 2:16–17; 7:10–11), knowing that Heaven is their destination. They are committed to praising God (Ps. 118:21), holding Christ and his interest in high regard (Song of Sol. 2:3). They are humble (Eph. 3:8). They delight in doing God's will (Ps. 40:8; 119:115) and his commands. They are confident that "he *hath begotten [them] again unto a lively hope*" (1 Pet. 1:3), and they declare, *"My beloved is mine, and I am his!"* (Song of Sol. 2:16).[181]

Joy: The Puritans and the Covenanters believed that "it is a contradiction to be happy and unholy."[182] Joy "is the fruit of faith and sanctification; it is a spiritual joy, a joy in God, through the Lord Jesus Christ, by whom we have received the atonement" (Rom. 5:11). It "is called the joy of the Holy Ghost" (1 Thess. 1:6).

Joy is an excellent blessing. It "has the marrow of blessing in it, so the psalmist sings, *'My soul shall be satisfied as with marrow and fatness, and my mouth shall praise the with joyful lips'*" (Psalm 63:5).[183] Scripture describes it as a lasting joy (Ps. 84:4) and a "joy of fat things" (Isa. 25:6). Its author is the Holy Ghost (Rom. 14:17), and its "object is God and his son Jesus Christ" (Phil. 3:1,3). The reason Christ gave for abiding in him was, *"that my joy might remain in you, and that your joy might be full"* (John 15:11). Joy "puts the heart in the right frame" for worship (James 5:13); those without it receive the cup of astonishment and desolation (Ezek. 23:33). Scripture associates great things with joy: (1) finding Christ (Matt. 2:10; 28:8), (2) performing service for God (Deut. 28:47), (3) suffering for Christ (Phil. 2:17), (4) saving of souls (Isa. 61:10), (5) offering of prayer (Phil. 1:4), and (6) communicating of the Word (Acts 13:51–52; Phil. 2:18). Scripture sets forth its excellency: it is called the *"great"* (Luke 2:10), *"exceeding"* (Jude vs. 24), *"unspeakable"* (1 Pet. 1:8), and *"everlasting"* (Isa. 61:7) joy. It is the people's strength, *"the joy of the Lord is your strength"* (Neh. 8:10), and the eternal state of those who *"enter into the joy of the Lord"* (Matt. 25:23).[184]

Joy is a promised covenant blessing. It is "one of the chief things of the kingdom that is promised" (Rom. 14:17) and "one of the chief fruits of the Spirit of Promise" (Gal. 5:22). Scripture promises salvation, faith, hope, the Christian life, and "through bearing in temptation": these cannot be without joy (Neh. 8:10; Ps. 51:12; Rom. 12:12; Phil. 1:20). Joy is "the flower and reward of every grace."[185]

These doctrines have many uses. First, learn to recognize true spiritual joy—it is "kindling fire from heaven and fuel of the Spirit." Second, "esteem it highly." It is "more than the gate of heaven, for it is heaven within the believer's gate; there is no blessedness without joy." Seek to have it by (1) turning godly sorrow to joy, (2) "making use of Christ for righteousness," (3) "acting faith upon promises," (4) "carefully following the ordinances," and (5) "remembering all former sweet experiences." Third, examine to see if you have it by these marks: It "is joined with knowledge" (Eccl. 2:26), "with the free spirit of God" (Ps. 51:12), and with other graces (holy fear, love, peace, long-suffering, gentleness) (Ps. 2:11; Gal. 5:22). It "is most inward and has all its springs in God" (Ps. 87:7). It "is pure and unmixed." It constantly abides (John 15:11), and "the statutes and commandments of the Lord will be matter of song to those who have this joy" (Ps. 119:54).[186] Fourth, do not foster in yourself those things that mar or interrupt joy. Do not seek to find its "root and spring" within yourself, for in doing so you will be "left to walk in the light of your own sparks." Fifth, believers should not be discouraged, for joy is promised, "even to mourners" (Isa. 61:3). On the other hand, those who do not have it "raise a scandal on the Christian life, which is itself a joyful life." Further, "if we have it not, we may blame ourselves; for *all the ways of God are pleasantness, and all his paths are peace*" (Prov. 3:17). Sixth, joy must be sought from the covenant; for *"with joy ye shall be able to draw waters out of the wells of salvation"* (Isa. 12:3).[187]

Comfort: Comfort, or consolation, is a "fair and sweet covenant blessing" that is only due to the "people of God" (Isa. 40:1). Specifically, it is only for weak-spirited, downcast, mourners (Isa. 61:2; Hos. 2:14; 2 Cor. 7:6). It is a "cordial, or a cure for the soul"; however, the words of comfort "must be spoken in, and received, before it can work its cure."

It is an excellent blessing. The entire Trinity is engaged in providing comfort: God authors it (Isa. 51:12; 2 Cor. 1:3); the Holy Ghost delivers it (John 14:16, 26; Acts 9:31); and Christ is its consolation (Luke 2:25; Phil. 2:1). Comfort is an excellent blessing with "effects, such as the establishing of the heart, the reviving of the spirit, and the quickening the whole man to duty." Consider how it uplifts the soul (Ps. 94:19; Isa. 50:4); prevails over suffering (2 Cor. 1:5); "makes man enjoy both God and himself"; and results from preaching of the Word (Acts 15:31; Rom. 15:4; 1 Cor. 14:3). Further, its excellency appears when we consider the "woefulness of sorrow and discouragement" when comfort is absent.[188]

God promises comfort for his people (Isa. 40:1; 51:3; 57:18; 66:13; Jer. 31:13). The "great promise of Christ" is "that he will send the Comforter" (John

15:26). The Scripture saints believed in the promise of comfort (e.g., David in Ps. 23:4). Scripture promises grace, hope, love, and faith; these cannot be without comfort (Rom. 1:12; Phil. 2:19; 2 Thess. 2:16).[189]

These doctrines have several uses. First, do not comfort those "who never were downcast." There is no comfort for those outside the covenant. Second, be careful to apply fully the right comfort to the "proper malady" in the "proper season." Third, reprove those who have a small esteem for comfort. Fourth, covet the consolations of comfort, for they are "the most rare and costly cordials in the world." It is not until we have our souls trodden down and "brought up again from the lowest pit" that we know their worth (Ps. 86:13). Fifth, seek comfort from the Covenant of Grace, wherein it is abundant.[190]

John Bunyan (1628–1688), a contemporary of John Nisbet, expressed the great comfort of hope in his book *Pilgrim's Progress*, written while imprisoned for refusing to stop preaching after the Outing in England. Christian, the hero of Bunyan's tale, is saved by the character Hopeful, as they attempt to cross the great river:

> Hopeful therefore here had much ado to keep his brother's head above water, yea sometimes he would be quite gone down, and then, e're a while, he would rise up again half dead. Hopeful would also endeavor to comfort him saying, "Brother, I see the gate, and the men standing by to receive us."[191]

The foundation of hope and comfort is faith in God's covenant promises, which are a great blessing to Christians during persecution. James Nisbet, along with the Covenanters, believed that it was "an article of grace's well-ordered Covenant" for Christians to face trials and afflictions: "God had one child without sin, but never any without suffering."[192] When troubled, James Nisbet fled to God for refuge, taking comfort that the Lord will fulfill his covenant promises:

> The most shocking afflictions that can befall me are but pieces of Time's misery, and streams of Marah's bitter waters, that all the Lord's noble cloud of witnesses have wade in and drank of before me (Heb. 11–12). In the midst of all my afflictions, I would still remember there remains a rest for the Lord's people (Heb. 4:9; Rev. 21:4). Of which rest none of his own can possibly come short because it is their covenanted inheritance.
>
> The Lord hath been graciously pleased to suit his people's suffering circumstances, and repeated trials, with many sweet and suitable precious promises, for faith, patience, and experience, to rest and feed on at all times, specially in the hour of temptation.[193]

As the priests' feet that bore the ark of God, Joshua (Josh. 4:10-11), stood firm in the midst of Jordan, until all the children of Israel, strong and weak, were clean passed over, so our merciful and faithful High Priest, Christ Jesus, the glorious antitype of these priests and that ark, stands in the midst of Death's Jordan, until he waft [waves] all his sons and daughters safe over to glory's enjoyment in the New Jerusalem.[194]

…That the great and wise Jehovah, while he sees meet to detain his people in this wilderness, hath been pleased graciously to suit his people's suffering circumstances and often repeated trials, with large and suitable encouragement for faith, patience, and experience to feed and rest on, held forth to them, in many great and precious promises. Wherewith, the whole book of God is wonderfully decked and be-spangled, as with precious pearls and sweet cups of kind consolation, from the beginning of Genesis to the end of the Revelation. The whole mass whereof is as a tree of life springing forth from the bosom of the infinite mercy of God, and bowing from thence downward to elect sinners; the branches whereof are richly laden with twelve manner of fruits for refreshing cordials, to refresh and solace the faintings, and weary passengers in their journey home to their Father's kingdom. Upon the receipt of which soul-enlarging consolations, they will in sometimes arrive to such a height of holy boldness and assured confidence, as to cry out, *"Nothing shall be able to separate us from the love of God which is in Christ Jesus; neither death nor life, principalities nor powers, things present nor things to come…. O death, where is thy sting? O grave, where is thy victory?"*[195]

Communion with God is the Last and Best Fruit: The "last and best fruit…is communion with God." In this communion, believers walk and dwell with God (Gen. 5:22; 6:9; 2 Cor. 5:15; 1 John 4:13), and God walks and dwells in them (Lev. 26:12). The communion between the Father and Christ provides the pattern for the communion between God and Christians: "Christ was the Father's delight; there was a most sweet communion betwixt them." Likewise, there is mutual delight between God and believers (Ps. 37:4; Prov. 8:30). Such close communion requires that there be union, "by the spirit they that are joined to the Lord are one spirit" (1 Cor. 6:17). It requires mutual communicating and corresponding (Isa. 64:1-2; Phil. 3:20). It requires mutual trust: "Christ looks upon believers, not as servants, but as friends." It requires mutual condescension: God promises, *"I will heal their backsliding"* (Hos. 14:4); man promises to *"deny himself"* (Matt. 16:24). It requires mutual familiarity, delight, sweet talk, and shared praises: Moses spoke to God face to face (Exod. 33:11); God rejoices over believers *"as the bridegroom rejoices over the bride"* (Isa. 62:5); the "spouse delights in him—'*his mouth is most sweet; yea, he is altogether lovely*'" (Song of Sol. 5:16).[196]

It is an excellent blessing. It is a high and excellent honor to be *"a people near unto him"* (Ps. 148:14). Communion with the triune God is an excellent thing: the Father is sworn by covenant to do all for our good (1 John 4:8), the Son sweetly and forever "makes us partakers of him" (Heb. 3:14; see also Prov. 8:30; John 17:21,23), and the Holy Spirit engages us in "a most inward and immediate fellowship." It "makes believers princes with God." If conversing with the wise improves men, "how much more will similar conversing with God do this?" Those with this fellowship have bold access with God (Gen. 18; Exod. 33:9–23; 2 Chron. 20:7; Isa. 41:8): they "may speak all that which is in their heart to him, and may expect great things from him in prayer." Their faces will shine as Moses' did (Exod. 34:29–30), and their soul will never weary from "delight in fellowship with God" (Matt. 17:4). Nothing can compare with "the fellowship of Christ with his bride"– "a bundle of myrrh unto her, lying all night betwixt her breast, when his hand in under her head, and his right hand is embracing her" (Song of Sol. 5:13; 2:6). No human relationship can be as satisfying.[197]

It is promised covenant blessing, wherein "God shall walk in and with them, and they shall walk with him" (Exod. 25:8; Lev. 26:11–12; Ps. 68:16; 132:13–14; Micah 4:5; 2 Cor. 6:16; Rev. 3:4). Fellowship with God, as our Father, Christ, as our head and husband, and the Holy Spirit, as our Comforter, must be by promise, for naturally man flees from God. Scripture promises holiness, forgiveness from sins, and conformity with Christ; these require communion with God. Further, the Lord directly promises it: "He will make his name known" unto his people, and he "will never leave or forsake his people" (Heb. 13:5).[198]

Nevay proposes several uses for these doctrines. First, if those who do not have this communion could know it, "nothing would be preferred unto it; and, they would take no rest until they were partakers of it." Second, those who desire communion with God must love holiness, "for this precious communion is the fruit of holiness: sin separates souls from God, but holiness brings the soul near God and God near the soul." In short, "holiness is God's image, and he loves to see it." Third, observe the "misery and madness" of those who "pour out their hearts, and spend their immortal spirits, which were made for communion with God, upon vanities and wickedness." Those without communion with God "die without hope" (Eph. 2:12).[199]

Fourth, examine if your communion with God has these marks. It must have "clear and distinct knowledge of Christ, and closing with him in covenant"; and it must have "spiritual apprehensions of God," with a communion that "tickles and delights the sensitive parts. " It must "delight in the law" (Rom. 7:22) and exhibit "boldness of access" unto God. It must have "antipathy to wicked fellowship, and cordial delight in the fellowship of the saints" (Ps. 16:2–3). It must have a "willingness to part with all, before we part with his fellowship," and a "love and longing for his appearing" (2 Tim. 4:8).[200] There will be restlessness when there are sad interruptions in this fellowship (Song of Sol. 5:6).[201]

Fifth, we must seek it through the covenant promises and not break it by having "fellowship with the unfruitful works of darkness" or by following false doctrines or worship practices (1 Cor. 10:20; Eph. 5:5–6,11). Fellowship with Christ and the Spirit requires conforming unto his life and his death, "drawing light and life from him" (Phil. 2:1; 3:10; Col. 2:6), and "maintaining fellowship with his suffering saints" (1 Pet. 4:14).[202]

Sanctification – Its Means

Prayer and praise are great covenant blessings that open the doors to all other blessings.

Nevay lists four *means* of sanctification: Hearing of the Word, Observance of the Sacraments, Prayer, and Praise. This section addresses the last two of these means, which are of no small value. Although the remnant suffered damage during the persecution when providentially deprived from hearing the Word and observing the Sacraments, they survived as a church through prayer and praise. As we have seen, James Nisbet's private reflections are ample proof that these two means of sanctification both preserved and defined the *Covenanters*.

Praise: Praise is "the showing forth and commending of the Lord's excellencies with admiration and adoration." This praising God "is sometimes expressed generally by showing forth his virtues (1 Pet. 2:9) or by loving and confessing to the Lord (Ps. 18)." It is also sometimes expressed by lauding (Rom. 15:11), blessing (Ps. 145:21), glorifying, extolling (Isa. 24:15), and exalting (Ps. 99:5) God. Proper praise "requires the whole man; the judgment, to esteem; the memory, to treasure up; the will, to resolve; the affections, to delight in God; the tongue, to utter; and the life, to express all his excellencies and free favors."[203] Praise is an excellent, good, and pleasant thing (Ps. 52:9; 54:6; 135:3):

(1) It is God's delight and dwelling place (Ps. 22:3). (2) It is angels' exercise (Isa. 6:1–3). (3) It is the exercise of a Spirit in a right frame (James 5:13). (4) It is the oil that makes the wheels go well in and about duty. (5) It is the

334 Lessons for Christians

fruit and flower that should grow up from every blessing. (6) It is an everlasting good, and eternity's work. (7) It is the Lord's end, Christ's end, and the soul's end, when it is right. (8) It is one of the great gospel sacrifices (Heb. 13:15). (9) Unto praise many promises are made (1 Sam. 2:30; Ps. 67:5–6). (10) The excellency of this exercise appears from the misery of those that have it not.[204]

Praise is covenanted and promised: *"This people have I formed for myself; they shall show forth my praise"* (Isa. 43:21). There "shall be so much praise in the church that her gates shall be called praise" (Isa. 60:18). Scripture promises joy, salvation, hope, the Spirit, and God's dwelling with his people: these must be with praise (Ps. 22:3; 42:11). God's glory is the great end of praise (Ps. 50:23), and praise itself is "Christ's great end in his work of redemption." Scripture abundantly promises it (Ps. 22:26; 66:2; 102:18; 145:4; Isa. 61:11; Rom. 15:1).[205]

Nevay identified the following uses for these doctrines. First, when we consider what true praise is, it is clear that those "who neither know him nor esteem him cannot but take his name in vain." Moreover, they cannot pay him his dues because his currency is praise. Second, praise is our great duty, and it "requires high thoughts of God, and low thoughts of ourselves." Of all duties, it is most expected. It "makes us priest unto God," and "by it God is glorified, and our will made comfortable to God's." Although, "the debt is never payable, yet what we find within our heart to pay is accepted." Third, we should examine if our praise is true. The marks of sound praise are much self-denial and thankfulness offered with strong resolutions, a fixed heart, a full spirit, and a sweetness. There must also be a "still working up like new wine" that accompanies a single-minded focus on God. Fourth, take comfort and turn to the covenant promises, wherein the spirit of praise is abundant.[206]

James Nisbet filled his memoir with page after page of praise, which comprised the large part of his private devotion. Please note that he was a Presbyterian. Do Presbyterians today use the same language in expressing their love for God, or do they rightly deserve the name, the "frozen chosen"? Christ's praise should be continually on our lips.

Prayer: John Bunyan exhorted Christians to "Pray often; for prayer is a shield to the soul, a sacrifice to God, and a scourge for Satan."[207] Charles Spurgeon declared, "On his knees, the believer is invincible."[208] According to Nevay, Scripture variously describes prayer:

It is calling upon the Name of the Lord (Gen. 4:26). It is wrestling with God, with weeping and supplication (Gen. 32:24; Hos. 12:4). It is bringing of desires and groans before God (Ps. 38:9). It is seeking of God's face (Ps. 24:6). It is heart and flesh crying out for the living God (Ps. 84:2). It is asking, seeking, knocking (Matt. 7:7). It is to faint not, to use importunity, to cry day and night (Luke 18:1, 4–5, 9).

Briefly, prayer is an offering up of our desires unto God, the pouring out of the heart before him (Ps. 62:6), according to his will (1 John 5:14), by the help of the Spirit (Rom. 8:26), in the name of Christ (John 16:23), with confession of sin (Ps. 32:5), and thankful acknowledgment of God's mercy (Phil. 4:6).[209]

The excellency of prayer is seen in that it is the means by which we converse with God and engage God's help according to the promises. "It was a great part of Christ's exercise in his lifetime and, in a sublime way, his exercise still" (Heb. 7:25).[210] Through it we obtain great things: health (Isa. 38:14–15, 21), strength and boldness (Judg. 16:28; Acts 4:29), children (Gen. 25:21), public gifts (1 Kings 3:9–12), power over physical objects (Josh. 10:12), deliverance from enemies (2 Sam. 15:31; 2 Kings 6:18, 10; 2 Chron. 20:12–17; Neh. 1:11; Dan. 3:25; Acts 12:5, 7). There are many promises made to praying people: to them "all things are sanctified" (1 Tim. 4:5); Satan is daily overcome; joy, acceptance, prosperity, peace, and salvation are promised (Ps. 122:6–7; Isa. 56:7; Rom. 10:13); the Holy Spirit is for the asking (Luke 11:13); and in what those in prayer agree will be done for them.[211]

Prayer is a "promised and great covenanting blessing." God "promises that his people will pray, and that he will answer" (Jer. 29:12): *"They shall come weeping, and with supplication will I lead them"* (Jer. 31:9). "To pour forth the spirit of praise and supplication" (Zech. 12:10), He also promises. It is obvious that prayer is a gift because *"we know not what we should pray for as we ought"* (Rom. 8:26). For this reason, those things necessary for prayer are promised: Scripture promises the Spirit to assist us, faith to enable us (Rom. 10:14), and obedience to bring us to it for strength. Prayer is the means by which we are kept from temptation (Matt. 26:41; Rev. 3:10), delivered from trouble (Ps. 50:15), enabled to enjoy communion with God and worship (Isa. 66:23). In fact, "it is put for the whole worship of God" (Isa. 56:7), and "we can make no use of the promises but by prayer" (Isa. 43:25–26; Ezek. 36:37).[212]

Consider the usefulness of these doctrines. First, before God will deliver his people from troubles, he requires sincere prayer from them (Exod. 14:15; Isa. 1:15; Jer. 11:14). Second, we must make our prayers with fervor, with our whole heart, and with the Spirit's inditing. Prayers must be consistent with the will of God, upon which we patiently and submissively wait.[213] Third, prayer is the "key to all the treasures of heaven,"

and "we can make use of no promises but by prayer."[214] It is certain that
"if we find in our heart to pray (2 Sam. 7:27), God will find in his heart to
answer." Although it does not always appear that God answers prayer,
"the believer's prayer is ever answered in the main ends of it, the glory
of God, the church's good, and that which is best for them." Fourth, to
those who do not feel fit to pray because of the lack of spirit, words,
ability, or concentration, Nevay gives the following advice: (1) Sometimes it is necessary to wrestle and wait on the Spirit of Supplication,
given to all whom God has adopted. (2) "It is not the words which make
prayer; sometimes there are but groans" (Isa. 38:14; Rom. 8:23): "God needs
not the words; the sacrifices of God are a broken spirit" (Ps. 51:17). (3)
"Prayers are not heard for their perfection, but for Christ's sake." (4)
Remain focused: "The Spirit's help is at hand.... Admit no thoughts,
though otherwise good, if they concern not the present duty."[215] Fifth, for
those outside the covenant, there is no hope in prayer because "no man
calls Jesus Lord but by the Holy Ghost" (1 Cor. 12:3).[216] Sixth, those "who
desire to pray aright must go in to the covenant and fetch it from thence;
and to the mediator therein: he teaches to pray (Luke 11:1), go to the promises for prayer, and then with prayer to the promises again, and that will
be a sweet and blessed round." Seventh, it is folly to "think it is an easy
thing to pray": "It is neither in our hand nor heart unless it be given us
to pray as Christ prayed in much communion with God" (Luke 9:29).[217]

Hope manifests itself in the life of Christians through prayer. For a
Christian to approach God with confidence in prayer, he must believe
the promises contained in the Word, as did David who "hoped in his
Word" (Ps. 119:49-50). According to Andrew Gray, the Christian must take
a specific "promise in his hand and present it to God, and say fulfill this
promise, because thou wilt not deny thy name, but art faithful."[218] Gray
contended that the experience of observing the Lord accomplish his
promises leaves divine impressions of his love on our souls, leads to a
discovery and appreciation of God's majesty, strengthens our heart and
interest in God, and builds hope and spiritual joy (Ps. 28:7).[219] Gray insisted that prayers must be offered without ceasing (1 Thess. 5:17), with a
deep impression of God's deity, with a humble and contrite spirit, with
faith and confidence that God is a hearer of prayer (Ps. 65:2), and with
fervency (Ps. 39:12).[220] He identified the following impediments to prayer:
praying for our lust (James 4:3) or with entanglements of our heart (Ps.
66:18), praying with formality or indifference (Mal. 1:14) or without wrestling, praying without employing the Holy Ghost as author (Job 37:19) or
Christ as mediator (Matt. 22:12), and failing to pray when led by the Spirit

(Song of Sol. 5:2) or with a humble spirit (1 Pet. 5:5).[221] David promises that those who seek the Lord in prayer *"shall be abundantly satisfied with the fatness of thy house, and thou shalt make them drink of the rivers of thy pleasures"* (Ps. 36:8). It is also through prayer that the city of God is made glad (Ps. 46:4).[222]

James Nisbet took the advice of Nevay and Gray to heart. The most striking characteristic of James Nisbet's memoir is that he seems to be continually in prayer. Perhaps the many close escapes from death fashioned within him a living hope in a living God. Perhaps the prayers of the Covenanters, which he witnessed first hand during his youth, irreversibly comforted and edified his soul, as he relates in his memoir:

> The way how they employed and improved their time, except when flying and shifting from place to place to escape their enemy's fury and cruelty, was spent in earnest and fervent prayers to the Lord, in bemoaning and bewailing their own sins [and the sins of others]. [They did so to] deprecate the Lord's wrath, that his anger might be turned away, and that he would pity, spare, and raise up a remnant to be a seed to serve him in these lands, according to his pattern showed them in his Word. In this, they were pathetically earnest and importunate with the Lord, as though they would take no denial, but often cried, "O that he would return!" O that he would return, and revive his work with power, light, and life, and help them … from all defection, error, and extreme, on the right and left hand. [They prayed] that he would mightily assist them, theirs, and all his own people everywhere with quickening, renewing, restraining, strengthening, comforting, and preserving grace and mercy, that they might be all borne up, and borne through, under all trials and all temptations assaulting them from the Devil, the world, and the flesh. [They prayed] that they might be richly furnished with divine aid and assistance to resist unto blood striving against sin; they being ever helped, though grace, to live [in, to, and for] him. [They prayed] that he would glorify himself [in, by, and upon] them, in a way of grace and gracious disposal so as they might be greatly helped to live to him in all sincerity and uprightness of heart; and when called to it, to die for him in all faithfulness and constancy.
>
> What watering with tears! What holy and vehement breathings of soul! What heavy and heart-rending groans for a body of sin and death! What mighty wrestlings with the Lord that he might cause his face to shine upon them and return to these lands in mercy! What self-judging and self-condemning of themselves! What bitter bewailing of sins personal, general, and national! What crying for the spirit of God, in all his saving and quickening operations in them [and…] for light and truth…! What holy and constant resolves to be for the Lord and his way, and

not for another, cost what it would…! What holy, constant, pressings and strivings to be made partakers of his fullness of grace…! What shining beauty was in their faces when thus employed! What melting and yearning of bowels! What cheerfulness and extension of voice, and yet the tears running as rain down their cheeks! What weighty and unforethought sentences and expressions proceeded out of their mouths, as if dictated by the Spirit of God, to the great amazement of those who were witnesses! And what earnest pleadings with the Lord to be ever counseled of him under all emergencies of providences that he might see fit to tryst them with! Thus, they would have been employed several hours, sometimes whole days, sometimes whole nights, sometimes three days and three nights, all spent in earnest prayer to the Lord and mighty wrestlings with him; only now and then interlaced with reading a portion of the Scripture and singing psalms, and refreshing their bodies with meat and drink once in the twenty-four hours; sometimes oftener, and sometimes not so often.[223]

Evidencing the life-changing influence of these experiences are some extracts from James Nisbet's manuscripts concerning prayer and the need to turn to prayer in time of affliction:

Whether the Lord really answers my prayer, answers me with silence, or with terrible things in righteousness; yet still my duty is to stir up myself and persevere in crying to him, by fervent prayer and supplication. [I pray] that he may bring me nearer and nearer to himself, by the blood of his covenant, and make me taste and feel, by faith, that all what he has revealed of himself in Scripture to be to and for his people.[224]

[We should] do as Hezekiah did with Senacherib's blasphemous letter; he answered not a word but spread it out before the Lord; which thing is our duty also, to make all our requests known to God by prayer and supplication, until he finish our course with joy and [translates us] over to the blessed land.[225]

At his own time, he will cause his sweet and lovely voice to be heard, saying to them, "Be not afraid; it is I, who am coming trampling upon the waves of your afflictions to save and deliver you." Thus, many times he answers the prayers of his people.[226]

13

Lessons for Citizens

All nations whom Thou hast made shall come and worship before Thee. –Ps. 86:9

Lesson #4: We must fulfill our biblical obligation to make disciples of all nations and to be the light and salt of the world. We can learn much from the successes and failures of the Covenanters in church and state relations. As we will see, there is nothing wrong with their objective to be a Christian state, a militant church, and obedient citizens. Unfortunately, to avoid repeating their mistakes, the modern church has abandoned these objectives. Fortunately, God's kingdom will triumph; hence, Christians should endeavor to achieve the proper relationship between church and state.

Church and State – Their Common Obligations

States, being moral agents, derive their authority from God and are obligated to promote good and punish evil, according to God's Word, being careful to honor Christ and protect his church. The church is obligated to Christianize and to hold the state accountable.

The Revolution Settlement was a turning point in history. Within a year of the Revolution Settlement, John Locke's *Essay Concerning Human Understanding*, one of the most influential books next to the Bible, inaugurated the Age of Reason and Enlightenment. No longer would man perceive truth as absolute–each man was now his own God. This new age not only witnessed the general dismantling of a united church, but it also established the self-governing modern state–no longer "subservient to God's authority and direction."[1] The later part of the seventeenth century marks the "first time in a thousand years in Western history, a deliberate attempt was made on a grand scale to organize a religiously neutral civilization–a political, economic, ethical and intellectual structure independent of Christianity."[2] The net result was an unwritten treaty of peace, which continues to this day, between the church and its enemies–both within and without the church.

The relationship between church and state was dear to the heart of the Scottish church.[3] In the final analysis, the issue that split the Scottish church concerned the necessity of biblical requirements for civil leaders. Florence McCoy remarks concerning the Covenanters: "No city of God on earth has yet been achieved. The splendor of Scotland's ministry was that they tried. The tragedy was not that they failed. Failure was inevitable. The tragedy was that even as they crowned their covenanted king in Scone, they did not know that they failed already."[4] They should have heeded the warning of Buchanan: "A king is created for the benefit of the people, and that nothing derived from heaven can be a greater blessing than a good, or a greater curse than a bad king."[5] Instead of a greater blessing from God, the Covenanters received a curse as their chosen king set about to destroy the foundation of the church. It is not surprising that the Covenanters stumbled so badly when they relied on an earthly king, rather than Jesus Christ, to oversee their covenant. They should have heeded Calvin's advice, "Even though all the princes of the earth were to unite for the maintenance of the gospel, still we must not make that the foundation of our hope."[6]

Were they wrong in wanting a king to execute their covenant? The simple answer might be that the church has no business trying to influence the political realm. Did not Jesus say, *"My kingdom is not of this world"* (John 18:36a)? It is true that Jesus' spiritual kingdom is not of this world, but to conclude that Jesus' kingdom should not influence the world is biblically unsound because believers are called to be the "salt and the light" of the world. One of the chief means of influence is through Christian leaders. In Psalms 72:1–17, Solomon lists twenty benefits of Christ's kingdom (i.e., his Church in Heaven and on earth).[7] Many of the benefits and promises of Christ's kingdom involve godly magistrates and the great blessings that they provide his people. Although godly magistrates are not the core of Christ's kingdom, they certainly are the outer crust through which Christ blesses his people.

Although the Scottish church may have erred in asking too much of the state, the modern church asks too little—a far worse error. Do nations and civil leaders have any obligation to God? Should churches endeavor to transform nations into Christian nations? To answer these questions it is necessary to examine the biblical requirements for the church and state relationship. The following five principles embody these requirements. The first of these asserts the necessity for separation of church and state; the other four assert the necessity of meeting mutual obligations. In discussing each principle, the opinions of James

Thornwell, a pre-Civil-War era Presbyterian minister, provide a sanity check. Thornwell's lighthouse of clear, biblical thinking is a welcome sight to those who venture into the sea of opinion regarding church and state relations.

Principle #1: *The church and state are of entirely distinct and have immiscible natures and purposes; however, they share many mutual obligations.* Most Reformed confessions emphasize that the church and state have completely different origins, objects, ends, principles, officers, and means. None debate the necessity for separation of powers. The church is an internal-spiritual entity; the state is an external-temporal entity. They can and must operate completely independently and separately. In every aspect, each party must not intrude into the other's primary sphere: magistrates must not preach the gospel; ministers must not wield the sword. Any intrusion or obstruction of the primary sphere of the other body is fatal to both bodies. Although all Reformed confessions demand independence, they also stress the mutual obligations of church and state to God, as illustrated by the Second *Book of Discipline*.

> The magistrate neither ought to preach, minister the sacraments, nor execute the censures of the kirk, nor yet prescribe any rule how it should be done, but command the ministers to observe the rule commanded in the Word, and punish the transgressors by civil means: The ministers exercise not the civil jurisdiction, but teach the magistrate how it should be exercised according to the Word.[8]

Secular sources also emphasize the necessity of separation. During the early history of America, Alexis De Tocqueville (1805–1859) analyzed the American relationship between church and state. Many of his observations and projections are applicable today. Concerning the great hazard of religion establishing a permanent bond with a state, Tocqueville observed, "Alone, it [religion] may hope for immortality; linked to ephemeral powers, it follows their fortunes and often fails together with the passions of a day sustaining them." He warned that in making such alliances, religion "sacrifices the future for the present, and by gaining a power to which it has no claims, it risks its legitimate authority." Through alliances with states, religion becomes subject to future changes in law that can undermine or mislead future generations and risks alienating other nations and peoples to which it is not allied. There is a real danger of religion becoming "mingled with the bitter passions of the world" which could result in alliances with the enemies of true religion. To Tocqueville, the early American model is the only proper relationship between church and state, and the great strength of American religion is due to the "complete separation of church and state."[9]

Although Tocqueville extolled the separation of powers, he also recognized the overarching influence of religion in church and state relations. He remarked that religion was "the first of their [Americans] political institutions" although it "never intervenes directly in the government." Illustrating this point, he describing of a court case where the judge dismissed a witness because the witness did not believe in God. The judge remarked that he was not "aware that there was a man living who did not believe in the existence of God; that this belief constituted the sanction of all testimony in a court of justice; and that he knew of no cause in a Christian country, where a witness had been permitted to testify without such belief."[10] Tocqueville cautioned, "If religions are to be capable of maintaining themselves in democratic ages, it is not enough that they remain within the spiritual sphere."[11]

Unfortunately, over the last three centuries, there has been a complete reversal regarding the mutual obligations of church and state. Today, states consider the people, not God, as the sole source of power. Today, churches are at peace with God's enemies. Both church and state have abandoned all the mutual obligations that the Covenanters treasured. For this reason, and the fact that these mutual obligations are scriptural requirements, it is necessary to examine the slow erosion that has robbed society of these important truths.

Although the concept that the church and state have a mutual responsibility to hold each other accountable is foreign to the modern sensibility, it is in perfect alignment with the beliefs of Scottish Presbyterians (e.g., Knox, Melville, Henderson, Rutherford, and Gillespie) before the Revolution Settlement. Undoubtedly, the Scottish Commissioners to the Westminster Assembly would have testified against the so-called religious peace and unbounded toleration that characterize the modern church and the "American" system. George Gillespie warned that those who in the name of "their great Diana, liberty of conscience" refuse to allow discipline in the church and assist the sects "in seeking after toleration ... will answer this to God and their own conscience."[12] Christian magistrates, he contended, should follow David's example: *"I will destroy all the wicked of the land; that I may cut off wicked doers from the city of the Lord"* (Psalm 101:8).[13] However, he is careful to clarify, "God would have the camp of Israel altogether holy and clean (Deut. 23:9–14). Clean from whom? Not so much from the wicked heathens ... as from the wicked Israelites."[14] Samuel Rutherford in his *Free Disputation Against Pretended Lib-*

erty of Conscience severely criticized the religious liberty expounded by
early Americans such as Roger Williams (1604–1683):

> So the Americans and wildest Papists keep the peace of their towns and
> cities safe and distinct, where there is no spiritual heavenly peace.

> Toleration of many religions is contrary to peace, if one of them be the
> only true way, the rest are all false ways, the mixture of the two contrary
> seeds, the seed of the Serpent, and the seed of the woman must be
> against peace; and Paul exhorting to union and Christian peace, thinks
> many religions to be tolerated, to be contrary to peace.

> Peace is commanded in the New Testament, no word of toleration of di-
> vers religions, which are the seminaries of discord between the seed of
> the woman and the Serpent's seed....[15]

Nowhere is the abandonment more inexcusable than in America. In
early America, the church and state were separate, distinct, and co-
ordinate bodies. John Cotton (1584–1652), an influential minister in the
infant colony of New England, emphasizing the mutual roles and inter-
dependence of the parties involved, insisted that "authority in magistrates, liberty in people, and purity in the church" do "mutually and
strongly maintain one another."[16]

Unfortunately, through changes in the constitutions of both church
and state, early Americans soon abandoned these mutual obligations.
Although the founding fathers did not intend to obliterate these mutual
obligations, they did not boldly declare them. In the word of James
Thornwell, "In their anxiety to guard against the evils of religious establishment ... they virtually expelled Jehovah from the government of the
country."[17] Consequently, compromised ecclesiastical and civil constitutions hinder the restoration of the proper church and state relationship.

As previously stated, in 1789, the Presbyterian Church in the U.S.A.
made significant modifications to the *Westminster Confession of Faith* that
greatly weakened any responsibility of the civil magistrate concerning
moral or religious issues. The original version of Chapter 23, concerning the duties of the civil magistrate, requires the civil magistrate–

> to take order, that unity and peace be preserved in the church, that the
> truth of God be kept pure and entire, that all blasphemies and heresies
> be suppressed, all corruptions and abuses in worship and discipline pre-
> vented or reformed, and all ordinances of God duly settled, adminis-
> tered, and observed. For the better effecting whereof, he hath power to
> call synods, to be present at them, and to provide that whatsoever is
> transacted in them be according to the mind of God.

In contrast, the revised version only requires the civil magistrate—

> to protect the church of our common Lord, without giving the prefer-
> ence to any denomination of Christians above the rest, in such a manner
> that all ecclesiastical persons whatever shall enjoy the full, free, and un-
> questioned liberty of discharging every part of their sacred functions,
> without violence or danger. And, as Jesus Christ hath appointed a regu-
> lar government and discipline in his church, no law of any common-
> wealth should interfere with, let, or hinder, the due exercise thereof,
> among the voluntary members of any denomination of Christians, ac-
> cording to their own profession and belief. It is the duty of civil magis-
> trates to protect the person and good name of all their people, in such an
> effectual manner as that no person be suffered, either upon pretense of
> religion or of infidelity, to offer any indignity, violence, abuse, or injury
> to any other person whatsoever: and to take order, that all religious and
> ecclesiastical assemblies be held without molestation and disturbance.

Even though the revised confession still stresses several important obligations of the state, it is illustrative of the gradual abandonment of ac-
countability. Most modern Presbyterians are unaware of these changes.
Many others believe the change was necessary to protect the church
from an Erastian state. Hetherington refutes this allegation: "The General Assembly [of the Scottish church] never would have ratified the *Confession of Faith* if they had understood it to contain any such Erastian taint
as some in modern times have affected to discover in it."[18] The confession itself validates this conclusion by clearly holding forth Christ as
head of the church and boldly proclaiming that the civil magistrate
"may not assume to the powers of the keys of the kingdom of heaven."[19]
This confession revision, which regards toleration as a higher virtue
than the adherence to the Word, is irrefutably inconsistent with the principles of Calvinism as understood by the early Reformers.[20]

The changes in the confession took place during the same period as
the framing of the U.S. Constitution and Bill of Rights. The intent of
these civil instruments was never the radical exclusion of religion from
secular society. Proper interpretation of these documents requires recog-
nizing that they represent a treaty among sovereign states forged by a
nation of Christians. Concerning these points, James Thornwell accurately contended, "The rights of Congress [granted by the Constitution]
are only the concessions of sovereign states."[21] Thornwell was rightly
concerned that the federal government "may forget that it is a servant,
and aspire to be lord." Thornwell captured the true intent now trampled
by shameless federal government: "The combination of the federal prin-

ciple with the sovereignty of states is the only arrangement which can maintain free institutions on a broad scale. This combination can secure freedom to a continent; it might even govern the world."[22] James Madison (1751–1836) agreed: "The powers reserved to the several states will extend to all the objects which, in the ordinary course of affairs, concerns the lives, liberties, and properties of the people, and the internal order, improvement, and prosperity of the state."[23] Despite their intent, neutrality of wording by our founding fathers in civil and ecclesiastical creeds has set the stage for destruction of both church and state.

Principle #2: *States are obligated to acknowledge God as the source of their authority. Churches are obligated to educate the state regarding these obligations. Both share the common end to advance the glory of God and the common good.* Are governments accountable to the people or to God? Do churches have no obligation to mankind? Do the moral responsibilities of people not carry over into the responsibilities of society? These questions are at the heart of all disputes regarding church and state relations. To answer these questions, we must understand the consequences of a government accountable solely to the people. The works of two authorities, one secular and one ecclesiastical, provide insight into these difficult issues.

The opinion of the majority is a fragile foundation upon which to build liberty. The unfortunate reality is that the America that Tocqueville wrote about no longer exists. In Tocqueville's day, the Christian religion was the majority opinion: "In America, the majority has enclosed thought within a formidable fence." Tocqueville warned that the "irresistible power" of the majority "is a continuous fact and its good use only an accident." Further, he warned of the despotic nature and power of the majority:

> Under the absolute monarchy of a single man, despotism, to reach the soul, clumsily struck at the body, and the soul escaping such blows, rose gloriously above it; but in democratic republics that is not at all how tyranny behaves; it leaves the body alone and goes straight to the soul.[24]

Tocqueville pondered, "If ever freedom is lost in America, that will be due to the omnipotence of the majority driving the minorities to desperation and forcing them to appeal to physical force." He asked, "How can a society escape destruction if, when political ties are relaxed, moral ties are not tightened? And what can be done with a people master of itself if it is not subject to God?" The reality is that Christianity is no longer the religion of the majority, and this trend will have dire consequences on our "precious freedom of religion."

Thornwell contended, "The fundamental error of our fathers was that they accepted a partial for a complete statement of truth." Although they "clearly saw the human side," they failed to recognize the "Divine side–that all just government is the ordinance of God, and that magistrates are His ministers who must answer to Him for execution of their trust."[25] James Thornwell, like Tocqueville, warned of the great hazard of pure democracy (a government accountable only to the people). He cautioned that one of the greatest threats to our freedom is "the tendency to sink our institutions into pure democracy."[26] In a properly constituted government, the representatives "are appointed, not to ascertain what the will of the people actually is, but what it ought to be."[27] The people appoint them; the law guides them. Just as true church is one governed by God's law, a true state is one governed by law.

Thornwell epitomized the original Southern Presbyterian tradition that maintains a high wall between the encroachments of the church and state in either direction, yet maintains the necessity of the biblical church and state obligations. He stated that he "never introduced secular politics into the instructions of the pulpit," leaving it to "Caesar to take care of his own rights." He argued that he had "no authority to expound to senators the constitution of the state, nor to interpret for judges the law of the land," contending that "in the civil and political sphere the dead must bury their dead."[28] Though it is easy to take the above quotes out of context, the truth is Thornwell, like the Covenanters, held the state accountable to perform its biblical obligations. According to Thornwell:

> A state which does not recognize its dependence upon God, or which fails to apprehend, in its functions and offices, a commission from heaven, is false to the law of its own being.

> A state which should undertake to accomplish the ends of its being, without taking into account the religious element in man, palsies its own arm. Subjects that have no religion are incapable of law.

> A state must have a religion in order to be truly obedient, and as it is the true religion alone which converts obedience into a living principle, it is obvious that a Commonwealth can no more be organized which shall recognize all religions, than one which shall recognize none. The sanctions of its law must have a center of unity somewhere.[29]

The conclusion that states are accountable to God is in direct conflict with the Anabaptist notion that Satan is in control of the state.[30] The truth is that states are in rebellion against God, and so are churches that do not hold the state accountable.

As a moral being, the state is accountable for its sins; therefore, it must confess them. Thornwell, on the eve of the Civil War, expounded the core problem and only solution to this dilemma:

> We are too apt to restrict the notion of sin in its proper sense to the sphere of the individual; to regard it as altogether private and personal, and not capable of being predicated of the mal-administration of the state. But if the state is a moral institute, responsible to God, and existing for moral and spiritual ends, it is certainly capable of sin. It may endure, too, the penalty of sin....
>
> Sin must either be pardoned or punished; confessed or forsaken, or it will work death. Sin has been the ruin of every Empire that ever flourished and fell.... The first duty, therefore, which as a Christian people, we should endeavor to discharge this day is to confess our national sins with humility and penitence.[31]

Thornwell would agree with Nevay's advice to the persecuted remnant: "You do well to mourn, not only for your own but [also] for the sins of others, which, by not mourning for them, may become your own: Particularly, you have to mourn for your unfruitfulness in the gospel."[32]

Principle #3: *The state is obligated to promote good and punish evil, according to the Word.* Paul (Rom. 13:1–5) and Peter (1 Pet. 2:13) clearly teach that the state is to punish evil and promote good. The question is whether the state is given liberty to define good and evil, or is it imperative that the state derive its laws from the Word of God? The Reformers, such as Calvin, all held that the moral law (Ten Commandments) remains in effect for both the church and society: "The moral law ... is the true and eternal rule of righteousness prescribed to the men of all nations and of all times."[33] In contrast, many modern Christians contend that states are not obligated to frame their laws according to the moral law because Paul did not condemn but appealed to Roman law. Such reasoning ignores the following facts: (1) Paul zealously sought to convert kings, and thus nations; (2) good and evil are defined by God's Word not man; (3) Paul and Peter demanded that states promote good and punish evil, and (4) Scripture clearly sets Christ in authority over all powers. The warning to Israel applies to any nation in which the Word is openly preached: *"Hear the word of the LORD, ye children of Israel: for the LORD hath a controversy with the inhabitants of the land, because there is no truth, nor mercy, nor knowledge of God in the land"* (Hos. 4:1).

Calvin stated that the object of civil government is "that a public form of religion may exist among Christians, and humanity among

men." Government not only must maintain order and enable men to
meet their needs but also must ensure "that no idolatry, no blasphemy
against the name of God, no calumnies [slander] against his truth, nor
other offences to religion, break out and be disseminated among the
people."[34] Calvin stressed the important obligation of civil magistrates:

> The duty of magistrates, its nature, as described by the Word of God,
> and the things in which it consists ... extends to both tables of the law....
> Thus all have confessed that no polity can be successfully established
> unless piety be its first care, and that those laws are absurd which disre-
> gard the rights of God, and consult only for men.... Christian princes
> and magistrates may be ashamed of their heartlessness if they make it
> not their care.[35]

Although most would agree that states must enforce the second table
(man's duty to man), or at least most of it, few agree with Calvin and
the Reformers concerning the need for the state to punish violations of
the first table (man's duty to God). To the Reformers, first table sins reflect far greater hazards to society than second table sins. For example,
Calvin considered idolatry as the "sin on account of which God so often
punished his chosen people, afflicting them with sword, pestilence, and
famine, and, in short, all kinds of calamity; the sin on account of which,
especially, the kingdom, first of Israel, and then of Judah, was laid
waste."[36] To Calvin, there are things far worse than a government that
discourages toleration, and he challenges the church and state to action:

> A dog, seeing any violence offered to his master, will instantly bark;
> could we, in silence, see the sacred name of God dishonored so blas-
> phemously? In such a case, how could it have been said, *"The reproaches
> of them that reproached thee are fallen upon me"* (Ps. 69:9)?[37]

> It is indeed a bad thing to live under a prince with whom nothing is law-
> ful, but a much worse to live under one with whom all things are law-
> ful.[38]

> There is something specious in the name of moderation, and tolerance is
> a quality which has a fair appearance, and seems worthy of praise; but
> the rule which we must observe at all hazards is, never to endure pa-
> tiently that the sacred name of God should be assailed with impious
> blasphemy; that his eternal truth should be suppressed by the devil's
> lies; that Christ should be insulted, his holy mysteries polluted, unhappy
> souls cruelly murdered, and the church left to writhe in extremity under
> the effect of a deadly wound. This would be not meekness, but indiffer-
> ence about things to which all others ought to be postponed.[39]

Although the moral law is binding on all men, are the Old Testament punishments for violations of the moral law still binding? According to the *Westminster Confession of Faith,* punishments should be comparable to the "general equity" of those outlined in the Bible rather than those specified for the nation of Israel.[40] Even when Scotland, in 1560, legislated severe penalties for punishment of sins such as adultery, the laws "were largely ignored by the secular magistrates, leaving enforcement to the newly created ecclesiastical courts [following Knox's *First Book of Discipline*]."[41] In summary, the judicial laws of the nation Israel have expired, but the moral law has not. Nations should heed the advice of John Cotton who proposed that the laws of the infant colony of New England be based on the judicial laws from the law of Moses only so far "as they were of moral (i.e., perpetual and universal) equity."[42]

The essence of Thornwell's conception of the state is that the state is a *moral agent*; therefore, it is subject to the consequences of sin and "bound to do its duty [obey moral law] under the same sanctions which pertain to the individual."[43] However, the state must exercise care in applying Scripture. Thornwell offered two guiding principles in applying the Scripture in civil matters. First, the state must acknowledge Scripture as true. By accepting scriptural principles, Thornwell means "that the state may itself believe them to be true, and regulate its conduct and legislation in conformity with their teachings."[44] It must pass no laws "inconsistent with the will of God, as revealed in the Holy Scriptures."[45] Ideally, the state acts through sanctions rather than by law.[46] However, Scripture "is not a positive constitution for the state; in that relation, it stands only with the church." Second, Thornwell proposes that the formula according to which the state accepts Scriptures is "Nothing shall be done which they forbid." The state only has a negative, restraining power; it has no authority over the consciences of men.[47] According to Thornwell, as long as citizens are peaceful and not "injurious to the public welfare, no human power has the right to control his opinion or restrain his acts."[48] He opposed laws that do "violence to any man's conscience," and he supported laws that "protect its [religion's] outward institutions, such as the sanctity of the Sabbath."[49] Thornwell would agree with George Gillespie that the magistrate "is keeper, defender and guardian of both tables, but neither Judge nor Interpreter of Scripture."[50] In the words of Matthew Henry, the state's objective is "preservation, but not the propagation, of true worship."[51] Rutherford would agree that in a Christian society the magistrates aim in using the sword is not to force men to "external worship or performance" as a service to God but to protect men (i.e., their souls) from harm as a service to society.[52]

The deficiencies of Roman law did not deter the obedience of Christ and the apostles. However, the degree to which a state departs from God's law is a threat to Christian peace and freedom. Our goal should be to achieve, through Christ, the twenty promised blessings (see Ps. 72:1–17) of Christ's kingdom, many of which involve godly magistrates and practices. Historically, as James Froude observes, the first signs of Calvinism in operation has been "to obliterate the distinction between sins and crimes, and to make the moral law the rule of life for states as well as persons."[53] Only Calvinism "builds batteries which sweep the whole ground of sin with such horrible artillery.[54]

Principle #4: *States are obligated to honor and acknowledge Jesus Christ, and mold their institutions and behavior in conformity with Christian principles.* Scripture plainly teaches that Christ is head of all things for his church (Eph. 1:21–22; 1 Pet. 3:22). The state has forgotten its biblical obligation to "kiss the Son lest he become angry, and you perish in the way, for his wrath may soon be kindled" (Ps. 2:10, 12). Because God has given all authority to Christ (Matt. 28:18), it is the duty of the state to acknowledge Christ. A state that fails to do so is subject to the wrath of God. On the other hand, the failure of the church to be the light and salt of the world and hold the state accountable is more reprehensible.

The Two Kingdom theory, held by the majority of Reformers, best explains this important church and state relationship. According to this theory, "Christ has a kingdom administered by and in ecclesiastical ordinances, and a kingdom administered by his divine power, without ecclesiastical ordinances." In one kingdom, Christ, as the eternal Son of God, "exercises Sovereignty and Dominion over all things, even as the Father does ... for he and the father are one." In the other kingdom, Christ, as Mediator, rules to govern his elect. This dual government raises an important question, "Should a Christian magistrate serve Christ as he is Mediator and king of the church?" Gillespie answers: "Certainly he ought and must; and God forbid but that he should do so. But how? Not as ... magistrate, but as ... Christian."[55] Rutherford clarifies that the Christian magistrate is not subordinate to Christ as Mediator but as King. Although, the magistrate's job is not to promote Christ's spiritual kingdom,[56] both kingdoms share a common purpose, the glory of God. James Nisbet articulates the important relationship between these two kingdoms: "[Christ] having the government on his shoulders, doth wisely order his providential kingdom, for the advancement of his spiritual kingdom and the welfare of his people."[57] Typically, when the bible speaks of the kingdom of God it means the church (on earth and in Heaven), for which, Christ rules over all things.

To Thornwell, the real issue is not the relation between states and the church, but the relation between states and Christ. Although Thornwell opposed the establishment of a single denomination over another, he clearly supported a Christian government: "The state realizes its religious character through the religious character of its subjects; and a state is and ought to be Christian, because all its subjects are and ought to be determined by the principles of the gospel."[58] To the point, states must acknowledge Jesus Christ. Thornwell insisted that it is not enough for a state "to acknowledge in general terms the supremacy of God; it must also acknowledge in general terms the supremacy of His Son." Jesus "is the ruler of the nations, the King of kings, and the Lord of lords."[59] Thornwell argued that "the religion of the state is embodied in its constitution," and that it is legitimate for the state to have a religion (i.e., Christianity). Neutrality is impossible. Magistrates would not have to profess belief (even a Jew could be a magistrate) but only acknowledge that Christianity was the "religion of the state."[60] Further, the state must mold its institutions in conformance with Christian principles.

Although Thornwell sought less protection of the church than did the Covenanters, their beliefs regarding this topic are not inconsistent. They both held the state accountable as a moral agent to recognize Christ as king and to protect Christianity. Thornwell, like Christ, focused his attack on the false church, not the errant state, for Christ's zeal is for the house of the Lord. Exclusively attacking the externals of civil society was not the way of our Lord when on this earth; however, his silence is not an endorsement.

Thornwell contended that the gospel is the only solution for the state. Therefore, Christians should avoid conflicts that distract from the primary object of Christianity. The power of the gospel is the only force that can change the inner man and eventually transform the outer world. These changes can only take place in the context of the church, and reformation must begin with God's people. Thornwell discouraged the church in supporting crusades and the causes of voluntary organizations, not because such actions are improper, but because such actions are the responsibility of the church.[61]

Unfortunately, after the Civil War and during the painful reconstruction process, the Southern Presbyterians adopted an increasingly spiritual and isolated perspective on church and state relations. They adopted the philosophy of Stuart Robinson, a Civil War-era Presbyterian minister, who essentially disallowed interactions between church and state. This apolitical church doctrine was attractive to Southern Presbyterians, stranded by the Confederacy and abused by the meddling federal government. Such a doctrine not only provided a convenient moral cover for the rationalization of slavery but also served as a unifying force for the eventual reuniting of Southern and Northern Presbyterians. Thus, the Southern Presbyterian tradition of an apolitical church was born and within a few decades, historians rewrote history to attribute such doctrines to Thornwell and the pre-Civil War theologians.[62]

Interestingly, the American churches that descended from the Covenanters and Seceders were not silent on slavery as was the southern church; in fact, some were radical abolitionists. One branch, the Associate Synod, forbid its members from holding salves; consequently, it ceased to exist in the south. Another, the Associate Reformed churches reluctantly allowed slaveholding but attempted, without success, to train slaves to evangelize Africa. They also protested a bill to prevent slaves from learning to read, while the main southern church remained silent.[63]

Although modern Southern Presbyterian philosophy has much to commend it, it falls far short of Thornwell's clear thinking. Further, it fails to proclaim the full obligations of both the church and the state. It fails to preach "Christ as king and the government on his shoulders," for which Nevay warned the Indulged.[64] As currently implemented, it fails to speak out boldly on moral issues where clear violations of God's moral law exist, such as abortion.

In summary, Thornwell contended that his proposals do not imply "a single element of what is involved in a national church."[65] All his proposals deal with the relationship of states to Christ rather than to the church. Although abandoned by modern Christians, Thornwell's view of church and state is commendable.

Principle #5: *When God transforms a state into a Christian nation, the people, state, and church should covenant to establish and preserve the true religion.* What business does the state have in these matters? This controversial question lies at the heart of the difference between the teachings of Thornwell and the Covenanters. Thornwell would reject any role of the state over and above that previously mentioned. Clearly, the more proactive role of the state is only valid in a covenanted land; such lands are not a work of man but of God. Until the church attains unity in truth, the state should not attempt it. Until that time, it is the duty of every Christian in his place and station to combat false religion.

The goal of the Scottish church was complete victory of the Word. To them, a Christian nation with leaders zealous to promote true religion was a desired blessing from God. The Scottish church, based on the biblical pattern of Asa and Hezekiah, expected the magistrate to encourage reformation and protect the true religion. Under Knox, the *Scottish Confession of Faith of 1560* clearly defined the responsibilities of the civil magistrate:

> We affirm that chiefly and most principally the conservation and purgation of the religion appertains; so that not only they [magistrates] are appointed for civil polity, but also for the maintenance of the **true religion**, and for suppressing of idolatry and superstition whatsoever: as in David (1 Chron. 22–26), Jehosaphat (2 Chron. 17:6; 19:8, etc.), Hezekiah (2 Chron. 29–31), Josiah (2 Chron. 34–35), and others, highly commended for their zeal in that case, may be espied.[66]

The Westminster divines echo this philosophy. The *Larger Catechism* question number 108 requires, "The detesting, disapproving, opposing all false worship, and according to each one's place and calling, removing it and all monuments of idolatry."[67] In short, it is the duty of every Christian citizen to combat false religion. According to James Bannerman, "Without some religion, no society on earth, it is admitted by all parties [no longer true a century later], could exist at all; and without the *true religion*, no society can exist happily [always true]." He contended that *true religion* is "the only force strong enough to insure obedience and respect for the law—the only bond that can bind together the discordant elements of human society, and give peace between man and man." Consequently, "the magistrate is bound, by a regard to his own interest, and for the sake of the grand object for which the state exists at all, to make the care of religion one of the first duties he has to discharge towards his people."[68]

Unfortunately, the modern Christian has lost this vision. In fact, our forefathers lost it when they lowered the ideal standard for society from *true religion* to *religion*. Our contribution has been to remove the need for *religion* altogether. We continue to ignore Knox's warning to England to consider the fate of Israel as "a glass" to daily "behold what shall be the final end of those that do abuse the long-suffering of God calling all to repentance."[69] Is Knox's advice of no practical value to nations and national leaders today? Why does the Bible call Christians to witness to kings? Was it for the salvation of the king, or was it for the salvation of nations? The evidence of God's judgment of Israel cries out warning to us. How much longer will God tolerate a nation such as ours?

The more proactive role of the state envisioned by the Covenanters requires important safeguards. With these safeguards, the concept of Christian nations is viable; without them, it is doomed.

First, the state must not exercise power over spiritual matters. Some argue that the Covenanters, in their zeal for reformation, went too far in granting power to the state. Stuart Robinson contends that the greatest error of the Scottish church was not their doctrine of the church but their doctrine of the state.[70] He argues that "admitting the power of the state in spirituals as in some sort coordinate with that of the church" was the "leaven" that "worked gradually the corruption of their pure gospel theory of the church."[71] Although the Covenanters granted great powers to the state about matters affecting the church, it was not over spiritual matters. In the words of George Gillespie, the magistrate "is occupied about the outward things of the church," and the minister "is occupied about the inward or spiritual part of civil government."[72] The outer matters involved here include (1) regulation of matters common to both holy and civil societies (e.g., marriage); (2) restraint of "pernicious enemies to true religion and the church"; (3) preservation of true religion; (4) restoration of true religion when "decayed and corrupted"; (5) punishment of violators of civil ordinances based on the moral law; (6) regulation of synods within civil bounds; (7) provision of ministers and support where appropriate.[73]

In the era of the Scottish Reformers, such power in the hands of the magistrate was a matter of fact. The Reformers freely granted these powers, but only over external matters. By allowing the magistrate to "take order" in external matters, the Westminster Confession of Faith does not grant him jurisdiction in these matters, but only specifies "objects which he is entitled and bound to aim at, and to effect by such methods as are competent to him, without invading the jurisdiction of the church."[74] For instance, although they granted the magistrate the right to call synods, they strictly limited the synods to spiritual matters–the exclusive province of the church. They considered such civil power as mutually supportive of one true church in the land, and they saw the denial of these powers as a direct threat to the maintenance of true religion and civil peace. In summary, the state has no authority over spiritual matters. Church and state must remain separate and independent, each working in its own sphere, as they were in the Old Testament.

Second, rulers must perform their duty, as clearly commanded, prophesied, and limited in Scripture.[75] Rutherford pondered, how can the example of Old Testament saints "be good divinity then and bad now?"[76] "What the patriarchs and godly princes of Israel and Judah were obliged to do as rulers and princes, and not as such rulers who were privileges types of Christ," he posited, "that all kings and rulers under the New Testament are obligated to do." For example, the extraordinary acts of David and Joshua in subduing all the Canaanites were typical. Other acts were of ceremonial or judicially temporary nature, such as the complete destruction of man and beast in captured cities (Deut.13). Nevertheless, in most cases what lawful rulers did was "of common equity by the law of nature."[77] For instance, the magistrate's task is not to eliminate but to remove the "high places" of false religion.[78]

Although the Old Testament saints were under a "stricter tutelage," the "sword did force not the conscience of any then more [so] than now." To plead that Christ's silence and meekness forbids the magistrate from punishing evildoers, Rutherford declared, "has no foot except it so run."[79] Rutherford insisted the church as well as Christian magistrate should protect men (i.e., their souls) from that which seduces souls, infers diverse faiths, promotes doubting in religious matters, destroys the hope and comfort of Scripture, and forbids all means of removing heresies, because these are "not of God."[80] Such is duty of every Christian in their place and calling. The modern mind, convinced that non-fundamentals of religion are unimportant and that fundamentals are debatable, finds this hard to swallow. The Reformed belief is that not only are fundamentals knowable, non-fundamentals are even more so, but no less important. Does not the command to every Christian to receive not a false teacher (2 John) imply the ability of Christians, including Christian magistrates, to so judge?[81]

The magistrate must insist upon the Word and the clear principles contained therein. To protect against the magistrate intruding into spiritual matters, the Scottish church developed clear lines of responsibility for both church and state. The *Second Book of Discipline* clearly emphasizes the manner in which each party holds the other responsible: "The civil power should command the spiritual to exercise and do their office according to the Word of God. The spiritual power should require the Christian magistrate to minister justice, and punish vice, and to maintain liberty and quietness of the kirk within their bounds."[82] Properly, the magistrate controls no spiritual matters; he only insists upon the Word. Nevay and the Covenanters, expounding on the practice of Hezekiah and Josiah, insisted that the magistrate not limit ministers except "to act according to that which was written in the Book that was found" (2 Kings 22:12–13, 18; 23:3, 24; 2 Chron. 34:21).[83] Conversely, the magistrate is obligated to limit false teachers (2 Kings 23:5).[84] The most detrimental aspect of the 1789 revision to the *Westminster Confession of Faith* was the denial of the Word as a common guide for church and state.

Third, the church, not the state, is responsible for establishing true religion; the state is responsible for protecting the Christian religion as established by the church, provided it is consistent with the Word. Thornwell and the Covenanters would agree that magistrates should be "nursing fathers" to the church (Isa. 49:23).[85] They both agree that the real danger is when a state acts as father rather than the nursing father of the church. Isaiah clearly refutes any Erastian state controls that would usurp Christ's rights: *"And kings shall be thy nursing fathers, and their queens thy nursing mothers: they shall bow down to thee with their face toward the earth, and lick up the dust of thy feet; and thou shalt know that I am the LORD: for they shall not be ashamed that wait for me"* (Isa. 49:23).[86]

One of the chief points of contention raised by the Society People after the Revolution Settlement was their concern that the state rather than the church established Presbyterianism. History validates the Covenanters' concerns regarding the hazard of Erastian influences (e.g., patronage) on the church. In America, the church failed to establish a unified-Christian religion for the state to protect. James Bannerman offers two important rules that are essential to ensuring the proper relationship: (1) the church must settle upon a confession of faith, and (2) the state must legally recognize the "freedom and powers of the church."[87] Under these terms, and with the will of the people as established by law, the state can take action to preserve and promote reformation of true religion as outlined in the original Westminster Confession as previously discussed. Those who contend that no endorsement of religion from the state is preferable suffer from the delusion that the state can be neutral. There are few threats greater to religion than an avowed neutral state. Such establishment, as long as it does not violate Thornwell's construct, previously discussed, is desirable. Again, foundational to a Christian nation is a reforming Christian church: *"The Gentiles shall come to thy light, and kings to the brightness of thy rising"* (Isa. 60:3).[88]

Under the fourth safeguard, the church and state may freely cooperate in building the outer walls of a Christian society, but any state help in rebuilding or supporting the temple must be under the direction of the church. The state must always remain distinct from the church and never exercise power within the church. In order to understand the role of church and state, it is essential that one examine how the Old Testament and New Testament relationships are similar and different. The Old Testament (Zechariah 4) portrays the church (Joshua) and state (Zerubbabel) leaders symbolically as two olive trees that nurture the Jewish church, represented by a lampstand. The Covenanters patterned the cooperative effort by church and state to reform the church after the cooperative effort by Zerubbabel (civil magistrate) and Joshua (high priest) to rebuild the temple (Ezra 5:2; Haggai 2:15) after the exile. A few decades thereafter, through similar cooperation, Nehemiah and numerous able priests cooperated to rebuild the outer walls. Many Covenanters, including James Durham, cited these relationships as typifying the ideal church and state relation of Christian nations.

In contrast, the New Testament (Revelation 11) depicts the relationship symbolically as two olive trees and two candlesticks. These depictions differ only in their outer form. Although Christ's control over civil and providential matters is less visible, it remains. Even in the Old Testament, it was not the power of the earthly priest and kings that nurtured the church: God clearly declares that it is *"Not by might, nor by power, but by My Spirit"* (Zech. 4:6) that the work is done. Yet, Christ works through men. In both the Old and New Testament church, church and state are distinct with no blurred lines of authority. Christ, as king, is the only basis for unity. Although, in Ezra's day, church and state cooperated to build the temple, the priest oversaw the work (Ezra 3:8–9). Only in the case of an apostate church may the state facilitate reformation (e.g., call assemblies), then only as a catalyst. Once the temple is rebuilt, as in Nehemiah's day, both church and state may cooperate to rebuild the outer wall (analogous to civil legislation for a Christian society). Only then should the people of a nation engage in covenant commitments.

Fifth, with the consent of the governed and the leading of God, a Christian state must covenant to establish and preserve the true religion. Men will never be at peace until their consciences conform to the Word. Although God alone is Lord of our conscience, God ordained civil and ecclesiastical authority limits on our consciences. To deny these limits is to deny God.[89] In a nation that swears a covenant to God, it is lawful to enforce the terms of the covenant as each has sworn to do according to their respective places. For instance, it is lawful to restrict those in public trust to those who have sworn the covenant (see Ps. 75:10). In support of this position, note that Asa deposed his own mother for idolatry (2 Chron. 15:16), but he did so only after the nation swore the covenant. Hence, the

Protestors rightly insisted on Christian leaders in a covenanted land. Although it is not lawful to force heathens to embrace the Christian faith, according to Rutherford, it is lawful to restrain them from "spreading their blasphemies to hurt and seduce the souls of the people of God."[90]

The guidelines promulgated in the Westminster standards were for covenant-keeping Christian nations. These guidelines are traceable to John Calvin. Concerned that among the professing Christians "there is no more agreement than if we professed religions entirely different," Calvin urged rulers to provide "discipline to check" the rise of diversified sects. Calvin feared that if the church broke apart into numerous sects that "it would be vain to seek remedies."[91] To avoid this, he exhorted the leaders to "unite in a holy league":

> There is nothing in which men ought to feel a deeper interest, nothing in which God wishes us to exhibit a more intense zeal, than in endeavoring that the glory of his name remain unimpaired, his kingdom be advanced, and the pure doctrine, which alone can guide us to true worship, flourish in full vigor. How much more, therefore, does it become princes to make these things their care, to design, commence, and prosecute them to a close, seeing God has honored them with a communication of his name, that they may be on earth the guardians and vindicators of his glory.[92]

Although it is well past the point where it would be vain to seek remedies, the state's responsibility to honor Christ remains. Knox emphasized the need for covenant commitment more so than Calvin did:

> That whenever he taketh into his protection, by the covenant of his Word, any realm, nation, province, city, so that of mercy he becometh to them conductor, teacher, protector, and father; that he never castest off the same care and fatherly affection which is in his Word ... until they do utterly declare themselves unworthy of his presence.[93]

It was this high view of the covenant relationship that sparked and inspired the Scottish Covenanters to initiate the *Solemn League and Covenant*. Are Christians obligated to engage in covenants? The answer is clearly yes. The real question is whether Christians should join or separate from an immoral state. Paul clearly directs us not to form alliances with lawless parties: "*Be ye not unequally yoked together with unbelievers; for what fellowship hath righteousness with unrighteousness? and what communion has light with darkness?*" (2 Cor. 6:14). Hence, it is improper for Christians to form an alliance with a state that is not inherently Christian. It is beyond doubt that America, as now constituted, is not a Christian nation.

The situation today is entirely different from that in Scotland where a nation of Christians covenanted together to honor God.

Gillespie would not recommend that we attempt to form a covenant with our fellow citizens today. It is unlawful to make "mixed covenants, partly civil, partly religious," Gillespie contended. He argued that God forbade the Israelites from making a covenant with the Canaanites to "avoid ensnaring the people of God" (Exod. 23:32; Judges 2:2; 1 Kings 11:2; Ps. 6:8; 106:35; Ezek. 16:26). Gillespie reminds us that God forbade Judah to enter military alliances with the ungodly nations, including the Northern Kingdom (see 2 Chron. 19:2; 25:7-8). Citing 1 Corinthians 5:10–11, he stressed that this prohibition applies in particular to "scandalous [unrepentant] Christians." Although we may associate (provided the association does not yoke or bind us) with heathens, we must "not even to eat with such persons" who claim to be brothers yet are unrepentant sinners. Gillespie contended that mingled alliances with unbelievers teach us evil works, expose us to great temptations, rob us of the potential works that God bestows on a holy people, and tempt us to break our covenant commitments. The resultant disobedience could be hazardous because God is committed to the purging of rebels and transgressors.[94]

Even when the majority of the citizens are Christians, covenants pose other risks. James Guthrie, in *Causes of the Lord's Wrath against Scotland*, postulates that entrusting the king "with the cause and people of God, while he was continuing in his former disaffection to, and enmity against" the covenant to have been a "high provocation" of God.[95] In the final analysis, it was not the concept of a covenant but the alliance with the ungodly that led to failure in Scotland.

In summary, a Christian nation is a desired and promised blessing from God that we should seek. Although it is appropriate for a Christian people to covenant with God, it is inappropriate for a Christian people to enter a covenant with an immoral state. The Covenanters, in the *Solemn League and Covenant*, found the right balance. They believed that the rights of God extend into both the ecclesiastical and civil spheres. They had a vision that the goal of the Great Commission was the conversion of nations. They rightly understood that Scripture teaches, "The world is but a scaffold for the church."[96] They saw in God's promises (e.g., Ps. 72:8–11; Isa. 65:16–25; Zech. 14:16–21; Rev. 11:15) the promise of a new-world order in which the lion would lay down with the lamb. They believed that such a condition is the inevitable result of the advancement of the kingdom: *"Of the increase in his government and peace there shall be no end"* (Isa. 9:7a). The advance of which is for the asking: *"Ask of me and I will make the na-*

tions your inheritance" (Ps. 2:8a NKJ). They had crossed over into Promised Land and would not stop converting nations and fighting idolatry (using only spiritual weapons of course) until the whole world was saved or until Christ returned. This is why King Charles had them killed and why modern Presbyterianism knows not the voice of its forebears. Yet, they strongly believed in separation of church and state. They strongly believed the church was a spiritual entity, and all its power was spiritual. The difference was that they believed that the spirit of God was not in retreat but in advance. Unlike modern Christians, who are at peace with God's enemies, they were at war. They saw Christian nations as the inevitable result of the gospel's progress.

Their standard was the Word; they would settle for nothing less. Neither should we. Our goal as Christians should be to conquer the land using the power of the Word, not the sword. Just as in the Old Testament, the only stopping point is complete victory over God's enemies. This means bringing nations to Christ. Of course, this is the work of God, but he works through his people, the church. Just because the current focus of the church is correctly on building the temple, it does not mean that God will not some day enable the building of the outer walls. Our view of church and state relations must be broad enough for both eventualities. However, without victory in uniting the church, there is no reason to presume victory in uniting the state. Reform of the state can only take place after reform of the church. How can the church demand that the state honor Christ and uphold the moral law when it dishonors Christ's authority and truth and ignores much of the moral law. The Bible promises that judgment will begin first in the church. Given the scriptural pattern to first rebuild the church, the early Southern Presbyterian tradition, which focuses on first reforming the church, has a lot to commend it. However, we must never lose sight of the broader goal of transforming nations. In the meanwhile, Christ will work through his *stars* (Rev. 1:20) to reform his church.

Church and State – Their Common Citizens

A Christian society requires sincere Christian voters and magistrates. Individual Christians are obligated to obey lawful, higher powers and to Christianize the state.

A more complex question than the relation between the church and state is the proper relation between the Christian and the state. Contributing to this question's importance is that fact that Christians are members of both kingdoms. Although the witness of Christ and apostles seems clear on this subject, it is difficult to apply in all situations, particularly when national leaders break all the rules. The refusal of the Society People to recognize the post-Settlement state as lawful contributed to James Nisbet's decision to disassociate from them.

Owning Authority: Did the Covenanting remnant err in disowning the authority of the king in their declarations (e.g., *Apologetical Declaration*)? As the following evidence indicates, there are legitimate reasons for disobeying or for disowning the authority of some rulers.

First, the Bible, in passages such as Romans 13, requires that Christians submit to legitimate authority, but it does not require that believers obey commands inconsistent with God's law. The term "governing authorities" in Romans 13 really means "higher powers."[97] Therefore, our instructions are simple: "Let every soul be subject unto higher powers. For there is no power but of God: the powers that be are ordained by God." With this guiding principle, it is not difficult for Christians to decide issues of civil disobedience. Calvin reaches a similar conclusion:

> But since Peter, one of heaven's heralds, has published the edict, *"We ought to obey God rather than men"* (Acts 5:29), let us console ourselves with the thought that we are rendering the obedience, which the Lord requires when we endure anything rather than turn aside from piety. And that our courage may not fail, Paul stimulates us by the additional considerations (1 Cor. 7:23) that we were redeemed by Christ at the great price which our redemption cost him, in order that we might not yield a slavish obedience to the depraved wishes of men, far less do homage to their impiety.[98]

Second, not all rejection of authority is wrong. Was the remnant less justified in rebelling against authority than were the American Revolution patriots in 1776 or the Great Britain's revolutionaries in 1688? The underpinnings of the reasoning that permits Christian citizens to overthrow a tyrant rest on the works of Buchanan, Knox, and Rutherford. Buchanan, in his work *The Rights of the Crown of Scotland,* presents the following chain of logic to support the authority of the people to rise up against a tyrant. To Buchanan, the law is the voice of the people and "serves to direct and moderate" the king's "passions and actions." If a king deviates from the "mutual compact that subsists between a king and his subjects," then the actions of the king dissolve the compact. In doing so, the king becomes a tyrant and enemy of the people. This trail of logic ultimately leads to the conclusion that the people have the right to fight against and destroy, if necessary, enemies of the people, such as

a tyrant. Buchanan further contended that unrepentant tyrants are subject to excommunication.[99] Even the very words of King Charles's
grandfather King James support Buchanan's reasoning:

> A king governing in a settled kingdom, ceaseth to be a king, and degen-
> erateth into a tyrant, so soon as he leaveth to the rule by his laws, much
> more when he beginneth to invade his subjects' persons, rights, and lib-
> erties, to set up an arbitrary power, impose unlawful taxes, raise forces,
> and make war upon his subjects, whom he should protect and rule in
> peace; to pillage, plunder, waste, and spoil his kingdom; imprison, mur-
> der, and destroy his people in a hostile manner, to captivate them to his
> pleasure.[100]

Nevertheless, Knox, Calvin, and the Covenanters˙ believed that any
rebellion against a king's civil authority solely based on a his wickedness
is inconsistent with Scripture:[101]

> Remembering always, beloved brethren, that due obedience be given to
> magistrates, rulers, and princes, without tumult, grudge, or sedition; for,
> how wicked that ever themselves be in life, or how ungodly that ever
> their precepts and commandments be, ye must obey them for con-
> science sake; except in the chief points of religion; and that ought you to
> obey God than man; not to pretend to defend God's truth or religion
> (you being subjects) by violence or sword, but patiently suffering what
> God shall please be laid upon you for constant confession of your faith
> and belief. –Knox[102]

Although individuals should not take it on themselves to rebel
against tyrants, a people may. Further, Scripture does not require that
individuals "own" tyrannical authority as legitimate, as was required of
those persecuted in Scotland. Scripture requires we give unto God and
Caesar those things due them, but, as Alexander Shields reasoned, a tyrant "perverts both the things of God and Caesar." Consider how ab-
surd the assertion is that Romans 13 requires obedience to tyrants: "Let
every soul be subject to *tyrants*, for they are ordained of God as his ministers of justice."[103] The question is when is a magistrate a tyrant? To
Shields, a magistrate may be a tyrant if he gains power by force or

---

˙ "So far as public obedience is concerned," Calvin insists that even a magistrate "of the worst character … is to be held in the same honor and reverence as the best of kings." In his commentary on
1&2 Peter, Alexander Nisbet (1623–1669) states, "The wickedness of those to whom in God's
providence Christians are tied in any relation does not exempt them from making conscience of the
duties of that relation toward whom they are tied, the grounds of our duty being not the qualification of the person to whom we owe it, but the command of God obligating us to it." Nisbet worked
with Dickson, Durham, and other Scottish ministers to develop a set of scriptural commentaries.

fraud, pursues his own lusts instead of the nation's good, treats his subjects as slaves, abandons the rule of law, employs strangers to oppress the people, violates his oath of office, deprives people of the true religion, corrupts the youth, or fails to defend his subjects. One or two of these marks may not make a tyrant, but the habitual pursuit of them does. For example, David committed acts of tyranny but was not a tyrant.[104] Although Caesar gained control through conquest, he ruled by law as recognized by Christ and the Apostles. In contrast, Shields posits that Charles II and James II, who possessed most of these marks, were tyrants. Shields concurs that the magistrate's religion does not lesson the obligation of obedience, but by the law of his day a magistrate could not be Catholic, particularly one intent on overturning the law of the land. The Magna Charta states, "The king can do nothing but by law."[105]

Although we may yield in civil matters to tyrants until the Lord provides the means for their conversion or overthrow (Micah 7:9), we should follow the pattern of David, who patiently bore Absalom's usurpation (2 Sam. 15:26) until able to prevail against him.[106] The discriminating guide must always be the glory of God rather than the wickedness of man. To their credit, where the Society People disowned the tyrant Charles II, they placed limits on taking this power on themselves: "Yet they may not lawfully arrogate to themselves that authority which the tyrant hath forfeited, or act judicially either in civil or criminal courts; only they may do that which is necessary for securing themselves, liberty and religion."[107]

The third, their declaration was an act of self-defense. The primary intent of the declaration was not to call Christians to arms but to warn those who were shedding the blood of saints. McCrie both condemns and rationalizes the Covenanter's actions:

> We cannot but condemn the step taken by the sufferers as calculated, notwithstanding all their qualifications, and in spite of all the precautions they might use, to open up the door to lawless bloodshed, and to give encouragement to assassins. At the same time it is impossible to condemn them with great severity, when we reflect that they were cast out of the protection of law, driven out of the pale of society, and hunted like wild beast, in the woods and on the mountains to which they had fled for shelter.[108]

In particular, there are biblical grounds for defense of one's religion. In support of their position, Shields cited the biblical example of the revolt of the city of Libnah against Jehoram's attempt to force them into idolatry (2 Chron. 21:10): "Hence, if it be lawful for a part of the people to revolt from a tyrannical prince, making defection from the true religion; then it is duty to defend themselves against his force."[109] Defense of one's religion was the reason cited by Sir John Churchill (1650–1722) when he thwarted King James's attempts to convert England to Catholicism by joining forces with King William during the Revolution in 1688.[110] In response to those who refuse to allow the Christians to take up arms in self-defense, McCrie answers:

> Away with such pusillanimity! Scotland has ever been a loyal nation; but touch her on the point of conscience and it will be found that, like her emblematic thistle, she cannot be touched without impunity. She has ever been more anxious to secure her religious rights than to enjoy civil privileges; her love of liberty has hitherto been entwined with her love of religion; and if these twin-sisters should ever be disserved, we fear that the blow that divides them will prove fatal to both.[111]

Fourth, in his letters, Knox approved of rebellion in the case of a hypothetical-covenant-keeping king who violates his covenant promises: a "prince, king, or emperor who should go about to destroy God's true religion once established, and to erect idolatry … [should] be adjudged to death according to God's commandment.[112] Charles was such a covenanted king, who had sworn allegiance, albeit earlier in his life, to keep the covenants. The Covenanters refusal in a covenanted land to own the authority of a king who was in "opposition to the work of God" had previously been the position of the Scottish government. Hence, they considered themselves as "lawful" citizens. Evidencing this statement is the approval by the Committee of Estates of a remonstrance by the West-Kirk (a commission of the church) in 1650, which declared the kirk's and the kingdom's refusal to own King Charles "otherwise than with a subordination to God, and so far as he owns and prosecutes the cause of God" and the covenants.[113]

Fifth, and most importantly, is what the term "disowning authority" really meant as expressed by one of the martyrs, John Wilson. To Wilson, it was not possible to "own" the authority of a king who had taken Christ's authority as head of the church on himself. To the Covenanters, owning such authority was blasphemy.[114] Thus, the Covenanters would acknowledge the civil authority of the most corrupt king (e.g., Nero or Caesar) but would not acknowledge the authority of any king who attempted to be head of the church.

In truth, God, not us, is their judge. On the one hand, the teachings of the *Westminster Confession of Faith* are clear: "Infidelity, or difference in religion, doth not make void the magistrates' just and legal authority, nor free the people from their due obedience to them."[115] When the individual takes up the sword, he should do so with great fear and trepidation because God will hold him accountable. On the other hand, I propose that the guilt of modern man in neglecting to honor Christ as *"head over all things to the church"* (Eph. 1:22) is far greater than that of the Covenanters who refused to honor the authority of a tyrant who was intent on destroying true religion. The only threat greater to peace than a government that does not acknowledge God's authority is a government that commandeers God's authority. In the final analysis, Christians must acknowledge the civil authorities established by God and make it their duty to transform states into biblical governments that recognize and honor Christ and his church. The alternative is to have unbiblical states transform Christians. There is no middle ground.

Civil Duty of Christians: Not only is it the duty of Christians to submit to lawful commands and to honor magistrates; it is also their duty to pray for magistrates, support the state financially, serve as magistrates, fight just wars, and most importantly, serve as Christian voters and leaders. Tocqueville emphasized the important role of leaders in enabling states to fulfill their obligations:

> The only effective means which governments can use to make the doctrine of immortality of the soul respected is daily to act as if they believed it themselves. I think that it is only by conforming scrupulously to religious morality in great affairs that they can flatter themselves that they are teaching the citizens to understand it and to love and respect it in little matters.[116]

Tocqueville's advice echoes that of the great reformers concerning the important role of national leaders. Similarly, George Buchanan equated national leaders to physicians: "As the physician of the body ought first to have expelled all noxious humors, ought not the physician of the state to imitate him, and to exterminate universally all corrupt morals?"[117] According to Buchanan, a ruler is best able to apply this medicine through the example of his own life as any father does to his children. There is no greater influence than the example set by leaders: "Let a king, therefore, constantly resolve in his own mind, that, as he stands in a public theatre, exhibited as a spectacle to every beholder, all his words and actions must be noted and subject to comments."[118]

From 2 Samuel, Nevay derived a number of foundational principles regarding the requirements for leaders:

> *The God of Israel said, the Rock of Israel spake to me, He that ruleth over men must be just, ruling in the fear of God. And he shall be as the light of the morning, when the sun riseth, even a morning without clouds; as the tender grass springing out of the earth by clear shining after rain (2 Sam. 23:3–4).*[119]

First, those who give orders to others "must be ready to take orders from him that is above them." Second, "the Holy Ghost is no leveler, he is for one above another, for a ruler above men." The modern impulse to achieve perfect equality among men is destructive to the home, the state, and the church. To Nevay, this impulse to level was an Anabaptist fancy. Third, "rulers must be ruled by law" with the end "to be a minister of God for good to people." Fourth, "the essential and absolutely necessary property of a ruler, is, that he must be just." Fifth, "magistrates and rulers should rule in fear of God." Given that fear of God is the foundation of wisdom and justice, is it possible for a leader or judge to be just if he does not fear God? Moreover, "this is against the admission of profane men to be magistrates," because holiness is a "necessary qualification of a magistrate, as well as a minister." Nevay concludes, from verse four, that a just ruler is "like the shining light" and "righteousness and holiness does put states in a right complexion; so helps them to grow." We should pray for rulers who seek the Lord, such as Asa: *"The Lord gave him rest on every side, and he built and prospered"* (1 Chron. 22:18; 2 Chron. 14:7). This is because *"the LORD is with you, while ye be with him"* (2 Chron. 15:2). If this is our desire and prayer, we will seek rulers who bring a "bright morning" on the land. However, "What we want of comfort from the government of men, make it out by faith, from the government of Christ."[120]

The Civil Obligation of Ministers: One last point requires clarification. The Scottish church zealously restricted ministers from excessive involvement in civil affairs. The Second Book of Discipline specified that ministers "should exercise not the civil jurisdiction, but teach the magistrate how it should be exercised according to the Word." It allowed ministers, however, to "assist their princes in all things agreeable to the Word, provided they neglect not their own charge."[121] Their primary obligation is to their flock–a humbling obligation that requires their full dedication.[122] For those who are not ministers, what is our excuse?

14

Reformation

With continual weeping they shall come, and seek the LORD their God. They shall ask the way to Zion, with their faces toward it, saying, "Come and let us join ourselves to the LORD in a perpetual covenant that will not be forgotten."
—Jer. 50:4–5 NKJ

*L*esson # 5: Christians must covenant with God and should covenant with one another to seek reformation of their lives, churches, and society in accordance with the Word of God.** Scotland, England, and America are no longer Christian nations. According to a recent survey, slightly over one-fourth of the U.S.A. respondents claimed regular weekly church attendance.[1] Attendance in England is even lower. Further, the numerous diverse sects that exist today are far from a united church. The primary building block of church and the state, the family, is withering away. Truth goes undefended. We desperately need to break the church's downward spiral—now over three hundred years old.

Reformation Is a Covenant Obligation

We look in disappointment at the limping church, but little do we comprehend that the church limps from crushing the serpent (Gen. 3:15). In reality, the limp is an "emblem of triumph."[2] In this continuing struggle, God uses adversity to strengthen his church. Robert Leighton once said, "Adversity is the diamond dust Heaven polishes its jewels with."[3] We should take comfort, as did the Scottish church, that God would overcome and save us from the fowler's snare (Ps. 124:7). As depicted in Psalm 124, our enemies appear as great floods that engulf us and as clever men that trap us with well-laid snares. Nevertheless, we shout with joy and assurance that the Lord will deliver his people. It was from greater depths that Christ formed the Scottish church. It rose to breath-catching heights that will be but small hills to some future generation.

We can learn a lot from the Covenanters. Jesus Christ was truly at the center of their lives, church, and society. Unlike today's Christians, they equally emphasized doctrinal purity, evangelical outreach, and cultural influence. How many modern Christians have the mastery of doctrine and Scripture evidenced in John Nisbet's last testimony? How many modern ministers match Renwick's evangelical zeal? How many churches fulfill their obligation to transform society and its culture? Who can deny the Covenanters' true Christianity, with its perfect balance of faith, hope, and love? Who can deny that their primary focus was Jesus Christ, evidenced by the fact that they considered his lordship a matter worth martyrdom? The problem is not with them but with us. We should emulate them, particularly their faith, because *all true Christians are Covenanters.*

True Christians, as depicted below, are not satisfied with closing with Christ just as Savior, but only with closing with Christ as revealed in all of his offices by Scripture. All the dangerous heresies are traceable to inadequate recognition of one or more of the offices of Christ. For instance, the root cause of legalism is failure to comprehend fully the priestly office of Christ. As human beings, it is impossible for us to perfectly comprehend Christ as a whole; consequently, many Christians settle for a stereotypic impression of Christ. Although it is impossible to comprehend Christ fully, Spurgeon advised, "I cannot grasp the ocean in my span, yet may I bath therein with sweet content."[4]

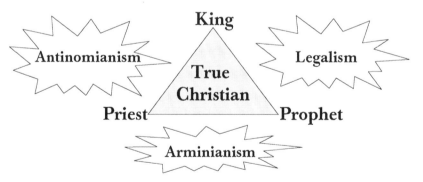

At best, our souls can dwell on each of his titles and offices repeatedly until we grasp that *"He is altogether lovely."*[5] Closure requires that we pursue the Apostle Paul's prayer for the Ephesians (Eph. 1:17-19) that through a spirit of wisdom and knowledge of Christ, we comprehend the calling (prophetic office), the inheritance (priestly office), and the power (kingly office) of Christ. Reformation is the process whereby men and churches strive for a balanced closing with Christ. If our closing is off-centered, then our Christian witness is off-centered. For example, from striving to defend Christ's kingly office and from lack of exposure to preaching and the sacraments, the Covenanting remnant drifted off-center. In contrast, modern Christianity, which over-emphasizes the priestly office, offers us a stereotype of Christ. Reformation settles for nothing less than embracing and proclaiming all of Christ.

Now that we have examined what we can learn from the Covenanters and have established the real covenant on which any virtue in the Covenanters is derived, we can now discuss, within the proper context, the practice of covenants initiated by humans, such as the *Solemn League and Covenant*. Were the Covenanters wrong in engaging in the *Solemn League and Covenant?* The short answer is "No"! God uses such covenants as a means of reforming his church. It is likely that real reformation of his church will not take place until the Lord lays it on the hearts of Christians to pledge themselves to reformation of their lives, church, and society. Such covenants are not properly a agreement between man and God, but rather a "solemn, promissory commitment to faith or troth on the part of the people concerned" to be "faithful to the Lord in accordance with his revealed will."[6] The Covenanters believed that closing in covenant with God "is a matter of the greatest concernment in all the world: it is the life of our soul" (Deut. 32:47).[7] To them, the absence of an oral commitment was like a wedding without the exchange of vows.[8]

God established the necessity and pattern of such covenants in his Word. In obedience to God, the Israelites renewed their covenant with God at various times throughout the Old Testament. It was binding to the visible church as well as to strangers in the land (see Deut. 24:10–13; Josh. 24:1,25; 2 Chron. 15:9,12,15; Jer. 11:10).[9] The covenants made by the Old Testament saints provide a scriptural pattern for us today. Isaiah prophesizes the continued use of covenants in the New Testament era (Isa. 44:5). Paul describes how the Corinthians "gave themselves to the Lord" (2 Cor. 8:5).[10] External corporate covenants made in this biblical fashion typically precede internal covenanting that leads to real spiritual change. Samuel Rutherford contended that just as "faith comes from hearing the sent preacher," "external covenanting goes before internal covenanting as the means before the end."[11] Further, the book of Psalms is a written covenant wherein God, believers, and the church make numerous "I will" and "We will" promises.

Please note that the *Solemn League and Covenant* does not require perfect obedience; it only requires sincere and earnest commitment to reformation. It is this knowledge-based heart commitment, rather than a commitment to words and phrases, that the Lord desires. We can learn much from James Nisbet's attempt at personal covenanting:

[In early 1686], I again renewed my personal covenant with more de-liberation, and, as I thought, suitable preparation, than formerly. I wrote it out in a fair copy and put my name to it; but afterwards, finding my treacherous heart and sinful nature altogether misserving me to live up with mind and soul to the terms thereof. For [I found that] after the highest spring-tide of a promising frame and disposition, there ordinarily succeeds the lowest ebb of unframedness and indisposition, accompa-nied with sore temporary afflictions. Upon which I laid aside my formal covenant and concluded there was an absolute necessity for me to be making continual application to the blood of Christ Jesus and spirit of his grace for daily washing away of the guilt, power, and filth of sin. This was an exercise that I am ever to put in practice, whether my frame and disposition be good or bad, and I am ever to close with the great Mediator, as party-contractor with God the Father.... There is no resting for me on a frame how large and heavenly so ever, but alone on the fountain of free grace, treasured up in the Lord Jesus Christ. Therefore, I am ever to be in the exercise of a humble believing application to him and [of a] firm reliance upon him in the use of the means of Grace, leav-ing the success to him in whom are all my springs. In this I am to act as a wise mariner at sea, who improves the fresh gales while they continue; and when storms and contrary winds come, yet he doth not give over, nor all up for lost, but steers on his course as he may, to the best advan-tage.[12]

In essence, covenants simply acknowledge our scriptural obligations. In such covenants, the covenanters acknowledge God as their God, con-fess their sins, and engage themselves to the duties associated with being the people of God.[13] Although such covenants are not essential to salva-tion, when accompanied by "sincere heart closing" with Christ, they convince us of our bargain with and dependence upon Christ.[14]

Was it wrong for the covenanting remnant to insist upon continued adherence to the *Solemn League and Covenant* after the Revolution Settle-ment when some of the conditions of the covenant no longer applied? Does the *Solemn League and Covenant* perpetually bind the descendants of the covenants? Nevay contends, "No earthly authority can loose these bonds." However, human covenants only bind us in all time to the eter-nal, moral truths of God, contained in his Word. Although one may make vows consistent with the Word, one may only vow "what he is able and resolved to perform." Even the most vocal supporters of covenanting concur: "These covenants bind us to nothing to which we are not previously bound by the divine law."[15]

On the other hand, with few exceptions, the entire covenant is morally biding. More importantly, reformation of church, state, and person requires a covenant commitment. The root cause of the decline of Presbyterianism since the Revolution Settlement is the abandonment of a covenant commitment to reformation. Without zeal and sincere commitment, truth falls. The Westminster standards presumed that all church officers and most members had sworn the *Solemn League and Covenant*; hence, the standards included no requirement for such a vow. Knox's church had similar covenant commitments. In both cases, these covenant vows were much more binding and broadly based that a simple vow to adhere to a doctrinal standard. It is indefensible to argue that vows of subscription to the standards are unnecessary because of the standard's silence regarding such vows. Nevertheless, most modern Presbyterian denominations have rendered subscription vows meaningless through Declaratory Acts or ambiguous language. What is needed in nothing short of a covenanted reformation.

As Covenanters, Christians have an obligation to follow the Old Testament example and covenant to reform their lives, society, and the church. In the remainder of this chapter, I challenge you thoughtfully to consider making three covenant promises, derived from the articles of the *Solemn League and Covenant*. They parallel the discussion presented in the previous chapters concerning our obligation in each sphere. Those that engage in covenant relations must do so with solemn determination because breaking covenant promises strikes at the heart of Christianity.

Reformation of the Church

We sincerely, really, and constantly, through the grace of God, endeavor, in our several places and callings, the reformation and preservation of religion in doctrine, worship, discipline, and government, according to the Word of God and the example of the best Reformed churches.[16]

Reform the church; reformation of the individual and the state will follow. As we have seen, reformation of the state requires reformed leaders and voters. Reformed people are the product of a reformed church. Although the Lord may initiate reformation through individuals, it is the Lord's pattern to first reform his church and then use his church to reform the people. According to Gillespie, reformation must start with the church: "Set before you also the example of the Jews, when the prophets of God did stir them up to the building of the temple, Ezra 5:1–2. They say not, 'We must first build the walls of Jerusalem to hold out the enemy,' but the text saith, *They began to build the house of God.*"[17] The needed reformation requires Christians solemnly dedicated to eliminate false doctrines and practices in church worship, government, and discipline. It requires a restoration of the attainments of the three reformations as described by John Dickson: "The primitive martyrs sealed the prophetic office of Christ with their own heart's blood; the reforming martyrs sealed his priestly office with theirs; and last of all, our [Covenanting] martyrs have again so sealed his kingly office."[18] Reformation settles for nothing less than all of Christ. Only as the church leans of Christ can it come out of the wilderness (Song of Sol. 8:5–7).[19]

First, reformation of doctrine must be according to the Word. The standard is zero toleration of heresy. The Covenanters owe much to John Calvin, who emphasized the primacy of the Word. It is ironic that Calvinism is the antithesis of modern, human-focused thinking considering, "It is in Calvinism that the modern world strikes its roots; for it was Calvinism that first revealed the worth and dignity of man."[20] This unworldly thinking called Calvinism, which focuses on God rather than man, can truly move mountains and transform the world: *"The sea saw it, and fled: Jordan was driven back. The mountains skipped like rams, and the little hills like lambs"* (Ps. 114:3–4). Such reformation requires more than vague assent to the Word; it requires adherence to doctrinal standards that provide a shared interpretation of the Word. The Westminster standards provide this needed standard for reformation. Nevertheless, no matter how reformed a church is, it must always be willing, as was the Church of Scotland, to engage with other churches to identify a shared set of standards consistent with the Word. It is the duty of the most reformed church to condescend in promoting reformation, yet it is equally their duty not to marginalize but to magnify God's Word.

The heart and driving force of reformation must be to the glory of God, which can only be according to Scripture. Calvin rightly emphasized the "true source of faith and also of unbelief":

The source of unbelief is this—when men confine God's power to their own understanding; and the source of faith is—when they ascribe to God the praise due to his infinite power, when they regard not what is easy, but being satisfied with his word alone they are fully persuaded that God is true, and that what he promises is certain, because he is able to fulfill it.[21]

Second, reformation of worship is, according to Calvin, "the beginning and foundation of righteousness." Without it, everything a man or a society does "is empty and frivolous in the sight of God."[22] Scripture commands few things more clearly. For example, the overwhelming majority of the "I will" promises in Psalms pertain to worship. Although Calvin accentuated the importance of worship, John Knox applied the principles of worship so vigorously that he transformed an entire nation. Knox is truly worthy, although not fully recognized, of the title, "Father and Founder of English as well as Scottish Puritanism. " Knox developed the Puritan principles during his ministry in northern England and then applied these principles to small congregations of Scottish and English exiles in Geneva and Frankfort. In matters of faith, these small congregations were "perfectly joined together in one mind and one judgment,"[23] and they formed the nucleus of the Puritan and Covenanter movement that shaped English, Scottish, and American history. Such congregations were no larger than the small band at Pentecost that turned the Roman Empire upside down. If God moves to reform the church, he will use such congregations. Let us pray for this transformation in our lifetime.

Third, without a commitment to proper church government and discipline, reformation is not possible. To the covenanting ministers such as John King, one cannot be a child of God unless the church is his chief joy.[24] This joy requires *the church to re-establish the notes and marks of the true church as attained during the Second Reformation*. We should heed the words of the Scottish Commissioners regarding religious diversity:

> Nothing is so powerful to divide the hearts of the people as division in religion; nothing so strong to unite them as unity in religion; and the greater the zeal in different religions, the greater the division; but the more the zeal in one religion, the more firm union. In the paradise of nature, the diversity of flowers and herbs is pleasant and useful; but in the paradise of the church, different and contrary religions are unpleasant and hurtful.[25]

The tragic error of the modern church is the neglect of church unity and government—leading to the rise of interdenominational organizations to fill the void. This error stands in deep contrast with the *Solemn League and Covenant*. For this error, Zechariah's warned Israel in Zechariah 11:7–14. This passage describes how the people's refusal to heed the Shepherd's rule gives just cause for the Shepherd to first break his staff named "Beauty," symbolic of uniting truth and government, and then to break his staff named "Bands," symbolic of the uniting bands that hold his people together. Regarding this passage, Matthew Henry remarked, "When the staff of Beauty is broken, the staff of bands will not hold long. An unchurched people will soon be an undone people."[26]

Regarding separation from a church, we should follow the advice of the Puritan Richard Byfield, "We must separate from them that hold not Christ, in all things, wherein they hold not Christ, *and no farther*."[27] James Nisbet's advice is similar:

> In all ages of the church, [we] see that they never stated separation from their brethren upon differences of judgment and practice, except where sins of error, defection, and backsliding from the Lord and his ways, were willfully persisted in contrary to clear truth, and an express command.[28]

Fourth, maintenance of the above requires a covenant commitment.

Last, church reformation requires prayer. It is not enough for Christians to pray for themselves and their families, they must also pray for the church, particularly for church unity and reformation. Only Christ can build his church, and he bids us to pray that his kingdom come. It was Christ's prayer and promise to his church that John Knox wanted to hear one more time before his death. It should be the first item of our daily prayers. Thomas Cartwright (1535–1603), an English contemporary of John Knox, emphasized that prayer is the driving force of reform: "Pray for reformation by the power of the Word preached."[29] Calvin emphasized the continual need for prayer: "As the kingdom of God is continually growing and advancing to the end of the world, we must pray every day that it may come: for to whatever extent iniquity abounds in the world, to such an extent the kingdom of God, which brings along with it perfect righteousness, is not yet come."[30] The Puritans and the Covenanters hoped, as previously discussed, for a great outpouring of God's grace to all nations as a product of prayer: *"Ask of me, and I shall give thee the heathen for thine inheritance, and the uttermost parts of the earth for thy possession"* (Ps. 2:8). This hope through prayer is embodied in the very definition of *Thy kingdom come* provided in the *Larger Catechism* Question 191: "... We pray, that the kingdom of sin and Satan may be destroyed, the gospel propagated throughout all the world, the Jews called, the fullness of the Gentiles brought in; the church furnished with all gospel-officers and ordinances, purged from corruption, countenanced and maintained by the civil magistrate...."[31] Jonathan Edwards, citing Zech. 8:20–22 and 12:10, contended that the millennial age will be brought on when God pours out a "Spirit of grace and supplication" in which "one city will go to another" to entreat and seek the Lord, leading to "many peoples and powerful nations" to do likewise.[32]

According to Alexander Peden, the church and those in prayer are one in the same: "Where is the church of God in Scotland at this day? It is not amongst the great clergy. I will tell you where the church of God is. It is wherever a praying young man or young woman is at a dyke-side in Scotland—there the church is."[33] Perhaps, if the Protestors and Resolutioners had focused more on prayer, they would have achieved the same level of unity in truth achieved at the Glasgow Assembly. The unity of the Glasgow Assembly would not have been possible without praying leadership, as evidenced by Baillie's commendation of Henderson: "Among that man's other good parts, that was one, a faculty of grave, good, and zealous prayer, according to the matter in hand; which he exercised, without fagging [fainting], to the last day of our meeting."[34]

Reformation of Church and State

We covenant to obey, honor, and pray for lawful civil and ecclesiastical authority, and also endeavor to pursue all legal means to hold leaders of church and state accountable for their mutual biblical obligations.[35]

It is significant that the fall of the Scottish church coincides with the rejection, by the Resolutioner majority, of the necessity of national leaders to be God-fearing men. Today, by gradual steps, such rejection of biblical guidelines has led us to the modern American concept of freedom, which knows no spiritual bounds. The more we seek this type of liberty, the less free we become because true freedom is not possible without freedom from the slavery of sin (John 8:36; Gal. 5:1).[36] When will people comprehend that the concept of a neutral state is a dangerous myth? John Dickson, one of the covenanting ministers, labeled the condition of church and state after the Revolution Settlement as a "grave of neutrality." He saw no escape and warned that "our principles are so slippery, and the truths of God so superficially rooted in us, that when we are thrown into the furnace, many of us shall melt into dross."[37] Those who think that God's wrath will be vented first on the evil leaders of nations should ponder the fact that the Lord promises to refine his church (Mal. 3:3) and visit judgment first on church leaders (Ezek. 9:6).

In short, any deficiency in the state is traceable to a deficiency in the church. The church must influence culture. Our desire and prayer should be for the Lord to enable us to covenant with fellow Christians to hold our nation accountable to fulfill its biblical obligations to God, from whom it derives its power and authority. Four fundamental changes must occur for this to happen in a land: (1) the church must achieve unity in truth; (2) the church must make disciples of many in the land; (3) the family must be restored as the foundational civil unit; and (4) the state must acknowledge God as the source of its authority.

To overcome these four human impossibilities requires only one thing; it requires a God-given zeal for the truth. Failure to overcome is traceable to a lack of belief (1 John 5:5). A God-given zeal for truth manifests itself though use of the three weapons of overcomers: *"And they overcame him by the blood of the Lamb, and by the word of their testimony, and they loved not their lives unto death"* (Rev. 12:11).[38] Are not these the three objects (i.e., God's mercy, Word, and authority) of Satan's assault?

Overcoming through truth requires that the stars God gave his church shine, proclaiming the Word from every pulpit and exhibiting it in every action. This requires prayer for God-given leaders as described by David in his last words. It also requires that we consider openly unrepentant leaders as malignants, as did the Covenanters. Such leaders require reforming churches filled with reforming Christians, whose zeal is for the Lord's house and his holy Word. Unless reformation flows from a whole-hearted, covenant commitment, it will not succeed. More importantly, only through prayer and God's right arm can *Christians and churches fulfill their biblical obligation to be the light and salt of the world.*

Sometimes I wonder if the Covenanters were not the scouts who first ventured into the Promised Land of Christian nations. Because the people feared the giants, they sought to stone the scouts rather than follow them. After all, how could they, mere mortals, abide in the same land with such giants (e.g., governments)? Consequently, the church has chosen to wander in the wilderness. Whether one holds that the millennial reign of Christ began with his Resurrection, the Protestant Reformation, or is coming soon, it matters not; our obligation remains unchanged. Who knows? Perhaps, modern Christians now dwell in the rich pastures of Midian, content to dwell across the river from the Promised Land with half a promise. Possession of the land requires Christians not to rest in their struggles until they overcome God's enemies. The promise of Christian nations is for the asking: *"Ask of me, and I shall give thee the heathen for thine inheritance, and the uttermost parts of the earth for thy possession"* (Ps. 2:8). The warning of Moses to those who would choose Midian over the Promised Land applies to us today: *"But if ye will not do so, behold, ye have sinned against the LORD: and be sure your sin will find you out"* (Num. 32:23).

Perhaps victory will come one city at a time. Although Christians may legitimately debate the premise of one-church nations, rejection of one-city or one-province churches is unquestionably unscriptural. The dominant organization of Christians in the New Testaments was not denominations under one government, but churches in each city under one government. This requires unity in truth: there is no substitute. Reclaiming cities for Christ must precede reclaiming nations for Christ.

Reformation of church and state requires complete focus on the one thing important, as expressed by Renwick before his execution: "Ye that are people of God, do not weary to maintain the testimony of the day in your stations and places; and whatever you do, make sure of an interest in Christ; for there is a storm coming that will try your foundation. Scotland must be rid of Scotland before the delivery comes...."[39] It also requires we heed Calvin's warning, "For we are not of the church of God, unless we separate ourselves from the world, and from the subtleties thereof."[40] Our goal is not to build the nation but to build the church. The church is ever but a camp (Rev. 18:4) , whose sword is the Word.

Reformation of the Christian

We desire to be humbled for our sins and the sins of society and of the church; to prayerfully and humbly seek God's face, asking that he strengthen us by His Holy Spirit; and to amend our lives, witnessing dedication to personal sanctification and reformation of religion.[41]

Who were the Covenanters? James Nisbet describes them as men obedient to the Word; always in prayer; transformed by the power of grace; always witnessing for the truth; sincerely in love with one another; and breathlessly captivated by their beloved, altogether lovely Christ.[42] He closes his description of them with this epitaph:

We die witnessing against every thing in practice and principle that is contrary to thy holy will, revealed in thy blessed and unerring Word. We die most willingly, freely, and cheerfully, that we may seal with our blood all thy precious truths, which thou hast appointed in thy Word for a ground of faith and for matter of practice. [These] great things of thy law we look upon, O our Redeemer, as the shining pearls and rich jewels of thy mediatorial crown. They are the great things of thy law, every one of which [is] more glorious than mountains of prey and hills of frankincense, because they are thine, and because they came forth from thee: they are the intimations and declarations of thy good and divine will! Thou royal bridegroom and well beloved of our souls, we bless and praise thee forever and ever that thou hast caused the sweet and joyful news of them to be heard in our land, and to be heard in our ears, and to be heard in our hearts and souls. Amen.[43]

They were men, as we should be, sincerely and zealously in pursuit of God's covenant blessings. We, as James urged, should emulate them:

> The pious and religious practices, and holy soul-breathings of that persecuted people, were so many, that if all were recorded, they would have filled a large volume, of which this is a small taste; in which relations, I have, for matter and method, kept as near their own words as possible.... Lord, endue me with much of the all of saving grace, that I may ever conscientiously copy after these noble cloud of witnesses, by faith in the Lord Jesus Christ, till I come to the full and naked embraces of himself, and to the endless communion of those my glorified relations and religious companions. Amen.[44]

The Covenanters sought to *fulfill their covenant obligations and duty to be the people of God*. They understood that those in covenant with God must live for Him rather than themselves (1 Cor. 6:19-20). They saw themselves as called for this purpose (Matt. 5:16).[45] However, their commitment was more than to be a godly person; it was a commitment to be a godly people (1 Pet. 2:9-10). Having tasted God's healing of their souls, they sought his healing in all aspects of their lives: "*If my people, which are called by my name, shall **humble themselves**, and **pray**, and **seek my face**, and **turn from their wicked ways**, then will I hear from heaven, and will forgive their sin, and heal their land*" (2 Chron. 7:14).

First, following the biblical road map requires that we be truly *humbled for our own sins and the sins of society*. Although the covenanted reformations in Scripture started with the recognition of sin and duty by a single individual, the ultimate aim was corporate reformation. None stopped short, as does the modern Christian, at personal reformation. John Nisbet, in his dying testimony, pleaded that the faithful mourn for their own sins and the sins of society. Must God humble us with twenty-eight years of persecution before we do likewise?

> Now it is my last request and soul's desire that all who have made Moses' choice to suffer affliction with the people of God, rather than enjoy the pleasures of sin for a season, and are true lovers of Zion's righteous cause; that you set much time apart, and mourn, and afflict your souls, for your original sin, heart plagues, sins of persons and families, sins of kings and kingdoms; and for all the dreadful apostasies, hateful compliances, and sinful sidings of ministers and people with the enemies of God and godliness, and mourn that there is not more faithfulness and

zeal for the cause of God amongst his people (Ps. 51; Ezra 9; Neh. 9; Jer. 9; Lam. 3; and Ezek. 9 to the end).[46]

Second, we must *prayerfully and humbly seek God's face, asking that he strengthen us by his Holy Spirit.* James Nisbet learned that seeking God's face is a daily struggle, which he pursued daily through self-examination and prayer. Table 14.1 provides a summary of the questions he recommends that we daily ask ourselves as we examine our soul's condition. His questions cover all the covenant blessings.

How does your soul hold up against James's Spiritual Checklist? I confess mine is lacking. We cannot transform ourselves; God must do it. Righteousness is totally outside us; it is in Christ alone. Our job is to humbly examine and prayerfully confess our need for his transforming work. If we hunger and thirst for righteousness, he will fill us. James Nisbet's memoir provides an excellent pattern for employing all the means of grace (prayer, praise, the Word, and the sacraments) to seek God's face. Must God deprive us of preaching and of the sacraments, as James was, to appreciate them? Must God allow us to suffer persecution for us to appreciate prayer and praise? As we leave his memoir behind, I ask that you consider his closing prayer.

O Lord, enable me, by grace, conscientiously to examine myself impartiality anent all these foresaid [checklist] points, and in every other thing, wherein thy glory and my true interest and concern may lie. Ever draw me with the sweet and kind cords of thy infinite love up through the warm streams of the meritorious blood of the Lamb of God. For thy rich mercy's sake, hand in and seal unto my soul the full and free pardon of all my scarlet and crimson-colored sins, and breathe peace alongst therewith, saying unto me, "Because I live, thou shall live also." O for much of that peace which passes all understanding! O cherish, warm, and refresh my soul with the comforting influences of grace, saying unto my soul, "Eat, O friend, drink, yea drink abundantly, O beloved"; and thereby ever cause my soul [to] echo back again unto thee, "O Lord, *my beloved is mine, and I am his!*" O King of Saints, ever appear to be good and gracious unto all thy people, far and near, through the world! O Lord, accommodate thyself unto all the circumstances of their case, spiritual and temporal! And O King of Zion, evermore appear for thy work and interest, to defend and protect the same from all her enemies, and keep from all errors, extremes, sins, and defections of whatsoever kind! O magnify thy wisdom, power, grace, and goodness, in granting all these things; and to thee, O Lord, the only living and true God, Father, Son, and Holy Spirit, be glory for ever! Amen.[47]

Table 14.1
James Nisbet's Spiritual Checklist

Checklist
Am I leveling all the actions of my life to the glory of God...?
Am I ever-resisting sin [in] my heart, and bearing witness against it in my life...?
Am I ever searching if I be savingly convinced of my lost state and condition...?
Am I fully and sweetly persuaded that Jesus Christ is my only ... remedy?
Am I ever-striving in the use of all the means of grace ... to embrace ... [Christ]?
Am I willing to have him for my Lord and Lawgiver, as well as Lord and Savior?
Am I ever seeking to be a debtor to free grace...?
Am I ever seeking to get atheism and ignorance rooted out, and saving illumination, flowing from Christ's prophetic office, implanted in my heart and soul? Am I ever seeking [delivery] from the condemning power of sin, by virtue of Christ's priestly office? Am I ever seeking [delivery] from the power and tyranny of sin, by virtue of Christ's kingly office?
Am I ever studying the spirituality of the law as a schoolmaster, leading me to Christ, who is the end thereof to all who believe in him?
Am I ever taking the law for a rule to square my life conversation...?
Am I ever thirsting after the pardon of ... sin, and [Christ's] intercession ... therein?
Am I ever hating all sin, and prizing holiness at all times?
Am I greatly grieved when iniquities prevail against me? And do I run to the blood of Christ for daily washing?
Am I greatly grieved when the Lord withholds ... [his] face?
Am I ever seeking to have a present Lord with me at gospel ordinances, that he may he glorified, and my salvation promoted?
Am I studying, in the Lord's strength, ever to be a martyr for [God's] truth...?
Am I ever searching Scripture what I am to believe concerning God, and what I am to practice as a real Christian?
Am I ever seeking of the Lord ... to be strong in faith ... and to get all my doubts cleared by the light of his Word and help of his Spirit?
Am I ever seeking [the Lord's help] to get all my fears prevented?
Am I ever taking heed lest I fall, remembering, blessed is he that feareth always?
Am I ever endeavoring to glorify the Lord ... [by using] the means of grace when he is hiding himself, as when he is, in some measure, present?
Am I striving to take the beam out of mine own eye, rather than censure others?
Am I ever hating and keeping at a distance from the vicious practice and sinful ways of the wicked, but pitying and loving their persons?
Am I ever exercising a holy indignation against myself for all my sinful miscarriages, and a holy jealousy over myself for all times to come?
Am I ever seeking to be brought out and from under a covenant of works, and to be bought to and established in grace's freest and well-ordered covenant?
Am I ever preparing for death, judgment, and eternity, and ... [reminding myself] that I must give an exact account of all my thoughts, words, and actions?
Am I ever seeking to have my mind sanctified and brought to my lot?
Am I ever seeking ... the Lord's [help] to comply ... and to submit to his ... will?
Am I ever acknowledging the Lord in the whole of my ways?
Am I ever setting the Lord before me and living under ... [an] impression of him?
Am I ever seeking that the cause of the Lord's people, and the condition of his work and interest, may ever lie near my heart...?[48]

Third, we must turn from our wickedness and *amend our lives, witnessing dedication to personal sanctification and reformation of religion.* Our pattern is Christ, who had a body like us, yet "he never tasted one of the pleasures of sin."[49] In this regard, let us learn from John Nisbet, whom his friends described as "a **strict observer** of the Sabbath, a **great examiner** of the Scriptures, a **great wrestler** in prayer," and a **humble contender** "for truth (which he termed precious)."[50] His last testament calls us to duty:

> Wherefore it is the unquestionable and indispensable duty of all who have any love to God, to his Son the Lord Jesus Christ, to the thriving of his kingdom, to their own soul's salvation, and to the following generation; to act a close, constant, and needy dependence on the Lord Jehovah's all-sufficiency, for light, for counsel, for direction, for strength and stability, to make conscience in bearing testimony for him, for his persecuted truth, work, and interest in these lands....[51]

In summary, the way of the Covenanters requires faith evidenced by seeking God's face through the examination of his Word, love evidenced by willingly observing his Word, hope evidenced by wrestling with God in prayer, and the presence of his Holy Spirit evidenced by a humble contending for truth. These are the marks of a true Christian, yet without Christ these are but the "shell of heavenly things."[52] In the words of Robert McCheyne (1813–1843), "In yourself you will never stand righteous before Jehovah." To stand before Jehovah requires that one possess a heart broken "from its own righteousness" and "its love of sin," thus enabling the sinner "like a weaned child" to consider precious "the only one in all the world on whose face God can look and say, '*He is altogether lovely.*'"[53] Those who have thus closed with Christ must lean on Christ to leave the wilderness of this world and to enter the enclosed, well-watered, and fruit-bearing garden of his love (Song of Sol. 4:12; 8:5–7), which he bestows by grace alone. Those who thus accept God's covenant promise, following the pattern of David (2 Sam. 23:5), must become both his spouse, by covenant engagement, and his sister (Song of Sol. 4:12), as he transforms them into his image.[54] If you know not this garden, I pray that you, too, will accept God's promise: *"Incline your ear, and come unto me: hear, and your soul shall live; and I will make an everlasting covenant with you, even the sure mercies of David"* (Isa. 55:3–4).[55] If you have already closed with Christ, then take comfort in the words Samuel Rutherford offered Alexander Henderson: "God has called you to Christ's side, and the wind is now in Christ's face in this land; and seeing you are with him you cannot expect the lee side, or the sunny side of the [hill]."[56]

Conclusion

I close this book with thanks to the Lord. Books seemed to rain from heaven with answers to questions that the Lord laid on my heart. In the greatest moments of doubt and confusion, the Lord opened doors where minutes before all I saw were the walls. The struggles of my life and church all seemed perfectly timed to lead me to fresh insights.

In the final analysis, all modern ills, spiritual and temporal, are traceable to our continuing departure from the principles of the Second Reformation. Although I commend James Nisbet for joining the Scottish church, I must bear witness against the Church of Scotland and its American children for abandoning Reformed principles. In particular, I am convinced that the Lord will not bless a church at peace with his enemies. Our departure from truth has led to our undernourished condition as a church; truth, as Thornwell argued, is the only food that the soul can digest.[57]

It does no good to blame society or the church for our deficiencies before the Lord because Christ holds men, not churches and states, accountable. In the words of Hugh Miller, "Churches, however false and detestable, are never to be summoned to the bar of judgment.... To Christ, as his head and king, must every man render an account."[58]

The great heresy of our times is that all men are children of God. Those within the church have lost their identity as a people of God, united in spirit and purpose. We have adopted the half-truths of our fathers for which Judah faced punishment: *"Because they have despised the law of the Lord, and have not kept his commandments, and their lies caused them to err, after which their fathers have walked"* (Amos 2:4b). Nevertheless, Christ loves his church, and he will see to it that his bride is prepared (Eph. 5:27) for the great banquet. Based on the history of God's people, the needed corrections will result from either prayer or persecution, leading the people to renew their covenant promises. Let us pray that God's kingdom come, and let us covenant to fulfill our obligations to be his people. When persecution comes, let us pray that we would stand as firm as did the Scottish Covenanters. When covenanting comes, let us praise the Lord, for only in him will we stand firm. Let us ever strive to make it possible for our children to utter one of James Nisbet's praises, "O my soul! Bless and praise the Lord that I was born in a land where the glad tidings of the everlasting gospel are published and pressed with so much purity and plainness."[59] This should be our prayer, *"Turn us again, O God, and cause thy face to shine; and we shall be saved"* (Ps. 80:3).

NOTES and INDEX

Notes

Notes

Introduction

[1] James Durham, A *Commentary Upon the Book of the Revelation* (London: Company of Stationers, 1658), vol. 2, pp. 328–350 (hereafter cited as Durham, *Revelation*).

[2] Loraine Boettner, *The Reformed Doctrine of Predestination* (Philadelphia: The Presbyterian and Reformed Publishing Company, 1973), pp. 335–336 (hereafter cited as Boettner).

[3] Charles Hodge, *Systematic Theology* (New York: C. Scribner, 1887), vol. 1, p. 545.

[4] John Calvin, quoted in *An Introduction to Reformed Tradition*, ed. John Leith (Atlanta: John Knox Press, 1981), p. 151 (hereafter cited as Leith).

[5] John Calvin to Thomas Cramer, quoted in *Alexander and Rufus: or A Series of Dialogs on Church Communion*, ed. John Anderson (Associate Synod of North America, 1862), p. 151 (hereafter cited as *Alexander and Rufus*).

[6] Samuel Rutherford, *Fourteen Communion Sermons by Samuel Rutherford*, ed. A. A. Bonar (Glasgow, 1878), p. 59.

[7] Daniel Defoe, *Memoirs of the Church of Scotland* (reprint, Perth: James Dewar, 1844), pp. 318–323 (hereafter cited as Defoe, *Memoirs*).

[8] Sir William Petty refers to 80,000 new Scots in 1672, cited in *Political Anatomy of Ireland*, cited by J. G. Simms, *Jacobite Ireland*, 1695–91 (London, 1969), p. 11, cited by William Lyons Fisk, *The Scottish High Church Tradition in America* (Lanham, Maryland: University Press of America, Inc., 1995), p. 30.

[9] Thomas McCrie, introduction to *A Vindication of the Scottish Covenanters* (Glasgow: Andrew Young, Printer, 1824) (hereafter cited as McCrie, *Vindication*).

[10] Robert H. Bork, *Slouching Towards Gomorrah* (New York: Regan Books, 1996), 342–3 (hereafter cited as Bork).

[11] Bork, p. 5.

[12] Johannes G. Vos, *The Scottish Covenanters: Their Origins, History, and Distinctive Doctrines* (Pittsburgh: Crown and Covenant Publications, 1980), p. 118 (hereafter cited as Vos, *Covenanters*).

[13] R. C. Sproul, "The Conscience," *Table Talk*, vol. 21, no. 7 (July 1997): p. 6.

[14] Cornelius Van Til, *The Reformed Pastor and Modern Thought* (Phillipsburg: Presbyterian and Reformed Publishing Co., 1974), p. 199 (hereafter cited as Van Til).

[15] John Calvin, *Institutes of Christian Religion* paraphrased by Hans Hillerbrand, *The Protestant Reformation* (New York: Harper and Row, 1968), p. 181.

[16] Van Til, p. 199.

[17] Charles H. Spurgeon, a sermon entitled "A Defense of Calvinism," published in *C. H. Spurgeon Autobiography*, ed. Susannah Spurgeon and Joseph Harrald, 2 vols. (Edinburgh: The Banner of Truth Trust, 1973 reprint), vol. 1, p. 162 (hereafter cited as Spurgeon, *Defense*).

[18] Spurgeon, *Defense*, vol. 1, p. 168.

[19] Spurgeon, *Defense*, vol. 1, p. 168.

[20] Boettner, pp. 335–336.

[21] Egbert Watson Smith, *The Creed of Presbyterians* (Richmond: John Knox Press, 1960), p. 54 (hereafter cited as Smith, *Creed*); John Fiske, *The Beginnings of New England; or, The Puritan Theocracy in its relations to the civil and religious liberty* (Boston and New York: Houghton, Mifflin and Company, 1890), p. 58; Smith, *Creed,* p. 56.

[22] Samuel Rutherford, *The Due Right of Presbytery; or, a Peaceable Plea for the Government of the Church of Scotland* (London: 1644), p. 148 (hereafter cited as Rutherford, *Peaceable Plea*).Rutherford.

[23] James Nisbet, "A True Relation of the Life and Sufferings of John Nisbet in Hardhill," written in 1719 and published in Wodrow Society, Publications, vol. 7, part 2, reprinted in *Select Biographies*, ed. William K. Tweedie, 2 vols. (Edinburgh, 1845–1847), vol. 2, pp. 407–408 (hereafter cited as Tweedie).

[24] James Nisbet, *The Private Life of the Persecuted* (Edinburgh: William Oliphant, 1827), p. vii (hereafter cited as Nisbet, *Private Life*).

[25] G. K. Chesterton, *Orthodoxy* (Garden City: Doubleday, 1959), p. 95.

[26] Robert McWard, "The Poor Man's Cup of Cold Water: ministered to the saints and sufferers for Christ in Scotland who amidst the scorching flames and fiery trial" (1678), Microfilm: Early English Books, reel 1289:20, p. 58. McWard was one of the many Scottish ministers banished to Holland during the persecution. In Holland, he was active in supporting the cause of the persecuted Presbyterians.

[27] John Howie, *The Scots Worthies* (reprint, Edinburgh: Oliphant, Anderson, & Ferrier, Carslaw edition) (hereafter cited as Howie, *Worthies*).

[28] James Anthony Froude, "Calvinism: An Address to the Students at St. Andrews," *Short Studies on Great Subjects* (New York: Charles Scribner's Sons, 1884), 4 volumes, vol. ii, p. 52 (hereafter cited as Froude, *Calvinism*).

Chapter 1
The Breaking of the Bronze Serpent

[1] William Binnie, *The Psalms: Their History, Teachings, and Use* (London: Hodder and Stoughton, 1886), p. 387 (hereafter cited as Binnie, *Psalms*).

[2] Ian Finlay, *The Lowlands* (New York: Hastings House, 1967), p. 2 (hereafter cited as Finlay, *The Lowlands*). "I Byde It" is the Nisbet Motto; the Loudoun motto is similar.

[3] Leyburn, James G., *The Scotch-Irish: A Social History* (Chapel Hill: The University of North Carolina Press, 1962), p. 70 (hereafter cited as Leyburn, *Scotch-Irish*).

[4] John Hill Burton, *The History of Scotland*, 8 vols. (Edinburgh and London: William Blackwood and Sons, 1899), vol. 3, pp. 249–250; James King Hewison, *The Covenanters: A History of the Church in Scotland From The Reformation to the Revolution*, 2 vols. (Glasgow: John Smith and Sons, 1908), vol. 1, p. 8 (hereafter cited as Hewison).

[5] David Wright, *The Bible in Scottish Life and Literature* (Edinburgh: Saint Andrews Press, 1988), p. 17; Walter Bower, "De Combustione Jaconi Resby Heretici Apud Perth" (1406), cited in David Laing, *The Works of John Knox* (Edinburgh: James Thin, 1895 reprinted in New York: AMS Press, Inc. 1966), vol. 1, pp. 495–496.

[6] John Knox, *John Knox's History of the Reformation in Scotland*, edited by William Dickinson (reprint, New York: Philosophical Library, Inc., 1950), vol. 1, pp. 8–11.

[7] Wright, *The Bible in Scottish Life and Literature*, pp. 156–161.

[8] Matthew 6:9–13 translated by Murdoch Nisbet into Scots around 1520 from Purvey's translation of Wyclif's Bible, printed in *Thomas Law, The New Testament in Scots* (Edinburgh and London: William Blackwood and Sons, 1905), p. 34 (hereafter cited as Thomas Law, *New Testament in Scots*).

[9] Roland H. Bainton, *Here I Stand – A life of Martin Luther* (Nashville: Abingdon Press, 1983), pp. 41–44 (hereafter cited as Bainton).

[10] Bainton, pp. 49–50.

[11] Bainton, p. 50.

¹² Bainton, p. 90; B. K. Kuiper, *The Church in History* (Grand Rapids: Wm. B. Eerdmans Publications Co., 1991), pp. 196–202 (hereafter cited as Kuiper, *The Church in History*).

¹³ B. B. Warfield, an article entitled *Calvin as a Great Theologian and Calvinism Today*, pp. 23–24. Quoted in Boettner, p. 334.

¹⁴ W. Beveridge, *A Short History of the Westminster Assembly* (Edinburgh: T. & T. Clark, 1904), p. 6 (hereafter cited as Beveridge, *Short History*).

¹⁵ Thomas McCrie, *The Story of the Scottish Church from the Reformation to the Disruption* (Glasgow: Bell and Bain Ltd., 1874), reprinted by Free Presbyterian Publications, p. 14 (hereafter cited as McCrie, *Scottish Church*).

¹⁶ Smith, *Creed*, pp. 97–98; Nathaniel McFetridge, *Calvinism in History* (Philadelphia: Presbyterian Board of Publications, 1882), p. 124 (hereafter cited as McFetridge, *Calvinism in History*); James Nisbet, *A True Relation of the Life and Sufferings of John Nisbet of Hardhill, His Last Testimony to the Truth; with a short account of his last words on the Scaffold, December 4, 1685* (Edinburgh: Printed by Robert Brown, 1718), p. 3 (hereafter cited as James Nisbet, *True Relation*).

¹⁷ John Knox, *The History of the Reformation of Religion Within the Realm of Scotland*, abridged version entitled *The Reformation in Scotland*, ed. by C. K. Guthrie (Edinburgh: The Banner of Truth Trust, 1982), p. 73 (hereafter cited as Knox, *The Reformation in Scotland*).

¹⁸ A. G. Dickens, *Thomas Cromwell and the English Reformation* (New York: Harper & Row, Publishers, 1969), pp. 109–123.

¹⁹ Boettner, p. 371.

²⁰ Kuiper, *The Church in History*, pp. 222–229.

²¹ John Green, History of the English People, 5 vols. (New York: John B. Alden, 1885), vol. 3, pp. 58–59 (hereafter cited as Green, *History of the English People*).

²² Sir James Stewart and Rev. James Stirling, *Naphtali, or, The Wrestlings of the Church of Scotland for the Kingdom of Christ* (Edinburgh, 1667), pp. 11–12 (hereafter cited as Stewart, *Naphtali*).

²³ David Laing, *The Works of John Knox* (Edinburgh: Bannatyne Club, 1864), vol. 6, p. 285. The practice of singing Psalm 124 began in 1582 upon the return of an exiled minister.

²⁴ John Brown, *The Psalms of David, in Metre* (1560; reprint, Dallas: Presbyterian Heritage Publications, 1991), Ps. 124:1–4 (hereafter referred to as the *Scottish Psalter*).

²⁵ Peter Lorimer, *The Scottish Reformation: A Historical Sketch* (New York: Robert Carter and Brothers, 1861), pp. 218–221 (hereafter cited as Lorimer, *The Scottish Reformation*).

²⁶ Thomas McCrie, *The Life of John Knox the Scottish Reformer*, abridged from McCrie's *Life of Knox* (Philadelphia: Presbyterian Board of Publication, 1839), p. 121 (hereafter cited as McCrie, *John Knox-abridged*).

²⁷ James Kirkton, *The Secret and True History of the Church of Scotland* (Edinburgh: James Ballantyne and Co., 1817), pp. 21–22 (hereafter cited as Kirkton); John Knox, quoted by Jasper Ridley, *John Knox* (New York: Oxford University Press, 1968), p. 326; McCrie, *Scottish Church*, pp. 49, 51.

²⁸ Hewison, vol. 1, pp. 7, 27–29.

²⁹ Knox, *The Reformation in Scotland*, p. 279; Hewison, vol. 1, p. 31; McCrie, *Scottish Church*, p. 53.

³⁰ Knox, *The Reformation in Scotland*, pp. 275–276, 278; Hewison, vol. 1, pp. 8–9.

³¹ Knox, *The Reformation in Scotland*, p. 338, 277.

³² John Knox, et al., *The First Book of Discipline*; James Cameron, *The First Book of Discipline* (Edinburgh: The Saint Andrews Press, 1972), Head 5, p. 131 (hereafter cited as *First Book of Discipline*); W. Fred Graham, *Later Calvinism—International Perspectives*, vol. 22 of *Sixteenth Century Essays & Studies*, ed. Charles G. Nauert, Jr. (Ann Arbor: Edwards Brothers, 1994), pp. 193–194 (hereafter cited as Graham, *Later Calvinism*).

³³ Mary Black Verschuur, *Enforcing the Discipline of the Kirk: Mr. Patrick Galloway's Early Years as Minister at Perth*, within Graham, *Later Calvinism*, p. 219; Anthony Ross, "Reformation and Repression," *Essays on the Scottish Reformation, 1513–1625*, ed. David McRoberts (Glasgow: Burns, 1962), pp. 390, 394.

³⁴ *First Book of Discipline*, Head 7, pp. 165–167; Michael Graham, *The Civil Sword and the Scottish Kirk, 1560–1600*, (hereafter cited as Graham, *The Civil Sword*) within Graham, *Later Calvinism*, p. 219.

³⁵ Kuiper, *The Church in History*, p. 240; Hewison, vol. 1, pp. 63, 65, 68–70.

³⁶ McCrie, *Scottish Church*, p. 61; John Knox cited in McCrie, *Vindication*, p. 184; John 17:21 (NKJV).

³⁷ Hewison, vol. 1, p. 78; James Howell to Lord Clifford, 1639, *Epistolae Ho-Elianae- Familiar Letters, Domestic and Forren* (London, Thomas

Guy, 1673), vol. 1, p. 261 [sic], cited by Hewison, vol. 1, p. 339.

[38] Hewison, vol. 1, pp. 81–82; Gordon Donaldson, *Scottish Historical Documents* (New York: Barnes & Noble, Inc., 1970), pp. 143–150 (hereafter cited as Donaldson); McCrie, *Scottish Church*, p. 67.

[39] Hewison, vol. 1, pp. 98–104; McCrie, *Scottish Church*, pp. 70–72; Hewison, vol. 1, p. 99.

[40] McCrie, *Scottish Church*, pp. 75–76; Hewison, vol. 1, pp. 111–121; Donaldson, pp. 153–155.

[41] Hewison, vol. 1, p. 115; David Calderwood, *The History of the Kirk of Scotland*, 10 vols. (Edinburgh: Wodrow Society, 1842–49), vol. 4, p. 246 (hereafter cited as Calderwood); Hewison, vol. 1, pp. 120–121.

[42] McCrie, *Scottish Church*, pp. 81–83; Hewison, vol. 1, pp. 128–134.

[43] McCrie, *Scottish Church*, p. 88; Henry Hallam, *The Constitutional History of England from the accession of Henry VII to the death of George II* (London: J. Murray, 1827), vol. 1, p. 181; Andrew Melville, cited in Thomas McCrie, *Life of Andrew Melville,* (Edinburgh: William Blackwood, 1824), vol. 1, pp. 391–382 (hereafter cited as McCrie, *Melville*).

[44] Hewison, vol. 1, pp. 141–145; McCrie, *Scottish Church*, pp. 89–91; Hewison, vol. 1, pp. 144–148.

[45] John Richard Green, *A Short History of the English People* (New York and London: Harper & Brothers Publishers, 1898), pp. 472–473 (hereafter cited as Green, *Short History*).

[46] Hewison, vol. 1, pp. 148–149; George Buchanan, *The Rights of the Crown in Scotland* (hereafter cited as Buchanan, *Rights*), translated by Robert MacFarlan and reprinted in Samuel Rutherford, *Lex, Rex* (Harrisonburg: Springle Publications, 1982), pp. 261, 280–281 (hereafter cited as Rutherford, *Lex, Rex*); Hewison, vol. 1, p. 183.

[47] Hewison, vol. 1, pp. 153, 175.

[48] McCrie, *Scottish Church,* pp. 109–110; Hewison, vol. 1, p. 194; John Calvin, *Commentary on the Book of Psalms,* Translated by Rev. James Anderson (Grand Rapids: Baker House Books, 1989), comments on 92:1, vol. II, p. 495 (hereafter cited as Calvin, *Commentary on Psalms*).

[49] Hewison, vol. 1, p. 195; McCrie, *Scottish Church,* pp. 110–111; Calderwood, vol. 7, pp. 257–279.

[50] Hewison, vol. 1, pp. 196–203; McCrie, *Scottish Church,* pp. 113–114.

[51] Bishop Gilbert Burnet, quoted by Hewison, vol. 1, p. 206; Hewison, vol. 1, p. 148; Samuel Rutherford to Mr. J. R., June 16, 1637, *Rutherford's Letters* (London: Third Edition, 1675), p. 200 (hereafter cited as Rutherford, *Letters*).

[52] Kirkton, p. 18.

[53] McCrie, *Scottish Church,* pp. 128–135, 138, 152–153; Samuel Rutherford to Lord Loudoun, March 9, 1637, *Letters,* p. 41.

[54] Hew Scott, *Fasti Eccleslae Scoticanae: The Succession of Ministers in Parish Churches of Scotland From the Reformation, A.D. 1560, to the Present Time,* (Edinburgh: William Paterson, 1866–71), vol. 2, part I, pp. 183–184 (hereafter cited as Scott, *Fasti*).

[55] James Nisbet, *A True Relation,* p. 4.

[56] Nisbet, *Private Life,* pp. 124–127.

[57] Nisbet, *Private Life,* p. 128.

[58] Hewison, vol. 1, pp. 209–210, 240. Everett H. Emerson, *English Puritanism from John Hooper to John Milton* (Durham: Duke University Press, 1968), pp. 34–41.

[59] James Barr, *The Scottish Covenanters* (Glasgow: John Smith and Son, 1946), p. 17 (hereafter cited as Barr); McCrie, *Scottish Church,* pp. 139–140.

[60] William Hetherington, *History of the Westminster Assembly of Divines* (Edmonton, Canada: Still Waters Revival Books, 1993), p. 393 (hereafter cited as Hetherington, *Westminster Assembly*).

[61] Samuel Rutherford to John Nevay, June 16, 1637, *Letters,* p. 196.

[62] Andrew Bonar, Preface to *Letters of Samuel Rutherford* (Edinburgh: Oliphant Anderson & Ferrier, 1904), pp. 1–2; T. M. Lindsay, "A Literary Relic of Scottish Lollardry," *The Scottish Historical Review* (Glasgow: James Maclehose and Sons, 1904), vol. 1, p. 270.

[63] Edwin Palmer, *The Five Points of Calvinism* (Grand Rapids: Baker Book House, 1972); Arthur Custance, "Calvin and Calvinism," *The Sovereignty of Grace,* online 1996 <http://www.custance.org>.

Chapter 2
The Rise and Fall of Truth and Unity

[1] Kirkton, p. 31; McCrie, *Scottish Church*, p. 141; Hewison, vol. 1, pp. 243–245; Kirkton, p. 31.

[2] Hewison, vol. 1, pp. 250–251; Samuel Rutherford to Alexander Henderson, March 9, 1637, *Letters*, p. 40, cited by W. Beveridge, *Makers of the Scottish Church* (Edinburgh: T & T Clark, 1908), p. 119 (hereafter cited as Beveridge, *Scottish Church*); Beveridge, *Scottish Church*, p. 118; Hewison, vol. 1, pp. 252–253.

[3] Donaldson, pp. 194–201; Hewison, vol. 1, pp. 265–266; McCrie, *Scottish Church*, pp. 145–146.

[4] Florence McCoy, *Robert Baillie and the Second Scots Reformation* (Berkeley: University of California Press, 1974), p. 37 (hereafter cited as McCoy, *Robert Baillie*).

[5] McCrie, *Scottish Church*, pp. 145–146; Barr, p. 20; Hewison, vol. 1, p. 282.

[6] King Charles I to Marquis of Hamilton, 11 June 1638, printed in Alexander Peterkin, *Records of the Kirk of Scotland, Containing the Acts and Proceedings of the General Assemblies, from the Year 1638 Downwards…* (Edinburgh: John Sutherland, 1838), p. 68 (hereafter cited as Peterkin, *Records*); David Stevenson, *The Scottish Reformation 1637–1644* (New York: St. Martin's Press, 1974), p. 99 (hereafter cited as Stevenson, *Scottish Reformation*).

[7] McCrie, *Scottish Church*, p. 154; Barr, pp. 20–21.

[8] McCrie, *Scottish Church*, p. 156; McCoy, *Robert Baillie*, pp. 53–54; Marquis of Hamilton to King Charles I, 22 Nov. 1638, *Hamilton Papers*, 1880, p. 59 cited in Hewison, vol. 1, p. 298; Hewison, vol. 1, p. 300.

[9] McCrie, *Scottish Church*, pp. 158–159.

[10] McCoy, *Robert Baillie*, p. 55; McCrie, *Scottish Church*, p. 160.

[11] Peterkin, *Records*, p. 147; McCoy, *Robert Baillie*, pp. 55–56.

[12] McCrie, *Scottish Church*, pp. 159–164; Hewison, vol. 1, pp. 306–313; McCoy, *Robert Baillie*, pp. 56–60.

[13] Robert Baillie, *The Letters and Journals of Robert Baillie*, A. M., Principal of the University of Glasgow, mdcxxxxii–mdclxlii. David Laing, ed., 3 vols. (Edinburgh: Bannatyne Club, 1841–1842), vol. 1, pp. 156–157 (hereafter cited as

Baillie, *Letters*); McCrie, *Scottish Church*, pp. 164–165; *Scottish Psalter*, Ps. 133.

[14] Gilbert Burnet, *The Memoirs of the lives and actions of James and William, Dukes of Hamilton and Castleherald* (London: J. Grover for R. Royston, 1677), vol. 1, p. 203 (hereafter cited as Burnet, *Memoirs*).

[15] McCoy, *Robert Baillie*, p. 62; J. C. McFeeters, *Sketches of the Covenanters* (Philadelphia: Second Church of the Covenanters,1913), p. 106.

[16] Baillie, *Letters*, vol. 1, p. 211.

[17] Peterkin, *Records*, vol. 1, pp. 228–229; Stevenson, *Scottish Reformation*, p. 153.

[18] Mathieson, *Politics and Religion: A Study in Scottish History from the Reformation to the Revolution*, 3 vols. (Glasgow: James Maclehose and Sons, 1902), vol. 2, p. 13 (hereafter cited as Mathieson); McCrie, *Scottish Church*, p. 176.

[19] Hewison, vol. 1, pp. 334–338; McCoy, *Robert Baillie*, p. 66.

[20] Mathieson, vol. 2, p. 15; McCrie, *Scottish Church*, p. 187.

[21] Hewison, vol. 1, pp. 345, 352.

[22] McCrie, *Scottish Church*, p. 191; Thomas Carlyle, "Cromwell," *Carlyle on Heroes, Hero Worship, and the Heroic in History* (Boston: Ginn & Company, 1901), vol. 1, p. 85; McCoy, *Robert Baillie*, p. 75

[23] McCrie, *Scottish Church*, p. 189; Kuiper, *The Church in History*, p. 251.

[24] Hewison, vol. 1, pp. 366–368; Ninian Hill, *The Story of the Scottish Church from the Earliest of Times* (Glasgow: James Maclehose and Sons, 1919), p. 167.

[25] Edward Clarendon, *The History of Rebellion and Civil Wars in England* (Oxford, Printed in Theater, 1702–1704); vol. 1, p. 184.

[26] From a letter, written by Kirk in response to a query for closer alliance from the English church, cited in Hewison, vol. 1, p. 360.

[27] Hetherington, *Westminster Assembly*, p. 321.

[28] Donaldson, p. 208–210; Hewison, vol. 1, pp. 479–481.

[29] Baillie, *Letters*, vol. 2, p. 2.

[30] McCoy, *Robert Baillie*, p. 94.

[31] Hetherington, *Westminster Assembly*, pp. 347, 348.

[32] Beveridge, *Short History*, pp. 99–103.

[33] Calvin, *Commentary on Psalms*, Commentary on Ps. 81:3. vol. ii, p. 312; John Girardeau, *Instrumental Music in the Public Worship of the Church* (Richmond, Whittet & Shepperson, 1888), pp. 63–64 (hereafter cited as Girardeau).

[34] Hetherington, *Westminster Assembly*, pp. 136–150; McCoy, *Robert Baillie*, p. 108.

[35] Hetherington, *Westminster Assembly*, pp. 175, 194, 199–200.

[36] "Reasons of the Dissenting Brethren," p. 124 cited in Hetherington, *Westminster Assembly*, p. 218. Any who question the legitimacy of the Presbyterian form of government should read Thomas Goodwin, et al., "The Reasons Presented by the Dissenting Brethren Against Certain Propositions concerning Presbyterial Government ... Together with the Answer of the Assembly of the Divines to those Reasons of Dissent" (London: Printed by T. R. and E. M. for Humphrey Howard, 1648). Both the pros and cons are laid out in Scripture proof form with the winner clearly being the Westminster divines. The early Congregationalists imputed the office of ruling elder to the magistrate.

[37] Baillie, *Letters*, vol. 2, p. 266; Hetherington, *Westminster Assembly*, pp. 233–234.

[38] Hetherington, *Westminster Assembly*, p. 287; John Seldon, cited in Hetherington, *Westminster Assembly*, p. 202.

[39] Hetherington, *Westminster Assembly*, p. 267.

[40] George Gillespie, *Wholesome Severity Reconciled with Christian Liberty or, the True Resolution of the Present Controversie Concerning Liberty of Conscience* (London: 1644), pp. 39–40.

[41] Gillespie, *Treatise of Miscellany Questions* (Edinburgh, 1649), p. 124 (hereafter cited as Gillespie, *Treatise*); Preface to the *Confession of 1560* cited in Beveridge, *Short History*, p. 118.

[42] *The Confession of Faith*, printed in *The Confession of Faith; The Larger and Shorter Catechisms, with the Scripture Proofs at large: Together with The Sum of Saving Knowledge* (Glasgow: Free Presbyterian Publications, 1985), chapter xx.2, p. 86 (hereafter cited as *Westminster Standards*); Hetherington, *Westminster Assembly*, pp. 330–331.

[43] Mathieson, vol. 2, p. 65; Mark Napier, *Montrose and the Covenanters, Their Character and Conduct* (London: James Duncan, 1838), pp. 237–238.

[44] McCrie, *Scottish Church*, pp. 210–215.

[45] Kuiper, *The Church in History*, p. 252; Mathieson, vol. 2, p. 74; Hetherington, *Westminster Assembly*, p. 328; Smith, *Creed*, pp. 72–73.

[46] Mathieson, vol. 2, p. 70.

[47] John Buchan, *Montrose, a History* (Boston and New York: Houghton Mifflin, 1928), pp. 261–262 (hereafter cited as Buchan, *Montrose*); Mathieson, vol. 2, p. 70.

[48] Interloquitur of Parliament (January 10, 1646) cited in Buchan, *Montrose*, p. 261 footnotes.

[49] Mathieson, vol. 2, pp. 70–71.

[50] Act of Scottish Parliament, December 23, 1646, cited by Mark Napier, *Montrose and the Covenanters* (London: James Duncan, 1888); Mathieson, vol. 2, pp. 70–71: see footnotes on these pages.

[51] David Stevenson, "The Massacre at Dunaverty, 1647," printed in *Scottish Studies* (Aberdeen: The University Press), vol. 19, 1975, pp. 27-37.

[52] Newton Nisbet, *Nisbet Narrations* (Charlotte: Crayton Print Co., 1961), p. 15.

[53] Hetherington, *Westminster Assembly*, pp. 308–309; Samuel R Gardiner, Introduction to *The Constitutional Documents of the Puritan Revolution 1625-1660* (Oxford: Clarendon Press, 1906), pp. xliv–xlix (hereafter cited as Gardiner, *Documents*).

[54] Maurice Ashley, *James II* (London: J. M. Dent & Sons LTD, 1977), p. 25 (hereafter cited as Ashley, *James II*).

[55] William Anderson, *The Scottish Nation; or the Surnames, Families, Literature, Honours and Biographical History of the People of Scotland* (Edinburgh: Fullarton, 1860–1863), vol. 2, pp. 694–695 (hereafter cited as Anderson, *Scottish Nation*); Peterkin, *Records*, p. 571; Baillie, *Letters*, vol. 3, p. 49 [Hewison, vol. 1, pp. 445–446].

[56] David Stevenson, "Church and Society under the Covenanters," *Scotia: American-Canadian Journal of Scottish Studies* (Norfolk: Institute of Scottish Studies, 1977), vol. 1, no. 1 (April 1977): pp. 25–31.

[57] Hetherington, *Westminster Assembly*, pp. 309–311; Beveridge, *Short History*, p. 143.

[58] Ronald Hutton, *Charles the Second King of England, Scotland, and Ireland* (Oxford: Clarendon Press, 1989), p. 37 (hereafter cited as Hutton).

[59] McCrie, *Vindication*, p. 271.

[60] George Gillespie, "The Testimony of Mr. George Gillespie Against Associations and Compliance with Malignant Enemies of the Truth and Godliness," printed in *The Works of Mr. George Gillespie*, ed. W. M. Hetherington (Edinburgh: Robert Ogle and Oliver and Boyd, 1846), vol. 2, p. 2 (hereafter cited as Gillespie, *Works*).

61 Thomas Hobbes, *Leviathan, or the Matter, Forme, & Power of a Common-Wealth, Ecclesiasticall and Civill* (London: Andrew Cooke, 1651), chapters 21, 27, 29, 42 and 18.
62 Oliver Cromwell to Scottish General Assembly, printed in Thomas Carlyle, *Oliver Cromwell's Letters and Speeches: With Elucidations* (London: Chapman and Hall, 1845), Letter 88, vol. 2, p. 20.
63 Alexander Smellie, *Men of the Covenant* (London: The Banner of Truth Trust, 1975), pp. 27–28 (hereafter cited as Smellie).
64 McCrie, *Scottish Church,* p. 236.
65 Sir James Turner, *Memoirs,* extracts from J. G. Fyfe, *Scottish Diaries and Memoirs, 1550–1747* (Stirling: Eneas Mackay, 1928), pp. 219–220.
66 "The Remonstrance of the Presbytery of Sterling Against The Present Conjunction with the Malignant Party to the Commission of the Kirk at St. Johnston" (Edinburgh: Evan Tyler, 1651), pp. 4–8.
67 McCrie, *Scottish Church,* p. 238; Vos, *Covenanters,* pp. 56–59.
68 S. A. Burrell, *The Apocalyptic Vision of the Early Covenanters,* The Scottish Historical Review, vol. 43, no. 135 (April 1964).
69 A Reply To the late Printed Answer Given to the Letter, Directed by the Protestors to their Brethren, Who are for carrying on of the Public Resolutions, and for the Authority of the late Pretended Assembly" (printed in 1653), pp. 36–38, 61. The Protestors defend themselves by pointing out that elders had been moderators in previous assemblies. This exchange conveys the Resolutioner's prelatical leanings.
70 James Durham, *The Dying Man's Testament to the Church of Scotland; or, A Treatise concerning Scandal* (Edinburgh: Christopher Higgins, 1659), p. 311 (hereafter cited as Durham, *Scandal*).
71 Kirkton, pp. 63–64.
72 Hewison, vol. 2, p. 57.
73 W. M. Hetherington, *History of the Church of Scotland from the Introduction of Christianity to the Period of Disruption, May 18, 1842,* 2 vols. (Edinburgh: John Johnstone, 1848), vol. 1, p. 399 (hereafter cited as Hetherington, *History*); Green, *Short History,* pp. 604–608; Roger Pepys, cited by Green, *Short History,* p. 620.
74 Hutton, p. 149; King Charles I, quoted in Hewison, vol. 2, p. 70; Hutton, p. 166.

75 David Laing, *Memoir of the Life and Writings of Robert Baillie,* printed in supplement to Baillie, *Letters,* vol. 1, p. lxxii.
76 McCrie, *Scottish Church,* p. 255; Robert Wodrow, *The History of the Sufferings of the Church of Scotland from the Restoration to the Revolution,* 4 vols. (Glasgow: Blackie & Son, 1836), vol. 1, p. 93 (hereafter cited as Wodrow, *History*); Kirkton, pp. 74–93. Kirkton provides an excellent step by step description of the demise of the covenanted laws of Scotland.
77 McCrie, *Scottish Church,* pp. 256, 258.
78 Jock Purves, *Fair Sunshine* (Edinburgh: The Banner of Truth Trust, 1990), p. 18 (hereafter cited as Purves).
79 Stewart, *Naphtali,* pp. 203–204; Hewison, vol. 2, p. 90.
80 Hewison, p. 262; Kirkton, p. 134; McCrie, *Scottish Church,* p. 266.
81 Thomas Hobbes, *Behemoth: The History of the Causes of the Civil Wars of England,* ed. William Molesworth (reprint, New York: Burt Franklin, 1969), p. 30 (hereafter cited as Hobbes, *Behemoth*).
82 Hetherington, *Westminster Assembly,* pp. 312–319; Green, *Short History,* p. 622.
83 Kuiper, *The Church in History,* p. 244; Leyburn, *Scotch-Irish,* p. 34; Sir Walter Scot, introduction to *The Legend of Montrose* (Boston, 1923).
84 Nisbet, *Private Life,* p. 125.
85 John Nisbet, "His Last and Dying Testimony," (hereafter cited as John Nisbet, "Dying Testimony"), printed in James Nisbet, *True Relation,* p. 17.
86 James Nisbet, *True Relation,* p. 4.

Chapter 3
The Burning Bush

1 Alexander Shields, *A Hind Let Loose* (Glasgow: William Paton, 1797), p. 129 (hereafter cited as Shields, *Hind*); Kirkton, p. 64; Vos, *Covenanters,* p. 74.
2 Bishop Gilbert Burnet, *Gilbert Burnet's History Of His Own Time, From the Restoration of Charles II to the Conclusion of the Treaty of Peace at Utrecht, in the Reign of Queen Anne* (London: printed for T. Davies, 1766), vol. 1, pp. 217, 221 (hereafter cited as Burnet, *History*).
3 Crichton, *Memoirs of Blackader,* p. 105.
4 Andrew Crichton, *Memoirs of Rev. John Blackader* (Edinburgh, 1823), pp. 97–104

(hereafter cited as Crichton, *Memoirs of Blackader*).

[5] *Scottish Psalter*, Psalm 27:5.

[6] Thomas Gillespie, "Peden's Farewell Sermon," printed in John Wilson, *Wilson's Tales of the Borders and of Scotland: Historical, Traditionary, and Imaginative*, revised by Alexander Leighton (London: Walter Scott, 1889), pp. 114–122.

[7] Shields, *Hind*, p. 124; Alexander Witherspoon, ed., *The College Survey of English Literature* (New York: Harcourt, Brace, 1951), p. 303.

[8] Nisbet, *Private Life*, pp. 12–17; McCrie, *Scottish Church*, pp. 277–280; Hewison, vol. 2, pp. 177–178; Defoe, *Memoirs*, p. 208.

[9] Hutton, p. 247; Hetherington, *History* (1857 Edition), p. 408.

[10] Nisbet, *Private Life*, pp. 12–17; McCrie, *Scottish Church*, pp. 277–280.

[11] Hutton, pp. 201, 196, 214–225.

[12] Hobbes, *Behemoth*, p. 128.

[13] Crichton, *Memoirs of Blackader*, pp. 147–148; James Nisbet, *True Relation*, p. 4.

[14] Crichton, *Memoirs of Blackader*, pp. 130–134.

[15] Crichton, *Memoirs of Blackader*, p. 149.

[16] Crichton, *Memoirs of Blackader*, p. 180.

[17] John Owen cited in Howie, *Worthies*, pp. 327, 328.

[18] Hewison, vol. 2, p. 184; Howie, *Worthies*, pp. 331–332; McCrie, *Scottish Church*, pp. 280–281.

[19] Howie, *Worthies*, p. 262; Burnet, *History*, vol. 1, p. 391; Anderson, *Scottish Nation*, vol. 3, p. 256; Burnet, *History*, vol. 1, p. 391.

[20] Kirkton, pp. 218, 282–283.

[21] Hugh McKail, quote from last public sermon on Canticle 1:7 printed in Stewart, *Naphtali*, p. 364; Hewison, vol. 2, p. 180; Wodrow, *History*, vol. 3, p. 232.

[22] Sir James Stewart, *Jus Poluli Vindcatum* (London, 1669), pp. 10–13, 62–67 (hereafter cited as Stewart, *Jus Poluli Vindicatum*).

[23] Robert Lewis Stevenson, *The Pentland Rising* (reprint, Heron Books:1969), pp. 455–456; James Nisbet, *True Relation*, pp. 4–5.

[24] Nisbet, *Private Life*, pp. 41–45.

[25] Smellie, p. 276.

[26] Stewart, *Naphtali*, pp. 168–169, 274–280.

[27] Stewart, *Naphtali*, p. 282.

[28] Stewart, *Naphtali*, pp. 283–286; Hewison, II, p. 208; Purves, p. 33.

[29] *Scottish Psalter*, Psalm 31:1–5.

[30] Hewison, vol. 2, pp. 213–214.

[31] Hewison, vol. 2, pp. 230–235; Shields, *Hind*, pp. 146, 147.

[32] Crichton, *Memoirs of Blackader*, pp. 198–206.

[33] Ailesbury's Memoirs (Roxburgh Club, 1890), vol. 1, pp. 14, 18, cited in Hewison, vol. 2, pp. 216, 227; Charles II, cited in Hutton, p. 247; Hewison, vol. 2, p. 217.

[34] McCrie, *Scottish Church*, pp. 301–303; Hewison, vol. 2, pp. 225–227.

[35] Quote from Hutton, p. 267; McCrie, *Scottish Church*, pp. 304–305; Hewison, vol. 2, pp. 222, 231–232.

[36] Antonia Fraiser, *Royal Charles: Charles II and the Restoration* (New York: Alfred Knopf, a Division of Random House, 1980), pp. 270, 275.

[37] Burnet, *History*, vol. 1, p. 410.

[38] Hewison, vol. 2, pp. 235–236.

[39] Shields, *Hind*, pp. 151–152.

[40] Defoe, *Memoirs*, p. 219.

[41] Defoe, *Memoirs*, pp. 220–221; Wodrow, *History*, vol. 2, pp. 409–411; Shields, *Hind*, p. 150.

[42] Smellie, p. 278.

[43] Wodrow, *History*, vol. 3, p. 50.

[44] Wodrow, *History*, vol. 3, pp. 66–67.

[45] Nisbet, *Private Life*, pp. 45–49.

[46] Nisbet, *Private Life*, pp. 49–52.

Chapter 4
Drumclog and Bothwell Bridge

[1] Alexis De Tocqueville, *Democracy in America* (Anchor Books: New York, 1969), p. 258 (hereafter cited as Tocqueville).

[2] Finlay, *The Lowlands*, p. 24.

[3] Nisbet, *Private Life*, pp. 52–53.

[4] John Howie, introduction to Appendix VI, *Biographia Scoticana: or a Brief Historical Account of the Most Eminent Scots Worthies* (Glasgow: W. R. McPhun, 1827), p. 622 (hereafter cited as Howie, *Worthies* (1827 edition)). The compilers of the Appendix to *Scots Worthies* considered this account a "description of the facts, all of which might and many of which we know did, take place on the occasions."

[5] Thomas Brownlee, reprinted in Howie, *Worthies (1827 Edition)*, Appendix VI, pp. 622–628.

[6] Howie, *Worthies*, pp. 506–507.

[7] John Nisbet, from an unpublished manuscript cited by Howie, *Worthies*, pp. 506–507; Wodrow, *History*, vol. 3, p. 69.

[8] Nisbet, *Private Life*, pp. 124–125.

9 Kirkton, pp. 377–378.

10 Wodrow, *History*, vol. 3, pp. 70–71. Wodrow speaks of only soldiers defending Glasgow; other accounts contend that citizens also participated.

11 Wodrow, *History*, vol. 3, p. 91.

12 Wodrow, *History*, vol. 3, pp. 90–92.

13 McCrie, *Scottish Church*, p. 329.

14 Wodrow, *History*, vol. 3, pp. 91–93.

15 Wodrow, *History*, vol. 3, pp. 94–95.

16 Howie, *Worthies*, p. 598.

17 Lt. Col. John Blackader, *Memoirs*, p. 214, cited by Hewison, vol. 2, p. 292.

18 McCrie, *Scottish Church*, pp. 338–340.

19 Howie, *Worthies*, p. 411.

20 McCrie, *Scottish Church*, p. 332.

21 John Blackader cited in Andrew Crichton, *Memoirs of Blackader* (Second edition), p. 220; John Blackader quoted by T. Ratcliffe Barnett, *The Story of the Covenant: Fifty years of Fighting Faith* (London: Oliver and Boyd, 1928), p. 199.

22 Crichton, *Memoirs of Blackader*, p. 211.

23 Crichton, *Memoirs of Blackader*, p. 218.

24 John Nisbet, "Dying Testimony," p. 19.

25 Wodrow, *History*, vol. 3, p. 199.

26 Wodrow, *History*, vol. 3, p. 199.

27 Wodrow, *History*, vol. 3, pp. 103–105.

28 Wodrow, *History*, vol. 3, pp. 106–107.

29 Thomas Brownlee, reprinted in Howie, *Worthies (1827 Edition)*, Appendix VI, pp. 629–633.

30 Wodrow, *History*, vol. 3, pp. 110–111.

Chapter 5
Truth Preservation

1 Alexander Shields, sermon printed in *Sermons delivered in Times of Persecution in Scotland*, ed. by James Kerr (Edinburgh: Johnstone, Hunter, & Company, 1880), p. 605 (hereafter cited as Kerr, *Sermons*).

2 Patrick Walker, *Six Saints of the Covenant*, 2 vols. (London: Hodder and Strouguton, 1901), vol. 2, p. 131 (hereafter cited as Walker, *Six Saints*); Wodrow, *History*, vol. 3, p. 123.

3 The Indemnity was issued on July 27, 1678. Wodrow, *History*, vol. 3, pp. 118–119; Patrick Walker, *Biographia Presbyteriana* (Edinburgh: D. Speare and J. Stevenson, 1827), vol. i, p. 47 (hereafter cited as Walker, *Biographia*); Nisbet, *Private Life*, pp. 28–29.

4 Howie, *Worthies*, p. 466.

5 Hewison, vol. 2, p. 319.

6 Nisbet, *Private Life*, pp. 53–58.

7 Nisbet, *Private Life*, pp. 29–30.

8 Barr, p. 55; Hewison, vol. 2, p. 331; Howie, *Worthies*, p. 429.

9 John H. Thomson, *A Cloud of Witnesses* (reprint, Harrisonburg, Virginia: Springle Publications, 1989), pp. 144, 138 (hereafter cited as Thomson, *Cloud*).

10 Thomson, *Cloud*, pp. 124–125; Hewison, vol. 2, p. 346.

11 *Scottish Psalter*, Psalm 74:7–12.

12 Ashley, *James II*, pp. 130–145; Hutton, *Charles the Second*, pp. 382-414; Hetherington, *Westminster Assembly*, p. 405.

13 Thomson, *Cloud*, p. 306.

14 Nisbet, *Private Life*, pp. 60–63.

15 Nisbet, *Private Life*, pp. 63–68.

16 Nisbet, *Private Life*, pp. 68–69.

17 Nisbet, *Private Life*, pp. 58–60.

18 Walker, *Six Saints*, vol. 1, pp. 52–53; Wodrow, *History*, vol. 3, p. 356.

19 Walker, *Six Saints*, vol. 1, p. 54; Thomson, *Cloud*, p. 10.

20 William Anderson, A sermon entitled *The Voice of Renwick* (London, 1882), p. 8.

21 Hewison, vol. 2, pp. 356–357; Howie, *Worthies*, pp. 471–472, 475.

22 Michael Shields, *Faithful Contendings Displayed*, ed. by John F. Howie (Glasgow, 1780), p. 5 (hereafter cited as Shields, *Faithful Contendings*) [ESTC Reel 5187].

23 Walker, *Six Saints*, vol. 1, pp. 84–93.

24 John Howie, preface to Shields, *Faithful Contendings*, pp. xv–xviii; McCrie, *Scottish Church*, p. 184.

25 John Howie, preface to Shields, *Faithful Contendings*, p. xi; Shields, *Faithful Contendings*, p. 13.

26 Thomson, *Cloud*, p. 239; Thomas Houston, *The Life of James Renwick* (Photocopy edition reprinted by Still Waters Revival Books of introduction to *The Letters of Renwick* (Paisley: Gardner, 1865), p. 36 (hereafter cited as Houston, *Renwick*).

27 Shields, *Faithful Contendings*, pp. 18–19; Wodrow, *History*, vol. 3, p. 51.

28 Richard Greaves, "The Rye House Plotting, Nonconformist Clergy, and Calvin's Resistance Theory," printed in Graham, *Later Calvinism*, pp. 517–518 (hereafter cited as Rye House).

29 Shields, *Faithful Contendings*, pp. 21, 31–32.

30 Shields, *Faithful Contendings*, p. 42.

[31] Thomson, *Cloud*, p. 303; Hewison, vol. 2, pp. 367–368.

[32] Ian B. Cowan, *The Scottish Covenanters 1660–1688* (London: Victor Gollancz Ltd., 1976), p. 112 (hereafter cited as Cowan, *Scottish Covenanters*).

[33] Accounts by historians favorable to the Covenanters likely exaggerate Claverhouse's lawlessness. The evidence suggests Claverhouse executed only those that he was legally empowered to execute based on the laws at the time, but those he turned over for trial typically ended up dead. The net result was the same. Defoe, *Memoirs*, pp. 238–239; Charles Terry, *John Graham of Claverhouse – Viscount of Dundee 1648–1689* (London: Archibald Constanble and Company Limited, 1905), pp. 210–211 (hereafter cited as Terry, *Claverhouse*).

[34] Thomson, *Cloud*, pp. 231, 236; Hewison, vol. 2, pp. 382, 385.

[35] Nisbet, *Private Life*, pp. 69–74.

[36] Nisbet, *Private Life*, pp. 74–79.

[37] Hewison, vol. 2, pp. 391, 408.

[38] Wodrow, *History*, vol. 3, p. 453.

[39] Thomson, *Cloud*, pp. 290–291.

[40] Thomson, *Cloud*, p. 289.

[41] Thomson, *Cloud*, p. 590.

[42] Thomson, *Cloud*, p. 317.

[43] Nisbet, *Private Life*, p. 83.

[44] Nisbet, *Private Life*, pp. 79–82.

[45] James Renwick to Loudoun, September 1683, printed in Nisbet, *Private Life*.

[46] Shields, *Faithful Contendings*, p. 100–101.

[47] Smellie, p. 399.

[48] Nisbet, *Private Life*, pp. 83–90.

[49] Nisbet, *Private Life*, pp. 90–91.

[50] Nisbet, *Private Life*, pp. 91–94.

[51] Wodrow, *History*, vol. 4, p. 6.

[52] Scott, *Fasti*, vol. 2, p. 184; Robert Law, *Memorials; or The Memorable Things That fell Out Within This Island of Britian from 1638 to 1684* (Edinburgh: Archibald Constable and Co., 1819), p. 260; Thomson, *Cloud*, pp. 289–298.

[53] Hewison, vol. 2, p. 423; Spottiswood, p. 61.

[54] Hewison vol. 2, p. 420; Wodrow, *History*, iv, pp. 231–279.

[55] Rye House, pp. 505–524; Thomas Sprat, *A True Account of the Horrid Conspiracy Against the Late King, His Present Majesty, and the Government* (Thomas Newcomb, 1685), pp. 107–113, 20–76, 81–82 (hereafter cited as Sprat, *Horrid Conspiracy*); John Owen, *A Brief and Impartial*

Account of the Nature of the Protestant Religion (London, 1682), p. 12.

[56] Howie, *Worthies* (1827 Edition), Supplement, p. 549; Hewison, vol. 2, pp. 421–422.

[57] Hewison, vol. 2, p. 422; Wodrow, *History*, vol. 4, pp. 65–66; Thomson, *Cloud*, pp. 365, 371, 569.

[58] William Wilberforce, *Real Christianity*, ed. James Houston (Portland: Multnomah Press, 1982), pp. 98–99 (hereafter cited as Wilberforce).

[59] Smellie, p. 398; Wodrow, *History*, vol. iv, p. 65; Hewison, vol. 2, pp. 423–424, Howie, *Worthies*, pp. 490–493.

[60] Shields, *Faithful Contendings*, pp. 143–144.

[61] McCrie, *Vindication*, pp. 160–161.

[62] Howie, *Worthies (1827 Edition)*, Supplement; Hewison, vol. 2, p. 442.

[63] Nisbet, *Private Life*, pp. 94–100.

Chapter 6
Killing Times

[1] Hewison, vol. 2, p. 453.

[2] Nisbet, *Private Life*, pp. 101–102.

[3] Scott, *Fasti*, vol. 5, p. 239.

[4] Shields, preface of the *Hind*, p. v; Gen. 30:7; 49:21; Deut. 33:23; Josh. 19:32–39.

[5] Alexander Shields, *A True and Faithful Relation of the Suffering of the Reverend and Learned Mr. Alexander Shields, Minister of the Gospel* (1715), pp. 45–65 (hereafter cited as Shields, *Memoirs*).

[6] Shields, *Memoirs*, pp. 80, 79, 90, 135.

[7] Shields, *Memoirs*, p. 71.

[8] Shields, *Memoirs*, p. 140.

[9] Shields, *Faithful Contendings*, pp. 282–285.

[10] Barr, p. 163; *Scottish Psalter*, Ps. 27:5–6.

[11] John Brown was executed on May 1, 1685. Claverhouse turned the younger Brown over to the military authority at Mauchline to do with as he pleased. On May 6 the younger Brown was executed, likely after a trial (in name only) by a jury consisting of soldiers. Terry, *Claverhouse*, pp. 205–207; Mark Napier, *Memorials and Letters Illustrative of the Life and Times of John Graham of Claverhouse, Viscount Dundee* 3 vols. (Edinburgh: Thomas G. Stevenson, 1842), vol. 2, pp. 456–459 (hereafter cited as Napier, *Claverhouse*).

[12] Hewison, vol. 2, pp. 476–477.

[13] Shields, *Faithful Contendings*, p. 166.

[14] Shields, *Faithful Contendings*, pp. 168–182.

15 Shields, *Faithful Contendings*, p. 169.

16 Nisbet, *Private Life*, pp. 114–115.

17 Nisbet, *Private Life*, pp. 100–101.

18 Hewison, vol. 2, p. 471.

19 Nisbet, *Private Life*, pp. 102–110.

20 Nisbet, *Private Life*, pp. 110–112.

21 Nisbet, *Private Life*, pp. 113–114.

22 Nisbet, *Private Life*, pp. 115–116.

23 Nisbet, *Private Life*, pp. 116–119.

24 Nisbet, *Private Life*, pp. 127–128.

25 *Scottish Psalter* (Psalm text added).

26 Nisbet, *Private Life*, pp. 119–120.

27 Nisbet, *Private Life*, pp. 128–131.

28 Barr, p. 117; Howie, *Worthies*, p. 498; Tweedie, vol. 2, pp. 384–395; Howie, *Worthies (1827 Edition)*, p. 471 n.

29 Barr, p. 117, Howie, *Worthies*, p. 498; Tweedie, vol. 2, pp. 384–395; Howie, *Worthies (1827 Edition)*, p. 470 n.

30 Howie, *Worthies*, pp. 499–500.

31 Nisbet, *Private Life*, pp. 121–124.

32 Howie, *Worthies*, pp. 500–501.

33 Howie, *Worthies*, pp. 500–503.

34 John Nisbet, "Dying Testimony," pp. 12–24.

35 John Nisbet, "Dying Testimony," pp. 23–24.

36 Tweedie, vol. 2, pp. 389–390.

37 James Nisbet, *True Relation*, p. 24.

38 *Scottish Psalter* (Verses not listed in Nisbet, *Private Life*), Ps. 34:1–6.

39 James Nisbet, *True Relation*, p. 24.

40 Wodrow, *History*, vol. 4, p. 235.

41 Nisbet, *Private Life*, pp. 131–134.

42 Nisbet, *Private Life*, pp. 141–143.

43 Nisbet, *Private Life*, pp. 134–136.

44 Nisbet, *Private Life*, pp. 136–143.

Chapter 7
Nowhere to Look but Up

1 Bainton, p. 189.

2 Nisbet, *Private Life*, pp. 143–152.

3 Charles Thomson, *Notices of the Martyrs and Confessors of Lesmahagow* (Glasgow: W. Lang, 1832), p. 11.

4 Nisbet, *Private Life*, pp. 152–154.

5 Shields, *Faithful Contendings*, pp. 244–245.

6 Shields, *Faithful Contendings*, pp. 242–243, 265.

7 Shields, *Faithful Contendings*, p. 243; McCrie, *Vindication*, p. 164.

8 Hewison, vol. 2, p. 500; Walker, *Six Saints*, vol. 1, p. 292.

9 Nisbet, *Private Life*, pp. 179–184.

10 Nisbet, *Private Life*, pp. 154–179. In his meditations, he attributes the works of John Brown of Wramphray (1610–1679) for convincing him of the importance of trials. Brown was banished at the same time as Nevay.

11 Andrew Gray, *The Works of Andrew Gray* (Ligonier, Pennsylvania: Soli Deo Gloria Publications, 1992) (hereafter cited as Gray, *Works*).

12 Nisbet, *Private Life*, pp. 165–168.

13 Nisbet, *Private Life*, pp. 168–171.

14 Nisbet, *Private Life*, pp. 171–172.

15 Nisbet, *Private Life*, pp. 172–176.

16 Nisbet, *Private Life*, pp. 176–179.

17 Nisbet, *Private Life*, pp. 152–179.

18 Hewison, vol. 2, pp. 503–504; Shields, *Faithful Contendings*, pp. 311–316; Hewison, vol. 2, p. 506.

19 Nisbet, *Private Life*, pp. 186–196. James listed these five points under two heads (1–3 & 4–5).

20 Houston, *Renwick*, p. 38.

21 Nisbet, *Private Life*, pp. 196–198.

22 Shields, *Faithful Contendings*, p. 322.

23 Howie, *Worthies*, pp. 539–549.

24 Nisbet, *Private Life*, pp. 198–202.

25 Nisbet, *Private Life*, pp. 224–225.

26 Nisbet, *Private Life*, pp. 225–228.

27 Shields, *Faithful Contendings*, p. 343; Wodrow, *History*, vol. 4, p. 457.

28 Nisbet, *Private Life*, pp. 224, 228–230.

Chapter 8
Revolution Settlement

1 Shields, *Faithful Contendings*, pp. 366–367.

2 Stephen Webb, *Lord Churchill's Coup* (New York: Alfred A. Knopf, Inc., 1995), p. 125 (hereafter cited as Webb).

3 Nisbet, *Private Life*, pp. 230–231.

4 Shields, *Faithful Contendings*, p. 376.

5 Shields, *Faithful Contendings*, pp. 338–388.

6 Shields, *Faithful Contendings*, p. 392.

7 Hetherington, *History*, vol. 2, p. 183.

8 Hewison, vol. 2, p. 524; McCrie, *Scottish Church*, p. 400.

9 Shields, *Faithful Contendings*, pp. 403–404.

10 Shields, *Faithful Contendings*, p. 419; McCrie, *Scottish Church*, p. 401.

11 Fred Lieburg, *From Pure Church to Pious Culture: the Further Reformation in the Seventeenth-Century*

Dutch Republic, within Graham, *Later Calvinism*, pp. 409–429 (hereafter cited as Lieburg).

[12] Defoe, *Memoirs*, p. 327.

[13] Hewison, vol. 2, pp. 527–530; McCrie, *Scottish Church*, pp. 404–405.

[14] *Records of Parliament*, July 14, 1690, cited in Napier, *Claverhouse*, vol. 3, pp. 467–468; McCrie, *Scottish Church*, p. 406.

[15] Hewison, vol. 2, p. 531; Major R. Money Barnes, *The Uniforms and History of the Scottish Regiments* (London: Sphere Books Limited, 1972), p. 40 (hereafter cited as Barnes, *Regiments*); Preface to Nisbet, *Private Life*, p. vii; McCrie, *Scottish Church*, p. 400.

[16] Hewison, vol. 2, p. 531–532; McCrie, *Scottish Church*, pp. 408–409; McCrie, *Scottish Church*, p. 409; Barnes, *Regiments*, p. 40.

[17] Hewison, vol. 2, p. 532; Shields, *Faithful Contendings*, p. 419.

[18] Smellie, p. 504.

[19] Nisbet, *Private Life*, pp. 231–235.

[20] Shields, *Faithful Contendings*, p. 421.

[21] Shields, *Faithful Contendings*, p. 462.

[22] Walker, *Six Saints*, vol. 1, p. 147.

[23] Nisbet, *Private Life*, pp. 235–238.

[24] Nisbet, *Private Life*, pp. 238–240.

[25] Wodrow, preface to *History*, p. x; Wodrow, *Analecta*, vol. 3, p. 518; Thomas Law, *New Testament in Scots*, pp. xxii–xiv.

[26] Nisbet, *Private Life*, pp. 240–246.

[27] Howie, *Worthies*, p. 471.

[28] Howie, *Worthies*, pp. 597–598.

[29] Scott, *Fasti*, vol. 5, p. 239.

[30] Francis R. Hart, *The Disaster of Darien/ The Story of the Scots Settlement and the Causes of its Failure 1699–1701* (Boston and New York: Houghton Mifflin Company, 1929), p. 144 (hereafter cited as Hart, *Darien*); John Prebble, *The Darien Disaster, A Scots Colony in the New World 1698–1700* (New York: Holt, Rinehart and Winston, 1969), p. 238 (hereafter cited as Prebble, *Darien*); Hart, *Darien*, pp. 135–136.

[31] Wodrow, *History*, vol. 3, p. 233; Prebble, *Darien*, pp. 303; Hart, *Darien*, pp. 144–145.

[32] Wodrow, *History*, vol. 3, p. 232.

[33] Wodrow, *History*, vol. 3, p. 335.

[34] Wodrow, *History*, vol. 3, pp. 51, 52.

[35] Wodrow, *History*, vol. 3, p. 68.

[36] Houston, *Renwick*, pp. 59–62; James Dodd, *The Fifty Year's Struggle of the Scottish Covenanters 1638-1688* (London: Houlston and Sons, 1868), p. 376.

[37] Houston, *Renwick*, pp. 59–62.

Chapter 9
The Ongoing Struggle

[1] Nevay, *The Nature, Properties, Blessing, and Saving Graces, of the Covenant of Grace* (Glasgow, 1748), p. 265 (hereafter cited as Nevay).

[2] John Miller, *The Glorious Revolution* (London and New York: Longman, 1983), p. 65.

[3] Richard Ashcraft, *Latitudinarianism and Toleration: Historical Myth Versus Political History*, published in book by Richard Kroll, *Philosophy, Science, and Religion in England 1640–1700* (Cambridge: Cambridge University Press, 1992), p. 153.

[4] James H. Tully, *John Locke: A Letter Concerning Toleration* (Indianapolis: Hackett, 1983), p. 44, reprinted in J. Wayne Baker, *Church, State, and Toleration: John Locke and Calvin's Heirs in England, 1644–1689*, within Graham, *Later Calvinism*, p. 441. The footnote is summarized from Baker, *Church, State, and Toleration*, within Graham, *Later Calvinism*, pp. 525–543.

[5] John Nevay to the Congregation of Loudoun, Oct. 22, 1669, printed in Nevay, p. 471.

[6] Iain H. Murray, *The Puritan Hope: Revival and the Interpretation of Prophesy* (Edinburgh: The Banner of Truth Trust, 1971), p. 96 (hereafter cited as Murray, *Puritan Hope*).

[7] James Wood, *The Doctrinal Differences which have agitated and Divided the Presbyterian Church: or Old and New Theology* (Philadelphia: Presbyterian Board of Publications, 1853), p. 47 (hereafter cited as Wood, *Doctrinal Differences*).

[8] Smith, *Westminster Assembly*, p. 244.

[9] Samuel Smith, "The Westminster Symbols Considered in Relation to Current Popular Theology and the Needs of the Future," published in J. Henry Smith, *Memorial Volume of the Westminster Assembly, 1647–1897* (Richmond: The Presbyterian Committee of Publications, 1897), pp. 244–247 (hereafter cited as Smith, *Westminster Assembly*).

[10] Murray, *Puritan Hope*, p. 210.

[11] Smith, *Westminster Assembly*, pp. 233, 238.

[12] Pierre du Moulin, cited by Brian Armstrong, *Calvinism and the Amyraut Heresy* (Madison, Milwaukee, and London: The University of Wisconsin Press, 1969), pp. 85–89.

[13] John Murray, "Atonement and the Free Offer of the Gospel," *The Collected Writings of John*

Murray (Edinburgh: The Banner of Truth Trust, 1976), pp. 59–85.

[14] Charles Spurgeon, "Immeasurable Love," *Metropolitan Tabernacle Pulpit* (London: The Banner of Truth Trust, 1971), vol. 31, pp. 391–395.

[15] Robert M'Cheyne, *Robert Murray M'Cheyne: Memoir and Remains*, ed. Andrew Bonar (London: The Banner of Truth Trust, 1966), p. 369 (hereafter cited as M'Cheyne).

[16] John Calvin, *Commentary on the Catholic Epistles*, translated by Rev. John Owen (Grand Rapids: Baker House Books, 1979), 1 John 4:10, pp. 240–241.

[17] John Calvin, *Concerning the Eternal Predestination of God*, translated by J. K. S. Reid (London: James Clarke & Co., 1961), p. 56 (hereafter cited as Calvin, *Predestination*). Use fee paid.

[18] Samuel Rutherford to [Brethren in] Aberdeen, 1661, *Letters of Samuel Rutherford*, ed. Andrew Bonar (Edinburgh: Oliphant Anderson & Ferrier, 1904), Letter no, 364, p. 706.

[19] John Calvin, *Commentaries on the Epistles to Timothy, Titus, and Philemon*, translated by Rev. William Pringle (Grand Rapids: Baker House Books, 1979), 1 Tim. 2:4, pp. 54–55.

[20] John Calvin, *Commentaries on the Epistle of Paul to the Hebrews*, trans. by John Owen (Grand Rapids: Baker Book House, 1979), comments on Heb. 3:9, pp. 419–420.

[21] John Calvin, *Commentary on the Book of the Prophet Isaiah*, trans. by William Pringle (Grand Rapids: Baker Book House, 1979), comments on Isa. 6:10, vol. 1, p. 217.

[22] Calvin, *Predestination*, pp. 76–78, 105–108. Verses on election are from pp. 68–79.

[23] Calvin, *Predestination*, pp. 105–108.

[24] Calvin, *Predestination*, pp. 122–124.

[25] Calvin, *Predestination*, pp. 93, 103–105.

[26] Calvin, *Predestination*, pp. 92–96.

[27] Calvin, *Predestination*, pp. 100–101.

[28] Calvin, *Predestination*, p. 120.

[29] Calvin, *Predestination*, pp. 81–86.

[30] Wood, *Doctrinal Differences*, pp. 204, 205.

[31] Robert Shaw, *The Reformed Faith: An Exposition of the Confession of Faith of the Westminster Assembly of Divines* (Inverness: Christian Focus Publications, 1973), comments on chapter xxi, sec. 1 and 2 (hereafter cited as Shaw, *Exposition of the Confession*).

[32] John Murray, *Redemption Accomplished and Applied* (Grand Rapids: Wm. B. Eerdmans Publishing Co., 1978), pp. 69–70.

[33] William Young, Preface to Nevay, pp. ix–xi.

[34] Calvin, *Predestination*, p. 130.

[35] Calvin, *Predestination*, pp. 126–127.

[36] Charles Hodge, *A Commentary on 1&2 Corinthians* (1857; reprint, Edinburgh: The Banner of Truth Trust, 1994), 2. Cor. 13:5, p. 681; Robert Dabney, *Discussions: Evangelical and Theological* (reprint, Edinburgh: The Banner of Truth Trust, 1967), vol. 1, pp. 215–217 (hereafter cited as Dabney, *Discussions*). Davidson's (an early Scottish Reformer) Catechism defines faith as a hearty assurance…"

[37] John Calvin, *The Institutes of the Christian Religion*, translated by Henry Beveridge (Grand Rapids: Wm. B. Eerdmans Publishing Company, 1997), sec. iii.2.14–19, pp. 482–486 (hereafter cited as Calvin, *Institutes*).

[38] *The Confession of Faith*, printed in *Westminster Standards*, chapter xviii.3 (hereafter cited as *WCOF*).

[39] John Knox, preface to *The Works of John Knox*, ed. David Laing (Edinburgh: James Thin, 1895 reprinted in New York: AMS Press, Inc. 1966), vol. 5, p. 26.

[40] *The Shorter Catechism*, printed in *Westminster Standards*, Question 86; Dabney, *Discussions*, p. 185.

[41] *WCOF*, chapter xviii.2, 4; Dabney, *Discussions*, p. 194.

[42] George Hutchinson, *The History Behind the Reformed Presbyterian Church, Evangelical Synod* (Cherry Hill, New Jersey: Mack Publishing Company, 1974), p. 213; Robert Adams, *The Scottish Church 1500-1920: A Graphic Chart* (Edinburgh: T & T Clark, 1923), foldout.

[43] James Reid, *Kirk and Nation: The Story of the Reformed Churches of Scotland* (London: Skeffington, 1960), p. 107.

[44] Shaw, *Exposition of the Confession*, p. 270.

[45] Ian Donnachiie and George Hewitt, *A Companion to Scottish History: From the Restoration to the Present* (New York: Facts on File, 1989), p. 195.

[46] Thomas Halyburton, *The Works of the Rev. Thomas Halyburton* (London, Thomas Tegg & Son, 1835), p. 798.

[47] Herbert S. Skeats and Charles S. Miall, *History of the Free Churches of England, 1688–1891* (London: Alexander & Shepherd, 1891), p. 250 (hereafter cited as Skeats, *Free Churches*).

[48] Jeremy Goring et al., *The English Presbyterians* (London: George Allen & Unwin Ltd., 1968), pp. 20, 103–104, 120, 135, 137, 180.

[49] Skeats, *Free Churches,* pp. 250, 248.

[50] Fred Hood, *Reformed America: The Middle and Southern States, 1783-1837* (University of Alabama: University of Alabama Press, 1980), pp. 29–45.

[51] Wilberforce, pp. 103, 109.

[52] James Macleod, *Scottish Theology* (Edinburgh: The Banner of Truth Trust, 1974), p. 157.

[53] Hugh Miller, *The Headship of Christ and the Rights of Christian People* (Edinburgh: William P. Nimmo, 1873), p. 45 (hereafter cited as Hugh Miller).

[54] John Buchan and George A. Smith, *The Kirk in Scotland 1560-1929* (Edinburgh: T. and H. Constable Ltd., 1930), pp. 53–63 (hereafter cited as Buchan and Smith, *The Kirk of Scotland*).

[55] Hugh Miller, p. 400.

[56] J. H. S. Burleigh, *A Church History of Scotland* (London: Oxford University Press, 1960), pp. 295–307 (hereafter cited as Burleigh, *Church History*).

[57] Buchan and Smith, *Kirk in Scotland,* pp. 77–79.

[58] R. A. Finlayson, "How Liberal Theology Infected Scotland," online 1997 <http://www. freechurch.org.finlay son.rtwl.hmtl>.

[59] Gordon Donaldson, *Scotland: Church and Nation Through Sixteen Centuries* (Naperville, Ill.: SCM Book Club, 1960), p. 100; Burleigh, *Church History,* pp. 364–399.

[60] Buchan and Smith, *Kirk in Scotland,* pp. 88–95; Ian Hamilton, *The Erosion of Calvinist Orthodoxy: Seceders and Subscription in Scottish Presbyterianism* (Edinburgh: Rutherford House Books, 1989), pp. 186–195 (hereafter cited as Hamilton, *Erosion*).

[61] Hamilton, *Erosion,* pp. 186–195.

[62] John Kennedy, *Hyper-Evangelism,* online 2000 <http://members.aol.com/RSISBELL/hyper1. html >.

[63] Charles H. Spurgeon, sermon preached on February 5, 1882, "A Home Question and a Right Answer," *The Metropolitan Tabernacle Pulpit: Sermons preached and revised in 1882* (London: The Banner of Truth Trust, 1971), vol. 28, pp. 110-112; Iain Murray, *The Forgotten Spurgeon* (1966; reprint, Edinburgh: The Banner of Truth Trust, 1998), pp. 166–190.

[64] Charles H. Spurgeon, sermon preached on October 16, 1887, "Behold the Lamb of God," *The Metropolitan Tabernacle Pulpit: Sermons preached and revised in 1887* (London: The Banner of Truth Trust, 1969), *Sermons,* vol. 33, p. 575; Iain Murray, *The Forgotten Spurgeon* (1966; reprint, Edinburgh: The Banner of Truth Trust, 1998), pp. 138–150.

[65] Charles H. Spurgeon, *An All Around Ministry* (1960), p. 373, cited by Iain Murray, *The Forgotten Spurgeon* (1966; reprint, Edinburgh: The Banner of Truth Trust, 1998), pp. 152–165.

[66] A. C. Cheyne, *The Transforming of the Kirk* (Edinburgh: The Saint Andrews Press, 1983). Note: The Declaratory Statement containing this clause was adopted in 1879.

[67] "The Church of Scotland: History and Structure," online 1997 <http://www.churchnet. uscm.ac.uk.cos.history.html>.

[68] George H. Morrison, *Memoirs of the Life, Time, and Writings of the Reverend and Learned Thomas Boston, A. M.* (Edinburgh and London: Oliphant Anderson & Ferrier), p. 225n. Cited in Vos, *Covenanters,* p. 162.

[69] *Act, Declaration, and Testimony, for the Whole of Our Covenanted Reformation, as Attained to, and Established in, Britain and Ireland; Particularly Betwixt the Years 1638 and 1649, Inclusive,* by the Reformed Presbytery (Philadelphia: Rue & Jones, 1876), p. 154.

[70] Matthew Hutchinson, *The Reformed Presbyterian Church in Scotland: Its Origin and History, 1680– 1876,* pp. 198–199.

[71] John C. Johnston, *Treasury of the Scottish Covenant* (Edinburgh: Andrew Elliot, 1887), pp. 171-177; Vos, *Covenanters,* p. 205; [Patrick Walker was a member of the Secession Church].

[72] Patrick Adair, A true Narrative of the Rise and Progress of the Presbyterian Church in Ireland (Belfast, 1966), pp. 103-105 cited in William Lyons Fisk, *The Scottish High Church Tradition in America* (Lanham, Maryland: University Press of America, Inc., 1995), p. 30 (hereafter cited as Fisk, *High Church Tradition*).

[73] Several sources including Patrick Walker cited by Fisk, *High Church Tradition,* p. 30.

[74] George M. Marsden, "Introduction: Reformed and American," (hereafter cited as Marsden) *Southern Reformed Theology,* ed. by David F. Wells (Grand Rapids: Baker House Books, 1989), p. 3; paraphrasing Nicholas Woltersorff, "The AACS in the CRC," *The Reformed Journal,* no. 24 (December 1974), pp. 9–16.

[75] Marsden, pp. 4–11.

[76] L. P. Bowman, *The Days of Makemie, or the Vine Planted A. D. 1680–1708* (Philadelphia, 1885), p. 415 (hereafter cited as Bowman) cited in Morton H. Smith, *Studies in Southern Presbyterian Theology* (Phillipsburg, New Jersey: Presbyterian and Reformed Publishing Company, 1962), p. 20 (hereafter cited as Smith, *Studies*).

[77] Marsden, p. 4.

[78] *Records of the Presbyterian Church in the United States of America: 1706–1788* (New York: Arno Press & The New York Times, 1964), pp. 94–95.

[79] Leonard J. Trinterud, *The Forming of an American Tradition, a re-examination of colonial Presbyterianism* (Philadelphia: The Westminster Press, 1949), p. 48 (hereafter cited as Trinterud, *American Tradition*).

[80] Smith, *Studies*, pp. 24–27.

[81] B. K. Kuiper, *The Church in History*, p. 345.

[82] Stephen Berk, *Calvinism versus Democracy* (Hamden, Conn.: Archon Books/The Shoe String Press, 1974), p. 58 (hereafter cited as Berk).

[83] William Sprague, *Annals of the American Pulpit* (New York, 1857), vol. 2, p. 38; Berk, p. 65.

[84] Robert Ellis Thompson, *A History of the Presbyterian Churches in the United States* (New York: The Christian Literature Co., 1895), p. 34.

[85] Berk, pp. 9–12.

[86] Marsden, pp. 4–5.

[87] Randall Balmer and John Fitzmier, *The Presbyterians* (Westport, Conn: Greenwood Press, 1993), p. 27 (hereafter cited as Balmer, *Presbyterians*).

[88] Ibid, pp. 30–32.

[89] Ibid, p. 33; Milton Coalter, *Gilbert Tennet, Son of Thunder* (New York: Greenwood Press, 1986), p. 120.

[90] Balmer, *Presbyterians*, p. 36.

[91] Trinterud, *American Tradition*, p. 193.

[92] Iain H. Murray, *Revival and Revivalism* (Edinburgh: The Banner of Truth Trust, 1994), p. 74 (hereafter cited as Murray, *Revival*).

[93] McFetridge, *Calvinism in History*, p. 152.

[94] Berk, pp. 15–17.

[95] B. K. Kuiper, *The Church in History*, p. 356.

[96] Morton H. Smith, "The Southern Tradition," *Southern Reformed Theology*, ed. by David F. Wells (Grand Rapids: Baker House Books, 1989), p. 19.

[97] Boettner, p. 382.

[98] Smith, *Studies*, p. 47.

[99] Berk, p. 65.

[100] James G. Leyburn, "Presbyterian Immigrants and the American Revolution," in *Journal of Presbyterian History*, ed. by James H. Smylie (Philadelphia: Presbyterian Historical Society, 1976), vol. 54, no. 1 (spring 1976): p. 29 (hereafter cited as Smylie, *Journal*).

[101] James L. McAllister, "Francis Alison and John Witherspoon: Political Philosophers and Revolutionaries," in Smylie, *Journal*, vol. 54- no. 1 (spring 1976): p. 43.

[102] John Witherspoon, quote reprinted in "Presbyterians and the American Revolution," in Smylie, *Journal*, vol. 52, no. 4 (winter 1974): p. 356.

[103] Quote from a 1770 commencement debate proposition supported by John Witherspoon, reprinted in "Presbyterians and the American Revolution," in Smylie, *Journal*, vol. 52, no. 4 (winter 1974): p. 357.

[104] John Witherspoon, cited by Paul Carlson, *Our Presbyterian Heritage* (Elgin, Il.: David C. Cook Publishing Co., 1973), p. 14.

[105] William Tennent III, "To the Ladies of South Carolina," in the *South Carolina Gazette and Country Journal*, 2 August 1774, p. 1, reprinted in "Presbyterians and the American Revolution," in Smylie, *Journal*, vol. 52, no. 4 (winter 1974): p. 374.

[106] J. R. Sizoo, quoted in Boettner, p. 384.

[107] William Tennent III, "Speech on Dissenting Petition, Delivered in the House of Assembly, Charleston, South Carolina, Jan. 11, 1777," in David Ramsey, *The History of Independent or Congregational Church in Charleston...*, (Philadelphia: J. Maxwell, 1815), pp. 53–8, 60–4, reprinted in "Presbyterians and the American Revolution," in Smylie, *Journal*, vol. 52, no. 4 (winter 1974): p. 449.

[108] "Presbyterians and the American Revolution," in Smylie, *Journal*, vol. 52, no. 4 (winter 1974): p. 474.

[109] Berk, pp. 44–45, 85–90.

[110] Murray, *Revival*, pp. 149–157.

[111] Murray, *Revival*, p. 173.

[112] B. K. Kuiper, *The Church in History*, pp. 355–357; Murray, *Revival*, p. 173.

[113] Murray, *Revival*, p. 170.

[114] Murray, *Revival*, pp. 176–177.

[115] Murray, *Revival*, pp. 365–371.

[116] Smith, *Studies*, pp. 32–33, citing S. J. Baird, *A History of the New School and of the Questions*

Involved in the Disruption of the Presbyterian Church in 1838 (Philadelphia, 1868), p. 166.

[117] Smith, *Studies,* pp. 33–35, citing *Minutes of the General Assembly of the Presbyterian Church U.S.A,* 1838–1847, pp. 387–388.

[118] Smith, *Studies,* pp. 40–41.

[119] *Minutes of the General Assembly of the Presbyterian Church C.S.A,* 1861, pp. 51–60, cited by Morton Smith, *How is the Gold Become Dim* (Jackson: Steering Committee for a Continuing Church, Faithful to the Scriptures and Reformed Faith, 1973), p. 10 (hereafter cited as Smith, *Gold*).

[120] Louis Berkhof, *Systematic Theology* (Grand Rapids: Wm. B. Eerdmans Publishing Co., 1946), p. 553 (hereafter cited as Berkhof).

[121] Lefferts Loetscher, *The Broadening Church: A Study of Theological Issues in the Presbyterian Church since 1869* (London: University of Pennsylvania Press, 1954), pp. 5–13.

[122] Ibid, pp. 42–47, 87–88; In 1902 the PCUS also declared warrant in belief that deceased infants are within the Covenant of Grace (Digest PCUS, p. 8).

[123] Ibid, pp. 98–99, 120.

[124] Ibid, pp. 134–135.

[125] John Gerstner, "American Calvinism until the Twentieth Century Especially in New England," *American Calvinism,* ed. Jacob Hoogstra (Grand Rapids: Baker House Books, 1957, pp. 46–54.

[126] *A Digest of the Proceedings of the General Assembly of the Presbyterian Church in the United States* (Richmond: Presbyterian Committee on Publications, 1945), p. 248 (hereafter cited as Digest PCUS); Ernest Thompson, *Presbyterians in the South, Volume Three: 1890–1972* (Richmond: John Knox Press, 1973), p. 494 published as vol. xiii of *Presbyterian Historical Society Publication Series.*

[127] Digest PCUS, p. 4.

[128] Minutes of the 1937 General Assembly of the Presbyterian Church U.S., cited in Smith, *Gold,* pp. 233–241.

[129] *The Confession of Faith of the Presbyterian Church in the United States* (Richmond: Presbyterian Committee of Publication, w/revisions through 1944), new chapter on the Gospel, chapter X, section 2, p. 65 and new chapter on the Holy Spirit, chapter IX, section 3, p. 62.

[130] Minutes of the 1937 General Assembly of the Presbyterian Church U.S., cited in Smith, *Gold,* p. 241.

[131] Smith, *Gold,* pp. 57–58, 26–29.

[132] Ray King, *A History of the Associate Reformed Presbyterian Church* (Charlotte, the Covenant Life Curriculum, 1966), p. 100.

[133] J. I. Packer, *Fundamentalism and the Word of God* (Grand Rapids: Wm. B. Eerdmans Publishing Co., 1976), p. 29 (hereafter cited as Packer, *Fundamentalism*).

[134] A summary of regrets by J. G. Machen contained in Packer, *Fundamentalism,* p. 36.

[135] Packer, *Fundamentalism,* p. 35.

Chapter 10
Lessons from the Covenant

[1] Stuart Robinson, *The Church of God as an Essential Element of the Gospel and The Idea, Structure, and Functions Thereof* (Philadelphia: Joseph M. Wilson, 1858), reprinted by Greenville Presbyterian Theological Seminary in 1996, pp. 58–59 (hereafter cited as Robinson, *The Church of God*).

[2] Robinson, *The Church of God,* pp. 36–37.

[3] Nevay, pp. 27–29. Note: in the remaining sections, footnotes are inclusive of the material in a given paragraph.

[4] Nevay, p. 30.

[5] Nevay, pp. 30–31.

[6] Nevay, pp. 32–33.

[7] Nevay, pp. 34–35.

[8] Nevay, pp. 29, 31, 33, 35.

[9] Nevay, pp. 37–39, 40–44. Although Nevay lists Moses as Mediator of the old dispensation, Rutherford rightly assigns Christ this title in Samuel Rutherford, *The Covenant of Life Opened: or a Treatise of the Covenant of Grace* (Edinburgh, 1654), p. 80 (hereafter cited as Rutherford, *Covenant of Grace*).

[10] Nevay, pp. 38–39.

[11] Rutherford, *Covenant of Grace,* p. 80.

[12] Calvin, *Institutes,* sec. ii.10.2, p. 370.

[13] Nevay, pp. 39, 40–43.

[14] Nevay, p. 50.

[15] Nisbet, *Private Life,* pp. 157–160.

[16] Nevay, pp. 50–51. Supplemented with other references.

[17] Nevay, pp. 45–47.

[18] Nevay, p. 48.

[19] Nevay, pp. 47, 49–49, 51–52.

[20] Nevay, pp. 53–54.

[21] Nevay, p. 54.

[22] Nevay, p. 55.

[23] Nevay, pp. 55–56.

[24] Nevay, pp. 56–57.
[25] Nevay, pp. 57–58.
[26] Nevay, p. 59.
[27] Nevay, p. 60.
[28] Nevay, pp. 61–62.
[29] Nevay, p. 62.
[30] Nevay, p. 62.
[31] Nevay, pp. 62–64.
[32] Nevay, p. 65.
[33] Nevay, p. 66; Reference to verse 14 added.
[34] Nevay, pp. 66–67.
[35] Nevay, p. 67.
[36] Nevay, p. 68.
[37] Nevay, pp. 69–71.
[38] Nevay, p. 71.
[39] Nevay, p. 87.
[40] Nevay, p. 88.
[41] Nevay, p. 92.
[42] Nevay, p. 87.
[43] Nevay, pp. 88–89.
[44] Nevay, p. 89.
[45] Nevay, p. 89; Heb. 3:19 added to keep 4:1 in context.
[46] Nevay, pp. 89–93.
[47] Nevay, p. 92.
[48] Nevay, pp. 93–94.
[49] Nevay, p. 94.
[50] Nevay, p. 103.
[51] *WCOF* vii.3 states that the Covenant of Grace "require[s] of them faith in him, that they may be saved." *WCOF* xi.1, and elsewhere, teaches that God calls and justifies men "not for anything wrought in, or done by them, but for Christ's sake alone; not by imputed faith itself, the act of believing, or any other evangelical obedience to them, as their righteousness." *WCOF* xi.2 states, "Faith, thus receiving and resting on Christ and his righteousness, is the alone instrument of justification." *The Larger Catechism*, printed in *Westminster Standards*, Questions 73 and 32.
[52] *The Larger Catechism*, printed in *Westminster Standards*, Question 73.
[53] Charles Bell, *Calvin and Scottish Theology* (Edinburgh: The Handsel Press, 1985), pp. 76, 85, 93, 100, 113, 132.
[54] John Flavel, "Vindiciarum Vindex," printed in *The Whole Works of the Rev. Mr. John Flavel*, 6 vols. (London: W. Baynes and Son, 1820), vol. 3, pp. 528–530 (hereafter cited as Flavel, *Works*); John Owen, "The Death of Death," *The Works of John Owen*, ed. William Goold, 10 vols. (reprint, Edinburgh: The Banner of Truth

Trust, 1965), vol. 10, p. 235 (hereafter cited as Owen, *Works*); Thomas Watson, *A Body of Divinity* (reprint, Edinburgh: The Banner of Truth Trust, 1974), p. 156 (hereafter cited as Watson, *Divinity*).
[55] John Flavel, "Vindicarum Vindex," printed in Flavel, *Works*, vol. 3, pp. 526–539.
[56] Watson, *Divinty*, pp. 156–157.
[57] Gray, *Works*, p. 137.
[58] Rutherford, *Covenant of Grace,* p. 90.
[59] Rutherford, *Covenant of Grace*, pp. 91–92.
[60] Berkhof, pp. 280–281.
[61] Nevay, pp. 95–96.
[62] Nevay, pp. 96–97.
[63] Nevay, pp. 97–99.
[64] Nevay, pp. 99–101.
[65] Nevay, pp. 101–102.
[66] Nevay, pp. 102–103.
[67] Nevay, pp. 104–109.
[68] Nevay, pp. 109–112.
[69] Nevay, pp. 112–118.
[70] Nevay, pp. 118–120.
[71] Nevay, pp. 121–125.
[72] Nevay, pp. 125–129.
[73] Nevay, pp. 129–135.
[74] Nevay, pp. 135–137.
[75] Nevay, pp. 138-142.
[76] Nevay, pp. 143-146.
[77] Nevay, pp. 146–149.
[78] Nevay, pp. 149–154.
[79] Nevay, pp. 155–160.
[80] Nevay, pp. 160–163.
[81] Nevay, pp. 157–168.
[82] Nevay, pp. 173–175.
[83] Nevay, pp. 176–177.
[84] Nevay, pp. 179–180.
[85] Nevay, p. 181; promises extracted from Exod. 6:7; Jer. 32:38; Ezek. 38:27; 2 Cor. 6:17.
[86] Nevay, pp. 181–186.
[87] Rutherford, *Covenant of Grace*, p. 75.
[88] John Murray, *The Covenant of Grace* (Phillipsburg: Presbyterian and Reformed Publishing Company, 1988), pp. 31–32 (hereafter cited as Murray, *Covenant of Grace)*.
[89] Nevay, pp. 190–193.
[90] Nevay, pp. 194–196.
[91] Nevay, p. 197.
[92] Calvin, *Institutes*, sec. iii.4.18, p. 549.
[93] Nevay, p. 200.
[94] Nevay, pp. 201–203.
[95] Nevay, pp. 200–201, 203–204, 206–207.
[96] Nevay, pp. 209–215; Nevay lists 8 steps, which are abridged into six for clarity.

97 Nevay, p. 211.
98 Nevay, pp. 210–214.
99 Nevay, pp. 215–216; Verse reference added to Song of Solomon.
100 Nevay, pp. 211–212; 214–217.
101 Nevay, pp. 218–219.
102 Nevay, pp. 216–220.
103 Nevay, p. 225.
104 Nevay, pp. 220–226.
105 Watson, *Divinity*, p. 242.
106 Nevay, pp. 393–394.
107 Nevay, pp. 395–386, 399.
108 Nevay, pp. 396–398.
109 Nevay, pp. 399–400.
110 Nevay, p. 399.
111 Nevay, pp. 401–402.
112 Nevay, p. 403.
113 Nevay, pp. 402–404.
114 Nevay, pp. 405–407.
115 Nevay, pp. 402, 404–405, 407–409.
116 Nevay, pp. 410–411.
117 Nevay, pp. 412–414.
118 Nevay, pp. 416–417.
119 Nevay, pp. 411, 414–418.
120 John Nisbet, "Dying Testimony," p. 17.
121 Nevay, pp. 419–420.
122 Nevay, pp. 420–421.
123 Nevay, pp. 422–424.
124 Nevay, pp. 420, 422–425, 426–427.
125 Gray, *Works*, p. 118.
126 Nevay, pp. 428–429.
127 Nevay, pp. 430–432.
128 Nevay, pp. 432–435.
129 Nevay, pp. 435–436.
130 Nevay, p. 437.
131 Nevay, pp. 437–439.
132 Nevay, pp. 439–440.
133 Nevay, pp. 440–442.
134 Nevay, pp. 442–443.
135 Nevay, p. 444.
136 Nevay, pp. 444–445.
137 Nevay, pp. 444–446.
138 Nevay, pp. 447–448.
139 Nevay, pp. 448–449.
140 Nevay, p. 449.
141 Nevay, pp. 449–450.
142 Nevay, pp. 450–451.
143 Nevay, pp. 451–452.
144 Nevay, pp. 452–455.
145 Nevay, p. 455.
146 Gray, *Works*, pp. 424–426.
147 Gray, *Works*, p. 119; see also Jer. 31; 32; Ezek. 11:36.
148 Nevay, pp. 456–457.
149 Nevay, p. 458.
150 Nevay, pp. 458–459.
151 Nevay, p. 460.
152 Nisbet, *Private Life*, pp. 160–161.

Chapter 11
Lessons for the Church

1 *The confessioun of faith professit, and beleuit, be the Protestantes within the realme of Scotland* (Edinburgh: Jhone Scott, 1561), (hereafter cited as *The Scottish Confession of Faith*).
2 *The Book of Church Order of the Presbyterian Church in America* (Atlanta: The Office of the Stated Clerk of the General Assembly of the Presbyterian Church in America, Fifth edition), Section 2-2 (hereafter cited as *PCA BCO*). The PCA emphasis on discipline is evidenced by definition of a particular church—one that submits to the lawful government of Christ's kingdom.
3 *WCOF*, chapter xxv.2, p. 107.
4 James Bannerman, *The Church of Christ* 2 vols. (Edinburgh: The Banner of Truth Trust, 1974 edition), vol. 1, pp. 59–61 (hereafter cited as Bannerman, *Church of Christ*).
5 Bannerman, *Church of Christ*, vol. 1, pp. 6–15.
6 Bannerman, *Church of Christ*, vol. 1, pp. 16–17.
7 Bannerman, *Church of Christ*, vol. 1, p. 56.
8 *Westminster Standards*, pp. 44, 246, 191–193, 404, 410.
9 James Wood, "The Testimony of James Wood," printed in Stewart, *Naphtali*, no page number.
10 *WCOF*, chapter xxv.3, p. 108.
11 *WCOF*, chapter xxv.4, p. 109.
12 James Ramsey, *The Book of Revelation* (Edinburgh: The Banner of Truth Trust, 1995 reprint), p. 99 (hereafter cited as Ramsey, *Revelation*).
13 Ramsey, *Revelation*, pp. 81–84.
14 Ramsey, *Revelation*, pp. 99–111.
15 James Nisbet, *Private Life*, pp. 224–225.
16 Nevay, p. 11.
17 John Knox, *John Knox's History of the Reformation in Scotland*, ed. William Croft Dickenson (London: Thomas Nelson and Sons, 1949), vol. i, p. 91.
18 Peter Lorimer, *John Knox and the Church of England* (London: Henry S. King & Co, 1875),

pp. 56–59 (hereafter cited as Lorimer, *John Knox*).

[19] Lorimer, *John Knox*, p. 61.

[20] Durham, *Revelation*, vol. 1, p. 263.

[21] Durham, *Revelation*, vol. 1, p. 262.

[22] Ernest Kevan, *The Grace of Law: A Study of Puritan Theology* (Grand Rapids: Guardian Press, 1976), pp. 119–121 (hereafter cited as Kevan, *The Grace of Law*).

[23] Richard Byfield, "Temple Defilers Destroyed," *A Short Treatise Describing the True Church of Christ and the Evils of Schism* (London: Ralph Smith, 1653), pp. 38–39 (hereafter cited as Byfield, *Temple Defilers*).

[24] Packer, *Fundamentalism*, p. 60.

[25] Calvin, *Institutes*, sec. iv.8.8, p. 394.

[26] Gillespie, *Treatise*, pp. 58, 60, 47, 49.

[27] Gillespie, *Treatise*, pp. 47, 49.

[28] Lorimer, *John Knox*, pp. 69–71; 257–259.

[29] Rutherford, *Peaceable Plea*, p. 226.

[30] J. Ligon Duncan, "Owning the Confession: Subscription in the Scottish Presbyterian Tradition," PREMISE vol. ii, no. 1 (January 28, 1995), p. 5, online <http://www.capo.org/premise/archieve.html>.

[31] T. David Gordon, "The Church's Power: Its Relation to Subscription," PREMISE vol. ii, no. 1 (January 28, 1995): p. 5.

[32] John Nisbet, "Dying Testimony," p. 18; 2 Tim. 3:16; 2 Tim. 1:13; Heb. 6:1.

[33] Smellie, p. 35.

[34] Durham, *Revelation*, vol. 1, pp. 263–264.

[35] Durham, *Revelation*, vol. 1, p. 265.

[36] Durham, *Revelation*, vol. 1, p. 265.

[37] McCrie, *John Knox–abridged*, p. 192.

[38] Nevay, p. 312.

[39] Alexander Drysdale, *History of the Presbyterians in England: Their Rise, Decline, and Revival* (London: Publication Committee of the Presbyterian Church in England, 1889), p. 493 (hereafter cited as Drysdale, *Presbyterians in England*).

[40] Murray, *Puritan Hope*, p. 232.

[41] James Nisbet, *Private Life*, pp. 224–225.

[42] Martin Luther, preface to "Letter of St. Paul to the Romans," printed in *Word and Sacrament*, vol. 35, *Luther's Works*, edited by Helmut T. Lehmann (Philadelphia: Muhlenberg Press, 1960), p. 372 (hereafter cited as Luther, *Romans*).

[43] Luther, preface to *Romans*, p. 372.

[44] Durham, *Revelation*, vol. 1, p. 263.

[45] Durham, *Revelation*, vol. 1, p. 260.

[46] Durham, *Revelation*, vol.1, p. 265.

[47] Durham, *Revelation*, vol.1, p. 261.

[48] Durham, *Revelation*, vol.1, p. 261.

[49] Durham, *Revelation*, vol.1, pp. 261–262.

[50] Durham, *Revelation*, vol.1, p. 262.

[51] Durham, *Revelation*, vol.1, p. 262.

[52] Jonathan Edwards, "True Grace Distinguished from the Experience of Devils," printed in *The Works of Jonathan Edwards*, 2 vols. (Edinburgh: The Banner of Truth Trust, reprinted 1976), vol. 2, p. 48 (hereafter cited as Edwards, *Works*).

[53] John Flavel, *Christ Altogether Lovely*, printed in Flavel, *Works*, vol. ii. pp. 214–224. He cites Song of Sol. 5:16; Psalm 14:2; 73:26; Prov. 8:11; Col. 1:19; 1 Cor. 1:30; Job 4:21.

[54] John Owen, "Meditations and Discources Concerning the Glory of Christ," Owen, *Works*, vol. 1, p. 288.

[55] McCrie, *John Knox–abridged*, p. 192.

[56] Calvin, *Institutes*, sec. iii.6.4, p. 4.

[57] Durham, *Revelation*, vol.1, pp. 260–261.

[58] Durham, *Revelation*, vol.1, p. 261.

[59] Durham, *Revelation*, vol.1, p. 261.

[60] John H. Primus, *Holy Time Moderate Puritanism and the Sabbath* (Macon, Georgia: Mercer University Press, 1989), p. 180.

[61] John Nisbet, "Dying Testimony," p. 15.

[62] Gray, *Works*, p. 66.

[63] Thomas Watson, *Heaven Taken by Storm* (Morgan, Pennsylvania: Soli Deo Gloria Publications, 1997 edition), pp. 28–29 (hereafter cited as Watson, *Heaven Taken by Storm*).

[64] Nevay, p. 1.

[65] Nevay, p. 8.

[66] Binnie, *Psalms*, pp. 386–387.

[67] Nevay, p. 7.

[68] Martin Luther, preface to *Revised Edition of the German Psalter, A.D. 1531,* translated in Binnie, *Psalms*, p. 396.

[69] Nevay, pp. 8–10.

[70] Augustine, cited in Binnie, *Psalms*, p. 383.

[71] Nevay, p. 7.

[72] Martin Luther, preface to the *Revised Edition of the German Psalter, A.D. 1531*, translated in Binnie, *Psalms*, p. 399.

[73] Watson, *Heaven Taken By Storm*, p. 17.

[74] Nevay, pp. 374–377; Synthesized from Nevay's description of right hearing and his marks of the hearing ear.

[75] Nevay, pp. 376–377.

[76] Nevay, pp. 378–379.

[77] Nevay, pp. 19–23.

[78] Nevay, pp. 23–26.

[79] Nevay, pp. 25–26.

[80] Robinson, *The Church of God*, p. 113.

[81] Augustine paraphrased by Calvin, *Institutes*, iv.14.6, vol. 2, p. 495.

[82] Nevay, pp. 380-381.

[83] Beveridge, *Scottish Church*, p. 142.

[84] Calvin, *Institutes*, sec. iv.17.40, vol. 2, p. 598.

[85] Nevay, p. 380.

[86] Nevay, pp. 381–382.

[87] George Gillespie, *Aaron's Rod Blossoming* (London: Kings Arms in Paul's churchyard, 1646), pp. 436–475 (hereafter cited as Gillespie, *Aaron's Rod*).

[88] Gillespie, *Aaron's Rod*, pp. 504–519.

[89] George Gillespie, *Aaron's Rod*, Summary of contents for book 3, chapter 15.

[90] Gillespie, *Aaron's Rod*, pp. 541–542.

[91] Gillespie, *Aaron's Rod*, pp. 540–541.

[92] Gillespie, *Aaron's Rod*, p. 541.

[93] Gillespie, *Aaron's Rod*, p. 541.

[94] Calvin, *Institutes*, sec. iv.17.43, vol. 2, p. 599.

[95] Charles Hodge, *Systematic Theology*, 3 vols. (Grand Rapids: Wm. B. Eerdmans Publishing Company, 1977 reprint), vol. 3, p. 616.

[96] Lorimer, *John Knox*, p. 37.

[97] Lorimer, *John Knox*, p. 32.

[98] Lorimer, *John Knox*, pp. 156, 158.

[99] Lorimer, *John Knox*, pp. 156–157.

[100] Lorimer, *John Knox*, pp. 234–235.

[101] Nevay, p. 381.

[102] Nevay, p. 218.

[103] J. A. Ross Mackenzie, "The Covenant Theology–A Review Article," published in *Journal of Presbyterian History* (Lancaster, Pa.: Department of History of the United Presbyterian Church in the U.S.A., 1966), vol. 44, p. 204.

[104] Walker, *Six Saints*, 1, p. 144.

[105] John Flavel, "Vindiciarum Vindex," printed in Flavel, *Works*, vol. 3, pp. 544–45.

[106] John Calvin, *Commentary on a Harmony of the Evangelists, Matthew, Mark, and Luke*, translated by William Pringle, Luke 1:50, vol. 1, p. 56 (hereafter cited as Calvin, *Harmony*).

[107] Nevay, pp. 72–75.

[108] Nevay, pp. 72–77.

[109] Nevay, pp. 78–82.

[110] Nevay, pp. 82–84.

[111] *WCOF*, chapter xxviii.3.

[112] Nevay, p. 85.

[113] *First Book of Discipline*, Head 9, pp. 185–186.

[114] H. A. White, *Southern Presbyterian Leaders* (New York, 1911), pp. 55–56; Smith, *Studies*, pp. 48–49.

[115] Nisbet, *Private Life*, p. 141.

[116] Nisbet, *Private Life*, p. 126.

[117] Rutherford, *Peaceable Plea*, pp. 287, 301.

[118] Wilhelm Niesel, *The Theology of Calvin* (Grand Rapids: Baker Book House, 1980 edition), translated by Harold Knight, p. 198.

[119] Calvin, *Institutes*, sec. iv.12.1, vol. 2, p. 453.

[120] Calvin, *Institutes*, sec. iv.3.2, vol. 2, p. 317.

[121] Calvin, *Institutes*, sec. iv.2.4, vol. 2, pp. 306–309; John 18:37; John 10:14, 4, 5.

[122] Durham, *Revelation*, vol.1, p. 84.

[123] General Assembly of 1651, "Causes of The Lord's Wrath Against Scotland, Manifested in the Late Sad Dispensations," (hereafter cited as Guthrie, *Wrath*). reprinted from the Edition of 1653 in Gillespie, *Works*, vol. 2, pp. 11–17. Actually writen by James Guthrie or Archibald Johnson.

[124] Crichton, *Memoirs of Blackader*, pp. 35–41.

[125] Calvin, *Institutes*, sec. iv. 11.1, vol. 2, p. 438.

[126] Jerome quoted in Calvin, *Institutes*, sec. iv.4.2, vol. 2, p. 328.

[127] Robinson, *The Church of God*, pp. 65–68, 98–100; Robinson cites Exod. 3:15-16; 4:29-31; 12:3, 21; 14:7-11; 17:5-6; Deut. 17:9-12; 2 Kings 6:32; Exe. 8:1; Jer. 26:8, 17; Acts 15:4, 6, 22, 23; 16:4; Eph. 1:4-23; 4:4-16; 5:23-24, 25-32; Rom. 12:4-8; 1 Cor. 12:27-28; Col. 1:18; 1 Tim. 4:4-12; 5:17; Heb. 13:3-17; 1 Thess. 5:12.

[128] Ambrose quoted in Calvin, *Institutes*, sec. iv.11.6, vol. 2, p. 444.

[129] James Hensley Thornwell, *The Collected Writings of James Henley Thornwell*, ed. John B. Adger and John L. Girardeau, 4 vols. (Richmond: Presbyterian Committee of Publications, 1871–1889), vol. iv, p. 218 (hereafter cited as Thornwell, *Collected Writings*); Ludger G. Whitlock, Jr., *James Henry Thornwell*, in *Southern Reformed Theology*, ed. David Wells (Grand Rapids: Baker Book House, 1989), p. 66.

[130] Calvin, *Institutes*, sec. iv.9.3, pp. 404–405.

[131] John Calvin, *The Necessity of Reforming the Church*, printed in *Selected Works of John Calvin* (Grand Rapids: Baker Book House, reprint 1983), translated by Henry Beveridge, vol. 1, p. 170 (hereafter cited as Calvin, *Necessity*).

[132] Drysdale, *Presbyterians in England*, pp. 346–541.

[133] John Nisbet, "Dying Testimony," p. 19.
[134] Thornwell, *Collected Writings*, vol. iv, p. 135.
[135] Gillespie, *Treatise,* p. 56.
[136] Calvin, *Necessity*, vol. 1, p. 214.
[137] Calvin, *Necessity*, vol. 1, p. 214.
[138] Alexander Shields, *Church-Communion Inquired Into* (Edinburgh: William Ceray, 1747), p. 4 (hereafter cited as Shields, *Communion*).
[139] Shields, *Communion*, pp. 5, 7.
[140] Shields, *Communion*, p. 11.
[141] Durham, *Scandal*, p. 312.
[142] Shields, *Communion*, pp. 21–22.
[143] Durham, *Scandal*, pp. 324–328; Shields, pp. 24–33.
[144] Calvin, *Institutes*, sec. iv.12.11, vol. 2, p. 460.
[145] Shields, *Communion*, pp. 33, 27–28, 23–24.
[146] Shields, *Communion*, pp. 24, 41, 42.
[147] Shields, *Communion*, pp. 24–26.
[148] Shields, *Communion*, p. 48.
[149] Shields, *Communion*, pp. 55–57, 62–65.
[150] Shields, *Communion*, pp. 65–67.
[151] Shields, *Communion*, pp. 68-69.
[152] Shields, *Communion*, pp. 69–71.
[153] Shields, *Communion*, pp. 72–74.
[154] Durham, *Scandal*, pp. 64, 390–391.
[155] Shields, *Communion*, pp. 74–75.
[156] Shields, *Communion*, pp. 75–78.
[157] Durham, *Scandal*, pp. 393–399.
[158] Durham, *Scandal*, pp. 399–408.
[159] Shields, *Communion*, pp. 79–80.
[160] Shields, *Communion*, pp. 81–82.
[161] Shields, *Communion*, pp. 82–84.
[162] Shields, *Communion*, pp. 84–86.
[163] Shields, *Communion*, pp. 86–88.
[164] Durham, *Scandal*, pp. 314–320.
[165] Shields, *Communion*, pp. 88–91.
[166] Shields, *Communion*, pp. 91–94.
[167] Shields, *Communion*, pp. 94–98.
[168] Shields, *Communion*, pp. 98–110.
[169] Durham, *Scandal*, pp. 425–432.
[170] Rutherford, *Peaceable Plea*, p. 255.
[171] Thomson, *Cloud*, pp. 313–314.
[172] John Nisbet cited in Howie, *Worthies*, pp. 506–507.
[173] John Nisbet, "Dying Testimony," p. 21.
[174] Douglas Bannerman, *The Scripture Doctrine of The Church Historically and Exegetically Considered* (Grand Rapids, Baker Book House, 1976 edition), pp. 434–436.
[175] Bannerman, *Church of Christ*, vol. 1, p. 20.
[176] Bannerman, *Church of Christ*, vol. 1, p. 21.
[177] Durham, *Revelation*, vol.1, pp. 540–541.
[178] Rutherford, *Peaceable Plea*, pp. 92–109, 118.

[179] Rutherford, *Peaceable Plea*, pp. 131–139.
[180] Rutherford, *Peaceable Plea*, pp. 242–267.
[181] Rutherford, *Peaceable Plea*, pp. 289–295.
[182] *WCOF*, chapter xxv.2, pp. 107–108.
[183] 1 Timothy 3:15; Matthew 28:19-20; and Matthew 16:18.
[184] From the founding speech to the First General Assembly of the PCA, "A Message to all Churches of Jesus Christ throughout the World from the General Assembly of the National Presbyterian Church," printed in *PCA Digest Position Papers 1973–1993* (Atlanta: Presbyterian Church in America, 1993), Part V, p. 10. This speech is excerpted from the speech given over a century earlier at the founding of the Presbyterian Church CSA.
[185] From "Biblical, Historical, and Contemporary Concepts of Church/State Relations," received as information by the 15th General Assembly (1987), printed in *PCA Digest Position Papers 1973–1993* (Atlanta: Presbyterian Church in America, 1993), Part V, p. 116.
[186] Byfield, *Temple Defilers*, pp. 3–7.
[187] Byfield, *Temple Defilers*, p. 5.
[188] James E. Ostenson, Incorporation of PCA Churches–Exhibit A, "Articles of Incorporation of First Presbyterian Church, Inc., A Non-profit Corporation."
[189] US Code Title 26 Section 501 (c)(3). Note: The omitted statement (indicated by…)does not apply to churches.
[190] Byfield, *Temple Defilers*, p. 12.
[191] Walter Chantry, *God's Righteous Kingdom* (Edinburgh: The Banner of Truth Trust, 1980), pp. 142–146.
[192] Stuart Robinson, *Theology Without a Church*, 1:20, October 29, 1863, quoted by Preston Graham, Jr., "The Spirituality Doctrine of the Church in the Border States During America's Civil War," PREMISE vol. iv, no. 2 (June 30, 1997): p. 5.
[193] Robinson, *The Church of God*, p. 67.
[194] Binnie, *Psalms*, pp. 292–299.
[195] Ernest Thompson, *Presbyterians in the South: 1607–1861* (Richmond: John Knox Press, 1963), vol. 1, p. 72.
[196] M'Cheyne, pp. 251, 595, 597.
[197] Stuart Robinson, "The Churchliness of Calvinism," *Report of Proceedings of the First General Presbyterian Council convened in Edinburgh, July 1877* (Edinburgh: Thomas and Archibald Constable, 1877), pp. 62–68.

Chapter 12
Lessons for Christians

[1] Simon J. Kistemaker, *New Testament Commentary, Exposition of the First Epistle to the Corinthians* (Grand Rapids: Baker Books, 1993), p. 470.

[2] John Calvin, *Calvin's Commentaries: The First Epistle of Paul the Apostle to the Corinthians,* translated by John Fraser (Grand Rapids: Wm. B. Eerdmans Publishing Company, 1976), p. 282.

[3] Saint Augustine, *The Enchiridion, Addressed to Laurentius; Being a Treatise on Faith, Hope, and Love,* printed in *A Select Library of the Nicene and Post-Nicene Fathers of the Christian Church,* ed. Philip Schaff (Grand Rapids: Wm. B. Eerdmans Publishing Company, 1980), vol. 3, p. 237 (hereafter cited as Augustine, *Enchiridion*).

[4] Gray, *Works,* p. 62.

[5] Gray, *Works,* pp. 340–341.

[6] Nevay, pp. 227–229.

[7] Nevay, pp. 232–233.

[8] Nevay, p. 233.

[9] Nevay, pp. 234–235.

[10] Gray, *Works,* p. 322.

[11] Gray, *Works,* pp. 317–318, 333–336.

[12] Gray, *Works,* p. 334.

[13] Gray, *Works,* pp. 313–317.

[14] Gray, *Works,* pp. 338, 319–320.

[15] Gray, *Works,* pp. 340–348.

[16] Gray, *Works,* pp. 348–356.

[17] Gray, *Works,* p. 365.

[18] Gray, *Works,* pp. 356–361; Acts 17:31.

[19] Gray, *Works,* pp. 365–372.

[20] Gray, *Works,* p. 375.

[21] Gray, *Works,* p. 335.

[22] Nevay, pp. 236–237.

[23] Nevay, pp. 237–238.

[24] Nevay, p. 238.

[25] Nevay, p. 238.

[26] Nevay, pp. 239–240.

[27] Nevay, p. 231.

[28] Nevay, p. 241.

[29] Nevay, p. 244.

[30] John Nisbet, "Dying Testimony," pp. 12–17.

[31] Nevay, p. 254.

[32] Nevay, p. 255.

[33] Nevay, pp. 255–256.

[34] Nevay, pp. 259–260.

[35] Nevay, pp. 256–259.

[36] Nevay, pp. 260–262.

[37] Gray, *Works,* p. 135.

[38] Gray, *Works,* p. 128.

[39] Gray, *Works,* pp. 116, 157.

[40] Gray, *Works,* pp. 116, 64.

[41] Gray, *Works,* p. 174.

[42] Gray, *Works,* pp. 45, 48.

[43] Gray, *Works,* p. 30.

[44] Gray, *Works,* p. 33.

[45] Augustine, *Enchiridion,* chapter 18, p. 243; chapter 31, pp. 247–248.

[46] Calvin, *Institutes,* sec. iii.2.9, vol. 2, p. 477.

[47] Nevay, p. 283.

[48] Nevay, p. 284.

[49] Nevay, pp. 285–287.

[50] Nevay, pp. 290–291.

[51] Nevay, p. 284.

[52] Jan Anderson and Laurel Hicks, *Introduction to English Literature* (A Beka Book: Pensacola, 1996), pp. 336–339 (hereafter cited as Beka).

[53] Nisbet, *Private Life,* pp. 160–165.

[54] Nevay, p. 284.

[55] Nevay, p. 287.

[56] John Flavel, "Christ Altogether Lovely," printed in Flavel, *Works,* vol. ii, pp. 214–224.

[57] Gray, *Works,* p. 392.

[58] Patrick Walker, "The Life and Death of Mr. James Renwick," Walker, *Biographia,* pp. 264–265.

[59] Nevay, p. 292; S. of Sol. 1:7; 2:8–10, 16; 3:1, 4; 5:2, 4–6; 6:2, 3; 7:10, 11.

[60] Nisbet, *Private Life,* pp. 208–209.

[61] Nisbet, *Private Life,* pp. 213–222.

[62] Nevay, pp. 287, 289.

[63] Nisbet, *Private Life,* pp. 208–211.

[64] Lorimer, *John Knox,* p. 42.

[65] Lorimer, *John Knox,* p. 155.

[66] Spiros Zodhiates, *The Epistle of James and the Life of Faith,* vol. 2, *The Labor of Love* (Grand Rapids: Wm. B. Eerdmans, 1959), p. 173.

[67] Augustine, *Enchiridion,* chapter 19, p. 243.

[68] Augustine, *Enchiridion,* chapter 20, p. 244.

[69] Nevay, p. 289. Nevay discusses both the love of goodwill and the bountiful nature of love but does not specially link these concepts.

[70] Nevay, p. 288.

[71] Nevay, p. 284.

[72] Augustine, quoted in Calvin, *Institutes,* sec. ii.8.5, vol. 1, p. 320.

[73] Spiros Zodhiates, *The Epistle of James and the Life of Faith,* vol. 1, *The Work of Faith* (Grand Rapids: Wm. B. Eerdmans, 1959), p. 139.

[74] Kevan, *The Grace of Law,* p. 22.

[75] Kevan, *The Grace of Law*, p. 265.

[76] Nisbet, *Private Life*, pp. 203–204.

[77] John Dod and Robert Cleaver, *A Plaine and familiar Exposition of the Ten Commandments* (London: 1603), pp. 8–9.

[78] Jeremiah Burroughs, *The Saints Treasury* (London: 1654), p. 95.

[79] Thomas Edwards, *Baxterianism Barefac'd Drawn from literal Transcript of Mr. Baxter's* (London: 1699), pp. 153–158.

[80] Van Til, p. 231.

[81] Thomas Watson, *A Divine Cordial*, printed in W. W. Woodward, *A Pious Selection* (Philadelphia: W. W. Woodward, 1815), p. 112.

[82] Nisbet, *Private Life*, pp. 211–214.

[83] Nevay, p. 291.

[84] Nevay, p. 292.

[85] Nisbet, *Private Life*, pp. 208–209.

[86] Nisbet, *Private Life*, pp. 215–216.

[87] Nisbet, *Private Life*, p. 248.

[88] Nevay, pp. 263–264.

[89] Nevay, p. 265; Calvin, *Institutes*, sec. iii.9.5, vol. 2, p. 29.

[90] Nevay, pp. 265–266.

[91] Nevay, pp. 268–270.

[92] Nevay, pp. 264–265, 270.

[93] Nevay, pp. 267–268.

[94] Nevay, pp. 268, 270–272.

[95] Richard Cameron, Sermon in Kerr, *Sermons*, p. 457.

[96] Nevay, pp. 434–435.

[97] Durham, *Revelation* (1680 edition), vol. 2, pp. 326–328, 332–333, 342–343, 349, 395–396, 460–462, 468–469.

[98] J. N. Darby quoted in Murray, *Puritan Hope*, p. 201.

[99] Nevay, pp. 434–435.

[100] Nevay, pp. 246–247.

[101] Gurnall, *Complete Armour*, pp. 293, 309.

[102] William Gurnall, *The Christian in Complete Armour; A Treatise of the Saints' War against the Devil*, 2 vols, (Edinburgh: The Banner of Truth Trust, 1979 reprint), vol. 1, p. 315 (hereafter cited as Gurnall, *Complete Armour*).

[103] Nevay, pp. 246-247.

[104] Nevay, p. 250.

[105] Nevay, pp. 250–251.

[106] Nevay, pp. 248-250.

[107] Nevay, pp. 251–254.

[108] Nevay, pp. 273–275; Reference to Mal. 3:16 added.

[109] Nevay, pp. 276-277.

[110] Nevay, pp. 279–281.

[111] Nevay, p. 47.

[112] Nevay, pp. 273–275.

[113] Nevay, pp. 279-280.

[114] Nevay, pp. 281–282.

[115] Augustine, *Enchiridion*, chapter 1, p. 237.

[116] Nevay, pp. 292–293.

[117] Nevay, pp. 294-296.

[118] Nevay, pp. 298-299.

[119] Nevay, p. 294.

[120] Nevay, pp. 296-297.

[121] Nevay, pp. 299–300.

[122] Watson, *Heaven Taken by Storm*, pp. 1–37.

[123] Watson, *Heaven Taken by Storm*, p. 52.

[124] Nevay, pp. 306–307.

[125] Nevay, p. 309.

[126] Nevay, pp. 306–307.

[127] Nevay, pp. 307-308.

[128] Nevay, p. 308.

[129] Nevay, p. 310.

[130] Nevay, pp. 301–302.

[131] Nevay, pp. 303–304.

[132] Nevay, pp. 304–305.

[133] Nevay, pp. 301–303, 304–305.

[134] Gray, *Works*, p. 65.

[135] Nevay, p. 311.

[136] Nevay, p. 312.

[137] Nevay, pp. 313–314.

[138] Nevay, p. 317.

[139] Nevay, pp. 317-318.

[140] Nevay, pp. 315–317.

[141] Nevay, pp. 318–319.

[142] Gurnall, *Complete Armour*, p. 337.

[143] Nevay, pp. 319–320.

[144] James Durham, *Heaven Upon Earth* (Edinburgh: Andrew Anderson, 1685), pp. 147–165 (hereafter cited as Durham, *Heaven Upon Earth*).

[145] Durham, *Heaven Upon Earth*, pp. 1–15.

[146] Durham, *Heaven Upon Earth*, pp. 184–233.

[147] Nevay, pp. 320–341.

[148] Nevay, pp. 322–324.

[149] Nevay, pp. 326–328.

[150] Nevay, p. 324.

[151] Nevay, pp. 322–324.

[152] Nevay, pp. 325–326.

[153] Nevay, pp. 327–329.

[154] Gray, *Works*, p. 64.

[155] Nevay, pp. 330–331.

[156] Nevay, pp. 331–333.

[157] Nevay, pp. 321–338.

[158] Nevay, pp. 266–267.

[159] Nevay, p. 339.

[160] Nevay, pp. 339–340.

[161] Nevay, pp. 341–342.

[162] Nevay, pp. 344-345.

[163] Nevay, pp. 343–344.

[164] Nevay, p. 346.

[165] Nevay, p. 345.

[166] Nevay, p. 347.

[167] Gray, *Works*, p. 383.

[168] Nevay, p. 348.

[169] Nevay, pp. 349–350.

[170] Nevay, pp. 351–352.

[171] Nevay, pp. 349–350.

[172] Nevay, pp. 352–353.

[173] Nevay, p. 347.

[174] Nevay, p. 353.

[175] Nevay, pp. 354–355.

[176] Nevay, pp. 354–355.

[177] Thomson, *Cloud*, p. 371.

[178] Augustine, *Enchiridion*, chap. 7, pp. 238–239.

[179] Spurgeon, *Defense*, vol. 1, p. 175.

[180] Gray, *Works*, pp. 197–200.

[181] Gray, *Works*, pp. 203–205.

[182] Richard Baxter, *End of Doctrinal Controversies which have Lately Troubled the Churches by Reconciling Explication, without much Disputing* (London: 1681), p. 205.

[183] Nevay, p. 357.

[184] Nevay, pp. 357–359.

[185] Nevay, pp. 360–361.

[186] Nevay, p. 359.

[187] Nevay, pp. 360–361.

[188] Nevay, pp. 361–363.

[189] Nevay, p. 364.

[190] Nevay, pp. 362–364.

[191] John Bunyan, *The Pilgrim's Progress* (Westwood, New Jersey: Barbour and Company, 1985), p. 182.

[192] James Nisbet, Extract from "Ebenezer in a Furnace," printed in Nisbet, *Private Life*, pp. 273–274 (hereafter cited as Nisbet, "Ebenezer").

[193] Nisbet, "Ebenezer," pp. 274–276.

[194] Nisbet, "Ebenezer," p. 276.

[195] Nisbet, *Private Life*, pp. 155–157; Rom. 8:38, 39; 1 Cor. 15:55.

[196] Nevay, pp. 365–367.

[197] Nevay, pp. 368–370.

[198] Nevay, pp. 371–372.

[199] Nevay, pp. 367–370.

[200] Nevay, pp. 370–371.

[201] Nevay, pp. 368–370.

[202] Nevay, pp. 370–372.

[203] Nevay, p. 389.

[204] Nevay, p. 390.

[205] Nevay, p. 391.

[206] Nevay, pp. 390–391.

[207] Beka, pp. 336–339.

[208] Charles Spurgeon, *The Greatest Fight in the World* (Pasadena: Pilgrim Publications, 1990), p. 5.

[209] Nevay, p. 384.

[210] Nevay, p. 384.

[211] Nevay, p. 385.

[212] Nevay, p. 387.

[213] Nevay, p. 384.

[214] Nevay, pp. 385, 387.

[215] Nevay, pp. 386–387.

[216] Nevay, p. 388.

[217] Nevay, pp. 388–389.

[218] Gray, *Works*, pp. 160–161.

[219] Gray, *Works*, pp. 163–165.

[220] Gray, *Works*, pp. 222–225.

[221] Gray, *Works*, pp. 228–235.

[222] Gray, *Works*, pp. 237–242.

[223] Nisbet, *Private Life*, p. 204.

[224] Nisbet, "Ebenezer," pp. 268–269.

[225] James Nisbet, "Letter on the Great Difference Between Stoic Silence and Christian Composure," printed in Nisbet, *Private Life*, p. 280.

[226] Nisbet, "Ebenezer," pp. 270–271.

Chapter 13
Lessons for Citizens

[1] Greg L. Bahnsen, *Theonomy in Christian Ethics* (Nutley, New Jersey: The Craig Press, 1977), p. 4.

[2] James H. Nichols, *History of Christianity 1650–1950: Secularization of the West* (New York: Ronald Press Co., 1956), p. 6.

[3] Buchan and Smith, *Kirk in Scotland*, p. 55.

[4] McCoy, *Robert Baillie*, p. 138.

[5] Buchanan, *Rights*, p. 267.

[6] John Calvin, quoted by J. H. Merle D'Aubigne', *History of the Reformation in Europe in the Times of Calvin*, (1876 edition), vol. 7, p. 41, cited in Introduction to Murray, *Puritan Hope*, p. xii. Also see Ps. 118:9.

[7] David Dickson, *A Commentary On The Psalms* (Edinburgh: The Banner of Truth Trust, 1985 reprint), pp. 437–442.

[8] *The Second Book of Discipline* (1578), chapter 1, sec. 21; Robinson, *The Church of God*, pp. xxi–xxii.

[9] Tocqueville, pp. 295, 297–298.

10 Tocqueville, pp. 292–293.

11 Tocqueville, p. 445.

12 Gillespie, *Treatise,* p. 82.

13 Gillespie, *Treatise,* p. 74.

14 Gillespie, *Treatise,* p. 82.

15 Samuel Rutherford, *A Free Disputation Against Pretended Liberty of Conscience* (London: Andrew Cook, 1649 edition), pp. 331–334 (hereafter cited as Rutherford, *Free Disputation*).

16 John Cotton, "Copy of Letter from Mr. Cotton to Lord Say and Seal in the Year 1636," printed in John Norton, *The Life and Death of Mr. John Cotton, Late Teacher of the Church of Christ, at Boston in New England* (London, 1658), p. 417 (hereafter cited as Norton, *Cotton*).

17 James H. Thornwell, "Relation of the State to Christ," printed in Thornwell, *Collected Writings,* p. 555 (hereafter cited as Thornwell, "Relation of the State to Christ").

18 Hetherington, *Westminster Assembly,* p. 307.

19 Bannerman, *Church of Christ,* vol. i, pp. 174–175; *WCOF,* chapter xxx.1 and xxiii.3, pp. 101, 120.

20 Leyburn, *Scotch-Irish,* p. 146.

21 James H. Thornwell, "Sermon on National Sins: a fast day sermon, preached in the Presbyterian Church, Columbia S.C., Wednesday, November 21, 1860," printed in Thornwell, *Collected Writings,* pp. 526–527 (hereafter cited as Thornwell, "National Sins").

22 Thornwell, "National Sins," pp. 527–529.

23 James Madison, "Federalist Paper no. xlv," *The Federalist Papers,* ed. Clinton Rossitner (New York: Penguin Books, 1961), pp. 292–293.

24 Tocqueville, pp. 255-256.

25 Thornwell, "Relation of the State to Christ," p. 550.

26 Ibid.

27 Thornwell, "National Sins," p. 534.

28 Thornwell, "National Sins," p. 511.

29 Thornwell, "National Sins," pp. 514–517.

30 John Eidsmoe, *God and Caesar: Christian Faith and Political Action* (Westchester, Il: Crossway, 1984), pp. 13–14.

31 Thornwell, "National Sins," pp. 521–523.

32 Nevay to Old Congregation in Scotland, Oct. 22, 1669, Nevay, p. 472.

33 Calvin, *Institutes,* sec. iv.20.15, vol. 2, p. 663.

34 Calvin, *Institutes,* sec. iv.20.3, vol. 2, p. 653.

35 Calvin, *Institutes,* sec. iv.20.9, vol. 2, pp. 657–658.

36 Calvin, *Necessity,* vol. 1, p. 188.

37 Calvin, *Necessity,* vol. 1, p. 189.

38 Calvin, *Institutes,* sec. iv.20.10, vol. 2, p. 661.

39 Calvin, *Necessity,* vol. 1, p. 198.

40 *WCOF,* chapter xix.4, p. 81.

41 Graham, *The Civil Sword,* p. 237 (abstract).

42 John Cotton cited in Norton, *Cotton,* p. 22.

43 Thornwell, "National Sins," pp. 521–522.

44 Thornwell, "Relation of the State to Christ," p. 552.

45 Jack P. Maddex, "From Theocracy to Spirituality: The Southern Presbyterian Reversal on Church and State," *Journal of Presbyterian History* (Philadelphia: Presbyterian Historical Society, 1976), vol. 54, no. 4 (winter 1976): p. 445 (hereafter cited as Maddex, "Presbyterian Reversal").

46 Thornwell, "National Sins," p. 519.

47 Thornwell, "Relation of the State to Christ," pp. 552–554.

48 Thornwell, "Relation of the State to Christ," p. 552.

49 Thornwell, "National Sins," p. 518.

50 Gillespie, *Aaron's Rod,* p. 250.

51 Mathew Henry, cited by Greg L, Bahnsen, "M. G. Kline on the Theonomic Politics: An Evaluation of His Reply," *The Journal of Christian Reconstruction,* vol. 6, no. 2, winter (1979–1990).

52 Rutherford, *Peaceable Plea,* pp. 51–57.

53 Froude, *Calvinism,* p. 13.

54 Henry Ward Beecher, *Leading Thoughts of Living Thinkers,* cited by McFetridge, *Calvinism in History,* p. 121.

55 Gillespie, *Aaron's Rod,* pp. 198, 200, 187.

56 Rutherford, *Free Disputation,* p. 331.

57 Nisbet, "Ebenezer," p. 272.

58 Thornwell, "National Sins," p. 517.

59 Thornwell, "Relation of the State to Christ," p. 551.

60 Thornwell, "Relation of the State to Christ," p. 554.

61 Maddex, "Presbyterian Reversal," p. 441.

62 Maddex, "Presbyterian Reversal," pp. 446–453.

63 Fisk, *High Church Tradition,* pp. 75–80.

64 Nevay, p. 471.

65 Thornwell, "Relation of the State to Christ," p. 555.

66 *The Scottish Confession of Faith,* chapter 24, Paragraph 2.

67 The *Westminster Larger Catechism,* printed in *Westminster Standards,* Question 108, p. 193.

68 Bannerman, *Church of Christ,* vol. 1, p. 131.

69 Lorimer, *John Knox,* p. 217.

[70] Robinson, *The Church of God*, p. 58.
[71] Robinson, *The Church of God*, pp. 127–128.
[72] Gillespie, "One Hundred and Eleven Propositions Concerning the Ministry and the Government of the Church," (Edinburgh: Robert Ogle and Oliver and Boyd, 1844 reprint), p. 13, printed in Gillespie, *Works*, vol. 1 (hereafter cited as Gillespie, "Propositions").
[73] Gillespie, "Propositions," pp. 12–16.
[74] Shaw, *Exposition of the Confession*, p. 270.
[75] Rutherford, *Peaceable Plea*, p. 145, 209-218.
[76] Rutherford, *Peaceable Plea*, p. 275.
[77] Rutherford, *Peaceable Plea*, pp. 177-188.
[78] Rutherford, *Peaceable Plea*, p. 484.
[79] Rutherford, *Peaceable Plea*, pp. 189-209, 292.
[80] Rutherford, *Peaceable Plea*, pp. 145-177.
[81] Rutherford, *Peaceable Plea*, p. 319.
[82] *The Second Book of Discipline* (1578), chapter 1, sec. 17; Robinson, *The Church of God*, p. xxi.
[83] John Nevay to the Congregation of Loudoun, Oct. 22, 1669, printed in Nevay, pp. 470–471.
[84] John Nevay to the Congregation of Loudoun, Oct. 22, 1669, printed in Nevay, pp. 470–471.
[85] Rutherford, *Lex, Rex*, p. 105; Isaiah 49:23.
[86] Buchan and Smith, *Kirk in Scotland*, p. 65.
[87] Bannerman, *Church of Christ*, vol. 1, p. 112.
[88] Isa. 60:3; Al Hembd, "Josiah, Erastianism, and National Covenanting," online, part 3, page 2 of 7.
[89] Bannerman, *Church of Christ*, vol. 1, pp. 159–170; *WCOF*, chapter xx.4, p. 87.
[90] Rutherford, *Free Disputation*, p. 250.
[91] John Calvin, *Necessity*, vol. 1, pp. 221–222.
[92] John Calvin, *Necessity*, vol. 1, p. 228.
[93] John Knox cited in Lorimer, *John Knox*, p. 215.
[94] Gillespie, *Treatise*, pp. 71, 82, 74, 78.
[95] Guthrie, *Wrath*, p. 29.
[96] Charles Spurgeon, *Sermons of Rev. C. H. Spurgeon* (New York: Sheldon & Company, 1872), Series 9, p. 180.
[97] James M. Wilson, *Civil Government: An Exposition of Romans xiii.1–7* (Philadelphia: William S. Young, 1853), pp. 15–18.
[98] Calvin, *Institute*, sec. iv.20.32, vol. 2, p. 676.
[99] Buchanan, *Rights,* pp. 276–280, 282.
[100] McCrie, *Vindication*, p. 152.
[101] Calvin, *Institutes*, sec. iv.20.25, vol. 2, pp. 670–671; Alexander Nisbet, *An Exposition of 1 & 2 Peter* (1658; reprint, Edinburgh: The Banner of Truth Trust, 1982), p. 101.
[102] John Knox to the Congregation in Berwick, reprinted in Lorimer, *John Knox,* p. 259.

[103] Shields, *Hind*, pp. 320–324, 378.
[104] Shields, *Hind*, pp. 326–334.
[105] Shields, *Hind*, pp. 340–410.
[106] Shields, *Hind*, pp. 336–343.
[107] Michael Shields to Friends in Ireland, printed in Shields, *Faithful Contendings*, p. 302.
[108] McCrie, *Vindication*, p. 162.
[109] Shields, *Hind*, p. 700.
[110] Webb, p. 125.
[111] McCrie, *Scottish Church*, p. 175.
[112] Reprinted in Lorimer, *John Knox*, p. 219.
[113] "West Kirk to Committee of Estates," August 13, 1650 and a declaration of Committee of Estates, 1650 printed in *A True Narrative of the Proceedings of His Majesties Privy-Council in Scotland, for Securing the Peace of the Kingdom, in the year 1678* (London, 1678), pp. 4, 5.
[114] Thomson, *Cloud*, p. 314.
[115] *WCOF*, chapter xxiii.4, p. 103.
[116] Tocqueville, p. 546.
[117] Buchanan, *Rights*, p. 257.
[118] Buchanan, *Rights*, p. 257.
[119] Nevay, p. 13.
[120] Nevay, pp. 16–18.
[121] *The Second Book of Discipline (1578)*, chapter 1, sec. 22–23, p. xxii.
[122] Stewart, preface to *Naphtali*.

Chapter 14
Reformation

[1] "National Church Attendance Drops," *Equip for Ministry*, vol. 3, no. 4 (July–August 1997): p. 14.
[2] George Grant, "Against the Tide: Four Alternative Movement," PREMISE vol. II, no. 7, (August 27, 1997): p. 9.
[3] Beka, pp. 336–339.
[4] Charles Spurgeon, *Sermons of Rev. C. H. Spurgeon* (New York: Sheldon & Company, 1872), Series 9, p. 324.
[5] Ibid, 329. Song of Solomon 5:16.
[6] Murray, *Covenant of Grace*, p. 11.
[7] William Guthrie, *The Christian's Great Interest* (London: Dorman Newman, 1667), p. 153 (hereafter cited as Guthrie, *The Christian's Great Interest*).
[8] Guthrie, *The Christian's Great Interest*, pp. 154–157.
[9] William Roberts, "On the Duty of Covenanting and the Permanent Obligations of

Religious Covenants," sec. 11 of the *Reformed Presbyterian Catechism* (1853); online 1998 <http://www.swrb.com/newslett/actualnls/Pres CatCov.htm>.

[10] *Alexander and Rufus*, p. 357.

[11] Rutherford, *Covenant of Grace*, pp. 107–108.

[12] Nisbet, *Private Life*, pp. 154–155.

[13] *Alexander and Rufus*, p. 382.

[14] Guthrie, *The Christian's Great Interest*, pp. 150–151. Rutherford differentiate between two sorts of covenanting: "one external, professed, visible, and conditional; the other internal, real, and absolute." The elect engage in both types of covenanting; the visible church, including infants, engage (or are engaged) in the former type only.

[15] WCF (Ch. 22); *Alexander and Rufus*, p. 361.

[16] Derived from the *Solemn League and Covenant*, sec. 1 and 2.

[17] George Gillespie, "A Sermon preached Before the Honourable House of Commons at Their Last Solemn Fast," March 27, 1644, printed in Gillespie, *Works*, vol. 2, p. 2.

[18] John Dickson, quoted in Howie, *Worthies*, p. 594.

[19] M'Cheyne, p. 383.

[20] Green, *History of the English People*, vol. 3, p. 114.

[21] John Calvin, *Zechariah & Malachi*, vol. 5 of *A Commentary on the Twelve Minor Prophets*, first translated and edited by John Owen (Edinburgh: The Banner of Truth Trust, 1986), comments on Zech. 8:6, p. 198.

[22] Calvin, *Institutes*, sec. ii.8.11, vol. 1, p. 324.

[23] Lorimer, *John Knox*, p. 224.

[24] John King, cited from a sermon by John King, *A Collection of Very Valuable Sermons*, ed. John Howie (Glasgow, 1780), p. 44; King cited Psalm 137:6 as a proof text. [ESTC 5187].

[25] "Arguments given by the Scottish Commissioners of Scotland unto the Lord of Treaty, persuading Conformity of Church Government, as one Principal means of a Continued Peace between the Two Nations," cited by Hetherington, *History*, vol. 1, p. 356.

[26] Matthew Henry, *Matthew Henry's Commnentary on the Whole Bible* (Peabody, Mass.: Hendrickson Publishers, 1991), comments on Zech. 11:14, p. 1588.

[27] Byfield, *Temple Defilers*, p. 32. [emphasis added]

[28] Nisbet, *Private Life*, p. 146.

[29] Benjamin Brook, *The Lives of Puritans* (1813 edition), vol. 1, p. 383.

[30] Calvin, *Harmony*, Matt. 6:10, vol. 1, p. 320; Murray, *Puritan Hope*, p. 90.

[31] *The Larger Catechism*, printed in *Westminster Standards*, Question 191, pp. 274–275.

[32] Jonathan Edwards, "A Humble Attempt to Promote Explicit Agreement and Visible Union of God's People, in Extraordinary Prayer, for the Revival of Religion and Advancement of Christ's Kingdom on Earth," printed in Edwards, *Works*, vol. ii, pp. 281–282.

[33] Alexander Peden, sermon printed in Kerr, *Sermons*, p. 565.

[34] Baillie, *Letters*, Let. x. vol. 1, p. 101 cited in James Reid, *Memoirs of the Westminster Divines* (Edinburgh: Banner of Truth Trust, 1982, p. 298.

[35] Derived from *Solemn League and Covenant*, sec. 3, 4, and 5.

[36] John Ewing, Mss. Sermon, vol. 1, reprinted in "Presbyterians and the American Revolution," in Smylie, *Journal*, vol. 52, no. 4 (winter 1974): pp. 478–479.

[37] John Dickson, quoted in Howie, *Worthies*, p. 595.

[38] Durham, *Revelation*, vol. 2, p. 348.

[39] James Renwick, quoted in Howie, *Worthies*, p. 547.

[40] John Calvin, "The Sure Foundation," printed in *The Mystery of Godliness and Other Selected Sermons* (Grand Rapids: W.B. Eerdmans Pub. Co., 1950), p. 86.

[41] Derived from *Solemn League and Covenant*, sec. 6.

[42] Nisbet, *Private Life*, pp. 203–224.

[43] Nisbet, *Private Life*, p. 222.

[44] Nisbet, *Private Life*, pp. 223–224.

[45] Donald K. McKim, *Encyclopedia of the Reformed Faith* (Louisville: Westminster/John Knox Press, 1992), p. 87.

[46] John Nisbet, "Dying Testimony," p. 21.

[47] Nisbet, *Private Life*, pp. 263–264.

[48] Nisbet, *Private Life*, pp. 259–264.

[49] M'Cheyne, p. 154.

[50] Tweedie, p. 407.

[51] John Nisbet, "Dying Testimony," p. 17.

[52] M'Cheyne, p. 19.

[53] M'Cheyne, pp. 297, 298, 300, 436, 437.

[54] M'Cheyne, pp. 378–382.

[55] Murray, *Covenant of Grace*, pp. 23–24.

[56] Samuel Rutherford to Alexander Henderson, March 9, 1637, *Letters*, p. 40.

[57] James Thornwell, *Discourses in Truth* (New York: Robert Carter & Brothers, 1855), p. 64.
[58] Hugh Miller, p. 383.
[59] Nisbet, *Private Life*, p. 141.

Where possible and required, quotes are used with permission; all rights reserved.

INDEX

F

I

See publisher's website at http://christianfocus.com
See author's website at http://www.covenanters.com

Reformation Flag
Courtesy of Bill Reid

About the author:

Edwin (Ed) N. Moore is a Ruling Elder at Grace Presbyterian Church in Aiken, South Carolina. He is the happily married father of three children. After graduating from Clemson University with a B.S. degree in Chemical Engineering in 1972, Ed has worked at the Savannah River Site in a variety of assignments including plant operation, design, and startup. He currently serves as a Senior Advisory Engineer in the Strategic Planning and Integration Department. Ed is active in his church, and he has spent his spare time during the last four years researching *Our Covenant Heritage*. He claims no special qualifications for authoring this book; the true experts are those whom Moore quotes. Not published for centuries, these sources include memoirs, treatises, and sermons from those who actually suffered intense persecution for the cause of Christ's Truth and His Church. Moore can only say with the Covenanter Alexander Shields that religion is in a sad condition when God uses pitiful creatures such as himself to do His work.